HARPER'S
BIBLE
COMMENTARY

HARPER'S BIBLE COMMENTARY

William Neil

HARPER & ROW, PUBLISHERS

1817

New York, Hagerstown, San Francisco, London

Author's Note to the Paperback Edition

The publication of this commentary as a paperback both in the U.S.A. and U.K. almost fifteen years after its first appearance in hard covers encourages me to believe that over these years it has been found service-able by many people and that there is still a felt need for a small commentary of this kind.

Amid all the changes in the modern world the Bible has still its ancient power to speak to the hearts and minds of men and women everywhere, for as Isaiah said: "The word of our God will stand for ever" (Isa. 40:8).

Nottingham
March 1975

WILLIAM NEIL

HARPER'S BIBLE COMMENTARY. *Copyright © 1962 by Hodder & Stoughton Ltd.
Printed in the United States of America. All rights reserved. No part of this book
may be used or reproduced in any manner whatsoever without written permission
except in the case of brief quotations embodied in critical articles and reviews. For
information address Harper & Row, Publishers, Inc.,10 East 53rd Street, New
York, N.Y. 10022.*

This book was originally published in England under the title
WILLIAM NEIL'S ONE VOLUME BIBLE COMMENTARY.

ISBN: 0-06-066091-0

LIBRARY OF CONGRESS CATALOG CARD NUMBER: 63-7607

First Harper & Row paperback edition published in 1975.

85 18 17 16 15 14 13 12 11

PREFACE

"WHEN THE miner finds the gold he throws away his tools." This remark, interjected by a young American in a student debate in which I took part many years ago, on the value of scientific study of the Bible, has stuck in my mind and seems to me to have become more and more relevant as time has gone past. Obviously the use of scientific methods by biblical scholars over the last century and more has paid handsome dividends. Literary criticism, textual study, historical inquiry, archaeological and anthropological investigation have enhanced our understanding of the Bible beyond all recognition.

No praise can be too high for the patience and reverence of scholars of all branches of the Church who have been concerned to illuminate by their efforts some aspect or other of the record of "the faith which God entrusted to his people once and for all". A veritable host of modern "books about the Bible" testifies to the eagerness of those who have tried to translate into ordinary language the conclusions of these experts in their various specialisms.

However, as one of these writers of "books about the Bible" I have been disturbed from time to time by the comments of readers that they find themselves more interested in "books about the Bible" than in the Bible itself. This is obviously a major failure on the part of "popularisers" of the Bible. Unless all that is written about the Bible is an inducement to the reader to turn to the Bible itself it is largely misdirected effort.

Accordingly it seemed that the obvious next step was for someone to write a "book about the Bible" that could not be read without reading the Bible itself. This is what I have now tried to do. I hope it will be impossible for anyone to make much headway through these pages without having a copy of the Bible at his elbow which he is reading at the same time. This book is thus not an introduction to the Bible or a substitute for reading the Bible but an aid to studying the Bible.

Many bigger and better one-volume commentaries are already in existence. If they have any fault it lies in their unwieldiness. It has been possible to provide a complete commentary on the Bible of this small compass only by omitting all but the barest minimum of critical detail and background information, and it is assumed that readers who are looking for that kind of material will turn to these larger commentaries.

But—and this brings us back to our starting point—there does seem to be a danger in large-scale commentaries that the very profusion of background information and critical comment is for the ordinary man who wants to understand the Bible something of a deterrent. Is it not possible at this stage in biblical studies to take for granted the general conclusions of biblical scholars over the past century and to concentrate on the theological teaching of the Bible, what it has to say about the meaning and purpose of life, about God, ourselves and the world we live in? Having used scientific tools to find the gold may we not now cast the tools aside and concentrate on the treasure?

The reader of this commentary will therefore find none of the usual separate essays on topics such as biblical chronology or the synoptic problem, nor indeed detailed treatment of vexed questions of authorship, variant readings and so on. Instead he will find an attempt to provide a running commentary from *Genesis* to *Revelation* which is based on the assumption that the biblical writers were primarily theologians and not anthropologists, scientists or even historians, that the Old and New Testaments are part of one and the same revelation and that they cannot be understood apart from one another.

I hope that this book will serve as an introduction to deeper study of the Bible. For those who wish to go further the S.C.M. Press "Torch" series of commentaries on individual books of the Bible is warmly recommended. The order of books in the English Bible has been followed, and this commentary is designed to be read together with any version of the Bible, although suggestions are made in the text as to the use of modern translations. Partly because the normal order is followed, and partly to make it possible for an individual book of the Bible to be studied by itself, a certain amount of repetition has been inevitable.

My unacknowledged debt to previous commentators and to biblical scholarship in general is obvious on every page. I owe the expression of a particular debt of gratitude, however, to Professor Robert Davidson, M.A., B.D., of the University of Glasgow for his careful reading of the typescript and for his many helpful criticisms and valuable suggestions.

WILLIAM NEIL

Nottingham
August 1961

THE BOOKS OF THE BIBLE

Old Testament—continued

APOCRYPHA

THE BOOKS OF THE BIBLE
NEW TESTAMENT

Other abbreviations

A.V.	—	Authorised Version
R.V.	—	Revised Version
R.S.V.	—	Revised Standard Version
LXX	—	Septuagint

OLD TESTAMENT

GENESIS

THE WORD *Genesis* means "beginning", and it seems at first glance that what the Bible is dealing with in this book is the story of the beginning of everything: the world, mankind, civilisation, and in particular, the origin of the nation whose story is told through the rest of the Old Testament. Actually the Bible is dealing with something much more profound. We can get factual information about all these things from physicists, geologists, biologists, archaeologists and historians—at least so far as they know the answers.

The Bible is concerned much more with theology, that is, it is a book about God and his dealings with men. It does not speculate about the existence of God. That is something we can neither prove nor disprove. It rather focuses our attention on certain aspects of life and the world around us, records certain things that have happened in history, claims to interpret their meaning, and then compels us to make a choice. It forces us to conclude that the interpretation of life which it offers is complete nonsense, or to accept that interpretation with all its implications for ourselves.

The Bible does not stand or fall by the accuracy of its information, because it is not a textbook of science, or history or archaeology. It stands or falls by what it has to say about the purpose of life, the meaning of the world we live in, and the reality that lies beyond it. It claims to provide the clue to the mystery that surrounds our existence, to tell us who we really are, where we should be going, what we ought to be doing, and how we can do it.

One way of looking at the Bible is to think of it as a divine drama, with God as the chief character. It is not a spectacle for us to sit back and enjoy or criticise, however, for we are all taking part in the drama ourselves. The theme of the drama is the Acts of God—past, present and future. It begins with a prologue; then come three acts, followed by an epilogue. The prologue, which is contained in the first eleven chapters of *Genesis*, sets the stage for the whole drama. Act I is the rest of the Old Testament. Act II is the gospels. Act III is the rest of the New Testament. The epilogue is the book of *Revelation*.

Briefly, the prologue paints the picture of the world as God meant it to be, and then shows us the appalling mess that we have made of it. The three acts tell the story of what God has done, and is still doing, to enable us to get out of the mess. The epilogue paints the picture of the end product, when men and things become what God intended them to be.

When we say that *Genesis* means the "beginning", then, we should think of it rather as the book that begins the story of God's intervention to save us from the consequences of our own pride and folly. As we read it, we should look primarily at its religious and moral teaching, and only incidentally at background details (*II Tim.* 3: 14–17). But first comes the prologue to the story.

In the Beginning God
(1: 1 – 2: 4a)

WE DO NOT know how the universe started. Science has various theories about it, but no one knows for certain. We must not expect that the writer of the first chapter of *Genesis*, whose ideas were those of over two thousand years ago, thought any more scientifically about the origin of sun, moon, stars and of the earth itself, than did his contemporaries. He is content to think of some kind of chaos or disorder as the first stage (1: 2), out of which comes an ordered and harmonious universe. His chief interest is not in how this happened—which is what modern science is concerned with—but in making plain his conviction that it did not happen by accident.

We may disregard the various steps in the process. The writer divides it into six days. These do not mean "days" of twenty-four hours, or "years", or even "stages". This is a poem and

not a timetable. The writer lets his imagination play upon the theme of the created world and its mysteries, that were as obscure to him as they are to us. He sees the orderly succession of night and day, the sequence of summer and winter. He scans the starry heavens, and the teeming life of land and sea. He contemplates man, with his purposeful control of the natural world. And he writes this great hymn of praise, because he sees behind it all the mind and purpose of a Supreme Power, whom he has already come to know in his own experience, and whose guiding hand he has seen in the movements of history.

The writer was a devout member of a community which regarded every seventh day as a day not only of rest but of recreation in the deepest sense. It was the day above all others when people gathered together to worship and pray and learn the will of God. It was the day when, above all, they acknowledged the sovereignty of God over their lives, when they confessed their failures, gave thanks for God's goodness, and sought his help. The seventh day was in a real sense the Lord's Day.

It is not surprising, therefore, that the writer of this magnificent hymn of Creation chooses to think of the ordinary creative working week of six days as a reflection of the great creative acts of God "in the beginning". They culminate in the seventh day, on which he pictures God resting and refreshing himself, and contemplating his work with satisfaction (1: 31 – 2: 3), as a man, conscious of having done a good job for six days, would rest and recreate himself and commune with the Creator.

There is obviously nothing in this dramatic poem which conflicts with anything that biologists can tell us about the evolution of living creatures, or with what geologists have to say about the age of the earth, or with what astronomers may conjecture about an expanding universe. Science is looking at the problem from a different angle. It would not have alarmed the author of this chapter to be told that the earth was millions of years old, although it would no doubt have perturbed Archbishop Ussher, who calculated in 1654 that the Creation of the world had taken place in 4004 B.C.

Nor would this old writer have been greatly concerned to be told about the millions of galaxies, compared with which our solar system is very small fry. Indeed he was firmly of the opinion, like all his contemporaries, that the earth was a flat disc mounted on pillars, and that beneath the earth and above the solid dome of the sky were the waters of the great deep. But this kind of knowledge was incidental. He was much more interested in theology.

So we are right to see in the first four words of this chapter the really essential point in the biblical view of Creation. The Bible invites us to believe that the universe, by whatever process it has come into its present state, and however long that process has taken, is not the result of chance or accident, or of some impersonal evolutionary development, or of some blind groping life-force, but that it has its origin in the mind and purpose of the Supreme Being, whose nature and actions are disclosed in the drama that is to follow. Before there was a universe at all, the Bible tells us, there was God. Whatever is, is there because God willed it. He is the power behind and within everything that exists.

When we remember that the ancient Egyptians viewed Creation as an act of sexual self-abuse on the part of the Creator, and that the ancient Mesopotamians viewed it as the by-product of a conflict between numerous squabbling gods and goddesses, we cannot fail to recognise the profound insight which lies behind the Hebrew concept of Creation by divine command. The universe and all that it contains comes into being because: "God said, Let there be . . ." Here already the Bible introduces a theme which recurs again and again: the Word of God. The created world is the product of the mind of God. He expresses his purpose in a rational way, a way that men can understand. Later, the prophets of Israel declare the purpose of God for the world by using the same phrase: Thus saith the Lord. St. John, too, harks back to this creation story when he speaks of Jesus as the Word made flesh (*John* 1: 14), the purpose of Creation summed up and expressed in a human life (cf. *Heb.* 1: 1–2).

There are two other important assertions in this chapter. The first is that "God created man in his own image" (1: 27). The Bible sees man, as distinct from the other animals, in a special relationship to God. Whatever the word "image" implies, it certainly means that men in their own sphere are god-like. The psalmist speaks of man as the crown of creation (*Ps.* 8), controlling the forces of nature, exploiting its natural resources. The author of this chapter sees man's status and function in the same way: privileged to run the world, but responsible and accountable to its Creator.

But if man alone is made in God's image, human personality has a value which is unique. Men and women may not be treated as goods and chattels, or as cogs in a machine, or as tools of the state. The Bible has a high view of man because it has a high view of God. It sees him as capable of great things. Above all, the idea of the image of God suggests that there is in man, unlike any other creature, the possibility of responding to God. He may do so or not, for he is free to choose. There is in any event a point of contact, an awareness of God, which St. Augustine has well expressed: "Thou hast made us for thyself, and our hearts are restless till they find rest in thee."

The other important claim that this Creation story makes is in 1: 31: "God saw every thing that he had made, and, behold, it was very good." This picture of the Creator gazing round on his handiwork with approval has great significance for our attitude to the world. If God made it, and delighted in it, it is not for us to spurn the material things of life, as if the Bible inculcated some kind of rarified spirituality which disdains the good things of this world. The Bible has certainly much to say about the wrong use of material things, but here we are reminded that this is God's world. If things have gone wrong in it, that is no part of God's work or will.

Man's Opportunity and Failure
(2: 4b – 3: 24)

FOLLOWING THE great liturgical hymn of Creation with which the book of *Genesis* opens, comes, surprisingly enough, what seems to be a duplicate account of the same event. Quite clearly the second Creation story was not written by the author of the first. The style is quite different. In chapter one there is a magnificent restraint in the description of God's creative acts. The process is sketched rather than described in detail. God is pictured as the great Original, who utters the divine fiat and his will is done.

By contrast, the second Creation story reads like an old-fashioned fairy tale. God moulds man like a potter (2: 7), plants a garden (2: 8), strolls in it of an evening (3: 8), and makes clothes for Adam and Eve (3: 21). The process of Creation is different, as is the order in which the various items appear. The first story begins with the creation of light (1: 3) and ends with the creation of man (1: 26), while the second begins with the creation of man (2: 7) and ends with the creation of woman (2: 22).

As long ago as 1753, Jean Astruc, physician to Louis XV, reached the conclusion that there were two separate narratives of Creation, from two different sources, and dating from two different periods. He further saw that these two elements were not confined to the Creation story, but that they could be traced right through the book of *Genesis* and beyond it. Since Astruc's day, scholars have consistently confirmed his theory and developed it. As we shall see, two further strands are added, one beginning at *Gen.* 15, and the other appearing in the book of *Deuteronomy*. These four strands, whether they were written documents or made up of fragments of oral tradition, were woven together to form the Pentateuch, the name given to the first five books of the Old Testament.

It is important to recognise that two of these strands are present in these early chapters of *Genesis*. They account for the contradictions and inconsistencies in the stories of the Creation and the Flood and elsewhere. The older source, which refers to God as "the Lord", and can thus be easily detected, is responsible for the vivid lively narratives, while the younger source, which refers to God as "God", is more concerned with genealogies, details of ritual and ceremonial. The older source, probably dating from the ninth century B.C., is generally known as J or Jahwist, from the name it gives to God, Jahweh (Jehovah), blended in places after *Gen.* 15 with another version, the E or Elohist tradition, whereas the younger source is for obvious reasons called P or the Priestly source, and dates roughly from the fifth century B.C.

In the Creation story, then, the editors have incorporated two accounts: first, the liturgical poem in chapter one (P), and then the older traditional narrative in chapters two and three (J). That should help us to understand that we cannot dismiss the second Creation story as a fairy tale, or merely as a primitive attempt to answer such questions as: Why the world? Why are there men and women? Why do we wear clothes? The second story is clearly meant to be regarded as a sequel to the first, and not as a repetition of it. Its inclusion cannot be justified unless it has something to add. When we examine it, it emerges that far from this being a rather naïve account of the origin of things, such as would be produced at a primitive stage of civilisation, it is in fact as highly theological and profound in its insights as is the first story. It is no more to be taken scientifically or literally than its predecessor, but it has certainly to be taken seriously. For having painted the picture in *Gen.* 1 of the world as God meant it to be, the Bible goes on now in *Gen.* 2–3 to paint a picture of the world as it is.

Adam and Eve are, of course, not intended to be regarded as historical characters. This is not the story of the first man and the first woman and what happened to them, but the story of every man and every woman since human life began. The Hebrew words for Adam and Eve mean Man and

Life, so perhaps if this wise old theologian had been writing today he might have entitled these two chapters: "The Story of Mr. and Mrs. Everyman." As we read these chapters, with their deep insights and profound understanding of human nature, let us remember that this is our story. Adam and Eve are you and I.

There are countless subtleties and nuances in this portrayal but the main lines are painted with a broad brush. We are shown God's good earth, the Creator's handiwork, with man charged with the task of developing it and keeping it in good order (2: 15). At his side, as his companion and sharer of his life, is woman (2: 23). The world and its resources lie open before them. Communion with God is theirs (the tree of life—2: 9), as also is the whole gamut of human experience.

Men and women may select from the field of experience what they will. Freedom of choice is open to them. But this freedom has its dangers. The ultimate standards of good and evil are not theirs to settle. They must recognise their limits as creatures under authority, and that it is God's prerogative to determine what is right and what is wrong. This is a function they must not usurp. If they attempt it, the consequences are fatal (2: 17).

But this is the very thing that men and women try to do. The temptation to make their own standards of right and wrong, to flout God's authority, to run the world in their own way proves irresistible. Pride is their undoing,

the pride that makes them want to be on a level with God (3: 5). Inevitably disaster follows. Human relationships are tarnished (3: 7); the world becomes a hostile place (3: 17-19); worst of all, a barrier divides man from God (3: 24).

Much ink has been spilt over the question of whether this picture is intended to represent that at some point, early in the history of the human race, something went wrong and man took the downward path, which he has ever since followed. This is the traditional theological doctrine of the Fall. It assumes that man lived originally in a state of innocence and perfect communion with God, that the world was then in fact a Paradise. Perhaps it is not a sufficient argument against this view that it is singularly difficult to do much more than assert it as a dogma to be accepted or rejected.

On the other hand, if we are not prepared to say that sin came into the world at the instigation of a talking serpent, in other words, if we recognise the poetic and symbolic nature of the whole story, it is not by any means clear that the Bible is talking about a historical or prehistorical event at all. Surely the truth that the Bible is conveying to us is much more that as long as there have been men and women on the earth they have used their freedom in the wrong way, by putting themselves at the centre instead of God, by refusing to recognise that this is not their universe but God's, and that it must be run in God's way and not man's way.

Man who is made in the image

of God, capable of making the right response to God, and living in the right relationship to him, consistently distorts the image and frustrates God's purposes. The pride that makes Adam and Eve impatient of restraint and eager to be rid of any authority beyond their own, lies at the root of man's failure and perennial downfall. That is equally true today, and the Bible would tell us that it has always been so.

If we may think of Creation as in one sense an event in time, in that nothing exists that has not been brought into being by God, we may think of it in another sense as an eternal act, in that God is continuously creating new life and energy. Similarly the truth behind the Fall may be twofold. We repeat in our own lives every day the story of the Fall; our human pride and our separation from God are too painfully real to allow us to forget them. But may we not also say that in the dim beginnings of man's evolution from the animal kingdom, there came the point when his behaviour was no longer conditioned by reflexes or instinctive reactions, when he could in fact make rational choices. By choosing the lower way rather than the higher, the easier way rather than the harder, the selfish way rather than the unselfish, he began to follow the path which all of us since then have followed, and started off mankind on its rake's progress to destruction.

These two chapters (2–3) will repay careful and thoughtful study. They are a treasure house of insights into human nature,

our relations with one another and with God. Notice how well the two sides of our being are reflected in 2: 7. We are of the earth, earthy (in Hebrew, man— *adam*—comes from the ground— *adamah*—cf. *I Cor.* 15: 47) but God has breathed something of himself into us. The Garden of Eden is the symbol both of the beauty of God's created world and of our proper status in it as God's custodians, responsible to him for its care and maintenance (2: 8–15). True marriage is beautifully described as an unselfconscious relationship (2: 25) where a man and a woman find that they become part of each other, almost as if they become a joint personality (2: 24). Jesus set the seal of his approval (*Mark* 10: 2–12) on this old writer's conception of marriage as a lifelong partnership, woven into the very basic fabric of society.

The serpent (3: 1) is the perfect symbol of temptation. It is not surprising that later, when the demonic character of evil was recognised, and personified in the symbol of Satan, the serpent in the Fall story should be thought of as Satan in disguise (*Wisd.* 2: 24). Notice how he persuades the man and the woman that God's warning that violation of his laws will bring disaster cramps their freedom, preventing them from realising their true greatness and from occupying their proper status in the universe (3: 2–5). "Glory to man in the highest" is a refrain as old as man himself.

It is sometimes thought that the Bible represents sin as primarily a matter of sex. This seems to be suggested by the emphasis on "nakedness" (2: 25; 3: 7), but in a series of symbols such as we find in these chapters, fig leaves cannot be meant to be taken any more literally than serpents. The lesson surely is that failure to recognise the obedience of God as our highest obligation destroys the free and spontaneous relationship with one another which we ought to have. The sense of sin disrupts human society, separating us from one another, as certainly as it separates us from God. The man and the woman are no longer at ease in each other's company, just as they feel out of harmony with God (3: 10).

Note how adroitly our evasion of responsibility is characterised. The man blames the woman; the woman blames the serpent. Indeed the man practically accuses God: It was you who gave me the woman in the first place! (3: 12–13). Men have always tried to shuffle out of responsibility for their failures. We blame our instincts, our environment, our parents, our wives or our neighbours, and if all else fails we can always blame God.

But the price has to be paid. The world is at war with itself. The joy has gone out of life, the harmony has been broken. Man's self-will has marred the Creator's fair design. It is unlikely that this old writer had any clearer idea than we have ourselves as to why there should be a tragic side to the beauty of the earth: the struggle for existence in the animal world, ruthlessness, torture and sudden death. But he maintains that this is not in the purpose of the Creator. It is an intrusion into his plan. The plight of the serpent and its enmity with man (3: 14–15), by which he symbolises the whole mystery of man's relation to the natural world, the suffering of dumb creatures, the groaning and travailing of the whole creation as St. Paul puts it later (Rom. 8: 22), is somehow the result of a cosmic breakdown. Not only mankind but nature itself is in constant rebellion against God. Pain and cruelty, disease and decay, are no part of a world which the Creator saw to be "very good". Once more the Bible offers not an explanation but a conviction.

An even deeper note is struck in 3: 15. It may have been fanciful for early commentators to see in the words "it shall bruise thy head", a promise of the coming of Christ, the seed of a woman, who would triumph over Satan and destroy the power of evil. But if the serpent symbolises not merely the lower forms of animal life but the embodiment of cunning, temptation and guile, these words are at once a recognition of the constant battle between mankind and his evil impulses, and a hope of ultimate victory for man. He may have to hobble along the way of life, bruised in the heel, hindered by evil, but evil itself is doomed to a worse fate, crushed to death under man's foot. Whatever was in the writer's mind on this point we are right to think that with the coming of Christ and his victory over evil, the victory of Man as man was meant to be, these old words have come strangely and wonderfully true (Rom. 16: 20).

Again we are brought face to face with the mystery of pain in 3: 16. Marriage and children are seen as part of the beneficent design of the Creator (1: 27–28) but the agonies of childbirth are no part of God's will. Why new life should come into the world at the cost of a mother's suffering, and sometimes her own life, we do not know, and the Bible does not tell us. But in this tale of Eve, the pains and subsequent cares of motherhood are regarded as in some way connected with the disorganisation of the divine pattern which sin has occasioned.

Man pays the penalty for his disregard of God's laws in that his life becomes a burden. Work in the divine plan was to be creative and pleasurable (1: 28–29; 2: 15) but as a result of man's pride his best efforts are laboured and sorrowful. His problems multiply, his tasks loom menacingly over his head. His back-breaking toil brings him no more than enough to keep life in being, and at the end of it the earth from which he came receives him back for ever. It we translate this picture into modern terms, its truth remains even with a five-day week and automation. For the sweat of the brow substitute the monotony of mechanised industry, or the frustration of trivial occupations or the sense of futility and helplessness that makes so many question the whole trend and structure of modern society.

Modern man, in this atomic age, with all his ingenuity and resources, is still out of harmony with the world and with his neighbour. We do not need to look far

in the international, social or economic fields to find the curse of Adam. We not only know from our own experience that the sin of Adam is our sin and that we pay the price, but we also find ourselves burdened with the legacy of wrong choices, pride and selfishness which the past has bequeathed to us, and which bedevils every attempt to put the world to rights.

So the picture would appear to be black indeed, though no more black than our knowledge of history and of the world today would confirm, and certainly no more black than we deserve. Man is given his opportunity; he is made in the image of God; but he abuses his freedom, flouts the laws of God, and brings upon himself disaster, pain and death. Thus, unerringly, this old biblical tale of the Fall illuminates the contemporary scene and speaks to our condition.

Yet already we are given a hint that despite our stubbornness and folly God will not give us up. Man may have been in constant rebellion against God, but he still bears traces of the divine image. He is still potentially a child of God, with the breath of God's life in him. So for the first time the characteristic pattern of God's attitude towards us is outlined, a pattern which we shall trace right through the Bible. God is Judge, and his judgment will not allow us to play fast and loose with the moral order of his universe. We must pay the price of our failure to live according to his will. But he is also the God of mercy and forgiveness, who will not forsake us or leave us to our deserts.

This pattern is revealed tellingly in the concluding verses of this *Genesis* story. Adam accepts God's judgment because he can do no other and knows it to be right, but something tells him that this is not God's last word—an empty future, futile endeavour and death to end it all. He still has hope, and signifies it by calling his wife Eve, a name implying the promise of motherhood and new life (3:20). In this we may perhaps see that element of hope in man at all stages of his existence, which has somehow refused to believe that despite his failure and the mystery that surrounds him of pain and decay and death, this world is nothing more than a meaningless chaos in an empty universe.

Adam's hope is well founded. The symbol of the coats of skins which God made for the man and the woman (3:21) implies God's providential care for all mankind. Sinful, wayward, wilful, ignorant though they be, all men everywhere are God's concern. He keeps them in life and shields them from the thorns and thistles (3:18) which they have brought upon themselves. Paradise is not for us. We are unfit to live in full communion with God, which means to share his eternal life (3:22). We have godlike power which we cannot be trusted to use right. So man is banished to his joyless tasks and condemned to live estranged from God until death overtakes him. A barrier stands between him and the perfection that might have been his (3:24). But he has not been written off, for God still cares. It is on this fact that the whole story that the Bible records is founded.

Too much importance cannot be attributed to these three chapters of the prologue, which expound the theological doctrines of Creation and Fall. Their narrative form, replete with symbol and image, answers more perfectly than any doctrinal formulation the purpose in the mind of the writer. He is setting the stage for the drama that begins in *Gen.* 12, and while it is true that there are eight more chapters in the prologue, and that all have their own contribution to make to the total picture, nonetheless the essential themes have already been stated: God's design and man's disorder, God's grace and man's sinfulness, God's judgment and man's punishment, man's hope and God's compassion.

In a sense it is a one-sided picture: a world without the Gospel and mankind without a Saviour. As Christians we know that God does not leave man to reap the full consequences of his betrayal. He does not stop at compassion. He steps in to rescue man from his plight. He plans to save him from himself, because he is God and for no other cause, and beginning with Abraham, the plan for man's salvation comes into action. By the grace of God we live under the Gospel.

But the Bible pulls no punches. It insists that first of all we should see ourselves as we are and that we should recognise God as he is. We must see ourselves as stupid, twisted creatures, capable of every crime from simple folly through lechery and lust to murder. We must be shown that God is no benevolent cosmic sponge, prepared to wipe away our worst excesses and absorb them with genial tolerance.

We have to be shown that a holy God hates sin and that he cannot gloss it over. He takes it seriously and expects us to do the same. Therefore through these ancient stories of the prologue he lets us see ourselves as we are and the punishment we deserve. We are not under condemnation because once upon a time the first man and the first woman failed God, but because we ourselves are Adam and Eve and their failure is ours. What they deserve we deserve, but for the love of God. We are to be shown what that love means in action, but first we must be told the full tale of our tragic human situation in the remaining chapters of the prologue.

Murderers All

(4: 1–15)

THE FASCINATING tale of Cain and Abel presents a variety of problems. It does not follow altogether naturally on the last verses of the preceding chapter. Cain's fear of reprisals (4: 14) and his marriage (4: 17) imply a world more thickly populated than by Adam and Eve and their two sons. Unless we take refuge in the sorry shift that 4: 14 refers to Cain's younger brothers and 4: 17 to his sister, we must recognise that trivial questions as to where Cain found his wife belong to the outworn controversies of eighteenth-century rationalism and can only arise if the story is mistakenly regarded as historical.

Similarly, it is a thin interpretation of the significance of this tale that would see it as an attempt to account for the age-old conflict in the Near East between the settled agricultural communities (Cain) and the nomadic pastoral tribes (Abel), or to explain the origin of sacrifice, or of the blood-feud among warlike clans, or the fierceness of one of them in particular, if the later Kenites (15: 19) take their origin from Cain.

Nor does it do justice to the narrative to connect it with the Babylonian New Year Festival, and see in it the Hebrew form of a ritual slaying whereby the fertility of the crops may be ensured for another year, with Cain taking the part of the sacrificing priest who must be banished for a time as technically unclean, but must not be harmed since he is under divine protection.

How many—if any—of these motifs were present in the original form of the story it is now impossible to say. It would seem to be an ancient tale with traces of a variety of different backgrounds, but clearly as it stands it is intended by the compiler of the prologue to reinforce the teaching of chs. 1–3. It repeats the theme of the Fall but at a faster tempo. Disobedience by the father now develops into murder by his son. The rebellious Adam which is in us all is now revealed as the murderous Cain.

The universal quality in Cain's action bears no relation to whether he was a shepherd or a farmer. He is the type of man, any of us, all of us, who resents the success or good fortune of others. In Old

Testament times this would be called the blessing of God. Cain broods over what he feels to be the injustice of life. He is not getting a fair deal. Moffatt's translation sheds light on the obscurity of 4:7: "Why are you downcast?" asks the Eternal, "If your heart is honest, you would surely look bright? If you are sullen, sin is lying in wait for you, eager to be at you —but you ought to master it."

But Cain does not master sin. Sin masters Cain. Petulance develops into hate and hate begets murder. Then follows the accusing voice of conscience and the perennial cry of man's guilty irresponsibility: "Am I my brother's keeper?" (4:9). This is the cry that has echoed down the centuries over the graves of the victims of humanity's crimes, the victims of greed and violence. Civilisation, of which we are all part and from which we all benefit, has left a bloody trail of war, slavery and industrial exploitation. The Bible will not allow us to pretend that we have no share in this. The guilt sits squarely on all our shoulders, murderers all, at best by proxy.

Then once again the bell tolls. God's condemnation of man's inhumanity to man is proclaimed (4:11). The world is poisoned because of it and man is doomed to "go stumbling and straying over the earth" (4:12). With unerring insight the Bible exposes the shallowness of our reproachful plaint: "Our punishment is more than we can bear. We are estranged from God and hated by our fellowmen" (4:13–14). Yet once again the unexpected, undeserved mercy of God interpose with a message of hope.

The first foreshadowing of the Good News of God's care for man despite his failure has already been given in the story of the Fall. By every standard of human justice man as Adam brings disaster on his own head by his wrong choices yet God will not let him go (3: 21). By the same standards, man a Cain, hating his brother man to the point of taking his life, merits a like fate. But once again, more strongly because the sin is greater, the forgiving love of God is proclaimed. Cain deserves death but God steps in to save him from his deserts (4:15).

We are being led to the point where for the first time the Old Testament introduces the conception of a covenant between God and man, which is indeed the master theme of the Bible. The very word "testament" itself means covenant. This distinctive relationship between God and man, uniquely expressed in the Bible, takes on even greater depth and meaning as the Old Testament unfolds God's plan and passes for its fulfilment into the New Testament. We shall see how in the stories of Noah (*Gen.* 9), Abraham (*Gen.* 17) and Moses (*Ex.* 19), the conception of this relationship is enriched and intensified, how Jeremiah (31: 32–34) pins his faith on an even closer relationship between God and his people than prophets and priests had hitherto dreamt of, and how finally Jesus comes to effect the New Covenant (*Mark* 14: 24), the perfect way for man to reach fulfilment of his being in unbroken fellowship with his Creator.

But here, as in 3: 21, the theme of God's plan to save the proud and self-willed being that man has made himself is already tentatively sounded, without the other side of the coin in the covenant-idea—man's response in terms of obedience to God—being specifically emphasised. The Bible is rather saying to us at this early stage that the forgiveness of God is stronger than the perversity of man, and that in spite of ourselves God will love us back into the relationship of perfect sonship for which he created us (2: 16–17). Although it is clear that the old writer of *Genesis* had no knowledge of the Cross of Christ, and no thought of the sign of the Cross as being God's protective mark on Cain (4: 15), which was presumably some kind of tattoo, the Christian Fathers were right in their intuitive identification of the one with the other.

The Cross of Christ is indeed the seal of God's forgiveness for the sin of the Cain that each of us carries within himself. When the author of the epistle to the *Hebrews* (12: 24) speaks of the "sprinkled blood whose message is nobler than Abel's", he is proclaiming in the same terms as the author of *Genesis* that God's love superimposes on the just law of revenge (4: 10) the divine Gospel of forgiveness (4: 15).

The Perils of Civilisation

(4: 16–24)

So MAN with his brother's blood on his hands goes out from the place where he has known fellowship with God (Eden), into the wider world, the place of his wandering (Nod), and proceeds to build himself cities and to cultivate the arts and crafts. Presumably the list of names in this passage represents the traditional founders of the various branches of civilised life as they were preserved in the folk-lore of the Hebrew nation. If we regard them as no more than another instalment in a record of origins based on some kind of historical interest, we should have to ask why the editor took the trouble to include these details, since in the next chapter but one all civilisation is going to be wiped out by the Flood.

We should further have to ask why the editor gives us two lists of genealogies, with some apparent duplication, in chs. 4 and 5. It is hardly a sufficient answer to say that ch. 4 contains the J version of primeval history and that ch. 5 contains the P version. That is of course true as far as it goes, but are they both preserved side by side in the Bible simply because the final editor of *Genesis* did not know which was right, or because he regarded them both as ancient and worthy records which he dare not interfere with?

Surely we must give the compiler of *Genesis* more credit for subtlety and theological concern. Notice that it is Cain, the symbol of man's inhumanity to man, who breeds a progeny that builds cities and begins to develop the fabric of civilisation. Yet we cannot regard this as a forthright condemnation of all progress on the part of the Bible, for man is put into the world to develop it and to exploit all its natural resources (1: 28; 2: 15). Nor can we say that it is merely the prejudice of a pastoral people against the world of trade and commerce, for the nomadic shepherd (4: 20) features in the list with the musician and the smith (4: 21, 22).

Rather should we see this as the red light which the Bible places over all human activity. Civilisation and material progress are inevitable but fraught with danger. The evil impulse that Cain could not control, that led him to murder, crouches like a wild beast (4: 7) at the door of civilisation itself. The arts and crafts, commerce and industry, come under the judgment of God and by their very complexity offer greater opportunities for abuse and malpractice. Greed and extortion, dishonesty and deceit, cruelty and oppression are part of the warp and woof of civilised life. They need not be and should not be, but the Bible rightly links the fratricide of Cain with the cutthroat struggle for existence that disfigures human society.

It is no accident that the compiler concludes his suggestive sketch of the lineage of civilisation from Cain with the bloodthirsty hymn of hate of Lamech (4: 23–24). In a day when the best brains of science are dedicated on the one hand to the cure of disease and the prolongation of life, and on the other to the production of the best and quickest means to destroy the world we live in, this biblical insight into the perilous character of man's efforts to build society in the land of Nod, adrift from God, appears sombrely only

too relevant. Such a world is not beyond God's care. Cain still lives under the protective sign of the Cross, for Christ died for all. But the Bible puts a large question mark against all human endeavour that is not directly related to God.

The Way of Salvation
(4: 25 – 5: 32)

THEN INTO this world, the world of Adam as we know it, estranged from God and only too readily following the path first trodden by Adam's eldest son, comes the possibility of renewal and redirection. The symbolism of the birth of a third son to Adam and Eve is highly significant. The first son was a murderer, inheriting the worst of his father's tendency to selfwill and bringing it to its inevitable conclusion. The second, Abel, was his victim, the type of innocent suffering which has paid with blood and tears throughout all human history the price of man's hatred and violence against his brother man.

The third son is to take the place of Abel, to act as a counterpoise to Cain. As we learn from the next few verses, this son bears the image of his father (5: 3) as his father bears the image of God (5: 1). He is called Seth, which means "set" or "appointed", and it is his son Enosh, a name which simply means "man", like "Adam", who is associated with the beginning of worship (4: 26).

It is as if the Bible were saying to us: you are all Adam, on the one hand made in the likeness of God, bearing his image, and on the other hand proud, self willed and disobedient. You are all Cain, joint heirs with him of Adam's failure, bearing the same passionate murderous heart as Cain, sharing his fratricidal guilt, caught up in the toils of a world at best indifferent to God, at worst in open violation of his laws. But you are also all Seth, joint heirs with him of Adam's glory, the glory of the image of God, set apart in the world to witness to God, and to maintain his ways among men.

Seth is in one sense, then, the foundation member of a people of God, a divinely appointed community not outside or apart from the world but within it. This would seem to be indicated by the fact that several of the names of the descendants of Cain in ch. 4 are repeated in the list of the descendants of Seth in ch. 5. We may indeed from the Christian point of view see here the beginning of the idea of a Church, for the Bible goes on to trace the line of Seth through Noah to Abraham, who is regarded by both St. Paul and the author of the epistle to the *Hebrews* as the founder member of the Israel of God, the Christian Church (*Gal.* 3: 7; *Heb.* 6: 13–20).

Seth is no more a historical figure than Adam or Cain. Whether any of the characters in chs. 4 and 5 ever existed is a matter of no moment. The Bible is not concerned here with scientific truth but with theological truth. It is putting before us the world we have to live in, dominated by the figure of Cain and all that he represents. Into this world God introduces a new element, a tiny germ of promise. A son of Adam, who shares his father's weakness but unlike Cain remains true to the image of God in which he is made, however defaced by sin it may be, points the way to the faithful minority who strive against the pull of sin to remain obedient to God. This minority which never fails to bear witness to God throughout the ups and downs of the story that the Old Testament tells, is here symbolically founded in the dim origins of humanity's existence on earth. From the beginning, the Bible would say to us, there has been a choice between the way of life and the way of death. We can follow the path of Cain, and attach ourselves to his hell-bound crew, or we can join the company of Seth, which takes the precarious but rewarding road of Abraham, Moses and the prophets, the road which leads through Christ and his Church to the heavenly Eden, which is our true home.

The list of names in ch. 5, then, is more than a genealogy from the P source which is included because it gives fuller details than the list in ch. 4. Superficially it is just that. The P source with its zeal for factual detail prefers to give us the names and ages of the ten patriarchs from Adam to Noah, who bridge the gap between Creation and Flood. Obviously the ages of the patriarchs are as irrelevant as Archbishop Ussher's date of Creation which was based upon them. The concern of the P source is to divide ancient history into epochs, leading up to the greatest event in

Israel's history, at least in the eyes of the priestly writers, which was the foundation of Solomon's Temple.

Two factors may explain why the total ages of the ten patriarchs come to the formidable number of 8,575 years. One is the common assumption of folk-lore, not peculiar to the Hebrews, that the great men of old lived much longer than ordinary mortals. The other is that there appears to be some correspondence between a Babylonian list of ten kings who lived before the Flood, which as we shall see was described in Babylonian mythology in a form very similar to that in *Genesis*, and this Hebrew list of patriarchs. Probably both lists have some kind of common origin, although the total reigns of the ten Babylonian kings come to 432,000 years!

But the biblical genealogy from Adam to Noah (5: 1–32) does much more than provide us with chronological tables. It was not for this that the priestly editors included it, but rather to assert the unbroken line of witness, to recite the roll of honour of the people of God. The J source gave it in embryonic form in 4: 26. Seth, the man's of God's appointment, is followed by Enosh, the man of worship. The P source in ch. 5 re-emphasises that this is the line of those who are true to the image of God (5: 1, 3), and then proceeds to trace the line through Enoch, who walked with God (5: 24), and Lamech, who is of a different character from his namesake in 4: 24, to Noah, of whom we are told in 6: 8 that he found grace in the eyes of the Lord.

So in a world estranged from God, dominated by the spirit of Cain, the Bible would say to us that right from the beginning of man's story there have been those who responded to God according to their lights, before the further revelation of his purpose to Israel and his final revelation of himself in Christ. There have always been some who have known that man is made in God's image. Through no merit of their own, but by the appointment of God, they are the material which God will use in his plan for the salvation of the rest of the world. But now the Bible turns from this word of hope to contemplate the darker side of our human situation.

The Demonic Power of Evil
(6: 1–4)

THIS STRANGE, abrupt fragment unconnected apparently with what precedes it, seems to transport us into a fairy-tale world which is ill-adjusted to the stark reality of the following verses (6: 5–7). Yet nothing could be more erroneous than to dismiss this passage as a fanciful interlude in which amorous angels rub shoulders with legendary giants.

The background, is, of course, pure mythology, as much as that of Jack-the-giant-killer, Hercules or the Titans. It is true that there is further reference to giants or Nephilim in *Num.* 13: 33, which seems to imply a racial memory of pre-Semitic inhabitants of Canaan of considerably greater stature. This may be a reference to megalithic culture, and it has been suggested that the bedstead of Og, king of Bashan, who is cited as the last of the giants (*Deut.* 3: 11) was in fact a dolmen (see p. 134).

In the earlier part of the passage, however, the theme is one, common to various mythologies, of sexual intercourse taking place between divine beings and mortal creatures. It is of the calibre of the story of Leda and the swan. The sons of God, i.e. angelic beings or demi-gods who are by nature immortal, produce as a result of their irregular union with earthly women, superhuman progeny who constitute the mighty men of old and provide rich material for legend and saga.

But why is this apparent relic of paganism included in the Bible? The ingenious writer of the inter-testamental book of Enoch saw in the story the origin of sin. The evil that is in the world springs in his view from these "fallen" angels who became the denizens of the demon world, and thereafter instigated all the troubles that flesh is heir to (cf. *Jude* 6– p. 534). There is no suggestion in the passage, however, that this was in the mind of the compiler of *Genesis.*

Clearly we are intended to understand 6: 1–4 as a prelude to 6: 5–7. We are being told that the condition of the world that merits its total annihilation, that makes the Creator regret that he ever brought it into being, is more than the product of human waywardness. The whole cosmos is at loggerheads with God. Evil has become endemic, a monstrous, supernatural, all-pervasive pollution. The atmosphere is saturated with it. There is no escaping it.

The sin of the world is not the sum total of the peccadilloes of its inhabitants. There is a poison in the heart of it which suffuses and taints every aspect of life, so that nothing that man can do is pure or holy. His best intentions are thwarted, his noblest aspirations are stillborn. He builds mighty empires which crash in ruins. Power corrupts the high-souled idealist. Cynicism dogs the footsteps of the reformer.

It is not simply that our self-righteousness debases our piety or that our smugness defeats our charity, our state is far more perilous. We are all caught up in the paradox of progress and civilisation, so that things good in themselves like national pride, scientific development, expansion of trade, development of backward countries, and improvement of living standards bring as many curses as blessings in their train, if they do not end in total disaster for all whom they seek to benefit.

It is this desperate canker at the heart of all human activity, to which we can give no other name than a demonic corruption of the whole fabric of existence, which this myth of the fallen angels seeks to express. The Bible offers no metaphysical explanation. Modern psychology may attempt to account for it, partially at best, with the concept of the unconscious, and the accumulation of wrong choices which any society and each member of it has to accept as a legacy from the past. The Bible chooses to express it in this mysterious piece of symbolism, whose very obscurity serves only to enhance the truth of its insight.

We must spend our days, make our plans and build our brave new world with the certainty that our best endeavours will end in disaster, because of the demonic forces which threaten at every moment to engulf us. The "men of renown", supermen, self-styled saviours of society, the Napoleons, Hitlers and Stalins, thrown up by history because of our failures, serve their countries and at the same time destroy them because of this same demonic power which possesses them.

It is to man in this hapless plight that the Bible speaks. But it demands that first we recognise ourselves as we are and the world as it is, that we see in desperation and disillusionment the hopelessness of our case. Man cannot save himself: the world cannot save itself. No human panaceas, educational, scientific or social, can remedy our situation for we have "to struggle not with blood and flesh but with . . . the potentates of the dark present, the spirit-forces of evil in the heavenly sphere" (*Eph.* 6: 12).

The Judgment of God on the World

(6: 5–7)

LEFT TO itself the world merits nothing less than destruction. No more realistic words have ever been spoken about human kind than those in 6: 5, "the wickedness of man . . . great in the earth: and . . . every imagination of the thoughts of his heart . . . only evil continually". Self-willed, murderous, diabolical—man's character has been sketched in the

stories of Adam, Cain and the Nephilim. Now it is summed up trenchantly in words which permit of no evasion. Has such a creature the right to live, and to enjoy the good earth upon which God has placed him?

The answer of the Bible is: No. It pictures God as grown weary of man and his devilries, grieved and sick at heart to see how man has distorted the image of his Maker, how he has failed to realise God's purpose in Creation. The Bible makes no bones about it. Man deserves to be written off, lock, stock and barrel, and God is prepared to do it. There is only one thing that makes him stay his hand, of which the Bible now proceeds to tell us.

The One and the Many

(6: 8–9)

NOAH HAS a twofold significance in the prologue. First, he is presented as standing in the direct line of the saving community, the people of God in Christ, who see themselves in the biblical imagery as members of a fellowship that traces its ancestry from the New Testament back into the Old Testament; from the book of Acts, through the apostles, to Isaiah's faithful remnant and Abraham, and beyond that to the symbolic figures of Shem, Noah, Enoch and Seth.

Noah is neither a Christian nor a Jew. He belongs to the prologue, not to the Acts of God, in his plan for the salvation of the world through Israel. But as the symbol of the righteous man, who seeks to practice the obedience of God according to the law written in his heart (*Rom.* 2: 15), who trusts in God despite all appearances to the contrary (*Heb.* 11: 7), and who endeavours to be true to the image of God which all men bear, he is regarded by the Bible as belonging by right to the company of God's people. We may think of him in this sense as the type of the devout and charitable man in any religion outside the Hebrew-Christian tradition, whether Hindu, Mohammedan or Buddhist.

But in another sense Noah represents a profound and important element in biblical theology. God deems mankind worthy of extinction, but he makes a new beginning possible by means of one good man. Just as he is prepared to spare the infamous city of Sodom if but ten righteous men be found in it (*Gen.* 18: 23–32), so we can see here the biblical principle whereby the obedience of one is the means of salvation for many, a concept which lies at the heart of our Lord's redeeming sacrifice.

The significance of the story of the ark does not lie in the realm of history but of theology. Mankind may be corrupt and deserving of nothing but to be blotted out, but the mercy of God is such that for the sake of one good man the race is granted a second chance. For Noah's sake his family is spared, and the eight souls who survive the Deluge in the ark to witness to God's name, typify not only the salvation from the world which the Church offers to all but also, beyond that, the redemptive power of the Church in the midst of the world. (Cf. *I Pet.* 3: 20–21.)

The Flood
(6: 10 – 8: 20)

IT SHOULD hardly be necessary to repeat that in the prologue we are dealing with stories, parables, symbols and images and not with history. The details, therefore, of the measurements of the ark, the cubic capacity of its interior in relation to the housing and feeding of its numerous and varied occupants, the problem of the collection of the animals before the Flood and their redistribution after it, are as irrelevant as the periodic canards which claim that the skeletonic framework of the ark has been found on some Armenian mountain.

The Flood story is the Hebrew version of a much older Babylonian myth, which relates the adventures in similar terms and in almost exact parallel of one Utnapishtim, a Babylonian worthy who is warned by the god Ea of an impending deluge, builds an ark and is saved in the same manner as Noah. The details of the story as contained in the Babylonian epic of Gilgamesh can be found in any of the archaeological textbooks. There are major differences in the Hebrew version in respect of the religious and moral implications. Unlike the Babylonian tale it has moreover an outspokenly monotheistic tone. But basically the *Genesis* story is taken from the common fund of Near Eastern tradition and is used by the biblical writers in characteristic fashion to teach a religious lesson.

Evidence was found at Ur in 1929 by Sir Leonard Woolley, that a flood of some magnitude had covered that part of Mesopotamia in early times, possibly about 4000 B.C. It would seem as if the Persian Gulf had for a time—perhaps in association with earth subsidence or other seismic activity —encroached on the land at its northern end and submerged previously existing civilisation there. Archaeological evidence in Egypt, however, produces an unbroken record of civilisation throughout this period so that the flood was obviously a local one. If we were to take the *Genesis* story literally we should have to allow for the submersion of the whole earth to a depth of five miles. No doubt the story of the Flood, whether in its Babylonian or Hebrew version, goes back to this ancient occurrence, but in its present form it has lost contact with history entirely.

In the narrative there are certain inconsistencies, e.g. in the numbers of clean and unclean animals which enter the ark (cf. 6: 19–20 and 7: 14–15 with 7: 2–3) or in the length of time that the Flood lasted (cf. 7: 11 and 8: 14 with 7: 12; 8: 10, 12). These are due to the fact that the editor of *Genesis* has combined the J tradition with the P tradition, interweaving their versions which differ in these and other incidental respects.

The story should not be read as an allegory, as if every item in it had some religious significance. It should be read as a whole, and treated as a dramatic and splendid tale which vividly portrays the total annihilation of the human race as a judgment upon its corruption, but which points through the divine preservation of Noah and his sons to the sequel which is now to be related, and which indeed is the real point that the story is being used to illustrate.

God's Covenant with Mankind (8: 21 – 9: 17)

IN 4: 15 we saw the first suggestion that despite man's perversity God still cares for him. Cain's murderous act is punished but his life is spared. This merciful attitude is, however, misunderstood and abused. The bloodthirsty song of Lamech (4: 23–24) and the parable of the Nephilim (6: 1–4) show humanity in its rake's progress turning its back on God, presuming on his leniency, and marching steadily downhill to perdition until even the merciful Creator has had more than he can stomach. Instead of repenting of his sins in face of God's clemency, man exploits it. He has to be shown that God is in earnest about sin, that he is no sentimental heavenly Father Christmas.

The point of the Flood story is not that mankind was once obliterated and then given a fresh start. To say that would be to bring the Bible down to the level of Greek mythology. The Flood is the symbol of God's timeless judgment on us as we are, twentieth-century man no less than man in the ancient world, a foreshadowing in our Lord's mind of the final Assize which we must all face (*Matt.* 24: 37–39). Extinction is what we deserve and what man has always deserved. That we are not destroyed is due only to the fact that there are some Noahs n every age, who "walk with God" and make the human race worthy of preservation.

In the *Genesis* story God makes a covenant with Noah, which like all the biblical covenants is an act of God's pure grace by which he involves himself with man, taking upon himself obligations and laying obligations on man. God for his part recognises that man is naturally prone to evil (8: 21), and that the high purpose of Creation is inevitably frustrated by man's wrong use of his freedom. He will nevertheless accept man on these terms and permit him to exist, providing for him the beauty of an ordered universe and a generous guarantee of the necessities of life (8: 22).

He will recognise that in his present fallen state man must kill in order to live, and that a relationship of fear must exist between the natural world and human beings (9: 2–3). The fellowship of man and beast that God had intended (1: 29–30) is not yet possible (cf. *Isa.* 11: 6). Furthermore man must now come under the rule of law. He cannot be trusted to respect his neighbour's rights. He must therefore be kept on the straight path by fear of the consequences. The man who takes his brother's life must henceforth pay for it with his own (9: 6).

So the Bible brings us face to face with the world that we know. It is not the world as the Creator intended it to be, but it is the kind of world that man's abuse of his freedom has made inevitable. It is not a world where man responds to God and to his neigh-

bour in the spontaneous relationship which God purposed, but a grey world of second-bests, a world where compromise and self-interest are involved in every action. The moral ambiguities of politics, the tyranny of suspicion and fear, the necessity for penal laws, the machinery of government, all indeed that goes to make up the fabric of civilised life is summed up in the symbolism of this covenant with Noah. But for the existence of the minority represented by Noah there would be no life on the planet at all. For his sake by the mercy of God life is allowed to go on, but it is a fallen world of tarnished men who are only prevented from destroying each other by fear of retribution.

So the Bible with deft sure touch puts life as we know it in its proper perspective. We have lost our chance of Paradise in this world, and we are condemned by our own persistent distortion of the image of God to live in the half-light of frustrated hopes. But let us not imagine that this is the Bible's last word. The covenant with Noah is like all God's covenants, a covenant of grace. It is an unmerited favour to a world that has gone sour and that has rottenness at its heart. The message of the rainbow (9: 13) is a vivid promise of better things to come. It takes the place of the war-bow, the symbol of God's vengeance. It is the sign of God's mercy when the Deluge of his Judgment is over, the mark of the covenant of God's peace (*Isa.* 54: 9–10).

As the symbol of this first

covenant with mankind it expresses God's providential care for "every living creature of all flesh" (9: 15), and his recognition of the value of ordinary human decency as symbolised by Noah. But God cannot be content with a created world that is doomed to live permanently at odds with itself, restrained only by the rule of law and the authority of government. It was not for this that he created man. If man cannot find his way back to God by himself he must be shown the way, and indeed the whole story of the Bible from *Genesis* 12 onwards tells us how God has done that very thing.

So the covenant with Noah points forward to the succession of covenants by which the Bible indicates God's acts to bring men back to the status of sonship which he had destined for them from the beginning. The Bible now shows us, and our own experience confirms it, that without such direct intervention by God in our affairs a society founded even on the virtues of a Noah has little future.

The Drunkenness of Noah

(9: 18–29)

THE BIBLE would not for a moment suggest that Noah or the type that he represents is "naturally" good. Noah like everyone else comes under the condemnation of 8: 21. But he does represent those in all ages who are true to the image of God which is in every man, and who live by the light of conscience. He is the "preacher of righteous-

ness" of *II Pet.* 2: 5. The Bible reminds us that it is God who has made all such men, and has revealed something of himself and his purpose to them, and given them some sense of the difference between right and wrong. They have responded to what they have understood of that revelation and for this, like Noah, they find favour with God. The Bible now seeks to show us in this and the following parable (11: 1–9), that however worthwhile such "natural" goodness may be, man's response to general revelation of this kind is not enough to save a fallen world.

It cannot have been carelessness on the part of the compiler of *Genesis* which made him introduce at this point a story which has so many loose ends. Clearly this is a fragment of folk-lore—or perhaps two independent fragments loosely woven together—which is designed to account for Israel's later occupation of the land of Canaan and dominance over its inhabitants. It explains why Shem, the eponymous ancestor of the Semites, of whom the Hebrews formed a part, is blessed, while Canaan, regarded here as the grandson of Noah, is cursed.

But it is not merely for this reason that the story is included here. The curse upon Canaan and the blessing upon Israel could have been represented in a variety of ways without making it depend upon what Luther called this "apparently foolish and utterly useless story" of Noah's drunkenness. The Christian Fathers, or at any rate some of them, fled from its unedifying details and chose to regard it as an allegory of Christ's Passion. Christ drank the cup of bitterness and died among his own people (in his tent). His death (nakedness) was foolishness to the unbelievers (Ham), but the power and wisdom of God to "them that are called, both Jew and Greek" (Shem and Japheth). This is far-fetched exegesis indeed.

More akin to the mind and times of the Old Testament is the interpretation which would connect this story with the drunken debauchery which was part of the Canaanite fertility-cults to which Israel later succumbed. In representing Noah's degradation the story is both prophetic and condemnatory. All this is no doubt true.

But we must ask further why is the "preacher of righteousness" displayed in this unattractive role after he has been the means of ensuring that mankind should not be exterminated. Surely it is not just to emphasise that even the virtuous are fallible, but to point in symbolic form to the need for the special revelation which will be given to the sons of Shem beginning with Abraham.

If we are to take Noah as the symbol of the just man within the wide covenant that embraces all mankind, this story must be included at this point to illustrate the limitations of even the best efforts of secular society to develop its resources, without the guidance of God's special revelation through prophet, psalmist and above all, for Christians, through his Son. Noah as an individual behaves no worse than many Jews and many

Christians. The symbolism is, however, not concerned with individual folly but is concerned to illustrate the inevitable failure of any human undertaking which is not directly inspired by the revelation of God's will as contained in holy scripture.

It is no accident that Noah's activity as the supposed originator of viticulture links up rather with that of the progeny of Cain, the founders of the various arts and crafts of civilisation, who inherited the seamy side of their ancestor's character (see pp. 25–26). For the suggestion here is that the world of Noah is still the old world of Cain under a new name, still prone to abuse God's good gifts, still unable to escape the sorry consequences of its own inner weakness and the perversity of human nature.

Noah, the husbandman, plants a vineyard which produces wine intended to gladden the heart of man (*Ps.* 104: 15). But because of man's radical deformity of nature a thing good in itself is twisted into something depraved and revolting. Intoxication and indecency may be taken as examples of the abuse of any gift of God, such as alcohol or the sex instinct, which is characteristic of a society which knows no higher motive than fear of the consequences.

The Bible is showing us here that life under the covenant of Noah, governed by the rule of law and the principle of self-preservation, is an inadequate foundation on which to build a society of mature and responsible men and women, who are at least beginning to measure up to the status of sonship to God for which they were created. Some may feel that not the least significant feature of this unlikely incident, involving Noah and his sons, is the suggestion at this early stage that the descendants of Japheth, i.e. what we now know as western civilisation, should yet be brought to the knowledge of the truth by Israel, the descendants of Shem, the one who knows the name (Hebrew—shem) i.e. the nature, of God (9: 27).

The World and its Peoples
(10: 1-32)

FROM this point until the end of the prologue (11: 32) the compiler's main interest is to bridge the gap between Noah and Abraham. He has demonstrated in the parable of Noah's drunkenness the inadequacy of the Noachic covenant, and he will do so further in the parable of the Tower of Babel (11: 1-9). The relationship between God and man, and between man and his neighbour, as symbolised by the covenant with Noah, is sufficient to maintain human society in equilibrium, to guarantee its future and to evoke some kind of civilised behaviour. But God is not content. He must have the deeper response of faith and love on the part of man to match his own unbounded lovingkindness. Nothing less than the return of wayward man in repentance and renewal to his Creator, like the Prodigal Son (*Luke* 15: 11-32), will fulfil the original design of a loving Father.

But unlike the Prodigal, man has as yet no clear picture of the Father to whom he must return. He cannot "come to himself" until he has learned "the breadth and length and depth and height" of God's love (*Eph.* 3: 18). This he cannot do because of the perversity of his nature. God himself must intervene and show him the way.

We may take as a parallel, for indeed it is the same biblical pattern, our Lord's public ministry in Galilee, where when he had found to his sorrow that both he himself and his mission were largely misunderstood, he took the Twelve apart and instructed them intensively, so far as they were able to grasp it, in the nature of his Messiahship, teaching them how alone men could be brought into loving obedience to himself. Beginning with the Twelve as a nucleus, he would build his Church and through his Church bring the whole world to God.

So in these chapters of *Genesis* the divine plan is unfolded. Out of the races of mankind God will select one group, out of this group one tribe, out of this tribe one man, and Abraham, the son of Terah will be chosen as the foundation member of a community which God will make his own. They are to be the nucleus of a people of God to whom God will reveal his will and purpose. It will be their task and mission to bring the light of the knowledge of God into a sin-darkened world, and to win back that world for God.

They will be shown amid the changes and chances of life and in the ups and downs of history what constitutes the true obedience of God. With them he will make new covenants which deepen the relationship between himself and this people that he has chosen to be his special instrument of revelation. As the story of the Old Testament unfolds we shall see how once again the perversity of man's nature frustrates God's plan of salvation, and how in the end, so great is God's love to man and so strong his will to save him from the consequences of his folly that he sends his own Son to reconcile the world to himself.

These two chapters of genealogy therefore (10–11) are no mere happy hunting ground for archaeological or anthropological research. They are consciously setting the stage for the first act of the drama when God summons Abraham from Ur of the Chaldees to be the basis of his first move to break the power of evil that still, even after the judgment of the Flood, holds sway in the hearts of men.

In *Gen.* 10, prior to the singling out of God's chosen people, we are given a picture of the repopulation of the earth after the Flood, in which the three sons of Noah are represented as the ancestors of the three great ethnic groups which were known to the Hebrews. Presumably this information, as well as the sub-division of these groups, came to them through trade and war. It would seem that the P tradition here depends on older material, perhaps dating from about 900 B.C. It is astonishing that at this early date the scope of Hebrew knowledge was so

extensive. The contents of this chapter may thus be said to represent the geography and ethnology of the ancient world as known to the Hebrews at that period, the nations, tribes and places being personified as descendants of Noah.

Generally mankind is divided into three ethnic groups, the Hamites, representing roughly the African peoples, the Japhethites, covering Asia Minor and beyond to the north, and the Shemites representing the peoples of the Near East. These three racial types are then divided into nations, called here "sons", and these nations in turn are broken down into tribes or towns, represented as "grandsons". The "world" is bounded by Armenia in the north, Ethiopia in the south, Iran in the east and Greece in the west. Tarshish, possibly Tartessus in Spain, is here as always in the Bible a vague shadowy outpost of civilisation in the far west (10: 4; cf. *Jonah* 1: 3). Even within this area we are given far from an exhaustive list of countries and peoples, and there are various dubious allocations. The list has some antiquarian interest but little scientific value.

From a theological point of view, however, the purpose of its inclusion here is that Noah's world is still God's world. It is not beyond his providence. He may select the line of Shem for his special revelation but all the nations are in his care also. It is for their sake that Israel is chosen. Even Nimrod (10: 8–10) who is here represented as the ancestor of the Assyrians and Babylonians, and who as a "mighty hunter" and a "mighty one in the earth" perfectly presages the war-lords of these empires in later days, is described as exhibiting his prowess "before the Lord".

The Tower of Babel
(11: 1–9)

THEN, having paved the way for the choice of Abraham, the descendant of Shem (11: 10–32), the compiler inserts the highly significant parable of the Tower of Babel. Superficially this would appear to be a little story from the J tradition which accounts for the origin of different languages and the name of the city of Babylon. But we have already been told in the previous chapter that the nations had their own tongues (10: 5, 31), and Babylon has been accounted for (10: 10). Apart then from the fact that no one would now accept this incident as a satisfactory explanation of the origin of languages, it is quite clear that once more the Bible is not teaching science but theology.

It is indeed a parable of the utmost significance and in a sense the climax of the prologue. The theme is not new, it is basically the same as that of the story of the Fall : man's defiance of God. But here the setting is amid the bricks and mortar of city life instead of the idyllic greenery of Eden. For the nomadic Hebrews, migrants from the desert, the city states of Babylonia (Shinar) represented the acme of cultured life, and we can detect behind this tale the first impact which these ancient centres

of civilisation must have made upon pastoral tribesmen. Doubtless too behind the figure of the tower lies the reality of one of the many ziggurats, or temple towers, which studded the Mesopotamian plain in ancient times. These artificial mounds crowned with their sanctuaries must have been visible for miles around. Perhaps it was an unfinished or ruined ziggurat that formed the basis for the story.

In its present form, however, and particularly from its position in the prologue, it is designed like the story of the Drunkenness of Noah to be a critique of all man's attempts to build up a civilisation without reference to God. Mankind is represented as being on the march. Civilisation is advancing (11: 2). Man's inventive genius is symbolised by his discovery of the art of building with manufactured bricks and bitumen (slime), instead of using the more primitive natural stones (11: 3).

But where does man's inventiveness lead him? Not to build to the glory of God but to the glory of man. A true son of Adam, he wants to be God himself. Man wants to run the world in his own way. He wants to put himself at the centre of his civilisation on a pedestal inscribed with his name: "Glory to MAN in the highest" (11: 4). But there can be only one God and one Creator. Man is a creature and his destiny is to seek to know the will of God and in humility to be obedient to it.

So in the story God comes down in judgment upon man for his presumption and overrules his schemes and plans. Man's common purpose becomes a wrangle of warring interests. Confused babbling replaces intelligent planning. Chaos and disorder reign where harmony and understanding should have prevailed. Man can no longer co-operate with his neighbour and Utopia is stillborn (11: 5–9).

There is no doubt that in introducing the name of Babylon (Babel) and identifying it with this mythical city, the Bible intends us to understand under that name the fine flower of any secular civilisation. It was not for the beauty of its avenues, its palaces or its temples that the biblical writers so often mentioned Babylon. They saw underneath its beauty the cruelty and oppression, the violence and vice upon which it was built and by which it was sustained in power. In the New Testament it is a synonym for Imperial Rome (*I Pet.* 5: 13; *Rev.* 18). Likewise there is no doubt that by the confusion of tongues whereby men could no longer understand each other's speech, we are meant to see a symptom of the deeper disharmony that prevents unity and common understanding, when civilisation sets itself the task of building up its fabric in disregard or defiance of God.

The parable is thus the final indictment of any society, in Noah's world or in the twentieth century, capitalist or communist, which seeks to build its prosperity without reference to God's will. Its noblest endeavours are bound to fail and its high-souled idealism is doomed to vanish in face of the harsh reality of man's own twisted nature. Whatever he sets his hand to becomes distorted by

his lust for power, by his uncontrollable vanity and overweening pride. The demonic element in him hurtles him on to self-destruction. The dice are loaded against him not by his stars or by fate or by God, but by his own corrupt will.

The New Testament proclaims the only solution in the parable of the common language at Pentecost (*Acts* 2: 1–13) which is in effect the Tower of Babel turned upside down. Whereas by the pride of man and his perversity he is unable to understand his neighbour and to co-operate with him in building up a civilisation that will last, by the power of the Spirit the curse of Babel is reversed, and men of all nations find themselves bound by a common understanding of God's will in Christ. But in the dispensation of God that stage in the divine plan lies far ahead and man must learn through Israel's experience the bitter truth about himself. So in the last few verses of this chapter the Bible turns our thoughts towards God's design to save us from ourselves by the choice of Abraham.

The Choice of Abraham
(11: 10–32)

IT is difficult to say at which point in this genealogical list we first make contact with fully historical characters. Shem (11: 10) obviously stands for the racial group of Semites to which Israel belonged, just as Eber (11: 14) represents the particular subdivision of that group, Hebrews, of which the people of the Old Testament story formed a part.

No doubt some of the names of Abraham's immediate ancestors were handed down by tradition but it is impossible to say whether these names imply tribes, cities or individual persons. Part of the difficulty lies in the Old Testament conception of "corporate personality" which is unfamiliar to western minds. The Hebrews thought of individuals as being so closely bound up with the existence of their tribe, city or nation that it is not always easy to say whether the Bible is referring to a single person or to the unit of which he formed part.

Similarly there is no certainty as to the place of origin of the people of the Old Testament. They were clearly of Semitic stock, known as Hebrews, and formed part of the nomadic peoples who from time immemorial had herded their sheep and cattle in the Near Eastern desert. Such arid scrubland provided no more than a marginal existence for these bedouin tribes, in contrast to which the well-watered lands of Mesopotamia, Palestine and Egypt, together constituting the Fertile Crescent, had always proved a tempting bait to small or large migrations of nomads.

A steady succession of such migrations in the days before biblical history begins had filled the Fertile Crescent with a mixed population who had built up a high standard of civilisation in Mesopotamia and the Levant. When the Hebrews appear first on the stage of history about 2000 B.C. they constitute in comparison with the established commercial and cultural life of their neighbours a nomadic tribal group of a relatively primitive character. It is not known whether they formed part of a migration which had drifted into the Fertile Crescent from Arabia or whether they originally came from the east or from the north, but when they emerge into the light of day they are settled near the ancient Babylonian city of Ur in modern Iraq (11: 28) over 100 miles from the top of the Persian Gulf.

It is highly unlikely that they lived in the city itself, although local guides to the ruins of Ur confidently point out Abraham's house, since the whole background of the subsequent narrative of their fortunes suggests a purely pastoral origin. Indeed there is some reason to believe that the tradition linking their early days with Ur may be wrong, since Haran, in north-west Mesopotamia, was the scene of the earliest stage of their existence of which we have any reliable record (11: 32).

A Semitic tribe of unknown origin, appearing for the first time in history in what is now the Kurdistan region of Turkey, is thus at the end of the prologue introduced as God's choice to be recipients of his special revelation of himself and his purpose and to be the means whereby he will bring mankind back to himself. "How odd of God to choose the Jews!" In human terms the choice is as inexplicable and improbable as that God's fullest revelation of himself should have come in a village carpenter, and that his Church should have been founded on a dozen obscure Galileans, mostly fishermen.

History and Interpretation

WHATEVER uncertainty there may be about the historicity of Abraham's ancestors and many of his descendants, there can be little doubt that Abraham himself was a real person. It is difficult not to feel as we read these chapters of *Genesis* 12–50 that we are now in an entirely different atmosphere from that of *Gen.* 1–11. We have passed from a description of the world as God intended it to be and as man has in fact made it, a picture conveyed in story, symbol and poetic image, to a relatively sober account of the selection of a historical person, Abraham, to be the founder-member of a historical community, the people of Israel, who are destined to be the bearers of God's revelation to the world.

Admittedly there is no archaeological evidence for the existence of Abraham or indeed of any of the patriarchs who follow him, and some scholars would claim that we do not reach solid historical ground until the time of Moses and the Exodus. Admittedly too the earliest written records of Israel's history of which we have any knowledge date from about a thousand years later than Abraham, and the present form of the narratives as we find them in *Genesis* dates from several centuries later still. Clearly then we must not expect to find historical accuracy in the

modern sense in these chapters, either in the incidents or in the dialogues. Stories of the great men of the past grow in the telling, recorded conversations depend on the inspired imagination of the story-teller, and legends come to be attached to sanctuaries and local place-names.

On the other hand let us not forget the retentive memories of oriental story-tellers or the controlling influence of the community acting as a brake on any deviation from the accepted form of a story. These biblical narratives of Abraham and the later patriarchs were handed down by oral tradition through the centuries, before the Hebrews had occasion to write a connected story of God's providential ordering of their early fortunes. Traditions of this kind preserved by priests at local shrines or recounted by professional story-tellers would in all probability vary their form but little.

We shall err on the side of caution if we say that historically speaking the rest of *Genesis* from ch. 12–50 gives us in bold outline the earliest stage of Israel's history as it was known in the days of the monarchy about 1000 B.C. Abraham, Isaac, Jacob and Joseph at least are recognisably varied characters, and we are given a sufficiently clear impression of each of them to think of them as real persons, although we cannot vouch for the historicity of any of the stories that are attached to their names or any of the words they are supposed to have uttered. No doubt many of the other characters in the narratives are likewise historical but it is not always easy to tell whether we are reading personal history or tribal history.

Similarly the general movement of the tribe of Abraham from Mesopotamia into Canaan, its pastoral mode of life among the uplands of that country during several centuries, and the ultimate migration into Egypt of at least part of the people seems reasonably certain. Archaeological discoveries in the area have confirmed the general background of social and economic conditions which the narratives reflect.

But it is not for this bare framework that we read the Bible, and it was not to provide us with a textbook of ancient history that the Bible was written. When the authors of the book of *Genesis* collected and edited these stories of their early days as a nomadic tribe, it was with the conviction that from the moment that their ancestor Abraham had been moved to leave Haran and to set out on his journey to Canaan, the hand of God had been upon him and upon the life of the people he founded.

Whatever information the Bible gives us that is not directly concerned with this call of God and response of Abraham and his descendants is incidental. Stories and conversations are recorded for their religious and moral significance, and we cannot hope to disentangle the historical basis from the religious interpretation. This, however, should not unduly alarm us, because although the revelation of God recorded in the Bible is a historical revelation, and the Acts of God take place on the plane of history, the significance of these acts can only be conveyed by the insights of the theological commentator, in this case the priests and prophets of Israel who were responsible for the writing of the Pentateuch.

The Call of Abraham
(12: 1–3)

WITH THE call of Abraham the curtain rings up on Act I of the divine drama. The stage has been set by the prologue. Our human situation has been depicted in all its desperate need. There is no way out for the world's teeming millions unless God provides it. The message of the Bible is that God has created the way. Beginning with Abraham he will build up a community, the Israel of God, whose task it will be to witness to him in the world. It will never be synonymous with the nation of Israel, because even the people of God's choice share in the common failure of mankind. But there will never be lacking within the historical national group that calls itself Israel at least a few who will respond to God as Abraham responded, and who will bear the name of God on their hearts throughout the centuries that lie ahead in the story that the Old Testament will tell.

As Christians we must recognise that the Old Testament is our story but we must at once add the qualification that not all of it is our story. If the Old Testament held the final answer to the world's plight there would have been no place for Christ and his Church. God's Messiah came and was rejected by Israel as a nation, but the line of Abraham's obedience and response to God was continued by the twelve Israelites whom the Messiah chose to be his disciples, and upon whom he founded the new Israel, the Christian Church. Through their witness the Church expanded and the Gospel has been proclaimed to the whole world, so that Jews and Gentiles together form the Israel of God, of which Abraham was the founder, inheriting the promises made to him and the mission appointed for him, together with the ever deepening insights into the wisdom and love of God which were given to his successors.

Accordingly, if as Christians we seek to enter into our heritage it must be with the recognition that the Bible is one continuous story from *Genesis* to *Revelation*. We must not regard the Old Testament in Carlyle's phrase as "Hebrew old clothes" but as the preparation for and prelude to the Gospel, as the promise of which we know the fulfilment. As participators in Act III of the divine drama we must not treat these early chapters of our own story as a quarry for archaeological or anthropological research. There is undoubtedly a vast field of interesting and fruitful study for the ancient historian and the archaeologist in the stories of patriarchs, priests and kings. But as members of the people of God, we must look to the Old Testament to give us rather foreshadowings of the Gospel, evidence of the same pattern of God's saving activity in the world, embryonic tokens of the same themes as we have come to know in the fulness of his revelation of himself through Christ.

Since as a fact of history the people of the Old Testament as a whole rejected the Gospel, and Jesus and his disciples judged that many beliefs and practices in the Old Testament had been superseded by the Gospel, much that we find in its pages must have little or no direct value for Christian people. It is therefore a mistaken devotion which would seek to find in every incident and saying in the Old Testament some direct bearing upon Christ and the Church. If Christ is the true Vine whose roots stretch down into the deep soil of Israel's past, it is equally true that many of the lower branches are dead wood which were cut off by the Lord himself. Let us not be afraid to acknowledge the presence in the Old Testament of much that has a relevance only for practising Jews or for literary and historical critics.

In reading the Old Testament as Christians, that is as participators in the same drama, we must be guided by the writers of the New Testament and by our Lord himself. We cannot go far wrong if we allow ourselves to be led by Paul and the other New Testament writers to single out for our special attention those themes, incidents and words of the Old Testament which through their knowledge of the mind of Jesus and his purpose for his Church, the New Testament writers reckoned to be of paramount significance. We shall thus study the Old Testament story, beginning with the call of Abraham, not as if we were investigating the origin and development of some Near Eastern cult, but retrospectively from the standpoint of the Church today.

We shall expect to find, since it is all part of God's revelation of himself to us, perceptions of the same truth about God and ourselves as we already know from the Gospel, albeit often imperfectly understood or expressed. We shall expect to find the same mixture of saints and sinners, and saints who are also sinners, as we find in the New Testament and in the life of the Church. Remembering that the God of the Old Testament Church is also the God and Father of our Lord Jesus Christ, and that the final editors of the Old Testament were no primitive Levantine nomads, but highly trained theologians who could use simple tales to convey profound and startling insights into the mysteries of God's way with men, we shall not dismiss the stories of the patriarchs as fragments of ancient folk-lore, but try to see them as the Old Testament compilers saw them, as vehicles of some aspect of God's revelation, and above all as the New Testament writers saw them as harbingers of Gospel truth.

For Christians, therefore, as for Jews, the meaning of Abraham's departure from Haran and his migration with his tribe into the land of Canaan is not exhausted by saying that he was responding to economic pressures, and the terms of God's promise to him are not explained by attributing them to the wishful thinking of a landless nomad. Nor does it concern us

as twentieth-century Christians what precisely was the conception of God held by a Semitic sheikh of the second millennium B.C. What does concern us is that both St. Paul and the author of the epistle to the *Hebrews* follow the writer of *Genesis* in regarding this departure of Abraham from Haran as the historical beginning of the mission of Israel, old and new, to be a people of God and a means of blessing for the whole world.

Here is the man, "the father of all" (*Rom.* 4: 16), through whom God purposed to save mankind. Summoned by God to a high destiny, that of being the founder of a great community through which new life and hope would come to all the "families of the earth", this landless, childless man went out "not knowing whither he went" (*Heb.* 11: 8), trusting only in the God who had bidden him, becoming thereby through his obedient faith the kind of man on whom God could build his Church. Into a world which lay under the curse of Adam, a world unable to extricate itself from the toils of its own making, God sends the possibility of the renewal of its life through his Church.

Abraham becomes the type of those in all ages of the Church's history who live in the world but are not content with things as they are or with themselves as they are. They listen to the voice of God which calls them back to him and dedicate themselves to his service and the service of their fellow men. Unlike the men in the story of the Tower of Babel they do not seek to build a city or a civilisation to the glory of man, for they have responded to a call which makes them, like Abraham, landless wanderers in this world. They know that everything built by man's misguided efforts is bound to topple and crash, so they look for "a city which hath foundations, whose builder and maker is God" (*Heb.* 11: 10).

The Promised Land

(12: 4–14: 24)

ABRAHAM, then, sets out into the unknown, in effect the first missionary of the Church, leading his tribe to the land of the promise. Canaan, the country to which he was guided, and which he was told was to be the land of God's people (12: 7) was already occupied by a native pagan population. But he consecrates it to God as the Holy Land for all time by building altars and worshipping the true God there. In so doing he symbolically claims the whole earth for God to be his Holy Land (12: 4–9).

We may imagine Abraham and his tribe, camping in the hill country of Canaan, unmolested by the inhabitants who cling to the more civilised cities of the plain. In true nomadic fashion they settled with their flocks and herds for some time in each place, gradually moving southward to fresh pastures. Famine, the perennial problem of the nomad, drives them down into Egypt, with its rich Nile lands, the granary of the ancient Near East.

The point of the story in 12: 10–20 which reflects no credit upon Abraham, and is repeated in the same form but with different background in chs. 20 and 26, is theological. Sarai or Sarah, Abraham's wife, is passed off as his sister and becomes an inmate of the pharaoh's harem. Abraham is compensated with material possessions. The sequel in the story conveys in a vivid way that God has determined that the promise must be fulfilled and that nothing must be allowed to prevent that. Thus Abraham must not be killed by concupiscent Egyptians and Sarah must not be permitted to remain in the pharaoh's harem. The people of God must be preserved and delivered from the threat of extinction, a pattern which is to be repeated at the Exodus and again in the experience of the Holy Family (cf. *Matt.* 2: 13–15).

A sombre note is introduced in ch. 13 where Abraham and his nephew Lot decide to separate. Lot is given the choice of territory in which to pasture his sheep and cattle, and selects the rich lands of the Jordan plain. Abraham is left with the highland hills, but this becomes the heart of the land of the promise, whereas Lot's preference for the alluring prosperity of the land adjacent to the cities of the plain leads him to pitch his tent "towards Sodom", a choice which he will live to regret (ch. 19).

We may leave to the experts the identification of the participants in the campaign of which we have a glimpse in ch. 14, in which Abraham emerges as Lot's rescuer (14: 12–16) and a disinterested ally (14: 21–24). This irruption of world politics into Palestine, involving its petty kings or chieftains, presages the role that the land of the promise will play throughout biblical history. A pawn in the game that is played consistently by its more powerful neighbours, the Holy Land is to be the scene of an unending series of wars, invasions, rebellions and civil strife.

But at the heart of this narrative, as it were amid the clash of arms, comes the strange meeting between Abraham and Melchizedek (14: 18–20). Here for the first time we encounter Jerusalem, the holy city, around which so much of the biblical story revolves. This is to be the city of David, the home of the Temple, the scene of the Crucifixion and Resurrection. The psalmists will sing of Zion as the very dwelling place of God and in the epilogue to the Acts of God, the book of *Revelation*, when the writer thinks of the consummation of God's purpose at the end of time it is in terms of a New Jerusalem coming down from heaven (*Rev.* 21).

Whatever be the motive of the compiler of *Genesis* in including this incident or of the author of *Psalm* 110 in associating it with the office of the messianic king (*Ps.* 110: 4), it was the writer of the epistle to the *Hebrews* who first gave a Christian interpretation of its significance (*Heb.* 7), albeit of doubtful value. Under his guidance some commentators, ancient and modern, have claimed that we can see in this mysterious priest-king of Salem a prefiguration of the priestly office of Christ.

Before the coming of the Jewish priesthood through Aaron, Melchizedek is represented as exercising a universal type of priesthood which in the eyes of the author of *Hebrews* is revived and fulfilled by Christ. "I have existed before Abraham was born", said our Lord himself (*John* 8: 58), and the Christian fathers saw in the bread and wine which Melchizedek offers to Abraham with his blessing a pointer to the New Covenant in Christ's body and blood, which fulfils but also in a Christian sense precedes the covenant with Abraham described in the following chapter.

God's Covenant with Abraham (15: 1 – 17: 27)

THE covenant idea has been already introduced in the story of the Flood (9: 9). God symbolically entered into a relationship through Noah with the whole of mankind, whereby he undertook to preserve the life of man and obliged him to recognise a moral order in the universe. Now the creation of a special people of God within mankind, inaugurated by Abraham, is to be symbolised by a second covenant. There are two forms of this covenant, the more dramatic account from the J tradition in ch. 15 and the more ritualistic from the P tradition in ch. 17.

In both cases the terms of the covenant are to confirm God's choice of Abraham and to mark a special relationship between God and Abraham's progeny. The New Testament would of course have us regard this covenant not as one which concerned the racial ut the spiritual descendants of Abraham (*Matt.* 3: 9; *Gal.* 3: 7). It is not fulfilled until the New Covenant through Christ includes Gentiles as well as Jews (*Gal.* 3: 4). The promise of an ultimate issue as numerous as the stars in the sky (15: 5) or of the fatherhood of many nations (17: 4, 6) becomes in this sense a prophecy of the expansion of the Church, and the setting apart of the Holy Land as the home of the people of God 15: 7; 17: 8) suggests a token of the Church's ultimate possession of the whole earth in the name of Christ the King.

The significance of the dividing of the animals in the ancient ritual of the J story (15: 9–17) goes back to the old idea that the life of an animal resided in its blood (cf. 9: 4–6). By the shedding of its blood in ritual sacrifice its life is made available for some dedicated purpose. In the case of a covenant of this kind between two parties the sacrificial animal is divided in halves and the two parties pass between the dismembered body cf. *Jer.* 34: 18). The idea behind this is that the two parties are thus bound together in a sacred bond by the unifying third factor, namely the liberated life of the consecrated victim into which they enter. Variations of this basic idea lie at the root of all such sacrificial ritual in the Old Testament, and it is sublimated in the New Testament teaching on the meaning of the sacrifice of Christ, where the liberated life of the Risen Saviour, who offered himself to God, binds God and man together in a new and deeper covenant relationship (*Heb.* 9: 15–22).

Here in the *Genesis* story it is only God who passes symbolically between the sacrificial victims. This is because the two parties to the covenant are not equals. It is an act of God's grace to bind his people to himself. In the awe-inspiring symbolism of the rite, God is represented as a "smoking furnace" and a "burning lamp", as he will later be portrayed as a "pillar of cloud" and a "pillar of fire" when he delivers his people from bondage (*Ex.* 13: 21–22). The prophecy of the Egyptian bondage here (15: 13) is of course not a forecast but retrospective knowledge many centuries after the event.

In the second version of the covenant with Abraham in ch. 17 circumcision is made the sign of the bond between God and his people, as the rainbow had been the sign of the covenant with Noah. Circumcision was probably originally part of a marriage rite in the ancient world, but it was emphasised particularly by the Jews in Babylon during the Exile as the distinguishing mark of God's chosen people in a land where the practice was not customary, and this passage is doubtless prompted by that situation.

In Palestine in earlier days, however, it seems to have been the general rule among the Semitic peoples in contrast to other racial groups such as the Philistines (e.g. *II Sam.* 1: 20). Thus its association with the covenant was not merely in the interests of racial exclusiveness although that was a constant danger. It was regarded as an outward sign of inward grace, a mark of a life consecrated to God (*Deut.* 30: 6; *Jer.* 4: 4). By New Testament times, however, it had become so closely associated with Jewish national pride, presumably because the practice had lapsed among their neighbours, that St. Paul is at pains to point out that Abraham was accounted righteous by his faith in God (15: 6) before circumcision was instituted (*Rom.* 4: 9–12) and he includes uncircumcised Gentiles as heirs of this covenant if they share Abraham's faith (*Gal.* 3: 8–9).

The main obstacle to the fulfilment of the promise, however, still remains. Abraham has no son. Where then is the justification for the changing of his name from Abram, "the Father (God) is exalted", to Abraham, said to mean "father of a multitude of nations"? (17: 5). By law Abraham's steward would be his heir and this is the subject of his complaint to God (15: 2–3). God's reply is to teach Abraham, and us through Abraham, a lesson in patience. What God has promised he will fulfil, even though it seems impossible of fulfilment. So the purpose of the narrative until the birth of Isaac is to contrast man's impatience with God's wise providence.

Whether the birth of Ishmael in ch. 16 was once intended to account for the origin of the wild bedouin tribes (16: 12) or not, that is clearly not the purpose of its inclusion here. The intriguing domestic triangle described in this chapter is not recorded even for its human interest, although it has that in plenty, but to illustrate the radical requirements of faith. No makeshift device, proposed and executed by human wits, can hasten the inexorable certainty of God's will in God's own time. Sarah and Abraham wish to hurry things along, to provide the promised heir, to show God how to do his job (16: 1–2). Despite St. Paul's suggestion that Abraham's two sons Ishmael and Isaac represent the old and new covenants, and that Hagar stands for Mt. Sinai where the covenant with Moses, now superseded, was sealed (*Gal.* 4: 22–25), it seems abundantly clear that the compiler of *Genesis* had another perfectly adequate reason for including this story.

The Bible consistently teaches us that God does not work according to man-made laws. It would almost seem as if one of the main messages of the Bible is to convince us that it is precisely what we should not expect that God does, precisely the people who should not choose that God chooses, precisely the moment that we should not judge appropriate in which God acts. We have already seen that God chose not Cain, the first-born, but Seth; not cultured Babylonia, but primitive Israel. Now he passes over Ishmael, despite Abraham's entreaty (17: 18), and tells him that in his own good time he will provide the son who will inherit the promise.

The Son of the Promise
(18: 1 – 21: 34)

So at the beginning of ch. 18 (1–15), the Lord himself with two attendant angels visits Abraham as he sits at his tent door, and despite Sarah's incredulous laughter, which echoes Abraham's own (17: 17), the aged couple are told of the impending birth of Isaac. Against all the normal rules of nature, and despite man's good intentions, God chooses his own way in his own time to further the divine plan. "Is anything too hard for the Lord?" (18: 14).

Then as if to re-emphasise the need for divine intervention to save the world from its headlong rush to destruction, the biblical spotlight is turned on to the fate of Sodom and Gomorrah (18: 16 – 19: 38). At some point in history these twin cities on the plain by the Dead Sea must have suffered a dramatic and sudden disaster, in all probability, as the story suggests, as a result of earth movement coupled with volcanic activity (19: 24 – 25, 28). It is not clear whether the inhabitants were particularly renowned for the type of sexual perversion described in the narrative, or whether this was originally a variation of the Flood motif, implying the total destruction of mankind with sodomy as a mark of human depravity in general (cf. *Luke* 17: 26–29). This appears to be suggested by the valiant attempt of Lot's daughters to continue the human race at all costs (19: 30–38), and by the parallel between the deliverance of Noah and his family and Lot and his daughters, presumably in this case because of Lot's disapproval of his neighbours' behaviour (*II Pet.* 2: 6–8) and his kinship with Abraham (19: 29).

At all events, just as the fate of Lot's wife (19: 17, 26)—possibly originally a legend attached to an appropriately shaped rock-salt formation in the neighbourhood of the Dead Sea—has become proverbial as a warning against disobedience (*Luke* 17: 32), so the fate of the two cities becomes a biblical synonym for the judgment of God (*Isa.* 13: 19; *Lam.* 4: 6; *Amos* 4: 11; *Matt.* 10: 15). The implication of Abraham's moving intercession for the doomed cities (18: 23–32) is that not even ten righteous souls could be found in them to justify their preservation. Abraham's concern, however, reveals him as a worthy father in God of the future divine community (18: 19), and illustrates a biblical insight into the nature of God's mercy which is to be of great significance (see p. 31).

The story in ch. 20 which is the E (Elohist) version of 12: 10–20 and repeats its motif, stressing the divine determination that nothing must stand in the way of the promise, is followed in 21: 1–8 at last with the birth of a natural son to Abraham and Sarah. The suspense and protracted delay have been intentional. When human hope is at the point of exhaustion God shows his hand. The son of the promise is born and is named Isaac, "laughter", a reference to the incredulous reaction of his aged father and mother (17: 17; 18: 12), but also to the joyous welcome which his birth occasioned (21: 6).

The sequel in 21: 9–21, which suggests an act of spite on the part of a triumphant Sarah, is on the contrary a lesson on the love of God. It was Sarah's suggestion (16: 1–2) that divine Providence should be assisted by contriving an heir in human terms for Abraham. She must now be shown as recognising her mistake. Hagar and Ishmael must be removed from the scene, as the symbols of man's good but misguided intentions. But God will not let them suffer. Hagar and Ishmael are also his children, as were Noah and his offspring. Although they are not within the covenant of the promise they are not outside of God's care. Ishmael has his own role to play (21: 18), even if it is not that which Abraham and Sarah in all innocence projected for him.

The last few verses of ch. 21 (22-34) show Abraham, still a landless nomad in the country of the promise, staking his first claim, striking root for the first time as it were, by planting a tree to the glory of God at Beersheba, which was to become traditionally the southern outpost of the Holy Land (*Judg.* 20: 1 etc.).

The Sacrifice of Isaac

(22: 1-24)

ABRAHAM's faith has been rewarded (*Rom.* 4: 17-22). The birth of Isaac gives an earnest of the promised people, and the tamarisk at Beersheba is at least a pointer to a more permanent settlement in the promised land. Isaac is generally referred to in the commentaries as a colourless personality. Certainly when we compare him with Abraham and Jacob it is impossible to form a clear picture of him. Few stories are recorded about him, pre-sumably because there was little known of him that was worth recording, and in those stories in which he does feature he is generally a minor participant in the narratives dealing with his more notable father or son.

Yet the Church has always seen in Isaac, both in the manner of his birth and in the story of his sacrifice, which provides the Good Friday lesson from the Old Testament, a figure of messianic significance. We should, however, be ill-advised to follow the Christian Fathers along the path of allegory which led St. Augustine, for example, to see in the ram caught in the thicket (22: 13) Christ wearing the crown of thorns, and to find in the faggots which Abraham prepared for the sacrifice (22: 6, 9) a foreshadowing of the Cross.

But we cannot bypass the New Testament itself, where our Lord in the midst of a highly significant utterance (*John* 8: 31-59) connects the birth of Isaac with himself, and where the epistle to the *Hebrews* associates the sacrifice of Isaac with the Crucifixion and Resurrection (*Heb.* 11: 17-19). There is no need to claim for the compiler of *Genesis* some kind of magic power of foreseeing future events, or to suggest that the idea of the coming of Christ is anywhere present in the minds of the originators of these ancient traditions.

In biblical thought, however, there is a direct line of continuity between Abraham, the father of the people of God, and the Messiah, who in St. Matthew's gospel is described as the son of Abraham (*Matt.* 1: 1). Christ is the Head of his Body, the Church (*Eph.* 1 : 22–23) which consists of all who are sharers of Abraham's faith (*Gal.* 3 : 7). Isaac is the first fruits of the promise, the pledge of the ultimate life and witness of the Church. Does not our Lord then identify himself with Isaac in *John* 8 : 56?

In the long controversy in that chapter in which Jesus seeks to disabuse the minds of his Jewish antagonists of the idea that racial descent from Abraham counts for anything in the sight of God, he claims that Abraham "rejoiced" to see his day (*John* 8 : 56). Surely this is no vague allusion to some preview that Abraham may have had of the future messianic age but a direct reference, based on our Lord's profound knowledge of the Old Testament, to the birth of Isaac, the child called "laughter", the joyful evidence that God's promise had come true. Our Lord sees in the birth of Isaac, the only begotten or beloved son of his father—the same word is used in the Old and New Testaments (22 : 2; *Mark* 1 : 11), and means "unique" in the sense that he is the child of grace and not of nature—the first sketch of a pattern which Jesus is aware that he has now perfectly fulfilled.

Similarly in the story of Isaac's sacrifice, we do the Old Testament writers an injustice if we see no more in it than an attempt to provide divine sanction for the abolition of human sacrifice, or even an example of a supreme test of faith. At the very least it is certainly that. The child of the promise has at last appeared, and

Abraham has had every reason to rejoice. But hardly has the child begun to grow up, when the incredible command comes to his father to kill him. Nothing would appear more finally and utterly to make nonsense of the promise that God planned to make of Abraham a great nation, nothing would seem more clearly to indicate that the Almighty had perpetrated a gigantic hoax.

We are not invited, however, to criticise Abraham for even conceiving that God could demand so cruel a deed as the slaying of Isaac, on the contrary we are invited both in this chapter and in the comment on it in the epistle to the *Hebrews* (11 : 17–19) to see this as the supreme example of faith. So great is Abraham's trust in God that he is prepared to believe in his power to fulfil his promise, even if it means bringing a dead body back to life. The author of *Hebrews* sees in this a parable of the Resurrection (11 : 19), for God did indeed raise Christ from the dead in order that the promise made to Abraham should be fulfilled in his Church.

But this story is more than an illustration of how God tests our faith, and more than an example of how strong our faith in him must be. Can we read this chapter with its picture of the loving father and the obedient son, its theme of costly sacrifice, and of the provision by God of an offering of his own appointing (*Rom.* 8 : 32), without recognising here the same images as we find woven together in the perfect self-giving of our Lord's Death? We need not try to create artificial parallels in incidental details in order to see the story as a whole as an illuminating preface to John the Baptist's words: "Behold the Lamb of God, that taketh away the sin of the world" (*John* 1 : 29).

Abraham's faith is vindicated. He is now described as "the friend of God" (*Jas.* 2 : 23) by virtue of his faith and his obedience. By solemn oath God reaffirms (cf. *Heb.* 6 : 17) the promise, and the blessing upon Abraham and the Church that is yet to be (22 : 16–18). Was our Lord thinking of God's guarantee to Abraham that the people of his choice would "possess the gate of his enemies" (22 : 17), when he promised his Church that "the gates of hell" should not prevail against it? (*Matt.* 16 : 18). At all events, the great assignment of the missionary task of the people of God and the assurance of ultimate victory are proclaimed with equal clarity both here in *Genesis* and later in the gospels.

Abraham's Foresight and Death

(23 : 1 – 25 : 18)

THE INTEREST of the narrative now switches to Abraham's grandson Jacob, whose story occupies virtually the second half of the book of *Genesis* (25 : 19–50 : 26), for Isaac, as we have seen, is briefly passed over and the story of Joseph (ch. 37–50), finds its climax in the death of his father Jacob. Before Jacob's story begins, however, we are told of the death of Sarah (ch. 23), of the quest for a suitable wife for Isaac

(ch. 24) and of the death of Abraham (25 : 1–18).

By purchasing the cave of Machpelah (23 : 16–19), Abraham secures his first fragment of the land which had been promised to him when he set out from Haran. He had spent his whole life in Canaan as a landless stranger, and now for the first time as he nears his own end he succeeds in buying only enough of it to bury his wife and himself. The importance of the purchase, however, in the long history that is yet to be unfolded is that more than four centuries of exile and servitude in Egypt lie immediately ahead. Yet when the Israelites return from bondage to take possession of the land of Canaan, they will be returning to a country where their great forefather Abraham lived as a wandering stranger, but where at least he was buried in a piece of ground that they could call their own.

Before Abraham dies he ensures that his son Isaac will not marry into the pagan people that surround the tribe, and the lovely story of the wooing of Rebekah, so beautifully told that one might almost believe that the Bible *was* designed to be read as literature, brings a wife for Isaac back from the early homeland of the Hebrews (ch. 24).

The list of names in 25 : 1–18 which credits Abraham with a large second family is once more tribal and not individual history. These, together with Ishmael's descendants, purport to account for the origins of neighbouring peoples, while the Bible firmly proceeds to trace the fortunes of the single line of the family of Abraham, which God has chosen out of all others to witness for him in the world.

The Paradox of Jacob

To pass from the stories about Abraham to the stories about Jacob is to plunge from the mountain top, where the saints commune with God, to the chaffering and haggling of the market place, where the meanness and trickery of man obscure the light of God, and distort his image in which the Bible assures us we are all made.

Whatever element of idealisation later veneration for the father of Israel has contributed to the biblical picture of Abraham, his character emerges as that of a man who, by implicit obedience to what he conceives to be the will of God, and by unwavering trust in God's power to achieve his purpose, is wholly admirable as an example of piety and integrity, and who still four thousand years after his day impresses us as being entirely worthy to be regarded as the "father of us all", the recipient of the promise, and the founder of the world-wide people of God. Where Abraham falls short of the gospel ethic (e.g. ch. 12), we feel that it is attributable to his time and the ways of bedouin life, and that he is rightly judged by the author of *Hebrews* to belong to those of whom "God is not ashamed to be called their God" (*Heb.* 11: 16).

By contrast his grandson Jacob would seem to belong more properly to some oriental hall of fame, where the places of honour are reserved for those who have most fully exhibited the qualities dearest to the heart of the bedouin, native cunning, quick wittedness, and a flair for unscrupulous bargaining. Alike in his dealings with his more gullible brother Esau and his equally crafty uncle Laban, Jacob suggests the popular hero of Hebrew folk-lore, the type of Israelite whom later generations looked back on as possessing *par excellence* the characteristics of his race.

If we may think of Abraham as the type of Israelite that priests and prophets exhorted the nation to be, and perhaps the type that the ordinary Israelite in his best moments wanted to be, we may think of Jacob as the kind of man the ordinary Israelite knew that he was, the kind of human material with which priests and prophets had constantly to struggle.

To the average Hebrew, Abraham must have appeared as a venerable but somewhat remote figure, whose holiness and charity raised him to a plane untenanted by lesser mortals, and gave him the right to be called father of his people before God, but Jacob must have seemed much more the father of his people on the secular level, first bearer of the name Israel (32: 28), progenitor of the twelve tribes, beloved embodiment of his people's virtues and also of their weaknesses.

At first glance it may surprise us that the Bible allows this verdict to stand, and that it apparently condones the attribution of this high honour to a man whose very name means deceit and guile. Esau would indeed appear to have been a much more admirable character, a simple, honest extrovert, a man of generous impulses and quick emotions. Yet the New Testament epitaph on Esau dismisses him as an impious profligate (*Heb.* 12: 16), while our Lord himself brackets Jacob with Abraham and the prophets as occupying an honoured place in God's eternal Kingdom (*Luke* 13: 28).

It is clear from the clue which the Bible gives us in 25: 23 and 36: 1, that at some stage in their composition the Jacob-Esau stories served a wider purpose than that of recording a conflict between two brothers, and that since Jacob is Israel and Esau is Edom, we must see in the initial relationship, the changing fortunes, and the ultimate separation of the two brothers, a reflection of the historical relationship between the two countries of Israel and Edom. It is claimed by some commentators that an exact correspondence can be traced between the ups and downs of the fortunes of the two brothers, and the development of political relations between the two countries. At all events the biblical identification of Esau with Edom, which throughout most of Old Testament history was at loggerheads with Israel, might account in part at least for the unfavourable view of Esau by the author of *Hebrews*, but it would not account for Jesus' estimate of Jacob.

Whatever may have been the political connotations of the Jacob-Esau stories, either original or imposed, it was no political motive that secured their inclusion in the Bible. Moreover, although the tone of many of the Jacob stories is ethically dubious, and the P tradition which contributes the most markedly "religious" element to *Genesis* is conspicuously absent in this section, nevertheless the final editors of *Genesis* who were no less "religious", must have included such "secular" stories here as elsewhere in the Bible because they served a theological purpose.

The Bible never asks us to believe in an irrational God, although it equally never suggests that we can always understand God's reasons for doing what he does. Sometimes in retrospect we seem to be able to see the guiding hand of Providence in specific events in history, as in our own lives, but even then it is not always clear. The Bible teaches us to accept this partial understanding as part of our human limitation, and to emulate the saints and prophets who lived by faith in the hidden good purposes of God.

But at the same time the Bible teaches us that God cannot be untrue to himself, and that if he has designed the universe in such a way that man can only live wholesomely and happily upon it by doing justly, loving mercy, and walking humbly (*Micah* 6: 8) in accordance with God's revelation of his will, then these principles are not valid today and invalid tomorrow, but are the revealed purpose of God for all time and in all societies. Man may at various stages of his development be unable to hear what God is saying to him, but the divine law remains unchanging.

Accordingly, when we are confronted in the Bible, as we are in the Jacob stories, with what appears to be divine approval of people whose actions are by Christian standards immoral, we must neither make the mistake of condoning these actions as if their presence in the Bible made them automatically right, nor on the other hand conclude that God is himself irrational. If we are invited to admire Abraham as a model of piety and integrity, we do so willingly because in the light of the Gospel that is what he was. But if immediately thereafter we are introduced to his grandson Jacob whose conduct is highly unethical by Christian standards, we must seek to understand why our Lord is content to name them both in the same breath.

To do this we must come to terms with the biblical concept of election or choice. God chose Israel out of all the nations to be the means of revelation. But it was not an irrational choice. Israel had no inborn flair for religion, but it did throw up a series of notable men from Abraham onwards who responded to God's summons, and were able to see at least in part something of the mystery of God's ways and the majesty of his glory. Jacob finds his place in this succession not by lineal descent, still less by an arbitrary divine edict, but because he too, despite his crafty cunning, was all his days a seeker after God and in the end became a man of God.

Whatever historical basis there may be in the Jacob stories we cannot now say, but as he is presented to us in the Bible here at the beginning of the record of the people of God's choice, it is as if the Bible were saying to us that God does not only choose the godly Abrahams of this world for his people but the wily cowardly Jacobs, the common stuff of sinful humanity, and makes them into his children. The Bible does not ask us to admire Jacob without reservation, but to see ourselves in him, and to learn what God can do with such unpromising material.

We are being told at this early stage that the Church is no preserve of the godly, and that therefore self-righteousness is the last sin of which we ought to be guilty. The Church is a community of sinners whom God has called, whose hearts he has touched, and who, like Jacob, stumbling, falling, rising and falling again, hold fast in life to the vision they have been granted and on which they are prepared to stake their lives.

Jacob's Treachery
(25: 19–34)

THE STORY of Jacob begins with the same emphasis on the divine interest in his birth as we have seen in the case of Isaac. His mother Rebekah is barren, and it is only as a result of Isaac's urgent petition that a child is born to inherit the promise (25: 21). This is the Bible's way of impressing on us that at every stage in the growth of the community which God has appointed to serve him, nothing but his grace could have made that growth possible. Twins are born and Jacob is the younger. The vivid description of his attempt to be born before his brother, which earns him his name, "heel-catcher" or "supplanter", is indicative of the consuming passion which possessed him from then on, to be the one who would inherit the blessing given to Abraham.

Esau, his shaggy brother, was clay in his hands, and his doting mother Rebekah gave him every encouragement. Isaac's preference for Esau is depicted as cupboard love (25: 28), and the day soon comes when Jacob's craftiness persuades Esau to trade his birth-right, which of course includes the promise made to Abraham, in return for a dish of stew. What the Bible is conveying in this homely parable is that Esau was a shallow character, quite unfit to stand in the succession of Abraham. This was the unforgivable sin in the eyes of the author of *Hebrews*. Esau had no faith in the destiny that God had promised to Abraham and his descendants. He was prepared to barter it for the satisfaction of a momentary appetite. On the other hand there is no suggestion that Jacob's part in the affair was anything but despicable.

The Theft of the Blessing
(26: 1 – 28: 9)

CHAPTER 26 contains another variation of the wife-sister story already encountered in chs. 12 and 20. This time it is con-cerned with Isaac and Rebekah and serves to reiterate the recurring motif of God's overruling of the chances and changes of fortune, to ensure that nothing should interfere with the divine plan. The promise has been handed on to Isaac (26: 3), and no human hand (26: 7) must be allowed to prevent him from passing on the blessing to him whom God has appointed. In this case no miraculous intervention is required. God secures Isaac's safety by "natural" means, and the patriarch finds his fortunes prospering. He signalises his sense of the divine protection by following in Abraham's footsteps both in good works and worship (26: 18, 25). Esau meanwhile further reveals his unfitness to receive the promise by marrying pagan wives (26: 34).

It is against this background that the dramatic and moving story of Jacob's masterpiece of trickery is now recorded. Blind old Isaac resolves before he dies to hand on the precious blessing to his favourite son Esau. Rebekah is determined that the blessing shall go to the apple of her eye despite Jacob's reluctance, a reluctance which is based on fear of Isaac's wrath and not on moral scruples (27: 12). Jacob, however, agrees to his mother's plot, passes himself off as his brother and with lies and hypocrisy (27: 20) secures the old man's blessing. The father's horror and Esau's bitter tears when the truth is discovered cannot undo what has been done. The irrevocable blessing has been given to Jacob, thus for the second time his brother's deceiver.

In these early stories the blessing of God is thought of in terms of material prosperity (27: 28–29), although later in the Old Testament it is more deeply understood as consisting of such gifts as wisdom and righteousness. Our Lord gives it an even deeper connotation in the Sermon on the Mount (*Matt.* 5: 2–12). But in this case as in the case of Jacob's own blessing of his grandsons (48: 14–20), or Balaam's blessing of Israel (*Num.* 23), the blessing is regarded as prophetic and certain of fulfilment. The giver of the blessing is communicating power from God, and once given it cannot be recalled.

Esau vows to be revenged (27: 41), and Rebekah engineers Jacob's flight to safety with her relatives at Haran, on the pretext of finding a wife among his cousins (27: 46 – 28: 1). Before his departure, Isaac gives the promise of Abraham to the usurper, as he must (28: 3–4), while the luckless Esau seeks to make amends for his pagan marriages by adding one of Ishmael's daughters to his harem (28: 9).

God's Summons to Jacob

(28: 10–22)

So JACOB sets out for Haran with the guilt of his deceit upon him, and the ill-gotten promise as his only possession, with little likelihood of his ever being able to enter into his heritage. His brother's vengeance awaited him whenever he would set foot again in the Holy Land. Rebekah may have thought that Esau's wrath was a passing mood (27: 44), but even after twenty years Jacob was still to fear it (ch. 33). It was then as he journeyed northward, a fugitive and an exile, that the hand of God fell upon him.

This strange story of Jacob's dream has not exhausted its significance when we see it as the explanation of why a Canaanite sanctuary called Luz became an Israelite sanctuary called Bethel (28: 19), or when we look beneath the surface and detect the steps of a pagan temple behind the symbol of the ladder, and the customary sacred stone or *massebah* behind the symbol of the pillow (28: 18). Nor is it enough to see in the story a message of the nearness of heaven to earth, and the possibility of communion with God wherever we may be. The story must be seen in the context of the record of the people of God, whatever subsidiary elements may be found in it.

In this sense it becomes the first stage in Jacob's conversion. There must have been in this strange twisted nature some deep and passionate yearning for God, to make him stake life and honour on securing the promise. No one can have known better than he how unworthy he was to wear the mantle of Abraham. Yet God knew him better than he knew himself. God saw that there was in this crafty trickster the stuff that saints are made of. It was because of this that Esau's honest naïveté had lost him the blessing, that Isaac's misjudgment of his sons had been overruled, that even Rebekah's intrigues had been used in the divine purpose. Jacob had the root of the matter in him, and he must be schooled and moulded, punished and disciplined, to bear the high role for which God had destined him.

At Bethel God makes him his own, and confirms the promise. Jacob knows from that moment what it is to be apprehended of God. Like Abraham he is bound upon a venture of which he does not know the outcome, but God has set his seal upon him and shown him something of the glorious mystery of his calling. Jacob's response (28: 20–22) is not as it appears on the surface the old trickster bargaining with God, but the incredulous reaction of a man who cannot believe that God has chosen such a guilty sinner as he to be the instrument of his purpose. Nothing seemed less likely than that he would ever cross the threshold of the land of the promise again or reach his home in safety. How could the arch deceiver be sure that he was not deceiving himself?

Jacob's Punishment
(29: 1 – 31: 55)

JACOB'S arrival at Haran and meeting with Rachel his cousin are beautifully told. The narrator ironically suggests that it was not only the exhilaration of love at first sight that gave Jacob strength to lift the heavy stone from the mouth of the well, but the prospect of a handsome dowry (29: 10). There was to be no dowry, however, for the wily Hebrew had met his match in his uncle Laban. Once more Jacob's patient pertinacity is revealed in his readiness to serve seven years without pay for the hand of the girl he loved. "And they seemed unto him but a few days, for the love he had to her" (29: 20).

But at the end of it he finds himself outsmarted by Laban, and saddled with the older sister Leah whom he did not want. Laban had carefully refrained from telling him of an old Syrian custom (29: 26). Jacob nevertheless gets his Rachel after the wedding festivities, but he has to work a further spell of seven years for nothing to be able to call her his own. Doubtless in these fourteen years as a penniless dependant Jacob had ample time for reflection. Leah and his wives' two maids, who in those days could act as proxies in case of barrenness, provided him with ten sons and a daughter. The sons are represented as progenitors of ten of the twelve later tribes of Israel.

But the beloved Rachel had no children, until once more divine intervention (30: 22) assisted by mandrakes, a fruit which was believed to induce conception (30: 14), led to the birth of Joseph who was destined to be the next bearer of the promise. At this point Jacob began to think of returning home (30: 25). Laban is unwilling to let him go, for his farm had prospered under Jacob's shrewd management (30: 27). The sequel is a classic of oriental sharp practice (30: 31–43). Laban's tactics are simple cunning (30: 35–36), but Jacob outwits him by adding skill in cattle breeding. At the end of six years (31: 41) Jacob has made himself a wealthy man, while Laban, having come off worst in the bargain, is left with a weakened herd of livestock and several resentful sons (31: 1).

Jacob decides that it would be prudent to leave, a decision which is confirmed by divine command (31: 3), and gathering together all his gear he takes his departure in Laban's absence (31: 20). When the wrathful Syrian overtakes him, Jacob is only saved by divine intervention (31: 24), and by Rachel's lie about her foolish theft of the family mascot (31: 34–35). Now he can afford to be righteously indignant, and the pent up bitterness of twenty years' bondage and hardship pours out in full flood (31: 36–41). Nothing but the hand of the God of Bethel, who had accepted his years of affliction as a penance, could have brought his sojourn in Haran to such a successful issue (31: 42). Laban accepts the inevitable with a good grace. They agree to separate in peace and by solemn oath to respect each other's rights, a parting which probably picturesquely represents the establishment of a frontier between Israel and Syria (31: 44–53).

Jacob's Conversion

(32: 1–32)

As JACOB enters the promised land, an encounter with mysterious angelic figures heightens the tension within him. Do they portend judgment or blessing? (32: 1–2.) He learns that Esau is on his way to meet him with a large accompanying force. Prudently he makes his disposi-

tions in case of hostile attack, humbly he abases himself before God, confessing his utter unworthiness and acknowledging God's mercy. Then having invoked divine protection, he sends his peace-offering on its way to mollify his brother, sees his family and his belongings across the river Jabbok in safety, and remains himself alone on the farther side (32: 3–23).

Then he experiences the second great spiritual crisis of his life, in a sense the complement of his dream at Bethel. For twenty toilsome years he has been chastened and disciplined. Now he receives the divine approval as worthy to re-enter the land of the promise and play his part in God's unfolding purpose. Again we may find in this ancient story traces of the various elements that have gone towards its making: the demon of the river who challenges the right of travellers to pass, the tabu on this part of an animal in primitive dietary law.

But clearly as the story stands now we are meant to see in this obscure and mysterious incident the crisis of Jacob's conversion. He wrestles throughout the long night with God for his blessing. The Bible merely hints at the agony of a tormented soul which cannot rest until it finds forgiveness and peace with God. By daybreak, a new Jacob has been born, no longer named the Deceiver, but Israel, Perseverer with God, God's warrior, called to be the father of the tribes of Israel, and raised to the honoured patriarchate with Abraham and Isaac.

Jacob does not become a saint

overnight, but he has seen God face to face, and by the grace of God he will grow to the full stature which his role demands. But the significance of the story is that the cunning twister that was Jacob died and was buried at Peniel (32: 24–32; cf. *Hos.* 12: 3–5). There could be no greater contrast between two characters than between those of Abraham and Jacob, the one as we should say "naturally" good and the other "naturally" rotten. Yet the Bible shows us here, as the history of the Church has so often confirmed, that some of God's greatest saints have earned the right to bear that name only when by God's grace they have fought and won their battle against the power of evil within them which had well nigh destroyed them.

Jacob's Return

(33: 1 – 37: 1)

THEN follows Jacob's dreaded meeting with his brother, which contrary to his guilty apprehensions becomes a real reconciliation. Jacob can only account for the magnanimity of his brother by seeing the hand of God at work again (33: 10). To his self-abasement (33: 3) he adds the gift of half his possessions, trying thereby to atone for the theft of the blessing (33: 11). The brothers part friends, Esau returns to his own territory in the south, while Jacob after a short stay at Succoth, crosses the Jordan and like his grandfather Abraham buys a plot of the Holy Land, this time near Shechem, right in the very heart of Palestine. This too was to become a patriarchal sepulchre when Joseph's bones were interred in Israelite soil after the Exodus (*Josh.* 24: 32).

But this was all of the land of the promise that Jacob, like Abraham, was allowed to own. He too was destined to remain a wanderer, and indeed to die on alien soil (49: 33). The apparently irrelevant story of Dinah (ch. 34) makes it plain that this was part of the divine plan. If we read this story as a simple tale of rough justice meted out by Simeon and Levi to the man who had dishonoured their sister, or even as early tribal history disguising the attack of these two clans on the town of Shechem we should fail to discover its true significance.

Jacob has at last after twenty years re-entered the promised land. He has by weary penance expiated the wrongs done to his brother. Their reconciliation is the proof of God's forgiveness. Enriched in spirit and dedicated to God he is ready to begin the up-building of a people of God in the land of God's choice. Whatever be the historical basis of this story it is used here as a parable to teach us that in the wisdom of God the time was not yet ripe. Jacob had bought his little plot but he must be content with that token of the future right of Israel to make the Holy Land its own. Both Jacob and his descendants must await the day when, after the searching and sifting experience of Egyptian bondage and the Exodus, and after the new revelation given to Moses of God's nature and purpose, the people of God would be forged into a weapon fit to take possession of the Holy Land. They have yet to learn what it means to be God's chosen people.

The lesson of ch. 34 is that God does not permit any short cuts, and that there is no royal road to the Kingdom. Here were the native Canaanites, out and out pagans, and as we know from later references in the Bible and from the evidence of archaeology, devotees of a religion which was the direct antithesis of all that the God of Abraham demanded. They were prepared to welcome Jacob and his household, to allow them to settle there, to trade with them, to intermarry with them, to become one people. They were even prepared to undergo circumcision as a meaningless symbol if it would please these strange but obviously prosperous nomads. For Israel to accept on these terms might have been one way of achieving ultimate control of the land of the promise, but it was not God's way. The people of God must maintain a distinctive witness.

If Jacob toyed with the idea of assimilation as a serious possibility, he was soon to learn that Providence had a different plan. God used the violence of Simeon and Levi to ensure that Jacob did not succumb to temptation although they themselves later have to pay the penalty for their crime (49: 5-7). In all this we may see a foreshadowing of the mission of the Church in the world today, and a warning against attempting to win the whole earth for God by lowering our standards and cheapening God's demands.

So Jacob has to set out again to the south, towards Hebron, where Isaac, now in sight of death, still pastures his flocks within reach of his father's tomb (35: 27). Before leaving Shechem Jacob sets his own household in order, most of them pagans from Haran, by confiscating their idols and charms and burying them for ever (35: 4). At Bethel he renews his vows and hears again the words of the promise (35: 6-15).

Rachel dies in childbirth on the way and Jacob calls this son Benjamin, the twelfth and, with Joseph, the dearest of his children for Rachel's sake. When he reaches Hebron he has the further sad duty of burying his father (35: 29). Chapter 36 describes the final agreement of Esau (Edom) and Jacob (Israel) on their respective pasture areas, and gives a list of the Edomite chieftains.

The Story of Joseph
(37: 2 – 50: 26)

THE SUPERB story of Joseph, a masterpiece of narration, is inserted into the record of Jacob. The figure of the old patriarch broods over the adventures of his sons in Egypt, and the book of *Genesis*, and with it the period of the patriarchs, ends with the handing on of the promise by Jacob to Joseph and his son (48: 15-16) before his death (49: 33).

Unlike the stories of both Abraham and Jacob, the story of Joseph is not made up of a collection of ancient traditions of independent origin, but forms a coherent and continuous narrative, which bears every indication of having been a unity from the start and whose meaning unlike the others is generally apparent on the surface. Apart from two minor insets (chs. 38 and 49), the Joseph story is a highly moral tale of the innocent victim of jealousy and ill-will, who turns the tables on his persecutors by succeeding despite them and returning good for evil.

Young Joseph, the spoiled darling of his father, brought up to regard himself as a cut above the rest, did not endear himself to his brothers by telling tales on them or by interpreting his dreams to them. It was hardly cause, however, for them to plot his death or finally to sell him as a slave (37: 2–36). His initial good fortune in Egypt soon deserted him, and he found himself in prison as a reward for his refusal to betray his employer's trust (39: 1–23). His flair for interpreting dreams came to his aid, however, and by a strange turn of fate he found himself grand vizier of Egypt (40: 1–41: 46).

Not only so, he found himself also in a position to take revenge on the brothers who had wronged him and who now came as suppliants from Canaan, then in the grip of famine, to buy the corn which Joseph's shrewdness had accumulated in the pharaoh's granaries (41: 47–42: 6). After some oriental cat and mouse play, which must have delighted the ancient story-teller's audience, Joseph discloses his identity to the wicked brothers, now sorely chastened men (42: 21), magnani-

mously forgives them with promise of further help, and the happy ending sees Jacob and all his household migrating to Egypt and settled, with the pharaoh's sanction, in the district of Goshen to the east of the Nile delta (42: 7–47: 12). In a footnote, the business acumen of Joseph is underlined and the peculiar system of land tenure in Egypt is attributed to him (47: 13–26).

Old Jacob is now at the point of death, but before his passing he ensures that he will be buried with his forebears in the cave of Machpelah (47: 27–31), and that the blessing and promise are properly transmitted (48: 1–22). Jacob's impressive funeral (50: 1–13) is followed by a brief notice of Joseph's own death, and his prophecy that Egypt would not be the permanent home of his people, as a token of which his mummified body was preserved against the day of their deliverance (50: 14–26).

It is too easy to dismiss the Joseph story as a romantic tale designed to bridge the gap between the nomadic period in Canaan, covered by the stories of Abraham, Isaac and Jacob, and the great event of the Exodus from Egypt under Moses to which the Bible now turns. The fact that Joseph's fracas with Potiphar's wife is paralleled in the Egyptian tale of "The Two Brothers" is no argument against the authenticity of a situation which can hardly be described as unique, and which merely concerns one section of the narrative. There is no more reason to suppose that there was not an actual historical Joseph than that there was no real Abraham or Jacob, and in Joseph's case there is much less reason to think that we are reading tribal history in the guise of personal adventures.

But we must admit ignorance here as in the other patriarchal stories in *Genesis* as to the historicity of the individual events described. Archaeology can confirm that the background details in the Joseph story are accurate, that the Egyptian customs described are authentic, that the geographical locations are appropriate, and so on. But apart from the biblical narrative, which, we must remember, is oral tradition handed down for centuries and not contemporary writing, we have no confirmatory evidence.

We do not know, for example, whether the migration to Egypt involves merely the seventy souls mentioned in the record (46: 27), or whether it represents a much larger and prolonged tribal migration. If it consisted of such a small number it is difficult to see how that number could grow to the dimensions suggested in *Ex.* 12: 37, where the total of men, women and children leaving Egypt would appear to be in the region of two millions. Doubtless the latter figure is an exaggeration, and equally probably the former figure is an understatement. There is good reason to believe that most of the Semitic nomads who entered Canaan at the time of Abraham remained there, and that only part of them settled for a time in Egypt, and later became the spearhead of the invasion of Canaan under Joshua after the Exodus.

Nor can we say with certainty when all these events may have taken place. It is believed that the native dynasty of Egypt was overthrown by invading Semites, known as Hyksos, approximately about 1700 B.C., and that these usurpers remained in control of Egypt until approximately 1550 B.C., although even these dates are not universally agreed. It may well be that a migration of Hebrews into Egypt was more possible in that period than at other times within the second millennium B.C., and that the pharaoh of the Joseph story was in fact a fellow-Semite, and therefore more likely to appoint a non-Egyptian as his prime minister. Similarly the expulsion of the Hyksos, and the resumption of power by the native Egyptian rulers may account for the change in the fortunes of the Hebrews, and explain their bondage under a pharaoh "who knew not Joseph" (*Ex.* 1: 8).

In this case, if with a liberal margin we fix a date somewhere about 2000 B.C. for Abraham, we may think of the patriarchal period covered by *Genesis*, during which the Hebrews led a semi-nomadic existence in Palestine, as covering approximately three centuries. At the end of that time the section of the tribes with whose history the Bible is concerned migrate to Egypt, say, somewhere between 1700–1600 B.C. This would allow for a stay in Egypt lasting approximately four centuries, if we take the date of the Exodus as approximately 1290 B.C.

In the present state of our archaeological knowledge of this period, and remembering that the

Bible is not primarily concerned with dates and facts, there must remain a vast number of unanswered questions as to the actual course of events in this early period of Israel's history. This need not trouble us any more than it troubled the biblical writers themselves. They were well aware that their primary concern was to trace in such traditions as had come down to them the guiding hand of Providence in all their affairs, and to see God shaping the beginnings of their national story in preparation for the great day of the Exodus, when they knew they had been singled out and set apart for some momentous purpose which they could at that stage only dimly grasp.

If we are content to suspend judgment on the historical issues of this period, it does not in the least detract from the importance of the *Genesis* stories as affording us insights into the recurring themes and patterns which we shall meet throughout the Bible. This is as true of the Joseph stories as of those of Abraham and Jacob. All alike must be seen through the eyes of the final editors of *Genesis* who cherished and preserved them, because they found in them evidence of the redemptive love of God.

The dominant theme of the Bible is God's plan to save the world from itself, by the choice and providential guidance of a community which would act on his behalf against the massed forces of greed, hate, cruelty and the rest of the sins that disfigure mankind. This theme is clearly reflected in the Joseph story. The clue is in

45: 5 and 50: 20: "Now therefore be not grieved nor angry with yourselves, that ye sold me hither; for God did send me before you, to preserve life" (45: 5). "But as for you, ye thought evil against me; but God meant it unto good, to bring to pass, as it is this day, to save much people alive" (50: 20). Joseph incarnates the experience and the redemptive work of the people of God. Chosen to inherit the promise made to Abraham that through him and his seed God's rich blessing would come to the nations, Joseph's fortunes prospered no matter what evil chances befell him. "The Lorde was with Joseph and he was a luckie felowe", as Tyndale happily translated 39: 2.

Despite the malevolence of his brothers, the pique of a jilted lady and the perils of high office, his success is assured. God overrules the evil of man to further his purposes, for it is quite clear from the text that it is God's glory and not Joseph's that the Bible is concerned with. Joseph's promotion and material wellbeing are incidental. He is but an instrument in God's hands to save life—the lives of Jacob and his family, involving the safeguarding of the promise and the lives of the whole Egyptian people. The pattern of Joseph's life-story is thus of the same pattern as the life story of the Israel of God, who despite her own suffering and the power of evil, is enabled by God to fulfil her mission of saving the life of the world.

It is for this reason that the Church has always connected the story of Joseph with the experience of our Lord, who was crucified by

THE STORY OF JOSEPH 65

his brothers but raised up by his heavenly Father to be the means of blessing and salvation for the world. As Christians, we believe that in Christ the promise made to Abraham has been fulfilled. As son of Abraham and embodiment of the true Israel, our Lord becomes finally the one through whom all the nations of the earth are to be blessed. The missionary vocation, which was God's will for Israel, is accepted on Israel's behalf by the Messiah whom they would not acknowledge. Through him it now falls to the Church to extend the blessing to the world.

Once again therefore it becomes abundantly plain why the New Testament writers saw in these stories of the patriarchs the dim beginnings of the story of the Church. They belong as the author of *Hebrews* tells us (11: 39–12: 2), to the great cloud of witnesses who ran their race in faith as we must also run ours. They believed in the promise although they did not see its fulfilment, and although its fulfilment came in God's good time in a way which they did not expect. Yet they too had their "eyes fixed upon Jesus as the pioneer and the perfection of faith" in that they saw as the crown of God's purpose for them the lion of Judah (49: 9), who is identified in the majestic vision of the book of *Revelation* with the Lamb that was slain for our redemption (*Rev.* 5: 1–14).

The Blessing of Jacob (49: 1–28), which is an early poem incorporated into the Joseph story, professes to outline the destinies of the tribes of Israel, personified as Jacob's twelve sons. The introductory sentence (49: 1) arrests our attention by the use of the phrase "in the last days", which regularly in the Old Testament is applied to the end of time and history, when God's will and purpose will be made manifest to the world (e.g. *Isa.* 2: 2–4). In this context it is the prophecy concerning Judah (49: 8–12) which has for us the deepest significance.

Each of the tribes is allotted its portion of the land of the promise but Judah is given a "sceptre" and a "ruler's staff" (R.V.). Whatever we make of the phrase "until Shiloh come", which is obviously meaningless as it stands, and may originally have meant "until he who is his comes", there does seem to be in it a clear messianic reference. The blessing promised to Judah implies future dominion for that tribe, and the appearance in it of one who will receive "the obedience of the peoples" (R.V.) in a setting strongly suggesting Paradise restored.

"Till he come" is a phrase which has a familiar ring for Christian ears (*I Cor.* 11: 26), and here in what is probably one of the earliest fragments of Hebrew poetry, inserted into the midst of these ancient stories of the patriarchs, superficially so much part of irrelevant Jewish pre-history, appears the beginning of the hope which we shall encounter right through the Old Testament of the coming of God's ambassador, the Messiah, who will be sent to save the world by inaugurating a new order and a new relationship between God and man. The ancient poem is not thinking in terms of Jesus but of David and his descendants, the most illustrious scions of the tribe of Judah, and it looks for the Messiah as coming from among them. But as Christians we cannot forget that our Lord was given the title of "son of David" in the gospels (e.g. *Matt.* 21: 9), and that through Joseph, the husband of Mary his mother, he not only numbered David among his ancestors but also Pharez, the son of Judah, whose birth is the climax of the apparently unconnected story of Tamar in ch. 38 (*Matt.* 1: 1–16).

We must not leave the fascinating stories of the patriarchs without pausing to notice the significance of the incident in 48: 1–22, the parable of the crossed hands of God. Old Jacob on the point of death wishes to pass on the blessing and the promise to Joseph and his sons, Manasseh and Ephraim, Manasseh being the elder. Joseph brings his children forward for the blind old man's blessing, expecting his father's right hand, the hand of blessing, to be laid on the elder son's head. But Jacob crossed his hands, "guiding his hands wittingly" (48: 14), and gave the blessing to the younger boy, despite Joseph's protests.

In the event, the tribe of Ephraim was to become sufficiently important to be synonymous with the northern kingdom after the disruption following Solomon's death, but the real lesson that the Bible is teaching us in this story is once again to recognise the sovereign power of God. God does not choose the servants of his purpose by man-made standards. "Man looketh on the outward appearance, but the Lord looketh on the heart" (*I Sam.* 16: 7). Therefore he chose not Ishmael but Isaac, not Esau but Jacob, not Reuben (cf. 35: 22; 49: 3–4) but Joseph, not Manasseh but Ephraim. Primogeniture, racial lineage, or other human yardsticks mean nothing in the sight of God. Those who are chosen for his blessing are those whom he knows to be fittest to receive it.

So the patriarchal period ends with the custodians of the promise happily settled in Egypt. But it is the calm before a storm as the opening verses of the book of *Exodus* proceed to tell us. Nevertheless, whatever vicissitudes may be in store for them, the children of Israel have nothing to fear. The future of the people of God is safeguarded by God's word to Jacob at Beersheba (46: 1–4) "I will go down with thee into Egypt; and I will also surely bring thee up again". History shows that this was no empty assurance.

EXODUS

THE SECOND book of the Old Testament has as its focal point the event which the biblical writers regard as not only the real beginning of Israel's history, but also as the most significant moment in it. Prophets and psalmists (e.g. *Hos.* 11: 1; *Ps.* 77: 13–20) look back upon it as the signal proof that God had chosen Israel for his own and singled it out to be the means of blessing for the whole world. New Testament writers see in it an Act of God which has strong kinship with the Death and Resurrection of Jesus (e.g. *Luke* 9: 31—"Decease" = "Exodus"; *I Cor.* 5: 7).

On the sober plane of established historical fact little enough was involved. A few thousand Hebrews made their escape from forced labour in Egypt under the leadership of one of their own members, Moses, and became the nucleus of an aggressive and nationally conscious tribal group which later was to gain control of Palestine. Neither the escape nor the existence of Moses is confirmed by any evidence apart from that of the Bible, far less the dramatic nature of the escape and its prelude, or the supernatural powers of the leader.

On the other hand the record of the Exodus is so deeply embedded in biblical tradition, that it is impossible to see how the Old Testament could ever have been written if there had been no Exodus. No proud and independent people are likely to invent a chapter in their history which proclaims their national origins as having their root in slavery, especially when their yoke was broken by no spirited rebellion and indeed almost against their will. Yet in later days Israel positively glories in the story of its bondage and its own powerlessness to save itself. Similarly, whatever doubt there may be about many of the deeds and attributes of Moses, there can be no doubt that at this point in Israel's history a personality of the first magnitude made an impact upon the people in such a way as to give a new direction to their religion, their law and their national policy. As has often been said, if Moses did not exist we should have to invent someone to take his place.

Nevertheless, it remains true that we can say little with certainty about the Exodus beyond the fact that it happened. We do not know how many people were involved. We cannot tell when it happened. Two schools of thought suggest as possible dates the middle of the fifteenth century or the beginning of the thirteenth century B.C., with a preponderance of opinion in favour of the latter.

We do not know the circumstances of the Israelites' departure, how far the plagues in the biblical record affected the situation and what they were, if indeed they happened at all. Nor can we satisfactorily account for the tradition that the fugitives made their escape across the sea-bed dryshod, while their pursuers were engulfed by the returning waters. Was it volcanic action, or a strong wind? And was it at the Gulf of Suez, the Bitter Lakes, the Gulf of Aqaba, or where? Was the holy mountain to which Moses led the people in the Sinai peninsula, or on the mainland beyond it?

To all these and many other questions that the historian would wish to ask there is no unequivocal answer. For we are faced in the book of *Exodus*, as in the book of *Genesis*, not with a factual historical record but with a narrative which is so entirely composed of a mixture of historical events, theological interpretation of these events and the legendary accretions that naturally accumulate around any dramatic occurrence, particularly one of such momentous significance, that it is no longer possible for us to disentangle them.

If we wished to make a cautious assessment in terms of historical probability, we should have to say something like this: The Hebrews who had settled in Goshen found themselves confronted, some time after the days of Joseph, with a total reversal of their former happy position as welcome immigrants. A pharaoh with a bent for building construction, probably Rameses II, and with no sentimental attachment to Semites like his predecessors the Hyksos, conscripted the able bodied men for slave labour in the development of his building reconstruction schemes in the Delta.

Restive under this yoke, the Israelites responded to the suggestion of Moses that they should stage a mass escape. An unusual incidence of national calamities in the shape of plagues contrived to aid their plan, and in the general confusion they fled. Pursued by Egyptian forces, once again coincidence came to their assistance. Faced with an insurmountable barrier in the shape of an arm of the sea or a lake, which threatened to deliver them again into the hands of their masters, a powerful wind, or earth movements, or some other natural cause made it possible for them to cross in safety while, as their pursuers were following them across, the water returned and engulfed them.

The ancient song of Miriam in the heart of the book of *Exodus* (15: 21), which is the oldest and possibly a contemporary record of the event, conveys the dramatic and unexpected suddenness by which a way of escape opened up. Whatever happened, it made an indelible impression on the minds of the people, and the colourful narratives that enlarge on the event in the first part of the book indicate how time and imagination have assisted to enhance the wonder of the occasion.

But we have only to attempt a reconstruction of the event in this way to see that, no matter how much we recognise that only a concatenation of unusual happenings could have given rise to the Exodus-tradition, no bald historical analysis can tell us very much about what the Exodus meant, or why it plays the major role that it does in both the Old and New Testaments. Certainly we must satisfy ourselves that this is no fairy-tale, that the Exodus did take place. But equally important with the event is the significance which the Bible attaches to it. For with one accord priests, prophets and apostles would say that it was in this experience of the Exodus that Israel as a people first encountered God, and that it was in the Exodus that God showed them for the first time that they had been chosen for some high divine purpose.

The Bible does not see the Exodus merely as the escape of Israel's sorely-tried ancestors from Egypt, but as the direct intervention of God in their affairs, whereby they were saved from a living death and the prospect of slow extermination, and by marvellous means which were none of their own doing, were snatched from the hands of their enemies and put on the way to a new life. It was not an exit but a deliverance, an Act of God by which he showed that the faith of the patriarchs had not been in vain, that the promise was no empty hope.

The real meaning of the Exodus for us, therefore, is not to be found in any attempt to sift history from interpretation but, as in the stories of the patriarchs, to take the narrative as it stands, and try to learn from it why the Bible consistently regards the Exodus as of supreme importance in the story of the people of God. It is tempting to find the answer sum-marised in the first few verses of the book (1: 1-5). There we are given the names of the twelve sons of Jacob, who are represented as the forefathers of the twelve tribes of Israel. At the same time the number of Jacob's household is recorded as seventy, which was the number of the Gentile nations known to the Jews (Gen. 10). Consequently the number seventy is sometimes used in the Bible in such a way as to suggest that the world at large is intended (e.g. the mission of the Seventy in Luke 10, a token of the Church's mission to the Gentiles), as op-posed to the number twelve which suggests the Jews only (e.g. the mission of the Twelve in Luke 9, a token of the Church's mission to the Jews).

Is it altogether fanciful to think that the final editors of Exodus, by prefacing the book with these num-bers were indicating subtly that whatever the Hebrews of the time thought about the Exodus, the later theologians of Israel saw its real meaning as the beginning of Israel's mission to the world? At all events the Exodus was for them their commission and consecration as the people of God, for these sorry fugitives from Egyptian soil carried with them the destiny of Israel to bring the whole world to the know-ledge and service of the one true God.

House of Bondage

(1: 1 – 2: 25)

THE BOOK begins by painting the backcloth for the dramatic events that are to be described. Some time has passed since, under

Joseph's auspices, his kinsmen had fled southwards from famine-stricken Canaan to the land of plenty, and had settled in the pasture lands of Goshen. Their numbers have grown and their fortunes have prospered. But a new pharaoh, to whom if he were a native Egyptian, the name of Joseph would be anathema, and the presence of a strong Semite minority in his territory a cause of anxiety and alarm, decided to break their spirit and provide himself with cheap labour at the same time, by setting them to work on his building projects.

Rameses II is known to have enlarged the cities of Avaris-Tanis, the capital of Egypt, and Pi-Tum, at the beginning of the thirteenth century B.C. and these are probably the towns which the Bible calls Raamses and Pithom (1: 11). A famous wall painting in the tomb of Rekhmire, a grand vizier of Egypt in the fifteenth century B.C., shows a group of earlier Semitic captives making and laying bricks with an Egyptian taskmaster in charge.

In the case of the Hebrews in the biblical story, however, ill-treatment did not check their numbers (1: 12), and the pharaoh resorted to more dramatic methods which were equally unsuccessful (1: 15-21). His edict calling on the Egyptians virtually to exterminate the Hebrews slowly by killing off all male infants (1: 22), is the prelude to the appearance of the chief character in the drama of the Exodus, and indeed one of the great figures in world history. The refusal of the midwives to co-operate with the Egyptian ruler, and the deter-

mination of Moses' mother to save her son from the massacre (2: 1-10), are both illustrations in picturesque biblical idiom of God's overruling providence which ensures that no power of evil can frustrate his good purposes. The promise must be fulfilled and Moses must be spared, since he is destined to be the next instrument in the grand unfolding of the divine plan.

So the author of *Hebrews* properly speaks of the action of Moses' mother in concealing his birth as a proof of her faith (*Heb.* 11: 23), being a wiser man than Calvin, who reckoned that to abandon the child among the bulrushes was rather an example of collapse of faith. The child in the ark and the child in the manger (*Luke* 2: 7; *Matt.* 2), both preserved from the violence of despots, the pharaoh and Herod, in order to execute God's will for men, speak to us of the gentleness by which God achieves his purposes in face of the ruthless weapons of human power. Even the very daughter of the pharaoh himself is unwittingly made to play a part in thwarting her father's evil intentions to the glory of God. The little ark with its precious cargo is rescued, and Moses is brought up in the pharaoh's own house.

For the second time an ark becomes the symbol of the Church, built to ensure the survival of a witness to God in a fallen world. Whether there is any historical truth in the story of the ark in the bulrushes is immaterial. The Bible is teaching us theological truth, and we learn nothing of that by dismissing the tale as a replica of the much older story of the birth of Sargon, king of Akkad, recorded in a Babylonian inscription.

The book of *Exodus* passes swiftly over the boyhood of Moses. Josephus, the Jewish historian, however, has a tale that on one occasion young Moses threw the pharaoh's crown on to the floor. It is possibly the truth behind this tradition to which the author of *Hebrews* refers when he speaks of Moses disdaining the advantages of a royal upbringing, and choosing rather to throw in his lot with his own people. In so doing he not only proved himself to be a man of faith, since there seemed little sign at that stage of anything but extinction ahead of the Israelites, but also he identified himself with Christ, whom the author of *Hebrews* sees as sharing, in his messianic role, the afflictions of the people of God throughout the Old Testament story (*Heb.* 11: 24–26).

So this man with the Egyptian-sounding name becomes the champion of his oppressed countrymen (2: 11–14). But his hot-tempered killing of a brutal Egyptian overseer did less than might have been expected to commend him to his own people (*Acts* 7: 25). They doubtless distrusted him as being not quite one of themselves, and they resented his interference in their affairs. Moses has to flee from the consequences of his crime, and becomes an exile in Midian, which lies in the region of the Gulf of Aqaba.

Again the author of *Hebrews* singles out this flight as an example of Moses' faith, and not of fear as the narrative suggests (2: 14–15). He may have meant that Moses' motive in fleeing the country was not fear for his own skin, but a prudent withdrawal in confidence that God's hour for him had not yet struck. Beyond the visible and temporarily all powerful king, he saw the eternal invisible Lord of history (*Heb.* 11: 27).

The Call of Moses
(3: 1–12)

MOSES' passion for justice, and his chivalry in coming to the aid of the chief priest of Midian's daughters, leads to his marriage with one of them, Zipporah, and to his settling as shepherd in the home of his father-in-law (2: 15–22), who is variously named Reuel (2: 18), Jethro (3: 1), and Hobab (*Judg.* 4: 11). We have seen already that it was the practice of the Hebrews to give meaningful names to people and places (e.g. Isaac = laughter; Jacob = deceiver; Bethel = house of God). Moses names his son Gershom (2: 22), meaning "a stranger there", as if to remind himself constantly that his destiny is with his own troubled people and not in the happy security of Midian. God's summons to him comes in the parable of the Burning Bush (3: 2).

We need not pause to question whether the holy mountain which features henceforward in the Exodus story was called Horeb, as here, or Sinai (19: 18, etc.), or both, or where in fact it was situated. Ancient tradition regards the names as alternatives, and identifies the site with the present-day Jebel Musa, the Mountain of Moses, in the south of the Sinai peninsula. Nor need we be exercised to find some rationalisation of the bush itself, either by explaining the flames as red berries with the sun shining on them, or by attributing them to some kind of natural gas or oil.

In biblical imagery fire is symbolic of the Presence of God (19: 18; *Ezek.* 8: 2, etc.), representing his glory, his righteous judgment and his zeal. This story of the burning bush, therefore, is simply the biblical way of describing Moses' encounter with God. The bush itself which burned but was not consumed may represent the ever-living presence of God, or it may be a tiny herald of the holy mountain itself (19: 18). Whatever be the precise significance of the symbol of the bush, it is clear that the meaning of the incident is that God calls Moses, as he called Jacob at Bethel, and summons him into his service.

He is to leave the security and peace of Midian, and return to share the hardships and hazards of his own captive people. It is no light assignment that he is given, nothing less than the task of liberating his countrymen from their bondage and leading them to the land of the promise, the land of "milk and honey". But he will not be alone, for God will be with him (3: 12). Like Jeremiah in later days (*Jer.* 1: 6), Moses felt himself quite unfitted for the task (3: 11).

YHWH

(3: 13–15)

IN HIS speech to the Sanhedrin, in which he summarises Old Testament history, St. Stephen describes Moses as "learned in all the wisdom of the Egyptians" (*Acts* 7: 22). Certainly his upbringing at the Egyptian court which there is no reason to doubt must have familiarised him with the best that could be said for the range of mythological gods and goddesses, the animal worship and cult of the dead which constituted Egyptian religion in his day.

He would also be aware of the unsuccessful effort of Akhnaten almost a century before the Exodus, to abolish the corrupt priesthood and the degrading polytheism that surrounded his throne, by instituting a religious reformation. The basis of this was the substitution of the worship of Aten, the sun, for the multiplicity of deities associated with the old state religion of Amun. This attempt to introduce monotheism was short-lived, but some scholars have seen in it the source of the distinctively monotheistic faith of the Old Testament.

In view of Moses' Egyptian background there may indeed be some connection between the two, but there are certain fundamental differences which make it necessary for us to look elsewhere for the origin of the characteristic faith of Israel, which these verses tell us was born at the time of the Exodus. According to the narrative (3: 14), God reveals his name to Moses as I AM or I WILL BE (R.V. margin). In the following verse (3: 15), he describes himself as THE "LORD"—a word for which the Hebrew consonants are YHWH. This word is related to the Hebrew word for I AM, and has been anglicised eventually into

Jehovah. A little later (6: 3), we are told that before the days of Moses, God was not known as Jehovah or YHWH but as God Almighty, El Shaddai (R.V. margin).

This difficult passage raises a host of problems, some of which in our present stage of knowledge are quite insoluble. A major difficulty is that the various streams of tradition which go to make up the Pentateuch do not agree on the important question as to whether Jehovah was in fact the name first used of God at the Exodus, or whether it had also been used by the patriarchs. The P and E traditions, with their emphasis on the religious significance of the Exodus, both imply that the new revelation of the name of God was given first to Moses, and do not use the name Jehovah until this point. The J tradition, on the other hand, uses the name Jehovah from the Creation story onwards (*Gen.* 2: 4). For J, the God of Adam, Noah and Abraham was Jehovah, the Lord, as he was for Moses and the prophets who came after him.

Partly due to this confusion, as well as to our ignorance of what the Bible means by the various names given to God before the Exodus [Elohim (*Gen*, 20: 3); El Elyon (*Gen.* 14: 18); El Shaddai (*Gen.* 17: 1)], assisted by our lack of accurate knowledge of the religious beliefs of the Hebrews during the patriarchal period, and the fact that all the stories of the patriarchs have been coloured by the theology of a much later age, we are unable to assess the full significance of the communication of the divine name at this juncture.

What is quite certain is that from this point in the narrative onward, the name of the God of Israel is the distinctive and unique word YHWH, which the Hebrews probably, pronounced as Yahweh, a name so sacred that in later days it was not allowed to be uttered, and when it occurred in public reading of scriptures was replaced by the word Adonai, meaning "the Lord". The God of the Old Testament psalmist and prophet, the God whom Israel learned to know and tried to serve, whom she came to recognise as Creator and Lord of all history, is this utterly holy and righteous God whose name no mortal man has the right even to whisper.

When we reflect on this conception of God which Israel held, setting side by side what YHWH meant to Isaiah, Jeremiah, Ezekiel, Amos and Hosea—a God who acts in human affairs—with the religious beliefs of any other nation in the ancient world—a medley of nature cults and mythologies—it is obvious that there is a radical difference which cannot be explained by gradual development from primitive beliefs, and which constitutes a unique faith among the religions of the world.

When we ask further how and when this unique faith and this distinctive conception of God came to Israel, we cannot be content to attribute its origins to the great eighth-century prophets. Amos and his successors never claimed to do any more than proclaim truths that their countrymen had neglected or forgotten. Again and again they point back to the Exodus as the moment when

Israel's unique faith was born, and we are irresistibly led to see the mind of Moses as the instrument which God selected to reveal this unique conception of himself to the people he had chosen, and through them to the whole world.

Obviously it was not given to Moses to comprehend all the truth about God and his will for mankind that was later grasped by the profound insights of psalmists, prophets and wisdom scribes. But as we read these stories in the book of *Exodus*, we shall see reflected in them in embryonic form the distinctive marks of the faith and obedience which make the religion of the Old Testament the swaddling clothes of Christ. Whatever the name YHWH means, whether "he who is", "he who will be", or "he who causes to be", it is a conception of God large enough to hold all the range and depth of meaning which the later insights and experience of Israel's saints will pour into it.

Such a conception of God as Moses was granted cannot be satisfactorily explained as a derivation from the short-lived Aten worship of his Egyptian background, still less as a simple adoption of the local deity of his Kenite father-in-law, as has been widely suggested. To be faced with the task of returning to Egypt, and rallying his countrymen under the auspices of a hitherto unknown God would surely have been an impossible assignment.

We must therefore take the text of *Exodus* 3:15 as it stands, and see this revelation to Moses not as paving the way for the introduction of a new God to Israel, but as a revelation of a new understanding of the God that Abraham and his descendants had always worshipped, in token of which God is given a new name, which from now on becomes the key to Israel's story as the people of YHWH. These dispirited serfs and exiles are to be summoned to go out again like Abraham, their forefather, into the unknown, trusting in the God whom Abraham served, but who will reveal to them through Moses truths about himself that Abraham and those who came after him only dimly grasped. The Lord of the universe, creator of Adam, deliverer of Noah, and summoner of Abraham, has now by his grace acted again, and raised the curtain for the next scene in the divine drama which records the story of man's salvation.

YHWH and the Gods of Egypt
(3:16–11:10)

IT WOULD seem as if Moses embarked on his gargantuan task with the conviction that if indeed his mission succeeded, and he was able to lead his people out of Egypt to the holy mountain where he had received his call, he would know for sure that the hand of God was behind the enterprise (3:12). But how could the pharaoh be persuaded to let the people go, and how could the people be persuaded to embark upon such a venture? If we are to take the next few chapters of *Exodus* literally, it would seem that the answer to both questions was wholly within the realm of the black arts.

Moses has a magic rod, which can change into a serpent. He can summon and banish leprosy and turn water into blood (4: 1–9). His elder brother Aaron has a similar device which is equally effective. This is sufficient to persuade the Israelite slaves that Moses and Aaron must be obeyed, since clearly they are endowed with supernatural power (4: 30–31). The pharaoh is more sceptical, even when his own magicians in competition with the brothers are unable to perform such startling tricks (7: 8–12). What does persuade him eventually, however, is a series of plagues brought about by the same kind of magic, which so disrupt the life of the Egyptian people that in the end the pharaoh reluctantly agrees to part with his cheap labour. Perhaps not surprisingly, the natives encourage the speedy departure of their uncomfortable neighbours with lavish gifts.

Can we disentangle a thread of historical fact from this obviously legendary recital; more important, what is its religious value? The historical question is complicated by the fact that the three strands of tradition—J, E and P—are closely interwoven in this section. The J tradition, which is of course the earliest, gives the most matter of fact account, e.g. that Moses' magic rod was his ordinary shepherd's crook. The E tradition, a little later in origin, enhances the element of magic, while the P strand as might be expected stresses the importance of Aaron, the priest.

If Moses was brought up in the court of Egypt, there is nothing improbable in the claim that he had easy access to the ear of the pharaoh. Nor is it impossible, similarly, that having been reared in such an environment he was well acquainted with the tricks of the Egyptian wizards and was able to outwit them. Similarly, although the round number of ten plagues is arrived at by the editor of *Exodus* by amalgamating the disasters described in the three traditions—J mentions 8, E and P both record 5, though not the same 5—there is none of them except the last which by itself is an incredible occurrence.

W. J. Phythian Adams, in *The Call of Israel* (1934), has a persuasive explanation which includes the plagues as part of a sequence of effects of volcanic action, located in the great geological fissure which extends from the Jordan Valley through the Red Sea to the upper reaches of the Nile. Volcanic activity at the sources of the Nile might account for the blood-like discoloration of the lower reaches due to volcanic mud, which being poisonous would account for the death of the fish and of the frogs, and the consequent spread of disease through flies. The plague of darkness would be caused by a pall of volcanic ash floating down the Nile Valley, which need not affect the Israelites in the remote area of Goshen (10: 23).

A less likely explanation has been offered more recently by I. Velikowsky, in *Worlds in Collision* (1950), who traces the unusual natural phenomena associated with the Exodus, including the plagues, to the erratic movements of the planet Venus which at about this time is claimed to have passed too close to the earth. Mostly, however, the plagues are reckoned to have been natural occurrences, which at this particular point in history may have happened with unusual intensity. Discoloration of the Nile water as it rises in flood, due to the presence of red marl carried down from the Abyssinian mountains; swarms of frogs, mosquitoes, flies and locusts; cattle disease and human skin-rash; dust or sand-storms darkening the sky during the Khamsin period—these are all features of the Egyptian scene familiar enough to the inhabitants of the Nile valley. The tenth plague, the death of the firstborn, may either have been originally the death of the pharaoh's firstborn, or an epidemic affecting children generally, including the crown prince.

At all events, however much we deduct from the narrative as inevitable exaggeration in retrospect, among people to whom these phenomena were no longer familiar, the basic facts would seem to be a combination of unusual natural disasters together with the opportunism of Moses, who not only seized the apparently heaven sent chance to free his people from their serfdom, but interpreted the catastrophes as an unmistakable sign that the God of Israel was behind them. From the point of view of history therefore we may think of Moses, returning from Midian convinced of his call to lead his people from slavery to freedom, using the

harsher conditions of bondage (5: 6–18) and the preoccupation of the Egyptians with their own plight, to encourage the Israelites to make their escape when the confusion was at its height.

Yet in the stories of the plagues as they are recorded in *Exodus*, the dominant theme is not the personal struggle between Moses and the pharaoh, in which the stubborn obstinacy of the king is broken by the supernatural forces deployed against him. The real antagonists are the God of Israel and the gods of Egypt (12: 12). Their servants the magicians are discomfited by the servant of YHWH as they themselves are mocked by the superior power of the Lord of Creation. The holy river Nile with its sacred croco-diles, the varied species of cattle which the Egyptians worshipped as gods, Amun-Re, the supreme sun-god himself, blotted out by the darkness which YHWH spread over the land, all are playthings in the hands of Israel's God. It is he too who hardens the pharaoh's heart to demonstrate his sovereign power over man and nature (9: 16), and to bring into even more vivid relief the underlying miracle of Israel's election to be his people (*Rom.* 9: 14–18).

In that curious and otherwise inexplicable little incident in 4: 24–26, Moses, the human instru-ment in God's plan, is circumcised by proxy, so that the continuity of the covenant with Abraham may be symbolically maintained (*Gen.* 17: 14), in preparation for the covenant at Sinai, to which the startling events of the Exodus are merely the preliminaries.

The First Passover

(12 : 1 – 13 : 16)

THE present account of the first passover, still celebrated in orthodox Jewish homes in commemoration of the Exodus, is a compound of later ritual practice and the onset of the tenth plague. The narrative would suggest as a basic historical fact an outbreak of some virulent disease to which the Egyptian children fell victims, and from which the Israelites, not improbably because of their relative isolation in the land of Goshen, were immune. In the retrospective enhancement of the marvellous nature of their escape from Egypt, it is not surprising that the story has taken on its present fanciful colouring.

Scholars are generally agreed that the origin of the passover is to be found much earlier than the Exodus in the traditional spring festival of nomadic people. The form of the ritual would suggest a feast of communion with a deity, associated with sacrifice as a propitiation, and the protective smearing of the tents with the blood of the victims. In the narrative of the Exodus, this has become attached to the greatest event in Israel's early history. Similarly the feast of unleavened bread, an ancient Canaanite rite later taken over by Israel, and the sacrifice of the firstlings of the flocks, also a general nomadic observance of thanksgiving to their particular god, are here likewise brought together and traced back to this specific occasion.

Clearly, however, we must take the narrative as it stands, and as it was understood by the theologically-minded compilers of the Old Testament. In this sense all these ancient and diverse elements are fused into a celebration of the mercy of God, who "passed over" and thus delivered his people from death, and opened up the way for them to new life. This was the real birth of the people of God, of Israel the firstborn of God's new community. Thus it is fitting that it should be celebrated with unleavened bread, symbolising the complete break with the past, and with a sense of urgency as befits those whose faces are now turned towards their promised land.

It is in this light that we can see the significance of St. Paul's words in *I Cor.* 5 : 7–8, and indeed of many other New Testament allusions. "Christ our passover is sacrificed for us." Surely this is no mere reference to the fact that our Lord died at the time of the Jewish feast, but a perception that in the Passion and Death of Jesus, the pattern of God's salvation of the world foreshadowed in the Exodus had now been perfected and demonstrated once and for all. Indeed the New Testament writers see Christ, the one true Israelite, as recapitulating Israel's experience.

Thus the writer of Matthew's gospel is not thinking in terms of mechanical fulfilment of prophecy when he associates the return of the Holy Family from Egypt, to which they had fled to escape the massacre of the innocents (*Matt.* 2 : 13–16), with the words of Hosea: "Out of Egypt have I called my son"

(*Hos.* 11 : 1). Christ, the firstborn of God's new creation, is delivered from death by the same Father who had delivered Israel, firstborn of his people, from a similar fate. But as Israel was delivered not for its own preservation but to become the servant of God's purpose, so the New Testament writers see the self-giving of Christ in his sufferings and Death as the culmination of God's plan for the salvation of the world, initiated at the Exodus and commemorated at the passover. It was in order that Christ should become the Paschal Lamb for all mankind, that Israel was set apart by this signal act of God's mercy.

So it is that in St. John's gospel, the Baptist acclaims Jesus as the Lamb of God (*John* 1 : 29), who enters Jerusalem on the day that the passover lamb was to be taken into the homes of Israel (*John* 12 : 1, 12; cf. *Ex.* 12 : 3–6), who was crucified as the paschal lambs were being slain for the feast (*John* 19 : 14) and whose bones must not be broken in accordance with the ancient ritual (*John* 19 : 36). In St. Mark's gospel Christ celebrates the passover with his disciples (*Mark* 14 : 12), attaching to it the highest significance (cf. *Luke* 22 : 15) which becomes apparent when he transforms it into the sacrament of his own body and blood offered for the New Israel (cf. 12 : 42 with *Matt.* 26 : 27–"all"). From that moment the passover of the Exodus story becomes the Eucharist of the Israel of God. The thread of continuity is unbroken, even to the sense of urgency with which the Church celebrates the Lord's death "till he come" (*I Cor.* 11 : 26).

The Baptism of Israel
(13 : 17 – 15 : 21)

IT WAS said at the time of the Darwinian controversy, when the ordinary layman—and some churchmen—rallied to the defence of the book of *Genesis* against the theory of evolution, that what they were defending was not so much the biblical view of creation, as Milton's fanciful embellishments of the biblical account in *Paradise Lost*. In the case of the climax of the Exodus story, when the fugitive Israelite slaves, having escaped death by plague finally escaped death by drowning, and found themselves in freedom and safety on the threshold of the promised land, we have not only to contend with the imaginative reconstruction of the event by modern film producers, but with the pious exaggeration of biblical tradition itself.

If we take the figures of 12 : 37 as they stand, giving an approximate total of two million men, women and children, to say nothing of the additional "mixed multitude" and the herds of cattle of 12 : 38, and combine this with the familiar picture of the Red Sea dividing at Moses' command, enabling the vast assorted concourse to pass dry shod between walls of water on either side, we are out of the realm of history or even miracle and into the world of children's story books.

First of all, as to numbers involved, neither the land of Goshen nor the peninsula of Sinai in which the fugitives took refuge could support more than a few thousand souls. This would tally with the fact that two mid-wives appear to have been suffi-cient to deal with the Hebrew birthrate (1: 15); that even allow-ing for the passage of four centuries (12: 41), which itself is doubtful on other grounds, the seventy odd souls of 1: 5 could hardly have multiplied themselves thirty thousand times; nor would such a gigantic caravan have been properly described as "the fewest of all people" (*Deut.* 7: 7).

We may then justifiably think of a mass escape of the able bodied men from the pharaoh's new towns, collecting their families on the way, and probably other dissident non-Israelite elements from the labour-gangs as well, totalling somewhere in the region of five thousand. Their primary aim is to get out of Egypt. To the east the way is barred by the Princes' wall, a chain of frontier posts guarding the normal route into Palestine, "the way of the land of the Philistines" (13: 17). The fugitives have no choice but to head south. They are thus flanked on the left by what is now the Suez Canal, the construction of which has so altered the original landscape that it is difficult to say at which point the Israelites were faced with a choice between the "sea" in front and the pursuing Egyptian chariots behind.

It seems more likely that the Hebrew words Yam Suph, "sea of reeds", would indicate an inland fresh-water lake rather than the Red Sea itself or one of its arms, whether the Gulf of Suez or the Gulf of Aqaba. It would appear no less miraculous to the Hebrews at the time if, as the oldest strand of tradition in the Exodus story claims, a "strong east wind" (14: 21) made a passage on foot pos-sible, perhaps across a shallow ford in the centre of the lake with deeper water on either side, while the chariots of the Egyptians stuck in the marshy ground and the returning waters engulfed them (14: 25–28).

Alternatively, volcanic action has been suggested, causing the bed of the sea or lake to rise, enabling the fugitives to cross, and subsiding with an accompany-ing tidal wave which destroyed the pursuers. On this view the pillar of cloud by day and of fire by night (13: 22) would be identified, like the later smoke and thunder at the holy mountain (19: 16–18), as characteristic features of the general volcanic interpretation of the strange events of the Exodus narrative.

The plain fact is that there is no certainty in the matter at all. A volcanic background to the Exodus events, while it seems to meet most of the difficulties and would certainly account for the deep impression made upon the minds of the Israelites, is ques-tioned on the grounds that geo-logical evidence does not indicate activity of this kind at this particu-lar place or at this particular point in history, nor is there any account of it in Egyptian records. Many will be content to think simply in terms of a dramatic escape from what appeared to be the tragic end of a great venture, and will not be overmuch concerned to know precisely where or precisely how God "made the waters to stand as an heap" (*Ps.* 78: 13).

The ancient fragment of the

Song of Miriam (15: 21), which has later been expanded into Moses, hymn of thanksgiving (15: 1–19), is echoed throughout the Old Testament (*Deut.* 11: 4; *Ps.* 78: 53; 136: 13–15; *Isa.* 63: 11–12), testifying to Israel's conviction that here above all was certain proof that God had laid his hand upon her and singled her out to be his people. It is perhaps in the light of this conviction that we can best interpret the pillar of cloud as the symbol of the Presence of God (cf. 33: 9–10; 40: 34–38), leading his people to the land of their destiny. But while he protects them he also judges them, hence it is also a pillar of fire, which at the same time confounds their enemies, to whom it is a pillar of darkness (14: 20).

This great act of deliverance by which God brought Israel from death to life, and sealed her for his own, stands at the beginning of the story of the people of God, but it is a theme which runs through the whole Bible as characteristic of God's will and power to save. Second Isaiah (i.e. *Isa.* chs. 40–55; see p. 248) sees it as of the same pattern as the Creation of the world, when God brought light out of darkness, order out of chaos, and, in his own day, hope out of despair as the Babylonian Exile ended and the way was opened up for Israel to return to Zion, the city of God (*Isa.* 51: 9–11).

In St. Luke's account of the Transfiguration, Jesus' approaching death is spoken of as his "*Exodos*" (*Luke* 9: 31), God's deliverance of mankind not from mortal enemies like Egyptians or Babylonians, but from sin and evil and death. St. Paul brings out the full significance of the Exodus when he likens it to Christian baptism. "All our fathers were under the cloud, and all passed through the sea; and were all baptised unto Moses in the cloud and in the sea" (*I Cor.* 10: 1–2). In this simile he pictures old Israel, under the protecting Presence of God, being led from slavery to freedom, from darkness to light, from death to life within the old Mosaic covenant, just as the members of the New Israel pass through the water of baptism from the death of sin to the life and liberty of the New Covenant in Jesus Christ.

"*I taught Israel to walk*"

(15: 22 – 17: 16)

IF UNDER the guidance of St. Paul we see the real meaning of the miracle of the sea as the baptism of Israel, the firstborn of God's people, we may look on the narrative that follows, which describes the experiences of the Israelites in the desert before they are allowed to enter the land of the promise, as a series of stories illustrating the lessons the child had to learn before it was ready for the task that had been laid upon it. Hosea well describes this journey through the wilderness as God's teaching Israel (Ephraim) to walk, leading it by the hand (*Hos.* 11: 3).

Assuming that the holy mountain to which Moses was guiding his motley caravan was the traditional Jebel Musa or Mountain of

Moses in the Sinai peninsula, the route of the column would seem to have followed the ancient track which led from Egypt to the turquoise mines of Serabit not far from the sacred mountain itself. There would now be no particular reason for haste, and the daily distance covered would probably be in the region of fifteen miles. The scrubland would offer little enough pasture for the cattle and the water holes would determine the camping spots. Some of the place-names mentioned in the biblical narrative can still be identified as oases.

Whatever romantic illusions we may have harboured as to the high sense of purpose and dedicated intention of the mass of the people who took part in this pilgrimage, they are certainly not shared by the final editors of the book of *Exodus*. There emerges, from the picture they present, a leader of outstanding resourcefulness and courage harassed and bedevilled by a querulous spiritless mob with no heart in the enterprise, always ready to reproach Moses for having induced them to leave the relative security and well-being of slavery, for hardship and starvation in the desert.

The parallel account in the book of *Numbers* (11: 1–6) is inclined to lay the blame at the door of the "mixed multitude" which had attached itself to the Israelites, but in the book of *Exodus* the contrast between the faith of Moses, who "endured as seeing him who is invisible" (*Heb.* 11: 27), and the lack of faith on the part of Israel is the real motif of the narrative. By a series of acted parables Israel is taught that the first requirement of the people of God is to trust in him come what may.

The incidents themselves are, like the plagues, susceptible of natural explanations. It is not unlikely that Moses had acquired the knowledge during his days of exile in similar terrain in Midian which enabled him to neutralise salt water (15: 25), and strike water from the porous limestone rock (17: 6). Similar "miracles" are vouched for in the Sinai area in recent times. Flocks of quails (16:13) migrating from Africa to Europe, and falling exhausted after their flight across the Red Sea, are still picked up by bedouin in this region. Manna (16: 14–31) is a honey-like exudation of the tamarisk tree which is still found as the narrative describes it, and is used for food by the Arabs.

But the motive of the narrative is not to provide us with a handbook to the geology and biology of the Sinai Peninsula. Nor is it of much moment whether some of the incidents belong more properly to a later stage in the journey to Canaan. Israel is being prepared for the vital moment at Sinai when the covenant with Abraham is renewed under Moses. The timid and distrustful child must learn that the hallmark of fitness to do God's bidding is to rely on God's providence from day to day. The whole passage may be read as a commentary on the petition in the Lord's Prayer: "Give us this day our daily bread", i.e. enough for today, or on our Lord's words in the Sermon on the Mount (*Matt.* 6: 31–32): "take no thought, saying, what shall we eat? or what shall we drink? . . . for your heavenly Father knoweth that ye have need of all these things".

So when the people clamour for water (15: 24; 17: 2), or for bread (16: 3), and when there seems to be no likelihood of obtaining either, they are taught by their providential appearance that God will always supply his people's needs. Similarly the pitched battle with the Amalekites (17: 8-16) is doubtless intended to teach the lesson that sustained united supplication to God, symbolised by Moses' uplifted hands being supported by his brethren, will alone guarantee victory over Israel's enemies in days to come.

For the author of *Hebrews*, following *Ps.* 95: 8-11, the incident at Massah or Meribah (17: 7) finds its significance as a warning to his Christian readers not to fall into the error of the Israelites of old, who provoked God by putting his providential care of his people to the test and who doubted his word of promise. For this they were punished by being kept in the wilderness for forty years until they learned to have faith (*Heb.* 3: 7-19). St. Paul sees a deeper meaning in the manna and the water from the rock (*I Cor.* 10: 3-4). A Jewish legend had it that the rock that Moses struck followed the Israelites through the desert supplying them with water (cf. *Num.* 20), and St. Paul, thinking in terms of Christ as supplying the water of life (*John* 4: 5-14) identifies him with the rock by which Israel was sustained.

This is no mere playing with words but an expression of the conviction, common to the New Testament, that the beginning of the Christian story and of the saving work of Christ was not to be found in his birth at Bethlehem, but in the first chapter of Genesis, and above all in the schooling of the people of God's choice. Our Lord himself sets the seal on the Old Testament interpretation of the manna as bread from heaven (*Neh.* 9: 15; *Ps.* 78: 24-25), when he speaks of himself as the Bread of Life (*John* 6: 31-58). and in the sacrament of his body and blood the New Israel sees the fulfilment of this ancient Exodus story.

The Priest of Midian
(18: 1-27)

IT IS difficult to know quite what to make of the strange interlude involving Jethro, the priest of Midian, father-in-law of Moses, which is inserted after the series of acted parables in 15: 22-17: 16, and before the great revelation of the Law and the renewal of the covenant at Sinai which is described in 19: 1-25.

The caravan has now reached the region of the holy mountain where Moses was called to be a servant of YHWH in the symbolic experience of the Burning Bush (3: 1-12). The fact that he has accomplished his mission of leading his people from slavery to freedom is not regarded as a tribute to his own leadership, but to the power of the God to whom he dedicated himself at the end of his exile in Midian (3: 12). Now his father-in-law brings his wife and children to meet him and a solemn thanksgiving ceremony takes place.

Many scholars have noted that the impression left by this narrative is that Jethro is represented not so much as a humble convert to the worship of YHWH, moved by the tale that Moses has to tell of the marvellous deliverance that has taken place, but rather as a religious dignitary who is treated with marked respect by Moses (v. 7), and who acts as the celebrant at the ceremony which follows and at which Aaron, the priest, and the chief laymen of Israel are mere worshippers (v. 12).

It has been argued from this that in effect Jethro is the key to the problem of where Moses derived the new name for God which occurs for the first time, according to E and P, at the Exodus (3: 14–15; 6: 3). If YHWH was the god of Sinai, worshipped by the Midianites or Kenites (*Judg.* 1: 16), and if Jethro was his chief priest, Moses' father-in-law would be receiving no more than his due if he were treated with the utmost respect by all the Israelites, who had by this time learned that this powerful god had been responsible for the events by which they had been enabled to escape from Egypt.

The absence of mention of Moses as partaking in the ceremony of 18: 12 would imply that Moses had already, through his encounter with the god of Sinai at the Burning Bush, been incorporated into the cult of YHWH, into which Aaron and the chief representatives of Israel are now formally admitted by Jethro. The subsequent reorganisation of the judicial practice of the fugitives (vv. 14–26) would imply that Israel took not only the name of the god of Jethro but also the judicial system of the Kenites.

It is impossible to dismiss this view as derogatory to the exalted monotheism of the full flower of Israel's faith. We cannot credit Moses with the spiritual insights of the eighth-century prophets, still less with the universalistic faith of Second Isaiah (e.g. *Isa.* 40: 28). God discloses the mystery of his being in proportion to the readiness of minds sensitive enough to perceive it. Moses for all his gigantic achievements was a child of his times, and the insights of the later prophets, Jeremiah, Hosea, Isaiah and Ezekiel, were conditioned by the centuries of the experience of the people of God by which their knowledge of his ways and purposes was enriched.

There is therefore nothing inherently impossible in the idea that before YHWH became the God of Israel he was worshipped by the tribe of Midian, among whom Moses in his early days sought refuge from Egyptian justice, and that, in this eighteenth chapter of *Exodus*, the leaders of the Israelites acknowledge that the god whom Moses had come to know had been powerful enough to ensure the defeat of the hosts of Egypt, and was therefore a god well worthy of Israel's allegiance. The fact that in the rest of the Old Testament the part played by Jethro and the Kenites is ignored may simply mean that YHWH had become so closely identified with Israel and the Mosaic revelation that earlier associations were forgotten or regarded as unimportant.

But even if this origin of the name and "identity" of YHWH be conceded, it would still be quite wrong to speak of Israel as having "taken over" the god of the Kenites. There is a radical break between the conception of God as held by the prophets of Israel and developed by priest and psalmist, and that of any other Near Eastern people of which we have any archaeological evidence. Whatever the Kenites meant when they said YHWH, if indeed the above theory is correct, it was certainly not the same as was meant by Israel, even as early as the covenant of Sinai.

On any showing, the Old Testament pinpoints the Exodus as the beginning of a unique faith and singles out Moses as the creative mind which God used to mediate a new conception of himself, albeit under an old name, to the people of his choice. At the Burning Bush, Moses was singled out not by an imaginary tribal deity of an obscure Midianite clan, but by the Lord of Creation and history, the God of Jeremiah, Job, Isaiah and of our Lord Jesus Christ, who used, as he always does, the foolish things of the world to confound the wise (cf. *I Cor.* 1 : 18–29).

The God whom the Bible reveals may have entered history as the protector of a now long-forgotten unimportant tribe, but in his providential ordering of man's salvation it was to Moses that he first revealed the dim beginnings of what the name YHWH came to mean. It was to Moses that he revealed that whatever names the patriarchs may have used for God (6 : 3), it

was the same YHWH who had spoken to Abraham, Isaac and Jacob as had now spoken to their dispirited descendants in Egypt, and had laid his hand upon them to make Israel in a far deeper way the bearers of his truth to the nations.

However little even Moses himself may have grasped of the task that was being laid upon his disgruntled followers, nothing less than the renewal of the life of the world, it was clear to him that he had been summoned to a mammoth assignment, and that the God who had summoned him was no circumscribed local godlet but a living personal power, who could overrule the plans of princes and harness the forces of nature in obedience to his will. In this light we may perhaps best think of the significance of this odd prominence of Jethro, priest of Midian, as symbolising the transformation of Yahweh, god of the Kenites, into YHWH God of Israel, and, in the second half of the chapter, we may see the symbolic handing over of authority by Jethro, whose task it had been to make known the will of Yahweh, god of the Kenites, to his godchild Moses, involving the appointment of Moses as the supreme lawgiver whose role it will be to seek to know the will of YHWH, God of Israel, and to communicate it to YHWH's people.

The Covenant at Sinai

(19: 1–25)

NOW FOLLOWS with all solemnity the oath of allegiance which the Israelites swear to the

God who had chosen them and brought them from death to life. The first few verses of this chapter (vv. 3–8) crystallise the significance of the events at Sinai and of the covenant which is made there. In a sense this covenant is something new in Israel's experience, but it is also the same theme which we have seen already in the story of Noah (*Gen.* 8 : 20 – 9 : 17) and of Abraham (*Gen.* 15 : 18).

In the symbolism of the covenant with Noah, there is expressed the biblical conviction that God cares for all mankind, and that though man has deserved and still deserves nothing but just retribution for his persistent rebellion against God, God's love is so strong that he will not allow man to destroy himself. Then in the covenant with Abraham we saw the beginning of God's plan to save the world from itself by the choice of a particular community which would be his instrument of salvation. But Israel could not be the saviour of the world until it had itself come to know the saving power of God in a unique way. The experiences of the Exodus had provided this, and in their midst was a leader who could interpret for the people the significance of their recent deliverance.

Accordingly, the time is now ripe for an act of communal dedication, in which Israel acknowledges its adoption by YHWH and pledges itself to his service. The covenant with Abraham, father of the tribes, is now renewed with the tribes themselves. Again it is not an equal partnership. On the one hand there is enthroned the Lord of nature and of history; on the other this ill-assorted band of refugees out of which he will mould a nation. The terms of the covenant are in no sense a mutual bargain. God prescribes the task and the terms. Israel's role is to accept both in humility and obedience. They have been wonderfully delivered, borne on "eagles' wings" (v. 4), and now, face to face with God, they are given their assignment.

The whole earth belongs to the Lord, and all men are in his loving care, but Israel is to be his "peculiar treasure" i.e. special possession (v. 5), destined not for power or glory but to be a "kingdom of priests", a missionary people, set apart from the rest ("holy"), and consecrated to the supreme vocation of bringing the whole world to the knowledge of God (v. 6). This is the obligation that Israel accepts, and in the following chapters the method by which they are to achieve it is outlined for them.

More than one New Testament writer applies these words used of Israel in this chapter to the Christian Church, recognising that the missionary vocation of old Israel has now devolved upon the Israel of God. Thus the Church is a "peculiar people" (*Tit.* 2: 14) singled out as God's own; "priests of God" (*Rev.* 20: 6; cf. also 1: 6; 5: 10) charged with the office of mediating between God and the rest of the world, representing God to man and man to God. Above all the words of *I Pet.* 2: 5, 9 show how strongly conscious the Church was of having entered into the historical pattern of the covenant relationship with God, which even though it had been remade in Christ and had been given fresh significance by his words and works, was still as of old God's way of redeeming the world: "You are God's 'chosen generation', his 'royal priesthood', his 'holy nation', his 'peculiar people' —all the old titles of God's People now belong to you" (*I Pet.* 2: 9).

It is impossible, because of the composite nature of the narrative, to follow Moses' journeys up and down the holy mountain. It is equally unprofitable to speculate whether the smoke and flames, the rumbling and quaking, vividly suggesting a volcanic eruption, fit into a general volcanic explanation of the original events surrounding the Exodus (see p. 75), or whether YHWH was regarded here as so often in the early stages of Israel's history (e.g. *Josh.* 10: 11; *Judg.* 5: 20–21) as manifesting himself pre-eminently in storm and thunder, in lightning and raincloud. Nor do we learn much of the significance of this encounter of Israel with YHWH by criticising the anthropomorphic descent of YHWH from heaven (v. 18), or by classifying the prohibitions of vv. 12–13, 22, 24 as vestiges of primitive tabu.

This is much more a wonderfully effective impressionistic painting or a prose poem, which conveys precisely what the editors of *Exodus* intended: the awful Presence of YHWH, symbolised as before (cf. 13: 21; 16: 10) by cloud and fire; the imperious Voice of YHWH, conveyed by the image of the trumpet and the thunderstorm: and the utter Holiness of YHWH, which set a gulf between sinful man and holy God such as no common foot might bridge. It is a sombre picture and a true one, reminding us that the covenant relationship in which like old Israel the new Israel stands is no partnership between equals, but a relationship in which we must always recognise our place as that of creatures under the Creator, where the words that God speaks to us are not pleasantries that we enjoy listening to, but challenging uncomfortable words at which we may well tremble (v. 16; cf. 20: 19).

But it is not the whole picture, as the author of *Hebrews* in a magnificent passage makes plain (*Heb.* 12: 18–29). He contrasts the atmosphere of life under the old covenant with life under the New Covenant in Christ, using this picture of the giving of the Law at Sinai as symbolic of the gloom and darkness of the Law without the Gospel, or in modern terms, of the Old Testament without the New. Over against the message of the awfulness of an unapproachable God, he sets the proclamation of forgiveness through Christ. It is not a different God that the author of *Hebrews* believes in, but the same God who has now been more fully revealed as a God of love.

Yet, as if to prevent our misunderstanding of what the New Testament means by the love of God, the author of *Hebrews* concludes his contrast with words which indicate that the conception of God under the old covenant has not been cancelled but merely corrected. For the God of love and forgiveness whom the New Testament reveals in Christ must still be served "with reverence and godly fear". He is still "a consuming fire" (*Heb.* 12: 29). With this quotation from *Deut.* 4: 24 both the author of *Hebrews* and the compiler of *Exodus* would agree.

It is in keeping with the thought of *Hebrews* which connects the Voice of God (vv. 16, 19), symbolised by the trumpet on Sinai and the terror it instilled into the hearts of the Israelites, with the Last Judgment (cf. *Heb.* 12: 26 with *Ex.* 19: 16), that other New Testament writers introduce the trumpet or Last Trump into the imagery of the Second Advent of Christ (*Matt.* 24: 31; *I Cor.* 15: 52; *I Thess.* 4: 16; cf. *Rev.* 1: 10; 4: 1).

The Ten Commandments

(20: 1–17)

THE Ten Commandments are the terms of the covenant. This is to be the pattern of life for the people of God, the mark of his "peculiar people", and in agreeing to mould their lives on these basic principles they make their response of gratitude to God for their deliverance. It has often been suggested that the Ten Commandments could not possibly have originated at this early stage in Israel's history, and that they more properly belong to the age of the classical prophets five centuries later.

This is of course perfectly possible, in view of the fact that the final arrangement of the Pentateuch is several centuries later still. There is also added weight for this view, apart from other minor considerations, in the fact that in the later pages of the Old Testament there is no clear reference to these particular Ten Commandments as being a recognised foundation for the Law of Israel.

On the other hand there is no doubt that the Exodus, the covenant of Sinai, and the subsequent sojourn in the desert before the conquest of Canaan are regarded as the formative experiences which made Israel a nation, shaped its thought and gave it its distinctive self-consciousness. It would be surprising if the pedestrian regulations which follow the Ten Commandments (20: 22 – 23: 19), were sufficient to make the profound impact upon Israel's early life which impels later prophets and psalmists to look back to the desert days following the Exodus as the high water mark of Israel's obedience of God. In later tradition this period was always regarded as the time in Israel's history, before the insidious encroachment of Canaanite customs and religion sowed the seeds of the final downfall of Israel as a nation, when a simple faith in YHWH walked hand in hand with an austere code of morality. Something as startlingly novel and creative as the Ten Commandments is surely required to explain this tradition and to match the stature of the recent deliverance from bondage.

Nor is there anything inherently

improbable in such a code emerging at this stage in history and in such a setting. The life of a bedouin tribe, with its simple demands, its communal ownership of the necessities of life, its wholesome attitude to sex and generally uncomplicated existence was one in which such provisions as those contained in the Decalogue would seem in no sense unrealistic Indeed, we may hazard a guess that part of the background of Moses' call to the service of YHWH was the glaring contrast presented to his mind between the sensuous amoral polytheism, which he had come to know at close quarters in Egypt, and the healthy piety and morality which he found among the Kenite worshippers of Yahweh.

In their original form the commandments were probably much shorter, and therefore more readily memorised, than they are in their present form. It is possible that Moses' first enunciation of the basic Law of Israel in this absolute or apodictic form was on the following lines:

Thou shalt not worship any other god but YHWH
Thou shalt not make a graven image
Thou shalt not take the name of YHWH in vain
Thou shalt not break the sabbath
Thou shalt not dishonour thy parents
Thou shalt not murder
Thou shalt not commit adultery
Thou shalt not steal
Thou shalt not commit perjury
Thou shalt not covet

There was a time when the Ten Commandments were felt to be replaced by the commandments of Jesus, in particular by his summing up of the whole Law in the two great commandments "Thou shalt love the Lord thy God with all thy heart, and with all thy soul, and with all thy mind and with all thy strength" and "Thou shalt love thy neighbour as thyself" (*Mark* 12: 29–31) But Jesus is not superseding the Decalogue. He is bringing out its deepest meaning. Thus when he quotes the sixth and seventh commandments in the Sermon on the Mount (*Matt.* 5: 21–22, 27–28), he does not abrogate them in stressing that the new Law which he brings makes heavier demands on us. He aims to show not that the Mosaic code is wrong but that it is inadequate. Jesus does not destroy the Law, he fulfils it (*Matt.* 5: 17–20).

While it is therefore true to say that the positive approach to human relationships such as the Gospel enjoins, "thou shalt" rather than "thou shalt not", implies a more profound basis for behaviour than the negative injunctions of the Decalogue, it is not true that the Ten Commandments can be dismissed as part of the "Hebrew old clothes" that the New Testament has put out of fashion. On the contrary they are still a relevant working code for twentieth-century society.

At the forefront of the Decalogue, as its justification and foundation, stands the unquestioned authority of God: "I am the Lord thy God" (v. 2). This is surely a primary recognition of man's place in the universe, as opposed to the self-deception which claims that the reins of our destiny are in our own hands. "The earth is the Lord's" (*Ps.* 24: 1), not man's, and it is at our peril that we think or act as if scientific skills and educational panaceas will bring about the golden age. We are puny, helpless mortals, unable without divine guidance to run our lives or the life of the world on wholesome lines, and, more than that, unable without divine help, to bring any good thing to fruition.

It is this latter fact which is embodied in the second part of the preface. It is God who rescues us from bondage. As he rescued the Israelites from Egypt, it is his will that all men should be saved from the slavery of sin and self, from frustration and failure. In these words we see the pattern of God's purpose not merely for Israel but for all mankind. It was because it is God's will that man should not remain in the toils of his own fashioning, and that the gracious purpose of Creation should not be defeated by our twisted natures, that God chose Abraham to be the father of the new community, and now chooses Moses to be the voice by which men, through the insights given to this community, should learn the truth about God and themselves. We must learn through Israel—and this is our first lesson—that we are wholly dependent upon God and that it is his purpose to deliver us from ourselves. It is little wonder that the Jews regard this solemn and significant "preface" as the first of the commandments.

I. *Thou shalt have no other gods before me*

IN OUR reckoning, however, the first commandment is the one which forbids us to put anything in place of God. "Thou shalt have no other gods before me." The Bible knows full well that there is only one true God, but it knows equally well that man has always contrived to invent others. The word "God" has been described as an empty picture frame into which we can fit a variety of portraits, including our own. For ancient Israel the danger was that in place of YHWH the gods of their neighbours often seemed to offer a more alluring allegiance, and as the story of the Old Testament will tell, the main task of the keepers of the nation's conscience, from Moses onwards, was to expose the hollow pretensions of the various gods of the ancient world and to show their inadequacy.

For us today, the attraction of other gods is no less powerful. In western civilisation within living memory, one great Christian nation allowed itself to be seduced from the service of the God of Luther to the service of the god of racial purity, involving a massacre of innocents of unparalleled dimensions in the whole record of human bestiality. Another great nation makes the state its god, and some words of Berthold Brecht provide an illuminating commentary on the deification of amoral power:

Who fights for Communism
Must be able to fight and not to fight,

To say the truth and not to say the
Truth, to render and to deny service,
To keep a promise and to break a Promise, to go into danger and to
Avoid danger, to be known and to
Be unknown.
Who fights for Communism has of all
The virtues only one; that he fights for
Communism.

But let us not forget the democracies, our own included, which make material progress their god, or a better standard of living irrespective of the needs of other nations; or the individual Christains, all of us, who make gods of social success, private ambitions, wealth, pleasure, health or home. The first commandment would not deny that all of these—including racial pride and the omnicompetent state—have their value and their place in our allegiance, but they must never take primacy over the allegiance we owe to the God whom we fully know through Jesus Christ.

II. *Thou shalt not make unto thee any graven image*

ISRAEL lived in a world where every tribe and every nation made idols and images of almost every conceivable object (cf. *Rom.* 1: 20–25) to represent its gods. Alone among them the Hebrews had none, although this was not so until long after the time of Moses. The prophets had to fight hard against persistent infiltration of idolatrous practices borrowed from Israel's neighbours, and had no easy task to convince the people finally that YHWH was so far removed in wisdom and holiness from mortal man that no sculptor or painter could possibly depict him (*Deut.* 4: 16–19). When the Romans reached Jerusalem and penetrated into the Holy of Holies in the Temple, they were astonished to find no statue of the God who meant so much to these extraordinary people the Jews. It may be an artistic loss that Hebrew sculpture and painting was to all intents non-existent as a result of the prohibition in the second commandment, which covered not only images of God but of everything else that might be made into a god, but at the same time it is a mark of the seriousness of Israel's religious faith and her horror of the practical effects of idolatry among her neighbours.

For us today the relevance of the second commandment lies not so much in the danger of making the wrong kind of images of God in wood or stone—although it may be questioned whether some modern (and ancient) representations of the crucified Christ do not border on the realm of morbid psychology—but rather in warning us against harbouring the wrong kind of mental images of God. The conventional saccharine "gentle Jesus meek and mild" of many illustrated children's books is as one-sided a representation of the truth about God as the muscular "Elder Brother", the boy's hero. Both in isolation are as partial as the unrelieved dejection of the "Man of Sorrows". There was a deep wisdòm in the Hebrew prohibition. Our picture of God must be based on the whole Bible.

The commandment stresses two aspects that must not be omitted: God's sternness and God's love. Primarily the God that the Bible reveals is a loving heavenly Father, but he is also a "jealous" God, which is just another way of saying that we must not confuse love with easy-going tolerance. "God is not mocked" (*Gal.* 6: 7), and we cannot play fast and loose with the moral law without paying the price. The commandment would remind us that part of the price is that the sins of the fathers are visited upon the children. The time-honoured example of venereal disease is far less striking than the evil consequences of imperialism, slavery, and industrial exploitation, not on the descendants of the oppressed but on the descendants of the oppressors.

But to balance the baleful effect of the violation of God's laws the commandment reminds us also that the influence of a good life can still be operative "thousands" of generations later. The examples of Abraham, Moses, St. Paul, St. Francis and of modern saints like Shaftesbury, Wilberforce, Elizabeth Fry and Florence Nightingale point the way to the truth of this insight.

III. *Thou shalt not take the name of the Lord thy God in vain*

IT IS a truism to say that the Gospel of Jesus Christ means nothing to those who do not feel that they need a Gospel. If we have no sense of sin, no sense of failure, no sense that we are twisted, superficial creatures, complacent without cause, we cannot see the relevance of a message of redemption or want to hear the Good News of God's forgiveness. It is only when we recognise the gulf that divides us from God, how far we come short of the glory of God (*Rom.* 3: 23), how seldom our service of God is single minded, and how much good we could do but fail to do, that we are in the right frame of mind to listen to the word from the Beyond for our human predicament.

The third commandment is concerned with something much more vital than the casual oath which more often betrays poverty of vocabulary than deep-seated profanity. Its purport is rather to warn us against making light of the sovereignty of God over the whole field of life. The "name" of God, in the biblical sense, is the nature of God—the essential character of God—his power, his judgment, his mercy. To take God's name "in vain" is to refuse to take seriously the claim of God to command our obedience in social, political and economic affairs as well as in our private lives. It is to lack a sense of our responsibility to God, and consequently to lack a sense of failure.

This commandment is therefore primarily a condemnation of smugness and self-satisfaction, of disregard of God's authority. It reminds us that we are all guilty in ourselves or as members of society of disregarding the sovereign rights of God, and by warning us that we shall be held to account, it turns us towards the Gospel of forgiveness as our only hope.

IV. *Remember the sabbath day to keep it holy*

IN SOME ways this must seem the least relevant of the commandments in a generation which has achieved a five-day week and does not believe in a six day creation. Neither point invalidates the purpose of the commandment, and the fact that for Christendom the first day of the week, and not the seventh, is a holy day and that for different reasons, should prevent us from any narrow interpretation of this injunction, which is framed to fit the circumstances of a pastoral and agricultural society in a pre-Christian era.

Literal sabbatarianism is neither possible nor obligatory in twentieth century Christian society. When the Church ceased to be a Jewish sect and became a missionary movement in the pagan world, Sunday, the Lord's Day, the day of the Resurrection, replaced the Jewish Sabbath, and the early Christians saw no cancellation of the commandment either in the change of day or in the fact that most of them had no choice but to work on the Lord's Day (*Col.* 2: 16).

This fourth commandment implies that there is a rhythm in nature which makes a regular rest day incumbent upon the created world. The old golf professional at St. Andrews was not too wide of the mark when in a controversy about the pros and cons of Sunday golf he said to the advocates of Sunday play: "If you don't need a rest one day a week the greens do." But that is something quite different from a gloomy prohibitionism which would seek to interpret "rest" as enforced deprivation of healthful recreation.

The point of the commandment is not interference with legitimate pleasure, but protection of the worker's right to rest. It is the "manservant" and the "maidservant" who stand to benefit most, and who have benefited most, from what unscrupulous employers or an age of automation might have denied them. The guiding principle must be that no one should be forced to do without a day of rest to provide pleasure for others, or to make ends meet in an inflationary economy. Enforced Sunday overtime is as contrary to the spirit of the commandment as selfish denial to others of that right to Sunday recreation which we demand for ourselves. There is no simple answer in present day society to the question of Sunday entertainment and Sunday games. But the Bible would seem to offer us no little guidance.

We are to "remember the sabbath day, to keep it holy", i.e. to bear in mind its significance as a day set apart from the rest. It is a day when we do something different from what we do on the other six days, and for the office worker or shop assistant that will not mean necessarily doing the same thing as the open-air worker. For the hotel-employee or the bus driver in our complex society, the "sabbath day" may well be a

Monday or a Friday. But one day in the week and as far as possible Sunday, the Lord's Day, we are enjoined to keep "holy". That does not necessarily involve idleness or unrelieved meditation. The "sabbath" is intended to help us and recreate us, and most of us can neither afford to be idle nor indulge in constructive meditation.

Yet the biblical emphasis—however much we make allowance for the changed circumstances of the modern world—is on renewal and recreation through stillness and quietness. We need a quiet day each week. For some it may mean the open air, for others the fireside. For all there should be a conscious effort to dedicate part of the Sabbath specifically to the worship of God. Those who are readiest to denounce the continental Sunday can hardly have attended early mass at one of the great cathedrals and seen the crowds beginning their day of recreation with an hour of worship, or have experienced the sabbath peace of a French or German village. Anglo-Saxons have no monopoly of the proper use of Sunday.

In the version of the Ten Commandments given in *Deut.* 5 the ground for keeping the seventh day as a day apart is not that God rested from his creative work on that day, as in the present version in the book of *Exodus*, but that the sabbath should be a perpetual reminder of God's deliverance of Israel from bondage (*Deut.* 5: 15). It is in the same spirit of thanksgiving for deliverance, from the bondage of sin and self through Jesus Christ, that Christians who

take their faith seriously will not feel that the Lord's Day is properly observed unless they have spent part of it in the public worship of God. If we are in earnest about that part of our Sunday observance, there is little danger that we shall go far astray in our use of the remainder of the day. The author of *Hebrews* goes to the heart of the matter when he sees the sabbath rest (*Heb.* 4: 9), involving an encounter with God in public worship when we see God as he is, and ourselves as we are, as a foretaste of that life in the presence of God which awaits his people in the hereafter.

So ends the first table of the Law, so called because by tradition Moses wrote the Ten Commandments on two stone tablets (*Ex.* 32: 15). The first table has been concerned with our duty to God, the second table will deal with our obligations to other people.

V. *Honour thy father and thy mother*

A NOTED theologian was once asked why he believed in God. His unexpected reply was: "Because my mother taught me." Christian homes and godly mothers are the life blood of the Church, but the influence of any home and any kind of parents on a nation's children cannot be overestimated. Here lies the root of juvenile delinquency, false values, extravagance, irresponsibility and the other evidences of adolescent malaise. Yet the fault is as often with the parents as with the children. How can broken homes or quarrelling parents produce anything but maladjusted children? How can homes where there is no sense of obligation to society, no spirit of service, no example of stability, expect young people either to respect family life or honour the parents who deserve none?

The Hebrews had a strong sense of family obligation (*Ex.* 21: 15–17; *Deut.* 21: 18–21; *Mark* 7: 10–13) which is still noticeable even among unorthodox Jews. Again we must reckon with the changed circumstances of the modern world which have altered the patriarchal family system of the ancient Near East. But basically the biblical emphasis remains the same. We are not isolated individuals but members of a community, of a home, a village, a city or a nation. We are what we are because we enter into a legacy and a heritage which we have not created. Home, church, and community give us the foundations of our faith and our way of life. We are debtors to all three. This fifth commandment would call to our remembrance what we owe to parents and teachers, to those who make our laws and those who carry them out. We must honour those in authority over us because they in their turn are under the authority of God.

VI. *Thou shalt not kill*

THIS commandment is clearly concerned with private killing and not with judicial or mass killing. It is concerned with murder and not with capital punishment or with war. These questions are dealt with elsewhere in the Old Testament, and it is therefore not legitimate to use the sixth commandment in connection with discussions on the death penalty or pacifism. This commandment denies us the right to take the law into our own hands. It is opposed alike to suicide and mercy killing. Every man is made in the image of God, and this law of Moses for the people of God simply reinforces the basic natural law enshrined in the covenant with mankind symbolised by Noah (*Gen.* 9: 6). We have no right to destroy the image of God because it seems to our private judgment a proper thing to do. For this reason suicide is a sin although a merciful God will surely be no less compassionate than human justice, which recognises the mental confusion and black despair which so often precede self-destruction.

Likewise mercy-killing is a sin, even if it appears to us to be the kindest thing to terminate suffering or the prospect of a lifetime of insanity. Yet here again the commandment is directed to the individual. Given adequate safeguards, a responsible panel of doctors would perhaps not necessarily violate this commandment if they were convinced that a patient in agony was beyond recovery or medical aid and agreed to release him from pain. In this case they are acting not as individuals but in a sense on behalf of society, like judges or generals. Society is however rightly hesitant about authorising mercy-killing. There is so often an element of doubt and, perhaps more important, "mercy-killing" is a vague term and a dangerous weapon. Hitler no doubt considered his extermination of the Jews as coming under this heading.

If we are tempted to think that this sixth commandment is the one that most of us are least likely to break let us not forget that there are more ways of committing murder than by administering arsenic. The mass-murder in terms of malnutrition, tuberculosis, and sweated labour which lies at the door of the godly citizens who profited by the industrial revolution has happily vanished from our own land, but how much do we all profit still through our national economy from the same conditions overseas? And which of us can evade the searching interpretation of this commandment by our Lord in the Sermon on the Mount (*Matt. 5: 21–22*) or the unequivocal accusation of *I John* 3: 15?

VII. *Thou shalt not commit adultery*

PERHAPS at no time in the history of Christendom has this seventh commandment been less heeded. Fornication and adultery can hardly be described as new phenomena. What is new is that they have never before been so easy. There may have been times, for example in the age of Charles II, when sex was hawked around as blatantly as it is today. But there has not until now been a time when the gutter-press, the cinema and commercialised music could combine in unholy alliance to produce such a sex-laden atmosphere for young people to grow up in. Those who argue that the fact that homosexuality, prostitution, and premarital intercourse are now regarded as normal talking points by teenagers is a healthy reaction against the hypocrisy of Victorian Grundyism, might well be asked whether this is a mark of liberation or of decadence. It is ironical at this stage to hear a sustained plea for more sex-education and biological instruction in schools from some educationalists.

The truth is that the pendulum has swung dangerously far and threatens to wreck the clock—in this case the institution of marriage and the solidity of home life. When venereal disease no longer holds any terrors, and when illegitimacy can be safeguarded by the universal availability of cheap contraceptives, it is not more education that is needed but a new respect for self-control. There is no evidence that medical students, who presumably are better educated in sexual matters than most, are any less addicted to amorous adventures than their contemporaries in other walks of life.

No one can accuse the Bible of prudishness, or of failing to recognise the powerful biological urges that are no stronger in the twentieth century than they were in ancient times. But the Bible consistently sets its face against artificial stimulation of these urges, whether under the guise of religion as was the case in biblical times, or in the interests of money-making as in our own day. With unerring insight the Bible pinpoints a casual attitude to sex relations as a certain indication of the weakening of moral fibre in an individual or a nation. It is not for obscurantist or kill-joy reasons that prophet after prophet condemns incontinence or sexual malpractices.

Let us by all means have sympathy and understanding for the homosexual and the lesbian, but let us continue to regard both as abnormal. Let us accept the fact that prostitution, professional or amateur, will never be eradicated but let us do nothing which will make it more easily available. Let us talk less about the need for sexual self-expression and self-fulfilment, and more about the need for sexual self-discipline. Above all let us remember that the chief casualties in our "progressive" attitude to sex are impressionable youngsters, physically mature and biologically curious, but emotionally unripe and mentally unable to resist the pressures and titillations of prurient literature and box-office exploitation.

The seventh commandment sums up in its condemnation of adultery not only unfaithfulness in marriage, but sexual laxity in all its forms. Our Lord saw this clearly when he interpreted adultery not as sexual intercourse outside marriage but as lust in any form (*Matt.* 5: 27-28). The greatest obstacle to a return to a sane estimate of sex and its place in the life of the ordinary man and woman and in society as a whole is that we are bewitched by jargon. When shall we have the sense to see, and the courage to say that

companionship and not "sexual compatibility" is the foundation of a happy marriage; that "sex experience" is not essential for a healthy body and a healthy mind; that motherhood is not the only fulfilment of womanhood; that "love" in its Hollywood connotation means lechery, and that our "enlightened" modern attitude to sex is transforming us inevitably into the ghastly human stud-farm of Aldous Huxley's *Brave New World*?

VIII. *Thou shalt not steal*

STEALING is not confined to robbing a jeweller's shop window or extracting a wallet from a convenient coat pocket. In all these commandments we must reject the temptation to say: "This does not affect me." Stealing also includes making slight "adjustments" to our income tax returns and fiddling the expense account. Many of us have vivid recollections of the readiness of soldiers who would never dream of robbing a friend, to "win", "scrounge" or "flog" army property on the grounds that it could not be stealing to take what belonged to the War Office. In vast impersonal combines or nationalised industries the same tendency persists. But it all comes under the condemnation of this commandment.

Perhaps we do not steal property, but do we never steal time? Failure to do a full week's work for a full week's pay; time-wasting; the abuse of leisure—that is also stealing. Sharp practice on the stock exchange and the aim of the large-scale gambler to get something for nothing would likewise be included, although there is nothing immoral in legitimate financial speculation and little harm in the occasional "flutter". Yet in principle there is no difference between putting a shilling on a horse running in the Derby, and becoming a victim of the current obsession with football pools. Here is a vast streamlined organisation involving the employment of large numbers of people, demanding no skill in the competitors and offering rewards out of all proportion to the investment. There is surely here a blurring of the distinction between the luck of the draw, which motivates participants in raffles and spasmodic small-scale gambling, both of which are innocuous, and the plain greed which is encouraged by the vast unearned dividends in football pools. Men will always gamble, but there does seem to be a point beyond which it is difficult to distinguish gambling from stealing.

IX. *Thou shalt not bear false witness*

NO ONE who reads in the daily press accounts of criminal trials can doubt the relevance of this ninth commandment. The prescribed formula of swearing on the Bible to tell the truth has ceased to have any meaning for a large percentage of witnesses, as is evidenced by their conflicting statements. No longer does the fear of God or of his judgment— still less of punishment hereafter— lessen the natural tendency to say what is expedient rather than what is true.

It is chiefly against perjury that this commandment is directed, but it includes also slander and malicious gossip which can poison the life of a community. This is a sin of which religious people are particularly guilty. There may be more violence and brutality in frankly pagan circles or in society's underworld, but there is probably less harmful whispering. It may well be that the gossip which does damage springs basically from an interest in other people, which is in itself a good quality, and from the fact that a village or a small congregation is an intimate fellowship, not unlike a family, in which everyone feels himself concerned. It is perhaps a healthier phenomenon than the self-centred impersonality of the dweller in a block of flats, or the nominal adherent of a large parish, but it has its dangers. The commandment stresses our responsibility to guard our tongues and the epistle of James has much to say about the tongue as an "unruly evil, full of deadly poison" (*Jas.* 3: 3–10).

It would be wrong, however, to limit the force of the commandment to a prohibition of perjury or gossip. For in fact its main emphasis is on telling the truth, as Jesus emphasised in the Sermon on the Mount (*Matt.* 5: 37), and as James echoed in his epistle (*Jas.* 5: 12). Respect for the truth in day to day affairs is the only possible basis of a wholesome society. When trust and confidence vanish life becomes unworkable. Seen from this angle the ninth commandment is generally well honoured among Christians, and perhaps one of the greatest services the ordinary Christian man or woman can render to modern society is to be known as one for whom truth is sacred and lying is dishonourable, for no other reason than that such is the will of God. This more than any frenzied attempt to "do good", is probably the best compliance with our Lord's injunction to "let your light shine before men" (*Matt.* 5: 16).

There will be many occasions for Christians, as for others, when a "white lie" is not only permissible but obligatory. We must keep our sense of proportion and avoid the literalism of the Pharisees. In political life there is often no option but to tell a lie as the lesser of two evils, and in private life it is often kinder to conceal the truth, as in the case of serious illness. On the other hand there are times when to speak the truth in love (*Eph.* 4: 14–15) is a greater kindness, even if it makes unpleasant hearing. Conscience must be our judge, as it was for Micaiah ben-Imlah (*I Kings* 22: 1–18).

X. *Thou shalt not covet*

IT HAS often been pointed out that this tenth commandment is the one which comes nearest to our Lord's method of interpreting the obedience of God. It would be possible for many of us by following the letter of the law to claim an unblemished record. Theft, adultery, murder and the rest of the prohibitions of the Decalogue could be defined in such a strictly legalistic way that most ordinary citizens who have succeeded in keeping themselves out of the law courts and who have conscientiously observed the sabbath, supported their parents and abstained from worshipping idols might pride themselves on their virtue.

But the tenth commandment is of a different order. It is the only commandment with a specifically inward reference, although, as we have seen, the others are in effect only properly understood and complied with when they are treated in the same way. Moses did not intend to give his followers the opportunity to acquire merit by claiming that they had broken none of the commandments, for here is one which no one can avoid breaking. It takes us back to the profound insight of God's judgment on man in the story of Noah, that "every imagination of the thoughts of his heart is only evil continually" (*Gen.* 6: 5), and it takes us forward to Jesus' critique of the inadequacy of external standards of behaviour: "out of the heart proceed evil thoughts, murders, adulteries, fornications, thefts, false witness, blasphemies" (*Matt.* 15: 19).

Who has not coveted something beyond his grasp—power, money, social status, ability? This was the sin of Adam, in other words the root of human disobedience. "Coveting" does not mean a legitimate desire to better our standard of living, or to give our children a better opportunity than we have had ourselves, nor does it mean a recognition that other people have gifts and skills that we should fain acquire. It means greed, and black envy; it means grudging discontent; it means the first step towards ruthless acquisition of what does not belong to us. If the other commandments can be treated as an ethical system, capable of being followed by exercise of the will, this commandment points inward to the radical twist in human nature which can only be straightened out by a power that is not our own, as St. Paul clearly saw (cf. *Rom.* 7:7).

The Book of the Covenant
(20: 18 – 23: 33)

THE narrative of the Exodus is resumed briefly at 20 : 18, continuing the dramatic description of the scene at Sinai into which the Decalogue has been inserted. The primacy of the Ten Commandments is emphasised by the implication that these divine injunctions were heard by the whole community from the lips of YHWH himself, with all the accompanying signs of his power and majesty, which so terrified the people that they appointed Moses to be their mediator, to receive and transmit any further commandments. The picture conveyed is thus that of Moses ascending the mountain again into the mysterious darkness in which YHWH dwelt, later symbolised in the darkness of the Holy of Holies in the Temple at Jerusalem, and receiving from God the instructions which occupy the next three chapters (20: 18–21).

The laws that follow (20: 22 – 23: 19), commonly known as the "Book of the Covenant" (24: 7), reflect on the whole a settled agricultural existence as opposed to the conditions of a nomadic community. They are generally held to embody the common law of Israel during the period of the judges and the early monarchy. It is of no consequence to inquire how much, if indeed any of this legislation was promulgated by Moses himself. Many of the provisions are paralleled in Egyptian and Hittite laws, and particularly in the Babylonian Code of Hammurabi, dating from several centuries earlier, probably about 1700 B.C. It is unlikely that these laws in the "Book of the Covenant" were directly derived from the Babylonian Code. They rather represent the Hebrew version of the general legal system of the Near East at that time, perhaps being adapted from the common law of Canaan after the settlement of the tribes in Palestine. Their value for the ordinary reader of the Bible, apart from the legal historian, is that they present a vivid picture of the social life of Israel in the formative years of her growth into a nation.

Shrines are erected to YHWH (20: 24) at which offerings are made, including the firstfruits of the crops and the firstlings of the flocks (22: 29–30). A weekly sabbath rest day is observed (23: 12), and three great festivals are held each year (23: 14–16) Slavery and concubinage by purchase are an accepted part of the social structure, and laws are enacted to safeguard the rights of slaves and to ameliorate their conditions (21: 2-11, 20-21, 26-27). Strict retribution is exacted for murder and assault, on the principle of "life for life, eye for eye, tooth for tooth" (21: 23-25)—except in the case of a master illtreating a slave, where the penalty is less severe but more expensive (21: 26-27). Lack of filial respect is punishable by death (21: 15, 17). Some of the laws make provision for the protection of aliens, who had no legal rights (22: 21), and of widows and orphans (22: 22). The poor are safeguarded from unscrupulous money lenders (22: 25-27), and receive the benefits of a sabbatical year in husbandry (23: 10-11). Various other provisions deal with theft (22: 1-4, 7-8), trespass (22: 9) and dangerous animals (21: 28-36).

On the whole it is a humane code, and less severe than the Code of Hammurabi. The law of exact retaliation (Lex Talionis) is, despite its apparent bloodthirstiness, an advance on the practice of blood-feuds and tribal revenge, whereby innocent victims were made to pay the price of a kinsman's crime. While slavery is accepted as the norm, the slave has rights and a choice of freedom (21: 2). The death penalty for witches (22: 18), which was quoted with such dire results as late as the eighteenth century, reflects a situation where necromancy was a real and not an imaginary danger. Likewise the odd prohibition against seething a kid in its mother's milk (23: 19) was doubtless directed against the pagan black magic with which Israel was surrounded.

The "Book of the Covenant" ends with a promise and a warning (23: 20-33). If these laws are observed Israel will prosper. YHWH will send his angel before them to lead them into the land of Canaan. Those who resist their progress will be destroyed. Little by little the land of the promise will become their own, until their domain stretches from the Red Sea to the Mediterranean, and from the desert to the Euphrates. The condition is that they must have no traffic with the natives or with their religion, and a solemn warning is given that that way lies disaster.

Doubtless this promise is prophecy after the event. The angel, in the persons of Moses and Joshua, did indeed guide the Israelites to the promised land; their enemies were one by one eliminated and by the time of David, when this "Book of the Covenant" was probably codified, their territory had almost reached the promised bounds. But the condition had not been fulfilled. Israel had succumbed to the lure of strange and attractive ways, and a sensuous and corrupt religion, and long before this ominous proviso found its way into the narrative the snare referred to in v. 33 had tightened and strangled YHWH'S wayward people.

The Sealing of the Covenant
(24: 1-18)

WE RETURN now to the narrative of the events at the holy mountain. As in ch. 19 the description is composite. Three different sources of tradition have been combined, each of which taken by itself gives a coherent account of the movements of the actors in the drama. Woven together as they are, the cumulative effect is to obscure the details but to enhance the impressiveness. (Some readers might care to see for themselves how this dovetailing of the sources throughout the Pentateuch works out in this chapter, which may be taken as a good example of the process as a whole: the Jahwist tradition appears in vv. 1, 2, 9-11; the Elohist contributes vv. 3-8, 12-15a, 18b; the Priestly source supplies vv. 15b—18a.)

The total effect is to produce a parable of great beauty in a series of poetic images which convey the deep significance of this decisive moment in Israel's history. It is as if we were being shown a scene from a medieval morality play with Mt. Sinai as the stage setting. At the top of the mountain which is overhung by the cloud that symbolises the Presence of God stands Moses, ready to receive the commandments of YHWH; half way up the mountain are the senior representatives of Israel, the "cornerstones" (nobles) of the people, having glimpsed through the cloud the glory of the God of Israel and partaken of a sacramental meal; at the foot of the mountain, is the mass of the people surrounding the altar where by solemn ceremony they have been sealed as God's chosen instrument for the fulfilling of his purpose to recreate the world.

The whole narrative is replete with meaningful symbolism. The mission of Israel to the seventy nations of the Gentiles is suggested by the seventy elders who are granted the vision of God (vv. 1, 9-11). God himself writes the Decalogue on tablets of stone (v. 12) which then become the sacred evidence of Israel's covenant, to be borne with them on their journey to the promised land (*Deut.* 10: 5). The mysterious Presence broods over the mountain in silent stillness for six days, as if to show that this consecration of a people of God is the beginning of a new Creation, a means of renewing the life of the world that God had made and man had marred (v. 16). The symbol of the six days is given added significance in the gospels, when in the story of the Transfiguration this scene on Sinai finds its true meaning (*Mark* 9: 2-9).

But of course the most profound piece of symbolism is the erection of the altar and the ceremonial associated with it (vv. 4-8). The people have pledged themselves to obey the commandments of God (v. 3). As a sign and seal of this new relationship a sacrificial altar, presumably surrounded by the twelve pillars referred to, signifying the twelve tribes of Israel, becomes the place where YHWH and his people meet. The ancient theory of sacrifice was essentially based upon the idea of mediation. The sacrificial victim was the bridge between God and man. Since the life of the animal sacrificed was believed to reside in its blood (*Gen.* 9: 4), the killing of the sacrifice was held to liberate its life, represented by its shed blood. If the blood was then sprinkled on two contracting parties to a covenant, or if they passed between the two halves of the severed animal, the implication was that they were inevitably bound together by the life of the third party to the transaction, the sacrificial victim (*Jer.* 34: 18).

This is the symbolism of the covenant rite in the story of Abraham (*Gen.* 15) and it is so also here. Moses sprinkles some of the sacrificial blood over the altar, representing YHWH, and some of the same blood he sprinkles over the people. They are thus symbolically bound together with YHWH in a covenant relationship which cannot be broken. Their pledge of obedience and loyalty to YHWH is thus sacramentally sealed.

It is this relationship to God, based on the terms of the laws which Moses has enunciated and now proceeds to expand (chs. 25–31, 35–40), which Jeremiah holds to be inadequate when he looks forward to a new type of covenant (*Jer.* 31: 32–34) and it is the New Covenant he hoped for which Jesus sealed, with words clearly echoing those of Moses, on the night in which he was betrayed (*Mark* 14: 24). So deeply was the early Church conscious that this pattern of the covenant, particularly the covenant of Sinai, had been fulfilled and perfected by the self sacrifice of Christ, who had made God and man at one by the offering of his life, that the author of *Hebrews*, in quoting from memory the words of Moses on this occasion, instinctively begins to quote the words of Christ (*Heb.* 9: 20).

Tabernacle and Priesthood
(25: 1 – 31: 18)

THE next seven chapters (25–31) together with chapters 35–40 provide detailed instructions for the building of a shrine (the Ark of the covenant) which is to contain the stone tablets of the Ten Commandments, and for the construction of a Tent or Tabernacle to hold the Ark, together with regulations for the consecration and proper vestments of the high priest and his subordinates. Although Moses and Aaron with his family are specifically involved in these arrangements, and although some of the provisions may go back to the time of the Exodus, it is generally agreed that in its present form this body of legislation dates mainly from during and after the Exile, more than seven centuries later.

By that time the desert wanderings were over, Israel had been for hundreds of years a settled community in Palestine, had won and lost an empire, and had seen its Temple, the glory of Solomon's capital, sacked by Babylonian invaders, and its treasures carried off as spoils of war. Priestly exiles looking back with loving memory on the Temple worship they had known, and looking forward to the day when after a return to the Jerusalem that filled their dreams they would once again see the Temple rise in beauty from the ashes of pagan devastation, painted much of this picture, an idealised version of what had been and what was yet to be.

The prophet Ezekiel, likewise

in Babylonian exile, embarked on a similar project in which he described the perfect sanctuary which he hoped to see as the centre of Israel's life after the return to the homeland (*Ezek.* 40–48), but here the priestly writers turn their thoughts towards the glorious past and attribute the subsequent pattern of worship as they have known it to the voice of YHWH himself from Sinai, assigning the first construction of the Temple furnishings to the Israelites in the wilderness.

It does not materially affect the picture that is drawn for us here that it is historically impossible in a desert setting. The rich accoutrements of the priesthood, the precious stones and exotic spices, the rare woods and metals, to say nothing of their manufacture, accord ill with the situation in which this motley band of fugitives from Egypt living on the borderline of starvation found themselves at Sinai. Nevertheless as is usual in the Bible, the historical basis is there, however much embellishment subsequent tradition has imposed upon it.

There was in fact an Ark of the covenant at this early stage, but it was no doubt a simple wooden box in keeping with the circumstances of the Exodus (*Deut.* 10: 1). Its purpose was indeed to hold the tablets of the Testimony, a symbol of the sovereignty of YHWH to accompany the Israelites on their journey to Canaan and to remind them of the covenant they had sworn at the holy mountain (*Num.* 10: 33–36). There was also a Tabernacle or Tent of Meeting (27: 21 R.V.) in

which the Ark was housed, but it was doubtless a simple goatshair covering like any other bedouin dwelling, except that it symbolised the place where YHWH would meet his people (33: 7–11; *II Sam.* 7: 6).

In our attempt to trace the common purpose and continuity of themes and patterns which make the Bible a unity and not two distinct halves, one of which as Christians we can reject, it is undoubtedly easier to see the relevance for the twentieth-century Church in the symbolism of the simple Ark and the modest Tent of Meeting, than in the elaborate description given in these chapters of the appurtenances of Jewish ceremonial, Jewish priesthood, and Jewish sacrifice. All of these belong to the outward form of Old Testament religion which has been superseded by Christ, and which the New Testament writers regard as a deviation from the true line of faith and witness which runs from Abraham through Moses and the prophets to our Lord and his disciples.

We can easily feel ourselves bound in a community of faith with those who sought to hold fast to the moment of revelation at Sinai, when it seemed as if heaven opened and the voice of God proclaimed his will in the stark "thou shalt" of the Decalogue. To wish to preserve that memory in tablets of stone which would ever be a living witness to Israel's call and vocation is an impulse whose significance we can still share, and it is a moving reflection that the ancient palladium of Israel had within it for centuries, whether in the desert or later in Jerusalem itself, this symbol of the Word of God to man which the Church still acknowledges as binding on its members. Similarly as we picture Israel in its desert days assembling round the Tent of Meeting to hear the continuing commands of God, and to come face to face with him in worship, we can again feel the cords of tradition binding our own worship to theirs.

But this highly elaborated instruction for the exact dimensions of the Ark (25: 10), the width of the curtains for the Tabernacle (26: 2), the "curious girdle of the ephod" (28: 27), the "wave offering" of a ram's intestines (29: 22-24) and the morning offering of a lamb with "a tenth deal of flour mingled with the fourth part of an hin of beaten oil" (29: 40), is not only apparently irrelevant but in places revolting. Yet if there is anything that emerges from this unfamiliar and in parts unattractive recital, it is the passionate love of the compilers for "the glory and beauty" of the worship of God (28: 2), their deep sense that the purpose of all this elaboration is that men may "meet" and "commune" with God (25: 22; 29: 45), their conception that the function of a priest is to bear on his heart the needs of the people he represents (28: 29-30), and their recognition that the words that were inscribed on the high priest's diadem preside in spirit as well as in fact over the whole of the ceremonial: HOLINESS TO THE LORD (28: 36). There are, moreover, several points in the ritual where we may see, as so often in the Old Testament, a quest for truth which finds fulfilment under the New Covenant of Christ, and which helps us to understand more fully the significance of New Testament theology.

The instructions given here for the manufacture of the Ark of the covenant and for the other furnishings of the Tent of Meeting, however much these were carried into effect in the desert, reflect by and large the plan and equipment of the successive Temples in Jerusalem, beginning with that of Solomon. The pattern was repeated in the Temple of Zerubbabel, or second Temple. This took the place of Solomon's Temple, which had been destroyed in 587 B.C., and was now reconstructed after the Israelite community had returned from the Exile in Babylon. This second Temple was rebuilt and enlarged by Herod the Great shortly before the birth of our Lord, although the outer buildings were still in process of construction during Jesus' ministry (*Mark* 13: 1; *John* 2: 20). Once again the pattern was the same. Thus, while the instructions given in these chapters refer specifically to portable furnishings, such as could be carried for the remainder of the journey into Canaan, it was precisely this mobile sanctuary which was reproduced as a permanent erection in the heart of the Jerusalem Temples.

The Temple area at Jerusalem consisted latterly of a series of open courtyards surrounded by colonnades. The outermost court was available to all, including

Gentiles, but from that point, passing inwards, there was a progressive degree of exclusiveness attached to each court, until beyond the courts of the women, the male Israelites and then the priests, at the heart of the Temple area stood the Tabernacle (26: 1–30). This was divided into two unequal parts, separated by a veil or curtain (26: 31). In the outer and larger section of the building, the holy place (26: 33), stood the table of the shewbread (25: 23–30) and the great seven branched candlestick (25: 31–40).

Within the innermost part of the sanctuary, the Holy of Holies or Most Holy place (26: 33), stood nothing but the Ark of the covenant containing the tablets of the Ten Commandments (although these seem to have disappeared when the Temple was sacked in 587 B.C.). The covering of the Ark which is described in the Bible as the mercy-seat, was overshadowed by the wings of two sphinx-like figures known as cherubim (25: 10–21). In front of the Tabernacle stood the altar of burnt offerings (27: 1–8) and a vessel containing water for ritual ablutions (30: 18–21). At some stage in the history of the Temple an altar of incense (30: 1–10) had been installed in the outer sanctuary, and, according to the author of *Hebrews*, a pot of manna (*Heb.* 9: 4; *Ex.* 16: 32–34) and Aaron's rod (*Heb.* 9: 4; *Num.* 17: 1–11) had been deposited within the Ark beside the tablets of the Decalogue.

The symbolism of all this is crystal clear. At the heart of the religious life of Israel is the covenant relationship with God (the tables of the Testimony). The throne of the invisible Lord of the universe (the mercy-seat), shrouded in mystery (the cherubim), rests upon the historic tokens of his providential care for his people (the pot of manna) and of the authoritative priesthood (Aaron's rod). Cleansed from the contamination of the outside world (the laver), the ministers of YHWH offer on behalf of his people perpetual sacrifice of prayer (the altars), and thanksgiving for the fruits of the earth (the table of shewbread), in worship that never ceases because God is always present (the lamp). No one would wish to take issue with this grand and lofty conception, simple and moving, of the faith of Israel and of the obedience owed to God. The power of such worship to grip the hearts and minds of a people for centuries is evidenced not only in the devotional writings of the psalmists (cf. also *Ecclus.* 45: 6–22; 50: 1–21), but also in the readiness of all Jews everywhere at home and overseas to pay the traditional half-shekel each year for the maintenance of the services of the Temple (30: 11–16; *Neh.* 10: 32).

Charged with the proper ordering of this worship was the complex hierarchy of the priesthood, claiming lineal descent from Aaron, whose consecration and vestments, meticulously described here (28: 1 – 29: 35), indicate the care with which later generations followed what they believed to be the divine pattern delivered by YHWH to Moses. Modern minds recoil from the contrast between, on the one hand, the dignity and symbolism of the high priestly vestments—the precious stones each bearing the name of a tribe of Israel, which the high priest wore when he interceded on their behalf; and the Urim and Thummim, probably oracular stones, by which he declared God's will for the people (28: 15–30)—and, on the other hand, the blood and slaughter of helpless animals with the accompanying malodorous filth which the sacrificial element of Old Testament worship made inevitable, and which is reflected in the ritual described here (29: 10–25) for setting apart fallible mortals for the sacred task of bringing men into the right relationship with God.

But it is not on humanitarian or hygienic grounds that the New Testament condemns the practice of animal sacrifice. As we shall see more fully in the book of *Leviticus*, this was not only ancient practice but was fundamentally based on man's deep sense of his need to bridge the gulf between his own sinful state and the holiness of God. Thus, when the author of *Hebrews* deals with this and similar passages in the old Testament (*Heb*. 8: 1–10: 18), his condemnation is directed not against its unpleasant associations but against its complete inadequacy as a means of making the worshipper, whether priest or layman, at one with God. "It is not possible," he says, "that the blood of bulls and goats should take away sins" (*Heb*. 10: 4). Similarly he condemns the ineffectiveness of any high priesthood which depends on

human fallibility, on man's sinfulness and man's mortality (*Heb*. 7: 23–28).

Yet he sees, as we must also see, in the Old Testament high priestly office of intercession and atonement, of representing the people before God and declaring the will of God to the people, a pointer towards Christ, our great High Priest, who by his sacrifice of himself once for all accomplished what the ritual of the Temple attempted but failed to do.

The Golden Calf
(32: 1 – 34: 35)

ONCE again the sanctity of the sabbath has been stressed as a perpetual memorial of the covenant at Sinai (31: 12–17), and Moses, having received from the hands of YHWH the stone tables of Testimony "written with the finger of God" (31: 18), prepares to come down from the holy mountain. But in the meantime, i.e. during the forty days of Moses' absence (24: 18), there has been a catastrophic change in the situation which was described in ch. 24, when with solemn vows of allegiance the people had been bound to YHWH in the sacramental union of the covenant.

It is as difficult to try to disentangle the various strands of tradition that have been woven into the narrative of chs. 32–34, as it is to determine their historical basis. Perhaps the origin of the story of the Golden Calf is to be found in prophetic denunciation of the practice of bull worship in the reign of Jeroboam I (*I*

Kings 12: 28-33; cf. 32: 4). After the disruption of the kingdom that followed the death of Solomon, when ten of the tribes under Jeroboam separated themselves from Judah and Benjamin, which remained faithful to the house of David and accepted Solomon's son Rehoboam as their king, Jerusalem with its national sanctuary in the Temple was no longer accessible to the northern tribes. Accordingly Jeroboam established two shrines at Bethel and Dan, and in place of the throne of YHWH on the mercy seat of the Ark, installed in his sanctuaries figures of bulls on which YHWH was supposed to be enthroned.

Whether the bulls were in fact designed as thrones, a common enough concept in ancient religion, or whether they were intended to be regarded as symbolic of YHWH himself, their association with the fertility cults of Canaan was too obvious to escape the condemnation of the Old Testament historians who denounced them as rank idolatry. The bull, as a symbol of power and fertility, was commonly venerated in Canaanite religion, and connected with this worship, sacred prostitution and orgiastic dances were practised.

The appeal of this sensuous type of religion to the Israelites, once they settled in Canaan, was too strong to be resisted. Many of the features of Canaanite religion became incorporated in the religion of YHWH, and it required the concerted efforts of the prophets and more than one religious reformation before the Mosaic standards were restored.

It is possible that this story of the Golden Calf, or young bull, is inserted here as part of the prophetic campaign against all deviations from the traditional symbols of the Ark and the Tabernacle. The cause of the reformers would be strengthened if it could be claimed that bull worship was an ancient sin condemned by YHWH as far back as the Exodus. It is more likely that this is the historical origin of the story, than that the Israelites, so soon after the covenant, replaced YHWH with the cow-god Hathor of Egypt, in view of their unhappy associations with that country.

The shattering of the stone tablets of the Decalogue (32: 19) may possibly reflect a tradition that at some point the original tablets had been lost, and the "second" Decalogue (34: 17-26) is probably the J version of the Decalogue of 20: 1-17, which comes from the E tradition.

Perhaps all that we can say with any degree of certainty about the historical basis of these chapters is that there was a rebellion at Sinai against the authority of Moses, which had to be quelled by force, and that the rebellion was idolatrous in character (32: 26-28). But that is a poor substitute for this splendid and dramatic story which, taken as it stands and regarded not as literal history but as theological teaching, is full of illuminating insights, apart from being a masterpiece of the narrator's art.

We are told how the people get tired of waiting for their elusive leader. For almost six weeks he has been invisible, brooding alone with YHWH among the crags of Sinai. The feeling grows that this sombre man and his more sombre God take things too seriously. "Religion should be a joyous affair, so let us change our god and make one for ourselves." Aaron melts down their jewellery and fashions a golden idol. To this they offer sacrifice and celebrate a feast which becomes a sexual orgy (32: 1–6; cf. v. 25). Up on the mountain the Lord taxes Moses with the people's defection. *Thy* people—not *mine*, says YHWH—are corrupt and worthy only of destruction. Let me destroy them and I shall found a new people, not on Abraham but on you (cf. 32: 10 with *Gen.* 12: 2).

But Moses intercedes with the Almighty. Making no excuses for his idolatrous followers, he pleads for their preservation, not because they deserve it but because otherwise their deliverance from Egypt would be pointless in the eyes of the heathen. The Israelites, whatever they may do, are still the people of God's choice, they are still the people of the promise. So the Lord leaves the disciplining of his wayward flock in Moses' hands (32: 7–14). Then follows the magnificent picture of the arrival of Moses among the drunken revellers, like the avenging angel of the wrath of God; the smashing of the tables of the Testimony; the burning of the idol; the pitiful excuses of Aaron; and the bitter price that has to be paid for the crime (32: 15–28).

Again Moses climbs the mountain to intercede for his people, offering his own life for theirs (32: 32). YHWH will have none of it, and as part of their punishment condemns the Israelites to continue their journey to the promised land without him (33: 3). Moses removes the Tent of Meeting from among the tents of Israel as a sign of the Lord's disfavour, and from the pillar of cloud which descends upon it, the Lord speaks with Moses, and Israel worships in penitence from afar (32: 29 – 33: 10). As a result of Moses' renewed pleas, YHWH agrees to accompany the Israelites on their farther journey, and as a supreme mark of his favour allows Moses to glimpse his glory (33: 11–23).

Next morning, Moses, according to instructions, climbs the mountain again having prepared two fresh stone tablets to receive the words of God. The Lord makes a momentous proclamation of the attributes of his being: "merciful and gracious, long-suffering, and abundant in goodness and truth, keeping mercy . . . forgiving iniquity and transgression and sin"—but just in judgment. He promises despite the rebellion of the Israelites to bestow the promised inheritance of Canaan upon them, but warns them against any attempt to compromise the purity of their faith by any further idolatrous ventures (34: 1–16). There follows a second set of ten commandments (vv. 17–26), dealing mainly with religious observances, which Moses inscribes upon the tablets. Moses comes down from the mountain bearing the visible marks of his communion with YHWH. His transfigured appearance fills his kinsmen with awe, and he has to veil his face from them, only removing the veil when he enters the Tent of Meeting to commune with God (34: 17–35).

Is not this whole fascinating episode a parable of the mystery of Israel's election to be the people of God, of its glory and its failure, of the transience of the old covenant and the permanence of the covenant principle, of the strength of the Law and the inevitability of the Gospel? It is not enough to explain the violent contrast between the high honour which is destined for Aaron in ch. 28, and his abysmal failure in ch. 32—even to the ineptitude of his self-excuse in v. 24: "they gave me their gold; I put it in the crucible; and somehow out came a golden calf!"—by attributing the second narrative to an earlier tradition. The compilers knew their business too well to include both sides of the story if they did not intend both to have a meaning, and the second narrative to complement the first.

It is surely the realism of the Old Testament theologians that is here most evident. They are convinced of Israel's vocation, but they have no illusions that it is anything but the sovereign mercy of God that has singled them out, or anything but his grace that enables them in any way to fulfil their task. Left to themselves they are as idolatrous as any pagans. The priesthood, for all its solemn consecration, is as fallible as the laity. Had it not been for Moses, who brought with him from his encounter with God something of the glory of God himself (34: 29),

and the few in Israel who climbed with him into the heights where God dwells—the Elijahs and Isaiahs, the prophets and the psalmists of Israel—the Lord would have discarded this obstinate, self-willed shiftless people and left them to their deserts. The breaking of the covenant tablets is God's judgment on Israel, his assessment of their human worth; the renewal of the tablets is the token of his mercy, for the sake of the few who like Moses are unswerving in their obedience and single minded in their devotion.

But the Bible is a unity, and as Christians we must look at this parable not merely through the eyes of the prophets but also of the apostles. For us Aaron's apostasy is the failure of the ritual law which he represents to fulfil the covenant between Israel and God. The cult of the Law became idolatry. Temple, priesthood, sacrifice and ceremonial became a travesty of the proper obedience of God. The shattering of the tables of the covenant is for us a token that God's covenant with Israel, based on the Decalogue of true obedience (20: 1–17), was broken from the very beginning, and what was put in its place and slavishly followed was a decalogue of religiosity (34: 17–26). There is thus in the roles of Aaron and Moses in this story a commentary on the weakness and the strength of the Law and a reflection of the two-sidedness of Israel's legacy to us.

Aaron, the high priest to be, who is powerless to save the people from violating the covenant, and who is bound with them in an unholy fellowship of substitute-religion, represents the future failure of the priests and people of Israel to be the true servants of God that they were meant to be. Moses, on the other hand, condemns as it were in the name of Christ the failure of the people to be God's people, accepts their inability to fulfil the high covenant task embodied in the first Decalogue, and binds them to a second and lower type of covenant which makes less demands. But the Decalogue in principle remains intact, and comes into operation again when it is fulfilled in the Sermon on the Mount (*Matt.* 5:17).

Moses, too, as mediator between God and Israel, not defending their failure but maintaining their right still to be called God's people, points forward to the intercessions of psalmists and prophets yet to come, and to the great mediator of the New Covenant, the Prophet like unto Moses (*Deut.* 18:15, 18), our Lord Jesus Christ.

The real fulfilment of the prophecy in 34:10 of "marvels, such as have not been done in all the earth, nor in any nation" is for us the Life, Death and Resurrection of Jesus by which the covenant with old Israel was renewed and enlarged to include not only Jews but Gentiles, just as the fulfilment of the transfiguration of Moses (34:29) is to be found in the Transfiguration of Christ (*Luke* 9:29). The veil with which Moses had to cover his face, that is, the blindness which prevented old Israel from seeing the glory of God when the true Moses, the Messiah, came, has

now, as St. Paul says, been "done away in Christ", so that "we all, with open face beholding as in a glass the glory of the Lord, are changed into the same image" (*II Cor.* 3:7–4:4).

The Building of the Tabernacle
(35:1–40:38)

DESPITE the rebellion of the Israelites and their infatuation with a bogus faith, the divine plan is carried out. The covenant people build the Tabernacle as the symbol in their midst of the continuing Presence of YHWH and of their allegiance to him. The contents of these chapters (35–40) simply reproduce with minor variations the contents of chapters 25–31. The instructions given there to Moses are now faithfully carried out to the letter. Emphasis is laid on the willingness with which the people went to work to build the shrine—all "wisehearted" men (36:1), under the direction of craftsmen filled with the spirit of God (35:31), fashion the ornaments and prepare the sanctuary; "wisehearted" women weave the fabrics and the priestly vestments (35:25–26). They have to be restrained from excess of zeal. More than enough is offered (36:5–7).

At last the Tabernacle with its furnishings is complete. Moses anoints Aaron and his sons as the first priests, and the daily worship and sacrifice begin (40:17–33). The account ends with a picture of Israel ready to set out from Sinai on the way to the promised land, inspired and encouraged by the visible Presence of YHWH shrouding and filling the Tabernacle, a fiery cloud which never left them by day or night and which determined the rate of their progress (40: 34–38).

It is quite clear from his address to the Sanhedrin which ended in his martyrdom (*Acts* 7), that St. Stephen attached great significance to the fact that the original Tabernacle was portable. That symbolised for him the missionary vocation of Israel. Their call to be the people of God implied movement. They must go forward—into the unknown—with nothing to hold on to but the accompanying Presence of God. They were to be an onward-going outward-looking community, dedicated to the task of bringing the world to the knowledge of God. In Stephen's view they had ossified their mission by transforming the mobility of the Tabernacle into the immobility of the Temple at Jerusalem. "But Solomon built him an house" (*Acts* 7: 47).

As Isaiah and Jeremiah had proclaimed (*Isa.* 66: 1–2; *Jer.* 7: 4) and as Stephen underlined, the Temple and its worship became a fetish, an end in itself, which stultified the vocation of Israel to be a missionary people and turned them into an exclusive religious club. David had been a wiser man than his son in preserving the Tabernacle in its primitive form in his new capital at Jerusalem, but it was not until the Son of David came in the providence of God to fulfil all Old Testament hopes and promises that the real significance of the moving Tabernacle became plain.

When the Word became flesh, the Presence of God tabernacled among men in the lively words and works of Jesus. By his Death and Resurrection the living Presence came to dwell with his Church and to journey with them—again into the unknown—in the fulfilment of old Israel's task of bringing the world back to God.

LEVITICUS

THE THIRD book of the Old Testament is probably not only the most unfamiliar even to regular readers of the Bible, but is also the book which more than any other leads us into territory that we cannot regard as common ground for Jews and Christians, but rather think of as exclusively Jewish property. Even for some orthodox Jews, however, this book, so largely concerned with ritual and ceremonial connected with the Temple at Jerusalem which came to an end in A.D. 70, has more of an antiquarian interest than present relevance. The title of the book defines its chief interest as being levitical, i.e. it deals with the duties of the priests of Israel, who by law must belong to the tribe of Levi, and sets out a wide range of religious obligations incumbent upon the people which it was the business of the priesthood to superintend.

The setting of this body of legislation is represented as Mt. Sinai, and Moses is claimed to have been given these instructions by YHWH for the proper ordering of his worship. This framework is, however, clearly artificial, and the book of *Leviticus* in effect consists of a collection of civil and religious regulations, some of which may indeed come from the time, and perhaps even from the mind of Moses, but most of which

represent the current practice of over eight centuries later when the Temple and its worship had become the focal point of Jewish life. It is a matter for the experts to date the various elements in this book, but for all practical purposes it is best for us to think of it as reflecting the outlook and behaviour of the little theocracy that jealously guarded its distinctive traditions and its Temple ritual in the last four centuries of Old Testament times, when Israel had ceased to matter in the outside world and devoted its whole attention to the cultivation of its unique mode of life under the direction of its priesthood.

Why then should this pattern of behaviour for so late a stage in Israel's story, embracing all aspects of common life, involving personal hygiene and public health as much as the service of the altar, stand at this early point in the Old Testament? The answer may be found in two verses: "Just balances, just weights, a just ephah, and a just hin, shall ye have: I am the Lord your God, which brought you out of the land of Egypt" (19: 36); "Ye shall be holy: for I the Lord your God am holy" (19: 2).

When the various strands of tradition that constituted the Law of Israel were gathered together about 400 B.C., the Exodus was but a dim memory as an event, but its significance had grown with the passing of the years. The Israelites had founded and lost their kingdom; they had known the pangs of exile; and on their return to that fragment of their former territory which as vassals of the Persian empire they were allowed to occupy, their main concern was to repair and rebuild the shattered structure of their national life. Under the guidance of the prophets they had come to see their past defeats and disasters as the just judgment of God on their failure to fulfil their side of the covenant of Sinai. In repentance and self-condemnation they acknowledged their sins —their pagan practices, their social injustices, their political expediencies.

None of this, they resolved, must happen again. They must present to the world a picture of a consecrated people, an example of a community united in allegiance to the one true God, betraying by every single action their high sense of their calling to be a unique and dedicated commonwealth, whose task it was to lead all nations into the saving knowledge and service of God. That this high sense of mission and vocation, so clearly seen by minds of the calibre of Second Isaiah, was eventually strangled by nationalism, intolerance and exclusiveness—as the later pages of the Old Testament story will disclose—should not blind us to the nobility of the conception which lay behind them. Nor should the details of the pattern of everyday life and worship as we

find it expressed in *Leviticus*—at times repulsive, at times grotesque —blind us to the zeal and integrity with which the priestly mentors of Israel sought to bring the whole fabric of society under the sovereign will of God.

These were fallible men who had grasped the significance of the covenant relationship as the distinctive feature of Israel's existence as a people, and who sought with all the limitations of their time and horizon to order the entire life of the community on the basis of justice and holiness. The motive for both they found in the event of the Exodus and the revelation at Sinai. The shopkeeper must give value for the customer's money not because justice in the abstract is a good thing, but as the response of obedience to the God who had delivered the Israelites at the beginning of their story, in order that their reflection of his justice in their daily life might create a new pattern of honest dealing in the world at large (19: 36). Similarly, the whole life of the people must be a sustained act of worship, focused in the liturgy of the Temple, not because it is comforting or prudential, but because God had revealed himself as Holiness (19: 2), with all the depth of meaning which the prophets had read into this fundamental attribute, but which was indelibly written into the Exodus story at the Burning Bush and on the holy mountain (*Ex.* 3: 1–6; 24: 1–18).

Thus when the corpus of laws governing the service of the sanctuary and the ordering of society came to be assembled after the Exile, it was right that these provisions of varying age and significance should be associated with the name of Moses and located at this point in the Old Testament, since every statute, religious or civil, within Israel, served merely to underline the covenant relationship which traditionally had been established at Sinai, and expanded its basic obligations which had been enshrined in the Decalogue.

"Ye shall be holy"
(1: 1 – 15: 33)

IT IS in this light that we should read those sections of *Leviticus* which deal with the various types of sacrificial offerings to be made in the Temple. However involved the ritual, and however revolting the ceaseless slaughter of helpless birds and beasts, the basic purpose of it all is to maintain the covenant relationship, and to be a people at peace with God. Any crime must be punished, as in any other legal system, but for the people of God there was the further need to restore the right relationship with God which had been broken by the offence. Not only breaches of the moral code but also unconscious violations of ritual holiness, which was conceived to be the proper service of a holy God, must be made good in this way.

Thus there was developed the elaborate system of ceremonial law as we find it in *Leviticus*. Undoubtedly it is crude and barbaric at its worst and pedantic at its best. With the coming of the New Covenant in Christ it has no validity for Christians,

and the whole nauseating traffic of animal sacrifice has been roundly condemned as useless by the author of the epistle to the *Hebrews*: "It is not possible that the blood of bulls and of goats should take away sins" (*Heb.* 10: 4). Yet it is important to recognise the earnest desire of the formulators of the Law to treat sin seriously, to regard the whole fabric of life and not just the "religious" aspect of it as being the service of God, and to try to find some way of restoring the relationship with God which man in his pride and folly is constantly breaking.

We have seen (p. 101) that the whole practice of animal sacrifice was based on the principle that the life of man and beast resided in the blood. Death, involving the spilling of the blood, meant that the mysterious power which is life was liberated. The theory of animal sacrifice was that the animal became a third party to the transaction between the worshipper and God. By virtue of its life being freed from its body by the shedding of its blood, and by the sprinkling or smearing of its blood both on the altar and on the worshipper, or by the worshipper first laying his hand upon the head of the victim, a symbolic bridge was established between God and the person making the sacrifice. It was not even held that the person who made the sacrifice initially provided it. He only offered on the altar what God gave him to offer (17: 11). It is this basic idea that the animal victim is a divinely ordained and divinely provided mediator which lies behind the various types of sacrifice provided for in Leviticus —burnt offerings, sin offerings, guilt or trespass offerings and peace offerings.

It is not of great consequence to the ordinary reader of the Bible to distinguish between them. What is important is to recognise that whatever primitive origins the practice of animal sacrifice may have had—burnt offerings as nourishment for the god, or a sacrificial feast as a means of sharing the god's power—there is in all these sacrificial regulations the primary motive of mediation. It implies a recognition that to insist on high standards and lofty principles is no answer to the problem of man's plight. We cannot be at peace with God however impressive be our moral code, because of the accursed twist in our natures which frustrates our best intentions. Man needs help from beyond himself to be at peace with God, and the Jews thought they had found the answer in the mediatory effectiveness of animal sacrifice.

As Christians we know that only God could bridge the gulf between man's sinfulness and his own holiness, and that the mediator had to be one who was both God and man, willingly offering his life in sacrifice to enable man to be at one with God. Yet as we read these chapters of Leviticus let us not dismiss them as ancient superstition or mere hocus-pocus, but rather see in them a genuine attempt to grapple with the problem of man's need and man's failure, which neither priest nor prophet could finally solve but

only God's own Son. Similarly when we read the sacrificial language of the New Testament, our knowledge of Leviticus should save us from interpreting in any crude way such phrases as "the blood of Christ", which is his Risen Life liberated by death making his people at one with God (cf. John 6. 56; I John 1. 7), and should help us to understand better what St. Paul means by the "sweet smelling sacrifice" of a life dedicated to God (cf. Eph. 5: 2; Phil. 4: 18).

Leviticus should further not be regarded merely as a code of regulations providing for mechanical sacrifices which must be made with meticulous care. It should be seen in the context of the Psalms in which we may sense not only the music and pageantry which were associated with the liturgy, but also the joy and exaltation of the worshippers as they found themselves caught up by the holy mysteries into the very presence of God. We cannot read the Psalms without being reminded of the sacrificial system to which they formed the accompaniment, nor should we read Leviticus without hearing in the background the strains of praise and thanksgiving from hearts from which the burden of guilt had been lifted.

The book opens with a description of the prescribed ways of restoring the broken relationship with God, beginning with instructions for the correct method of making a "burnt offering" as an act of worship (ch. 1). It must be a domestic animal which is offered, and thus a costly offering, even to the poor man who can only afford a pigeon. The worshipper, by laying his hand upon its head (v. 4), symbolically offers his own life to God. Next, the "meal offering" (ch. 2) consisting of the produce of the soil, the labour of men's hands, is to be given as a token of homage and seasoned with salt as the oriental mark of friendship (v. 13).

The "peace offering" (ch. 3), as a means of establishing fellowship with God, is shared between the altar and the worshipper. By partaking of the animal of which God also receives a share, the worshipper is united to him in the symbolism of a common meal. Next, provision is made for cases where priests or laity have violated some item or ceremonial or moral law in ignorance (4: 1–5: 13). This is a wholesome recognition that human fallibility is universal, that priest and people are united in common failure to fulfil the law of God. The broken relationship must be restored by a "sin offering". But if there has been a conscious offence, restitution must first be made to the person who has been wronged before a "trespass or guilt offering" is made to God (5: 14 – 6: 7).

There follow regulations for the guidance of the priests who have to make these offerings, and a specification of their share of the slaughtered animals (6: 8 – 7: 38). The form of consecration of the priests is then described (8: 1 – 9: 24), followed by warnings against unauthorised practices by the priesthood including that of drinking when on duty (10: 1–20). The next section (11: 1 – 15: 33)

deals with ritual purity. Certain animals are to be regarded as "clean" and therefore fit for human consumption; others are to be regarded as "unclean" and may not be eaten. Similarly certain bodily conditions render a person "unclean" i.e. unfit to enter the sanctuary, until the priest has certified that he is "clean". Much, but not all of this makes sense. "Leprosy" including apparently various skin diseases, is dealt with at length (ch. 13–14) and public health must have benefited from the extreme care which is enjoined here to prevent infection from spreading. Similarly few would quarrel with the concern for personal hygiene in ch. 15.

The division of animals into "clean" and "unclean", however, is less convincing. Doubtless many animals and birds found their way into the "unclean" category on the grounds that they were sacred to one or other of the neighbouring tribes or nations. Others perhaps were associated with an ancient tabu. There is little point, therefore, in trying to justify this biblical discrimination against swine (11: 7) on the grounds that pork is fairly indigestible in any case, unless we are prepared to include bald locusts, beetles and grasshoppers on our menu (11: 22).

"Uncleanness" is thus not altogether a rationally distinguishable quality. It later became a fetish for strictly orthodox Jews, such as Pharisees, to avoid contamination with anything "unclean", which by that time had come to include all non-Jews.

Our Lord disposed of their obsession with ritual "cleanness" by pointing out in trenchant words that it is what comes out of the heart and not what goes into the stomach that defiles a man (*Mark* 7: 1–23), and demanded that they should recover a proper sense of proportion between ceremonial and moral holiness (*Matt.* 23: 25–26). It was in keeping with this that the Church, following the divine guidance which came to St. Peter in his vision of clean and unclean animals on the rooftop at Joppa (*Acts* 10: 1–16), eventually abolished the distinction not only between "clean" and "unclean" as applied to food but also as applied to Jews and Gentiles.

The Day of Atonement
(16: 1–34)

THE regulations which occupy the first part of *Leviticus* reach their culmination in ch. 16. The various types of offering whereby the Law sought to make fallible mortals at one with God, and thereby keep the covenant relationship intact, came to be focused in an annual ceremony covering the whole nation. This was the Day of Atonement, known simply as the Day, when the high priest on behalf of the community performed a ritual which was designed to restore the people to a proper state of peace with God. This was no free pardon for all offences. Crimes against God and man which had been committed with full knowledge and deliberation were punished in accordance with the statutes concerned. The Day of Atonement was designed rather to cover sins of omission and ignorance. This may be dismissed, if we choose, as an artificial arrangement which was only necessary because of the multiplicity of ceremonial laws, whereby it was impossible to avoid breaking some part of the Law in the ordinary business of living from day to day.

But there was surely a deeper intuition behind this solemn ceremony, involving the recognition that restitution and punishment as well as individual offerings by the guilty were not enough. There must be a united confession of sin by the whole community, and the community as such must be given absolution, since every man was involved in the sins of his neighbours and involved his neighbours by his own failure to be fully obedient to the will of God. The ritual was dramatic and meaningful.

The high priest first of all symbolically makes his peace with God, including in this act the whole priesthood, thereby acknowledging that the professed ministers of God had failed as much as the laity (16: 11–14). Then not only the people but the whole sanctuary and its appurtenances are symbolically cleansed of all impurity and made fit for the proper service of God (16: 15–19). The climax of the ritual is the act of confession of sin on behalf of the community, made by the high priest as he lays his hands on the head of a goat, offered by the people, after which the goat is driven off into the wilderness (16: 20–22). Again the symbolism is that of mediation, of priest and victim consecrated for this purpose by God (16: 10), who will remove from the shoulders of the people the sins that they cannot throw off by themselves and send them away to the demon world (*Azazel*—R.V. 16: 8) where they belong.

Here is indeed an Old Testament hope which finds fulfilment in Christ. The epistle to the *Hebrews*, which above all else in the New Testament shows how the whole purpose of animal sacrifice among the Jews was to effect a proper relationship with God without, however, having the power to accomplish it, sees the Day of Atonement as the direct pointer to the mediation of Christ. He as both High Priest and willing Victim took upon his own shoulders once and for all the sins of mankind and secured an effective forgiveness of man's sin not for a year but for ever (*Heb.* 9: 1–14).

The Pattern of Holiness
(17: 1 – 27: 34)

THE SECOND half of the book of *Leviticus* is a legal code, sometimes known as the Holiness Code. It consists of a collection of instructions of varying importance and covering various aspects of life, but all in one way or another subserving the idea of holiness, i.e. moral and ceremonial purity. Thus regulations for the proper offering of sacrifices (ch. 17) are followed by a list of forbidden sexual relationships including sodomy and bestiality (ch. 18).

Pagan religious practices are also prohibited (18: 21). Side by side with safeguards against food poisoning (19: 5–7), provision is made for the poor (19: 9–10) and fundamental moral principles are enunciated (19: 11–18).

Characteristic of this juxtaposition of items of differing importance is the location in the code of an injunction against wearing a garment made of linen and wool (19: 19), a mixture which seems to have been used in magic rites. This immediately follows the words which Jesus regarded as the second most important commandment of all: "thou shalt love thy neighbour as thyself" (19: 18 – cf. *Mark* 12: 31). It was indeed the failure of the Pharisaic legalists to distinguish between the important and the unimportant provisions of the Law, illustrated by such an unequal pair of injunctions as these, that earned Jesus' violent condemnation. Surely it was never intended by the formulators of these laws that they should be regarded as of equal significance.

The tragedy of later Jewish legalism, which had reached its peak in the time of Jesus, was that not only did the multiplicity of provisions contained in the Law come to be regarded as equally binding, but also that the traditional interpretation which had grown up round them had acquired the same status as part of God's will for man. When it came to be regarded as equally vital to wear the right kind of garment of unmixed materials as to love one's neighbour, and when a man could acquire an equal reputation for virtue by doing either, the Law had ceased to be a divine revelation and had become human nonsense. When Jesus said that he had come not to destroy the Law but to fulfil it (*Matt.* 5: 17), he meant that one of the purposes of his teaching mission was to restore the proper perspective in regard to the Law, to put first things first, and to recover the spirit of the Law, as opposed to the letter of the Law, in accordance with the divinely guided purpose of its original compilers.

Many of the injunctions contained in these chapters are designed to prevent superstitious practices which were common among neighbouring peoples (e.g. 19: 28; 20: 6), others are designed to ensure that nothing less than the best is offered to God in the sanctuary (e.g. 22: 17–24). There are ordinances for the observance of the sabbath and the various Jewish religious festivals (ch. 23), for the arrangements of the furnishings of the Temple (ch. 24),

for the observance of a sabbatical year every seven years to rest the land and for a year of jubilee every fiftieth year in which estates must go back to their original owners and all Hebrew slaves must be set free (ch. 25).

The promise is made that if these statutes are observed, prosperity and peace will be the lot of the chosen people in the land of Canaan, but if not, disaster and punishment will come upon them (ch. 26). The compiler knew only too well how this promise had been fulfilled. Yet once again the note of mercy is heard above that of judgment. If the people fail and pay the price, and recognise in penitence that the price they have paid is their just desert, God will not be unmindful of his covenant with his people and will not utterly destroy them (26: 40–45). Thus, apart from the appendix in ch. 27, this forbidding book ends with a message of hope, and points forward through the failure of old Israel to its rebirth in the Church.

NUMBERS

THE NAME which has been given to this fourth book of the Old Testament refers to the census which is represented as having taken place twice during the period between the Exodus and the conquest of Canaan (chs 1 and 26). This, however, is only one element of this interesting book, which also contains a variety of narratives dealing with the journey from Sinai to Canaan, as well as a fair amount of legislation. The Jewish name for this section of the Pentateuch or Torah is "In the Wilderness", which is a much more appropriate title since the total effect of the book is to paint a picture of this stage in the story of Israel.

Like the rest of the Pentateuch the present form of the book of *Numbers* dates about 300 B.C. at the earliest, i.e. more than nine centuries after the events it describes. Some of the narrative sections belonging to the J and E traditions probably existed in written form from the days of the monarchy onwards, but the specifically legal sections, consisting of the Priestly contribution to the Torah (P) come, like *Leviticus* and parts of *Genesis* and *Exodus*, from the days after the monarchy disappeared. During and after the Exile in Babylon in the sixth century B.C., Jewish scholars set about the task of gathering to-

gether the old traditions and practices of the people of Israel, adding such new provisions as they thought proper, to constitute a pattern of life for a community that had learned its lesson and was determined to be an exemplary people of God. In this blend of old and new, past history was coloured by experience and reflection to such an extent that we cannot expect to find in the book of *Numbers*, any more than in *Genesis* or *Exodus*, a reliable historical narrative of what exactly happened.

Doubtless parts of the narrative come from oral tradition which goes back to the events themselves. But no oral tradition can preserve with any accuracy over a period of several hundred years conversations, movements and events in what we should call today trustworthy historical detail. When, in addition, the stories have been worked over by editors who are primarily interested in finding ancient sanctions for present practices, and in the moral lessons of history rather than in the facts of history, it becomes very difficult, and indeed impossible to disentangle pious interpretation from basic happening.

We must therefore strike some sort of a balance in reading *Numbers* between treating it as a record of events, accurate in all respects, and dismissing it as so idealised a reconstruction of the past that history has disappeared altogether. While we cannot treat any of the individual statistics, incidents or conversations as historical in the modern sense, the picture as a whole preserves enough traditional material to enable us to get a reasonably clear impression of this important chapter in Israel's career.

The bare bones of history can be easily summarised. It would seem that Moses and his motley band, having escaped from Egypt and having at Sinai pledged their loyalty to one another and to YHWH who had delivered them, spent the next few decades in typical bedouin fashion living a sparse existence in the barren country which stretches north from Sinai to Canaan, centred in Kadesh-Barnea, south of Beersheba. The narrative reflects, no doubt accurately, an atmosphere of discontent, dissension and resentment against the authority of Moses, and more than one occasion of open rebellion. The Tent of Meeting containing the Ark of the Covenant is, apart from the power of Moses' own personality, the only factor that holds the group together.

Finally, after the first generation of fugitives has died out, a move is made towards better living conditions in Canaan, which, like the rest of the Fertile Crescent, appeared to these half-starved nomads to be "flowing with milk and honey". At the end of the period in the wilderness, however, Israel was no ill-assorted rabble but a compact fighting force. The period had been one of consolidation and developing unity, so that when the advance began it was carried through with determination and vigour. After an abortive attempt to enter Canaan by the direct route, the strength of the opposition compelled the Israelites to make a circuitous journey round the east side of the Dead Sea, skirting Edom and Moab. Their first real military success over the Amorite kingdom of Sihon gave them a foothold in Transjordan and brought them to the threshold of Canaan.

The Host of Israel
(1: 1 – 10: 36)

THIS meagre historical foundation, however, tells us little of the significance that the Israelites came to attach to this formative stage of their experience, of the lessons they learned from it, and of the guidance of God that they came to see in it. For this we must turn to the book itself, where we are at once plunged into an atmosphere of preparation for battle. All the fit men of over twenty years of age are being registered for military service (1: 3). It is very unlikely that there was at this early stage a clear division into twelve tribes, and it is quite impossible that this bleak territory could have supported over 600,000 warriors, implying a total population of about 2,000,000 souls (1: 46). As we have seen (pp. 78–79), a more likely total would be 5,000 or thereabouts. The tribe of Levi, in deference to subsequent practice, is not included in the fighting force (1: 47-53) but is set apart for religious duties in connection with the Tent of Meeting under the direction of Aaron (3: 1-4: 49).

The scene conveyed by the first few chapters is of the host of Israel encamped according to tribes in square formation (2: 1-34), and grouped around the Tent of Meeting which is guarded and tended by the Levites. Such was the idealised picture held in later days of the desert life of Israel, centred on the worship of YHWH and ready for the march upon the promised land.

As befits an encampment of the people of God, nothing that would defile it must be allowed to remain within it (5: 1-4) and moral offences must be punished (5: 5-31). Provision is made for men and women who wish to take special vows of holiness (6: 1-21), and the form of the priestly blessing of the people is appointed: "The Lord bless thee, and keep thee; The Lord make his face shine upon thee, and be gracious unto thee; The Lord lift up his countenance upon thee, and give thee peace" (6: 22-27). Offerings are made at the consecration of the altar and of the Tent of Meeting (7: 1-88), the Levites are set apart for their sacred office (8: 5-8: 26) and arrangements are made for a supplementary celebration of the passover (9: 1-14) so that everyone should be able to participate.

Now the sacred host is ready to advance. The mysterious Presence of YHWH descends upon the Tent of Meeting in the form of cloud by day and fire by night. The rising of the cloud from the Tent is to be taken as the signal for advance. Israel is to move forward at the beckoning of YHWH and to camp wherever and for as long as the cloud indicates (9: 15-23). Just under a year after they had reached Sinai the divine signal is given, the tents are struck and with pennons flying the host of Israel sets out for the promised land. The sacred Ark of the covenant, symbol of YHWH'S presence, precedes the column and acts as its guide and protector (10: 1-36).

This highly coloured picture of what later generations of Israelites liked to think was the manner of their forefathers' departure from Sinai—a mighty column of marching men, devout, enthusiastic and determined, with the Ark of God pointing the way—cannot however obscure the fact that there was another side to the canvas, and the realism of the priestly historians compels them to include this too. The caravan sets out and eventually reaches the promised land, but its story is not one of a triumphal progress. Discontent, disloyalty and cowardice are the keynotes of the journey through the wilderness, and in a series of vignettes all this is faithfully recorded. It is as if the compilers of the narrative were determined to confront Israel—and us—with the army of God's people, or the Church militant, as it should be and, by contrast, with the dismal reality of what it is.

In the Wilderness
(11 : 1 – 20 : 29)

TROUBLE first breaks out over food (11 : 1–35). Egypt may have been a house of bondage but the varied diet of fish and vegetables made the life of a slave more tolerable than this everlasting manna. The complaints are met by a reappearance of the quails (cf. *Ex.* 16 and p. 81), the grumblers being threatened with so much meat that it will come out of their nostrils (11 : 20)! Moses laments that his task is too heavy for him and he is given seventy elders from among the people to assist him (11 : 10–17). These men are apparently ecstatics, like the early type of "prophets" described in *I Sam.* 10 : 5. They should not be confused with classical prophets of the calibre of Amos and Isaiah. Far from feeling that his authority is diminished, Moses wishes to see similar signs of the presence of the Spirit in all God's people (11 : 29). His prayer was answered at Pentecost (*Acts* 2). Despite disaster by fire in the camp (11 : 1) and plague (11 : 33), both of which are regarded as judgments of God (the first perhaps by lightning and the second by indigestion!), the first stage in the journey is reached at Hazeroth (11 : 35), now Ain Huderah near the Gulf of Aqaba. The burial place of the victims of the plague is aptly dubbed: "Gluttons' graves" (11 : 34).

More trouble arises from the jealousy of Miriam, Moses' sister, and Aaron (12 : 1–16). Moses who is described as the humblest of all mortals (12 : 3)—which has, however, not been his most noteworthy characteristic so far— emerges from this trial with his authority vindicated. He is the only man with whom YHWH will speak face to face and not by dreams and visions as in the case of the "prophets" (12 : 6–8). Poor Miriam pays for her disloyalty with an attack of leprosy. "Leprosy" seems to have covered a variety of skin diseases, some fairly harmless (cf. *Lev.* 13–14), but clearly the cure here is regarded as solely due to the intercession of Moses. The whole chapter leaves many questions unanswered, e.g. Why was Aaron not punished also?, but the interest of the incident lies much more in this impressive estimate of Moses held several hundred years after his death.

From Hazeroth a reconnaissance party is sent out to report on the possibility of entering the land of Canaan from the south (13 : 1–20). Their orders are to find out the nature of the terrain, the strength of the inhabitants, and the possible resistance. They are gone for over a month and by the time they return the caravan has reached Kadesh, an oasis in the Negeb 150 miles from Sinai as the crow flies (13 : 26). They had penetrated north as far as Hebron, and as proof of the fertility of the land they had brought back among other things a giant vine from the Vale of Eshcol, which took two men to carry (13 : 22–27).

At the same time, however, they reported that the country was thickly populated with a variety of races and tribes, that walled cities abounded, and that the inhabitants were so tall that they felt like grasshoppers beside them (13: 28–33). The effect of this news is catastrophic. Despite the entreaties of Joshua and Caleb, who are in favour of advance in accordance with the command of YHWH and the desire of Moses, there is open rebellion against the leaders. The mob proposes to elect another chief who will take them back to Egypt, and Joshua and Caleb are on the point of being stoned to death (14: 1–10).

Then the avenging Presence of YHWH suddenly confronts the unruly throng from the Tent of Meeting. Only the vehement plea of Moses for the people who had wronged him stays the hand of the Lord from wiping out the chosen people and founding a new elect community on his most faithful servant. Moses calls to the mind of YHWH his own words (*Ex.* 34: 6–7) when he revealed his glory on Sinai, and, as Abraham had done for Sodom (*Gen.* 18), seeks the Lord's pity and forgiveness for this rebellious folk (14: 11–19).

YHWH pardons his people in response to the plea of Moses, but their punishment is to be that the whole generation of those who have rebelled against the will of God must die out in the wilderness, all, that is, save Joshua and Caleb, since only a new generation and possibly a more faithful one would be fit to enter the promised land. Too late, and despite this warning, an attempt is made to penetrate the mountains into

Canaan. It is done without the approval of Moses, and without the presence of the Ark. The invasion is repulsed by the natives of the region at Hormah (14: 20–45).

The narrative is interrupted by instructions for the making of certain offerings, and the distinction is made clear between sins of ignorance and sins "with a high hand". Into the latter category comes an unfortunate man who was found gathering sticks on the sabbath. The people are urged to decorate their outer garments with blue tassels to remind them of the commandments of God (15: 1–41). This is the hem of the garment referred to in the story of Jesus and the woman with the issue of blood (*Matt.* 9: 20).

Whether the major revolt of a faction of the Levites under Korah described in ch. 16 was associated with an earthquake or not, both of these things appear to have happened about this time. The authority of Aaron and the priesthood over all the subordinate Levites, and of the levitical priesthood over the people, is confirmed by the blossoming of Aaron's rod, which was then placed within the Tent of Meeting as a permanent reminder of the will of God in this connection (17: 1–13).

The status of the Aaronic priesthood is further defined and tithes, together with other offerings, are secured to them for their maintenance (18: 1–32). Contamination by contact with a corpse, which was strongly felt to entail ritual uncleanness—presumably based not on hygiene but on an ancient sense of the demonic mystery of death—is to be countered by a ceremony involving the ashes of a heifer, which the author of the epistle to the *Hebrews* regards as the acme of the futility of this type of ritual law (19: 1–22; *Heb.* 9: 13).

Now the death of Miriam (20: 1) is recorded, and the third parallel to the miraculous provision of food and drink at the time of the Exodus (*Ex.* 16–17) is introduced. Water from the rock follows manna and quails as a token of God's sustenance of his people despite their mistrust and contumacy (20: 7–11). On this occasion Moses and Aaron are included in the Lord's displeasure and both are told that they too will not live to enter the promised land (20: 12). This would no doubt be a means of explaining why it was that Moses, having led his people through so many trials and dangers should himself die before setting foot on Canaan's soil (*Deut.* 34: 5). Aaron, however, dies before him (20: 28).

Thus the second stage of the narrative of the journey from Sinai to Canaan comes to an end. We are to understand that about forty years have passed since the caravan set out in 10: 11. Most of that time has been spent in and around the oasis of Kadesh, now Ain Qedeis, which together with the adjacent oasis of Ain El-Qudeirat could well supply a nomadic community of a few thousands with the essential supply of water for their flocks and herds for a period of this length.

On the Threshold of the Promised Land

(21: 1 – 36: 13)

BUT NOW the caravan prepares to move for the last stage of the journey. The choice of Moses would have been to travel along the ancient "king's highway" which joined the Gulf of Aqaba with Syria, and passed along the east side of the Dead Sea. Astride this road however lay several kingdoms, and the first of them, Edom, refused permission to this nomadic migration to traverse its territory (20: 14–21).

It is difficult to know whether the successful attack on Canaan from the south centring on Hormah was a separate spearhead of invasion at this time, or whether it is a more flattering version of what has been recorded in 14: 40–45. At all events the main body proceeds to skirt the kingdom of Edom by taking a circuitous route through the more difficult terrain of Transjordan (21: 1–4).

It is at this point that the incident of the "Brazen Serpent" is introduced (21: 5–9). This may be an example of the ancient belief in sympathetic magic (cf. *I Sam.* 6: 5) by which the elevated brazen serpent would be reckoned to have the power to heal snake-bites; it may be designed to justify the subsequent destruction of the brazen serpent, Nehushtan, by Hezekiah when its honoured position in the Temple had come to attract superstitious veneration (*II Kings* 18: 4). The implication here is that healing power does not come from the brazen serpent but from YHWH, which was what

Hezekiah sought to emphasise (cf. *Wisd.* 16: 5-7.)

Our Lord used this story as a parable of his own Crucifixion (*John* 3: 13-15). In the Old Testament tale Moses neutralises the poison of the serpent's fangs by something which has a serpent's shape but none of a serpent's deadly venom. In the New Testament symbol, God sends his Son in the form of a sinful man, yet without man's sin, to destroy the power of sin for ever. As Christ is born under the Law to free us from the stranglehold of the Law, and endures death to take away the sting from all death, so the old serpent of *Gen.* 3: 15 is nailed to the Cross, and by the power of God is transformed into the gift of new life which is offered to us from Calvary and which draws the whole world to the feet of Jesus.

The route of the invaders is further described, partly in snatches of old ballads (21: 14-15, 17-18, 27-30), from which it appears that having avoided both Edom and Moab they were attacked by Amorites, under king Sihon, and by Og, king of Bashan. As a result of defeating both of these forces the Israelites found themselves masters of Transjordan (21: 10-35).

Archaeological evidence indicates that these petty kingdoms—Edom, Moab, and the territories of Sihon and Og—whose inhabitants belonged to the same wave of Semitic migration into the Fertile Crescent as did the Hebrews, had established themselves in this area slightly earlier than the Hebrew settlement in Canaan.

It was about the beginning of the thirteenth century B.C. that this area east of the Jordan rift was occupied by these peoples, which confirms the later date of the Exodus (see p. 67) and suggests that the events now being described took place about 1250 B.C. If the Israelites had attempted to pass along the "king's highway" before about 1300 B.C. there would have been no one to stop them (20: 17-18; 21: 22-23).

The Hebrews are now on the threshold of the promised land. Their tents are pitched on the hills of Moab looking over the Jordan and Jericho (22: 1) to the hills of Judah. The actual invasion of Canaan is, however, not described until the book of *Joshua*. The rest of the book of *Numbers* is devoted mainly to sundry legislative matters and preparations for the invasion, while the book of *Deuteronomy*, which follows it, purports to be an address by Moses to the host of Israel on the eve of their entrance into their promised inheritance.

The story of Balaam (22: 2-24: 25) comes at this point to emphasise the irresistible advance of Israel along the path which YHWH had mapped out for her. The apparent contradictions in the story (e.g. 22: 20, 22) are due to the fact that different versions have been woven into the same narrative. The Priestly tradition, as opposed to the JE tradition, represents Balaam in an unfavourable light (cf. 31: 8, 16). This accounts for his evil reputation in the New Testament (*II Pet.* 2: 15-16; *Rev.* 2: 14).

Balak, king of Moab, alarmed

at Israel's military successes attempts to overcome them by sorcery. He sends for Balaam, a well known wizard from the East, to put a curse on Israel which, in ancient belief, was, like a blessing, both irrevocable and effective. The moral of the tale is that even a heathen seer is impelled to proclaim that nothing can stop the people whom God has appointed to fulfil their destiny as masters of the promised land. Balaam, against his employer's wishes, insists on blessing Israel instead of cursing it. He can do no other. Even his intelligent talking ass recognises the hand of YHWH in the matter.

Once again the motif is the inexplicable grace of God, who despite the failure and rebellion of his people—and their unworthiness has been manifest on every page of the story of their journey from Sinai to Moab as the following chapter (25) clearly underlines —has nevertheless laid his hand upon them for his own majestic purpose. The divine plan will not be thwarted by man's folly and disobedience, although the price of folly and disobedience must be paid, as has also been made plain in story form in the preceding chapters.

In a sense the oracle of Balaam stands in the same line, and in part uses the same words, as the blessing given to Abraham and passed on by Isaac to Jacob (24: 9; cf. *Gen.* 12: 3; 27: 29). The blessing and the promise are by the will of God the only reason why this stubborn recalcitrant and altogether ungrateful people should not be left to

meet the fate they deserve. This is equally true of the Church which inherits the blessing and the promise. And indeed although the Star which Balaam's vision foretells (24: 17) doubtless refers to David—and perhaps the story itself dates from his day—Christian thought will see behind David the Messiah, and will treat the whole passage as a pointer to the ultimate victory of Christ and the Israel of God (*Rev.* 22: 16).

The narrative suggests that Balak, having failed to block the Hebrews' progress by magic, resorted to a more insidious method (31: 16). Such a ruthless massacre as is recorded in ch. 31 can only find its justification if we see the background of ch. 25 not merely as casual promiscuity between the men of Israel and the women of Moab and Midian. There is obviously more to it than that. The Ras Shamra tablets, discovered in the thirties at Ugarit in Syria, provide the clue. No greater contrast could be imagined than that between the austere and disciplined sex life of Israel's desert days and the licentious atmosphere of the fertility cults of Canaan with which the nomads now for the first time make contact.

The tablets of Ras Shamra give a clear picture of a religion common to the agricultural regions of Palestine and doubtless already adopted by the semi-nomads who had now settled on the fringe of the desert, in this case Moabites worshipping the god Chemosh. A highly developed cult with major gods and goddesses whose identity was clearly differentiated, followed a pattern similar to that of Egypt and Babylonia and indeed of the Fertile Crescent as a whole. In Canaan the chief god was El, a name used of God in *Genesis* (see p. 73) and connected with the normal Old Testament word for God, Elohim, the plural form denoting majesty.

The consort of El was Asherah (Asherat, Ashirat), a word frequently found in the Old Testament and generally translated "grove". When the Israelites entered Canaan they found their neighbours worshipping their gods in temples in the cities and on "high places" i.e. artificial temple mounds, in the villages. Associated with the "high place" and its worship was a sacred tree or carved tree trunk representing the goddess Asherah and therefore called by her name. The son of El and Asherah was Baal, the storm god, generally represented as a bull. Both the name and the symbol of the bull crop up frequently in the Old Testament, generally as objects of denunciation by the prophets.

This type of religion, common to the Fertile Crescent, highly sophisticated and accompanied by elaborate ritual, was based on a mythological interpretation of the sequence of nature. The death of vegetation in the autumn, followed by its rebirth in the spring, gave rise to the myth of the death and resurrection of the god. In Canaan it was Baal who owned the land and who was responsible for the life-giving springtime rain on which the farmer depended. Each place had its own little

Baal and its own little goddess, who were regarded as manifestations of the cosmic deities. Baal's sexual union with his sister and consort, Anath or Ashtart, was regarded as the basis of the fertility of the soil. It was believed that the ordinary worshipper by the process of imitative magic could assist the fertility of his own land by engaging in the reproductive act in the temples of the cities and the "high places" of the villages with male and female representatives of the god.

Sacred prostitution was thus part of normal Canaanite worship. This was later to prove a major threat to the integrity of Israel's allegiance to YHWH, but here it would seem that the Israelites first encountered the sensuous and demoralising practices of Canaanite religion before actually setting foot on Canaanite soil. The violence of Moses' reaction is a measure of his horror at this perilous development, which would undoubtedly have not only turned his men's thoughts in the direction of lingering among the attractions of a less arduous life than that which lay ahead, but would also have robbed their religion of one of its distinctive characteristics. A breakdown in the rigid sexual standard was but the first step to the Israelites' faith becoming indistinguishable in all other respects from the polytheism that surrounded them (25: 1–18; 31: 1–54).

After the plague (25: 9), which had been regarded as a judgment on the people for their deviation from the Law, another census is taken. The numbers are little

ON THE THRESHOLD OF THE PROMISED LAND 129

changed from the previous census in ch. 1, but none of the able bodied men registered then had survived, apart from Moses, Joshua and Caleb (26: 1–65). Laws of inheritance are drawn up with a view to apportioning the land of Canaan, and Joshua is appointed as Moses' successor but in secular matters only (27: 1–23). In religious matters Joshua is to be subject to the priesthood. No Israelite would ever again speak with YHWH "mouth to mouth" (12: 8) like his servant Moses, who was "faithful in all mine house" (12: 7), until in the fulness of time the Son of the house came to claim his inheritance and say "all things that I have heard of my Father I have made known unto you" (*John* 15: 15; *Heb.* 3: 1–6).

Various regulations are laid down in connection with public worship (28: 1 – 29: 40) and family responsibilities (30: 1–16). The tribes of Reuben, Gad and part of Manasseh stake their claim to the territories in Transjordan which had been wrested from Sihon and Og (32: 1–42), and a record of the route from Egypt to Moab is given in detail (33: 1–49). Although not many of the stopping places are now identifiable the general route is clearly indicated, and was fairly obviously determined by the location of water holes.

Instructions are given for the occupation of Canaan (33: 50–56); the extent of Israel's future territory is defined (34: 1–15) and the commissioners who are to allocate the land are named (34: 16–29). The Levites are to

have certain cities reserved for their exclusive use (35: 1–8), and six of these are to be cities of refuge in which persons who have been guilty of homicide may find sanctuary from tribal vengeance until they receive a fair trial (35: 9–34). The last chapter (36: 1–13) deals further with the law of inheritance.

St. Paul writes the footnote and suggests the proper interpretation of this formative period in Israel's history in his first letter to the Corinthians. He sees this period in the wilderness as the testing time of the people of God. Historians would rightly say that it was a period of consolidation, during which Moses hammered into shape—and into a formidable fighting force—the diverse elements which had followed him out of Egypt. St. Paul, thinking on a deeper level than the historian, treats the whole saga as a sustained parable. The temptations that caused Israel to stumble—and for which they were punished—are the same temptations as beset the Christian: lack of faith, discontent, greed, lust. Stories like those in the book of *Numbers*, St. Paul would say to us, are "written for our admonition". Israel is both our matrix and our mentor. God is speaking to us "upon whom the end of the ages has come" in these sometimes factual, sometimes fanciful stories of the childhood of the Church (*I Cor.* 10: 5–11).

In the same vein the author of the epistle to the *Hebrews* regards the forty years in the wilderness, which kept the Israelites out of their inheritance in Canaan, as primarily a punishment for their lack of trust in God. They refused to go forward into the promised land for fear of known and unknown dangers (chs. 13–14). Let this be a warning to the Church, says the writer of *Hebrews*. We too are on a pilgrimage, a new Exodus. Let us not shrink from the dangers that may lie ahead but rather go forward, putting our trust in God. For if we cling to the security of the present, or look back longingly to the security of the past, as did the Israelites, we too shall be denied entrance into the promised land, which for us is the presence of God (*Heb.* 3: 7 – 4: 11).

DEUTERONOMY

So FAR in the Pentateuch we have had, broadly speaking, two types of interest represented—narrative, and legal or ceremonial. The narrative sections are reckoned to date from the time of the monarchy, roughly somewhere between 1000 B.C. and 750 B.C. This was the period when Israel, in its heyday of expansion and success after the conquest of Canaan, recorded in writing the story of its origins and traced the hand of God in all that had happened to it. The story, as we have seen (pp. 16–17), is a blend of two interwoven traditions, one originating in the northern part of the country (the E or Elohist version) and the other in the south (the J or Jahwist version). Behind this blended narrative (JE) lie written records which are now lost but to which the biblical writers refer, such as the Book of the Wars of the Lord (*Num.* 21: 14) or the Book of Jasher (*Josh.* 10: 13), and behind these stretches the long period, as in any other literature, when song and story were handed down by minstrels and story tellers from generation to generation.

Distinct from this is the P or Priestly contribution, occasionally supplying another version of the JE narrative, but much more often concerned with ceremonial, genealogies and ritual law. This part of the Pentateuch, although containing elements which go back to the time of Moses or beyond it, comes in its finished form from the period when Israel had ceased to be a nation and had become a tiny community in and around Jerusalem under priestly government, but subject to one or another of the great world empires. The final editing of the Pentateuch by these priestly scholars was not completed before about 300 B.C.

This composite character of the Pentateuch is responsible for contradictions and discrepancies which appear in the narratives, and which at one time caused great distress to ordinary readers of the Bible since they could not understand how what they believed to be a miraculously infallible book could possibly have two inconsistent versions of the same story. We are now happily relieved of this burden, and as a result of scientific study of the Pentateuch over the past two centuries we have learned to distinguish between the Word which God has spoken and the fallible human minds that heard it and the fallible human hands that recorded it.

The book of *Deuteronomy*, like the book of *Leviticus*, does not present us to any great extent with this problem of sorting out the various component parts. It does however introduce the fourth strand which has gone to the making up of the Pentateuch (see

p. 17), and at least the central section of the book (chs. 12–26 and ch. 28) if not all of it, is generally attributed to an independent source which is not found anywhere else in the Pentateuch.

Unlike the three other elements in the Torah, the first appearance of the fourth element, known as D, can be accurately dated. It falls in time between JE and P. The story is a dramatic one and is recounted in *II Kings* 22. The year is 622 B.C. during the reign of king Josiah. By this time the northern part of the kingdom had been overthrown by the Assyrians and only the southern section, Judah, remained of the miniature empire which king David had established almost four centuries earlier. In religious matters, too, Israel had fallen upon evil days. Josiah's grandfather, Manasseh, who was by common consent one of the worst kings that the country had ever known, had so debased the religion of YHWH that it bore little resemblance to the faith of the Sinai covenant. Heathen worship was firmly entrenched in the sacred courts of the Temple; shrines and altars to the gods and goddesses of Canaan ranked with the worship of YHWH as part of the normal religious life of Israel; wizardry, necromancy and astrology had taken the place of the rigid simplicity of the Mosaic pattern of belief; sacred prostitution of both sexes had become part and parcel of Israel's religious practice (*II Kings* 21).

It would seem that Josiah had already begun to restore the fabric of the Temple, for it was in the course of repairs to the "house of the Lord" that Hilkiah the high priest discovered "the book of the law", which so moved the king when he heard its contents that he launched a religious reformation which cleansed the whole land of its heathen shrines and attendant immorality, arrogated to the Temple at Jerusalem the exclusive right of sacrificial worship, and made short shrift of the heathen priests and their idols (*II Kings* 23).

The reforms instituted by king Josiah correspond so closely to the policy advocated by the book of *Deuteronomy* that there can be little doubt that this was "the book of the law" which was found in the Temple. What is not so certain is when it was originally written and how it came to be so conveniently discovered. Manasseh's reign had followed the era of the great prophets and contradicted everything that they had stood for. Was this scroll, "the book of the law", which translates into practical terms the great principles enunciated by Amos, Hosea, Micah and Isaiah, the work of an underground prophetic resistance movement which composed it during Manasseh's reign, and was it conveniently planted or discovered when the times were more auspicious?

At all events the book as it stands is a triumphant confession of faith in YHWH as the only God of Israel, who had chosen this people and made his covenant with them at Sinai. Despite their melancholy record in the wilderness he had brought them to the good land of Canaan and now, in the framework of a valedictory address by Moses, the way of life is laid down which they must follow there as the response of thanksgiving and loyal obedience. In one sense this framework is artificial in that Moses was not the author of *Deuteronomy*. But the book represents the mind of Moses as it was understood by those who sought to reform the life of Israel in the seventh century B.C., and who claimed not to be advocating anything new, but rather a return to the fundamental principles of Israel's faith as they had been laid down by the great lawgiver. In this sense *Deuteronomy* is Moses' word to his people—and to us.

The name of the book, which means the second law-giving, was originally a mistaken understanding by the Greek translators of the Hebrew words in 17: 18. They wrongly took the Hebrew words for "a copy of this law" to mean "this second law", but in fact the book (chs. 12–26; 28) is well described in this way, since it is a second edition of the legal code contained in *Exodus* 20–23 called there the Book of the Covenant (*Ex.* 24: 7), enlarged and revised under the influence of the great prophets and incorporating their ideas. The difference between the Book of the Covenant and *Deuteronomy* is the measure of the effect which the prophets had on the life and thought of Israel.

The Meaning of the Exodus
(1 : 1 – 4 : 40)

THE first few chapters (1–11) purport to be two addresses or sermons (1 : 1 – 4 : 40 and 5 : 1 – 11 : 32) delivered by Moses to the tribes of Israel as they are gathered on the hills of Moab overlooking the Jordan valley, before making their entry into the promised land. Moses recapitulates the events that have taken place from Sinai onwards: the promise of conquest (1 : 6–8), the appointment of his own deputies (1 : 9–18), the report of the spies (1 : 19–25), the faintheartedness of the people (1 : 26–33), their condemnation to spend a generation in the wilderness (1 : 34–40) and their resolve to attack too late which ended in disaster (1 : 41–46).

Since this version of the approach to Canaan is written some considerable time later than the narrative which we have been looking at in the books of *Exodus* and *Numbers*, and since it dates from a time when Israel's military glory had vanished, it is not surprising to find that the reason given now (2 : 1–23) for the by-passing of Edom and Moab, and the failure to dispose of the Ammonites of Transjordan (which was in fact the superior strength of these peoples—*Num.* 20: 21; 21 : 24) is that the Edomites are the descendants of Esau (*Gen.* 36: 1), while the Moabites and Ammonites were descendants of Lot (*Gen.* 19: 37–38). From a purely historical point of view these were all kindred Semitic peoples who had originally formed part of the same racial migration as the Hebrews into the Fertile Crescent (see p. 126).

The victories over Sihon, king of the Amorites, and Og, king of Bashan, the allocation of their territories to the tribes of Reuben,

Gad and part of Manasseh, the appointment of Joshua and the impending death of Moses are recalled (2 : 24 – 3 : 29) more or less as they have already been described in the book of *Numbers*. The frequent reference to giants in this section, called Rephaim, Anakim, Emim and Zamzummim, meaning "ghosts", "terrors" and "howlers" (2 : 10, 11, 20), may imply that the previous non-Semitic inhabitants of the area before the nomadic invasions had been a taller race of men and that their memory persisted. The other possibility is that the Semites concluded from the size of the great stone graves from the megalithic age, which are found in considerable numbers in this region, that the early inhabitants must have been correspondingly huge. The "iron bedstead" of Og, king of Bashan (3 : 11), may have been a dolmen or a sarcophagus. A grave of this kind and of the biblical dimensions was discovered near Rabbath-Ammon, the modern Amman, in 1918. Stone graves are also found near Hebron, which would account for the report of giants by the spies in *Num.* 13 : 32–33.

Allowance in this rather highly coloured description of Israel's "glorious" past must also be made for the vivid imagination of the recorder. As in the pious exaggeration of the size of Israel's "army" which we have already encountered in the book of *Numbers* (see p. 121), so also we may take with some reservations the reference to wholesale extermination of hostile forces here and elsewhere in the early books of the Bible. No doubt battles were fought and on both sides men were killed. On occasion too, ruthless massacres were carried out, common in in the ancient Near East as sacrifices to a conquering deity —the *herem* (7 : 2–5; 20 : 13–18) or "ban" as the Hebrews called it —but we find most of these early enemies of Israel still plaguing them long after they are supposed to have been annihilated.

Similarly in the references to Canaanite "cities" with high walls and to unwalled "towns" (e.g. 3 : 4–6), the latter represents something more like a handful of huts and the former was considerably more modest than the name "city" suggests to us nowadays. A "walled city" was much more like a fort enclosing an area of anything from one to twenty acres. This was the permanent home of the headman or chief, called "king" in the Bible, who shared it with other officials and the important members of the community. Such people lived in solid houses, mostly one story, with open courtyards and on an average four to six rooms. The majority of the population—serfs and slaves—lived in mud huts outside the walls, and took refuge in the "city" only in time of war. Thus a "city" in the biblical sense as applied to Palestine both before and after the conquest is a relatively tiny affair compared with the great cities of Mesopotamia and Egypt.

The theme of chapter four is the marvel of Israel's call and covenant (4 : 1–40). The glory of the God of Sinai is extolled. YHWH who is the only God in heaven and earth (4: 39) spoke to the tribes in an indescribable setting of awe and majesty at the holy mountain, making them his own peculiar people, and summoning them to an obedience like that of no other folk. The Ten Commandments must be their rule of life in days to come. Above all the obedience of the invisible God demands purity of worship. No images of gods or goddesses, or of anything which might become an object of worship, or of sun moon or stars must ever be manufactured or owned. Should that ever happen the good land of Canaan which is about to be given to them will be wrested from them and they will find themselves dispossessed exiles in a foreign land. "YHWH thy God is a consuming fire" (4: 24). But that is not the Bible's last word about God here or elsewhere. He is a God who judges, but who is also merciful (4: 31). If Israel even at that late stage returns to the path of true obedience he will not forsake his people. He will always remember and fulfil his covenant (4: 29-31).

This stern prohibition of idolatry is of course only explicable in retrospect. By the time these words were written Israel had in fact become ensnared in the polytheism, immorality and corruption of Canaanite religion, and had in fact lost most of the good land already. In the view of the priests and prophets of Israel, which is expressed here in *Deuteronomy*, the root cause of Israel's downfall was its failure to preserve the monotheistic faith which had been revealed on Sinai,

and this was a profoundly true insight.

The prohibition of images, which made Israel the least distinguished of all the Near Eastern peoples in painting and sculpture, was based among other things on an unerring conviction that unless there is an absolute standard of obedience to one God morality becomes a casualty. Worship of images and idols separated religion from morality. In the Canaanite pantheon where gods and goddesses warred and wantoned, tricked each other and made sport with mortals, there was no possible common standard of conduct for ordinary folk to emulate and no particular reason for observing it. Only when right conduct could be seen as the proper obedience of one who was himself just, pure and holy did moral standards have any meaning. It was thus imperative for Israel to recognise that whatever might happen elsewhere they were the people of one God and of one Law which brooked no evasion. So long as this was heeded the people prospered, but when they broke the terms of the covenant disaster overtook them. Such was the Deuteronomic interpretation of history which we shall see applied to subsequent events as Israel's story is unfolded.

"The Lord our God is One Lord"

(4: 41 – 11: 32)

AFTER A brief reference again to the provision of places of sanctuary (4: 41-43), and as a prelude to the recapitulation of the Ten Commandments (5: 6–21), an important principle is enunciated which is of deep significance for the Church. It has been clearly stated more than once that the generation that heard the word of God at Sinai had perished almost to a man in the wilderness as a punishment for their lack of trust in God. Yet here we find the recital of the Decalogue prefaced by the assertion that the covenant was not made with dead men in days gone by but with us, "who are all of us here alive this day". It was with the successors of the generation that died in the desert that the Lord talked "face to face in the mount". The implication of this is of course that the revelation of God is timeless and that his words whenever they were spoken are addressed to us here and now (5: 1–4). Similarly, as in Old Testament times, each successive generation must repeatedly renew its allegiance to God and accept responsibility for doing his will.

The Ten Commandments of Ex. 20: 1–17 are then repeated (5: 6–21) with slight variations, e.g. that the reason for keeping the seventh day as a day of rest is no longer connected with Creation, but is now partly to protect domestic staff from exploitation and partly to preserve the memory of the great deliverance of Israel from death in Egypt (5: 14–15; cf. Ex. 20: 11). This refrain, "salvation from death (in Egypt) into new life (in Canaan), therefore thanksgiving through obedience" dominates this book. It is again the theme of chapter six, which

also contains the great confession of Israel's faith: "Hear, O Israel: the Lord our God is one Lord, (i.e. the only God for us). And thou shalt love the Lord thy God with all thine heart, and with all thy soul, and with all thy might" (6: 4–5).

The instructions to take this confession seriously (6: 6–9) led to the instructions themselves being taken literally, and devout Jews later showed their orthodoxy by wearing large-size phylacteries on their arms and on their foreheads (Matt. 23: 5) containing these words, and by attaching strips of parchment inscribed with the Shema (= Hear), as this confession (coupled with 11: 13–21 and Num. 15: 37–41) is called, to the doorways of their homes. Not only did Jesus reckon the opening words of the Shema to be the first of all the commandments (Mark 12: 29), coupling it with Lev. 19: 18, but he also used the words of 6: 13 and 6: 16 in rebutting two of his temptations (Matt. 4: 7, 10).

The seventh chapter enjoins the extermination of all the existing inhabitants of Canaan, with their cults. In the event neither of these things happened. As the book of Judges and subsequent narratives indicate, Israel's progress into Canaan was more by infiltration and intermarriage than by conquest. The prohibition of mixed marriages which is stressed here (7: 3) did not become a real possibility until Israel had shrunk into a small self-contained community in the days after the Exile and came then under the influence of Nehemiah and Ezra. Far from

destroying the religious appurtenances of their new neighbours the
Israelites adopted them, as
prophet after prophet bears witness. The point of such instructions here is to drive home the
lesson to the apprehensive rump
that Israel had become by the
time this was written, that they had
no one but themselves to blame.

Yet following this grim theme
comes one of the great passages
of the book (7: 6–8). Here, if
anywhere, is the key to the age old
question of why God chose Israel,
and here we are given the only
answer that the Bible ever gives
as to why God involves himself
with the Church or with mankind
at all, why he stoops down to
raise us up. The answer in all its
simplicity and mystery is that he
loves us.

Continuing this blend of past
history and future prospects, the
sermon refers (8: 1–20) to the
forty years in the wilderness, treating them as an object lesson in
God's providential care of his
people, including the bitter experiences. Even in a setting which
seems consistently to promise
material rewards for obedience,
the discipline of adversity is recognised (8: 5), and a warning is
uttered against ever regarding
these material rewards as anything
other than the evidence of God's
love. Again our Lord found in this
lofty interpretation of the wilderness experience the answer to another of his temptations (8: 3; cf.
Matt. 4: 4). Could there be a more
apposite word for our self-suffi-
cient scientific era than 8: 7–18,
and in particular v. 17?

In the ninth chapter Moses re-
cites the long list of Israelite rebellions against God from the time
they left mount Sinai. "Ye have
been rebellious against the Lord
from the day that I knew you" (9:
24). If they are now offered the
good land of Canaan and master
its various peoples, it is not for any
virtue of their own but because the
heathens are even worse than they
are (9: 5). In the midst of these
recollections and reflections comes
a magnificent passage (10: 12–21)
extolling the majestic love of God
and calling for love and charity to
the poor and needy as a fitting response. Circumcision would never
have become a national fetish if the
words of 10: 16 had been heeded.

The sermon, after dwelling with
obvious affection on the good land
so directly dependent on God
which is Israel's heritage (11: 11–
15), ends with a challenge and a
call for a decision. Before them
lies a blessing or a curse. To obey
God's commandments will bring
his blessing, to disobey will bring
his curse (11: 26–32).

The Book of the Law
(12: 1 – 28: 68)

THE following section (chs. 12–
26; 28) which forms the heart of
Deuteronomy is presented as part
of Moses' discourse which began
at 5: 1, but as it is quite different in
character, and indeed constitutes
an independent law code, it is
generally considered separately.
Since it lays down a pattern of
daily life for people living in towns
and villages of a Near Eastern
country over two thousand five
hundred years ago, there is not a

great deal of common ground between their way of life and ours except that we share the same basic needs and experiences.

We must not therefore expect to find a direct relevance in the contents of this body of laws and regulations to our twentieth century situation. On the other hand this is part of the warp and woof of the great tapestry of life which the Old Testament weaves, and through which runs the thread that leads from Abraham and Moses through priests and prophets to Christ and his Church. For our Lord and for the writers of the New Testament this was the hallowed tradition that had been handed down from the past. They quote its words and respect its authority. For us as Christians in the modern world though it is no longer the law under which we live, it is the law which is built on a faith which we share.

Behind these time-conditioned laws of *Deuteronomy* lies the unchanging summons of a holy God to a life of obedience on the part of his people. Our pattern of obedience must of necessity be different since we live in different times and in different places. But we are at one with the makers of these laws in that it is the same God we try to serve. In the light of the New Testament revelation we can see the shortcomings of many of the elements in this pattern of the good life, as it should be lived by a people who acknowledge the God of Abraham, Isaac and Jacob; a God who cares, a God who saves. But we can enter into and profit from the deep sense of love to God and neighbour which suffuses this code; we can respond to the insights of the prophets which these laws seek to translate into terms of everyday life; and we can learn from the men who framed these laws to see the obedience of God as something which involves every aspect of human activity. The fact that these statutes cover almost every conceivable thing in no recognisable order is the measure of how truly they reflect life as it has to be lived.

Many of the themes and provisions of this code are already familiar to us from previous sections of the Pentateuch, and we need not elaborate upon them. What is noticeable, however, is the new note of humanity underlying many of these ancient provisions, which is the mark of the new understanding of God which the prophets have communicated to Israel. Having come to see God more clearly as just and merciful, the makers of the Law stress not only justice, but justice tempered with mercy, in men's dealings with one another.

One of the most important provisions is the abolition of the variety of shrines and altars throughout the country which encouraged heathen practices, and the insistence on centralisation of sacrifice in one place (12: 1–32). What went on in the Temple at Jerusalem could be controlled, whereas the existence of a large number of independent sanctuaries, ostensibly dedicated to YHWH, inevitably meant that pagan rites filtered in, especially since they were no doubt built on the old sites of Canaanite holy places. Thus not only was the encroachment of polytheism and immorality repressed, but the way was prepared for the ultimate abolition of animal sacrifice entirely. It was easier to bear the loss of the Temple and its altar when the Romans destroyed it in A.D. 70, since by that time synagogues had become the regular place of worship of Jews everywhere and services which interpreted sacrifice as the offering of praise and prayer had become the norm.

It is only when we recognise the revolting nature of what the Bible calls "serving other gods"—which included human sacrifice and sacred brothels—that we can understand the drastic measures of 13: 1–18. Similarly some of the less intelligible prohibitions in the code refer to practices associated with heathen cults (e.g. 14: 1; 23: 1; 23: 18— "whore" and "dog" refer to female and male temple prostitutes). We may reckon that the ancient tabus (14: 1–21) have little bearing on twentieth century life, but we can learn from the charity which cares for widows and orphans in 14: 28–29. If it seems to us that the motive for openhandedness in 15: 10 has an element of self-interest in it, we must recognise that the motives of 15: 12–15 could not be higher. The great festivals are meticulously regulated (16: 1–16) but the alien and the hungry, including the dispossessed country priests, are not forgotten (16: 11, 14).

There is no doubt a glance over the shoulder at the opulent polygamous Solomon in 17: 14–17, but Israel is given here a charter for a consecrated constitutional monarchy which was matched by no other ruling system in the ancient world. David alone among all the kings of Israel before Josiah came near to fulfilling it (17: 18–20). Similarly many prophets claimed to speak in the name of God and a few in fact did (18: 20–22; cf. 13: 1–3) but the "Prophet like unto Moses" (18: 15, 18) remained one of the unfulfilled hopes of Israel until the coming of Jesus Christ (*John* 6: 14; 7: 40; *Acts* 3: 22).

Justice is stern (19: 21) but fair 19: 15), and innocent blood must not be shed (19: 10). War is cruel (20: 13) but must not be ruthless (20: 11), except against the "abominations" of the heathen (20: 16–18). Even then fruit trees which are "man's life" must not be destroyed to make weapons of war (20: 19–20). The status of women is advanced in a day and age when they were treated elsewhere as chattels (21: 10–14, 15–17; 22: 13–29) and it is worth noting that in the deuteronomic version of the Decalogue, coveting a neighbour's wife becomes a sin of more significance than coveting a neighbour's house (5: 21; cf. *Ex*. 20: 17).

Modern psychology would deplore the short shrift given to a wastrel son (21: 18–21), but in this and in similar cases of summary justice we ought to remember that prisons, clinics and remand homes were non-existent in the desert. It is laid down that a criminal who is hanged on a tree (after being stoned to death) is "accursed of God" (21: 23), a principle which St. Paul uses with effect to show that the crucified Christ, by becoming accursed under the Law for our sakes, exposed the falsity of the Pharisaic claim that to keep the Law in its entirety was the only way to salvation (*Gal*. 3: 10–13).

Good neighbourliness is commended (22: 1–4), and likewise kindness to birds and animals (22: 6–7; 25: 4). Public sanitation becomes a religious concern (23: 12–14). Humane treatment of runaway slaves (23: 15) and creditors (24: 10–13), as well as provision for the poor (24: 14, 19–21—as in the story of Ruth and Naomi; cf. *Ruth* 2: 2) are enjoined as incumbent on those who themselves have been rescued from hardship and slavery by the hand of God (24: 18, 22). Having dealt with divorce (24: 1–4) and the problem of inheritance (25: 5–9), this code of laws is rounded off on a note of thanksgiving (26: 1–19) and with a promise of blessing or curse according to whether it is observed or neglected (28: 1–68). The sombre prediction of war, siege, famine and cannibalism had been terribly fulfilled when the Assyrians attacked the northern kingdom a century before this "book of the law" was discovered (28: 49–57; cf. *II Kings* 6: 24–30).

This twenty-eighth chapter of *Deuteronomy* is a powerful proclamation of the moral order of the universe. It does not claim that the individual who observes the laws of God will always enjoy prosperity or that the criminal will always be found out, but it does say that there are certain laws according to which the world is run and that these are moral laws. Any society which runs contrary to these laws comes to grief, and conversely the society that observes them is assured of a future. Justice, fairplay, charity and integrity—as we have seen them commended in *Deuteronomy*—reap their reward

because that is the way the world is meant to be run. Behind the chances and changes of life there is a pattern which the Creator has laid down for the smooth running of the world he has made. We have a choice either to mould our community life in accordance with that pattern or to disregard it. The message of this chapter is that if we choose the latter we cannot expect to survive. Over and over again history has proved this to be true, from the downfall of Assyria to that of the Third Reich.

The Death of Moses
(29: 1–34: 12)

THE deuteronomic code, properly speaking, ends at chapter twenty-eight. Chapter twenty-seven appears to be a later addition which has been interpolated to make provision for a permanent record of the laws, and for a solemn ceremony of acceptance of them by the people. The covenant of Sinai is then reaffirmed in this new edition (29: 1–29), and the promise is made by Moses that even after failure to keep the covenant, true repentance will always be met with divine forgiveness (30: 1–20). Let the people of God remember that this covenant-obedience is no remote, abstruse impossibility but something written on their conscience, a practical choice between life and good or death and evil (30: 11–15). St. Paul applies these words to Christian obedience in *Rom.* 10: 5–10.

The last four chapters of *Deuteronomy* are really an appendix to the whole of the Pentateuch. In preparation for the final step which is to take Israel across Jordan to claim its inheritance, Moses hands over his authority to Joshua, knowing full well that the future choice of Israel will be disobedience and not loyal service to YHWH, that they will prefer evil to good and suffer death before they reach true life (31 : 1–30). Accordingly in two poems or songs, the so-called "Song of Moses" and "Blessing of Moses", the truth about Israel (or Jeshurun = the upright one) is summed up—wilful, ungrateful, faithless folk, deserving and receiving the just punishment for their disobedience (32: 1–43), yet still the people of God's choice blessed beyond their deserts, forgiven by his love, with the eternal God as their refuge and underneath them the everlasting arms (33: 1–29; cf. *Gen.* 49). With this magnificent contrasting picture of the people of God as they have always been, whether as old Israel or as the Church of Christ, *Deuteronomy* ends save for the death of Moses (34: 1–12).

The greatest of the prophets of Israel, having seen from mount Nebo the wonderful panorama of the land of the promise stretching beyond Jordan from Hebron in the south over Jerusalem to Hermon far in the north, dies in Moab and "no man knoweth of his sepulchre unto this day". Thus his spirit and inspiration would live on and accompany Israel on her way. His tomb could never become a symbol of a static revelation. He had found Israel enslaved and now she was free, with YHWH as her God and the words of the covenant as her guide. No man

before St. Paul in the whole pageant of the Church's story has been more wonderfully used by God to make known his will for the world.

It was partly because reverence and respect for Moses had become so firmly entrenched in Jewish minds, and not merely because of the words of 18: 15, 18, that the New Testament sees Jesus as the new Moses who leads his people in a new and greater Exodus out of the bondage of sin into the freedom of the Spirit and to the foretaste of the promised land. Like Moses he gives them a new Law in the Sermon on the Mount; like Moses on Sinai he reflects the divine glory at the Transfiguration; like Moses he establishes a New Covenant in the words of the Last Supper and creates a new Israel, the Church. This was by no means the only way that the early Church saw Old Testament foreshadowings becoming realities before their eyes in the words and deeds of Christ. As we shall see, the new Moses of the Pentateuch was also the Messiah of the psalmist, the Servant of *Isaiah*, the Son of Man of *Daniel*, the Wisdom of *Proverbs*, and the creative Word of *Genesis*.

As the author of *Hebrews* rightly said on behalf of the whole Church, Christ could not be merely a new Moses, since Moses was but a servant in the household of God whereas Jesus was the Son (*Heb.* 3: 1–6), but the whole of the Old Testament testifies that in the long story of God's preparation for the coming of Christ there was no more faithful or gifted servant in Israel.

JOSHUA

The Former Prophets

WITH the last chapter of *Deuteronomy* and the death of Moses, the first five books of the Old Testament known as the Pentateuch, the Torah or the Law come to an end. For the Jews this was—and still is—the most sacred part of their Bible. Next to it in order and importance comes the second section known to the Jews as the "Prophets", beginning with the book of *Joshua* up to and including *II Kings*, then continuing from *Isaiah* on to *Malachi*. *Joshua*, *Judges*, *I* and *II Samuel*, *I* and *II Kings* (the Jews did not include *Ruth* in this section) are together called the Former Prophets, while the books from *Isaiah* to the end of our Old Testament (except *Lamentations* and *Daniel*) are called the Latter Prophets.

When Jesus spoke of "the law and the prophets" it was these two great sections of the Old Testament to which he referred (*Matt.* 22: 40). Everything else in our Old Testament apart from the Law and the Prophets is known by the Jews as the "Writings", which include such books as the *Psalms*, *Proverbs* and *Job*.

It is most important to remember that in the original Hebrew Bible what we now call the "historical" books of the Old Testament were called "prophecy". It is also most important to understand what the Hebrews meant by prophecy and prophets. A prophet is not primarily a prognosticator who looks into the future and declares what is likely to happen. In the Old Testament a prophet is someone who speaks to his contemporaries in the name of God, declaring to them God's present demands, and interpreting the past, the present and the future in the light of God's purposes.

The so called "historical" books of the Old Testament are very properly called the Former Prophets, because they interpret history rather than record history. They are meant to edify and instruct. If we still call these books "historical", we should remember that they are quite different from modern history books as we know them. The best way to establish the difference is perhaps by quoting the example of king Omri and farmer Naboth. Omri, was a most notable king of Israel in the ninth century, a distinguished soldier who enlarged the bounds of his kingdom, maintained a formidable army and so impressed the warlike Assyrians that a century and a half later they were still calling Israel "the land of the house of Omri".

Yet this important potentate, whose reign would be accorded

respectful treatment in any normal history book, receives precisely six verses at the hands of the biblical historians (*I Kings* 16: 23–28). His less distinguished son Ahab, however, is given six chapters (*I Kings* 16: 29 – 22: 40) one of which is devoted to a completely insignificant peasant by name Naboth (*I Kings* 21) who owned a plot of land adjacent to the king's palace and refused to part with it.

The reason for the differing allocation of space in the Bible is clear. The Bible is not much interested in wars and battles, political changes and economic trends for their own sake, but only if they illustrate some religious truth, or can be shown in some way to be the hand of God at work. The reign of Omri in this sense, however important for secular history, was apparently of little consequence for the biblical type of history, and is dismissed in a few verses. His son Ahab, however, through his marriage with the notorious Jezebel, crossed swords with someone much more significant in the eyes of the biblical writers than foreign rulers, namely the prophet Elijah, and his reign is therefore allotted correspondingly larger space. A whole chapter is devoted to the story of Naboth's vineyard because it raises moral and social issues, which from a biblical point of view are much more important than dates of battles, numbers of troops and details of conquests.

It is in this light that we must read the historical books of the Old Testament from *Joshua* on-

wards. Not that they are unhistorical, for the Bible is a record of how God revealed his nature and purpose through things that happened in a particular part of the world at a particular time. The story that the Old Testament and New Testament tell is of how in the changes and chances of events God spoke to man. But the Bible emphasises the words that God enabled patriarchs, prophets, priests, kings and apostles to hear, rather than the bare description of the events themselves. It is concerned with what events mean rather than in chronicling them as they happened If some of the things that happened to Israel appeared to indicate that God was speaking louder than usual—as for example in the Exodus—they were given more prominence. If they did not appear to have this character, they were either not mentioned at all or given only sufficient mention to hold the story together.

We should not therefore expect to find a matter of fact account of what precisely happened on a particular occasion in the course of Israel's history, but much rather a narrative in which history is blended with reflection, fact with interpretation, statistics with theology. We should also expect to find that all the "historical" books are composed of these elements in different proportions. Some will have a higher percentage of "facts", others a higher percentage of interpretation. The books of *Chronicles*, for example, cover more or less the same ground and narrate more or less the same facts as the books of *Samuel* and

Kings. Yet even on a casual reading it is clear that the Chronicler is much more concerned with the theological significance of the facts than are the writers of *Samuel* and *Kings.* What emerges is therefore less historical in our modern sense although not necessarily less valuable.

There is the further point that the "historical" books are, like the books of the Pentateuch, composite documents. Each of them consists of material which may differ widely in date as well as in character. Some of the traditions may be as old as the events they describe, while some may date from not long before the books of the Former and Latter Prophets were finally edited and completed about 200 B.C. In answering any question as to the reliability of a particular narrative in these books, therefore, it would be necessary to ask not only whether it is written as a more or less factual record, or whether the element of interpretation bulks more largely, but also whether it seems to be an ancient tradition or a fairly recent addition.

Joshua and Judges

THESE questions arise forcibly in the case of the books of *Joshua* and *Judges.* Like *Chronicles* and *Kings* they cover more or less the same ground—in this case the conquest of Canaan. Both of them depend to a large extent on ancient tradition, in some cases as old as the events described, i.e. about 1250–1200 B.C. Both of them are written under the influence of the deuteronomic or prophetic view: (1) that the tribes of Israel were destined by God to inherit the land of the promise; (2) that they lost it again due to their own failure to keep faith with God in observing the terms of the covenant.

Judges, right at the outset, makes plain the point of view from which it is written (2: 10–23) and so, if not so specifically, does *Joshua* (1: 1–9). Yet the result is far from identical. The predominant impression left by *Joshua* is that after the host of Israel, i.e. numbering about two million (3: 1), crossed the Jordan under Joshua's leadership, they 'proceeded to embark as a united force on the total extermination of the inhabitants of Canaan, a task which they accomplished in five years (14: 10), after which the territory was distributed among the tribes, and before Joshua's death the Israelites were sole and undisputed masters of the promised land.

True, there are some comments in the book itself which accord ill with this general impression, and suggest that the conquest was not of such a whirlwind nature or so successful as the rest of *Joshua* implies. But when we turn to the book of *Judges,* it is indeed a vastly different picture that is given there. Far from being a dramatic saga of a conquering host, the impression given by *Judges* is of a piecemeal infiltration of the tribes, of individual settlement, of intermarriage with the natives, and of a long process, lasting perhaps a couple of centuries, during which Israel grew from being an ill-armed nomadic invasion into being the strongest united element in the country. From there it was but a step, as described in the books of *Samuel*, to the creation of a kingdom under Saul and its expansion under David, in whose reign Israel did in fact become mistress of Canaan and took possession finally of her promised heritage.

Since the references to this gradual infiltration and assimilation both in *Joshua* and *Judges* are obviously the true story, what are we to say about the whirlwind conquest under Joshua? Remembering that these "historical" books are much more prophecy than history, we shall have no difficulty if we regard *Joshua* as a foreshortened version of what later became an accomplished fact. *Joshua*, as it were, completes the story of the Exodus, and is as highly coloured as the narratives of the plagues and the crossing of the Red Sea.

It was neither inadvertence nor stupidity that prompted the compilers of *Joshua* and *Judges* to leave these two contradictory accounts of the conquest side by side in the Bible. Nor was it simply because they did not know which version was true. *Joshua* describes the conquest as a *fait accompli*, the fulfilment of the promise made to the patriarchs. It matches the picture which the Pentateuch has given of the formidable host of Israel making its way through the wilderness bent on taking over its inheritance. It matches too the later picture given by *Second Isaiah* and *Ezra* of the triumphant march of the exiles from Babylon back to the holy city, when a miraculous highway opened up for them across the desert (*Isa.* 40; *Ezra* 1–2). The final editors of the Old Testament left this impressive picture of the return from exile as it stands, although they knew perfectly well that what did in fact happen was much less spectacular.

For this is prophecy not history. The narrative whether of the Exodus, the Conquest of Canaan, or the Return from Exile is exaggerated, magnified, idealised, because it reflects the marvel of divine Providence. On the face of it, nothing was more unlikely than that the enslaved remnants of Jacob's descendants should ever leave Egypt alive, or that the few thousand straggling nomads who made their way through the wilderness should ever become the leading power in Palestine, or that the devastated Temple at Jerusalem and truncated territory of Judah should ever again after Nebuchadnezzar's campaign become the home of a self-conscious theocracy governed by the sacred Law. Yet these things did in fact happen, and the highly coloured narratives are the measure of the writers' conviction that nothing short of supernatural intervention could have brought all this about.

The hand of YHWH could be seen in each of these great and unexpected events. No ordinary prosaic record could do them justice So in such a book as *Joshua* it presented no more problem to the writers or readers of the Old Testament to attribute a miraculous whirlwind conquest of Canaan to YHWH'S chosen captain Joshua, than to attribute the whole of the Law to a single revelation given to God's chosen servant Moses on Sinai, while at the same time leaving every indication in the text that both the formation of the Law and the achievement of the Conquest were processes that must be reckoned in terms of centuries.

Joshua's Campaigns
(1 : 1 – 11 : 23)

LET us then look at the book of Joshua, bearing in mind that it is a mixture of promise and fulfilment, of hope and realisation, of prophecy and history. It opens with a picture of the tribes of Israel encamped on the far side of Jordan after the death of Moses. Joshua, who is described as Moses' minister, is promised complete mastery of the promised land from the Euphrates to the Mediterranean—rather more than the furthest extent of Israel in the days of David and Solomon. YHWH will bring this to pass and accompany his people on their way, on condition that the terms of the covenant are observed (1 : 1–9).

The two and a half tribes who had been allocated land in Transjordan are to share in this mighty invasion, and play their part before returning to their wives and families who are already settled there (1 : 10–18). Jericho being the nearest town across the river and the key to the heart of the promised land, spies are sent out to reconnoitre. They receive shelter and encouragement from Rahab, a local prostitute, presumably also an innkeeper, who like Balaam, shows by her words that even heathens are bound to recognise the power of YHWH (2 : 1–24; cf. Heb. 11 : 31). This story may possibly be designed to explain why a Canaanite comes into the family tree of David. Rahab thus also features in the pedigree of Joseph of Nazareth (Matt. 1 : 5).

Jordan is crossed by a miracle reminiscent of the crossing of the Red Sea. The Ark of the covenant which parts the waters is ceremonially borne across, and a memorial of the occasion is erected at Gilgal (3 : 1 – 4 : 24). It may be that behind this story lies an actual earth tremor which dammed the river as has happened on more than one occasion in recent times, and the tribal ceremony at Gilgal may serve to explain a well known landmark like Stonehenge in that area.

The troops are sacramentally circumcised; they celebrate the passover; the manna of the wilderness ceases whenever they eat their first bread made from the corn of the promised land; and YHWH in the guise of a mysterious angelic figure, "the captain of the Lord's host" appears to Joshua in a scene reminiscent of the episode of the Burning Bush. It is thus made plain that the promised land is holy ground (5 : 1–15). Nothing can withstand the Ark of YHWH, not even the stout walls of Jericho which fall not by siege but by a miracle (6 : 1–27). It is as fruitless to speculate whether they fell by earthquake or by undermining (cf. Heb. 11 : 30) as to wonder how Rahab's house was still on the wall after it had collapsed (2 : 15; cf. 6 : 22).

About thirty years ago archaeology appeared to have established the fact that Jericho had double walls which did in fact fall flat and outwards, and that the city was then burned as the narrative of *Joshua* describes. The date was even firmly fixed by Garstang at approximately 1400 B.C. Now it seems that not only should the date be considerably later, but that very little can be said about what Jericho's fortifications looked like in Joshua's day. Dr. Kathleen Kenyon has, however, established the fact that Jericho was a highly civilised city seven thousand years before Joshua crossed the Jordan, and must therefore be regarded as the oldest city in the world of which we have any evidence. In the biblical period it was a small walled town of about 6 acres with around 1,500 inhabitants.

Archaeological evidence also indicates that the town of Ai, whose capture is next described (7 : 2 – 8 : 29) cannot have been in existence in Joshua's day. It had been in ruins since about 2200 B.C. and was not rebuilt until after 1200 B.C. Since the word Ai in Hebrew means a ruin, and since 8 : 28 implies that Joshua made it so, we can only guess that what is said here about Ai refers to the neighbouring town of Bethel, or that the whole incident which is highly realistic belongs to some other campaign. The scene where Joshua holds up his spear until Ai is destroyed (8 : 18, 26) is reminiscent of Moses holding his rod aloft until Joshua himself had disposed of the Amalekites (*Ex.* 17 : 8–14).

The biblical recital is however more concerned with the story of Achan. Unknown to Joshua, this man had concealed part of the loot from the town of Jericho. Because of this, misfortune overtook Israel at Ai (7 : 5), and Achan, detected in his crime, had to pay the price by the death of himself and his whole family. The point of the story is that this was no ordinary invasion but a holy war in which the heathen must be exterminated but no profit must accrue to Israel. Jericho as the firstfruits of the Holy Land must be "devoted" to YHWH (see p. 134). Failure to observe the *herem* or ban (*Deut.* 20 : 16–18) brought a curse on the people until the sin was expiated. After the taking of Ai the instructions of *Deut.* 27 are faithfully carried out (8 : 30–35).

For us today we may see a foreshadowing of our Lord's words (*Matt.* 8 : 11-12; 21 : 31) in the story of Rahab, the Canaanite harlot, who by faith is incorporated into the people of God. By contrast Achan is the pure Israelite, whose sin brought expulsion from the holy community. There is also a healthy bluntness in the Lord's words to Joshua, who is prostrated with bewildered self-pity after the minor set-back at Ai. "Get thee up; wherefore liest thou thus upon thy face? Israel hath sinned" (7 : 5–11).

By a cunning stratagem the inhabitants of Gibeon save themselves from destruction, but are condemned to menial duties in the Temple yet unbuilt (9 : 1–27). To protect them against the resentment of neighbouring chiefs, Joshua fights a mighty battle in which Israel's arms are less decisive than divine intervention in the form of giant hailstones and an abnormally long day or night. "The Lord fought for Israel" (10: 14). It is implied that with the defeat of this coalition resistance crumpled in the south, and the whole of the Negeb as well as the hill towns now fell into Joshua's hands (10: 1-43). The triumphal progress continued northwards until from Hebron in the south to Hermon in the north, all the land that Moses saw from Moab was in Israel's power. No quarter had been given. The Canaanites were virtually annihilated and their cities sacked. "So Joshua took the whole land . . . and gave it for an inheritance unto Israel . . . and the land rested from war (11: 1-23).

History and Prophecy

(12: 1 – 24: 33)

The next chapters (12-21) are devoted mainly to the division of the territory of Cannan among the tribes and the establishment of tribal boundaries. Consternation is aroused by a report that the two and a half tribes in Transjordan have apparently set up a rival sanctuary to Shiloh, which has become the religious centre of the tribes in Canaan and where the Tent of Meeting has been erected (cf. 18: 1). Civil war is averted, however, by the assurance that the new shrine is to be no more than a witness to the common loyalty of all the tribes, that those beyond

Jordan as well as those within the promised land are one in faith and covenant (22: 1-34).

Joshua, now on the point of death, solemnly warns the tribes as Moses had done (*Deut.* 31) of the penalties for idolatry and compromise (23: 1-16) and confronts them once more with the choice of serving YHWH or the pagan gods of their ancestors or of their predecessors in Canaan. The people pledge their allegiance to YHWH and the covenant is renewed at Shechem. The book ends with the burial of Joshua and the interment of the bones of his ancestor the patriarch Joseph (*Gen.* 50: 24-26), who thus after these many centuries is laid to rest in the sacred soil of the land of the promise (24: 1-33).

So by and large it would appear that all was well with the Israelites, firmly entrenched in their heritage, in a land at peace, devoted servants of the God of Israel all the days of Joshua and his counsellors (24: 31). Yet we do not even need to go beyond the book of *Joshua* itself to realise that this is all future hope and not present reality. The land is far from conquered (13: 13; 15: 63; 16: 10; 17: 12; 23: 4), Israelites are living side by side with Canaanites, mixed marriages are a threat to national solidarity (23: 12), and the lure of "strange gods" is a danger to the faith of YHWH (24: 23).

To read thus between the lines in the book of *Joshua* is to arrive at the same conclusion as is more obviously suggested by the book of *Judges*, namely that if there is any historical basis in the book of

Joshua, it lies not in a wholesale conquest of Canaan and extermination of the population but in a limited attack under Joshua on the hill country of Judah, which probably left the invading nomads in possession of a small stretch of territory which was ill-defended, and which a poorly armed but resolute body of tribesmen, toughened by desert life, might well lay their hands on.

The land of Canaan at this point in history consisted of a collection of city-states, or independent republics, centred on strongly fortified garrison towns, ruled by local chieftains. Egypt was officially in control of the whole of the Mediterranean seaboard but for some time its suzerainty had been largely nominal. The local chiefs were in effect masters of their own house. Defended by stout walls and protected by armed forces with chariots (17: 18), these strongholds on the plain were much too hard a nut to crack for any nomadic band numbering a few thousands. On the other hand the highlands were much more open to attack from beyond Jordan, and it would seem as if Joshua's successes were gained in this quarter. Israel had now at any rate a foothold in the promised land, and as we shall see, outside events soon conspired to give her a chance to extend her domain.

In the heyday of the science-versus-religion controversy of last century, one of the problems that had to be explained by the defenders of a literal interpretation of the Bible was the incident in 10: 12–14 where Joshua made the sun stand still. Apart from the fact that the basis of the story is a fragment of a ballad from the lost book of Jasher (10: 13) (see p. 131) and thus obviously dramatic poetry and not history, it would seem now that this particular passage raises no more difficulty than the book of *Joshua* as a whole. It adds little to the historicity of the book of *Joshua* to explain this incident as a prolongation of the night by a black thunderstorm (10: 9, 11) or as caused by some astronomical aberration. The whole book is in fact one sustained "miracle" if we treat it as sober history, from the miraculous crossing of the Jordan and the collapse of the walls of Jericho, to the miraculously speedy subjugation of a powerfully armed people by desert tribesmen unskilled in normal warfare, and without more deadly weapons than clubs and slings, or bows and arrows.

Yet the moment we recognise this book as one of prophecy, it takes its place appropriately in the Old Testament canon as the prelude to the long and chequered story of Israel's rise to predominance in Canaan. It becomes both the epilogue to the Pentateuch, accurately claiming that what was promised was indeed fulfilled, that Israel did in fact inherit the good land, and also a curtain-raiser which, like a Greek chorus, reveals the plot which is now to be played out in detail in the scenes that follow of Israel's failure to respond with loyalty and obedience to the goodness of God, who had bestowed this gift upon his people.

150   JOSH. 10-24

The real purpose of the historical books of the Old Testament is
thus clearly adumbrated in the
book of *Joshua*. They are not to
provide material for students of
ancient history but to show how
a loving God offers his people a
rich and full heritage of life in the
right relationship to himself, and
how his people time after time
throw away their chances and end
in disaster. This is a lesson they
have to learn on the plane of history, in the experience of living,
which is the plane on which they
also come to learn the true nature
of the rich heritage that is offered,
and that it does not depend on
material success but on the life of
the spirit.

It is thus no accident that the
life of Joshua recapitulates in so
many respects the life of Moses, or
that so many features of the Exodus story reappear in the story of
the conquest. "As I was with
Moses so I will be with thee"
(1: 5). Joshua, whose name, like
Jesus (the Greek form), means
"God is salvation" is the type of
human saviour of his people as
was Moses. Both reflect the
character and purpose of God,
and both point forward to the
Joshua of the New Covenant who
fulfils their mission. As the
author of *Hebrews* saw, the
temporary "rest" that Joshua
achieved for his people in Canaan
was but a foreshadowing of the
rest through Christ that awaits the
people of God in the promised
land of the age to come (*Heb.* 4:
8-9; cf. *Josh.* 21: 44).

JUDGES

IF we may date the campaign described in the book of *Joshua*, by which Israel began to make its presence felt in Canaan, about 1250–1200 B.C., the book of *Judges* may be said to cover roughly the next century and a half. It appears to present a chronological account of the period it deals with but its chief concern is, like *Joshua*, not with a historical record but with theology. Yet it gives us, far more successfully than *Joshua*, a fascinating picture of the life and fortunes of Israel between the first arrival in Palestine and the establishment of the kingdom under Saul, which is described in the first book of *Samuel*.

The archives of pharaoh Amenhotep III and his son Akhnaten (see p. 72) which were discovered at Tell el-Amarna in 1887, contain a variety of correspondence from Canaanite rulers and Egyptian governors in Canaan in the 14th century B.C., in which among other things they ask for reinforcements to deal with constant attack from desert invaders whom they describe as Habiru. The Israelites attacking Canaan a century later under Joshua constituted one group of these seminomadic peoples which harassed the settled inhabitants of Palestine.

The first mention of Israel outside the Bible as a distinct group occurs on a victory monument erected by pharaoh Merneptan about 1220 B.C. In this inscriptioh he claims to have exterminated Israel, which may mean that he defeated them in some battle. The Bible makes no mention of the incident but it does raise the question as to whether the invasion under Joshua, which is the main concern of the Old Testament, was not merely the most significant of a variety of tribal movements into Canaan which later became consolidated into the confederacy of tribes that the books of *Samuel* and *Kings* describe as knitting together into a nation.

The foundation of the faith of Israel, and therefore of the Old Testament, was undoubtedly the Exodus. The experience of unexpected deliverance, the covenant of Sinai, the lessons of the desert wanderings, and the initial success of invasion under Joshua were the formative elements which forged the hard core of the nation that came to dominate Palestine. As we have seen, however, it is unlikely that this nucleus could have consisted of more than a few thousand hardy characters who were able to exist on the exiguous fare that the scrubland of the desert could provide.

We have also seen that the clear cut division of Israel into twelve tribes was a gradual development, and it is extremely difficult, in view of the length of time after the events of the Exodus period before the final story was written up, as well as the theological interests of the compilers, and the composite nature of the record, to tell how many separate tribes existed in the earliest stage of Israel's history, and which of them in fact were involved in the chain of events that started in Goshen and ended at Shechem.

Two things seem probable. One is that it was not only Joshua's group that made its way into Canaan, but that other tribal movements were taking place at the same time, resulting in Israelite settlements in the south and the north of Palestine as well as in the hill country of Judah. There would seem to have been an independent infiltration in the region around Hebron in the south as well as in the district near the Lake of Galilee in the north.

The other probability is that a larger proportion of the community which came to be called the tribes of Israel had never been in Egypt at all, but were the descendants of families which had drifted into Canaan in the time of the patriarchs and had remained there while the smaller group had migrated to Egypt in the time of Joseph. This Joseph-group, however, became the definitive element in the Old Testament story because of the Exodus experience. It was the descendants of this group who escaped under Moses, who made their way through the desert, and under Joshua established their claim to the highlands of Canaan.

The Ceremony at Shechem

(Josh. 24: 1 – Judg. 2: 9)

IT is noteworthy that in the book of *Joshua*, although detailed lists of conquests are given in the northern and southern districts of Canaan, little is said of campaigns in the central district around Shechem. When this fact is taken together with the impressive gathering at that town described in Josh. 24, the conclusion would seem to be that what happened at Shechem was much more significant than a repetition of an oath of loyalty on the part of the main invading force.

A careful reading of this chapter would suggest that what happened was that not only the invading force but the tribes of Israel who had never been out of the country and were now living in the Shechem area, sharing the customs and religion of Canaan, banded themselves together and became for the first time a numerically large and influential body. The charge to put away their "strange gods" (v. 23), the choice between YHWH and the gods of their forefathers or neighbours (v. 15), and the submission to the terms of the covenant (v. 24–25) are therefore no empty ceremonies, or repetitions of similar occasions in the past, but the acceptance by the settled and half-Canaanite tribes of Israel of the leadership of this new and successful invading force, together with the faith of YHWH and the standard of Mosaic law.

Some such amalgamation as this would explain both the social and religious background of the book of *Judges*. The general picture given there is not of a resolute army of nomads striving to establish themselves in a new country by making war on the inhabitants, as was the case in the book of *Joshua*, but of a relatively settled agricultural people leaving their fields to resist the attacks of other nomadic invaders from the western desert. It is noteworthy that in the various warlike encounters described in *Judges*, only on one occasion are the Israelites fighting the native Canaanites. On all other occasions they are resisting invasions of hostile forces from the other side of Jordan— Midianites, Ammonites, Moabites —who are now, like Joshua and his tribesmen, trying to obtain some of the "milk and honey" of the good land of Canaan for themselves.

Thus we may assume that once the initial wave of invasion was spent, which involved some conflict with the native Canaanites, the Israelites, now a much larger confederation of tribes, linked loosely to one another by blood and tradition, but more closely by a common religious allegiance, proceeded to settle down alongside the Canaanites, and because of their more recent virile nomadic strain established themselves by degrees as the military aristocracy of the country, determined to hold on to the land they had now acquired and in the process becoming its recognised defenders.

It is now really for the first time that the word Israel comes to have political significance. In the light of Joshua's ceremony at Shechem, we may think of the twelve tribes, the Exodus group and the larger settled group, now in the period of the Judges numbering perhaps 40,000 (5: 8), scattered in various areas throughout Palestine, forming a kind of federation known as an amphictyony. This kind of federation, which was not peculiar to Israel, meant that while the tribes were distinct and self governing, they were nevertheless bound by a common religious obligation; they met from time to time at a central sanctuary, they rallied to each other's defence in time of danger, and they observed a common law. In Israel's case this was of course the covenant of Sinai.

The book of *Judges* may best be regarded as a series of typical pictures from this stage in the story of Israel. It is by no means a systematic record of what happened between the days of Joshua and the emergence of Samuel and Saul as the next notable figures in the narrative. The last verse of the book (21: 25) sums up the situation: "In those days there was no king in Israel: every man did that which was right in his own eyes". This editorial comment reflects the independence of the tribes which is characteristic of the period.

The word "judge" in the case of this book has a quite different connotation from our understanding of it. We are not to imagine the century and a half after the death of Joshua as being dominated, as far as Israel was concerned, by a series of judicial administrators in full control of the tribes and accepted by them as duly appointed governors. There was far too much individualism among the nomadic elements of the confederacy, and far too little solidarity among the more settled elements, to tolerate any interference with their tribal life unless some major threat to their very existence forced them to accept the authority of one single man. It required such a threat to bring the monarchy into being as we shall shortly see. Nothing less would have done it.

But in this interim period what happened was that when any minor threat arose to the lives and property of a tribe, the most audacious, valiant and shrewd member of the tribe became, for the time being its leader and its champion. This is the meaning of the Hebrew word translated as "judge". Such a man might invite the assistance of neighbouring tribes, at all events he would be accepted for the duration of the danger period as the supreme commander, and once the danger was past he probably as often as not retired into the obscurity of his former position as a member of the tribe and came under the jurisdiction of the tribal council of elders.

We must think then as a background to the stories of the *Judges*, of some of the Israelites inhabiting the ruins of the towns on the hills of Judah which they had destroyed under Joshua, but of the majority scattered throughout a land which was still dominated by the Canaanite strongholds in the plains. An illuminating comment in the song of Deborah (5: 6) suggests that the main highways were so well policed by Canaanite troops that tribesmen had to use the hill

paths for safety, and the first chapter of the book indicates that the three main pockets of Israelite settlement were separated from each other by chains of Canaanite fortresses.

The book opens with what amounts to an epilogue to the book of *Joshua* (1: 1 – 2: 9). The personal names Judah, Simeon, Manasseh, etc., refer of course to tribes, not individuals, but it is not clear whether this section describes what happened before or after the death of Joshua, since his death is recorded twice (1: 1 and 2: 8). Possibly the implication is that during Joshua's lifetime single tribes had been making independent raids on the country, and that after his death some of the towns he had taken were recaptured by the Canaanites and had to be taken again .

Israel's Testing Time
(2: 10 – 3: 7)

THE real beginning of the book is at 2: 10, and from that point until 2: 23 the clue to the understanding of the rest of the book is provided. After Joshua's day we are told, there grew up a generation which "knew not the Lord nor yet the works which he had done for Israel . . . and served Baalim" (2: 10-11). This substitution of "strange gods" for the worship of YHWH was the reason why the promised land was withheld from Israel and why their enemies were allowed to plague them. Despite the fact that YHWH sent them "judges" or "deliverers" (again the salvation motif), the moment the danger was past they fell back into their "stubborn way" (2: 19). This same theme recurs as a refrain throughout the book.

This whole period therefore as seen by the compiler of the book of *Judges* is Israel's testing time, and the stories that follow are illustrations of how they were "proved", to see whether they would "keep the way of the Lord . . . or not" (2: 22). Thus the incidents that are recorded are placed within a theological framework which presents them as a sustained object lesson that what Amos, Hosea, Micah and Isaiah had taught had been proved true in the experience of early Israel as it was handed down in these ancient traditions. Obedience to the law of Moses and the spirit of Sinai, the compiler would say to us, invariably brought material success and prosperity, while disobedience invited disaster.

Such a facile rule-of-thumb criterion, which was of course challenged by Job and finally disposed of on Calvary, was at this stage and on a wide canvas by no means as superficial as when applied to an individual. Scattered as they were throughout the land of Canaan, living side by side with pagans, intermarrying with them, surrounded by a new and far higher type of civilisation, as archaeological evidence abundantly indicates, the ex-nomads were indeed under severe strain. They knew little or nothing about the arts and graces of settled city life, and, more important, since they were mainly outside the cities, they knew nothing of agriculture. They had

to learn how to grow crops, vines and olives, and the general art of husbandry. This brought them at once up against a problem.

YHWH the warrior God, the God of Sinai, of the desert and the mountain, was undoubtedly in their view more powerful than the gods of the Canaanites. But the gods of Canaan were well established, and above all they blessed or cursed the work of men's hands in the field. Did YHWH's power extend to ensuring good harvests, and would it make any difference to him if the local gods were placated as well? We may picture the Israelite family settling on the outskirts of some village and watching the natives making their way to the local "high place" to make offerings and ask favours from the god who presided over this particular piece of land. In such a setting it would seem natural for the settler, whatever his private allegiance might be, to insure himself against drought and starvation by incorporating the local god in his devotions.

As we have seen, however (pp. 127–128), not only was the religion of Canaan a fertility cult, but whether it was the highly developed pantheon of the city-states or the primitive Baal of the local shrine, its polytheistic character made nonsense of any standards of morality. To "serve strange gods" meant therefore not only that sensuous eroticism supplanted the virile austerity of the desert days, but that the authority of the absolute demands of the law of YHWH was weakened. If it was a degradation of worship to identify it with sexual intercourse with religious prostitutes, it was a deadly peril to morality to pay homage to a variety of deities among whom moral standards were non-existent.

The stories of the book of *Judges* and the running commentary by an editor who is imbued with the spirit of *Deuteronomy* indicate that the Israelites, as was to be expected, tried to make the best of both worlds. YHWH and Baal were worshipped side by side, and the practices of Canaanite religion became interwoven with the religion of Sinai. Even Gideon, one of the judges, has an alternative name Jerub-baal (7: 1). As late as the monarchy Saul, Jonathan and David give their children names which indicate that by that time Baal had become synonymous with YHWH (Ish-baal, I *Chron.* 8: 33, Merib-baal, *I Chron.* 8: 34, and Beel-iada, *I Chron.* 14: 7).

Yet the only thing that could hold the scattered tribes together was their common allegiance to YHWH and his covenant. Humanly speaking nothing could have prevented Israel in this situation from becoming completely assimilated in culture and religion to its Canaanite neighbours. The local Baals in all their diversity were a disintegrating factor, YHWH on the other hand stood between Israel and its disappearance into the racial and religious melting pot of the ancient Near East. In time of peace therefore the local Baals were in the ascendant, in time of danger YHWH the God of battle who had proved his power time and time again against Israel's enemies, from the pharaoh onwards, came

into his own. The prophetic compiler of *Judges* is therefore right to call this a testing time when YHWH afflicted Israel with "spoilers" and enemies (2: 14), for it was only in war that the tribes were forced into common action and were recalled to their common allegiance.

The Sword of the Lord
(3: 8 – 21: 25)

ACCORDINGLY in chapter three we are told of bedouin raiders from the desert who were thrown back by Othniel (3: 8–11), and of Eglon the fat king of Moab who ventured into Canaan and recaptured Jericho, the city of palm trees. Having disposed of the king, Ehud "blew a trumpet" to summon the tribesmen and the Moabites were massacred as they tried to escape back across the Jordan (3: 12–31).

The next incident is the only occasion on which the tribes are involved in battle with native Canaanites. The heroine of the story is Deborah, a prophetess with the power of a Joan of Arc, who rouses Barak to lead the northern tribes against Sisera, which he does successfully, and the unfortunate Sisera meets his death at the hands of another bloodthirsty lady. But far more gripping than the bald account of this affair in 4: 1–24 is the splendid song of Deborah in chapter five. This ancient ballad, probably contemporary with the battle, sheds valuable light on the actual conditions in Canaan at this time.

The opening invocation is to YHWH, the warrior God of storm-swept Sinai. Then comes a picture of the harassed tribesmen driven from their villages and in despair until, roused by the "mother in Israel", the tribes respond to Barak's summons. Blessings on those who rally to the fight mingle with taunts to those who stay away. Battle is joined near Megiddo and YHWH fights for Israel by sending a thunderstorm which turns Wadi Kishon into a raging torrent and sweeps the Canaanite forces to their death. The iron studded chariots of the enemy cannot save them now, the very "stars in their courses fought against Sisera". The treachery of Jael receives high commendation and the grief of the mother of Sisera gets scant sympathy. If the morality is questionable the poetry is superb.

Again danger looms up and YHWH comes into his own. Fierce camel-borne Midianites from the western desert ravage the land and drive the Israelites from their farms to take refuge in mountain caves (6: 1–6). The appointed champion in this case is Gideon, whose father, although a member of the tribe of Manasseh, has an altar to Baal on his farm. Gideon is summoned to lead the tribes by an angelic visitant and satisfies himself that he is to be YHWH's instrument by receiving a sign from heaven (6: 7–40). The Spirit of YHWH falls upon him—as it had fallen upon Othniel (3: 10) and as it would fall upon Samson and Saul—endowing him with super-human powers, and the neighbouring tribes rally

to the support of this obviously YHWH-possessed deliverer (6: 34–35).

The entertaining ruse by which Gideon and his three hundred carefully sifted warriors surprise the Midianites is fully described as it must have been told by story tellers in Israel down the generations (7: 1–25). Tribal rivalries are tactfully handled (8: 1–3) and Gideon with the valiant three hundred "faint yet pursuing" chase the Midianites back over Jordan. Surprise attacks by night were obviously here as elsewhere in the early history of Israel the most successful means of dealing with larger and better equipped forces and wholly in keeping with the Israelite nomadic tradition as far back as Abraham in the battle of the kings (*Gen.* 14).

Future developments are hinted at in the tribes' request to Gideon to become their king. Although he makes the correct reply for an Israelite that only YHWH may rule over Israel, it does not prevent him from making an image of YHWH which the commentator clearly regards as the cause of his son's fall from grace (8: 4–35). This man Abimelech, whose mother was a Canaanite, set himself up as king at Shechem, significantly with the support of the priests of the Baal-berith temple (9: 4), but the venture was short lived and the curse of his brother Jotham who told the fable of the trees that wanted a king, was tragically implemented (9: 1–57).

Once again danger threatens from the desert, this time it is Ammonites (10: 1 – 11: 40). The compiler has no doubt about the reason since the Israelites are now devotees of almost every god in Palestine (10: 6). This time the Spirit of YHWH falls upon a Gileadite by name Jephthah, who pledges a burnt offering of the first person to meet him on his return from vanquishing the Ammonites. In the event this turns out to be his own daughter, which may either indicate that human sacrifice was not unknown in Israel or that this may be an old story to account for the annual lamentation described in 11: 40. Injured pride which led to battle between two of the tribes, reminiscent of the clan feuds in Scotland, adds another element to the picture of Israel's life at this stage and gives us the origin of the word "Shibboleth" (12: 1–15).

The Samson-saga (13: 1–16: 31) is of a different character from the rest of the book. Samson is a Nazirite (*Num.* 6: 1–21) whose birth is unexpected but foretold by a heavenly herald (13: 1–25). In common with the other "judges" the Spirit of YHWH possesses him, but apart from that his behaviour is more reminiscent of Tarzan or Till Eulenspiegel. His expertise in handling lions and foxes is equalled only by his ineptitude in coping with women's wiles. He carries off the gates of Gaza, slays a thousand with the jawbone of an ass, and blinded and tormented dies with his persecutors amid the ruins of the temple porch which he has pulled down about their heads.

There is no obvious religious or moral value in the Samson stories. The Spirit of YHWH which enabled him to burst his bonds (15: 14) is on the same level of magic as the secret of his great strength which lay in his unshorn hair (16: 17–20). Presumably these were traditional stories told with great relish and acceptance at convivial village gatherings, and for the compiler there would be a sufficiently religious motif in the fact that Samson was a "good" Israelite patriot, despite his weakness for women, who took toll of the "bad" Philistines. The stories would also emphasise the value of Nazirite vows, and moral values are observed in a rough and ready way in that everyone more or less meets the fate he deserves—except Delilah.

It is perhaps of more moment to note the first substantial appearance in the narrative of the people who are to bulk more and more largely in subsequent pages of the Old Testament as Israel's most serious rivals for the control of the Levant. The Philistines formed part of a folk-migration of "sea peoples" from the Aegean who, unlike all other claimants for a share of the Fertile Crescent, did not approach it from the desert but in ships. They had settled on the coast of Canaan shortly after the Israelites were occupying the hill country under Joshua, about 1190 B.C.

They were apparently prodigious beer drinkers, to judge by the large numbers of beer mugs which have been found in their settlements (cf. 14: 10; 16: 25) but, more important, they were the first people in Canaan to process iron and bring the benefits of the Iron Age to the Levant. Apart from the undoubted advantage which this gave them for military purposes the possession of the secret of smelting gave them a tremendous economic advantage, which after their defeat by David accrued to Israel and became one of the grounds for Israel's expansion and prosperity during his reign.

At this early stage we find Israelites and Philistines living relatively at peace with one another. Samson has a Philistine wife and Delilah also belongs to that people. There is no suggestion at this stage that the Philistines are a greater menace to Israel than the other invading groups. But by the time the period of the judges comes to an end the Philistines have emerged as a threat to Israel's very existence.

The last few chapters of the book provide us with more illumination on social conditions in these times than on moral principles. The story of the man who made a private shrine out of some money he had stolen from his mother and then restored it for fear of her curse, who consecrated his own priest, and then lost both shrine and priest, is presumably included to explain the origin of the sanctuary at Dan which became a religious centre after the division of the kingdom (17: 1–18: 31). Similarly the ghastly fate of the Levite's concubine, strongly reminiscent of the story of the men of Sodom (*Gen.* 19), and the abduction of the "daughters of Shiloh", the Hebrew equivalent of the Rape of the Sabine Women, are obviously of less concern to the compiler than that the first action gave the tribes an opportunity to display their solidarity, and that the second showed that YHWH would not allow the sacred number of the twelve tribes to be reduced, whatever crime or folly any one of them had been guilty of (19: 1 – 21: 25).

RUTH

AFTER the blood and thunder of the book of *Judges* the book of *Ruth* has the idyllic quality of Millet's "Angelus", or of Burns' "Cottar's Saturday Night". It is a simple tale of tenderness and pity, its tone is one of broad sympathies and wide charity. Its setting is a peaceful countryside: its characters are honest peasants, hard working, neighbourly and contented. There is an air of genuine piety, honourable conduct and true love pervading the whole story making it one of the most attractive tales in any literature and certainly a welcome interlude at this point in the Bible.

It would almost seem as if we were being reminded that while political manœuvres and armed violence are part of the texture of life and the struggle for existence, side by side with them the life of the countryside goes on, the crops are sown and harvested, and ordinary folk carry on with the small affairs of the world and know the joys and sorrows of everyday.

This was, however, not the original setting of the book of *Ruth* since it falls within the third division of the Hebrew canon, the Writings. It was given its present place by the Greek translators because the events it describes are said to have happened in the days of the judges (1: 1). The Writings,

however, were not officially accepted into the Hebrew Bible until about 100 B.C. so that the story may date from long after the twelfth century. There are different views among scholars on this point and the evidence is fairly well balanced between some time before the Exile and some time after.

It seems hardly likely that the book was included in holy scripture simply because it was a pleasant story, and if we look for a religious motive it would appear to be the strong emphasis which is laid in the book on the fact that the heroine was not a pure Israelite but a native of Moab. According to the Law (*Deut.* 23: 3) no Moabite was eligible to belong to the religious community of Israel "even to their tenth generation". Like many other laws this was not generally enforced, but there was a period under Ezra and Nehemiah when racial purity became a fetish.

There was good reason for this. After the kingdom had crashed in 587 B.C. and the cream of the nation had been carried off in chains to exile in Babylon, the remnant in Palestine disintegrated and became barely recognisable as Israel. When the exiles returned to the homeland it became clear that only a radically tough policy of segregation and exclusiveness would preserve the identity of the people of God. This was undertaken in the fifth and fourth centuries B.C. at the instigation of Nehemiah and Ezra and their disciples. It involved among other things a ban on mixed marriages, hostility to foreigners, and an attempt to keep Israel as free from contact with the outside world as was humanly possible (*Ezra* 9: 1–2, 10–14; *Neh.* 13: 23–29).

The book of *Ruth* would suggest that this policy was not without its critics. Just as the book of *Deuteronomy* was produced as part of a prophetic resistance movement to the paganism of the reign of Manasseh (see p. 132), so this book may well have been the work of some unknown saint who shared the view of *Isaiah* 40–55 and the writer of *Jonah* (see p. 294) that God's mercy was wider than the rigid laws of the scribes and that Gentiles had also a place in his love.

Although the story is designed to expose the weakness of the case for nationalistic prejudice it is by no means a stormy polemic. Famine in Judah drives a family across the Jordan to Moab. That in itself would raise a frown on the faces of the advocates of "Israel for the Israelites". The two sons of the family die fairly soon after their father, which is not surprising since their Hebrew names mean "sickness" and "consumption". The mother Naomi is now left with two daughters-in-law, both natives of Moab, but while she naturally wants to return to her own country and expects her daughters-in-law to stay behind and marry Moabite husbands, one

of them, Ruth, chooses to throw in her lot with her mother-in-law and to forsake her own land and her own religion.

The moving words of Ruth to Naomi as she pledged her friendship are imperishable: "Whither thou goest I will go; and where thou lodgest I will lodge: thy people shall be my people, and thy God my God: where thou diest will I die, and there will I be buried: the Lord do so to me and more also, if ought but death part thee and me". When they reach Naomi's old home at Bethlehem poverty compels Ruth to glean from the fields what the humane law of *Deuteronomy* prescribed should be left for the widows and the needy (*Deut.* 24: 19). Doubtless it was with justice that Keats could speak of "the sad heart of Ruth when sick for home she stood in tears amid the alien corn".

However the tale has a happy ending. The field in which Ruth chances to glean belongs to a relative of Naomi's late husband. The old lady steps in and assists the bashful elderly Boaz to make up his mind to marry the attractive young widow. Naomi's chief interest is in keeping within the family a plot of land which would otherwise because of her poverty go to strangers. Boaz acquires it and also Ruth, in accordance with ancient custom, since a nearer kinsman who is more eligible to take over the land is not prepared to take the young widow as well.

The sting of the story, however, if such a pleasant tale may be said to have a sting, is in the tail. For the last few words make the author's point with admirable succinctness. The son of Boaz and Ruth, who thus in Israelite law is also regarded as the heir of Naomi and her dead husband, was called Obed, who was the father of Jesse, who was the father of David. The great king David, who stood in Israelite eyes next to Moses in honour and glory, was the grandson of a man whose mother was a Gentile.

So the policy of rigid Israelite racialism is challenged. Either the name of the greatest of their kings is tarnished by having Moabite blood in his veins or else there must be room for Moabites—and other Gentiles—among God's chosen people. For history includes not only Moabites but Canaanites as well, since Tamar (*Gen.* 38) and Rahab the harlot (*Josh.* 2) are also in the line of David and therefore of the Messiah (*Matt.* 1: 3, 5).

The occurrence in this little story of the Hebrew concept of the kinsman or *goel*, who according to law avenges a wrong done to his relative, stands surety for his debts thus releasing him from slavery, and is generally responsible for rescuing him from such other plight as he may be in, reminds us that it was from this social custom that the people of the Old Testament derived one of their most distinctive descriptions of God: the *Goel* or Redeemer of Israel (*Deut.* 7: 8; *Isa.* 41: 14). It is this same thought of rescue, release and deliverance that lies behind the Christian confession of Christ as the world's Redeemer.

I and II SAMUEL

"Not by Might, nor by Power . . ."

AFTER the interlude provided by the book of *Ruth*, the prophetic commentary on the rise and fall of Israel continues in the two books of *Samuel*. The refrain is always the same. The Israelites are a peculiar people unlike any other. Their call and their covenant single them out from any other nation as the chosen instruments of God's purpose, which they only learn bit by bit through the experiences that they undergo. Their vocation is one which only becomes clear to them as they learn to understand through priest and prophet the word that God is speaking to them. When they forget their call and covenant and behave like any other nation they come to grief. God teaches them through their folly and disciplines them through their failures.

In the period of the judges the lesson they had to learn was that amid the disintegrating forces of Canaanite polytheism, only a strong allegiance to the covenant bond with YHWH could prevent the people of God from losing their identity, and amid the decadent moral standards of their new neighbours only a rigid adherence to the austere pattern of the code of Sinai could ensure their survival as a distinctive community.

In the period that now follows—covered by the books of *Samuel* and *Kings*—it is not primarily the danger of 'strange gods' with their attendant amoral standards that Israel has to surmount, but the danger of playing at power politics and aiming to become a miniature empire. The monarchy, which was a necessary and inevitable stage in Israel's growth, had to be experienced so that the people of God might learn that the fulfilment of their vocation would come "not by might, nor by power, but by my spirit, saith the Lord of hosts" (*Zech.* 4: 6). They had to share the upsurge of nationalist feeling under Saul, the dream of expansion under David, the affluence of commericial enterprise under Solomon, to learn that these good things are also evil things and carry within them the possibility of self-destruction. In the end the people of God had to watch their proud hopes shattering, and see their promised land wrested from them, before they learned that it was not this kind of kingdom that God meant them to build.

Thus while as in the case of *Joshua* and *Judges* we find also that the later "historical" books are in fact prophecy rather than history, it is a more subtle commentary and interpretation of the events of the times that is offered, because the danger is more insidious and less obvious. When it was a conflict between black and white, between YHWH and Sinai on the one hand and the Baalim and Ashtaroth of Canaan on the other, it was fairly straightforward to denounce the latter and commend the former. The issues were relatively simple. Thus both Moses and Joshua could put the alternatives before Israel and ask them to choose.

But now the situation has changed. The Canaanites, who were after all Semites like the Hebrews and had merely arrived earlier and settled down sooner in Palestine than the Israelites, are now no longer mentioned as enemies or indeed as rivals. The two strains have amalgamated. Canaanites and Israelites are one. By intermarriage, treaty and trade the fusion is more or less complete. Israel has become the dominant partner in the transaction and the military leader. In the process many Canaanite customs have become Israelite customs, and in particular much of Canaanite religion has been incorporated into the religion of YHWH.

The choice has been made in favour of YHWH but YHWH is now very like Baal, and is even called Baal. As the word meant 'lord' or 'master' it was an easy switch. The prophetic historians who write their marginal notes, as it were, beside the story of the monarchy, are more concerned that the purity of the YHWH faith should be restored than that 'strange gods' should be avoided. At the same time they call attention to the dangers inherent in

the monarchy and in Israel's rise to power. Thus the story of Israel's success and failure as recorded from I Samuel to II Kings is told by the biblical writers from the standpoint of the great prophetic figures, who in this period exercise their right to criticise kings and commoners for their evasion of the obligations of a covenant people and for their lapses from the high doctrine and morality of Sinai.

"We will have a King over us"

SAMUEL, Nathan and Elijah are the precursors of the more significant classical prophets—Amos, Hosea, Isaiah, Jeremiah, Ezekiel and the rest—who constitute themselves the keepers of the nation's conscience, and who interpret events as they occur in the light of the revelation that comes to them in vision and ecstasy and in the clear-sighted intuitions of men who live close to God. In one sense they are sympathetic, for they are Israelites and share the hopes and fears of their countrymen, rejoicing in the bravery of a Saul, the shrewdness of a David and the brilliance of a Solomon.

In another sense they are critical for they see the ambiguities of the situation more clearly than their masters and are not afraid to speak their minds. Their courage is that of men who feel that what they say is not their own word but God's. Their critique of events is always prefaced by: "Thus saith the Lord". So as we read the story of the rise and fall of the monarchy in this section of the Old Testament the most striking feature is the ambivalency of the record. On the one hand there is the witness to the skill and wisdom of kings and statesmen, which turned Israel from a loose federation of tribes at the mercy of a variety of powerful enemies into a strong and compact national unit, now at last in full and legitimate occupation of the land which had been promised to the patriarchs. In all this the writers take proper pride just as they rejoice to see Jerusalem established as the new centre of national life, and the Temple with its permanent Tent of Meeting as the focus of the people's worship.

On the other hand, however, there is the equally strong element of disapproval. Opposite every stage of Israel's progress up the ladder of success the biblical writers place a large question mark. They see only too well the perils of prosperity, the dangers of complacency, the inhumanities of power. Their first loyalty is to YHWH and his covenant, and only after that can they share their countrymen's enthusiasm for Israel's rising fortunes. As prophet after prophet utters warnings and denounces dubious enterprises, we who read the story after these many years are prepared for the reverse side of Israel's meteoric success. When the kingdom splits and is truncated and finally vanquished we feel that the prophetic witness is vindicated.

Yet it is the glory and the mystery of the biblical revelation that Israel too had been prepared and forewarned, so that when the crash came it was seen not as the failure

of YHWH but as the failure of his people. It is because this prophetic critique was exercised not in retrospect but as the story was unfolding, that Israel in exile was able to see the hand of God shaping its destiny and teaching it the lesson it had to learn. It was because, Samuel, Nathan, Elijah and the rest had borne witness to the will and purpose of God in the day to day political and social scene, that when disaster overtook the nation people were prepared to listen to the prophets of a later day, Jeremiah, Isaiah and Ezekiel, when they told them that God was speaking to them as clearly in catastrophe as in victory, and that through catastrophe they would at last see the nature of their mission to be a peculiar people, like no other nation, since they had come to know the pitfalls of power and the perils of progress.

The early chapters of *I and II Samuel* (which may be reckoned for convenience as a single book) are dominated by the figure of the prophet himself, the last and greatest of the judges. He overshadows Saul whom he is responsible for anointing as first king of Israel, and even although the latter part of the book revolves round Israel's greatest and best loved king David, the grey eminence who fostered his early successes is still present in spirit and his words are not forgotten.

The background of the events that led to the choice of Saul as king can be briefly sketched. A major crisis faces the tribes, and indeed the whole land of Canaan. The Philistines, who had featured principally in the Samson stories a speaceful neighbours of Israel in the period of the judges, now develop territorial ambitions. Having settled on the maritime plain in their five principalities of Askelon, Ekron, Ashdod, Gaza and Gath they now in the middle of the eleventh century B.C. make a bid to become masters of the Levant.

There is no resistance from Egypt; the countries of the north are otherwise involved; the Canaanite city-states are powerless against this warrior stock. Nothing indeed stood between the Philistines and what might have become a new empire of the Near East except the tribes of Israel. Petty rivalries among the principalities of the Philistines may have added to their ultimate failure to achieve their aim, but undoubtedly the main hindrance came from the united front of the Israelite tribes which rose to defend the promised land in the name of YHWH.

There is little to suggest in the first few chapters of *Samuel* that the whole land was in the grip of the Philistines, and that Saul's election to be the first king of Israel was to a throne without a kingdom. The narrative disguises the catastrophe which overtook the tribes in 1050 B.C., when the religious capital which had been established at Shiloh for almost two hundred years since the days of Joshua was turned into a heap of ruins by the Philistines. It was still in ruins in the time of Jeremiah more than 400 years later (*Jer.* 7: 12; 26: 6, 9).

The archaeological evidence is that not only Shiloh but a number of other Israelite hill-towns were destroyed at the same time. The tribes therefore lost not only their central sanctuary, with the sacred Ark of the covenant (*I* 4: 11) but also most if not all of the highlands which had been in their possession since the days of the conquest. It was this threat to their very existence that made them ready for the first time to break with the nomadic tradition and tolerate a king. In such a crisis the role of a spokesman of YHWH was decisive, and therefore Samuel, who was both the last of the judges and the first great prophet since Moses, occupies the centre of the stage.

Samuel
(*I Sam.* 1: 1 – 7: 17)

The book which is called by his name opens with his birth (*1*. 1: 1–28). Once again as with Sarah, Rebecca and Rachel the implication is that divine intervention and not merely natural processes made Hannah a mother. Shiloh is the religious centre of the tribes and ordinary folk like Samuel's parents make an annual pilgrimage there. Only the well-to-do would normally eat meat, the peasants would on some special occasion attend the central sanctuary, sacrifice one or more animals and hold a feast. Religious sentiment and social gathering were combined. The parallel in modern times to this practice has been likened to celebrating Christmas and eating a Christmas dinner away from home.

The temple at Shiloh is presided over by Eli who is thus the religious head of the tribes, with apparently a hereditary system of high priestly government in operation. This is thus a half-way stage between the tribal judges and the monarchy. Hannah's silent prayer —an unusual practice since prayers were normally spoken aloud, which explains why Eli thought she was drunk—is answered, and the boy is named "Heard of God". He has been dedicated to the priesthood and destined to be a holy man before his birth. Hannah's messianic hymn of thanksgiving (2: 1–10) points forward to the Magnificat in *Luke*. 1: 46–55.

The contrast between the aged and ineffectual Eli, unable to control the corruption of his sons, and the zealous young temple ministrant (*I* 2: 11–26) is confirmed by a prophetic message to Eli (*I* 2: 27–36) and a divine visitation to Samuel (*I* 3: 1–21). Both of these pave the way for the disaster that wipes out Eli and his sons and leaves the way open for Samuel to become the religious and secular head of the confederacy. The Philistines march into the hills: the sacred talisman, the Ark of the covenant, is not only unable to protect Israel but is itself captured. The Israelites are vanquished, and Eli's sons are slain but it is the loss of the historic symbol of the Presence of God that kills the old man and brings the word "ichabod," "the glory is departed", into biblical vocabulary (*I* 4: 1–22).

But according to the narrative the Philistines have little joy of their trophy. Dagon, their corngod cannot stand in the same temple as YHWH. Plague breaks out wherever they try to install the Ark (*I* 5: 1–12). At last in despe-

ration they decide to restore it to Israel and there is a dramatic picture of the Ark, not simply being led back to Israel on an ox-wagon, but by the irresistible power of YHWH within it driving the milk-cows which are pulling it, willy-nilly and lowing with anguish, back into Israelite territory despite their natural instincts to return to their calves. The golden images of mice and emerods (boils) which accompanied it were by imitative magic supposed to neutralise the plague (*I* 6: 1–21). The Ark is then installed at Kirjath-jearim, the Israelites recognise that its loss and their defeat were due to their pagan practices, and under the guidance of Samuel, having put their house in order, their repentance is rewarded by divine intervention. Israel recovers its territory, and acquires the Philistine cities as well, while Samuel reigns supreme as judge of all Israel (*I* 7: 1–17).

All this however is largely wish-fulfilment and pious tradition. The evidence both of archaeology and the subsequent biblical record itself is that after the battle of Eben-ezer and the loss of the Ark, Israel was down and out. The Ark is not mentioned again until the time of David (*II* 6: 1–19), which suggests that it remained during these years in some Philistine temple and only came back to Israel when the Philistines were completely defeated by David. It does seem likely, however, that among the tribes of landless Israel, and in the absence of a settled priesthood at Shiloh, Samuel gradually became the undisputed arbiter of tribal differences, based on his home town of Ramah and visiting the main religious centres of the clans in turn (*I* 7: 15–17).

Samuel and Saul

(I *Sam* 8: 1 – 15: 35)

IT would appear that as a development of this there was the possibility that hereditary 'judges' might take the place of the hereditary high priesthood at Shiloh. Samuel's sons, however, were as unsatisfactory as Eli's and the thoughts of the tribes turned towards the possibility of a king (*I* 8: 1–5). The earlier 'judges' had been charismatic, i.e., their office was personal and depended on their obvious possession of the gift of the Spirit (charisma) of YHWH, as evidenced by the fact that when the Spirit fell upon them they were endowed with abnormal strength or courage as in the cases of Othniel, Gideon, Jephthah and Samson. Hereditary judges of a more judicial and non-charismatic type might well have been a possible form of tribal government.

It has generally been held that behind the book of *Samuel* as we have it lie two different traditions about how Israel came to have a king. In the older tradition Saul is represented as the choice both of Samuel and of the people and he is anointed king with divine approval and by public acclamation. This pro-monarchy tradition is normally reckoned to be a more reliable account of what actually happened than the anti-monarchy tradition which represents Samuel as warn-

ing the people of the perils of kingship, and only reluctantly agreeing to the election of Saul, whom he regards as usurping the place of YHWH, who alone is Israel's king. This anti-monarchy tradition, it is held, would date from the time when bitter experience had proved that kings wrought more harm than good and ultimately brought about Israel's downfall.

There are certainly two different pictures of Samuel, and two different attitudes to kingship in these early chapters of the book. In the one (*I* 7: 3–8: 22; 10: 17–25; 12: 1–25) Samuel is the venerable head of the commonwealth who tries in vain to dissuade the people from demanding a king when his sons prove unworthy successors. On divine instructions he paints a dismal picture of servitude, extortion and forced labour, but cannot move the tribal leaders from their determination to be "like all the nations" (*I* 8: 4–22). Saul is selected king at Mizpah by sacred lot (*I* 10: 17–25) and Samuel, making the best of a bad job, utters a general warning to king and people (*I* 12: 1–25).

When we turn, however, to *I* 9: 1–10: 16, 26–27; 11: 1–15, Samuel is described as a seer, which is explained as the old name for a prophet, who is presiding over a religious ceremony in an unspecified town. To this town comes a handsome young man Saul in search of some lost asses. The seer not only sets his mind at rest about this, but is divinely guided to anoint him king secretly as the future deliverer of Israel from the Philistines. On his way home Saul encounters a band of ecstatics and he too becomes possessed of the Spirit of YHWH and 'prophesies' i.e., becomes an ecstatic also, much to everyone's surprise.

His opportunity to show his mettle comes, oddly enough, not against the Philistines in the first instance but against desert Ammonites beyond Jordan. An impossible demand made by these nomads on the town of Jabesh-gilead comes to Saul's ears. The Spirit falls upon him and he hews in pieces the oxen with which he has been ploughing and sends them as a kind of fiery cross throughout the tribes of Israel (cf. *Judg.* 19: 29). They rally to his summons, Jabesh-gilead is relieved, and with divine approval and in Samuel's presence Saul is acclaimed king amid great rejoicing at Gilgal (*I* 11: 1–15).

These are obviously two different traditions which cannot be completely harmonised. But they are not so divergent as they appear at first sight, nor is there any real reason to think that the older narrative, which is undoubtedly the second, is necessarily wholly right and that the first is wholly wrong. The biblical editors by putting them side by side obviously felt that they were both right, at all events in principle. We shall not be far off the mark therefore if we think of the emergence of Saul as first king of Israel as the direct result of his charismatic leadership of the tribes at Jabesh-gilead. By popular acclaim he would be judged to be the man who could break the Philistine yoke and restore Israel's fortunes.

But there must have been many in Israel, including no doubt Samuel, who viewed with grave misgiving on religious grounds this departure from the historic dependence of Israel on YHWH alone as king. The point of view expressed in *I* 12: 1–25 (excluding the element of black magic in vv. 16–18) is not necessarily born of bitter reflection long after the event when the monarchy had proved to be Israel's undoing, but is rather the tempered judgment of the more conservative element in Israel who recognised that kingship, like 'strange gods' and other features of their neighbours' practices that seemed to indicate Israel's progress up the ladder of culture and civilisation, was fraught with grave peril for a people who were called not to be like other nations, but to be a unique community responsible directly to YHWH.

The die was cast, however, and to begin with it seemed as if the forebodings of the more conservative elements had been unjustified. The Philistines were so firmly in control of the land—and the monopoly of iron—that blacksmiths had even been prohibited or banished from among the tribes, so that an Israelite farmer had to go to a Philistine blacksmith to sharpen his implements. There was thus neither sword nor spear among the tribes to match the chariots and horsemen of the Philistine army (*I* 13: 19–22). Saul's tiny guerilla force after several years of nominal kingship amounted to six hundred men (*I* 13: 15).

The signal for revolt came from Saul's son Jonathan who killed a Philistine garrison-commander, not 'garrison' as in A.V. (*I* 13: 3). The Philistines took punitive action and massed in great numbers near Michmash. Many of the Israelites had to leave their farms and take refuge in caves and thickets (*I* 13: 6), many others were forced to join the ranks of the Philistines (*I* 14: 21). A daring raid by Jonathan and his armour-bearer on the deserted garrison of Michmash, assisted by an earthquake, throws the enemy into confusion. Saul profits by the consternation and rushes his small force into action. The Israelite levies in the Philistine army turn on their masters, other tribesmen appear from their mountain hides and the Philistines are routed (*I* 14: 1–23).

This battle was decisive. It restored the highlands to Israel and Saul had now a kingdom, albeit a small one. Israel for good or ill was now a nation. For Saul, however, it was but the beginning of his troubles. There was no question of his valour, and the rest of his life was spent in defending Israel against its foes. Not least of these were the Philistines against whom there was "sore war" all his days (*I* 14: 47, 52). But worse than the Philistine thorn in his flesh was the loss of Samuel's support.

The cause of this is variously described (*I* 13: 7–14) as Saul's arrogation to himself of religious duties which properly belonged to Samuel or (*I* 15: 1–35) as the king's failure to 'devote' the Amalekites, including their king and their cattle as he had been commanded. Modern sympathies would tend to be with Saul rather than Samuel, who carried out the law of *herem* (*Deut.* 20: 16) on the unfortunate Agag (*I* 15: 33).

Saul seems to have been concerned to abide by the Law when hungry troops broke the ancient tabu on eating non-kosher meat (*I* 14: 32–34), on the other hand he treated with scant respect a priest who was taking the auspices for battle (*I* 14: 18–19). ('Ark' here should be 'ephod', which is sometimes an image and sometimes a pouch worn by a priest containing objects—*urim* and *thummim*—used in casting lots. In either case the priest's function was by manipulation of the objects to give decisions, which since they were not reckoned to be subject to human intervention, were considered to be the decisions of YHWH.)

Saul certainly emerges from the record as a rough diamond—bold, brave, impatient and impulsive but genuinely devoted to YHWH and Israel. Yet Samuel must have judged him unfit for the task. "Rebellion" and "stubbornness" were no qualifications for a king of YHWH's people. Obedience was worth more than readiness to perform the outward obligations of religion (*I* 15: 22–23). The parting between Samuel and Saul is the stuff of tragedy. They never meet as friends again. But Samuel mourns for Saul with the sorrow of disappointed hope even as he casts around for his successor (*I* 15: 35 – 16: 1).

Saul and David

(*I Sam.* 16: 1 – 31: 13)

THE story of David which begins at this point is told much more sympathetically than the story of Saul. It is recorded that while he was yet a youth he was singled out by Samuel and anointed king (*I* 16: 1–13). From then on the drama lies in the rising star of David's fortunes seen against the sombre backcloth of Saul's declining power and increasing melancholia. Samuel has deserted him, therefore YHWH has deserted him. Brooding over this in his royal stronghold of Gibeah literally drives him mad. The one thing that calms him is music and young David enters his service as page and minstrel (*I* 16: 14–23).

The immortal tale of David and Goliath (*I* 17: 1–58), however splendid, appears to be an alternative and less likely story of how David put his foot on the first rung of the royal ladder. Someone else is given the credit for disposing of Goliath (*II* 21: 19), and Saul can hardly have failed to recognise his private musician (*I* 17: 58). What is certain, however, is that David found himself rapidly becoming a favourite, not only with the king's son Jonathan, but with the ordinary folk. The comparison drawn between him and Saul in popular ditties was more than the unstable mind of the king could bear. His madness became homicidal and he tried to rid himself of this dangerous young rival both by violence and cunning. David however emerged unscathed and with the king's daughter to wife for good measure (*I* 18: 1–30).

The last few chapters of the first book of *Samuel* dwell at length on the personal vendetta which Saul waged against his attractive son-in-law and which eventually drove David into exile (*I* 19: 1–20: 42). The stories that are told of David's exploits with his band of outlaws at the cave of Adullam, his acquisition of Goliath's sword, his pretence of madness to deceive the Philistines, his elusiveness and magnanimity are reminiscent of the annals of Robin Hood (*I* 21: 1 – 26: 25).

Saul's unpredictable mad fits eventually drive David to seek protection from the Philistines, and he is given the town of Ziklag from which he and his confederates proceed to harry the enemies of Israel, unknown to his apparently rather dull-witted Philistine patron (*I* 27: 1-12). Larger issues are however now impending. The Philistines mass a full scale attack against Israel, and their princes, more shrewd than David's protector, refuse to allow him to take his place in their ranks. He therefore returns to Ziklag and uses the opportunity of the Philistines' absence to wipe off an old Israelite score against the Amalekites, who are never heard of as a tribe again (*I* 29: 1 – 30: 31).

Meantime the hapless Saul, facing this Philistine invasion with the knowledge that YHWH has deserted him, in desperation consults the witch of Endor in the hope that the spirit of the dead Samuel might give him counsel and comfort (*I* 28: 1–25). The ghostly voice of the medium has

nothing but death to offer and the
sombre prophecy is fulfilled at
Gilboa where the flower of Israel
is massacred and once more the
tribes are without a kingdom. The
king takes his own life and had it
not been for the grateful homage
of some brave men from Jabesh-
gilead who remembered their bene-
factor (*I* 11), his dishonoured body
would have been left to rot on the
walls of Bethshan (*I* 31: 1–13).

David's Empire

(II *Sam.* 1: 1 – 8: 18)

THERE is no break in the narrative between the first book of
Samuel and the second book. The
story of the young Amalekite describing how he dispatched Saul
can hardly be a lie to gain favour
with David. This is an alternative
and probably more likely version
than Saul's suicide (*II* 1: 1–16).
At all events it is followed by the
ancient and magnificent Song of
the Bow (so called by reading
"song" for "use" in v. 18) which
is David's elegy on Saul and Jonathan, and the tribute of one great
man to another (*I* 1: 17–27). Saul
had been a complex character but
he had served Israel well as David
acknowledges, and he had given the
tribes their first taste of real unity.

David, who mingled personal
charm with considerable astuteness as has already been evident,
proceeded to build on these foundations. He first of all got himself made king over the Judah
territory in the south at Hebron,
doubtless with Philistine permission (*II* 2: 1–4). a move for which
he had previously paved the way

(*I* 30: 26–31), and attempted to
extend his power over the small
area of Transjordan which was
traditionally Israelite. Saul's late
commander-in-chief Abner, however, has different ideas and under
his patronage Saul's weak son
Ishbosheth becomes king of the
rump of Israelite territory at
Mahanaim in Transjordan, presumably also with Philistine approval, and claims the allegiance
of all the northern tribes. There
are now two tiny principalities in
Israel, neither of which could
properly be called a kingdom
(*II* 2: 5–11).

The name Ishbosheth means
"man of shame" (Hebrew: *bosheth*
=shame). Originally Saul's son
was called Ish–baal, "man of
God" (*I Chron.* 8: 33), Baal and
YHWH being at that time equally
valid names for Israel's God. Later
generations, however, under the influence of the prophets (cf. *Hos.*
2: 16) found it a shameful thing
that the pagan god of Canaan
should ever have been identified
with YHWH and altered Ish-baal
to Ishbosheth, and Merib-baal
(*I Chron.* 8: 34), perhaps "hero
of God", who was Jonathan's
crippled son, to Mephibosheth (*II*
4: 4). In the same way Gideon's
alternative name Jerubbaal (*Judg.*
7: 1) is transformed to Jerubbesheth
(= *bosheth*) (*II* 11: 21).

The incident in *II* 2: 12–32 may
be taken as a sample of what is
meant in *II* 3: 1 "There was long
war between the house of Saul and
the house of David". While David
is increasing his harem at Hebron
(*II* 3: 1–5), Abner quarrels with
Ishbosheth over another harem
problem (the Old Testament if it

sanctions polygamy can never be used as an advertisement for it!). As a result of this he throws in his lot with David, whose demand for the return of his first wife Michal is prompted not by affection but by political considerations. Abner meets a speedy end at the hand of Joab, David's nephew and general, who thus avenges his brother's death (II 3: 6–39). Ishbosheth is likewise assassinated and the way is now clear for David to become king of all the Israelites (II 4: 1–12).

There is a ceremony at Hebron where representatives of the tribes, sheikhs rather than "elders", accept David as their king. This was still a nominal sovereignty and might have remained so but for one of David's master-strokes of political genius. The stronghold of Jerusalem, which until now had been in the hands of a Canaanite tribe of Jebusites, for the simple reason that it was the most impregnable citadel in Palestine, was now captured by the use of scaling-hooks (A.V. "gutter") and David proceeded to make it his capital. The palace which he built forthwith was no doubt necessary for the increase in his female establishment (II 5: 1–16).

The strategic choice of Jerusalem as a capital was not only justified on the grounds of its commanding position (in the period of the judges it had been one of the chain of Canaanite fortresses which separated Judah from the rest of Israel) but also because it had been hitherto neutral territory. Neither north nor south, Israel nor Judah, could claim that it was the dominant partner. David's action was comparable to selecting Washington or Canberra as the seat of federal administration. An equally shrewd move was to make Jerusalem the religious centre of the tribes by recovering the Ark of the covenant and installing it with splendid ceremony and amid general rejoicing in the capital (II 6: 1–23). For the first time since Shiloh had been destroyed fifty years before, Israel had the shrine of the Exodus in its midst and YHWH dwelt among his people.

This could hardly have happened without first subduing the Philistines, who presumably had kept the Ark in one of their own sanctuaries. The record is, however, that during his reign David not only soundly defeated the Philistines, forcing them back into their five towns on the coast, but also conducted campaigns against neighbouring tribes and states until the new kingdom of Israel stretched from the Gulf of Aqaba in the south to well beyond Damascus in Syria to the north, and from the Mediterranean across Jordan into the eastern desert (II 5: 17–25; 8: 1–14). Apart from Philistia, therefore, and the Phoenician territory of Tyre and Sidon, the whole of the Levant from the Orontes to Egypt belonged to Israel. In addition to this David took steps to organise his little empire with himself at the head as the supreme authority and with delegated powers to the standing army, the priesthood, and the civil service (II 8: 15–18).

So the tribes are at last welded together into a nation like other nations, and Israel embarks on the stormy seas of political adventures.

By the absence of any other strong power in the Near East at that time, by the breaking of the monopoly of iron which the Philsitines had held and which kept the tribes impoverished, by conquest and by treaty, David, who had become king of undivided Israel about 1000 B.C., was able in the thirty odd years of his reign in Jerusalem to build a commonwealth which the later historians of Israel looked back upon as a golden age.

Not the least of his many diplomatic actions was the preservation of the Exodus tradition by housing the Ark in a tent (*II* 7: 2). Although Jerusalem was known as the city of David (*II* 5: 9) it thus became also the permanent sanctuary of the desert tradition, of Moses and Sinai, and of YHWH who had led his people from bondage and had now established himself in the heart of the promised land. Whatever element of calculation there may have been in this piece of symbolism, there is no doubt that David was like Saul a genuine believer in the traditions of Israel and a loyal—and more enlightened (cf. *II* 15: 24–26)—follower of Israel's God. But in establishing Jerusalem as Zion, city of YHWH, and paving the way by the installation of the Ark for the glory of Solomon's Temple, he earned for his dynasty the promise of the everlasting favour of YHWH (*II* 7: 1–29). When the monarchy finally collapsed and this became impossible, the fulfilment of the promise was transferred to the hope of a Messiah who would be David's son (*Luke* 1: 31–33; *Acts* 2: 29–31; 13: 22–23; *Heb.* 1: 5).

David's House

(II *Sam.* 9: 1 – 20: 26)

THERE is, however, far less in the Bible about David's military and political achievements than about his personal affairs. The fascinating so-called Court History of David which occupies *II* 9: 1– 20: 26 is reckoned to be a contemporary record and therefore among the oldest writings in the Bible. Doubtless it is included not only because it sheds a favourable light on the most loved figure in Israel's story, but also because in true biblical fashion it exposes the weaknesses of even the greatest men. David's faults are not a few and they are not glossed over. The realism of the recorder compels him to mirror faithfully the stages by which a reign of glorious promise became, through human weakness and despite its outward success, a tragic failure and a prelude to greater folly.

This Court History traces the decline of a bold young warrior king into a pitiable old man fleeing from his palace for fear of his own son, and the Bible makes it plain that the fault lay not in David's stars. All the various facets of the character of this brilliant monarch are exposed to the piercing rays of God's judgment. His strength and his weakness alike are compounded into a portrait which goes far to explain why David, despite the disapproval which much of his conduct aroused in the minds of later generations, still held so high a place in the affections of Israel. We may pause to marvel that such a revealing record should be permitted in an age when elsewhere kings were being worshipped as gods, and when the function of a court chronicler was to paint his royal master as a paragon of all the virtues. But this is the story of Israel, and Israel has a covenant with God.

Against a background of the campaigns that made and kept the kingdom, we are given first of all a glimpse of David's magnanimity— one of his noblest features—towards the household of Saul, and Jonathan's lame son becomes one of David's own family (*II* 9: 1–13). Then David falls from grace and a whole train of disaster is set in motion. Unlike his usual practice of leading his troops in person (*II* 10: 17), David on this occasion stayed in Jerusalem and had an adulterous affair with the beautiful Bathsheba who became pregnant by him. Failing in every effort to transfer paternity to the lawful husband David resorts to what amounts to murder (*II* 11: 1–27).

The scene (*II* 12: 1–14) where Nathan the prophet, successor to Samuel in the biblical record as the chief spokesman of YHWH, confronts David with his crime in the parable of the one little ewe-lamb, and points the accusing finger of God at the king with the words: "Thou art the man" is one of the great passages in the Bible. Where else in the ancient world— or for that matter in the modern world—could a man of God thus address a ruler? It is a mark of David's allegiance to the covenant—and of the power it wielded in Israel—that instead of summoning the guards he confesses

that he has "sinned against the Lord". If the penitential *Psalm* 51 is not from David's hand some such thought was surely in David's mind.

The chronicle dates the subsequent troubles within David's household from this crime. The first disaster was the death of the child for which David refused to mourn with a stoicism that was born of no expectation of life beyond death, but, as mostly throughout the Old Testament, of a conception of a shadowy existence in the abode of the departed under the earth beyond the jurisdiction of YHWH (v. 23). Joab, who has meanwhile been fighting the king's battles, loyally induces David to counteract the effect of his dalliance and crime upon the people by taking command of the army in the field. The apparently bloodthirsty treatment of the Ammonites in v. 31 is a mistranslation in the A.V. and means that they were conscripted for slave labour, not mutilated (*II* 12: 15–31).

The tragic story of David's indulgent love for his weak and treacherous son Absalom which clouded the old king's last years begins when Tamar, Absalom's full sister, was raped by her half-brother Amnon. In revenge Absalom had Amnon stabbed to death at a feast and fled the country (*II* 13: 1–39). David was inwardly pining for his exiled son, and the faithful Joab by a transparent ruse gave him an opportunity to permit Absalom to return to Jerusalem (*II* 14: 1–33).

No sooner was this vain and ambitious schemer restored to favour, however, than he set about undermining his father's authority

(*II* 15: 1–6). After four years (not 'forty' as in A.V.) he raised the standard of revolt at Hebron and large numbers rallied to his side. The old king, barefoot and weeping, left his capital and the Ark behind as Absalom and his army advanced on Jerusalem (*II* 15: 7–37). David and his retinue on their flight are treated with scant courtesy while Absalom and his chief adviser Ahithophel plan to destroy them (*II* 16: 1 – 17: 4). David, however, for all his age and distress had lost none of his traditional astuteness and by an excellent network of spies not only ensured that Ahithophel's plans were foiled but succeeded in escaping across the Jordan to Mahanaim where he was given shelter and hospitality (*II* 17: 5–29).

A pitched battle was fought between David's supporters and the army of Absalom in which Absalom's troops were routed and he himself, caught in an oak tree, probably by the neck rather than by his legendary long hair, was dispatched by Joab. The king was inconsolable: "O my son Absalom! my son, my son Absalom! would God I had died for thee, O Absalom, my son, my son! (*II* 18: 1–33). Joab's act and blunt condemnation of David's ill-timed grief lost him his command of the army. But David rallied himself and soon with the support of Judah and then of the remaining tribes returned to his capital (*II* 19: 1–43). A subsequent rebellion by one Sheba was dealt with by Joab who thus became once more commander in chief (*II* 20: 1–26).

Epilogue

(II *Sam.* 21: 1 – 24: 25)

So ends the Court History. The rest of the book appears to be made up of odd traditions which add little to the picture we have already been given of the life and times of David and the halcyon days of the kingdom. We are told of a blood revenge on Saul's sons by the Gibeonites (*II* 21: 1–14), of some of the exploits of David's knights-at-arms during the earlier campaigns (*II* 21: 15–22; 23: 8–39) including the splendid story of the water of Bethlehem (23: 13–17), and of a census (*II* 24: 1–17) which presumably took place in the heyday of David's power for the purpose of compiling a register for armed service and taxation and is represented as arousing YHWH's displeasure.

Apart from 22: 1–51 which is found elsewhere in the Old Testament as *Psalm* 18, two passages at the end of the book point forward to the future. David buys a plot of land from Araunah the Jebusite and builds an altar, which is later (*II Chron.* 3: 1) identified with the site of the altar in Solomon's Temple, now the Mohammedan Dome of the Rock (*II* 24: 18–25), and the last words of the "sweet psalmist of Israel", which really means "the favourite theme of Israel's poets", refer to the "everlasting covenant" with the house of David which became one of the elements in messianic expectation (*II* 23: 1–7; cf. *Ps.* 89: 3, 28, 34, 39; *Isa.* 55: 3; *Jer.* 33: 15–16).

I and II KINGS

Last Days of David
(*I* 1: 1 – 2: 11)

THE FIRST two chapters of the first book of the Kings can hardly be called inspiring. David's story is continued from the Court History (*II Sam.* 20: 26) and we find him now a decrepit old man still susceptible to pretty women and still holding on to the throne at about the age of seventy (*I* 1: 1–4). But others were less content than David apparently was to let the commonwealth drift, especially since there were two rival claimants for the succession: Adonijah, full brother of Absalom, and apparently equally spoiled, and Solomon, son of David's favourite wife Bathsheba, who now reveals herself as a formidable protagonist of her own flesh and blood.

On Adonijah's side the most notable support came from the ruthless old Joab whose chief concern is now the stability of the throne, while Solomon's claim has backing from, among others, Nathan the prophet. Between them Bathsheba and Nathan manage to persuade the old king to nominate Solomon as his successor, and while Adonijah is holding a feast to celebrate his accession Solomon is anointed king (*I* 1: 5–53). David's last words, which nowadays would be regarded as a senile and vindictive eagerness to pay off old scores, are more probably partly a desire to eliminate the possibility of civil war and partly a superstitious fear of the consequences of Absalom's unavenged death and of Shimei's curse (*I* 2: 1–11).

So, pathetically and ingloriously as the candid biblical record makes abundantly plain, the life of Israel's greatest king came to an end. Yet in his heyday David had been a brave soldier, a skilful general, a shrewd statesman and a generous friend. The blots on his character are not a few. His treatment of his enemies was cruel, but so were the times he lived in. His murder of Uriah judged by any standards was a shameful crime but David was man enough to stand up to Nathan's indictment and admit its truth. His treatment of the family of Saul and Jonathan was largehearted, as was his loyalty to Saul himself on the two occasions when his life was in his hands.

What weakness he had, such as his soft handling of Absalom's rebellion, was based on his strong affections. He was certainly no plaster saint but a man of very vital personality. His power of making friends must have been one of his most attractive features, witnessed to not only by his epic friendship with Jonathan, but by the fidelity of his henchmen, and, it would seem, of the whole people. Behind all this lay his zeal for YHWH and his cause, a zeal that was neither lip service nor political prudence but genuine piety. David was a democratic king, partly by nature and partly because the people would tolerate no other. He was as good an Israelite as they, and shared their hatred of domination to the extent of largely refraining from practising it himself. He had become king through a three-sided covenant, YHWH—the people—and himself (*II Sam.* 5: 3). In this relationship there was no place for the usual kind of eastern potentate. The king was at best first among equals.

The Son of David

THE two great figures of the Old Testament for ancient and modern Jews are always Moses and David; Moses who laid the foundation of Israel and David who built the fabric. He was indeed the man who extended the frontiers ot the Hebrews farther than they had ever been before and above all he was the man who made Jerusalem the holy city. For these reasons, as well as on personal grounds, much has been attributed to him by later piety that actually did not emerge until long after he was in his grave. He is credited with the planning of the Temple and with the authorship of the *Psalms*. In later days when amid the trouble and distress of war, oppression and exile the Hebrews longed for deliverance, they could think of nothing more glorious than that another David should arise and bring in a new and happier age.

We have already seen (pp. 174, 176) that breaking through the record of his reign the first notes are heard of the theme which in the end dominates Israel—the hope of a Messiah, God's anointed deliverer, who will one day come to liberate his people from servitude and despair. The messianic hope in the Old Testament is a vast tapestry into which is woven a multiplicity of threads of varying hue, and which leaves a number of loose ends. When Jesus comes to identify himself as the long awaited Messiah, he does not by any means slavishly accept as belonging to himself all that the Old Testament has to say about the deliverer, who bulks so largely in the hopes and prayers of psalmists and prophets.

Based on the promise of an everlasting throne for the house of David and faced with the reality of a series of kings who were unfit to occupy it, and, after the fall of Jerusalem in 587 B.C., with the reality of a non-existent kingdom, it was inevitable that this hope of Israel should centre on an idealised future ruler of the Davidic line and of Davidic dimensions—a warrior, statesman and liberator from the successive empires that held God's people in bondage. We shall hear this refrain echoing through the utterances of the prophets of the Old Testament and through the intertestamental period. We shall meet it again as part of the background of Jewish messianic expectation in New Testament times, as for example when blind Bartimaeus hails Jesus as the Messiah with the words: "Son of David, have mercy on me" (*Mark* 10: 47).

What is most striking, however, is that neither Jesus nor the Church regarded this particular strand of the messianic tapestry as having anything more than a genealogical significance. The only occasion on which our Lord identifies himself in any way with David is in the incident where the disciples are accused of plucking corn on the sabbath and Jesus recalls a similar incident from the life of David (*Mark* 2: 23–28; *I Sam.* 21: 1–6). Otherwise Jesus not only disregards the Son of David motif in his conception of his own role but goes out of his way to dissociate himself from it (*Mark* 12: 35–37).

The reason for this is clear. Jesus had his own ideas as to what God's Messiah should be and do, and very little that David was or did was included. The kingdom that Jesus came to found was not one that involved territorial demands or pitched battles. It had nothing to do with the subjugation of the Romans or of any other national unit but with the subjugation of evil among both Jews and Gentiles. To the Jews of Jesus' time the Messiah as Son of David would make it his first duty to restore to Israel the kingdom that it had lost, and by revolution and bloodshed recapture the glories of former days.

Nothing was further from Jesus' mind and intention. For him the Kingdom was the sovereignty of God over the whole life of mankind and his 'throne' was a Cross. So while the New Testament writers in the interests of missionary enterprise among the Jews stress Jesus' Davidic descent (e.g. *Matt.* 1: 1) and his association with Bethlehem the birthplace of David, their aim, in loyalty to the Master's intention, is to transform and reinterpret the Son of David theme into a deeper and more universal expression of what the Old Testament prophets were seeking after.

Solomon

(*I* 2: 12 – 4: 34)

IT was about 970 B.C. that Solomon came to the throne. As in the case of David his father, the record of his reign is ambivalent. On the one hand later generations for whom the Temple at Jerusalem was the very life-blood of their existence and the guarantee of Israel's unique witness, cannot but give Solomon credit for having been the architect of this greatest single factor in the preservation of Israelite tradition. Nor can they withhold just tribute to his remarkable astuteness which lost no opportunity to make Israel a byword for economic prosperity. Through his judicious financial and commercial enterprise the rustic kingdom of Saul, and the agricultural empire of David became a fabulously wealthy community which attracted attention far beyond the Levant. For this reason among others Solomon is credited with a wisdom which in some important respects was sadly lacking.

On the other hand the seamy side of his character is not

disguised: his love of luxury and ostentation; his enormous harem of foreign women whose religions he encouraged; his oppression of his subjects and his autocratic spirit. It is this seamy side that emerges first from the record. Although the first eleven chapters of the first book of the *Kings* deal with Solomon's reign they are far less a chronological account than a series of vignettes which, however, enable us to form an accurate picture of this remarkable monarch.

He inaugurated his reign with a blood-bath in which he disposed of Adonijah, his elder brother and rival for the throne, Joab, the most distinguished soldier Israel ever had, and Shimei the last significant survivor of the house of Saul. Abiathar, the last of the priestly house of Eli, was deprived of his office (*I* 2: 12–46). Having got rid of all likely sources of opposition he settled down to a reign of peace and prosperity. Benaiah became commander in chief of the army and Zadok was made head of the priesthood.

From this point we may try to piece together the fragments of tradition which the author, writing several centuries later, has included from the book of the Acts of Solomon (*I* 11: 41) which was no doubt a contemporary chronicle, and to which he and subsequent editors have added their comments. We are told of Solomon's flair for cementing political alliances by adding to his harem, and of his legendary wisdom (*I* 3: 1–15). His wisdom is then exemplified by his judgment in the case of the two mothers who claim the same child, from which it would appear that wisdom in this sense means rather oriental quick wittedness than speculative thought (*I* 3: 16–28).

He has an elaborate system of public administration, more so than David, with the ominous addition of regional commissioners. Following more or less the traditional tribal boundaries, Solomon divided his territory into twelve prefectures, each of which should be responsible for maintaining the king's household for a month every year. It is difficult to believe when we read of what it took to keep the king's household going for one day (vv. 22–23), that Israel and Judah had much left to themselves for "eating and drinking and making merry" (v. 20). In addition they had to support his considerable standing army and luxurious stables, a specimen of which has quite recently been excavated at Megiddo (*I* 4: 1–28). It is equally difficult to believe that the panegyrist of his wisdom in *I* 4: 29–34 included statecraft in his encomium.

Solomon is given credit for coining proverbs and composing songs. He may well have done both, as Moses was undoubtedly responsible for part of the Law and, more doubtfully, David for some of the *Psalms*, But the book of *Proverbs* and the *Song of Solomon*, which with *Ecclesiastes* and the *Wisdom of Solomon* are ascribed to the king, are like the Law and the *Psalter* not the work of any one man. The name of Solomon has been associated with *Proverbs* and *Canticles* in the same way as the names of Moses and David with the Law and the *Psalms*. Many laws, psalms and proverbs date from long after the time of their traditional authors but the biblical convention is to attach the whole collection to an appropriate and well-known name. For the same reason the book of *Isaiah* contains some utterances of that prophet but the most significant part of the book comes from an unknown author two centuries after Isaiah's day. Likewise the originally anonymous epistle to the *Hebrews* is credited to St. Paul.

Solomon's Temple

(*I* 5 : 1 – 9 : 9)

King Solomon is also depicted as an authority on natural history (*I* 4 : 33) but less attention is paid to that in the biblical record than to his construction and dedication of the Temple which occupies the next four chapters (*I* 5 : 1 – 8 : 66). For this purpose he enlisted the aid of Hiram king of Tyre. By a trade agreement Hiram provided timber, the renowned cedars of Lebanon, and skilled Phoenician craftsmen in return for wheat and oil. Solomon introduced forced labour among the Israelites to quarry stones and fell the trees and also to transport the stones and the timber to the site. If it is the case that an Israelite farmer had to give up four months every year to the king's corvée it is little wonder that resentment began to build up. The surprising thing is that the explosion was so long delayed (*I* 5 : 1–18).

None of this is in the priestly historian's mind however as he lovingly dwells on the details of the "house of the Lord". As distinct from Herod's reconstruction of the Temple in New Testament times when a complex series of courts—for priests, Israelites, women, and Gentiles—surrounded the central sanctuary, Solomon's Temple was one large enclosure which included his own palace and "the house of the forest of Lebanon", which seems to have been an assembly hall and armoury, as well as the Temple proper. This sacred part consisted of a single open court where the people congregated and which contained the altar of burnt offering (*II Chron.* 4: 1) with the Tabernacle reserved for the priests at one end of it. This building as described in the Exodus story (pp. 104–105) was divided into two compartments, the holy place and the Holy of Holies.

The size of the Tabernacle was only about 90 feet long by 30 feet broad and 45 feet high. It was really a royal chapel of Canaanite design attached to the palace. Adjoining it were a variety of rooms for administrative purposes. The Holy of Holies, called here "the most holy place" and "the oracle", was a complete cube and remained in utter darkness as the secret dwelling place of YHWH. Within the "oracle" was the Ark of the covenant guarded by two cherubim. The whole of the interior structure was of the finest carved wood and lavishly decorated with gold.

The craftsmen worked under the direction of a Phoenician expert, Huram-abi (A.V. Hiram), who cast two bronze pillars to stand at the entrance of the sanctuary, richly embellished, as well as an elaborate bronze water vessel and several smaller ones presumably used for ablutions. The furnishings, such as the table of shewbread, the candlesticks and the censers were of pure gold. Some of the stones may have been quarried and dressed underneath the rock on which Jerusalem stands, and the copper castings would undoubtedly be made at the foundries "in the plain of Jordan" of which archaeologists have found clear traces beside the copper mines, which were one of the chief sources of Solomon's prosperity (*I* 6: 1 – 7: 51).

When the Tabernacle was ready to receive it, the Ark containing the stone tablets of the Decalogue was brought from the site in the old city on which David had placed it and installed with proper ceremony. As in olden times the cloud of the Presence descended upon the Tabernacle and the glory of the Lord was seen again in Israel (*I* 8: 1–11). We may still capture some of the elation and exaltation that found expression in the prayer of thanksgiving, supplication and blessing which is much too good for Solomon and dates from long after his day, but which is put into his mouth on the occasion of the dedication of the Temple.

This prayer which is one of the high-lights of the Old Testament with its recognition of the majesty of God and also of his mercy, of human frailty and man's need of forgiveness, as well as of Israel's vocation to bring the world to the knowledge of God, is fit to rank with the best of Isaiah and finds an echo in every Christian heart. The feast which follows in which 'all Israel' takes part is of gargantuan proportions (*II* 8: 12–66). To conclude the story of the building of the Temple, a warning is given that if Israel is false to YHWH the land will be taken from her and the Temple will be destroyed. This of course is precisely what happened (*I* 9: 1–9).

The Copper-King
(*I* 9: 10 – 11: 43)

THE narrative now reverts to Solomon's secular activities. To meet the enormous cost of the exotic materials and lavish workmanship of his palace and of the Temple, Solomon had to cede to Hiram of Tyre twenty of his Galilean cities. Further public works which the king initiated are recounted, including improvements to Jerusalem, the rebuilding of various fortress towns, and the provision of granaries and stabling for his various garrisons of war-chariots. The statement that forced labour was imposed only on subject peoples and not on Israelites is contradicted by *I* 5: 13–18, and this present passage may refer to a period before the rebuilding of Jerusalem or to projects outside Jerusalem (*I* 9: 10–25).

Solomon also for the first time made Israel sea-conscious, and shipyards at Ezion-géber on the Gulf of Aqaba produced vessels which traded with Ophir, possibly Somaliland. Since the Hebrews were no sailors the Phoenicians supplied the captains and chief crew (*I* 9: 26–28). From Ophir Solomon imported expensive sandalwood, and his fleet of merchantmen (A.V. "navy of Tharshish") brought regular supplies of "gold, and silver, ivory, and apes, and peacocks (*I* 10: 11–12, 22).

It is only in recent years that archaeology has discovered how Solomon paid for all this. Part of the answer is that it was in his day that the mineral resources of Palestine were first exploited. The book of *Deuteronomy* contains as part of the description of the promised land a reference to it as "a land whose stones are iron, and out of whose hills thou mayest dig brass" (*Deut.* 8: 7–9). It now transpires that both iron and copper (brass) were extensively mined in Solomon's day. Nelson Glueck, who conducted excavations in the area, has described Solomon as "the copper-king" and has dubbed Ezion-géber "the Pittsburgh of Palestine". It had the biggest blast furnace in the Near East together with copper refineries and factories which produced a variety of tools and other metal articles for the home and export markets.

This then was the main source of Solomon's legendary wealth which transformed Israel from a peasant community into a top-rank industrial and commercial nation. When the queen of Sheba visited Solomon from her fabulous 'land of spice' in southern Arabia, "to prove him with hard questions" and "commune with him of all that was in her heart" it is more than likely that the purpose of her journey was a trade mission

and that hard economic bargains were driven on this occasion by a couple of very astute and progressive oriental rulers (*I* 10: 1–13).

"So king Solomon exceeded all the kings of the earth for riches and for wisdom". Little wonder that "all the earth sought to Solomon to hear his wisdom", if his wisdom could make them equally prosperous. Gold was the normal metal for the king's use and for his surroundings. Silver was "nothing accounted of". In addition to his export markets Solomon did a brisk trade as a middleman in horses and chariots, and levied tolls on the vast traffic of caravans which had to pass through his country on their way from Asia to Africa (v. 15). It is not unlikely (*Deut.* 17: 16) that he even sold some of his subjects to the Egyptians to buy horses for resale (*I* 10: 14–29).

Jesus sums up the grandeur and magnificence of this luxury-loving monarch when he dismisses "Solomon in all his glory" as less worthy of admiration than the common daisies in the fields of Galilee (*Luke* 12: 27). The biblical recorder traces Solomon's downfall to his foreign wives. Even if we deduct a large percentage of his thousand princesses and concubines—everything about Solomon seems to be on the grand scale—it would still amount to a considerable harem. He is accused in his old age of having encouraged them in their pagan religious practices by building them shrines and attending their ceremonies (*I* 11: 1–10).

For this he is threatened with the eventual disruption of his kingdom, and the loss of Edom and Syria from the empire which David had bequeathed him is treated as part of the divine punishment (*I* 11: 11–25). Before Solomon passes from the scene we are introduced to his successor over ten of the tribes, Jeroboam. This man, one of Solomon's labour overseers, as it would seem not for the first or last time with the encouragement of one of the prophetic party who disapproved of the royal ménage, staged a revolt which was unsuccessful and had to flee to Egypt. We are, however, now forewarned that on Solomon's death the kingdom will split, ten of the tribes following Jeroboam while Judah (with Benjamin) remains faithful to Solomon's son Rehoboam (*I* 11: 26–43).

The reason for the crash which followed Solomon's death and left his son with the rump of the kingdom was of course the unwisdom of Solomon's policies. Taxation and the corvée might have been endured had it not been obvious that all the king's activities were directed towards his own glorification and not the good of his people. His personal extravagance and love of ostentation coupled with his colossal entourage showed him up as a typical little oriental potentate, and there was too much of the nomadic spirit still in Israel to tolerate Solomon's kind of autocratic monarchy.

It was perhaps his misfortune that he was born into the purple. The early struggles and hardships that kept his father humble and always a people's man had been a closed book to Solomon. All he knew of court life was learned in the days when David was growing senile and life was cushioned. He came to the throne not by a covenant with YHWH and the people but by a court intrigue. His magnificence was paid for by the sweat of his people for whom he cared little.

Whatever grounds there may have been for the attribution of almost superhuman wisdom to this uninspiring but fascinating monarch, there can have been little real wisdom in a man who could so misjudge the temper of his people as to try to play the despot among men who were still at heart the proud and independent democrats of the desert. That the kingdom held together as long as it did is partly due no doubt to the fact that the tribal unit had been replaced by the prefecture—and of course by a more urban existence—and partly the fact that the blood-bath at the beginning of Solomon's reign had removed any alternative leadership and so discouraged opposition during his lifetime.

Kings and Prophets

SAUL had failed: David had failed: Solomon had failed. The kings and the kingdom had been weighed in the balance and found wanting. From the death of Solomon and the end of the undivided kingdom of Israel the story is a sad and sordid one of disruption, intrigue, war and corruption until finally the remnant of the high hopes of Israel crashed with the ruins of Jerusalem less than five hundred years after Saul became its first king. Israel had paid the price for playing at power politics, for aping the common run of nations, for mistaking culture for covenant, for becoming indistinguishable from any other of the petty principalities that staggered from one crisis to another in the ancient Mediterranean world.

But the Israelites were the people of God, a people with a call and a mission. They could not be left to disintegrate or to become assimilated to their neighbours. Saul's madness might make him unfit to govern his people; David's heart might be stronger than his head; Solomon's vanity might induce him to strive to bring his people into the mainstream of progress. It was not on figureheads like these, victims of their own passions and ambitions, that God would found his Kingdom. Yet Israel had wanted a king and mankind must learn through Israel's experience that valiance and astuteness and magnificence are not the foundations on which the well-being of God's peculiar people can rest.

The three kings of undivided Israel, each of them different, each of them exhibiting undoubted virtues, each of them in his own way desirous of making Israel a power among the nations, are written off as unfit for the task of leading the hearts and minds of their people along the way that God had appointed for them. Their successors—the kings of divided Israel and Judah—are for the most part condemned as even greater failures. The rest of the books of the *Kings*, which contains their story, covers the reigns of thirty-nine monarchs in thirty-six short chapters. This is the Bible's verdict.

Only one or two of the rulers of Israel and Judah who officially dominate the life of Israel, from the death of Solomon about 930 B.C. to the final disappearance of Israel as a national unit in 587 B.C., receive anything but condemnation at the hands of the biblical recorders. On the face of it their criterion may seem to have been an artificial standard of judgment. All the kings of the ten tribes of the north which seceded after Solomon's death to found the new kingdom of Israel are condemned because their religious focus was not Jerusalem, which now belonged to the southern kingdom of Judah.

But even the kings of Judah, with their seat in Jerusalem, the holy city, the city of the Ark and the Presence, are for the most part also dismissed as failures. If the prophetic historians, whose concern is that the Temple at Jerusalem and none other shall be the meeting place between YHWH and his people, cannot be called altogether impartial, they are on the other hand unerring in their insight that from the time of Solomon onwards there was movement in one direction only, and that downwards. Even the emergence of a Hezekiah or a Josiah could not arrest the headlong career of a people that had entrusted themselves to the wrong kind of leadership and that failed to see that the pursuit of wealth, power and prestige, and the false security that these things bring was not the path that the people of God must follow.

Yet it was a lesson that had to be learned and that could only be learned in the bitterness of experience and the collapse of disappointed hopes. Israel had to be convinced, as we through them have to be convinced, that it is to the Samuels and not to the Sauls, the Nathans and not the Davids, the Ahijahs and not the Solomons that the people of God must look and listen for the word that God is speaking. In the remaining chapters of the books of the *Kings* one figure stands out from the complex pattern of Israel's social and economic development—Elijah, a prophet of the calibre of Moses, who is ready to challenge kings or commoners if they deviate from the faith and practice of the covenant.

It would be wrong, however, to think that the sole witness was left to Elijah. He himself to his surprise found that there were many others as well as himself who in troubled and perplexing times would still hold fast to the Mosaic standards and to the revealed truth of Sinai (*I* 19: 18). But we may reflect that such nameless upholders of the faith of YHWH were supported, strengthened and guided by lesser prophets who, like Elisha, had inherited the mantle and spirit of Elijah—Micaiah-ben-Imlah (*I* 22: 1–28) and others of his kind. These were the men who gave Israel the leadership that its kings failed to give and who ensured that the values that Moses and Samuel and Nathan had stood for were not forgotten. These were the men who during the sad recital of Israel's decline and fall made it certain that out of the

disaster would come a new beginning and that a wiser, chastened Israel would arise out of the ashes of military defeat.

The Divided Kingdom
(*I* 12: 1 – 16: 28)

THE resentment and disaffection which had been brewing in Solomon's kingdom during his reign boiled over after his death when his son Rehoboam presented himself at Shechem for confirmation of his accession. This choice of a northern town for his coronation was no doubt motivated by the fact that the northerners were more restive, probably because they had· been more harshly treated. Shechem was the place where the twelve tribes had first found their unity under Joshua (*Josh.* 24), and it is now the scene of the split between north and south which disrupted Israel and brought that unity to an end for ever.

Ill-advised by his younger counsellors, Rehoboam, instead of offering to lighten the burdens which his father had imposed on the people, threatened them with 'scorpions' instead of 'whips' and was promptly disowned by ten of the twelve tribes who selected Jeroboam, the rebel leader of Solomon's day, to be their king. Rehoboam retired post-haste to Jerusalem where he had already been accepted as Solomon's successor by the tribes of Judah and Benjamin.

Even in David's day there had always been tension between Judah in the south and the larger territory of the ten tribes in the north. This had been encouraged even before David's day through the separation of north and south by Canaanite fortresses during the period of the judges. It might even go further back to the fact that Judah had been less influenced than the northern tribes by the Exodus element in Israel and may have consisted largely of decendants of patriarchal Israelites, who had never known the Egyptian bondage, and who had intermarried with native Canaanites. This may be the significance of *Gen.* 38.

At all events, possibly partly due to the hold that the capital city of Jerusalem exercised upon it, and partly due to its loyalty to the house of David, who was himself a Judahite, the southern kingdom remained faithful to the Davidic line, and when Jerusalem was finally destroyed in 587 B.C. three and a half centuries later, there was still a king of the house of David upon the throne of Judah. The northern tribes, which retained the title of the kingdom of Israel, though the Bible sometimes refers to them as "Ephraim" or "Samaria," had a succession of different dynasties before their disappearance in 722 B.C. a century and a half before the fall of Judah.

The story of the divided monarchy, for despite the disruption, the two little kingdoms were still one people, acknowledging YHWH, respecting the Mosaic tradition and bound by the same covenant, is told from this point on by writers who take the view that Jeroboam by the very first act of his reign committed an unforgivable sin and placed the northern kingdom beyond the pale for the rest of its history. Since Jerusalem was now the capital of the rival kingdom, Jeroboam had not only to constitute a new capital, which he did at Shechem, but had to provide a new religious centre. Since his kingdom was larger he selected Bethel, 12 miles from Jerusalem, and Dan in the far north, as the two chief sanctuaries of his realm and since he had no Ark of the covenant to serve as the symbol of YHWH's Presence he installed in each shrine a golden calf (cf. *Ex.* 32–34: pp. 106–107).

It is a mark of the syncretism which had overlaid the simple faith of the desert days that neither Jeroboam nor the people saw anything out of place in the fact that this bull-symbol, which was no doubt regarded as the throne of YHWH, was also the symbol of the fertility cult of Canaan. It was indeed a very suitable image for a half-Canaanite population, and was not Solomon's Temple itself to all appearances a typical Canaanite chapel? But to the later historians, who shared the conviction of *Deuteronomy* that Jerusalem and no other was the sanctuary of YHWH, and that anything that suggested the pagan rites of Canaan was anathema, this action was enough to put the whole subsequent history of the northern tribes under the ban.

In consequence no king of Israel after Jeroboam in the record of the books of the *Kings* is acquitted of sin. With monotonous regularity the verdict of the recorders is that "he did evil in the sight of the Lord". The verdict on the kings of Judah is not much more favourable, but some of them at least had the opportunity to receive commendation if they were responsible for some measure of religious reform. The kings of Israel had no such chance. In one sense this deuteronomic criterion is artificial. But in a deeper sense it is profoundly true. Jeroboam and his successors meant well enough. They were on the whole loyal to YHWH and the covenant, but they were playing with fire. It was no great step from admitting the possibility of a variety of symbols in YHWH-worship to admitting the possibility of a variety of gods.

As we have seen (p. 132), it was not until Josiah's day, three hundred years after Jeroboam, and a century after the northern kingdom had crashed, that the multiplicity of local sanctuaries and shrines throughout the land was abolished, and worship was centralised and controlled in Jerusalem. But the historians who wrote this record after Josiah's reformation were not altogether unfair in condemning the northern kings root and branch as doing 'evil', for it was not until golden calves and all the other pagan symbols and practices which had become identified with YHWH worship had been done away with that there was any possibility of a monotheistic faith and a moral code such as Moses had adumbrated and such as Judaism and later the Christian Church could accept as the foundation of their belief and practice (*I* 12: 1–33).

The recorder of Jeroboam's misdeeds does not, however, spare his own predecessors in Judah who under Rehoboam continued to frequent local sanctuaries with their Canaanite religious practices disguised as Yahwism, despite the fact that they had now the true dwelling place of YHWH in the Temple of Jerusalem, and who by consorting with male (and presumably female) cult prostitutes showed that they had degraded YHWH to the level of a fertility godlet. The invasion of Judah and Israel at this time by the Egyptians under Sheshonk I (A. V.–Shishak)—an inscription claiming his capture of 156 towns in Palestine can still be seen at Karnak—is regarded as fitting punishment (*I* 14: 21–31).

From now on the author of *Kings* attempts the impossible task of keeping pace with the history of the two kingdoms by a convention of dovetailing the two parallel accounts in accordance with a fixed formula. The reigns of the kings are introduced more or less as follows: "In the Xth year of A, king of Israel (or Judah), B became king of Judah (or Israel) and reigned for Y years". Then any events thought worthy of mention are inserted and the record concludes: "B did that which was evil (or good) in the sight of YHWH. And the rest of the acts of B and all that he did, are they not written in the book of the chronicles of the kings of Judah (or Israel)? So B slept with his fathers and C his son reigned in his stead".

We may take it that these chronicles of the kings of Israel

and Judah were like the book of the Acts of Solomon, contemporary records of their reigns which the compiler has used for his purposes. These purposes are, however, as we have seen, not historical, and in some cases little more than the length of the king's reign is noted. Invariably, however, an assessment of his reign is given on religious grounds and it is clear that it is the theological interest that is uppermost in the author's mind. As always in the Bible, history is treated rather as the arena in which the moral and religious issues that are at stake at a particular time have to be fought for.

Since we cannot share the Hebrew author's natural interest in the chronological framework of the kings of Israel and Judah, and are neither professional historians nor antiquarians, we may pass with a fairly light foot over the rest of the books of the *Kings* except where theological questions arise or where it is essential for the understanding of the narrative as a whole to fill in some background detail. We may therefore skim rapidly over the reigns of the next few monarchs of the two kingdoms until we come to Omri king of Israel, who as we have seen (pp. 142–143) deserved as soldier and statesman considerably more than the six verses that are allotted to him (*I* 16: 23–28).

Prophecy and Prophets

BUT Omri receives the attention which the author of *Kings* thinks is his due, despite the fact that he was responsible for transferring the capital of the northern kingdom to a virgin site at Samaria, which now becomes a city worthy to stand comparison with Jerusalem. The narrative, however, turns to deal at length with Omri's son Ahab and with Ahab's wife Jezebel, because it was through them that the greatest threat to the supremacy of YHWH worship arose since Israel became a kingdom.

Ahab became king about 870 B.C. and no doubt his father reckoned that he had made a prudential match for him with a princess of Tyre. This lady, however, a person of much stronger religious convictions than her husband, bid fair not only to eliminate the cult of YHWH completely from Israel, but also to rob the kingdom of everything that still, despite the strictures of the narrator, gave it some claim to be the upholder of the Mosaic tradition. The Bible disguises the critical nature of the issue by referring to the religious conflict which arose in Ahab's reign, and which brought on to the stage the prophet Elijah, as one between YHWH and "Baal".

Baal, meaning 'lord' or 'master' is used indiscriminately in the Bible of the chief god of the Canaanite pantheon or his local manifestation in any community, of heathen gods generally, of YHWH himself when the Israelites made no distinction, and in the Ahab narrative, where it stands for Melkart, chief god of Tyre, and Jezebel's native deity. The issue here is nothing less than an attempt of a domineering and fanatically religious foreign queen, with the connivance of any easy-going Israelite king, to substitute her own god Melkart for YHWH as the God of Israel. It is this challenge and peril to the faith and morality of Sinai that calls forth the violent reaction of Elijah.

Elijah is the greatest and best known of the succession of prophets who from the time of Samuel make their impact more and more felt in the life of Israel, until they reach their fine flower in the works of the writing prophets from Amos onwards. Sometimes a distinction is made between the writing prophets—or rather those prophets whose utterances have been collected in written form in the Old Testament —and those like Elijah of whom we learn through the narratives of the historical books. The latter are often given their Hebrew name of *nabhi* on the grounds that they are rather primitive types of ecstatics than men of the calibre of Isaiah or Jeremiah.

But the distinction is a fine one. Possibly all the Hebrew prophets were to some extent ecstatics and judged by twentieth century standards most of them were primitive. Some of them had an insight into the mind and purpose of God which is little short of New Testament standards, others are more like the dancing dervishes of Islam. It tells us very little about a prophet to say that he was an ecstatic who behaved at times like a mad-man, who 'prophesied' by uttering unintelligible noises, whirling in religious dance, cutting himself with a knife, lashing himself into a frenzy. All these things are recorded of what the Bible calls "prophets".

When Saul was secretly anointed king by Samuel he is described as associating with a band of these holy men (*I Sam.* 10: 10–11), and later we find him as a result of his contact with their contagious emotional condition stripping off his clothes and falling senseless to the ground where he lay naked for a night and a day (*I Sam.* 19: 20–24). Obviously behaviour like this was not regarded as proper for the son of a respectable citizen like Kish. In the question: Is Saul also among the prophets? we can detect the commonsense reaction of the normal person against the extravagant behaviour of religious fanatics. Yet, as we know, lying naked on the ground was not all that Saul did, although it may have been that sort of activity that exhausted the repertoire of his bizarre associates.

It would seem that this peculiar phenomenon which the Bible calls prophecy was in its early days in the time of the monarchy outwardly distinguished by this ecstatic behaviour common to many religions and not least the religion of Canaan from which prophecy of this kind probably came into Israel. But like many another religious practice that Israel borrowed it is more significant to notice what prophecy became rather than where it started. One of the last of the great writing prophets, Ezekiel, was also one of the most obviously ecstatic, yet it is of much less consequence to record this fact than to observe the profound understanding of God and man which pervades Ezekiel's utterances.

To 'prophesy' in the biblical sense—and this is as true in the New Testament Church, where it is called "speaking with tongues" (*Acts* 2: 1–13), as in Israel—may mean anything from incoherent gibberish to the divinely inspired sanity of an Isaiah or a John the Baptist. It was left to St. Paul finally to show that this charismatic possession that on occasion seized the 'judges' and the prophets, was not the only way that the Spirit of God laid hold of a man, although in Old Testament times it was the most convincing way for the spectator, but that wisdom, knowledge, faith and charity are equally gifts of the Spirit and proof of the indwelling God (*I Cor*. 12).

Primarily, however, the Old Testament prophet is a man of YHWH, albeit at times an unkempt and slightly comic figure. He may also be a patriot although his patriotism may often be to the Israel of God and not to the Israel of the king. Least of all is the true prophet a time-serving "yes-man", and the downfall and disappearance of prophecy as a potent influence in Israel came, apart from other reasons, when it was no longer certain that what a prophet said was what YHWH made him say and not what he was paid to say. Then the prophet became a "false" prophet in the eyes of every true Israelite, so that men who did indeed heard the word of the Lord were ashamed to be numbered with these lickspittle impostors and renounced the very name of prophet (*Amos* 7: 14; 13: 3–6).

It is noticeable how in the absence of proper leadership from the king, the troubled situation that follows the death of Solomon is more and more controlled by prophets and "men of God". It was a prophet Ahijah who had been the instigator of Jeroboam's rebellion (*I* 11: 29–39). Shemaiah, a "man of God", dissuades Rehoboam from embarking on civil war with the northern tribes (*I* 12: 21–24). A nameless "man of God" denounces Jeroboam at his new shrine at Bethel and is denounced by another nameless prophet for failing to keep strictly to the charge that God had laid upon him (*I* 13: 1–32). Ahijah who had sponsored Jeroboam's succession of Solomon, now having seen his fall from grace proclaims the fate of his whole house (*I* 14: 1–18). Jehu-ben-Hanani makes a similar pronouncement in the case of king Baasha (*I* 16: 1–4).

Elijah, Ahab and Jezebel
(*I* 16: 29 – 22: 53)

THUS IN this period it is the prophet or the "man of God" who reads the signs of the times, who is awake to danger, who warns and admonishes without fear or favour, and who is more ready to call the king to order than to bow the knee in homage. The outstanding example is Elijah, and we are fortunate in that we are given not a hasty sketch but a full length portrait. Doubtless because he was of outstanding character more stories have been told of him and included in the narrative than of most other prophets of the time. But we may think of him as embodying many of the characteristics of the prophetic class.

The record of Elijah is a mixture of popular stories which the writer of *Kings* has included in his narrative, and significant intervention in high-level political action. On the one hand he is the holy man of folk lore who is fed by the birds, who miraculously provides meal and oil for a poor widow, and brings her son back to life (*I* 17: 1–24), on the other hand he is the man who single-handed confronts and discomfits Jezebel's prophets, selects a successor for Ahab and for the throne of Syria, and denounces the king as Nathan denounced David for the murder of a humble Israelite (*I* 18: 1 – 21: 29).

When Elijah comes on the scene Israel is in the grip of one of its periodic droughts with consequent famine. Worse than that from the point of view of the faithful supporter of YHWH, Jezebel, in her fanatical determination to substitute Melkart worship, had had a large number of the prophets of YHWH in Israel exterminated. Elijah himself came from beyond Jordan, from the desert country where the YHWH tradition was still unimpaired by the insidious attractions of civilisation. He appears and disappears with dramatic suddenness, and always his presence denotes trouble for the reigning house. His dress is, like that of John the Baptist, a cloak of camel hair; his head is unshorn. With his iron constitution—and the nervous energy of a *nabhi*—he can out-pace a horse and fast for

days on end. The air of mystery that surrounds this meteoric character throughout the narrative is sustained to the end, when he does not die in the usual way but disappears heavenwards in a chariot of fire.

The Bible presents him in a series of sketches. He challenges the prophets of Melkart to prove the supremacy of their god over YHWH in a highly dramatic scene on mount Carmel. The mad cries of these ecstatics, their self mutilation, Elijah's ribald taunting of their slumbering god, and the denouement when the fire of the Lord falls and consumes the sacrifice, form one of the most vivid and exciting stories in the Old Testament. What actually happened it is impossible to say. It does not solve the problem to suggest that Elijah knew that the rain was coming and that lightning preceded it. What is clear, however, is that by the agency of Elijah, Melkart worship suffered a mortal blow, many of his prophets were massacred, and YHWH was reinstated as Israel's God (*I* 18: 1– 46).

He had proved that he could bring or withhold rain better than any Canaanite fertility god, and this together with Melkart's inability to save his prophets from slaughter was an argument that the ordinary man could understand. The little stories in ch. 17 would seem also to be parables illustrating YHWH's power to sustain the life of his people. In the barren desert (v. 6), in time of famine (v. 14), in face of death (v. 21), he proved himself to be the true giver of fertility to the land and health to the people. Elijah on Carmel was making Israel face up to a decision: "If YHWH be God follow him: but if Baal follow him". Under his influence Israel chose YHWH, although it was not until Jehu, prompted by Elisha, completed the extermination of the supporters of Melkart, that the victory was finally won (*II* 10: 18–28).

With his life in danger from Jezebel's fury, we next see Elijah seeking inspiration and courage at the holy mountain where Moses had received the word of God. There he is granted both. He learns that it is not in storm or fire that God speaks but in the silence and stillness of a receptive heart (A.V. "still small voice"). He learns too that he is not alone as a solitary defender of YHWH's cause, but that seven thousand as yet unrevealed witnesses for God stand with him in spirit. Ahab and Jezebel may flourish for a time but the cause to which this "troubler of Israel", as the king calls him (*I* 18: 17), has devoted his life will be brought by his disciple Elisha to its God-appointed end (*I* 19: 1–21).

After an interlude in which once more the influence of the prophets in political and military affairs is emphasised (*I* 20: 1–43) we next encounter Elijah making one of his dramatic appearances in Naboth's vineyard to defend the moral principles of Yahwism against the amoralism of any fertility cult. Presumably this superficially unimportant incident is recorded because it typified the ruthless autocratic policy of Jezebel—much more likely to be achieved under the auspices of Melkart than of YHWH—and in which Ahab was content to acquiesce. This stubborn peasant was nonetheless a man of Israel, rightly jealous of his tiny plot of the promised land which like all sons of the covenant he held in trust from YHWH, and no royal whim should deprive him of it. In Ahab's greeting: Hast thou found me, O mine enemy? we can detect the guilty conscience of a king who was still himself an Israelite, bound by the Law of Sinai, and who accepted the prophet's curse on the royal house as just and warranted (*I* 21: 1–29).

The last chapter of the first book of the *Kings* contains the revealing story of Micaiah-ben-Imlah. Ahab and his reluctant ally Jehoshaphat of Judah plan to rescue the town of Ramoth-gilead in Transjordan from the hands of the Syrians. All the court prophets, four hundred lackeys, officially supposed to declare the will of YHWH, complaisantly give the enterprise their blessing. But even Ahab recognises them as time-serving sycophants and sends for Micaiah because he knows that from this one man he will get the truth as YHWH discloses it to him, although he hates him for it.

At first Micaiah mockingly supports the representatives of the state religion. But Ahab will have none of it. "How many times shall I adjure thee that thou tell me nothing but that which is true in the name of YHWH?" In this question is revealed the power of the true prophet in Israel as opposed to the false prophets of the establishment. He might be a wild outspoken man from the desert like Elijah and walk with death for his companion, or he might be hated like Micaiah and rot his life away in some royal dungeon, but even the basest defaulter from the faith and covenant of YHWH acknowledged that from such men alone came the word of God, theirs was the voice from Sinai itself.

So in the story Micaiah foretells Israel's defeat and Ahab's death. "A certain man drew a bow at a venture" and Ahab's bloodless body was brought back to Samaria to be buried in the shadow of his splendid palace, inlaid with ivory, fragments of which are still found among its ruins (*I* 22: 1–53). Jezebel outlived her husband and saw two reigns before the prophecy of Elijah was terribly fulfilled that "the dogs shall eat Jezebel by the walls of Jezreel" (*II* 9: 30–37). The "troubler of Israel" himself, in keeping with his whirlwind life, disappears in like manner, saluted by his disciple Elisha as "the chariot of Israel and the horsemen thereof" (*II* 2: 11–12), so that after his day it was believed that in Israel's need he would come again to earth (*Mal.* 4: 5; *Matt.* 17: 10–11).

Elisha

(II 1: 1 – 13: 21)

ALTHOUGH THE passing of Elijah is not recorded until the second chapter of *II Kings*, his story more or less ends with *I Kings*. The first few chapters of the second book of the *Kings* deal principally with his disciple Elisha. In more ways than one the mantle of his master seems to have fallen upon him (*I* 19: 19). So many of the stories that are told of him resemble the Elijah narrative that it has often

been wondered whether there were in fact two prophets or whether Elisha and Elijah were not perhaps the same person.

But there is no need to suggest this when we remember the biblical conception of personality which is so different from modern western individualism. This curious overlapping of identity, sometimes called "corporate personality", which enables the Hebrew psalmist, for example, to speak of himself and his people as "I", or which allows the Hebrew historian to refer to a whole tribe or indeed the nation by the name of its traditional ancestor, is quite foreign to present-day convention. It is, however, entirely in accordance with the biblical scheme of recurring patterns. Just as the great themes of the Old Testament keep reappearing in different contexts and continue into the New Testament, so is there repetition and continuity in the great persons of the Bible.

Many of the characteristics and experiences of Joshua are, as we have seen, reminiscent of Moses (p. 150) and similarly much that has been recorded of Elijah is now paralleled in the life of Elisha. Both the Moses-Joshua pattern and the Elijah-Elisha pattern are by the same token continued via the messianic hope, which incorporates all the distinctive elements of Old Testament thought, into their New Testament fulfilment in Jesus Christ.

Elijah and Elisha divide the waters of Jordan by striking them with Elijah's cloak (*II* 2: 8–14), replenish a widow's cruse of oil (*I* 17: 8–16; *II* 4: 1–7), restore a child to life by the same method (*I* 17: 21; *II* 4: 34) and at their end are both described as the chariot and the horsemen of Israel (*II* 2 : 12; 13 : 14). Alongside this, however, is much that is different, so that we cannot speak of two identical prophets, but rather of Elijah 'overflowing' into Elisha as Moses 'overflowed' into Joshua.

Undoubtedly Elijah was the greater of the two, as Moses rises head and shoulders above Joshua. Many of the stories recorded of Elisha are trivial. This can never be said of Elijah. There is a dynamic courage in Elijah which enables him to face up to Ahab and Jezebel and which does not seem to have been communicated to Elisha. On the other hand Elisha plays if anything a more significant part in political affairs than Elijah had done, although his achievements are regarded as the fulfilment of Elijah's intentions.

The legends that occupy the first seven chapters of *II Kings* cannot be said on the whole to have much religious significance. They are presumably drawn from traditions preserved by the 'sons (disciples) of the prophets' who feature prominently in ch. 2. These are, like the "company of prophets" referred to in the Samuel-Saul narrative (p.190), resident communities or guilds attached to a particular sanctuary and fanatically devoted to the defence of national Yahwism. Here they appear to have centres at Bethel, Jericho and Gilgal, where the number of these cultic prophets is given as a hundred (*II* 4 : 43). Elisha is closely associated with them and we are reminded of the pious legends of the saints preserved by members of their orders.

First of all Elijah calls down fire from heaven to consume soldiers sent to arrest him. The real criminal is however Ahab's son who bypasses YHWH and seeks counsel from Baal-zebub, identified in New Testament times with Satan (*Matt.* 12 : 24 etc.) but here a Philistine deity at Ekron (*II* 1 : 1–18). The incident is recalled in the New Testament (*Luke* 9 : 54). It would seem that Elijah's character is already 'overflowing' into that of Elisha. Both prophets then make what seems to be Elijah's farewell tour of the centres of these prophetic guilds. Elijah is taken up to heaven from the region where Moses had died, and Elisha, having received a "double portion" of his spirit is able like his master to cleave the waters of Jordan and cross dryshod. He then decontaminates Jericho's water supply and with the assistance of a couple of ferocious bears disposes of some youths who had made fun of his tonsure, i.e. insulted YHWH (*II* 2 : 1–25).

Stimulated by music (v. 15), which apparently had considerable effect on the ecstatic (cf. *I Sam.* 10 : 5; 16 : 16; *II Sam.* 6 : 5, 16), Elisha devises a trick to deceive a Moabite army (*II* 3 : 1–27). On a more domestic level he saves a widow from debt and her sons from slavery by providing a miraculous supply of oil (*II* 4 : 1–7), and first promises that a wealthy and hospitable lady of Shunem shall have a child and then when the child dies of sunstroke restores it to life (*II* 4 : 8–37). In time of famine he prevents the prophetic community at Gilgal from being poisoned by baneful herbs and then multiplies loaves miraculously so that there is food enough and to spare (*II* 4: 38–44).

Undoubtedly the best of these excellent stories is the dramatic cure of Naaman and the transference of his leprosy to Elisha's dishonest servant Gehazi, which is recounted in *II* 5: 1–27. After an incident at the Jordan where some "sons of the prophets" are cutting timber to build themselves a bigger establishment and Elisha miraculously recovers a borrowed axe-head from the river (*II* 6: 1–7), the Elisha stories become more involved in the political events of his time. Before turning to these it may be worth noticing how many of the miracles of the last few chapters involve imitative magic. Poisonous water is made drinkable and suitable for irrigation by an admixture of an innocuous material like salt; the Shunammite's son is restored to life by breathing into his mouth and walking back and forth suggesting the action of a living person. A handful of harmless meal nullifies the effect of poisonous herbs, and the axe-head which has fallen into the river floats to the surface in imitation of the branch of a tree which the prophet has thrown into the water. In all these cases the idea behind Elisha's technique is the ancient belief that magic operates by imitation or sympathy.

Elisha now, however, turns his magic to a more patriotic use. A Syrian army is temporarily blinded and led into Samaria (*II* 6: 8–23). In time of siege and famine in the capital, where we are offered a terrifying glimpse of a beleaguered city reduced to cannibalism, Elisha is given credit for the mysterious horsemen and chariots whose imagined presence spread consternation among the enemy and raised the siege (*II* 6: 24 – 7: 20). He promotes a revolution in Damascus (*II* 8: 1–15) and engineers an even greater revolution in Israel by which Jehu, the proverbial furious driver, becomes king.

The whole of the royal household of Ahab's family is massacred including Jezebel, impudent to the last, and with them all the remaining devotees of her god Melkart (*II* 8: 16 – 10: 36). A similar religious purge took place in Judah (*II* 11: 1–21). Whatever Jehu may have meant by his "zeal for the Lord" (*II* 10: 16) as he drove into Samaria side by side with a representative of the prophetic party, this general upheaval in Damascus, Samaria and Jerusalem about 842 B.C. was as much religious as political and had the whole weight of the prophetic party behind it. It had been instigated by Elisha and those who shared his views, and it set the seal on Elijah's first successful challenge of Melkart-worship on Carmel several years before.

Unlike Elijah, Elisha died of a sickness, but true to type his magic survived even beyond death. It is recorded that when by chance an unknown corpse was buried in the same grave, whenever it touched the bones of the great wonder-worker it came to life again (*II* 13: 14–21). The value of legends such as surround the name of Elisha is that they witness to a personality who made no ordinary impact on his contemporaries: cf. St. Francis of Assisi. We may well think of the chief contribution of Elisha as being the furtherance of Elijah's work in ridding Israel of the perverted faith of the Tyrian Baal.

It was, however, a limited objective. The religion of YHWH retained many aspects of Canaanite worship in which both Elijah and Elisha acquiesced. The sacred bulls remained at Bethel and Dan as did the many shrines throughout the land with their sacred emblems of Canaanite fertility rites and their holy prostitutes. Minority groups still worshipped their national gods without protest from the prophets. At this stage all that was contended for—and achieved —was that as far as Israel was concerned YHWH of Sinai and no other must be Israel's God. It was left to a later generation of prophets to ensure that the Baal Israel called YHWH should indeed be the YHWH of Sinai, with all that that involved in faith and morality.

It is not to be wondered at that two men who in their day were reckoned to be worth all the chariots and horsemen of Israel put together, and who played so large a part in the shaping of the history of the people of God should feature, as a joint personality, in the thought of later Judaism (*Mal.* 3: 1; 4: 5) and of the New Testament. So strongly was the belief entrenched that Elijah would return before Messiah came that our Lord had to make it plain that in John the Baptist Elijah had indeed returned (*Luke* 1: 17; *Matt.* 11: 14), and that in contriving his murder Herod and Herodias had fulfilled the roles of Ahab and

Jezebel but with more effect (*Mark* 9: 11–13).

St. John's gospel (*John* 6: 30– 58) sees in the context of the Bread of Heaven motif not only a fulfilment by Jesus in the feeding miracles (*Mark* 6: 32–44; 8: 1–10: of the gift of heavenly manna in the Exodus story but of Elisha's barley loaves, which by the word of the Lord fed the prophets so that there was more than enough to satify their need (*John* 6: 9; *Ex.* 16; *II* 4: 42–44). Similarly in St. Luke's gospel, just as Elijah had followed Moses to the holy mountain and there received a direct revelation of God himself (*I* 19: 8), so both of them appear on the holy mountain of the Transfiguration when Jesus is revealed as the Christ of God, and share with the three disciples the foretaste of the glory of the Kingdom which will gather the saints of old and new Israel into one redeemed community (*Luke* 9: 28–36).

The Fall of Israel
(*II* 13: 22 – 17: 41)

THE LAST twelve chapters of the second book of *Kings* cover a period of roughly two centuries from about 800 B.C. to 587 B.C. By the end of the first of these two centuries the northern kingdom has ceased to exist and by the end of the second the southern kingdom is also within sight of its fall. Since the death of Solomon and the division of the kingdom around 930 B.C., relations between north and south have varied from temporary alliances to periods of war. At the same time intermittent warfare with Syria (Damascus) has also weakened the divided kingdom. A revolt in Moab (*II* 3: 4–27) is witnessed to not only by the Bible but by the Moabite stone, discovered in Transjordan in 1868 and now in the Louvre, a monument erected by king Mesha exaggerating, like comparable Assyrian records, the extent of his victory. But a more formidable foe now begins to make itself felt.

It is an odd convention that makes the history text-books refer to an outburst of military expansion in a nation as a 'revival' and a period when it threatens nobody as a 'decline'! In this period Egypt suffered a 'decline' and Assyria enjoyed a 'revival', which means that on the one hand the little states of the Near East were left in peace by Egypt but that Assyria began to become their nightmare. This vast war machine which has left as its memorial the most bloodthirsty record of a series of rulers whose one aim seems to have been to kill and destroy, began to afflict its neighbours and expand its territory soon after the death of Solomon.

The small fry of the Levant were no match for these ruthless war lords, whose boastful inscriptions of the devastation and death that they spread can still be read on tablets found among the ruins of their palaces and their victory monuments. A coalition of small states made an attempt to check Assyrian designs on the Near East and a notable battle was fought at Karkar on the Orontes in 853 B.C. The Bible makes no mention of this but Assyrian records indicate that Ahab of Israel deployed no fewer than 2,000 chariots and 10,000 foot soldiers, the chariots forming the largest contingent among the allies in this indecisive engagement. The black obelisk of Shalmaneser, now in the British Museum, also depicts king Jehu of Israel grovelling before the Assyrian king and describes the amount of tribute he had to pay in 841 B.C.

It is against the background of this growing threat to their very existence that we have to read in the last chapters of *Kings* the dismal story of how two of these tiny pawns in the game of Assyrian empire-building tried to escape the disaster that the prophets if not the kings saw looming ahead with deadly certainty. We are told (*II* 13: 7) that about 800 B.C. Israel could muster only ten chariots, fifty horsemen and ten thousand foot, so great had been the losses since Karkar only fifty years before, yet we find Israel and Judah still at each other's throats (*II* 14: 13–14) and apparently quite oblivious of their peril.

We have an abundance of Assyrian records from this period to fill out the sparse details given in the book of *Kings*, and in particular to provide for the first time an accurate chronology based on astronomical observations, as opposed to the rough and ready Hebrew method of calculating time, which makes it impossible to give more than an approximate date for any event before this period. But more important than Assyrian records we now also have the books of the prophets who lived through this Assyrian menace and spoke their minds as God guided them.

The author of *Kings* hints that the reign of Jeroboam II was a time of expansion and prosperity for Israel (*II* 14: 23–29). The reason for this was a temporary 'decline' in Assyria. But the book of *Amos*, who flourished at the end of Jeroboam's long reign about 750 B.C., indicates with a wealth of detail that this was Israel's Indian summer. The prophet paints a picture of a land lulled into a false sense of security by an economic boom and heedless of the signs of impending disaster, yet ridden with flagrant social inequality, extortion and injustice.

In the next chapter (*II* 15), king follows king in rapid succession and the Assyrian monster comes clawing at the door. Tiglath Pileser III, called Pul in the Bible (*II* 15: 19), has to be bought off and the book of the prophet *Hosea*, who followed shortly after Amos, emphasises the concern for the future which is now shared by all. Despite the fact that it led to the Assyrians nibbling off more than the fringes of the northern kingdom (*II* 15: 29), Israel's king in alliance with the Syrians thought fit at this time to attack Judah (*II* 15: 37).

The fall of Damascus in 732 B.C. which meant the end of Syria as an independent state, is mentioned as an aside (*II* 16: 9) but the author of *Kings* is more interested in the impoverishment of the Temple furnishings which was made necessary when Ahaz of Judah had to pay for help from Assyria against his northern neighbours (*II* 16: 1–20). The best authorities for this period in Judah are the books of the prophets *Isaiah* (chs. 1–39) and

Micah. Isaiah, unlike the majority of the prophets, belonged to the aristocracy, and from his vantage point as a counsellor of the king he influenced state policy from the inside. On this occasion he failed to dissuade the king from having any dealings with the Assyrians, and Tiglath Pileser was not slow to take advantage of the invitation to intervene in Palestinian affairs.

Samaria's turn came ten years later and in 722 B.C. the northern kingdom of Israel met the same fate as Damascus. Many of its people, almost 30,000 according to Assyrian records, were carried off in captivity to Assyria and settled in its dominions, while foreign captives were brought to replace them in Samaria. Not only therefore were the people of the northern kingdom no longer pure Israelites but their religion was no longer solely the religion of YHWH. Thus the Samaritans became a mixed and alien people with whom in later days good Jews would have no traffic, and the author of *Kings* in a diatribe against the northern kingdom traces its downfall directly to the apostasy of Jeroboam I two centuries before (*II* 17: 1–41).

The Fall of Judah

(*II* 18: 1 – 25: 30)

AFTER THE fall of Israel Judah lingered on. Considerable space in the record is devoted to the reign of king Hezekiah, one of the two rulers after the division of Solomon's kingdom who receive high commendation from the author of *Kings*. There was good reason for this because it was in his reign that a real attempt was made to purify the worship of YHWH of its pagan associations (*II* 18: 1–6). More space is however devoted to one of the best known incidents in Judah's history, which is recounted at length in *II* 18: 13 – 20: 20 and is probably an excerpt from a book of the Acts of Isaiah (cf. *Isa.* 36–39).

Assyria's triumphal progress was itself threatened by the rising new power of Babylon which eventually overthrew it. Hezekiah against Isaiah's advice toyed with the idea of invoking the aid of Egypt and joining the revolt of Babylon. The Assyrians were, however, far from ready to acquiesce in the dismemberment of their empire, and a punitive force under the redoubtable Sennacherib, having dealt with the rebels in Mesopotamia, descended on Palestine. This campaign is described in detail on a hexagonal prism now in the British Museum and Sennacherib's own account confirms in general the biblical record. In 701 B.C. detachments of his great army ravaged the puppet states of the Levant and one such detachment under an official called the Rabshakeh approached Jerusalem.

Meantime Hezekiah had prepared for a siege by constructing a tunnel to ensure an adequate water supply for the city. This aqueduct, over 1,700 feet long, with an inscription describing the remarkable feat of engineering whereby the tunnellers from inside the city walls met the tunnellers cutting through the rock from outside the walls, was discovered in 1880 by a small boy who fell into the Pool of Siloam. Isaiah describes the terror which seized Jerusalem as "the Assyrian came down like a wolf on the fold" (*Isa.* 10: 28–32). A parley is held between the Rabshakeh and the defenders but Isaiah encourages the king to stand firm.

Events proved him right. Either plague broke out in the Assyrian army or troubles further north required its presence. At all events the siege was raised and Jerusalem for the time being was spared the fate of Sennacherib's other victims. But Hezekiah had to pay a heavy tribute. It was in connection with this conviction, that YHWH would not allow his people to be wholly exterminated, that Isaiah formulated his doctrine of the "remnant" that would remain even if disaster overtook Judah (*II* 19: 31). This theme was to play a large part in the thought of both old and new Israel (*Isa.* 10: 20–22; *Rom.* 9: 27–33).

The reigns of Manasseh and his son Amon (*II* 21: 1–26) touched a new level of depravity in Judah's religious life. Nothing that any of the kings of Israel or Judah before them had done could compare with the infamous record of this ill-starred pair. The author of *Kings* regards them as worse than heathens and says that Hezekiah's reformation might never have happened. Shrines were multiplied, worship of foreign deities was encouraged, astrology and necromancy were practised and human sacrifice again made its appearance.

By contrast, their successor Josiah (*II* 22: 1 – 23: 30) is given the highest praise accorded to any king in Israel or Judah. For it was in his reign that the most thorough-going reformation of the state religion took place that has so far been recorded. To read *II* 23: 1–25 is to realise why the prophets Amos, Hosea and Isaiah thundered against the travesty that the worship of YHWH had become. It was not the work of Manasseh alone that had transformed YHWH into a Canaanite Baal and his sanctuaries into brothels. Every imaginable variety of superstition and black magic is recorded as having been part of the worship of YHWH of Sinai in 622 B.C.

Yet it should not be overlooked that in the violent switches between the kind of religious policy that satisfied the deuteronomic views of the compiler of *Kings*, and what he regarded as rank paganism and a crime in the eyes of YHWH, it was not merely the private convictions of the monarch that were operative. A vassal of Assyria as part of his submission had to recognise Assyrian gods, and conversely the expulsion of these gods was tantamount to an act of rebellion or a sign that the overlord had no power at the time to enforce his supremacy. Religion and politics were two sides of the same coin.

The cause of the reformation is described as the discovery of "the book of the law" in the Temple during some repairs and, as we have seen (p. 132), this is generally identified with the main part of the book of *Deuteronomy* which may well have been composed secretly during the reign of Manasseh by the prophetic party. Josiah died at the battle of Megiddo in 609 B.C. fighting against the

Egyptians for Judah's political and religious freedom at a critical time in world affairs. Assyria had been defeated in 612 B.C. by the new empire of Babylon and the prophet *Nahum* voices the exultation of all the victims of Assyrian brutality at the news of the fall of her capital Nineveh. Egypt, her ally, met the same fate a few years later. The way was now open for Nebuchadnezzar to become master of the world.

In the process the tiny state of Judah—a vest-pocket kingdom like the remaining Near Eastern principalities—was disposed of by the Babylonian war machine. The book of *Kings* gives us the bare bones; the book of *Jeremiah*, who lived through these days and saw Jerusalem crushed, gives us the flesh and blood. In 598 B.C. Nebuchadnezzar ravaged Palestine and took Jerusalem. The king Jehoiachin and the leading citizens with the craftsmen were deported to Babylon, and a nominee of the conqueror, Zedekiah, was put on the throne (*II* 24: 1–20).

This man, however, unexpectedly rebelled ten years later and Nebuchadnezzar laid siege to Jerusalem. In 587 B.C. the city was taken and burnt: the walls were broken down: the Temple treasury was pillaged: the king was captured and had his eyes put out before being carried in chains to Babylon. A second and greater deportation of the population took place and none was left but "the poor of the land". The book of *Lamentations* paints a vivid picture of Jerusalem's plight. Babylon appointed a regent, Gedaliah, who was shortly assassinated and the guerrillas fled to Egypt (*II* 25: 1–30). Thus to all intents and purposes Israel was finished and the promises made to Abraham and Moses were a dead letter. The land that was to flow with milk and honey now flowed with blood and tears.

I and II CHRONICLES

Church History

I AND II CHRONICLES, like *I and II Samuel* and *I and II Kings*, are really one book divided for convenience. Unlike the books from *Joshua* to *Kings*, *Chronicles* does not come under the category of Former Prophets in the Hebrew original, but is actually the last book in the Hebrew Old Testament, being regarded as a kind of supplement and placed among the Writings (see p. 142) since most of it has already been covered in *Samuel* and *Kings*. It forms the first part of what was originally a tripartite work by the same author, which might well be called the Religious History of the People of God. The second and third parts consist of the books of *Ezra* and *Nehemiah*.

Who the Chronicler was is uncertain. It has been suggested that it may have been Ezra himself. More probably it was some unknown writer living in Jerusalem about 300 B.C. and attached in some way to the Temple. He seems to have a special interest in its music. The distinctive feature of *I* and *II Chronicles* is that it covers the history of Israel from Adam to the end of the Exile almost exclusively from the religious angle, concentrating in particular on the Temple as the focal point of Israel's life.

By the time *Chronicles* was written the turbulent years of the divided monarchy were long past. The fall of Jerusalem, which brought the record of the Former Prophets to a close, in the last chapter of *II Kings*, was now seen not as the end of Israel's story but as its true beginning. Fifty years of exile in Babylon were over. During this time, under the guidance of great prophets like Ezekiel and Second-Isaiah (*Isa.* 40–55) the collapse of the kingdoms had come to be recognised as a necessary discipline imposed by God upon his recalcitrant people. The Exile had been followed by a return to the homeland and a complete reorientation of thought and action. The Temple had been rebuilt under the impulse of Haggai and Zechariah, the walls of Jerusalem had been restored by the leadership of Nehemiah, and the Law had become the national charter at the instigation of Ezra.

Israel was now a little theocracy without political ambitions or military importance. Its life was built around the Law and centred on the Temple. The real significance of its past history was therefore felt to lie not in its wars and diplomatic successes, its valiant kings and farsighted statesmen but in Israel's role as the custodian of the truth about God, as the inheritor of the promises, as the bearer of the Law. In a sense this had always been so, and, as we have seen in the books of the Former Prophets, the writing of biblical history was always subservient to theology and facts were seldom recorded for their own sakes but rather as features of a canvas whose total purpose was to illustrate and teach and admonish in accordance with the revealed will of God.

But in the work of the Chronicler this is carried a stage further because Israel was that much nearer a true conception of its mission and destiny. There is no wilful distortion of factual history in the work of the Chronicler any more than there is in the books of the Former Prophets, but rather an even more selective approach to history. It is now not merely a matter of omitting battles and political developments that seemed of secondary importance to writers whose concern was with the lesssons God had been teaching his people, but rather, in the case of the Chronicler, of a historian who is prepared to omit practically the whole record of the northern kingdom from the Disruption onwards because he considers that people who had cut themselves off from the meeting-place with the living God at Jerusalem were no longer part of his commonwealth.

The Chronicler has ample material for his narrative—the Pentateuch, the Former Prophets, and other sources oral and written—possibly the annals, commentaries and lives of the prophets which he repeatedly mentions as his authorities. Sometimes he quotes extracts from *Samuel* and *Kings* verbatim, at other times he adds details of an apparently reliable character which *Samuel* and *Kings* have not included. A fuller description of Hezekiah's tunnel is given, for example, in *II* 32: 30 than in *II Kings* 20: 20. More doubtful is the account of Manasseh's repentance and religious reform (*II* 33: 10–16), which may be true but may also be the Chronicler's escape from the problem of why such a notoriously wicked king should have reigned for such a long time.

But on the whole this is history written with such a strong religious bias that its factual value compared with *Samuel* and *Kings* is relatively small. From the point of view of obtaining a picture of the rise and fall of Israel as a state, with the dramatic clash of personalities, the impact of the prophets, the battle for power, the political tensions, the moral and religious conflicts, *Chronicles* has little or nothing to tell us that we have not already had more vividly and realistically and accurately recorded in *Samuel* and *Kings*.

The real value of the book is in its reflection of the attitude of mind which prevailed after the Exile when Jerusalem and its environs were all that was left of Israel's empire. Under the guidance of prophets and priests Israel was determined that never again would the scandals of the monarchy be repeated. Idolatry, necromancy and astrology were as much a dead letter as public immorality, flaunting luxury and royal despotism. The nation had become a religious community fulfilling God's charge to them at Sinai to be "a kingdom of priests and an holy nation"

(*Ex.* 19: 6) and therefore governed by the provisions of the Law or Torah administered by the priesthood.

That the sins of the flesh came to be replaced by the sins of the spirit—intolerance, self-righteousness and casuistry—was a gradual development which reached its peak in New Testament times. But in the meanwhile the Temple and its services were not only the symbol of the holy nation but the very life-blood of the men who set the tone for the whole existence of the people of God after the Exile. It is as one of these that the Chronicler rewrites the story of Israel. The kingdom that David had created, the genius with which he had made Zion its capital, and the piety with which he had installed the Ark as the focus of faith and the perpetual memorial of the covenant of Sinai had captured the hearts and minds of this purged and chastened Israel.

Politically the kingdom had vanished but the Temple and the holy city remained as tokens of the "sure mercies of David" (*Isa.* 55: 3), the pledge of the unique covenant and vocation of the people of God, the guarantee of the Presence of YHWH, and the hope of better things to come. Writing therefore from a time when the Temple had been restored to something of its former glory, and when a highly organised and strictly controlled priesthood ensured that ceremonial law and civil law alike conformed to the terms of the Torah, the Chronicler saw the whole history of his people as leading up to this joyous state and judged kings and commoners of past days according to whether they had hindered or advanced so obvious a fulfilment of the will of God.

"*The sure mercies of David*"

THE FIRST nine chapters of *Chronicles* consist of a selective genealogy of the people of God from Adam up to some time after the return from exile. It is in keeping with the Chronicler's viewpoint that Cain and his descendants are omitted as are the royal families of the northern kingdom. Special attention on the other hand is paid to the tribes of Judah and Benjamin, and to the tribe of Levi which by now has become the recognised priestly caste (*I* 1: 1–9: 44).

The remainder of the first book is devoted to the reign of David (*I* 10: 1–29: 30). Saul's death is mentioned only because it opens the way for David's reign, and the David who emerges is not the virile, fallible and attractive mortal whom we have come to know in *Samuel*. The Bathsheba affair is not referred to nor is Absalom's rebellion. The down-and-outs who surrounded David in his early days (*I Sam.* 22: 2) now become "a great host, like the host of God" (*I* 12: 22).

Glossing over the preliminary reign at Hebron, the Chronicler has David quickly installed in Jerusalem where his main concern is the recovery of the Ark and the organisation of a proper levitical priesthood. Excerpts from *Samuel* provide a thread of historical continuity in David's reign, but the

Chronicler is obviously more concerned with the arrangements which David makes before his death for the building of the Temple and the maintenance of its services.

Similarly in the case of Solomon, the rather shady intrigue by which he acceded to his father's throne is suppressed, and the predominant impression which the Chronicler wishes to leave is that this was the king whom God allowed to be the builder of the Temple which his great father had planned, under divine inspiration (*II* 1 : 1 – 9 : 31). The rest of the book (*II* 10 : 1 – 36 : 23) follows the fortunes of Rehoboam and his successors on the throne of Judah, largely ignoring the northern kingdom, and awarding praise or blame to each monarch on the same principle as the compiler of *Kings*, until the Exile brings the monarchy to a close.

Nevertheless although *Chronicles* cannot compete with *Samuel* and *Kings* on grounds either of historical accuracy or vivid narrative, it is of considerable importance as indicating a vital stage in the transformation of old Israel into new Israel, a halfway house, as it were, between Israel's conception of itself as a chosen nation and as a chosen community It is in *Chronicles* that we first encounter the idea of a Church, although in a sense Israel had always regarded itself as a worshipping congregation bound by covenant in a special relationship to God.

But we have seen how difficult it was for priest and prophet to keep this conception in the forefront of the minds of a people who were necessarily involved in the political and economic struggle for existence, who felt deeply the call of national independence and who were exposed to the insidious attractions of power and prestige on the one hand and sensuous polytheism and a low morality on the other. Now, however, many of these factors had ceased to operate. In its political backwater as a helpless vassal state, and above all through the experience of the Exile, Israel had had an opportunity to re-think its vocation and mission.

There was still a strong race-consciousness, intensified indeed rather than decreased, and there was still the hope of a revival of past glories. The lure of political and economic independence, the human desire for a large place in the sun and pride in their former hegemony in Palestine were never far absent from the popular mind and even from the thoughts of the religious leaders. But side by side with this, stimulated and encouraged by the work of Jeremiah, Ezekiel and Second-Isaiah, was the growing recognition that it was not in this direction that the true meaning of God's promises to Israel was to be found.

The best minds of Israel turned more and more to their religious vocation and their unique witness. They became more and more conscious that as they looked back over their past story, the element that mattered most was the line of obedience that linked them through David and Moses with Abraham, the friend of God. In this, rather than in the chequered pattern of political intrigue, military campaigns and material success, lay their true destiny. All these things were inevitably part of the picture, chapters in the story, but in retrospect not of the essence of a people of God.

In singling out David as the key-figure in this new conception of Israel's role, the Chronicler was not only interpreting the mind of his times but was saying something of profound significance for the Christian Church. For when we call ourselves the new Israel, and recognise the historic continuity that links the Church of the New Testament with the Israel of the Old Testament, it is not with the machinations of these petty oriental potentates whom the Chronicler largely disregards that we feel ourselves linked, but rather with the elements which he stressed, the legacy of Abraham, Moses and David, the Faith, the Law and the Worship.

However much we recognise that the animal sacrifices of the Temple, the rigid demarcation of priests and Levites, the meticulous observance of ritual feast and ceremonial law are part of the heritage of old Israel which was superseded by the new dispensation in Jesus Christ, we are still debtors to the Chronicler's conception of the nature of Israel as a worshipping community. We can still share his deep sense of the beauty of holiness, the ministry of music, and the solemnity of the house of God.

When he links the place of Abraham's sacrifice of Isaac on mount Moriah (*Gen.* 22) with the angelic appearance at the threshing floor of Araunah the Jebusite (*I:* 21), both events consecrating the site of the altar in Solomon's Temple (*II* 3: 1), we feel that this is no flight of fancy but a deep sense of the perennial mystery of sacrifice and the continuity of God's revelation in history which was ultimately fulfilled and transcended in the sacrifice of Jesus. When he puts into David's mouth the superb prayer in *I* 29: 10–19 we can well see how the legacy of Old Testament piety has enriched the worship of the Church and how the psalms that sprang from such a faith can still express the deepest moods of Christian devotion.

Above all in seeing the worshipping community of Israel as the true inheritors of the kingdom of David, with Zion at its centre, the Chronicler expressed and furthered the growing conviction of the coming of a messianic Kingdom with a messianic son of David as its governor. Whatever else Israel thought of as characterising that golden age to come its essence was always the religious side of David's achievements—the holy city, the sacred courts, the hymns of praise. This was the heart of the everlasting Kingdom into which the Church has entered as its heritage, and which from now on in the Old Testament features more and more in the story of Israel until it reaches its true evaluation in the proclamation of the Gospel of Jesus Christ.

EZRA-NEHEMIAH

Exile in Babylon

THERE IS A curious gap in the biblical record between the end of the second book of *Kings* and the beginning of the book of *Ezra*. As we have seen, First and Second *Chronicles*, which now separate *Kings* and *Ezra*, do nothing to fill the gap since the Chronicler covers the same ground as the Former Prophets. Yet it was in this period of fifty years during which they were in exile in Babylon that the people of the Old Testament underwent an experience which next to that of the Exodus was the most formative in their whole history.

It was in exile, deprived of the outward and visible tokens of God's Presence—the holy city and the sacred Temple—that they learned that God meant more to them in adversity than in prosperity. It was there that they learned finally that their vocation was not to be like other nations, and that the glamour of power and the lure of prestige alike were meretricious and tawdry. The message that the prophets from Amos onwards had been proclaiming for almost two centuries acquired a new reality. It became clear that the disaster which had overtaken Israel was no accident of history, far less the superior power of the gods of the Babylonians, but

the judgment of YHWH upon his wayward people from whom more had been demanded because so much more had been given.

When the Exile was seen as a discipline and a call to repentance it became a fruitful time of reflection and reorientation. It marked indeed the beginning of a new era for Israel. For it is from this death to the high hopes of David's kingdom that the rebirth of the old body politic into the body ecclesiastic, which we know from the pages of the New Testament, can be traced. Here the seed was sown of the conception of Israel as a Church, a kingdom of priests, a peculiar people. All the distinctive marks of later Judaism—as exemplified by the Pharisees and Sadducees of the gospels—find their origins in the Exile; the authority of the professional priesthood, the supremacy of the Torah, rigid legalism and ceremonial exactitude. It is to the Exile that we must look for the beginning of the synagogue, and the initial stages of the process that turned circumcision, sabbath observance and dietary laws into fetishes.

On all counts therefore the period of the Exile was one of supreme significance. Yet there is no straightforward record of the sojourn in Babylon in the Bible. It is not certain what proportion of the population of Judah was de-

Exile lead to:
authority of Priesthood
supremacy of Torah
rigid legalism
ceremonial exactitude
synaagogue
fetishes in rules

ported in 587 B.C. (cf. *Jer.* 52: 28–30 with *II Kings* 24: 14; 25: 11), how well or harshly the exiles were treated (cf. *Jer.* 29: 5–7 with *Isa.* 42: 22; 47: 6) or how many returned to the ruined city of Jerusalem fifty years later. We can read in the book of *Jeremiah* the warnings that the prophet uttered before the fall of Jerusalem, his insistence that the future of the people of God lay not in blind devotion to a doomed city and Temple but in acceptance of exile as an opportunity to reach a deeper understanding of their vocation. We can sense from such a psalm as *Ps.* 137 the dejection of those who found this too lofty a doctrine, and who sat down by the waters of Babylon and wept when they remembered Zion.

In the prophecies of Ezekiel, himself an exile, we hear the voice which more than any other, save the unknown prophet of the captivity whose utterances are contained in *Isiah* 40–55, turned dejection into hope and infused a sense of purpose into his despondent countrymen. Not all the prophets had been as pessimistic as Amos or as convinced of the inexorability of God's judgment on Israel. Hosea, Isaiah and Jeremiah had all encouraged the people to look for mercy beyond judgment and to think in terms of God's forgiveness revealing itself in an eventual return of a chastened and repentant people to the Holy Land.

Accordingly when Ezekiel issued his blueprint for a new kind of Israel (see p. 267), a community based on allegiance to the Law and centred on the worship of the Temple, a theocratic society conscious of its unique role, he was able to influence a sufficient number of people to seize the opportunity when it arose to implement his plan. When, in addition, the greatest of all the Old Testament prophets, Second-Isaiah, proclaimed that the day of deliverance was at hand, that God had pardoned his erring people and was ready to give them a fresh start, the stage was set for the return to Palestine which occupies the beginning of the book of *Ezra*.

World events had moved fast since Nebuchadnezzar had sacked Jerusalem in 587 B.C. and carried off its people to Babylon. A new power and a resolute monarch brought the short lived empire of Babylon to an end and in 539 B.C. Cyrus of Persia dealt with Babylon as Babylon had dealt with Assyria, and made himself master of the greatest expanse of territory hitherto ruled by one man in the ancient world. Judah in common with other provinces of the Babylonian empire became part of a Persian satrapy.

Unlike his predecessors, however, Cyrus preferred to leave his subject peoples in their own lands and at once set about restoring displaced minorities to their native countries. A clay cylinder now in the British Museum and containing the royal edict indicates that this humane policy extended to all exiles in his dominions. For the Jews, however, schooled by Second-Isaiah to see Cyrus' rise to power as the direct intervention of God to set his people free, this new possibility was tangible proof that the deprivations of exile had been accepted as penance and that this return to their homeland was the token of God's forgiveness.

Having already seen that the Chronicler interprets historical events in a highly theological fashion, we shall not be surprised to find that the book of *Ezra* paints a picture of the return of the exiles in glowing colours which require some toning down. Not only so but it is also fairly certain that the Chronicler, writing about two centuries after the events, confused the order of developments by making Ezra precede Nehemiah. This is easily explained when we note that in the period covered by the books of *Ezra* and *Nehemiah* there were on the throne of Persia six kings bearing the names of Darius, Xerxes (Ahasuerus in the Bible) and Artaxerxes. The Chronicler does not distinguish between Darius I and II, Xerxes I and II and Artaxerxes I and II.

If the arrival of Ezra in Jerusalem recorded in *Ezra* 7:1–8 was in the seventh year of Artaxerxes II and not of Artaxerxes I, it would mean that Nehemiah reached Palestine in 445 B.C. (the twentieth year of Artaxerxes I—*Neh.* 2: 1–11) to be followed by Ezra in 398 B.C. Not only does this eliminate a number of awkward problems in the two books under consideration but it harmonises with the picture of the situation given by the prophets Haggai and Zechariah (see pp. 301–303). On this view the historical sequence would be as follows: the Jews who returned to Palestine after the edict of Cyrus in 538 B.C. were too preoccupied with reestablishing themselves in a shattered city and its surrounding countryside to embark on any large scale rebuilding.

It was not until 520 B.C., with the advent of Haggai and Zechariah and the enthusiasm they instilled into the inhabitants, that the rebuilding of the Temple was undertaken and completed in four years. More than half a century elapsed before the rebuilding of the city walls was carried out under the inspiring leadership of Nehemiah, and almost another half century before Ezra came to Jerusalem and promulgated the Law as the basis of the life of the community. This solution of the vexed problem of the relationship between Ezra and Nehemiah is not without its own difficulties but on the whole it appears to square with the evidence better than any other.

Return to Jerusalem

(*Ezra* 1: 1 – 10: 44)

THE CHRONICLER naturally regards the imperial edict of Cyrus, permitting all exiles to return, as being directly prompted by YHWH and specifically designed to restore the Temple at Jerusalem. Those who choose to remain in Babylon are to contribute in kind towards the venture. According to Josephus many of the Jews in exile had prospered— clay tablets recording the transactions of a large Jewish trading firm of Murashu and Sons testify to their financial acumen among Gentiles even in those days—and they would obviously prefer the comforts of Babylonian civilisation to a precarious future in Palestine. The sacred vessels of the Temple are marvellously restored intact, although the narrative of *II Kings* 24: 13 had described how Nebuchadnezzar had melted them down for bullion. Sheshbazzar, possibly the Shenazzar of *I Chron.* 3: 18, and thus a son of Jehoiachin—or Jeconiah—(*II Kings* 25: 27) is leader of the returning exiles (*Ezra* 1: 1–11).

Although the numbers of returning exiles given in *Ezra* 2: 1–70 probably represent a total of small migrations over a long period rather than a spectacular response to the edict of Cyrus, it should be noted that the signs of the future rigid discrimination between priests and people are already present (vv. 61–62). Zerubbabel, a grandson of Jehoiachin, appears to have succeeded Sheshbazzar as the secular head of the community, while Joshua, as high priest, was the supreme ecclesiastical authority. At their instigation the altar of burnt offerings was restored among the ruins of the Temple in order that at least some of the ordinances of worship could be observed (*Ezra* 3: 1–6).

Two years later, the foundations of the Temple itself were laid amid scenes of rejoicing among the young mingled with sadness among the old, who wept for the departed glory of Solomon's masterpiece (*Ezra* 3: 7–13). To begin with, offers of help with the work were made by the neighbouring Samaritans, the descendants of the remnant of the northern kingdom, now assimilated to the mixed racial group which had been settled in that area by the Assyrians when Samaria was sacked in 722 B.C. This offer was scornfully rejected on the grounds that the Samari-

tans were no longer part of the covenant people (*Ezra* 4: 1–3), whereupon the Samaritans invoked the authority of the Persian army to veto any further building operations in view of Jerusalem's bad record as a trouble spot (*Ezra* 4: 4–24). The long term result of this action on the part of the returned exiles was that the Samaritans broke off all relations with the Jerusalem Jews, claimed to be the rightful inheritors of the Mosaic tradition, built a rival temple on Mt. Gerizim, and ended up as the sworn enemies of the Jews as the gospels testify.

The Chronicler thus accounts for the fact that it was not until 520 B.C., seventeen years after the return of the first exiles, that any serious attempt was made to restore the Temple. He rightly attributes the impetus towards this pious task as coming from the prophets Haggai and Zechariah (*Ezra* 5: 1–2), but the evidence of the prophets themselves contained in the books that bear their names is that the real reason for failure to undertake the rebuilding of the Temple was not opposition from outside but apathy within. It is doubtful whether even the foundations of the Temple were laid at any time before 520 B.C., far less accompanied by the scenes of enthusiasm and the frustrated zeal which the Chronicler feels must have been the appropriate attitude of a grateful but thwarted people.

The more reliable contemporary witness of Haggai and Zechariah, however, would point to the conclusion that the families of those Jews who had survived the devastation of 587 B.C. and had remained in Palestine, were in no mood to embark upon the rebuilding of their holy city, and that those who returned in 537 B.C. were too few and too preoccupied to undertake any large scale communal project. The damage caused by Nebuchadnezzar's troops had been enormous. Former enemies of Israel such as the Edomites had been quick to profit by their downfall and hastened to occupy their lands. The bitter resentment of the survivors is expressed by the prophet *Obadiah*.

Poverty, taxation, drought and famine had robbed the rump of Israel of any drive to do more than eke out a living on the few square miles that were left to them. The book of *Malachi* written shortly before the arrival of Nehemiah reflects the sombre plight of the Jews in Palestine in this period. Nevertheless both the Chronicler and the books of Haggai and Zechariah agree that by 520 B.C. once the necessary leadership was given the work of reconstructing the Temple was taken in hand and completed in four years. The Chronicler accounts for this happy issue by a reversal of the royal interdict (*Ezra* 5: 3 – 6: 19).

As a prelude to the arrival of Ezra the scribe from Babylon, the Chronicler sets the stage by noting that on the occasion of the first passover solemnised after the rededication of the Temple, a line was drawn between those Israelites who had returned from Babylon together with those who shared their exclusive attitude, and those Israelites who had not been in exile and who had contaminated themselves by associating and intermarrying with their Palestinian neighbours, "the people of the land" (*Ezra* 6: 20–22). It is clear from this and from subsequent developments that the ex-Babylonian element, like the ex-Egyptian element at the time of the Exodus, was to be the dominating influence in the constitution and outlook of the Israelite people.

According to the Chronicler, it is at this stage that Ezra comes to Jerusalem from Babylon, armed with special authority from the king of Persia, and accompanied by a large retinue of priests and attendants bearing a generous offering for the Temple (*Ezra* 7: 1 – 8: 36). As we have seen (p. 210) there is good reason to believe that Ezra's arrival in Jerusalem was some time later when the walls of Jerusalem had been rebuilt. It is assumed here that the walls are complete (*Ezra* 9: 9) although the book of *Nehemiah* describes their construction.

Ezra's first reaction on arrival is horrified amazement at the spectacle of Israelites having contracted mixed marriages with non-Jewish women (*Ezra* 9: 1–15). Moved by his righteous indignation, the whole community assembles· at Jerusalem and agrees to divorce all foreign wives and disown their children. Priests and people alike are guilty and the names of the offenders are recorded (*Ezra* 10: 1–44).

Nehemiah

(Neh. 1: 1 – 13: 31)

IT IS A relief to turn from this ecclesiastical bigot to the more attractive character of Nehemiah.

As one of his sources for the book of *Ezra*, the Chronicler had apparently at his disposal some memoir of Ezra written in the first person (*Ezra* 7 : 27 – 9 : 15). Whether or how much he altered this material is a matter for the experts, but there is general agreement that in the book of *Nehemiah* he has used personal memoirs written by Nehemiah himself and that this part of his work (*Neh.* 1 : 1 – 7 : 5 ; 13 : 4 – 31) has been faithfully incorporated without alteration.

Nehemiah describes himself as a personal attendant of the Persian king, but as one who had never forgotten the land of his fathers. Moved by what he had heard of the ruinous state of the holy city, intensified by some more recent attack, he sought and obtained permission and material help from the king to visit Jerusalem and rebuild its walls. Opposition from neighbouring Samaritans and uncertainty as to what support he might receive from the inhabitants of Jerusalem, compelled the new governor to inspect the state of the walls under cover of darkness (*Neh.* 1 : 1 – 2 : 16). Stirred by his appeal the people of Jerusalem and the surrounding district rallied to the task and the work was begun (*Neh.* 2 : 17 – 3 : 32). Threats of interference from various hostile elements in Palestine led by Sanballat, governor of Samaria, and all naturally strongly opposed to any resurgence of Jewish nationalist ambitions, were countered by arming the builders (*Neh.* 4 : 1 – 23).

Within the Jewish community itself, Nehemiah took strong measures to establish a contented society by putting a stop to usury and slavery and by setting an example himself as governor of Judah of renouncing the normal perquisites of his office (*Neh.* 5 : 1 – 19). Eventually, despite further threats from outside and some disaffection among the people themselves, the repairs to the walls were completed in less than two months (*Neh.* 6 : 1 – 7 : 5). The register of the exiles that follows (*Neh.* 7 : 6 – 73) is more or less the same as that in *Ezra* 2.

The Chronicler now leaves aside the memoirs of Nehemiah to describe the solemn ceremony at which the Israelites, secure within the walls of their holy city, adopt the Mosaic Law as their rule of life. It is unlikely that if Ezra had been in Jerusalem since the events described in *Ezra* 7–8 he would have waited until now to complete the mission which he had undertaken. We may therefore take it that the reading of the Law by Ezra, and its acceptance by the people as their charter (*Neh.* 8 : 1–6), was the purpose of his return from Babylon following on the completion of the restoration of the spiritual and secular symbols of Israel as the people of God.

What Ezra brought from Babylon and read, described as "the book of the law of Moses", was doubtless the codification of the ritual and ethical sections of the Pentateuch which had been compiled during the Exile. Now it becomes the very fabric of the community's existence and from this time on, i.e. approximately 400 B.C., the faith and practice of Israel are to be dominated by it. As a fitting conclusion to Ezra's promulgation of the Law, the feast of tabernacles is revived, linking the desert days of the Exodus with the new constitution (*Neh.* 8: 7-18).

The reading of the Law has brought home to Israel, more than the rebuilding of Temple and city, that theirs is a unique heritage. They can be true to it henceforward only if they keep themselves free of all contamination with the heathenism which brought disaster upon their forefathers. Accordingly in the great act of repentance described in *Neh.* 9-10 it is a people "separated from all strangers" (*Neh.* 9: 2) who confess their sins and the sins of their ancestors, who listen to a recital of the wondrous forbearance and mercy of God from the days of Abraham to this present time, who see his hand in all their story and who now in solemn covenant renew their allegiance to the God of their fathers.

The whole of ch. 9 in spirit and intention shows how succesfully the great prophets had done their work and how deep an impression they had made upon the national conscience. "Thou hast done right but we have done wickedly" (*Neh.* 9: 33) is the theme of the recital which ends by acknowledging that the present plight of God's chosen people, vassals of a foreign power, mere tenants in the land that once was their own, is just retribution for their failure to listen to the word which God had spoken to them through his servants the prophets.

Yet when we turn to ch. 10 to read the terms of the covenant which God's people now pledge themselves to observe, the striking difference between the nature of the service of God as outlined by the prophets and the service of God as understood after the Exile is at once apparent. The people pledge themselves "to walk in God's law which was given by Moses" (*Neh.* 10: 29) but the emphasis is not on the Ten Commandments, or on the basic principles of justice, mercy and humility which had been the burden of the prophetic message, but on racial exclusiveness and ceremonial obligations.

The marks of the people of God by which the world will know that they are a covenant community are to be abstention from marriages with all but racially pure Israelites, strict observance of the sabbath, regular payment of the tax for the upkeep of the Temple, and the due rendering of the proper offerings at the proper times, not forgetting the tithes for the priesthood (*Neh.* 10: 30-39). Following a record of the distribution of the population in Jerusalem and the district of Judah generally (*Neh.* 11), and a list of the priests and other ecclesiastical officials (*Neh.* 12: 1-26), the dedication of the wall which was completed in *Neh.* 6: 15 is celebrated with a service of praise (*Neh.* 12: 27-47).

For the conclusion of the book the Chronicler reverts to the memoirs of Nehemiah himself (*Neh.* 13: 4-31). From this it appears that Nehemiah had revisited the court of Persia in 433 B.C. i.e. twelve years after his arrival in Jerusalem (*Neh.* 13: 6). On his return to Jerusalem for a second term of office he finds that the more liberal element in the priesthood has violated the strict doctrine of apartheid, in particular by providing his old enemy the governor of Ammon with accommodation in the Temple precincts, that the proper offerings for the maintenance of the ministry of the Temple are not being made, that the sanctity of the sabbath is being violated, and that the rule on mixed marriages is being disregarded. On all these matters he takes appropriate action and on this note the Chronicler brings his tripartite volume to a close.

It may be noted that Nehemiah's attitude to mixed marriages does not extend to compulsory divorce, which is added reason for thinking that Ezra's more rigorist approach (*Ezra* 10: 1–3) was a subsequent development. It may also be suspected that these various abuses in *Neh.* 13 refer to the earlier days of Nehemiah's administration. It would be unlikely that an absence of what seems to be only a few months would be enough to undo the work of twelve years' vigorous government by this unusually forceful character.

A Holy Nation

WITH THE LAST chapter of *Nehemiah* the tale of Israel's vicissitudes comes to an end. The rest of the Old Testament consists of the Wisdom literature, psalms and prophecy. We have to wait until we reach the Apocrypha before the thread of history is taken up again, and by that time we are already in the period of the Hellenistic empire, founded on the conquests of Alexander the Great.

Until 331 B.C. therefore, when Alexander became master of the civilised world, the Jews remained as we have seen them in the pages of the Chronicler: a tiny unimportant fragment of the Persian empire, a rump of David's kingdom, without status, wealth or prospects.

Yet the Chronicler has done his work well. He has left us a picture of how the exiles reconstituted the life of the chosen people on the scanty acres of Palestine that remained to them, and how without royal house or means of defence they yet contrived to maintain their identity and cherish their unique heritage. It is clear from the pages of his work—implemented by the words of those wisdom scribes and prophets who fall within the ensuing period—that the pattern had been established which would from now on be followed until the next rebirth of Israel was heralded by John the Baptist.

The Exile had shaped the future. Permitted to live, so far as we can make out, in self-contained settlements in Babylon, the Jews of the Exile had had an opportunity to strengthen their national consciousness, to reflect on their past glories and to mould their life in accordance with what they believed to be the Mosaic tradition. Surrounded as they were by the wealth and splendour of Babylon they knew themselves to be the possessors of even greater treasures. When they had entered Canaan the Mosaic tradition had been hard put to it to withstand the allurements of a superior civilisation, and the tension between the beckoning finger of material progress and the restraining hand of an austere revelation had ended in compromise, and eventually in the triumph of those who wanted Israel to be like other nations.

But the loss of the kingdom and the commentary of the prophets had changed the situation. Even if "the poor of the land" who were left behind at the Exile reverted to paganism, and many of those who went to Babylon succumbed to the attractions of life in a prosperous empire, the hard core of those who were faithful to the covenant tradition, and who recognised the voice of the prophets as the voice of God, knew that they were the inheritors of a unique legacy which marked them out despite their unhappy state as custodians of something infinitely precious which must be preserved and handed on. They knew that despite the opulence that surrounded them they alone had the secret of true greatness.

It was this sense of being the bearers of a priceless heritage, which must at all costs be preserved, that motivated ultra-orthodox Jews of the calibre of Nehemiah and Ezra. That it issued in an exclusive policy which emphasised the differences between the people of God and the rest of the world by a frantic attempt to avoid the contamination of heathenism in any form—even to the shattering of family life—is a tragic comment on the fallibility of man's best intentions. The aim of the religious leaders of the community was indeed a noble one. The life of the returned exiles was to be based on the Law of God. The sins of greed and lust, of cruelty and in-

justice, which had brought just retribution on the Israel that had been must find no place in the Israel that was to be.

The new community of Judah, tucked away in a backwater of the Persian empire, was to be a spectacle for all the world of how a whole people could live in accordance with the revealed will of God. In the event, human nature being what it is, it was by concentration on such external trivialities as sabbath observance, payment of tithes and performance of ritual that the post exilic community sought to demonstrate its obedience. Moreover, by seeking to keep itself unspotted from the world, it became a harsh intolerant unloved pariah among the nations, a people to be shunned rather than emulated.

This was far from what the prophets, even Ezekiel, the father of Judaism, had envisaged. It was in the spirit of a Jeremiah or a Hosea that the writer of the little book of Ruth, which appeared about this time as a counterblast to the inhuman segregationist policy of Nehemiah and Ezra, drew his picture of the gentle Moabitess who in accordance with the law must be excluded from the congregation of Israel (Neh. 13: 1), and who yet mothered king David's grandsire. Such too was the protest of the writer of the contemporary book of Jonah who, in his tale of the dour unpleasant prophet who refused to countenance the admission of Gentiles into the company of God's people, has left us a merciless caricature of the Ezras of that and every other age of religious intolerance.

Yet in the providence of God

the folly and myopic zeal of godly men was turned to his own good purposes. In the Persian age and that which succeeded it, Israel would have been powerless to resist the encroachment of pagan religion and philosophy and of an indifferent morality, had it not been for the protection of the spiritual wall which Nehemiah symbolised by the stone and lime of Jerusalem's battlements. Within the confines of the holy city, and the hard shell of exclusiveness with which he and Ezra fenced in the life of the people of God, the heart of the prophetic age still beat strongly.

The obedience of God may have manifested itself in the meticulous observance of ceremonial and the trivial niceties of the moral law, but these were but the outer crust within which the broad humanity of the prophetic legacy lay waiting for the touch of one greater than Moses and the prophets to bring it out into the full light of day.

ESTHER

ONE OF THE many difficulties in reading the Bible today is that if we attempt to treat it as a continuous story from *Genesis* to *Revelation* of the choice and mission of a people of God, telling of the Acts of God in history and revealing his will and purpose for mankind, we run up against the fact that as well as being the prelude to the Christian gospel, the Old Testament is also the collected sacred writings of the Jewish Church. It therefore contains a generally developing narrative of events, which we have so far encountered from *Genesis* to *Nehemiah*, tracing the story from its beginning in the call of Abraham through the rise and fall of Israel as a nation until it reaches the point where Israel has become a religious community settled on a tiny fragment of Persian imperial territory in the fourth century B.C.

But the Jewish scriptures also contain the poetry, prophecy and wisdom literature of the Hebrews and this is what we find from now on until we reach the end of the Old Testament. This is also part of God's revelation and an essential element in the preparation for the coming of Christ, but there is no longer a continuous thread of historical development into which the various books can be fitted. It would be comparatively easy if we could say that what is left of the Old Testament consists of the religious writings of this small community in and around Jerusalem between the days of Nehemiah and Ezra and the advent of Christianity. But this is not so.

Some of the remaining books of the Old Testament undoubtedly fall within this period. *Esther*, *Job*, *Proverbs*, *Ecclesiastes* and *Daniel* all reflect in one form or another the way in which the thought of post-exilic Judaism was moving in the few centuries that remained before the Christian era. On the other hand the *Psalms* are a collection of hymns used in the services of the Temple at this time but dating, many of them, from the days of the monarchy. Similarly the prophets, from *Isaiah* to *Malachi*, cover a period from about 750 B.C., while Israel and Judah were still a divided kingdom, to somewhere in the third century B.C.

Thus we cannot any longer follow the historical thread which has guided us from *Genesis* to *Nehemiah* but must look at each book as we meet it, expecting to find some fitting into the background of the Jewish Church after the time of Ezra, while others, notably the prophets, will have to be seen in the light of chapters in the story of the people of God which have already been dealt with. The alternative to this method would have been to make some arbitrary chronological rearrangement of the order of the books of the Old Testament which would have raised as many problems as it solved. Let us therefore, as it were, leave the path which we have been following from the days of the patriarchs to the period of Ezra and Nehemiah. We shall come back to it at various points in the remainder of the Old Testament, principally in the book of *Daniel*, and shall rejoin it finally in the period of the Apocrypha which then leads straight into the New Testament.

Meanwhile we turn aside to look first at the book of *Esther*, which was presumably placed at this point in the Old Testament because it purports to deal with an incident in the Persian empire somewhere about the period covered in the books of *Ezra* and *Nehemiah*. In the same way the book of *Ruth*, although, as we have seen (pp. 160–161), it is a protest against the racial policy of Ezra and Nehemiah, is placed in the Old Testament after the book of *Judges* because the events it describes are supposed to have taken place "in the days when the judges ruled" (*Ruth* 1: 1).

It is difficult to understand how the book of *Esther* ever came to be included in the Old Testament. The puzzle is to find any trace of religious conviction in it. The name of God is never mentioned, the atmosphere is one of political intrigue and the action revolves round the whims of a despot. There is in *Esther* little charity and no mercy but an abundance of hatred and savage slaughter. It was admitted into the Jewish canon with considerable misgivings, since the religious sentiments contained in the additions to *Esther* in the Greek version of the Old Testa-

ment had to be relegated to the Apocrypha (see p.319). The Christian Church accepted it with reluctance; the New Testament does not refer to it; Luther wished it had never been written and most commentators since his day have deplored it.

It can only have surmounted the initial hurdle of admission into the Jewish canon because it purports to give the origin of one of the most popular festivals in the Jewish Church. *Esther* is not history although the historical background in the court of Xerxes I of Persia is realistic enough, but is a dramatic tale of the calibre of the Arabian Nights, full of colour and fantasy. It probably dates from the days of the Maccabees in the second century B.C. when a story with this kind of nationalistic flavour would have an undoubted appeal.

The narrative is straightforward and needs no comment. King Ahasuerus (Xerxes), having disposed of his queen selects the beautiful Esther as her successor. Haman, his pompous vizier, takes umbrage at the studied contempt of Mordecai a Jew who, unknown to the Persians, is the queen's cousin. Haman seeks to wipe out the affront by a wholesale massacre of the Jews but his plan is frustrated by the intervention of the queen, who discloses her race and saves her people. The tables are turned and Haman dies on the gallows he had prepared for Mordecai, while the Jews massacre those who had purposed their downfall. The rejoicing that followed was known as Purim (9: 26), and subsequently the festival was observed as a highly convivial occasion.

JOB

WHEN WE REACH the book of *Job* on our journey through the Bible, we come face to face with a problem which will affect us even more when we try to read the works of the prophets. It is beyond dispute that the English of the Authorised Version is superb. There is no need to enlarge on a subject which has so often been adequately dealt with and on which there has been general agreement since 1611. No revised version or modern translation, one may safely say, will ever rival the economy of diction, the arresting phrases, the flowing cadences and the austere dignity of what is in effect the masterpiece of William Tyndale. All subsequent English translations, including the A.V., bear the imprint of this tragic genius to whom the English speaking world owes a debt that it can never repay.

But it is equally beyond dispute that words change their meaning in the course of time; that as a result of the discovery of a vast number of ancient manuscripts and papyri, we are in a much better position than were the translators of the A.V. to know what the original Hebrew and Greek of the Old and New Testaments signify; and that the critical scholarship of the last century and a half has solved many of the difficulties which the text of the A.V. presents. In our reading of the Old Testament the problem of intelligibility has so far hardly arisen. Where a phrase or a sentence has seemed obscure the general flow of the narrative has made its meaning generally apparent. But when we pass from continuous narration, as for example in *Esther* to the involved discourses of *Job* or the disjointed utterances of the prophets, there is much to be said for sacrificing the beauty of language in the interest of better understanding.

There is little point in savouring the beauty of a well-turned phrase if it is not at all clear what the phrase means. Accordingly it may be suggested that on a first reading of a book like *Job* or one of the prophets a modern translation should be used. On a second reading or for detailed study one of the standard versions (A.V., R.V., R.S.V.) would provide the best of both worlds when read in conjunction with a detailed commentary, but to get the general meaning and theme in the first instance there is no better translation, pending the appearance of the Old Testament in the New English Bible, than that of James Moffatt.

Moffatt was sometimes arbitrary in changing the order of verses and chapters, but he worked on the healthy assumption that whatever has happened to the Hebrew and Greek text in the course of the last two or three thousand years it did originally make sense and was meant to be understood. Moffatt had an undoubted flair for language and a real insight into biblical thought. Many scholars would quarrel with his translation on points of detail, but his rendering of the more obscure parts of the Old Testament makes his version the best means so far open to us of reaching the heart of the message for us today of most of the remaining books of the Hebrew scriptures.

Even with the help of Moffatt's translation it is still not immediately plain what the book of *Job* is all about. It is obviously not entirely about the proverbial patience of Job (*Jas.* 5: 11), because most of the book is taken up with the attempt of Job's friends to quell the violence of his impatient outbursts against the injustice of his lot. Nor is it a studied examination of the question as to why an obviously good man like Job should be reduced to such a shocking plight. It gives no real answer to the perennial problem of the suffering of the innocent.

The book is the imaginative work of a master of dramatic poetry who, like Shakespeare, takes an old story from folklore or popular history and weaves it into the stuff of tragedy. It appears that Job was a traditional figure well known in Israel, most likely renowned for his patient endurance of various trials and finally vindicated by being restored to fortune. The motif is common enough in religious folktales, and is by no means peculiar to the Bible. This skeleton is taken by the unknown author of the book as we know it and is built up into a dramatic unity.

The book is carefully and systematically constructed. It opens with a prologue and closes with an epilogue, both in prose. The main body of the work consists of three cycles of dialogue in poetry. There are one or two obviously later interpolations which interrupt the rhythmic flow of the argument. These should be read separately: viz., the magnificent poem on wisdom (ch. 28), the redundant speech of Elihu (chs. 32–37) and perhaps also the poems about the hippopotamus and the crocodile (chs. 40: 15—41: 34). In ch. 27 before verse 7 the words: "then answered Zophar the Naamathite and said ..." should be inserted, i.e., the whole chapter is not a speech by Job but only down to verse 6. The introductory sentence to Zophar's speech has to be supplied.

Whether the date of the book is about the fifth century B.C. as is generally supposed, it is clearly written after the days of the great prophets. They had convinced Israel that God is both just and merciful, that obedience to him is rewarded and disobedience is punished. But since the Jews had no belief in life after death apart from some shadowy existence in the dim underworld of Sheol (see p. 234), any rewards and punishments must be handed out in this life or not at all.

It was easy enough to agree with this rough and ready solution so long as Israel was a nation. Any good fortune or disaster could be accounted for by the good or bad behaviour of the majority. But when after the Exile the nation had become a small community governed by the priesthood and comforming to the provisions of the Law of Moses, the prosperity or misfortune of the individual became a problem. Jeremiah and Ezekiel had both stressed the responsibility of every man for his own conduct, Ezekiel in particular insisting that each one suffered or prospered on his own merits alone (*Ezek.* 18: 20).

Thus the orthodox point of view at the time this book of *Job* was written was that if a man suffered disaster or misfortune it must be the result of his own sins, known or unknown, admitted or concealed. Material prosperity on the other hand was the reward of a virtuous life. For a man who was overtaken by affliction of body or estate, the remedy was to confess his sin, repent of his misdeeds and throw himself upon the mercy of God. It is this facile solution of the problem of pain which the author of *Job* rejects. If a man who is shown to be no better or worse than his neighbours becomes the victim of appalling disaster there may be no easy answer to the question of why this should happen. But in the person of Job the author of this book challenges the superficial explanation which was offered in his day.

Prologue

(1: 1 – 2: 13)

FIRST OF ALL we are given a picture of the patriarch Job himself, a native of Uz somewhere beyond Palestine, and therefore not a Jew. This man, a paragon of all the virtues (cf. *Ezek.* 14: 14, 20), was rightly, in accordance with popular belief, blessed with a lavish abundance of this world's goods. If therefore so godly and upright a man came to grief or suffered any affliction, the orthodox doctrine of "do well and prosper, do evil and pay for it" must be woefully false. According to the old folk tale disaster fell upon Job, but apart from ultimate restitution of his worldly goods and greater prosperity than before no explanation was given. Here, however, our author amends the folk tale by letting us into the secrets of the heavenly council where the reason for Job's subsequent misfortunes is disclosed.

YHWH in heavenly session is boasting to the Satan or Adversary, whose function at this stage seems to be largely that of a malicious trouble-maker, of the piety and worthiness of his servant Job. The wily sprite suggests that Job's piety is not without good reason. So prosperous a man may well indeed be a model of virtue. YHWH agrees to put Job to the test. The Adversary is to be allowed to shake the alleged props of Job's piety: his goods and chattels, his sons and daughters, everything but his own skin may be harmed and despoiled. So the scene is set for the drama that follows.

At the instigation of the Adversary, calamities one after another fall upon Job. His sheep, his cattle, his camels, his servants and finally his sons and daughters are struck down by an appalling series of accidents—lightning, hurricane and marauding bands. Job however bears all this with exemplary fortitude: "The Lord gave and the Lord hath taken away: blessed be the name of the Lord" (1: 21). But the Adversary is not satisfied. So long as a man has a whole skin he can bear anything: "All that a man hath will he give for his life" (2: 4).

So once again the heavenly council meets. The Adversary puts his case and is given permission to harry Job to the point of death. The good man is smitten with boils from head to foot, a particularly painful type of leprosy. His wife gives him little comfort. Her terse advice is to curse God and die. Job however denounces this as evil counsel and still utters no word of reproach against YHWH. His three best friends Eliphaz, Bildad and Zophar hear of his plight and hasten to comfort him. Their horror at the sight of him is so great that they sit with him upon the ground in silent sympathy for a whole week.

Thus ends the prose prologue and it is in this setting that we are to imagine the three cycles of dialogue that make up the bulk of the book. The rather fanciful picture of the transaction between YHWH and the Adversary should not obscure the fact that the poet is here putting forward a serious suggestion which we must consider in summing up the religious value of the book. He would have us believe that one reason for the sufferings of good men is to test the quality of their goodness, and that this is God's way of finding out how genuine are their professions of piety. To be devout and upright when things are going smoothly is easy. But can a man's faith stand

up to the buffets of disaster? Here the author of *Job* portrays at least one man who stands the test, retains his integrity and presents the classic example of disinterested goodness.

Each of the three cycles of dialogue that go to make up the book consists of six speeches. Job's friends speak in strict rotation and Job replies to each in turn. Between the prologue and the first cycle of speeches comes the outburst from Job which sets the drama in motion. As his friends sit silently beside him, the depth of their sympathy and horror at his plight clearly marked by their demeanour, Job's composure breaks down. He curses the day he was born and prays for death to end his suffering (3: 1–26).

First Cycle

(4: 1 – 14: 22)

HIS FRIENDS ARE convinced from the outset that if a man has been plunged into this state of misery and dejection his afflictions must be merited. God in his justice would not permit anything else. Job was obviously getting no more than he deserved. His passionate outcry was therefore highly improper. Eliphaz opens the debate in the most tactful manner possible. He is obviously moved by affection for Job and his speech is a masterpiece of delicacy. He stresses the universal beneficent rule of a wise Providence. The government of the world is in good hands. Surely then the proper thing for Job to do is to acknowledge that he has sinned, and throw himself on God's mercy. Let him look on his present ills as a discipline and things will all come right for him in the end (4: 1 – 5: 27).

But Job will have none of this. In his reply he charges Eliphaz with taking too casual a view of his plight. Why ask him to repent when he does not know what to repent of? He breaks out again into a desperate cry against the injustice of his lot and bitterly parodies the words of the psalmist—What is man that God should be mindful of him? (*Ps.* 8: 4) and asks: What is man that God cannot leave him alone? He calls God the great Spy upon mankind (6: 1 – 7: 21).

Bildad, the second friend, seizes on something that Job has said about God's injustice (6: 29) and summons up all the weight of human experience to refute it. He stresses God's discrimination. Job's children had obviously sinned, therefore they were struck down. Job cannot have sinned so grossly otherwise he would have suffered the same fate. Everyone knows that the good man flourishes and the bad man perishes. If Job is, as he says, guiltless let him rest assured that if he asks God to bless him prosperity will return (8: 1–22).

Job's reply is bitterly ironical. The only justice in God's dealings with man is the justice of the strong against the weak. Nobody can argue with God. Innocent and guilty alike are God's victims just as it pleases him. Providence is not the rule of justice but of universal injustice. In black despair Job accuses God of playing with him as a cat plays with a mouse, raising him up to great prosperity only to smash him in the dust, and asks for nothing more than a brief respite from his divine tormentor before the grave ends all his troubles (9: 1 – 10: 22).

Eliphaz is the gentlest and most tactful of Job's friends. Bildad is less patient. Zophar is the harshest and narrowest of the three. His reply to Job's latest outburst begins more abruptly and angrily than the speeches of the other two. His line of argument is that God sees deeper than man and that although Job thinks he is sinless the Almighty knows the black state of his soul and is punishing him accordingly. By turning his back on his sins and stretching out his hands to God Job will find that all will be well, and Zophar ends with a stinging reminder of the fate of those who have an opportunity to repent and do not take it (11: 1–20).

Job will listen to none of these specious arguments. Even the beasts of the field, he says, know that nothing can be hidden from God. But what is more significant than his universal knowledge is his unchallengable power, and this he uses to bring disaster or good fortune upon the earth and none can say him nay. But as for Job himself, come what may he will never admit that there is any justice in what has happened to him (12: 1 – 14: 22)

Second Cycle

(15: 1 – 21: 34)

IN THE SECOND cycle of speeches the three comforters adopt a second line of argument, this time not from the nature of God but from the experience of life. Their tone is now noticeably sharper and Eliphaz begins by claiming that even if the wicked prosper, the agonies of conscience that they suffer are worse than material downfall (15: 1–35). Job dismisses this as empty words. Beaten to his knees by the inexplicable anger of God and loathed by his fellow men, he appeals to God who alone can prove his innocence (16: 1 – 17: 16).

Bildad furiously returns to the attack on this godless rebel against the just judgments of Providence. No matter how wildly Job may protest it is certain beyond all doubt that the wicked get their deserts, and in Bildad's vivid portrait of the plight of the sinner the present condition of Job is clearly implied (18: 1–21). Job replies by asking his friends to pity him rather than harry and slander him.

He describes his pitiable state more movingly than ever before, yet through it all his sublime faith in God's ultimate justice leads him to the conviction, which he has already hinted at in 14: 13–15 and 16: 18–19, that there must be something more beyond death than the conventional belief in a shadowy Sheol (see p. 234). Though his body dies God will vindicate his innocence hereafter and beyond this mortal life he will yet see God. This is one of the few places (cf. *Ps.* 73: 23–28) in the Old Testament where there is any hint or hope that the grave may not be the end (19: 1–29).

Zophar says nothing new but says it with greater vehemence. Wickedness may go unpunished for a space but the vengeance of God brings certain retribution (20: 1–29). It is obvious now that Job's friends are seeking to wring from him a confession of guilt. Their lurid descriptions of the fate of the evildoers match the plight of Job. So far he has contented himself with reaffirming his innocence. Now, however, he dares to question whether there is any moral order in the universe at all. The wicked do not perish; they prosper and grow fat. They are not struck down by the wrath of God; they die in comfort in their beds (21: 1–34).

Third Cycle

(22: 1 – 31: 40)

HAVING FAILED to provoke Job into a confession of the guilt which he is convinced must have brought him to his present predicament, Eliphaz passes from insinuation to accusation. He charges Job with inhumanity, avarice, oppression and perversion of justice (22: 1–30). Job is still too absorbed in contemplation of the sheer irrationality of life to answer his abuse. The more he thinks of it the blacker becomes the picture of the sufferings of the honest poor, and the realisation that the criminal gets off scot-free (23: 1 – 24: 25).

At this point the text becomes confused and the pattern of the dialogue is broken in the A.V. We do well to follow Moffatt's version in attributing 25: 1 – 26: 14 to Bildad. He has nothing to add. His arguments are exhausted. He simply reiterates the greatness of God and the imperfections of human kind. Job too is reduced to reasserting his innocence (27: 1-6).

So far as we can make sense of this part it would seem that Job's short speech ends at 27: 6 and that 27: 7 begins the speech of Zophar which merely repeats the old argument of the fate of the evildoer (27: 7-23). The next chapter (28: 1-28), the magnificent poem about wisdom—one of the greatest passages in the Old Testament—breaks the continuity, and Job's final answer to Zophar, completing the cycle, comes in 29: 1 - 31: 40.

In ch. 29 he looks back upon the good old days of his prosperity when he was respected and honoured. This he contrasts in ch. 30 with his present pitiful state, and in ch. 31 he once more insists that his past life has been blameless. The standard of behaviour which he sets himself here is as high as anything in the Old Testament. It is part of the argument of the book that this was the kind of conduct expected from a man who claimed to be a good God-fearing Jew, and it is an ideal of which any society might be proud. It shows moreover how deep and lasting an effect the moral force of the teaching of the prophets had had on the life of Israel.

Chapters 32 – 37 appear to be an interpolation. A new speaker Elihu comes on the scene and his speech contains little that is fresh. It seems to have been introduced at a later date to enforce the argument that suffering is a moral discipline.

So Job and his friends are silenced. They have exhausted each other by the vehemence of their arguments. His friends are still persuaded that Job is guilty of some unknown but heinous sins; he on the other hand is as convinced that he is no more culpable than the common run of men. The great question mark remains: Why, if he has done no wrong, has he to bear this suffering? Job does not doubt at heart that the government of the universe is in wise hands. But the prosperity of wicked men baffles him as does his own misfortune. His mind is still perplexed and nothing his friends have said has helped to solve his problem.

Denouement

(38: 1 – 42: 6)

AT THIS POINT the poet introduces the only person who might give an answer: YHWH himself. His reply is in two parts, each followed by a short speech by Job, and it is best to regard 40: 15 – 41: 34 as a later interpolation. In magnificent and impressive language YHWH describes the marvellous intricacy and wonder of the created world (38: 1 – 40: 2). Job is overwhelmed at the power and majesty and infinite resource of the Creator. He confesses his sin of presumption in daring to argue with God (40: 3-5).

YHWH then asks him (40: 6-14) if now he thinks he could run the universe better than God himself and ironically invites him to try. Job's answer is one of complete penitence: not penitence for his sins as his friends had demanded, but penitence for questioning the ways of God and for impetuously doubting his providence (42:1-6). In the short prose epilogue (42:7-17), YHWH rebukes Job's friends for allowing their conventional orthodoxy to force them into lying arguments. Job is restored to greater prosperity than before and dies in honourable estate surrounded by his numerous offspring.

If we were to follow the advice of some scholars and detach the prose prologue and epilogue from the main body of the work we might well be at a loss to know what is the permanent religious value of the book of *Job*. Its literary and dramatic quality is in either case unquestionable, as is its elemental human interest. But since we do not now accept the orthodox Jewish view of that time that all suffering is the result of the sin of the sufferer, the elaborately constructed attack of the author upon this belief is for us a mere tilting at windmills.

Is the abiding message of the book then rather to be found in the spectacle of a man whose integrity is unshakable, who refuses to be beaten to his knees by arguments which he knows to be untrue and who will not recant against his conscience to satisfy the orthodoxy of the moment? This testimony to the power of the human spirit would indeed be timely in the era of the police state were it not that Job happily knew nothing of modern methods of extracting confessions.

Or are we to see the point of the book in Job's ultimate recognition of the inscrutable mystery of God's ways and in his penitent recognition of God's sovereignty? While

he cavils at God's providential ordering of men's affairs and beats his fists in vain against the gates of heaven he finds no peace of mind or respite for his tortured soul. But when he humbly acknowledges that the right relationship of man to God is one of unquestioning obedience and acceptance of the world as it is, his troubled spirit is at rest and adversity or success has now no power to smite him down or raise him up. He has learned that it is not through material things that man fulfils his being but in dependence and trust in God.

If we include the prologue and epilogue as we must, since whatever may have been the original scope of the book its present form in the Bible is what concerns us, we should have to reckon with the suggestion pictorially conveyed in the image of the heavenly council, that the book is teaching us that suffering comes upon us to test the quality of our faith. Job's final restoration to prosperity would then be a proper conclusion since he had emerged triumphantly from his testing time and was entitled to his reward.

Perhaps the answer to the difficulties presented by the book of *Job* is that the author or compiler had not merely one but several of these lessons in mind. Certainly the book offers no satisfactory solution to the problem of pain or of the moral order of the universe. It would, however, undoubtedly warn us against the danger of equating the religious orthodoxy of our time or any time with the mind and purpose of God. Job's well-meaning friends are so concerned to defend what they believe to be revealed truth, that they bludgeon him into refuting a God whom his conscience rejects as a caricature of the God whom the prophets had proclaimed.

The master hand of the author would also teach us to see in Job the eternal rebel that is in us all, bewildered by the apparent injustice of things as they are and tempted to claim that we could have ordered them better. Job's real sin is ~~man's~~ perennial sin of self-sufficiency, his partial and myopic view of life which sees no farther than his own concerns and questions the whole structure of God's government of the universe on the basis of his own limited experience.

In the end Job wins through from his despair to a true knowledge of God, when he recognises that the God he has been arraigning is a God of his own making. He finds peace of mind and spirit in a humble acceptance of his proper place in the scheme of things as a creature living by faith under a sovereign Creator whose ways are beyond man's understanding.

The paradoxes of the ways of God are part of the mystery of our being, and though we may see kinship between Job, Jeremiah and the Suffering Servant in *Second Isaiah*, it is only in the Crucifixion and Resurrection of Christ that the afflictions of Job reach their proper evaluation. We have reached the heart of the message of Job when we can say: "Nothing in my hand I bring, simply to thy Cross I cling" or echo St. Paul's words in *Rom.* 8: 35–39.

THE PSALMS

WE HAVE SEEN something of Hebrew poetry already in the old traditional folk songs and ballads of which traces are still to be found in the Pentateuch and in the later historical books (e.g. *Gen.* 4 : 23–24—The Song of Lamech; *Ex.* 15 : 21—the Song of Miriam; *Num.* 21 : 17–18—The Song of the Well; *Judg.* 5—The Song of Deborah; *II Sam.* 1 : 19–27—David's lament for Saul and Jonathan).

It is clear from these fragments that among the Hebrews as among other peoples, the subject matter of their folk songs was drawn from the major and minor experiences of daily life ranging from national victories to manual labour. But little of this type of poetry, except the *Song of Solomon* (see p. 246), has been incorporated in the Old Testament. This is hardly likely to have been because the poetic output of Israel was less than elsewhere in the ancient world. Indeed much of the prose of the Old Testament would pass for poetry, and if we are to judge from *Amos* 6 : 5 the Hebrews were known for their songs.

But whether or not their reputation rested on songs of a religious character as *Ps.* 137 : 3–4 would seem to suggest, the priestly editors of the Old Testament have seen to it that the poetry that has been handed down as the legacy of Is-

rael is primarily concerned with God's dealings with man, and the whole range of thought and emotion which is comprehended by the practice of the presence of God. When we talk of Hebrew poetry therefore, we turn instinctively to the book of *Psalms* which reflects in a way that is timeless the universal aspirations, doubts, fears and certainties of the human heart.

The Hebrew genius did not seem to lie in epic or dramatic poetry. It was essentially subjective, more apt to give tongue to its own emotions and aspirations in the first person than to interpret them through the characters of an Iliad or a King Lear. Hence it is in lyric poetry above all that it finds its best expression. Unlike western poets, however, the Hebrew poet was not concerned with either metre or rhyme. He was on the other hand extremely conscious of rhythm, and the chief characteristic of Old Testament poetry is the feature known as parallelism, which appears as plainly in the English translation as in the Hebrew original.

Essentially, this convention which operates in all Hebrew poetry and even appears sometimes in prose, consists of making each couplet or verse of two lines consist of two clauses of about equal length, the second line or clause completing or contrasting the first. There are naturally minor variations and deviations but on the whole this is the normal poetic form, and generally the most perfect specimens of Hebrew poetry are those which conform by and large to this pattern e.g., *Job* 28: 12–28; *Prov.* 8: 12–36; *Ps.* 104.

This parallelism must be remembered and looked for if the literary quality of the psalms is to be appreciated. But more important is the fact that the psalms formed the hymn book of the Jewish Church after the Exile. Most of them should thus be thought of in a musical setting. They were not meant for congregational singing. The part played by the congregation was that of singing the Amen and making occasional responses. The musical side was left to the professional choir and a very elaborate orchestra. Indeed the services of the second Temple must have been very splendid with a wealth of pageantry, colour and melody.

Such instruments as cymbals, trumpets, flutes, harps, drums and various others seem to have been used. The merry little *Psalm* 150, which rounds off the psalter, suggests that dancing—doubtless of a fairly sedate character—also formed part of the service. It is thought that many of the obscure Hebrew words which occur either in the title of some of the psalms or, like the word *selah*, within the text, indicate either directions to the musicians or the tune to which the psalm was to be sung.

Remembering that the psalms constitute a hymn book we shall not be surprised to find that like any modern hymnbook the con-

tents are of varing quality. Some of the hundred and fifty lyrics which make up the psalter surpass the best products of religious literature anywhere. Others are as uninspired as many of our hymns today. Like a modern hymnal too, the psalter is a compilation of ancient and modern, and in the manner of a present day hymnologist the final editor has made use of previous collections.

Usually the name of the collection from which a psalm is taken is given at the beginning e.g. 42 is from the Korahite hymnbook, 50 from the Asaphite. These were guilds of Temple musicians who had their own hymnaries from which various psalms were drawn. There was also apparently a hymnal known as the Chief Musician's collection from which several items have been culled (e.g. 66). Other psalms, called in the title Songs of Degrees or Ascents (e.g. 122), were processional hymns sung by pilgrims going up to the Temple at the great festivals, or, like 24, an ancient hymn accompanying the procession of the Ark into Jerusalem.

There is also a large number of psalms taken from a collection probably originally called the Hymns of David. The popular idea that David wrote all the psalms is false. Whether he wrote many of them or any of them is open to question. There is nothing in his life story to suggest that he wrote religious poetry. We are told that he was a poet and a musician but the only authentic specimen of his verse given in the narrative (*II Sam.* 1: 19–27) is of a secular character. If David wrote some of our present psalms we cannot tell which and it is of little use to speculate.

In characteristic Old Testament fashion, probably prompted mainly by the Chronicler, the name of the "sweet singer of Israel" became attached to them all as did the name of Moses to the laws and of Solomon to the proverbs (see p. 238). So it came about that any psalm that might bear some reference to incidents in David's life was immediately identified by some pious editor. *Psalm* 51 is a hymn of penitence for some grave sin, which the editor has assumed to be the king's affair with Bathsheba and which he indicates in the title. Many of the psalms which are ascribed to David are obviously of a very much later date.

Sometimes the same psalm occurs twice (e.g. 53 and 14, 70 and 40: 13–17). This is because different collections contained the same hymn before the final amalgamation took place. Moreover until recent times compilers of hymnaries had no scruples about altering, amending, abridging or expanding to suit their own denominational tastes. "In this way medieval Catholic poets are made to sing good Protestant songs, or Calvinists and Methodists to drop their shibboleths and express themselves in a manner acceptable to Unitarians. The familiar hymn: 'O for a thousand tongues to sing my dear Redeemer's praise' has been adapted to Buddhist use as 'O for a thousand tongues to sing my holy Buddha's praise, the glories of my teacher great, the triumphs of his grace'" (G.F Moore).

The editors of the psalms proceeded in the same way. Some of the psalms appear to be Hebrew adaptations of themes also found in Babylonian and Egyptian literature. *Ps.* 104 is so like Akhnaten's Hymn to the Sun that there must be some close connection.

So then behind the five divisions of the Psalter, indicated in the R.V. and no doubt introduced by the editors in imitation of the five books of the Torah, there lie these various smaller collections. But of course while the aim of the completed psalter was clearly to act as a hymbook and indeed also as a prayer book for worship in the second Temple, many psalms being used as accompaniments to the ritual, not all of them were composed for public use. Most of them are indeed of private origin, the thanksgiving, penitence or supplication of some unknown Israelite poet.

Although many of the psalms are doubtless as old as the monarchy, the psalter as we have it is predominantly post-exilic, edited in post-exilic times for post-exilic use. If we had to hazard a guess as to the date of the psalms in their original state we could hardly be more definite than to fix their composition somewhere between 1000—200 B.C. Some authorities would say that the range is more likely over a thousand years.

Psalmists and Prophets

IN A COLLECTION of such diverse origin it is obvious that it is no more possible to find a unified theological point of view in the psalms than it is in a modern hymnal. There was a world of difference between the religious background of David's day and that of the second or third century B.C. It is not surprising therefore to find considerable variation in the level of religious insight between one psalm and another or within the same composite psalm. But on the whole it may be said as in the case of the wisdom literature of Israel that Hebrew poetry likewise bears the mark of the classical prophets.

The tumult and the shouting had died: the convulsions of the social and political order had passed. Israel had settled down after the Exile to its new life in Palestine. The second Temple attracted the best that was in the community, and as in the great days of Christendom in Europe the ablest minds devoted their talents to the service of religion. Among such, those whose bent lay neither along legal nor philosophical lines betook themselves to private piety and devotional writing.

For the psalmists, religion was not so much something to be fought for like the prophets or argued over like the philosophers but to be accepted and reflected on with thankfulness. The psalter is therefore *par excellence* a devotional handbook. Although its ostensible purpose was to serve a liturgical purpose most of these ancient hymns like most modern ones are the outcome of some man's personal experience. They reveal all the moods of the human spirit from exhilaration to despondency, from confidence to despair.

The psalms have established a place for themselves in the worship and devotional life of the Christian as well as of the Jewish Church, for the very reason that in the universal quality of their heart-searchings the psalmists expressed the feelings not only of one nation but of all humanity. As a basis to all their meditation and reflection stands the Law of God: not merely the ceremonial legislation of the priests but the Law in its widest sense as the prophets understood it.

The uncompromising doctrinal and moral standards for which the prophets had fought and suffered had now become the established religious blueprint for Israel. But if all the psalms do not come up to this standard we may take it that where a psalm falls short of the prophetic level it may either be because it is partly of more primitive origin or because, as in our own hymnbooks, sometimes a writer's heart is stronger than his head.

It would be impossible within the compass of this commentary to provide an adequate exposition of each of the hundred and fifty psalms. But it is not necessary to do so. For while it is true that in some ways the book of *Psalms* presents the most difficult task of all for a commentator on the Old Testament, the problem is largely one of establishing the text, date and setting of each individual hymn. But if we are prepared to read and use the psalter as a handbook of devotion, as an aid to private prayer and meditation, we need not concern ourselves overmuch with these literary and historical questions. Undoubtedly, given time and patience, and the aid of a detailed commentary, anyone would find intensive study of the psalms a wonderfully rewarding venture.

But if we are content to by-pass these more technical problems there is no book in the Old Testament that reads more easily, particularly if we use a modern translation. Where there is so much that speaks directly to our needs we can well afford to turn a blind eye to the occasional obscurity, secure in the knowledge that the psalter has always been a guide and inspiration to myriads of plain folk throughout the centuries of the Church's story, who have never failed to find in its pages the right words to speak to their deepest experiences whether of joy or sorrow, and the gateway to a fuller knowledge of the God and Father of our Lord Jesus Christ.

It has been said that reading the Old Testament is like "eating a large crab, mostly shell". Often this thought must have crossed our minds as we made our way through the somewhat dreary stretches of the legal sections of the Pentateuch, or the less obviously relevant chapters of the troubled reigns of Israel's kings. It has often been difficult to sense the uniqueness of Israel's faith amid the ups and downs of Israel's fortunes from Abraham to Nehemiah, and to remember that owing to the arrangement of the various books that make up our Old Testament the distinctive contribution of the prophets which illuminates the historical scene is reserved to the end.

Only when we come to grips with the insights of Amos and Hosea, Jeremiah and Isaiah do we find the flesh that covers the bare bones of Israel's history and turns it into a living witness to the faith that the Christian Church has inherited. But even the prophets have their limitations. They speak to a particular situation. They are men of their time, involved in its affairs, and their message is essentially conditioned by the political and social happenings of their day.

So, of course, to some extent are the psalmists. But the psalms are a distillation of all that the prophets had taught with the added colour and warmth that come from personal piety displayed upon a smaller stage. If therefore we would see the Old Testament faith in all its depth and breadth and height, we shall find it nowhere better exemplified than in the psalms, and perhaps because of the greater detachment of the psalmists from the political conflicts that beset the prophets, their words have acquired that timeless and universal quality that have made them the spiritual powerhouse of Jews and Christians alike in all ages. When we have steeped ourselves in the thought that lies behind such psalms as 23, 24, 40, 46, 51, 103, 139 we shall know something of the spiritual foundation on which our Lord built his Church, and of the minds of the New Testament men who saw the Gospel as the culmination of the faith of their fathers.

The Message of the Psalms

THE DOMINANT note of the psalms is the praise of God, for his loving-kindness in choosing

Israel and establishing his covenant with her, for his righteousness in delivering her from her enemies in the past and promising a greater deliverance yet to come, and for his moral holiness which brings men to their knees in humility and penitence. This is the God who is Father of all created things yet who is near to all who call upon him. Therefore say the psalmists "Bless the Lord, O my soul; and all that is within me bless his holy name."

As for man, God has "made him a little lower than the angels" and has "crowned him with glory and honour", he has given him dominion over all his works and has "put all things under his feet" (8). What then must man do in return for God's goodness? The answer is partly given in 15 and 24: 3–5. Man must keep the Law which God has given him.

We may on occasion feel that there is an element of self-righteousness in the psalmists' outlook (e.g. 41: 11–12). If a man obeys the Law he is bound to receive his reward in terms of material prosperity and if the wicked seem to flourish it can only be for a short while. The problem that vexed the author of Job does not distress the psalmist of 37: 25. He is content to believe that if a man lives by the Law no harm can befall him. He deserves well of God. Yet to offset the danger of self-satisfaction there is the ever recurring note of penitence and humility (e.g. 51).

As in the rest of the Old Testament there is in the psalms no real hope of anything beyond this life. Ps. 16: 10, which seems to suggest

it, is rather a prayer against sudden death, and 17: 15 refers to earthly visions of God. Only in 73: 23–28, sometimes called the high water mark of Old Testament religion, does the idea of life after death find any expression. Otherwise the conventional view of Sheol, the cavernous subterranean abode of departed spirits, deprived of the possibility of access to God, marks the end of life's journey. But in 73, as in Job (see p. 225), the psalmist reaches out towards the belief that true communion with God cannot be broken by the accident of death. He has found eternal life here and now and knows that nothing can take it from him.

At this stage we may speak freely of a Jewish Church. The nation had ceased to exist and such identity as Israel now had derived from her religion. Life was focused on the Temple. Jerusalem was not so much the capital of what was left of David's kingdom as it was the city of God, the home of the sanctuary, the spiritual Mecca of all Jews everywhere. A psalm like 87 shows how deeply embedded in the people's hearts was the love of Zion, and the centre of Zion was the Temple, not only as the goal of pilgrimage for all Jews everywhere but as the object of the affection of every devout man.

One of the perennial tensions in Jewish religious life was between morality and the cult. The danger was always present that meticulous attention to the services of the Church should become a substitute for right conduct. It was against this danger that the prophets thundered. But in the psalms this problem seems to be less acute than elsewhere in the Old Testament. The good man sees his duty to God and society clearly in terms of ethical obedience, but equally clearly he sees his obligation to take his place as a worshipper in the Temple courts. He finds his personal relationship to God and his neighbours guided and strengthened by joining in the corporate worship of the Church.

Indeed in many places where it seems that a psalmist is expressing a longing for direct communion with God, it is in reality a desire to join with the throng of worshippers crowding into the Temple on some great festival (e.g. 42, 43). Though the Temple still had its animal sacrifices as the channel of worship and some of the psalms were used in this connection, more than one psalmist looks beyond this to something less material. "For thou desirest not sacrifice, else would I give it: thou delightest not in burnt offering. The sacrifices of God are a broken spirit: a broken and a contrite heart, O God, thou wilt not despise" (51: 16–17).

On first acquaintance the psalms may strike us as excessively nationalistic. The centre of the world is Jerusalem, the only true religion is Yahwism, and the only good race is the Jewish. Yet there was a large measure of justification for this. Life in Palestine after the Exile was a precarious existence. Enemies surrounded the Jews on every side, indeed the word "enemy" is one of the commonest words in the psalter. There is an undertone of constant danger, partly physical but also social and spiritual. In self defence Judaism had to insist on its distinctive customs and traditions and its national characteristics.

Doubtless it was this sense of insecurity that gave rise to so many imprecations against the ungodly, who were sometimes Gentiles and sometimes those within the Jewish community itself, who in the eyes of the psalmists flouted the will of God. This explains rather than excuses such violent denunciation as is to be found in e.g. 69 and 109, together with the general exaltation of the Jew and of all things Jewish. Yet side by side with this is to be found the recognition basic to the Old Testament that the Jews are the instruments of God's purpose to bring the world back to himself. It is in such words as those of 67 and 87 that the psalms stretch out beyond Judaism to God's concern for all mankind, and to the wider implications of Israel's role among the nations.

Part of the joyful thanksgiving of the psalmists springs from their deep certainty that the hand of God has been at work throughout the whole course of their existence as a people. Sometimes this sense of the Acts of God in history is expressed in hymns of thanksgiving for national triumphs (e.g. 136). Sometimes there is a ready recognition of the nation's failures as being due to disobedience of God's laws (e.g. 106). But the conviction remains that God has guided their destinies from the days of Moses until now and it is this that leads to the oft repeated certainty of an even more glorious future.

It is the more extraordinary that the less likely it seemed on the surface that any future at all lay in store for them as a nation—the smaller their territory, the greater the threat of suppression, the more numerous their foes—the more clearly burned this lamp of unquenchable hope that stubbornly refused to be extinguished. Well they knew that it was for God to decide when Israel would be restored and a descendant of David would reign again over a wider and happier nation.

But as the pressures intensified from without and as they became more and more conscious of their faithfulness to the covenant within, the hope grew ever stronger that the coming of a new order could not long be delayed. *Ps.* 102: 13 expresses this sense of urgency. Then at last the heathen opponents of God would be destroyed, Israel would recover its lost glory and be vindicated in the sight of all. The cities of Judah would be rebuilt and peace and plenty would reward God's faithful people. Nor would this age of blessedness be one of merely material wellbeing. Mercy, truth and righteousness would be the foundations of this golden age on earth (e.g. 85: 10–11).

It is in this context that we are to understand the psalms which speak of the king as the representative of God who would be instrumental in bringing this about. In days when the monarchy had ceased to exist the hope grew stronger of the advent of a new and greater David whose kingdom would embrace the earth, whose reign would be one of universal blessing, where the poor and needy would be cared for and all men would live in peace (72).

Although the psalms which speak of this son of David as the Anointed of YHWH, Son of God, and Priest (2, 110) doubtless had their origin in the royal enthronement festivals in the days of the monarchy, and show points of contact with the idea of divine kingship in other parts of the ancient Near East, nevertheless it was words like these that helped to build up Israel's hope in the coming of a messianic king. This hope our Lord claimed to fulfil, giving it however his own distinctive interpretation, and the New Testament writers, following his guidance, found in such psalms as 2 and 110 a rich quarry for their exposition of the significance of Christ.

PROVERBS

THE BOOK OF *Proverbs*, like the book of *Psalms*, though for different reasons, should be dipped into and savoured rather than read through as a whole. This is good counsel in the case of the psalter because of the diversity of its contents and because each psalm by itself provides enough food for reflection and leads inevitably to an act of prayer. The book of *Proverbs* on the other hand brings us down from the heights to the humdrum level of everyday conduct, and while this in itself is admirable and necessary, the repetition of the same themes and the pedestrian character of so much sustained moralising can be extremely tedious.

Proverbs belongs to the wisdom literature of the Bible which includes also the book of *Job*, *Ecclesiastes* and two books of the Apocrypha, *Ecclesiasticus* and the *Wisdom of Solomon*. Although these books are written in poetic form they are more like philosophy than poetry. Yet it is not the normal kind of speculative philosophy as commonly understood but something typical of the ancient Near East with a specifically Hebrew flavour. There is the characteristic biblical emphasis on theology throughout and when speculation enters into the question it is never for its own sake.

The authors of these books, known as wisdom scribes or wise men, were as distinctive a class in Israel as priests or prophets. Jeremiah (18: 18), writing some time before the Exile, says "the law shall not perish from the priest, nor counsel from the wise, nor the word from the prophet". Here then are three clearly designated orders: the priests whose business it was to expound the Law, the prophet who received messages directly from God to pass on to the people, and the wise man whose task it was to translate general moral principles into terms of every-day life.

Wisdom in the Old Testament sense has a special and limited use. In Israel's early days the wise man or woman was one who displayed unusual shrewdness or perspicacity or quick wittedness. The wise woman of Tekoa (*II Sam.* 14: 2–20) and the wise woman of Abel (*II Sam.* 20: 16–22) appear to get the title because they are noted for these qualities. Solomon's wisdom is exemplified by knowing what to do when two mothers claim the same child (*I Kings* 3: 16–28) and by having ready answers for the queen of Sheba (*I Kings* 10: 1–7). Joseph is accounted wise for being able to interpret the pharaoh's dream (*Gen.* 41: 39).

It is this practical, useful everyday aspect of wisdom rather than abstract metaphysics that is characteristic of all the wisdom literature of the Old Testament. By the time wisdom scribes had come to be regarded as an established class in society, their scope had extended but their function was still a practical one. They were not theologians in a specialist sense, although every writer in the Old Testament is in effect a theologian. But the wisdom scribes on the whole took the faith for granted and concerned themselves more with ethical behaviour.

They were not nationalists like the priests and the prophets; seldom do they mention Israel or Zion or YHWH's people. They rather concentrated on the underlying moral principles common to all nations and showed how they worked out in ordinary life. Their interest is in man, his nature, his habits, his virtues and his vices. Not unfairly they have been called the humanists of Israel. It is only where problems affecting humanity arise that they become at all speculative in a philosophical sense, as to some extent in the book of *Job*, or where the effects on society of human wisdom lead them to think of Wisdom personified as directing and inspiring the affairs of mankind at large.

It is not surprising that the wisdom literature reached its fine flower in the centuries following the Exile. It was a time for reflection. The firebrands of prophecy had long become grey embers. The nation, or what was left of it, was in a backwater. There was nothing to be gained by playing at politics. Religion in the hands of the priests had become an institutional affair. Consequently for gifted men with a religious bent there were only two main outlets left, either devotional meditation, which produced the psalms, or reflection on the human situation, which produced the wisdom literature.

It is probable that some of the wisdom literature is, like many of the psalms, older than the Exile; parts of the book of *Proverbs* may go back to Solomon's day. The fact that his name is attached to so many proverbs means little. He is credited with having coined three thousand (*I Kings* 4: 32) but whether, if this is so, any of them have found their way into our present book is uncertain. It has been suggested indeed that Solomon may have been responsible for introducing into Israel teachers of the particular type of moral aphorism that we find in the book of *Proverbs*. He was notably internationally minded and proverbs of the Old Testament variety were common in Egypt some time before Solomon.

This type of humanism may well have developed in Israel in court circles—as opposed to the priestly caste or the more proletarian background of the prophets—and there is every reason to believe that at the high level of culture to which Israel had attained in the later days of the monarchy, a much more varied literature of this type existed than we should suspect from the writings of the prophets and the historians.

The prophets make no mention of any body of wisdom literature in their day, but this is not surprising since the prosaic practical outlook of the wisdom scribes would not appeal to the prophets, and the international character of this type of writing would cause them some misgivings. The Chronicler draws a veil over what he possibly regards as a seamy side of Solomon's character and makes no mention of his gift for coining proverbs.

But the wisdom literature as we have it in the Old Testament and Apocrypha comes from the time when prophecy had ceased, and by then whatever wisdom writing had survived from before the Exile or had come from beyond Israel had received the distinctive hall mark of the great prophets. The background of the wisdom literature is the legacy of Amos, Isaiah, Jeremiah and Ezekiel.

The writers have no doubt that to serve God a man must live a good life. Equally they have no doubt that if he does live a good life he will get his reward in this world or be punished if he fails. It is this belief that goodness is a paying proposition that gives to the wisdom literature its characteristically utilitarian and prudential cast. The sensible man is the man who does what is right, the fool is the man who does what is wrong, not so much from the point of view of the wrongness of the act but because evil doing is invariably followed by retribution.

So long as this was taken by and large it was true enough as a philosophy of history for a nation or a community. But when the short span of an individual life was under review it was obvious that goodness was not always rewarded by prosperity and evil by misfortune. The orthodox solution was, as we have seen (p. 222), to say that if an apparently good man suffered it must be either on account of the sins of his fathers or on account of some secret sins of his own. It was

this unsatisfactory doctrine that drew the fire of the author of the book of *Job*.

On the other hand although there was a calculating, safety-first element in the wisdom literature this was not by any means all that the wise men of Israel had to contribute to the faith of the Old Testament. For it is due to them that the strong ethical side of the message of the great prophets was perpetuated and emphasised when there was a danger of its being smothered by the legalism of the priesthood. The wisdom scribes in fact developed the moral side of the Torah.

We have seen the two rival strains clearly in *Deuteronomy* and to some extent in *Leviticus*. The legalistic ritual element became stronger through the influence of Ezekiel and the Exile. Without the complementary emphasis of the wisdom school on rational moral conduct the Torah might well have become the dead wood of ceremonial law. But in the providence of God the moral conscience of the prophets was not only the basis of Jesus' ethical teaching, but was passed down as a legacy through the wisdom scribes to the Pharisees, and from both Jesus and the Pharisees through Paul into Christianity.

Trust in God and do the right

THE BOOK OF *Proverbs* itself is the least interesting and most pedestrian of the Old Testament wisdom books. It never rises above the level of the principle: Do good and prosper, do evil and suffer for it. Yet is it altogether just to question such a motive for right conduct? If this is a rational world and the Mind behind it is not only rational but righteous, that is, if there is indeed an ethical undertone in the universe, then the man who allies himself with it is surely not to be scoffed at. He does what is right because he believes that the nature of the world is such that in the ordinary course of events goodness will pay.

Admittedly to love goodness for its own sake or from a love of God is to live and act on a higher level, but the man who believes that justice is so inherent in the nature of things that goodness is bound to prove a good investment is not to be sneered at. If the alternative is amoral self-interest, as indeed it must be, then anything which discourages that cannot be wholly condemned. Nor is it as if "do good because it pays" was claimed to be the only motive. The wisdom scribes were as much men under God as priests or prophets, and for all three the ultimate ground for right conduct was the will of God. But in the book of *Proverbs* we are given practical instruction based rather on day to day experience than on religious sanctions, and above all guidance for the young who are advised on the various pitfalls that lie ahead of them.

The word 'proverb' seems to be used in the Old Testament in a wider sense than such proverbs as our own: "A rolling stone gathers no moss" and the like. Samson's riddles, Jotham's fable (*Judg.* 9: 8–15) and such a saying as: Is Saul also among the prophets? (*I Sam.* 10: 12), seem to be counted equally as 'proverbs' with the more familiar type quoted by Ezekiel: "The fathers have eaten sour grapes and the children's teeth are set on edge" (*Ezek.* 18: 2).

In the book of *Proverbs*, however, we find none of these primitive elements. It is a collection of stylished aphorisms, mostly of a distinct artistic pattern. These are obviously not the casual product of popular idiom but the carefully chiselled craftsmanship of professional writers. The book is like so much else in the Old Testament, a collection of collections. There are seven clearly distinguishable sections in the book as we have it, mostly introduced by a title such as the Proverbs of Solomon, the Words of the Wise, the Words of king Lemuel.

Whether any of the proverbs attributed to Solomon actually come from him or his times the bulk of the material is clearly post-exilic. The seven sections vary somewhat in character: one is a more or less sustained eulogy of Wisdom (1: 1 – 9: 18), another is a disjointed collection of moral axioms (10: 1 – 22: 16), another is an acrostic poem in praise of a virtuous woman, usually called "the A.B.C. of the perfect wife" (31: 10–31), while another seems to be largely borrowed from an Egyptian wisdom book, the Teaching of Amenemope, dating from before 600 B.C. (22: 17–24: 22).

The substance of the book is condemnation of wrongdoing in all its ramifications, which the wisdom scribes equate with folly. The 'fool' of *Proverbs* is not the ignoramus but the man who flies into rages, who idles his life away, who gathers gear by dishonest means, who is a prey to his own lusts. Much of the moralising of *Proverbs* is prosy, yet it is the ordinary unspectacular virtues that the moralist is concerned with. Kindness, diligence, honesty, chastity and sobriety are the warp and woof of character whether it be that of the plain man or the haloed saint.

Behind such simple but fundamental morality lies the religious sanction: "The fear of the Lord is the beginning of knowledge" (1: 7). Indeed it might be said that the motto of the book is: "Trust in God and do the right", but when Wisdom itself is the subject, the writers reach the point of treating it as almost a manifestation of God himself (3: 19–20; 8: 1–31). In such passages as these and *Job* 28: 12–28, we can see the breeding ground of St. Paul's ultimate equation of the Wisdom of God with Christ (*I Cor.* 1: 24), and of St. John's conception of the Logos (*John* 1: 1–14).

The book of *Proverbs* is full of shrewd observations and there is a galaxy of character studies in its pages: the busybody who "meddleth with strife belonging not to him" (26: 17), the idle fellow who says to himself "a little sleep, a little slumber, a little folding of the hands to sleep" (6: 10), the henpecked husband who prefers living on the rooftop to sharing a large house with a brawling wife (25: 24).

Many of the aphorisms have been taken into common use: "A soft answer turneth away wrath" (15: 1); "Hope deferred maketh the heart sick (13: 12); "Go to the ant, thou sluggard" (6: 6); "The wicked flee when no man pursueth" (28: 1); and one that is more familiar in its New Testament setting (*Rom.* 12: 20): "If thine enemy be hungry, give him bread to eat: and if he be thirsty, give him water to drink" (25: 21) As Moffatt's translation indicates, the reason for this charity is not to "heap coals of fire upon his head" (25: 22–A.V.) but in order to "quench blazing passions".

The writers have much to say about women of all varieties. The description of the adulteress (7: 6–27) is a classic, and the frequent wry references to shrews shed interesting light on the domestic trials of a professional wise man: "A continual dropping in a very rainy day, and a contentious woman, are alike" (27: 15); "As a jewel of gold in a swine's snout, so is a fair woman which is without discretion" (11: 22). The compiler, however, makes amends by concluding his book with the admirable description of the ideal wife (31: 10–31).

Thus side by side we find in *Proverbs* instruction for the young, including liberal application of the rod, utilitarian moralising suitable for all ages, a shrewd assessment of human nature, a keen eye for the life of town and country (e.g. 30: 15–31), sanctified common sense, and deep religious conviction. It is in this most "secular" of the wisdom writings that we stumble across the odd saying that at once raises the book from its matter-of-fact level and reminds us that this is part of the revelation to Israel: "The spirit of man is the candle of the Lord" (20: 27); "Where there is no vision, the people perish" (29: 18).

ECCLESIASTES

ECCLESIASTES is a book about which most people have mixed feelings. It almost failed to gain admission into the canon of the Old Testament when the Jewish Church made up its list of sacred scriptures at Jamnia in A.D. 90. Like *Esther* and the *Song of Solomon* it was among the last of the Hebrew writings to be accepted as suitable, but for different reasons. In the case of *Ecclesiastes* what gave rise to misgiving among the learned doctors was its apparent encouragement of scepticism and disillusionment.

This rather upsets some modern commentators too, and the book is criticised for its "cynicism", its "selfish materialism" and "agnosticism". It is generally agreed that *Ecclesiastes* as we know it is not the book that was originally written. Later hands than the author's have amended his work and interpolated more pious sentiments here and there throughout. It is by virtue of these alterations that *Ecclesiastes* was ultimately passed as fit to be included in the Hebrew Bible.

The author, who remains anonymous, is known by the Greek name Ecclesiastes, which is an attempt to translate the original Hebrew word meaning a "lecturer" rather than a "preacher". He seems to have been an elderly well-to-do Jew living in or near Jerusalem somewhere about 200 B.C., when the unsatisfactory rule of Persia had given place to the greater corruption of Greek administration. The book suggests a social order that has few redeeming features; injustice is rampant, oppression is severe and there is little hope on the horizon. The disguise of king Solomon which the writer adopts is of course a literary device; language, allusions and background make this clear.

Commentators are by no means agreed as to what constituted the original work and what must be regarded as later additions. Those who prefer to think of Ecclesiastes as a thoroughgoing sceptic and pessimist tend to attribute every vestige of religious sentiment to later hands. A more moderate view would on the other hand leave room for variations in a man's moods, and would credit Ecclesiastes with being neither an inspired visionary like the prophets nor an out-and-out fatalist like Omar Khayyam. May he not have been a man of a sober turn of mind who lived in a society which was in a parlous state, who saw life in all its cruelty and contradictions and yet out of his experience evolved a working philosophy for himself and his readers? Let us at all events take the book as it stands and look at it as a whole, without troubling too much to wonder what are the actual original words of Ecclesiastes, but trying rather to see what message the book in its present form has for us today.

Regarded in this light it becomes more than anything else a volume of memoirs, the memoirs of a man in the later years of life, reviewing his experiences and giving his verdict on the world as he sees it. He might have called it: "A Wanderer's Way". The first note he strikes is sombre but universally shared: Vanity of vanities, all is vanity (1 : 2). What is the good of life, what is it all for, why this struggle? It will be all the same a hundred years from now. The sun, the moon, the stars, the sea—they are all there as they have been from the beginning and so they will continue. While we poor mortals are like a puff of smoke or a breath of wind, a flutter of wings across the stage of life. Is this not a mood that is familiar to all of us?

Then in his *nom de plume* of Solomon, Ecclesiastes goes on to tell us how in one way and another he tried to find happiness. First he looked for it in learning. Nothing must be a closed book to him. He must know everything. He wanted to be the wisest man in the world, the most knowledgeable, the most cultured. He aimed at being a philosopher and an encyclopædia rolled into one, and in the end he had to confess failure. He found that "in much wisdom is much grief, and he that increaseth knowledge increaseth sorrow" (1 : 18). This is surely a true verdict that final happiness is as little to be found in amassing knowledge as in amassing money. We should all echo 12 : 12!

Then Ecclesiastes turned to pleasure. He rang the changes on the eternal theme of wine, women and song. He built himself houses and fancy gardens, employed a large staff, collected curios and antiques, and became the richest man in Jerusalem. Whatever he wanted he took; whatever caught his eye was as good as his. Then came the inevitable climax when everything turned to ashes in his mouth. Once again he registers "vanity and vexation of spirit".

This we may reflect is surely the experience of every man who sets out to have what he calls a "good time", which generally means having a very expensive time, a very silly time, and for anyone with a modicum of intelligence, rather a dull time. And what is Ecclesiastes' reaction? As we might expect: "therefore I hated life" (2 : 17). It is small wonder that the rabbis hesitated over including this book in the Jewish canon. This is the sort of thing we should not say —and yet how true it is to human experience.

A man hates life and curses creation when he finds himself thwarted in his desire for happiness. He sets his heart on one thing after another and they all fail him. "Therefore I hated life"—what else could he do? All his wealth and property, he reflects sadly, go to another. How is he to know that the fortune that cost him so many years of his life and so much hardship will not be squandered to the four winds by his heirs? Ecclesiastes is having *un mauvais quart d'heure* and he does not spare himself.

He looks round on the world

and sees things as they are, not merely as they ought to be. He sees the weak being oppressed and power in the hands of unjust men. He sees men envied and hated because they perform acts of kindness. He sees honest men going to the wall and tricksters prospering. And he says what many a man has said since his day: May God help you if you are alone when misfortune comes your way because the world will raise no finger to assist you. There is no sentimentality in Ecclesiastes' make-up. He wears no rose-coloured spectacles.

He saw that in life it is not always the swiftest man who wins the race, or the strong man who wins the battle. It is not always the ablest men who live in plenty or the most skilful men who get on best at their trade. For bad luck may overtake them all (9: 11). He tells the story of the poor wise man who saved his city and was promptly forgotten (9: 14-16). This is not the world of the story-books, but it is the world we have to live in, and it is the world that Ecclesiastes knew. "I have seen servants upon horses," he says, "and princes walking as servants upon the earth" (10: 7). Have not we all seen them too?

So Ecclesiastes is bitter as we all are at times with good cause. But we need not always be, says our author. In his famous passage on time (3: 1-8) he shows us that everything has its place. There is a time to laugh and a time to weep, a time to mourn and a time to rejoice, a time to despair and a time to hope. There is not a single good man on earth whose good deeds are without some sin (7: 20). This is something we must simply accept, together with all the other unpleasant truths that experience teaches us, including the fact of death. That is the one thing in this world of which we may be certain (2: 14).

But, he reflects, there is a time to be worried by the dark side of life and a time to look on the other side; a time to face facts and be depressed and a time to face other facts and take comfort. After all since we must die we must die, but a living dog is better than a dead lion (9: 4). While there is life there is hope.

Then, summing up his experience as a whole, he says some very wise things. The world is as it is and this we must accept. But we must not let it get us down. Go your way, says Ecclesiastes, eat your bread with joy and drink your wine with a merry heart. Take a pride in your appearance. Live happily with your wife and family as long as you have them and whatever you have to do do it with all your might (9: 7-10). Rejoice while you can, remove sorrow from your heart and put away evil from your flesh (11: 9-10).

Thus might the worldly wise Polonius have addressed Laertes. But Ecclesiastes' last word is not the philosophy of a courtier but of a man who has looked deeper into men and affairs than in polite exchanges. He is closing his memoir. He has, as he says, seen life from every angle. It holds no novelty for him. He has had his joys and sorrows, and he has not flinched from looking the facts fair and square in the face. Now the old warrior, making an apology for adding yet another book to the world's collection, gives his considered opinion of life in all its variety: "Let us hear," he says, "the conclusion of the whole matter: Fear God and keep his commandments: for this is the whole duty of man" (12: 13). With this impressive conclusion we reach the end of a singularly frank and honest book.

Ecclesiastes does not share the easy optimism of the book of *Proverbs*. He faces up to the problem of individual retribution, maintaining that misfortune does not necessarily overtake the wicked in his lifetime and that the path of the honest man is not rose-strewn. But he has no answer except that it is all a matter of luck and chance. On the other hand he shares the view of the authors of the *Proverbs* that death is the end of everything. The traditional Hebrew conception of the after life as Sheol, the abode of the shades, these ghostly replicas of men, still satisfies him. Men like animals "all go unto one place: all are of the dust and all turn to dust again" (3: 20).

This belief, the disordered times he lived in and probably a naturally sombre turn of mind, have combined to produce what no one would claim to be a wholly true philosophy of life. It is perhaps not unjust to call it a gospel of moderation in all things, designed for tired men living in chaotic times. There is no suggestion that one should do anything about the sorry mess that the world is in other than bear it with resignation. There is a paralysing discouragement of idealism and altruism and far too much self-interest. A man who was more interested in helping his neighbour than in seeking happiness for himself would not feel so strongly that all was vanity.

Ecclesiastes is a one-sided picture. Yet it is a picture that corresponds with many of our own moods when we see in the world what Ecclesiastes saw. It would seem that the Bible in its capacity as a looking glass of life has kept here a place, as Dean Bradley said, "for the sigh of defeated hopes, and for the gloom of the soul vanquished by the sense of the anomalies and mysteries of human life".

The beginning of the last chapter (12: 1–7), a superb allegory of the onset of old age and the progressive deterioration of bodily functions, is a literary masterpiece.

THE SONG OF SOLOMON

I F THE Old Testament were indeed the collected literature of a nation there would be nothing remarkable about the inclusion in it of the *Song of Songs*. Poems about love feature in the literary output of any civilisation. The Old Testament is, however, Hebrew literature edited and sifted by theologians, whose concern is that what is contained within its covers shall be sacred writings designed to edify and to regulate the life of the people of YHWH. There could be no place in such a lofty purpose for an anthology of poems which deal with sexual love and dwell sensuously on the physical attractions of the human body.

We may be grateful, therefore, that by virtue of the fact that these songs are capable of being interpreted allegorically, the rabbis, albeit with some hesitation, finally decided to include this book in the official list of Jewish scriptures (see p. 242). By identifying the two young lovers as YHWH and Israel, the erotic character of the poems could be given a religious significance, and, when the Old Testament became also Christian scriptures, the Church followed the Jewish example by making the lover Christ, while his lass became the Church, the soul or the Virgin Mary.

Doubtless the name of Solomon which was attached to the poems assisted their entry into the canon. But like the *Proverbs* which are attributed to him, these songs can hardly have formed part of his repertoire, although he is credited with 1,005 (*I Kings* 4: 32). Not only do they date from about the third century B.C., but the kind of love they describe is not the jaded lusts of the harem but the frank and honest passion of two ordinary young people.

It is sometimes suggested that these poems originally formed a drama revolving round Solomon's desire for Abishag (*I Kings* 1: 15; 2: 22), or that their background is the sacred marriage of a god and a goddess with its roots in paganism. It is simpler, however, to take them at their face value, and to be grateful that the Bible includes this little book which is not only unsurpassably beautiful as a piece of writing, but also sets the seal of divine approval on human love and affection despite the well meant attempts of Jewish and Christian ecclesiastics to transform it into something it was never intended to be.

If these were songs sung at a village wedding, where, as in Syria to this day, the bridegroom and bride are king and queen for the week's festivities, the mingling of apparently royal personages with simple peasants is easily explained.

ISAIAH

FROM THIS point until the end of the Old Testament we must come to grips with the message of the Hebrew prophets. We have already encountered them in various ways. Hardly a book in the Old Testament that we have already looked at has been uninfluenced by them, either in the substance of its teaching or in the actual drafting of its contents. The collection of books from *Isaiah* to *Malachi* covers a period of roughly five centuries, from 750–250 B.C., but of course as we have seen prophecy in Israel is far older (see pp. 190–191). In the early days of the monarchy bands of ecstatics were common enough and the impact on the community of individual prophets of the calibre of Samuel, Nathan, and Elijah was profound.

The difference between these earlier prophets and the later prophets from Isaiah onwards is not primarily one of function. All of them were men of YHWH and upholders of the Sinai tradition. Some were more articulate and some more fanatical than others. All of them claimed to be speaking on behalf of God, and none of them regarded the faith of Israel as a meditative pursuit to be engaged in within the cloister or the study but as something to be proclaimed, defended and fought for in the political and social stresses of his day. "Keeping politics out of the pulpit" was the last thing any prophet ever dreamt of doing.

What distinguishes the "latter" or "classical" prophets from their predecessors is simply that their utterances have been preserved and collected in written form. Not all that they said is of equal quality and not all the "writing" prophets can be called great. But among them and within the collected works of most of them, are to be found the men and the ideas that moulded Israel's faith and prepared the way for the coming of Christ and the institution of his Church.

In the Jewish scriptures the works of the prophets stand next in importance to the Torah, and occupy the central section of the Hebrew Bible. In our English versions the books of the prophets come last, and rather confusingly follow books which have obviously been influenced by them (e.g. *Psalms* and *Proverbs*), but since the prophets also shaped the form of the Torah there is little to choose between the Jewish and Christian order. Yet even within the prophetic section of the Old Testament itself the order of books is arbitrary, Amos for example being an earlier prophet than Isaiah, and the sequence seems to have depended on mechanical considerations of size rather than on chronology. Three large books —*Isaiah, Jeremiah* and *Ezekiel*— are followed by twelve short books which together made up a scroll of approximately the same length as one of the major three. *Lamentations* and *Daniel* were not included among the prophets in the Jewish original but formed part of the third section of their Bible, the Writings.

The book of *Isaiah* illustrates in an extreme form the character of these prophetic books in general. They are essentially collections of prophecies. Fundamentally the same process lies behind a prophetic book as lies behind a book of the Pentateuch or the psalter. Each book consists of isolated items of different dates and often of different authorship, assembled over a long period of years. Some of the prophetic books are more or less by the same hand throughout, like *Amos*, others, like *Isaiah*, are obviously the collected utterances of several prophets.

Since the prophets spoke to their own times it is often easy to detect obvious differences of authorship, as in *Isaiah*, although sometimes the verdict depends more on questions of style than on historical allusions. The books as we have them were not writtten wholly by the prophets themselves. It is not clear how far each of them was personally responsible for collecting his prophecies and how far they were collected by disciples either at the time or subsequently.

At all events a major difficulty in reading a prophetic book consists in the fact that we rarely find a consecutive narrative, or even a chronological sequence of oracles, but rather an anthology of fugitive pieces of different dates, referring to different situations, sometimes

by authors living in different centuries. The main substance consists of short public utterances, no doubt recorded on the spot by disciples, together with actual visions or experiences of the prophet, and sermon notes written or dictated by the prophets themselves, together with some biographical details.

The larger prophetic books in particular consist of collections of collections, small books containing a prophet's utterances joined together to make one large book, with no obvious break between the different oracles or the different collections, and with no apparent order or arrangement. The study of the text of the prophets is thus the work of a lifetime. All we can do is to avail ourselves of the considerable help of a modern translation, accept the general conclusions of the experts, and look for the salient points in each prophet's contribution.

First Isaiah

(1 : 1 – 39 : 8)

THE BOOK of *Isaiah* as we have it is the work of at least three prophets. The man who gave the book its name was an eighth century prophet living in Jerusalem and roughly contemporary with Amos and Hosea. His part of the book extends from chs. 1–39. From chs. 40–55 the prophecies are the work of an unknown prophet living in Babylon during the Exile, approximately two centuries later. For all we know his name may also have been Isaiah, but he is generally referred to as Second or Deutero-Isaiah. The concluding section of the book, chs. 56–66, consists of prophecies dating from the period after the Exile, spoken by someone living in Palestine, generally for convenience called Third or Trito-Isaiah.

When we bear in mind that many scholars on good grounds claim that within these three sections there are also many oracles which are not attributable to any of these three Isaiahs, we may be tempted to throw up our hands in despair. But the difficulty is no greater with Isaiah than with Moses. Moses was responsible for some of the laws of Israel, indeed the basic elements in the Torah. We may therefore speak justifiably of the whole of the Law as Mosaic, because all subsequent legislation was regarded as being promulgated in accordance with the fundamental principles laid down by him.

Similarly we must think of a prophet not so much as an isolated individual but as the founder of a school. His disciples in his own lifetime and for long after would regard themselves as bound by his teaching and called on to continue his work (cf. 8: 16). Whatever prophetic gifts they had they would reckon to use in the spirit of the master. Thus we must not think of the disciples of Isaiah as simply editing the words of the founder of the school, but of themselves enriching with fresh contributions the legacy he had left them.

If, as is not unknown in the fine arts, an apprentice should prove to be a greater craftsman than his master, pious veneration would see to it that his work would bear the master's name. We may thus regard the book of *Isaiah* as the dis-

tillation of three hundred years of prophecy inspired by Isaiah of Jerusalem, and containing among the work of his many disciples that of the anonymous spokesman of YHWH in Babylon, perhaps the greatest of the Old Testament prophets.

In trying to discover what the various prophets have to say, we ought in each case to turn back to the record of the times in which they lived so far as it is available in the historical books of the Old Testament. In the case of the first Isaiah (chs. 1–39) the background is Judah in the second half of the eighth century B.C. (see pp. 198–200). His career as a prophet begins on a note which is characteristic. In ch. 6 we are told how in the Temple at Jerusalem he had a vision of the holiness of YHWH. A sense of the otherness of YHWH, of his power and majesty, seizes and overwhelms him.

But for Isaiah it is more than the sovereignty of a remote ruler of the universe, it is the moral holiness of a God who cares, that brings him to his knees. It is a holiness that shows up his own life and that of his countrymen as something pitiably unworthy and unclean. He is filled with remorse and contrition but his penitence is rewarded, for by a symbolic act his lips are touched by YHWH's messenger and he is set apart to proclaim the Word of God. This vision takes place about 740 B.C., and for the next forty years Isaiah is in the centre of public affairs as the counsellor and adviser of kings and statesmen. He had received a call from God, like Moses and later St. Paul, and in his vision he finds the key to his life's work.

It is that conception of the moral holiness of God which leads Isaiah to denounce the injustices and wrongs of his time. His wrath is directed mainly against the rich for their oppression of the poor, for their perversion of justice, for their luxury and drunkenness (5:1-12). He attacks the widespread superstitious regard for religious ceremonial, and calls his countrymen to repentance and to the true service of YHWH (1:11-18). Chapter one may be taken as an introduction to the prophecies that follow and indeed as a summary of Isaiah's message.

But he knows full well that his cry is unlikely to be heeded and he warns his hearers of the approaching judgment of YHWH (1:19-20). This is of course Assyria. To the good patriotic Hebrew the rising power of Assyria was an affront to YHWH, but to Isaiah Assyria was the rod in YHWH's hand with which he would chasten his people (10:5-6). Yet such was Isaiah's conviction of the unique vocation of Israel and the special role of Jerusalem and its Temple, that he could not believe that YHWH would allow his people or his holy city to perish. Discipline there must be, but there would always be a faithful handful who would respond to God's challenge and so ensure a future for the chosen community (1:9; 10:20-22).

This conception of the "remnant", a theme which we have already seen hinted at in the stories of Noah and Elijah, and which is basic to St. Paul's conception of the Church as built upon the "remnant" of old Israel (Rom. 9:27; 11:5), is one of the outstanding contributions of Isaiah to Old Testament theology. With characteristic prophetic symbolism he calls his two sons by names which indicate his convictions both of God's impending judgment ("Spoilsoon, Prey-quick"—8:3-4), and of his supervening mercy ("A remnant-shall-return [to YHWH]"—7:3).

The short term effect of these convictions was that his advice on foreign policy was invariably in terms of avoiding involvement in political alliances. YHWH alone must be the rock on which his people's trust should be stayed. Nothing could stop Assyria from destroying Damascus and Samaria but Jerusalem would be spared, for when YHWH had used Assyria for his purposes he would crush it and humble its pride (10:1-22).

Isaiah's forecast of the fall of Damascus (732 B.C.) and Samaria (722 B.C.) proved correct, and when it came to be Jerusalem's turn to be besieged (701 B.C.) he was proved right again. Pestilence in the army or trouble in the empire drove Sennacherib back to Assyria in haste (see p. 200). While the situation was still tense, king Hezekiah sent a deputation in sackcloth and ashes to Isaiah in the hope that YHWH would save Jerusalem.

Doubtless this incident, recorded in II Kings 19 and also in Isa. 37 was the occasion on which Hezekiah promised some of the reforms with which he is credited in II Kings 18:3-5. Isaiah welcomed them joyfully. This was the sign of national repentance for which YHWH was waiting. Assyria having served its purpose could now be dispensed with and Jerusalem would be spared. So in a series of anti-Assyrian prophecies Isaiah sees Sennacherib sent packing with a ring in his nose and a bridle in his mouth (37: 29).

After this major triumph in 701 B.C. Isaiah is heard of no more. Tradition adds that he was sawn asunder in the reign of the notorious Manasseh, and perhaps the author of *Hebrews* in his roll of honour of Israel's martyrs refers to this (*Heb.* 11: 37). Many of the prophecies of *Isa.* 1–39, which may not have originated from this statesmanlike prophet of Jerusalem, have no obvious relevance for us today (e.g. chs. 13–23) and some (chs. 24–27) bear an apocalyptic character which is best examined when we look at the book of *Daniel* (see pp. 269–273).

But for dramatic quality there can be few equals of this master in the Old Testament. On a first reading, his oracles should be read through as a whole to gain an impression of their power. But special notice should be taken of the series of prophecies which look forward to a future time beyond the turmoil of political events through which Isaiah lived. He pictures Israel under a just and righteous ruler in a world at peace, with tyranny and oppression done away. He envisages nothing less than a new Creation where the warring elements in the world of nature as well as among men are reconciled. It is in effect a world in which God's purpose is at last fulfilled, where "the earth shall be full of the knowledge of the Lord, as the waters cover the sea" (2: 2–4; 29: 18–21; 32: 15–20; 32: 1–5; 9: 2–7; 11: 1–9).

Isaiah may have had in mind some future Davidic king and a restoration of the glories of David's kingdom, but his thoughts were surely being guided towards a hope that no human monarch could fulfil and to a Kingdom that reached beyond this world. To Israel, alone among the nations came this messianic hope, growing stronger the more the fallibility of kings and the inadequacies of their people became apparent. It was on words like these which sprang from no human questing for an answer to the complexity of the human situation, but came from a God whose will it was that men should learn to look to him alone for the answer, that the faith of Israel came to depend in the troublous times that lay ahead. In the providence of God it was words like these which taught the first Christians to see in Jesus the fulfilment of Israel's hope, and to recognise in the life of the Church that he founded the foretaste of the new order that Isaiah so confidently proclaimed.

Similarly, when in his words to king Ahaz he gave an assurance that within a few years after the birth of a royal prince, Israel's present dangers would be overcome and therefore the child might safely be named in faith: "God is with us" (7: 14–16), we need not think that because a fuller understanding of the Hebrew words now makes it plain that this is no prediction of the Virgin Birth of Jesus, St. Matthew was wholly mistaken in regarding this passage as if it were (*Matt.* 1: 23). Isaiah's prophecy was fulfilled in a deeper sense than he or St. Matthew knew when the Word was made flesh and "God with us" became a reality not only for Israel but for the world.

Second Isaiah

(40: 1 – 55: 13)

WHEN WE turn from the recorded utterances of Isaiah of Jerusalem (chs. 1–39) to those of his great disciple whose prophecies are collected in chs. 40–55 we are in a different setting and a different century. Judah has ceased to exist; Jerusalem is in ruins; Assyria has been replaced as the world empire by Babylon and Babylon itself is on the point of being supplanted by the new power of Persia under its remarkable ruler Cyrus. The scene is the Exile, the audience is the sometimes despondent, sometimes hopeful Jewish community in Babylon, separated by many miles of desert country from the rump of David's kingdom from which they had been forcibly deported in 587 B.C. (see pp. 208–210).

Towards the end of the harrowing half century that followed, a new voice of authority was heard, perhaps about 540 B.C. Jeremiah and Ezekiel had already taught the most responsive and sensitive elements in the exiled community to see in the shattering of their kingdom the just judgment of YHWH on the failure of the people of his choice, and to look on the Exile as a necessary discipline, a time for reflection and a chance of making amends. But not all the exiles were able to take so lofty a view. Many felt that YHWH had deserted them and that the gods of Babylon had proved more power-

ful. Most of them were doubtless weary of captivity and even if some had come to terms with the new environment many still wept when they remembered Zion (cf. *Ps.* 137).

Accordingly a message of encouragement and hope was timely and this is what Second Isaiah provides. The opening words of ch. 40 strike the note that dominates his work: "Console my people, console them—it is the voice of your God—speak to Jerusalem tenderly, proclaim to her that her hard days are ended, her guilt paid off, that she has received from the Eternal's hand full punishment for all her sins" (vv. 1–2). Indeed this first chapter of the prophecies of Second Isaiah, one of the greatest chapters in the Old Testament, may be taken, like the first chapter of First Isaiah, as an introduction and summary of his message.

The general theme of chs. 40–48 is the impending liberation of the exiles by Cyrus' conquest of Babylon, and that of the remaining chapters 49–55 is the return of the exiles to Jerusalem. But Second Isaiah sees in this far more than a turn of events in international affairs. It is YHWH who has raised up Cyrus to be the means of setting his people free, and it is YHWH who will enable him to complete his appointed task of subduing Babylon. Even if there was a resistance movement among the Jews to which Second Isaiah belonged and which was in contact with Cyrus, nevertheless these are still the words of an unknown member of a community of displaced persons in the heart of a once powerful empire, and the reference is to the man who will shortly control more territory than any world ruler had ever done before. For Second Isaiah, however, he is but an instrument which in the wisdom of YHWH, of whom Cyrus at this stage had doubtless not even heard. This is indeed the foolishness of preaching which in the wisdom of God saves them that believe (*I Cor.* 1:21).

When the Lord of history has used Cyrus for his purposes the way will be open for the exiles to return, and Second Isaiah pictures a miraculous highway opening up across the desert along which YHWH will lead his people home as a shepherd leads his sheep (40:3–11). Nothing less than such a vision would satisfy the prophet for to him this return of the exiles would be a second Exodus. Once more YHWH would save his people from a living death and offer them the possibility of new life. As he had brought order out of chaos and light out of darkness at the Creation, and cleft the hostile sea that barred the way to the promised land, so would he once again be strong to save (51:9–15) and once more Jerusalem would be the dwelling place of YHWH among his ingathered people (54:1–17).

With biting irony Second Isaiah taunts the Babylonians and ridicules the prognostications of their astrologers (47:1–15). The gods they serve, Marduk and the rest, are blocks of wood which men carve into shape after they have used the rest of the tree to cook their food and keep themselves warm (44:9–17). When the downfall of Babylon comes these paltry idols will be carried on the backs of their devotees to safety, impedimenta strapped to the mule-train. But YHWH is no helpless burden, for he himself has borne his people from childhood and will sustain them to the end (46:1–4).

Second Isaiah builds upon the insights of his master, Isaiah of Jerusalem. For the first Isaiah YHWH was God of Israel, greater than all other gods, but for Isaiah of Babylon there is only one God and all the rest are figments of man's imagination. "Is there a God beside me? . . . I know not any" (44:8). This is the high peak of Old Testament monotheism, implicit since the days of Moses but only now fully expressed. The God of Sinai is the eternal Creator, the ruler of princes, the lord of history, yet with it all the Shepherd who gathers his lambs in his arms. The majesty of God of which Ezekiel was so conscious, and the presence of God of which Jeremiah was so sure, are here in Second Isaiah sublimely united (40:10–15, 21–31).

Like Hosea and Jeremiah, Isaiah of Babylon is profoundly aware of the love that is in the heart of God towards mankind, and like Ezekiel he cannot see the impending return to the homeland as anything but a gracious act of a merciful God towards his wayward people. But there is a tenderness in the God of Second Isaiah that is lacking in the God of Ezekiel (55:6–7). God will forgive Israel because it is his nature to have mercy. Through no merit of his people but only by virtue of God's readiness to pardon, will Israel be given a fresh start and an opportunity to serve him in peace and freedom (44:22; 48:11).

More clearly than ever before, Israel's faith is seen by Second Isaiah to be a faith for the whole world and not a private possession of the Jews (45: 22–23). Israel's vocation is to be the bearer of God's revelation so that in days to come with Jerusalem rebuilt as the centre of true worship, and Israel as a living witness to God's saving power, Gentile nations yet unknown will flock to share in a new covenant relationship and in the blessing of YHWH's bounty (55: 1–5).

But, alas for Second Isaiah's hopes, almost a century and a half were to pass before Jerusalem had its walls and Temple and a people pledged to the obedience of the Law. As we have seen (pp. 209–210), the response to Cyrus' edict of liberation was lukewarm, and the rebuilding of the Temple had to wait for Haggai and Zechariah as the reconstruction of the city had to wait for Nehemiah. Not until Ezra's day was there any sign of Israel's common purpose or of its unity as the covenant people. Even then it was an exclusive and narrow conception of the covenant, which, despite the protests of such manifestoes as *Ruth* (see pp. 160–161) and *Jonah* (see pp. 294–295), saw little if any good in Gentiles and no obligation to share with them "the sure mercies of David" (55: 3).

Second Isaiah's achievement must be reckoned in longer terms. Such insights as he was granted were of a quality that awakened response only in the most sensitive minds, but it was due to him as much as anyone that Haggai and Nehemiah and Ezra were able to awaken any enthusiasm at all, and

that after the arid days of Judaism, the Gospel was able to speak in a language that had once been heard but in the meanwhile had been forgotten. The true fulfilment of Second Isaiah's prophecies came with Christ and his Church.

In the same sense we must look to the New Testament for the fulfilment of what is perhaps Second Isaiah's greatest contribution, the conception of the Suffering Servant. Discussion of this mysterious figure, described in four short songs (42: 1–4; 49: 1–6; 50: 4–9; 52: 13 – 53: 12) has occupied many critical volumes. The Servant has been thought to be, among a host of other suggestions, Jeremiah, the prophet himself, Israel, the faithful minority within the community, the ideal people of God. Possibly all of these, and more, were in the prophet's mind when he drew this picture of the perfect Servant of God who through his sufferings and death brought men to the knowledge of God.

It may be that the songs are slightly later than the rest of the prophecies and that they spring from Second Isaiah's disappointment. Cyrus did not give YHWH credit for his victories, neither did Israel joyfully accept YHWH's proffered chance of liberation and renewal. Perhaps out of the prophet's disillusionment came this conviction of Israel's future role, to be a people destined to suffer on behalf of others and thus to win the world for God. It was a prophecy that in the event Israel did not wish to understand.

But Jesus understood it, as did the apostles, and no words of Old Testament scripture played so large a part in early Christian theology as *Isaiah* 53: 1–12 (*Luke* 24: 13–34; *Acts* 8: 26–39). If the prophecies of the first Isaiah concerning the messianic king (see pp. 251–252) prepared the minds of the people of God for the coming of the Lord's anointed Messiah, it was Second Isaiah's conception of the Servant which Jesus made his own and fused with the author of *Daniel*'s conception of the Son of Man (*Dan*. 7: 13) to create his own unique interpretation of the kind of Messiah he chose to be. Thus the vocation that Israel rejected was fulfilled by the one true Israelite, and by the mysterious moving of God's Spirit the finger of this unknown and at the time unheeded prophet of the Exile points directly to Christ.

Third Isaiah
(56: 1 – 66: 24)

THE LAST section of the *Isaiah* collection, generally known as *Third Isaiah* (chs. 56–66), switches us back to Palestine but it is not the Palestine that the first Isaiah knew. It is rather the Palestine of Malachi (see pp. 305–306). Jerusalem is still in ruins (60: 10) although the Temple is rebuilt (56: 7). The time is therefore somewhere between Haggai and Nehemiah, i.e. between 516 and 444 B.C. (see p. 210). Although much in these chapters is reminiscent of Second Isaiah there is neither the glow of his enthusiasm nor the unity of his message. It seems likely that the work of several of his disciples has been assembled to form a conclusion to the scroll.

There is an air of despondency, not unexpected at a time when the remnant of Judah was suffering under Persian vassalage, when economic conditions were hard and when Israel's former enemies were taking delight in harrying a defenceless community, many of whom had fallen back into paganism. Second Isaiah would surely not have been concerned with so peripheral an aspect of obedience as the correct observance of the sabbath (56: 1–7), yet even within this legalistic framework there is a genuine desire to break down the barrier between Jews and proselytes which the later hardening process of Judaism tended to discourage (56: 3–5), and our Lord quotes a significant verse from this passage in his condemnation of the traders in the Temple (*Mark* 11: 17—see p. 376).

Despite the depressing environment, the light of prophecy was not dimmed and there are many splendid utterances in this concluding section (e.g. 57: 15 – 58: 14; 60: 1 – 62: 12; 63: 7 – 64: 12). When Christ came to his home town of Nazareth and preached to his former neighbours and friends, he chose as his text Third Isaiah's words in 61: 1–2 (omitting "the day of vengeance"), finding once more in the divine inspiration of these majestic oracles the key to his own mission (*Luke* 4: 16–21).

JEREMIAH

After the soaring heights of Isaiah's thought the book of *Jeremiah* is at first sight disappointing. It is certainly extremely confusing. There is no obvious order and no clear theme, except apparently that of sustained denunciation of everything and everybody. It is small wonder that the utterances of this prophet have introduced the word "jeremiad" into the English language. We tend to skim swiftly over the first half of the book which presents these problems, and hail with relief the fairly straightforward narrative of the major events in the prophet's life which begins at ch. 26. Perhaps it is best to start at that point and read through to 45: 5 before turning to the teaching of Jeremiah contained in the first twenty-five chapters. If we do this we shall undoubtedly revise our hasty judgment and recognise why indeed this much misunderstood prophet ranks among the greatest in Israel.

Jeremiah marks the final stage in the downfall of Judah (see pp. 199–202). He is in fact the best authority we have for the last days of Jerusalem, since his active life covered the closing forty years of the existence of the southern kingdom (626–587 B.C.; cf. 1: 1–3). Whatever reforms king Hezekiah had carried out in the state religion his successor Manasseh had undone. His reign (696–641 B.C.)

which was the longest in Judah's history was also the worst. All the indignation and horror that the editors of the book of *Kings* can command is summoned up to denounce the apostasy of Manasseh, who introduced pagan gods and pagan practices including astrology, necromancy and human sacrifice (*II Kings* 21: 1–17).

It was probably during his reign that within the underground movement which supported the ideas of the eighth century prophets, the laws of *Deuteronomy* were compiled (see p. 132). At all events in 622 B.C., during the reign of his grandson Josiah (639–609 B.C.), while repairs were being carried out in the Temple this "book of the law" was discovered, whereupon Josiah instituted a much more thoroughgoing reformation of the established religion than Hezekiah had done. Not only were all traces of foreign cults, doubtless many of them Assyrian, cleared out of the Temple, but every religious shrine in Judah apart from the Temple at Jerusalem was suppressed. There was now only one place in the land where YHWH could be publicly worshipped, and the syncretism from which the national religion had suffered in one way or another ever since the conquest of Canaan finally came to an end.

Outside Judah on the other

hand the prospect was dispiriting. The bugbear of First Isaiah's day, Assyria, was now herself on her last legs, which was no doubt why Josiah could risk offending her by sweeping away, among other abuses, the religious evidence of her political supremacy in the form of Assyrian cults, which Manasseh had been forced to incorporate in the state religion. The end of Assyrian domination, however, brought no relief to the harassed principalities of Palestine, including Judah, for the new star on the horizon, Babylon, having demolished Assyria and Egypt, turned her attention to the smaller fry and Jerusalem finally fell to Nebuchadnezzar in 587 B.C. Thus the two chief external factors in Jeremiah's life were the inspiring reformation of religion by Josiah at home, and the depressing certainty of invasion and exile abroad.

Jeremiah started on his prophetic mission, like First Isaiah, as the result of a vision. He came of a priestly family and his boyhood was spent in the village of Anathoth, just outside Jerusalem. His love of country life, so prominent in the allusions of his oracles, is one of his most attractive characteristics. Obviously neither Isaiah nor Jeremiah formulated his message exclusively on the basis of the vision that launched him into his public ministry. The vision served to clinch the thoughts that were already searching for expression in his mind and gave them the necessary impetus.

This is made plain by Jeremiah himself in the first chapter of his book, where he tells of the struggle that went on within himself before

he could find courage to take the vital step that committed him to be the spokesman of YHWH to his generation (1: 4–10). Here is the picture of a young man—perhaps at the time no more than twenty—sensitive, shy and thoughtful; well aware that the times were out of joint but dreading the inevitable conflicts that public life would force upon him. Yet he is seized willy-nilly by a stronger power than his own which forces down his protestations, summons him to action and gives him his commission to be YHWH's prophet.

Two other visions accompany his call. On a country walk he sees an almond tree in first blossom. From the tree the voice of YHWH speaks to him telling him that just as when branches appear to be dead there is still new life within them, so YHWH though he seems to be asleep is ever wakeful and will soon make his power felt. The second is a vision which a seething cauldron evokes of the trouble that is brewing for Judah by the judgment of YHWH and which will soon boil over (1: 11–19).

So this retiring, self-conscious man is dragged into the vortex of public affairs and subsequently endures greater tribulation and hardship than any other prophet. He has been called the Father of the Saints, and many have thought that his sufferings were in the mind of Second Isaiah when he wrote of the Servant of YHWH who bore the sins of his people (see p. 254). Jeremiah's life was indeed a prolonged agony in which both grief of mind and pain of body tested his faith and resolution.

He began to preach while the

country still suffered from the effects of the reign of the notorious Manasseh. Five years later came the specious reforms of Josiah, which Jeremiah seems to have welcomed joyfully and to have commended up and down the country (11: 1–14). It must have seemed to him at first that this was the answer to his repeated plea that YHWH's unfaithful people should repent of their idolatrous practices, and return to the God who had bound them to himself in love and loyalty at Sinai (2: 1–4: 4).

The prophet's enthusiasm was short lived, however, and despondency returned when he realised that the reforms amounted merely to a superficial trifling with the framework while at heart the nation was still at loggerheads with YHWH. He found that all that had happened was that instead of pinning their faith in the ritual of the local sanctuaries to save them, people now regarded the existence of the centralised worship of the Temple as a gigantic insurance policy covering the whole nation. There had been a change of external arrangements but no change of heart.

So during the reigns of Josiah's successors right up to the fall of Jerusalem, Jeremiah's whole life becomes a protest. As a result of a dramatic sermon in the Temple (ch. 7), he is charged with blasphemy and barely escapes with his life (ch. 26). Forbidden himself to enter the Temple, and having recourse to writing, he succeeds in having his prophecies read there as a manifesto by his faithful disciple and secretary Baruch, foretelling the disasters that YHWH will bring upon his obdurate people through the scourge of Babylon.

When the document reaches king Jehoiakim, he contemptuously slashes with a penknife each section of the prophet's work as it is read to him, and burns the scroll. Jeremiah and Baruch are, however, safe in hiding and the prophet has the last word by producing an enlarged second edition of his oracles with a special curse on Jehoiakim (ch. 36). On another occasion Jeremiah was put in the stocks (20: 2), on yet another he was flogged (37: 15), and it is not difficult to understand the reason for his misfortunes. He was against kings and nobles, priests and people. The tragedy for him was that he hated being in opposition, and yet like Luther he felt that he could do no other.

In 598 B.C. the first deportation to Babylon had taken place, and Jeremiah consistently maintained that there was no future for Judah. The Holy Land with its inviolable Temple had become a superstition —a religious talisman which made the genuine service of YHWH appear irrelevant. The real hope of true religion, said Jeremiah, lay with Judah in exile, uprooted from an illusory reliance upon stone buildings and historic altars (chs. 24 and 29). From exile they would return and found a new state, and a Davidic king would yet reign again over a purged and regenerate commonwealth (chs. 30–33). As proof of this conviction, even during the siege of Jerusalem, Jeremiah from his prison cell ostentatiously bought a plot of land in his native village of Anathoth (32: 1–15).

Since the downfall of Judah was the will of God, there was no point in resisting the Babylonian threat. She was bound to invade and the proper course for the people of YHWH was to surrender. To indicate God's impending judgment the prophet appeared in public wearing a yoke upon his neck (27: 1–11). This, of course, to king and commoner alike was sheer treason. Jeremiah was thrown into prison once more and then into a pit where he was left to die. Fortunately, an Ethiopian in the king's palace had more compassion than the prophet's countrymen, and, after interceding with the king, he hoisted Jeremiah out of his dungeon but not into freedom (chs. 37–38).

The prophet was still alive when Jerusalem was taken and eventually was carried off to Egypt after the murder of Gedaliah, the regent appointed by the Babylonians (chs. 40–44). Tradition says that there he was stoned to death. Jeremiah's life was thus one of apparent failure, of repeated disappointment, of suffering and mental anguish. It is not surprising that this man, whose life bears a closer resemblance to that of Jesus than any other Old Testament figure, should have been identified with him in New Testament times (*Matt.* 16: 14).

What then was Jeremiah's contribution to prophecy? Strangely enough, in view of his fame and importance, he added little that was new to the contributions of his predecessors. He has nothing more to say than Amos had already said about the right conduct that a righteous God demands of his

people. He merely underlines Hosea's emphasis on God's love and Isaiah's insistence on his moral holiness. In effect his chief contribution lies in the witness of his own life. He is the incarnation of the prophetic message, and it is this that makes him at once the most human and sympathetic figure in the Old Testament.

The patriarchs tend to be shadowy or idealised portraits, the kings and heroes are of mixed quality and the early prophets are cast in too unfamiliar a mould. But here is a man known to us by his own words and by the Boswellian pen of his faithful Baruch, who not only gives us an insight into a great soul but also a new revelation of what personal faith can mean. We feel that we know Jeremiah better than almost any other character in the Old Testament. In words which are wrung from him he confesses his doubts and fears, his distrust of himself (15: 10–21), his compassion for the very people whose doom he is impelled to foretell (8: 18–22), his anxiety lest he may after all have been mistaken in thinking that YHWH had spoken to him (20: 7–18).

It is without a doubt as a result of the experience of finding himself against his will an outcast from his own people yet being at the same time certain that this is what the obedience of YHWH demands, that Jeremiah makes what is perhaps his only original addition to earlier prophetic insights, his conception of the New Covenant (31: 31–34). Jeremiah did not treat lightly the covenant relationship which from the days of Moses had bound Israel to YHWH in terms of the Torah, but he saw its dangers and its inadequacies, and in particular, the ineffectiveness of the national renewal of the covenant at the time of Josiah's reformation.

It was possible for the people of his day to regard themselves as being in the right relationship to YHWH, so long as public worship in terms of ritual and sacrifice was offered regularly in accordance with the provisions of the Law. More than any other prophet, Jeremiah sees the weakness of formalism in religion, and insists that there must be within the framework of the worshipping community a personal commitment on the part of the individual believer. This is neither isolationism in the sense that worship resolves itself into a private and exclusive transaction with God, nor is it an outright rejection of ceremonial and the outward forms of religion, whether it be in terms of animal sacrifice or, in our own day, liturgical worship ranging from the Roman rite to the simplest form of public worship in a Protestant sect.

Jeremiah makes the distinction between the husks and the corn, between the shell and the kernel. He demands that within the worshipping community there should be a personal relationship to God on the part of each worshipper. But he cannot see this as an imme-

diate possibility. God's people must be disciplined and shown the folly of their ways, before repentance opens the way to God's forgiveness and his offer of a fresh start. It is as part of the texture of Israel's hope in a new era, when God's purpose for his world will be consummated, that Jeremiah looks for the day, as First Isaiah had done (*Isa.* 11 : 9), when men would be at one with God in the communion of perfect fellowship.

The significance of this prophecy for the Church can be measured when we remember that our Christian scriptures claim by their very name to be the record of its fulfilment. The title of the New Testament or New Covenant, for the Greek words may be translated either way, expresses the conviction of the Church that what Jeremiah hoped for came true in Jesus Christ. When our Lord at the Last Supper offered his disciples the cup as the sacrament of the New Covenant, he was claiming that through him this new personal relationship to God, of which Jeremiah spoke, was no longer a future possibility but a present reality (*Luke* 22 : 20; *I Cor.* 11 : 25). It was likewise in the light of this that the author of the epistle to the *Hebrews*, quoting Jeremiah's words in full, asserted that the day to which the prophet looked forward had now arrived (*Heb.* 8 : 8–13; 10 : 15–22).

LAMENTATIONS

THESE FIVE hymns dealing with the fall of Jerusalem in 587 B.C. were traditionally ascribed to Jeremiah, since he was the prophet most closely associated with that event and most likely to have written them. In the Hebrew Old Testament they come under the heading of the Writings, although in our English Bible they are included in the works of the prophets. They are now generally recognised not to be the work of Jeremiah or indeed to be all from the pen of the same anonymous author. It has been customary to understand them as little more than poems expressing the sense of desolation at the downfall of the holy city. They present no special problem; their form is that of acrostic dirges constructed on a conventional pattern, and they seem at first sight to add little—apart from conveying a vivid sense of the disaster, especially 2 and 5—to the religious content of the Old Testament.

They are, however, a striking expression of Israel's faith which was tested above all by the fall of Jerusalem and the Exile. They show how national disaster could, under the guidance of prophetic minds, come to be seen as part of the mysterious work of Providence, which still left room for future hope (3: 20–36). It is good that *Lamentations* should be used in the Church as appropriate reading for Holy Week. Much of the language used of Jerusalem's afflictions can be suggestively applied to the Passion of our Lord (e.g. 1: 12), and the third hymn might have been specially written for Good Friday.

It is even better that we should see in the liturgical use of these hymns in the Jewish Church during the Exile, evidence of how such prophetic insights of national guilt and renewal, of God's judgment and mercy, by being incorporated into public worship, taught the ordinary folk of Israel to turn despair into hope. Such hymns schooled them to recognise the purpose of God amid the collapse of all man-made plans and the shaking of all human foundations, and thus prepared their minds to receive a new message from God through such spokesmen as Ezekiel and Second Isaiah, who in their turn paved the way for the transmission of Israel's faith and the maintenance of Israel's hope through the dark days of the Return until Messiah should come.

EZEKIEL

JEREMIAH, before being carried off to Egypt as an unwilling guest of the rebels after the murder of Gedaliah, the regent appointed by the Babylonians to preside over the ruins of Judah in 587, had proclaimed his conviction that the future of the people of God lay in Babylon until the lessons of defeat had been properly learned. The first batch of exiles had already been deported by Nebuchadnezzar in 598 and among them was the prophet Ezekiel.

These early deportees doubtless expected their sojourn in Babylon to be a short one, although Jeremiah had warned them to adopt a more sober outlook (*Jer.* 29: 1-7, 28). Jerusalem was then still intact, and the popular view, encouraged by prophets of easy comfort, was that YHWH could not afford to let any serious harm befall it. Nebuchadnezzar, however, confirmed Jeremiah's prediction, and Jerusalem fell after the earliest exiles had been in Babylon just over ten years. To the average Israelite this meant that YHWH had been vanquished by Marduk, the chief god of the Babylonian pantheon.

Humanly speaking, had it not been for prophets of the stature of Jeremiah, Ezekiel and Second Isaiah, who convinced enough people that the sack of Jerusalem and the Exile were the voice of God speaking through history, the pageant of Israel's story would have ended in a whimper beside the canals of Mesopotamia. Such was not the will of God, however, and we have seen in the dirges of *Lamentations* how the true prophetic word infiltrated into common thought through the liturgy, and hope for the future replaced despair.

On the other hand the material lot of the average exile seems to have been relatively tolerable. Displaced persons were treated with more humanity in ancient times than is the case today. Judging by the letter of Jeremiah to the exiles referred to above, the Jews were allowed a large amount of freedom. Further, they appear to have been permitted to live in communities in Babylon (*Ezra* 2), which resulted, as with all racial minorities living together, in a heightened sense of nationalism and an increasing emphasis on national customs and traditions. Thus, while many no doubt in disgust defaulted from the worship of YHWH and attached themselves to the cult of Marduk, there was excellent opportunity, given proper leadership, for stimulating interest in Jewish life and Jewish religion.

This leadership was not lacking and there was a strong response. It was in Babylon that the Jews most noticeably acquired their sense of being different, of being a peculiar and indeed superior race. It was here that the nationalism which we have encountered in the books of *Ezra* and *Nehemiah* began to become a fetish, here that the Jews drew more and more within their own hard shell.

Their intolerance was up to a point legitimate. They were essentially a theocratic people whose national life was in theory at any rate governed by the religious sanctions of the Law. The men they listened to in the long run were not the politicians but the prophets, however much they subjected them to persecution and obloquy. The established church and the priesthood stood in the forefront of the nation, and they realised very well that for all their backsliding, their ethical and religious standards were far in advance of those of the Babylonians.

The Exile was not a repetition of the experience that Israel had had when the tribes came into Canaan after the Exodus, and found themselves among a vastly more cultured people than themselves whose ways of life they felt themselves obliged to adopt. However much they may have profited commercially by their contacts with the Babylonians—and the records of the great Jewish trading concern of Murashu and Sons found by archaeologists at Nippur witness to native Hebrew financial acumen—in cultural matters they had relatively little to learn, and in religious matters they were clearly the masters. Thus the inevitable tendency was more and more to close the circle, to emphasise the differences, to stress the national heritage and to despise every other.

The Temple had, of course, perished and with it went its animal sacrifices and their attendant ritual and ceremonial, but other brands of formalism took their place. The sabbath now becomes more and more a rigorously kept holy day, and the first stage of the synagogue undoubtedly dates back to this time when festivals and offerings in the Temple were no longer possible. Circumcision likewise became a patriotic rite. It had been an ancient custom common to all Israel's neighbours in Palestine, except the Philistines. Now that the Jews were among people to whom circumcision was an unknown practice it became vitally important to insist on it.

The same desire to be different from their neighbours led them to discriminate meticulously between such food as was permissible according to the Law and such as was not. Whatever the origin of these dietary tabus may have been, their observance now became an obsession. It was not a matter of avoiding certain animals which recent experience or ancient wisdom had classified as being in some way impure, but rather that certain animals should be openly shunned by all Jews in as ostentatious a manner as possible.

Yet this exclusiveness was the human and imperfect expression of profound religious conviction. This was the people of YHWH, bound in a covenant relationship to God such as no other nation had known or could know. How else were they to assert their distinctive role, their sense of a unique vocation, their pledge of complete obedience, unless by making it plain for all the world to see that in religion, morality and social behaviour they were determined to be no longer like "all the nations" but "a kingdom of priests and a holy nation" (*Ex.* 19: 6)?

This meant of course that the priesthood came more and more into prominence in Jewish life, no longer only as the ministers of the sanctuaries of YHWH, but first as the guardians of the Law, and later as the legal experts who developed what was to become a deadening and suffocating corpus of ordinances governing every aspect of daily life. Beginning with the laudable intention of expounding the distinctively Jewish observances of sabbath, circumcision and diet, this priestly concern to safeguard the heritage of Israel ended in later Judaism as a stranglehold on the community, killing the spirit of the Law by insisting on the letter.

It is in harmony with the increased importance of the priesthood that Ezekiel, the first of the two great prophets of the Exile, is himself a priest, and if we may judge from his early deportation to Babylon, a man already of some importance in 598 B.C. No book of prophecy in the Bible is better arranged than *Ezekiel*. Its very orderliness, as compared with any other prophetic anthology in the Old Testament, suggests that the original oracles of Ezekiel have been revised, augmented and otherwise edited to such an extent that it becomes difficult, if not impossible, to secure even some

measure of agreement among the experts as to the actual contribution of the prophet himself.

We may however bypass this particular problem, and be thankful that, unlike *Isaiah* and *Jeremiah*, this book begins at the beginning and ends at the end. Ezekiel's book starts with his call to prophesy, proceeds methodically to reproduce his prophecies in more or less chronological order, and concludes with his final oracle. Not only so, but the book is neatly divided into two halves, the first twenty-four chapters dealing with events up to the fall of Jerusalem, while the second twenty-four chapters contain oracles against foreign nations (chs. 25–32), and prophecies of the new Jerusalem (chs. 33–48).

Yet, in spite of these attractive features, the book remains for most people uninviting, and the prophet himself would be regarded by the majority of readers of the Bible as the least sympathetic of all the great prophetic figures. Part of the reason is that Ezekiel is the most "ecstatic" of the classical prophets. His psychic experiences seem to have been more abnormal than usual. He appears to have suffered at times from catalepsy and aphasia, and to have been subject to visions that read like nightmares. Part of the reason, again, is that his symbolism is sometimes offensive, and that his detailed plan for the rebuilding of the Temple fills several chapters with architectural specifications of little or no significance for today.

All this, however, is once more a superficial judgment, and Ezekiel stands out as one of the great prophets, not only on account of his importance as the spokesman of YHWH at perhaps the most critical point in Israel's history, but also because of the originality of his own thought and his contribution to the substance of Old Testament religion. What matters in the case of Ezekiel, as in the case of all other prophets, is not whether his behaviour strikes us as odd, or whether his expressions accord with modern taste, but whether the voice of God can still be heard speaking to us through him.

Ezekiel's account of his initial vision and call to be a prophet is bizarre, but magnificent. No one can fail to be awed by this strange man's conception of the majesty and glory of YHWH seated on his chariot-throne (ch. 1). The call came to him in Babylon, six years before the fall of Jerusalem (i.e. 593 B.C.), and from that time until the city was sacked, in his role as the "watchman" of YHWH, he poured out warning after warning, pronouncing the judgment of God upon the moral and religious failure of his people, and, like Jeremiah, attributing the impending catastrophe to God's outraged patience.

The prophet's method of indicating his commission and impressing his audience is characteristic. He metaphorically makes God's words his own by swallowing them (chs. 2–3). More than the other prophets he makes use of symbolism to drive home his message. He takes a clay tablet, draws a picture of Jerusalem on it and lays siege to it. He lies on his left side for 190 (LXX) days (presumably for a

symbols

certain time each day in some public place) to indicate the number of years that the northern kingdom must endure banishment, and then lies on his right side for 40 days to symbolise Judah's years of exile (ch. 4). He shaves his head and divides the hair into three. Each part is dealt with differently and their treatment points to the conditions which will obtain at the fall of Jerusalem: famine, massacre and deportation (ch. 5).

In ch. 8 he falls into a trance and finds himself carried to Jerusalem where he sees heathenism of all kinds being practised—the worship of foreign cults, of animals and of the sun. He castigates his countrymen for their public and private misdeeds, ranging over the familiar prophetic gamut of usury, oppression, murder, bribery, adultery, incest and a general breakdown of family life. Significantly Ezekiel includes sabbath breaking and eating non-kosher meat.

The false prophets who prate that all is well, and the fortune-tellers who befog the minds of the people with their superstitious nonsense, will meet their deserts (ch. 13). Even the combined merits of Noah, Daniel and Job could not save a people so sunk in their own corruption (ch. 14). The bride of YHWH has become a harlot (ch. 16), Samaria and Jerusalem have vied with each other to bring dishonour on their marriage vows (ch. 23).

Such conduct could not escape punishment. No magic circle existed around Jerusalem, no divine miracle would save them. This was YHWH's people, but consistently they had failed to keep their side of the contract ever since it was made in Egypt under Moses. Now at last YHWH's favour was to be withdrawn. Holding out the promise of forgiveness if there is true repentance, but with little hope that God's wayward people will respond, Ezekiel continues on this note of impending doom until Jerusalem falls. Fighting down his own personal grief at the death of his wife, the prophet rejects the conventional signs of mourning to bring home to his countrymen that the death of Israel, whom YHWH had taken to wife as part of himself, was to be the private sorrow of the Almighty but no occasion of his outward concern (ch. 24). On this note the first half of the book ends.

The next section of the prophecies (chs. 25-32) consists of oracles against Israel's neighbours—Ammon, Moab, Edom, Philistia, Tyre, Sidon and Egypt—who had contributed to her downfall or rejoiced over her humiliation. These are, however, collected and inserted at this point as a prelude to the restoration of the people of God to the homeland. In the ideal Jerusalem of the future which Ezekiel envisages, there must be no "prickly briers" surrounding it (28:24). The judgment of YHWH will have fallen upon Israel's enemies and for them there will be no reprieve.

With the beginning of ch. 33 the oracles strike a new note. The news of the fall of Jerusalem (33:21) vindicates Ezekiel's sombre forecast. Now his task is to hearten and encourage, to teach the stricken people that after

judgment comes mercy, after the Exile will come restoration. He repeats his former words (cf. ch. 18) that what YHWH desires is not death but life, provided his people mend their ways, and reaffirms God's promise to the exiles (cf. ch. 11) that Israel will be once again his people and serve him in the land that he had made his own.

In his famous vision of the valley of dry bones (ch. 37), he sees the scattered remnants of both Israel and Judah, dead because of their sins, but now miraculously restored to life by the forgiveness of YHWH. God takes away their hearts of stone and gives them hearts of flesh, endowing them with a new spirit that will respond to his word (36:26). The land will burgeon and prosperity will be assured. Under a perfect ruler of David's line, like Isaiah's messianic prince (*Isa.* 9:2-7), the sordid record of worthless kings and nobles will be blotted out and the world will know at last the sovereign power of YHWH.

It is not enough for Ezekiel's dream that Israel's ancient enemies should be disposed of. Pagan hordes from lands unknown, led by their prince Gog of the land of Magog, will descend upon the restored community. They too must be shown that YHWH is supreme, and learn in their destruction that no human power can thwart the will of God (ch. 38-39).

The climax of Ezekiel's picture of the Israel that is to be is his plan, dating from 573 B.C. (40:1), for the rebuilding of the Temple as the heart of the new community's life (chs. 40-48). With loving care he prescribes its dimensions, orders its ceremonial and ensures its ritual purity. As we make our way through these now tedious details, let us not fail to discern running through them the deeply spiritual purpose behind them. Although as a priest he reckoned that nothing less than this minutely regulated worship, free from all possible defilement, could wipe out the shame of the past, and safeguard the ritual holiness of a people called to be holy by a holy God, his whole conception is suffused by a devout sense of God's all pervading Presence.

Before Judah's judgment day, YHWH had washed his hands of Jerusalem and its Temple and had taken up his abode with the exiles (11 : 22-23). Now the glory of the Lord returns to his Temple and fills it with his Presence (43 : 1-5), from it flows the life-giving water that guarantees health to his people (47 : 1-12), and the city itself receives a new name which fittingly is Ezekiel's moving last word: The Lord is there (48 : 35).

Ezekiel's influence on subsequent Old Testament thought was of the highest importance. Contrasted with Jeremiah, Second Isaiah and even First Isaiah, his conception of God emphasises his complete otherness, remoteness and mystery. Much of his imagery is doubtless coloured by his Babylonian environment, but most of it is due to his own extraordinarily powerful and fertile imagination. Always his basic conviction is of the insignificance of man and the awful majesty and glory of YHWH. It was this insistence on the remoteness of God which led later Judaism, of which Ezekiel was the father, to introduce a host of superhuman intermediaries between mankind and the Creator. Ezekiel lays the foundations of such a development with his destroying angels in 9 : 1-11.

The seeds of the elaborate legalism, ceremonialism and ritualism of later Judaism (the Priestly Code P: see p. 131) are also to be found in Ezekiel. His blueprint for the new holy city and its Temple (chs. 40-48) paved the way for the rigidity and exclusiveness of the school of Ezra. Yet as we have seen (pp. 216-217), it was only by such strict safeguards that the living faith of the Old Testament was preserved from syncretism or disintegration and that it remained intact for rediscovery and restatement in the gospels and epistles.

In another respect, too, Ezekiel is a pioneer. Previous prophets had on the whole pictured the golden age which was the essence of Israel's hope, as being ushered in by the natural turn of political events under the direction of YHWH (e.g. Isa. 11 : 1-9). Ezekiel, however, introduces the supernatural element which in later years became predominant, when prophecy became apocalyptic, as in the book of Daniel (see pp. 271-273). The assault upon the restored community led by the mysterious Gog, already himself bordering upon incarnate evil, is destroyed not by force of arms but by earth-shaking cataclysm, by flood, fire and brimstone (38 : 18-22). Only thereafter can the real golden age begin.

It was also Ezekiel who first laid down unambiguously the principle of individual responsibility (18 : 1-

4). The traditional Israelite emphasis had been on community responsibility, whether of the family, the tribe or the nation. In the story of Achan's crime (*Josh.* 7) this had justified the annihilation of his whole family. In the prophetic denunciation of Israel, the whole people must suffer for the sins of their fathers. As the popular proverb had it: "The fathers have eaten sour grapes and the children's teeth are set on edge."

Jeremiah had refuted this doctrine, which left no hope for the individual burdened with the guilt of his ancestors, but he had linked the liberation of the individual with the promise of the New Covenant, as awaiting fulfilment in the age to come (*Jer.* 31 : 27-34). Ezekiel, however, declared it as a present truth that the sinner paid for his own sins only, and not for those of his contemporaries or of his forbears. His aim was clearly to offer hope to his countrymen that personal repentance opened the way for God's forgiveness, and that God would not condemn to destruction any man who turned to him whatever might be his society's crimes. But in so far as Ezekiel's doctrine that "the soul that sinneth, it shall die" also implied that suffering was a punishment for sin, a view which became part of orthodox belief, it raised a problem which was later challenged by the writer of the book of *Job* (see pp. 221-222).

As with the other prophet of the Exile, Second Isaiah, the measure of Ezekiel's prophecies does not lie in their literal fulfilment. His vision of a restored people of God was in some degree implemented by the time of Nehemiah and Ezra, but hostile neighbours were very much in evidence and when Gog appeared in the persons of Antiochus (see pp. 273-274) and Titus (see p. 315), it was the chosen people who suffered and not the enemy.

Yet Ezekiel's impact is not exhausted by his power over the men of his times, turning their despair into hope and creating a future for Israel, or even by his remarkable influence on the later thought of the Old Testament. Surely the Church can find in his vision of the new community protected by the Presence, suffused by the Spirit and worshipping the Name, inspiration for her present life and, as the seer of the Apocalypse recognised, also a divinely given pointer to a fuller revelation of the New Jerusalem of the age to come (*Rev.* 21-22).

DANIEL

THE BOOK of *Daniel* presents several features which can be not only puzzling but extremely misleading. The first half of the book reads like romantic fiction, while the second half is at first sight fantastic and incomprehensible. Without the clues provided by modern biblical studies *Daniel* can become a happy hunting ground for religious cranks, and it is not too much to say that no book in the Old Testament, except perhaps *Jonah*, can be more illuminated by a right understanding of its character, its purpose and its historical setting.

The Old Testament, as we have seen, is on the whole strongly anchored to this world. Hardly any poet or prophet ventures to hope for anything beyond this life. If such a hope is raised for a moment, as in *Job* or the *Psalms* (see p. 225), it is more a wistful longing than a developed conviction. There were various reasons for this. The Hebrew conception of the unity of the physical and psychical aspects of human nature implied that, when a man died, his intellect, emotions and aspirations died with him. His further existence in Sheol was that of a disembodied ghost or a shadow.

The cult of the dead, as practised by Israel's neighbours, was riddled with superstition and black magic to such a degree that the prophets, in any case concerned with the present disorders of society, preferred to direct attention to the claims of God here and now, rather than to encourage hopes that might lead to an unhealthy interest in what happened after death. As against this they generally offered a very solid compensation in the form of rewards and punishments bestowed by divine justice, in terms of material prosperity or adversity on this earth.

As time went on this view became less and less tenable. The life of the individual Israelite was always bound up with that of the nation, and there came a point when it was no longer possible to claim that either the nation or the individuals who composed it were being rewarded or punished with any semblance of justice. So long as the prophets could claim that national misfortunes were the result of collective sin on the part of the people, they could use public disasters to teach the need for repentance and reform. But after the Exile, when Judaism became the controlling element in the community life, when public practice and private conduct alike were regulated by the Law of YHWH, the problem became acute.

How could the fact be explained that when, at long last, after the lesson of defeat had been taken to heart, and as a sign of repentance the community had rid itself of all idolatrous practices, was observing the niceties of ceremonial and moral law, and acknowledged the leadership of YHWH's representatives, the high priests, nevertheless the promised rewards failed to materialise? Instead of becoming larger and more prosperous, as the prophets had promised, Israel had become smaller and more impoverished than ever. Instead of the glowing picture of peace and plenty that the prophets had painted, there was a drab landscape of hardship, oppression and persecution.

Thus the tendency grew, in the last few centuries before the Christian era, to give up completely any hope of seeing justice done in this world, either to the individual or to the community, and to substitute a new kind of hope in a sudden and dramatic supernatural intervention of God into human affairs, heralding a new order, coupled with a belief in vindication or retribution for the individual after death. The word used for views or beliefs about the ultimate end of history, or any order of being beyond the one which we know, including life after death, is "eschatology".

This feature of biblical thought, often unfamiliar and unintelligible to modern minds in its Jewish form, is an essential part of our understanding not only of the Old Testament but also of the New Testament. But it is not in any sense a feature which is found only in the Bible. All civilisations and peoples have their own eschatology, their own beliefs about what happens after death, or when time as we know it comes to an end.

Long before the days of the prophets the Hebrews had a traditional and popular expectation of a Day of YHWH. This was to be the day when their faith in YHWH would be vindicated, when the Lord would show his hand and right Israel's wrongs, confound their enemies, and exalt his people to their proper place as chief among the nations. The great prophets encouraged this hope in a Day of the Lord, but purged it of its nationalistic flavour.

They agreed that there would be a Day of YHWH, but added that it would not be an occasion for Israel's self-congratulation, but the hour when YHWH's righteousness would be vindicated, when God would judge and punish evil wherever it was to be found, whether in Israel or elsewhere, and would correspondingly reward the faithful (e.g. *Amos* 5: 18). When they pictured the sequel to the Day of the Lord as a golden age of justice, peace and plenty, with the hearts of the world turned towards a new Jerusalem as the source of light and truth, it was on the whole a picture painted in pigments that were in everyday use. In one sense they looked for a new Creation, but it was more like the old familiar world transformed. YHWH would, of course, be the power behind events, but political changes would bring it about and moral principles would govern it. Such was the character of "prophetic eschatology".

But after the days of the prophets, convictions about the final consummation of God's purpose for the world took on a new direction. This was partly because the good time coming, of which the prophets had spoken, did not materialise, and partly because of the influence of new ideas seeping in from the nations under whose dominion Israel had to live, whether as a community or in dispersion. Thus in the course of the five hundred years or so that followed the great eighth century prophets, the character of eschatology changed and became "apocalyptic".

We have only to glance at the second half of the book of *Daniel* in the Old Testament, or the book of *Revelation* in the New Testament, to be struck by their similarity. They are both "apocalypses", i.e. they claim to reveal what is to happen in the future, and to unveil what is normally hidden from human eyes. These two books are the only full-scale representatives in the Old and New Testaments of a class of writing—"apocalyptic eschatology"– which flourished intensively in the last two centuries B.C. and the first century of the Christian era. There is a whole library of Jewish and Jewish–Christian works, not included in the Old and New Testaments or in the Apocrypha, which deal more or less exclusively with this type of speculation.

Let us look for a moment at some of the characteristics of these apocalyptic writings, both biblical and non-biblical. Apocalyptic is the direct descendant of prophecy. Both apocalyptist and prophet claim to be revealing the will and purpose of YHWH. But while the prophet is a preacher, the apoca-lyptist is a writer; while the prophet hurls himself into the affairs of his times and tries to reform them, the apocalyptist, despairing of anyone being able to do anything about the times, so far are they out of joint, sits and broods over the future, until the vision comes to him of the disinte-gration of the present evil world and the birth of an entirely new and different one.

The prophet expects YHWH to use natural means to bring about the new order, the apocalyptist thinks in terms of upheaval, catastrophe and collapse, before any rebirth is possible. The prophets were on the whole optimistic about this world, the apocalyptists were pessimistic. In these five hundred years since the glorious eighth century figures, with their confident and triumphant faith in the future of Israel, for no other reason than that Israel was the people of YHWH, everything that had happened had, on the surface at any rate, exploded their predictions. Had the prophets been wrong? Had YHWH for-saken his people? This was the problem of thoughtful men in these two centuries or so before Christ.

One answer came from thinkers like Ecclesiastes, who advocated a grim trust in YHWH despite everything. The other answer came from the apocalyptists. The golden age of which the prophets spoke was no empty promise. It would certainly come and it must still be the mainstay of Israel's hope. YHWH had not forgotten or forsaken his people, but evil and corruption had so defiled the earth that nothing could be expected from it in its present state.

Soon this old and wicked world would come to an end in a cataclysm of violence and destruction. YHWH would break into history. Israel's enemies would be miraculously destroyed, as Ezekiel had foretold (see p. 267), and the reign of God would begin. Apocalyptic is thus the child of despair. Humanly speaking there is no hope. Only by a supernatural intervention on a cosmic scale can wrongs be righted, and the people of God established to do his will in peace and righteousness on a new earth, whose focus would be a new Jerusalem, come down from heaven.

When the prophets had spoken of the great Day of YHWH which would be the climax of history, they had been content to sketch the outline and leave the details to the imagination. The apocalyptists, however, now supply the details. Hence the total impression of these apocalyptic books is one of mystery and miracle, of supernatural wonders, of strange language and bizarre symbolism, of mystic numbers and camouflaged personalities. History ceases to be history and becomes merely a prelude to such extraordinary events that it becomes itself almost symbolic.

The apocalyptist lives in a world of visions, and the glimpses he gets of the future order colour his outlook on the world he lives in. A whole range of conventional, artificial and completely imaginary conceptions becomes his literary stock-in-trade. Strange animals in combat depict the conflict of nations, angels and demons recur in similar contexts, monsters with horns, wings and eyes generally bear the same interpretation.

An apocalyptist never writes under his own name. He is always supposed to be some ancient figure such as Enoch, Moses or Isaiah who, peering into the future from his own day, is represented as predicting the rise and fall of empires and the eventual golden age. This particular convention is of paramount importance for the understanding of such a book as *Daniel*. The anonymous apocalyptist assumes the name of Daniel, and writes as if he were living in Babylon at the time of the Exile, and foretelling the events of the ensuing four centuries. In fact, as we shall see, he is writing in the second century B.C. about events which have already happened, as if they were still to come. The only real element of prediction in the book is that of the impending end of the world, which in the usual manner of apocalyptic writings is reckoned to be not far off.

While the book of *Daniel* introduces us to fully fledged apocalyptic such as is found in the book of *Revelation, Second Esdras* in the Apocrypha, and in the extra-canonical literature of the period between the Old and New Testaments (see p. 311), it should be noted that in the writings of the prophets there are also occasionally passages of an apocalyptic character, in that they contain a type of supernatural "end of the world" prediction. Ezekiel's mysterious Gog vision (chs. 38–39), is the earliest of these, and similar specimens of what may be called an intermediate stage between prophetic and apocalyptic eschatology are to be found in *Isaiah* 24–27, *Joel* and *Zech.* 12–14.

Daniel is now generally agreed to have been the last of the Old Testament books to be written. In the English versions it is included among the prophets, but in the Hebrew Bible it is placed among the later Writings, which in itself is a pointer to a date after the age of prophecy had ended. The book can in fact be dated to within a few years, between 167 and 164 B.C.

As we traced the historical development of Israel's fortunes through the books of *Kings*, *Ezra*, and *Nehemiah* from the fall of Jerusalem through the Exile to the establishment of the tiny Jewish theocracy in and around Jerusalem, we last saw the people of God as vassals of the Persian empire. With local authority vested in the high priests, the spiritual walls of the Law shielding them from the impact of world affairs, and their size and economic difficulties preventing them from taking any part in them, the Jews in their political backwater can have registered little emotion when their Persian overlords were replaced by the succeeding world empire of Alexander the Great in 331 B.C.

On the death of Alexander, his empire was divided, and Judah came first under the control of Egyptian overlords and later under the sovereignty of the Syrian dynasty. With Alexander, the Hellenistic age began, when Greek language, customs and culture became the common coinage of the civilised world. Alone among the diverse racial groups that made up the Hellenistic empire, the Jews, staunch in their conviction of the uniqueness of their faith, rigid in the pattern of exclusiveness which Ezra and his followers had enforced, stoutly defended themselves against any infiltration of Greek customs or ways of thought.

In 175 B.C. Antiochus Epiphanes became ruler of Syria and overlord of Judah. He was an avowed Hellenist, determined to spread Greek culture throughout his territories, not least to bring the light of progress to what he must have regarded as the obscurantist and bigoted fanatics who inhabited Jerusalem. Encouraged by some support from sympathisers with his aims among the aristocratic priesthood of Jerusalem—the forerunners of the Sadducees—Antiochus to his chagrin encountered stubborn resistance amounting to rebellion on the part of the ordinary people, led by zealots who urged loyalty to the ancient faith and traditions of Israel. These patriots, who stood directly in the prophetic line, and were known as the Hasidim or "pious men", developed into the party of the Pharisees. It was thus at this stage in Israel's history that the two main religious parties that we encounter in the pages of the gospels—Pharisees and Sadducees —began to take shape.

Antiochus reckoned that nothing less than the sternest measures would meet the situation and bring the recalcitrant Jews to heel. He marched on Jerusalem and quartered his troops in the Temple. A strict ban was imposed on all distinctively Jewish practices. Circumcision, sabbath observance and the worship of YHWH were forbidden. The scriptures were publicly burned, and possession of a copy of the Torah was made punishable by death. The Temple was given over to the worship of Zeus, and pagan altars were erected not only in the Temple but throughout the land. The altar to Zeus in the Temple, described in Daniel as "the abomination of desolation", a Hebrew pun on its dedication to "the lord of heaven", was consecrated by the sacrifice of swine, and priests and people were forced to drink broth made of the swine's flesh.

In the eyes of devout and patriotic Jews, nothing so frightful as this had ever happened since the Creation. Revolt broke out in 167 B.C. led by Mattathias and his five sons, known as the Maccabees, which developed into a full scale war of independence. Already by 164 B.C. the guerrilla fighters had been so successful that Jerusalem was cleared of foreign troops, and the Temple was cleansed and re-dedicated to YHWH. The books of the *Maccabees* in the Apocrypha give an excellent account of this stirring period and provide an admirable introduction to the study of *Daniel* (see pp. 327–329).

It was probably at the beginning of this revolt in 167 B.C. that our book of *Daniel* appeared. Strongly patriotic in tone, the first half contains tales of the heroic past, recounting how Jews of old bore themselves in similar circumstances. The second half is a review of past history, ending with a prediction of the speedy end of the oppressive rule of Antiochus. The whole book is thus to be understood as a summons to action, a clarion call to the men of the times to quit themselves like heroes of old, who through threatened fire and slaughter kept their faith pure, together with a promise of a catastrophic end to the dynasty that held them in thrall.

The first six chapters therefore consist of legendary stories dealing with the adventures of a traditional hero Daniel and his friends during the Exile in Babylon. Ezekiel (14 : 14) mentions Daniel, together with Noah and Job, as being ancient worthies renowned for their integrity, and probably some of these tales were already familiar, being retold here for the occasion. The historical background is often inaccurate in detail, since it was several centuries removed from the author's day, but the stories are vividly narrated and in each case the application to the stirring times of 167 B.C. is clear.

The introduction tells how, among other bright well-born youths, Daniel and three friends were deported from Jerusalem to Babylon and there brought up as palace attendants of king Nebuchadnezzar. Daniel resembles young Joseph at the court of the pharaoh; he soon becomes popular with his new masters, he has the gift of interpreting dreams, and he rises to astonishing heights in his adopted land.

Chapter one shows Daniel and his friends in a vegetarian role. They refuse to eat the meat and drink the wine that come from the king's table for them, and insist on eating nothing but vegetables and drinking nothing but water. Despite this they put on more weight than those who ate the meat which, as was the custom, had been dedicated as a sacrifice to a pagan god. The point is obviously to encourage the Jews of Antiochus' day in their determination not to eat forbidden food, and to assure them that by God's protection those who kept the ceremonial law would be fitter in mind and body.

Chapter two tells of a dream king Nebuchadnezzar had which perplexed and worried him. To test his magicians he challenged them to tell him not only what the dream meant but what it actually was. When they were unable to do this the king ordered the execution of all the sages in the kingdom. This of course included Daniel, but Daniel was granted a vision which showed him both the king's dream and what it meant. As a reward the king made him his grand vizier.

Nebuchadnezzar had gone to sleep wondering what would happen after his death. In his dream he saw a colossal and magnificent image with a head of gold, breast and arms of silver, belly and thighs of bronze, legs of iron and feet of mingled iron and clay. This image was destroyed by a stone hewn by no human hands. It crumbled to dust while the stone became a mountain which filled the earth. Daniel gives an interpretation of the dream which shows that it is characteristic apocalyptic writing.

The dream is an allegory of the rise and fall of the four successive world empires, from Nebuchadnezzar's day until the time at which this book was written, culminating in their supersession by a kingdom of a different order. The golden head is Nebuchadnezzar's empire; the silver and bronze parts of the image are the empires of the Medes and Persians, which the author believed to have followed the empire of Babylon, although in fact there was no world empire of Medes as distinct from Persians; the iron legs are Alexander's Greek empire; the mixture of clay and iron in the feet indicates the division of part of Alexander's empire between Egypt (clay) and Syria (iron). The stone which smashes the image and then fills the earth is the supernatural Kingdom of God, which will replace the kingdoms of this world and which will be everlasting. The author's point is obviously that his readers are shortly to see this end event taking place.

Chapter three is a warning against allowing Antiochus to force any of YHWH's people into idolatry. The message is conveyed in the capital story of the fiery furnace. Daniel's three friends, who have shared in his advancement, choose to be cast into a furnace rather than worship an idol which Nebuchadnezzar had set up. Instead of being burned alive they are joined by an angel who protects them, and they emerge with their clothes not even singed. There is a splendid verse in this chapter (3: 17–18) that might have been spoken by Job. When the king threatens the men with the furnace they say: We are not alarmed. Our God can deliver us. But even if he does not, we still shall not worship the image.

In chapter four we are back in apocalyptic surroundings. The lesson is that God can bring even the proudest monarch low, and just as the story tells how he humbled Nebuchadnezzar, so now he can do likewise with Antiochus. Nebuchadnezzar again has a dream. This time it was of a great tree that reached to heaven and which was suddenly by order of an angel cut down. Daniel alone can interpret the dream which, he avers, relates to Nebuchadnezzar himself. He will suddenly be struck with madness, imagining himself to be an animal, and this madness will last for seven years.

Twelve months later it all happened as Daniel had foretold. The king, in a particularly boastful mood, suddenly heard a heavenly voice, went mad, proceeded to eat grass and live like an animal for seven years, at the end of which his reason returned and he became a humbler and wiser man. Whether Nebuchadnezzar ever suffered from madness or for such a time is very doubtful, but the story would gain added point from the fact that Antiochus, who called himself Epiphanes, meaning divine, was called by the wags of his day Epimanes, meaning madman.

Chapter five tells the story of the writing on the wall. Belshazzar, Nebuchadnezzar's son, gives a banquet at which he uses the sacred gold vessels from the Temple at Jerusalem as drinking cups. In the midst of the feast a hand appears writing on the wall. The words as read and translated by Daniel, who again alone knows the answer to the mystery, convey a message of the downfall of the Babylonian empire chiefly on account of Belshazzar's act of sacrilege. That very night the king is murdered. Historically the story has various flaws but it could not fail to make its point. Belshazzar's profanation of the sacred vessels was paralleled by Antiochus' desecration of the Temple, and the fate of the impious king in the tale would encourage the rebels of 167 B.C. to greater endeavour.

The last of the narratives in chapter six presents the immortal story of Daniel in the lion's den. Through the jealousy of his rivals, Daniel is put in the wrong by a decree forbidding prayer to be directed to any deity apart from the divine king. Daniel nevertheless continues his private devotions to the God of Israel, is thrown to the lions but is miraculously preserved. The purpose of the story is obviously to encourage the people to continue with private worship even although public worship had been forbidden by Antiochus, with the rider that if they are convicted for it they should behave with the courage of a Daniel.

At this point the stories end, and they are followed by six chapters of pure apocalyptic, which have proved to be fair game for successive generations of religious eccentrics. So long as these chapters are regarded as prophecies written about the time of the Exile, and prognosticating the unknown future, almost any interpretation is possible. Napoleon, Hitler, the Pope and many other historical personages have been detected, and wars from the English Civil War to World War II have been identified.

Only when we recognise that this is not prophecy about a remote future but largely lessons from the past, does the author's purpose become clear. Presumably himself one of the Hasidim, he wants to impress upon his readers that the whole pageant of history is controlled and unfolded by God, that the destinies of men and of nations are in his hand. To encourage the revolt against Antiochus he assumes the role of Daniel, and suggests that this prophet of the Exile could see stretching in front of him down the ages the various empires that rose and fell, and of whose general fortunes his readers were well aware.

By including the oppressive empire under which his countrymen suffered and by predicting its speedy downfall, to be succeeded by the everlasting Kingdom of God, he not only strengthened their confidence in the divine purpose behind all that had happened in the past, but also buoyed up their spirits with the hope that, as everything else had come to pass as the prophet had foretold, so too the heavenly Kingdom would soon become a reality. Divine judgment would fall upon Antiochus and all his evil works, and his monstrous empire would be replaced by the glorious new realm of God.

As we read these bizarre visions and some might add, distorted imaginings, let us not forget that every detail, however obscure to us now, had a significance for the people of those times; that allusions which are not clear to us even yet were probably perfectly intelligible to them, and that this apocalyptic medium was in fact the method by which, in the providence of God, when all apparent reason for hope had gone, Israel's faith in the future was maintained.

Chapter seven describes a vision of four beasts and the Ancient of Days. Verses 1–14 deal with the vision, while verses 15–28 give the interpretation. Out of the storm-tossed sea come four strange beasts. The fourth is a particularly fearsome monster, having ten horns, in the midst of which springs up another little horn with eyes and a large mouth. The little horn destroys three of the others. Then the scene changes and Daniel sees a vision of heavenly judgment presided over by the Ancient of Days. At this judgment the fourth beast is destroyed and the other three beasts are dispossessed. A human figure then appears and is given a kingdom which can never be destroyed.

Daniel asks one of the angels to explain the meaning of all this, and he is told that the four beasts are four kingdoms which succeed one another and are then followed by the eternal Kingdom of the saints of the Most High. The fourth beast interests Daniel most. This monster with fangs of iron and talons of bronze is the most ferocious and warlike of the empires. Its ten horns are its ten kings. The little horn is a king who destroys three other kings, harasses the saints, seeks to tamper with their holy seasons and the sacred law, and oppresses them for three and a half years. But divine judgment falls upon his empire and the Kingdom of the saints takes its place.

This is the puzzle which the author leaves his readers to solve, and it is not difficult to find a general answer. The four kingdoms are the same world empires as those in chapter two, Babylonian, Median, Persian and Greek, the Greek empire being the most formidable. The ten kings are Alexander the Great and nine successors. The little horn with the large mouth is, of course, the author's *bête noire*, Antiochus Epiphanes, while the three other horns which he destroyed were three contemporary rulers whom he had defeated in battle.

The Ancient of Days is God, in the guise of an old man with white hair seated on a chariot of fire, and it is by his judgment that the fourth beast is destroyed. The three and a half years are the duration of the persecution between 167 and 164 B.C. From a Christian point of view, however, it is the figure of one "like a son of man" in v. 13 which arrests attention, and indeed this passage is of fundamental importance for our understanding of the Gospel.

In the mind of the author of *Daniel*, this human figure is clearly representative of the faithful Israelites who will inherit the eternal Kingdom, appointed by God to supersede the kingdoms of this world. Man, as made in the image of God, and having the possibility of living in the right relationship of obedience, is contrasted with hideous beasts, who typify the greed, hatred and cruelty that govern the policies of godless oppressors. The son of man comes on the clouds of heaven because the Kingdom of the saints is from God, and not from the primeval watery chaos from which the powers of this world emerged.

It is thus a prophecy of the same order as First Isaiah's doctrine of the remnant (*Isa.* 1: 9), but its obvious messianic character led to later apocalyptic writers identifying the one "like a son of man" as the Messiah, who would come from heaven to inaugurate the Kingdom of God. We shall see how Jesus applied this conception of *Daniel* to himself, discarding the later apocalyptic connotation, and as he did with so many other Old Testament ideas, giving it his own distinctive interpretation (see. p. 371).

The second vision in chapter eight is that of the ram and the goat. Here again there is a survey of history leading up to the rise of Antiochus, ending with a prophecy of his doom. A ram with two horns, signifying the kingdom of the Medes and Persians, is attacked and killed by a goat with a conspicuous horn, i.e. the Greek empire under Alexander the Great. The conspicuous horn is broken, i.e. Alexander dies, and is succeeded by four other horns, i.e. the four divisions of the Hellenistic empire. Then there appears another little horn (Antiochus), who makes war on the stars (the Jewish faith), and abolishes the daily sacrifice (in the Temple).

In the very clear interpretation which the writer gives, Antiochus is picturesquely described as "a king of fierce countenance and understanding dark sentences" (8: 23), but his crime of usurping the status of the "Prince of princes", like that of the builders of the Tower of Babel, will assuredly bring down divine vengeance upon him.

Chapter nine deals with a problem that caused acute concern to faithful Jews in those troubled days. Jeremiah had indicated that the Exile would not be of short duration but would last beyond the lifetime of his hearers. He had actually given the figure of seventy years (*Jer.* 25: 11). As it transpired, this was a rough approximation of the length of the Exile, but according to Jeremiah after the seventy years of discipline divine favour would be renewed. Now, however, several hundred years later, there was still no sign of the promised deliverance. Instead, the people of God were still fighting for their existence.

Our author's contribution to the problem is to describe a vision of Daniel, in which the angel Gabriel, one of the patron saints of Israel, informs him that Jeremiah really meant seventy weeks of years, i.e. 490 years. This roughly brings the time of deliverance down to his own day, and would be precisely the type of message which was needed to encourage the people to brace themselves for a last effort. The chronology is not accurate, but the author makes it plain that the little community now stands within the last seven years of the period of discipline, and that the long night of darkness is almost spent.

The last three chapters of the book (10–12) form a unity. Daniel has a further vision, in which the angel Gabriel appears to him, and gives him ostensibly an account of what is to happen between the Exile and the final deliverance. In fact it is, of course, a historical survey in retrospect, disguised in veiled language and mysterious allusions. Where the writer comes close to his own times his account is detailed and accurate; where he describes Antiochus (11: 21–45), he speaks with deep feeling, and in 11: 40, which is obviously the point of time at which he writes, he leaves known facts and goes on to prophesy the precise fate of Antiochus. In this he guesses wrongly, as *I Macc.* 6 indicates.

Apart from historical interest, however, the author provides us with some new ideas which were to have great influence on subsequent thought. He has already been the first Old Testament writer to mention an angel by name (8: 16), and in this vision he takes the belief in the activities of angelic beings further by claiming that behind the rise and fall of empires there is a heavenly conflict. Guardian angels of Persia, Greece and Israel decide the issues on earth by fighting each other in heaven (10: 13, 20).

In his description of the unspeakable Antiochus, the author transforms him into an almost superhuman embodiment of evil. Antiochus thus becomes the prototype of the later apocalyptic figure of Antichrist. For Christians of subsequent generations, the worst of the Roman emperors, Caligula, who attempted to instal his own image in the Temple; Nero, who slaughtered the saints and sought to exterminate the faith, and Domitian, who likewise made havoc of the Church, seemed to incorporate the character of

Antiochus and to be Satan himself in human guise. Their assaults on the faithful, and the sense of history repeating itself, are reflected in *II Thess.* and *Revelation*.

In 12: 2 there is the clearest indication in the Old Testament of belief in a resurrection (cf. *Isa.* 26: 19). When the heathenish rule of Antiochus has ended and the kingdom of the saints has begun, those who have earned special merit for righteousness, such as the martyrs of the rebellion, will be raised from Sheol to enjoy everlasting life, while those who have been inordinately wicked, doubtless such an Antiochus, will be condemned to everlasting punishment. Cruder forms of this view, which developed greatly in the apocalyptic literature between the end of Old Testament times and the beginning of Christianity, led eventually to the medieval conception of the Last Judgment, with the bliss of paradise for the saints and the tortures of hell for the damned. New Testament teaching, however, as we shall see, while it develops Daniel's basic idea, lays more emphasis on the thought embodied in *Ps.* 73: 23–26 and *Job* 19: 25–27 (see p. 234).

HOSEA

WHEN WE turn from *Daniel* to *Hosea*, we step back five and a half centuries to the last days of the northern kingdom. Israel and Judah are still intact, the Exile lies yet in the future, and the trials and tribulations of the tiny theocracy in Jerusalem after the Exile, such as the book of *Daniel* has described, are not even dreamt of. The people of YHWH are, however, at this stage in their history in as parlous a plight. The eighth century, which was studded with the illustrious and creative prophecies of Amos, Hosea, Micah and First Isaiah, was also the century of the triumphant advance of Assyria into the Levant and of the downfall of Israel. In 722 B.C. the northern kingdom to all intents ceased to exist (see pp. 198–199).

It was in the middle of this century, about 750 B.C., that Amos, the first of the classical Hebrew prophets, startled and shocked the northern nation by the vigour with which he denounced his countrymen for their crimes in church and state, and sternly pronounced their impending doom in the name of YHWH. His conviction that the outraged righteousness of God would brook Israel's infamies no longer, allowed him to offer no easy way out. The northern kingdom must pay the price. In Amos' view there was nothing open to them but to accept the just judgment of God and face extinction at the hands of the Assyrians.

It was left to Hosea to proclaim that this was not the Almighty's last word, and it is his insight into the complementary truth of the mercy of God, that makes him both a greater prophet than Amos and a nearer kinsman of Christian evangelists. Despite the order of the prophetic books in the English Bible, which places *Hosea* first among the twelve small collections of prophecy which make up the fourth section of the Hebrew prophets after *Isaiah*, *Jeremiah* and *Ezekiel*, there is much to be said for reading *Amos* before *Hosea*, since he raises the curtain upon a new outburst of prophetic witness, and since the social and religious background against which both prophets are to be seen is better dealt with under the prior spokesman. It will be assumed, therefore, in what follows that *Amos* (see pp. 289–292) has already been read.

When we come to Hosea, twenty years have passed since Amos' dramatic appearance in the temple at Bethel. Israel is twenty years nearer its end. The luxuriant prosperity of Jeroboam's day has faded; king now follows king in a rapid succession that betokens a country hurtling to its doom. This way and that they might turn, seeking alliances here and there, anything to avert this darkening menace of Assyria, that cast an ever deeper shadow upon their future. What had been clear to the prophetic insight of Amos—the inevitability of Israel's downfall—had now become a nightmare to the politicians.

One day they try to circumvent the menace, next day they try to come to terms with it. Hosea rates them for their vacillation; he calls them a halfbaked bun—neither one thing nor the other; a silly dove fluttering first to Egypt hoping for an alliance, then to Assyria trusting in appeasement (7: 7-11).

Amos had been the prophet of justice. He came as an observer to the northern kingdom and objectively and dispassionately pronounced its fate. Nothing could save Israel from the consequences of social and private corruption; destruction and exile were all that she could look forward to. He had preached to men's consciences and had stressed the inexorability of YHWH's judgment. It was a true picture and one that needed to be painted, but the complementary truth had also to be stressed, that there was room for repentance in the divine economy. If YHWH is law he is also love. If there is punishment for wrongdoing, there is also opportunity for making amends.

The man who now redresses the balance is the prophet Hosea. He, no less than Amos, had a keen sense of the difference between right and wrong, and of the consequences of making false choices. But he had a sympathy and a tenderness that Amos lacked, and it was this that led him to see that the ultimate truth about God is not his sense of justice but his infinite love.

Hosea was himself a native of the northern kingdom. His view of the situation therefore, unlike Amos', was that of a member of the family; whatever happened he would stand or fall with his own countrymen. But deeper than the self-interested emotions that such a concern would awaken, lay the source of his understanding of human folly and of God's reaction to it.

The first three chapters tell the story of his own private tragedy, the heartbreak of an unfaithful wife, and in them we are shown how, from his own experience, Hosea was led to see the nature of God in a new light. So far as we can gather from the rather complicated and difficult text, the facts seem to be that after the birth of their first child, Hosea's wife Gomer became unfaithful to him. She bore two more children in his house of which he was not the father. Eventually she left him and became a temple prostitute, finally drifting into slavery.

It was out of his grief that Hosea's message was born. His broken marriage suggested an allegory of the broken relationship between YHWH and his faithless people. We have seen how the idea in Canaanite religion that Baal was lord or husband of the land, so that his marriage with the land guaranteed its fertility and ensured good crops, had led to sacramental fornication in shrines and temples, where worshippers through sexual intercourse with priests and priestesses of Baal sought to secure the benefits of this divine union for themselves (see pp. 127-128).

After the conquest, YHWH remained nominally the God of Israel, but in fact ceased to be recognisably the God of Moses, so completely had Canaanite religious faith and practice been absorbed into the religion of Israel. Baal and YHWH had become synonymous. So long as the idea that YHWH was the husband of the land held the field, the worship of Israel was bound to remain on the level of a nature cult.

Hosea, however, takes this idea and reinterprets it. YHWH is still the husband, but the husband not of the land but of the people. The relationship is moral not physical, and the marriage bond is sealed in mutual service. YHWH says: "I will betroth thee unto me in righteousness and in judgment and in loving kindness and in mercies . . . (and) in faithfulness" (2: 19–20). Israel had been unfaithful to the husband who had wed her in the wilderness, where the covenant between them had been one of moral obligation. She had played the harlot and betrayed YHWH's trust.

But YHWH will not give her up. "Israel, how can I let you go? . . . My heart recoils, all my compassion kindles" (11: 8). Yet she will not be restored without discipline. There will be a testing time indeed, but after repentance comes pardon, and the perfect union of YHWH with his people will be re-established. The wilderness covenant will be renewed, and

Israel will call YHWH: "My husband", and no longer, "My Baal" (2: 16).

Hosea had, like First Isaiah under different circumstances (see p. 250), given the children of his wife's unfaithfulness symbolic names: "No-Mercy" and "Not-my-People" (1: 6–9), referring to the judgment of God upon Israel. Now, says YHWH, "I will have mercy on her that had not obtained mercy, and I will say to them which were not my people: Thou art my people; and they shall say: Thou art my God" (2: 23). It is from this vision of what YHWH will do, that Hosea turns back to his own life. Since YHWH will forgive his one-time bride must he not be ready to forgive Gomer too? So Hosea buys his wife out of her degradation and she returns to his home.

But sterner tasks await the prophet than the settlement of his own affairs. He plunges now on to the darkening stage of national fortunes. In the next eleven chapters (4–14), he gives us a series of pictures of a nation in moral decay —a profligate court, a venal priesthood, perjury, murder, theft and adultery. He shows the consequences of corruption in the nation in terms of its political quandary—puppet kings, rival factions, loss of prestige abroad, weakened stock through sexual licence. Nothing is surer than that national collapse and exile loom ahead.

These chapters are extremely difficult. The Hebrew text is in places unintelligible, hence the obscurity of the English translation. There is no observable sequence in the series of short oracular utterances of which the main part of the book consists. The same themes recur with sometimes wearisome repetition. We cannot therefore do much more than gain an impression of the general tenor of Hosea's thought, and assess his contribution to the Old Testament preparation for the Gospel.

If Amos is the prophet of morality, Hosea is the prophet of faith. The concern of Amos is with right conduct. Hosea calls for the attitude of mind that gives rise to right conduct. Neither of them is primarily occupied with individuals. It is on the right relationship between YHWH and the community that Hosea insists. He speaks of it as that of husband and wife, or of father and child. Whatever figure he used, the prophet always saw this relationship as personal—YHWH teaching his child to walk, leading him out of Egyptian bondage, lavishing his love upon him and being repaid with nothing but ingratitude (11: 1-4).

The prophet's own experience doubtless helped to give him this deep insight into the nature of YHWH. If a mere man could still find it in his heart to want his wife despite her unfaithfulness, must not this same yearning for his wayward bride, albeit on an infinitely higher plane, be found in YHWH? But YHWH's love is no easy tolerance. Its ethical demands are even higher than those of a God of justice, for love demands no less response than love.

Thus Hosea does not urge his hearers to change their ways, he urges them to return to God, to put right their relationship to him in the belief that good conduct will follow of itself. So with religious observances: "I desired mercy and not sacrifice; and the knowledge of God more than burnt offerings" (6: 6). It is characteristic of the difference between the two prophets that while Amos sees no prospect for Israel but extinction, Hosea cannot believe that love will be defeated. The love of YHWH is stronger than death, and beyond the catastrophe which he recognises to be imminent, Hosea looks forward to the day when Israel will come to her senses and return to the pure and proper service of her God.

It is the more frustrating that the text of Hosea is so confused since he is so obviously, in company with Jeremiah and Second Isaiah, one of the great saints of Israel who lead us to the threshold of the Gospel. More clearly than in many other parts of the Old Testament, we can see the prophetic insight into the love of YHWH for Israel, the people of his choice, illuminating the same pattern of the love of Christ, the Bridegroom, for his Church, the Bride (*Eph.* 5: 22-33). The Church of the New Testament had no doubt that in its own creation the prophecy concerning the people who once were Not-My-People, and now again as the new Israel, both Jews and Gentiles, were called of God to be his children, had been marvellously fulfilled (*Rom.* 9: 24-26).

An even deeper note is struck in Matthew's gospel, where the evangelist finds in Hosea a prophecy of the flight of the Holy Family to Egypt (*Matt.* 2: 15). It shows little perception to accuse Matthew of a superficial or mechanical use of Old Testament prophecy in his use of Hosea's words: "Out of Egypt have I called my son" (11: 1), for basically what Hosea and the gospel writer were saying was the same. For Hosea, God had chosen Israel as his son, and proved it by leading him from the living death of Egypt to the new life of the promised land. For Matthew, Christ, the new Moses, had under God delivered the new Israel from greater bondage than Egypt into the promised land of life in his Risen Presence.

JOEL

WE KNOW nothing of Joel except the name of his father (1:1). From his interest in ritual we might guess that the prophet was attached to the Temple at Jerusalem, and his date appears to be about 400 B.C. The theme that binds the prophecies together is a spectacular plague of locusts which had stripped the land bare. This suggests to Joel the devastation which will be wrought when the Lord comes in judgment upon the world on the fearful Day of YHWH (see pp. 270–272).

In dramatic and vivid detail the prophet describes the depredations of the locusts (1: 1-20), which he sees as a presage of the coming judgment. Bringing darkness and terror, they sweep through the land like the consuming fire of God or like the avenging army of his wrath (2: 1-11). In the eyes of any prophet this meant that the people had sinned, but Joel proclaims that it is never too late to turn to God in penitence. If only the people will throw themselves on the mercy of God—"rend your heart and not your garments"—he will rid them of this plague (2: 12-17).

It would seem from the next words that the prophet's warning did not go unheeded. The people apparently gave some evidence of a change of heart by a national day of prayer, whereupon Joel predicted a reversal of their mis-

fortunes and promised fertility and abundance, with recompense for "the years that the locust hath eaten" (2: 18-27). Not only so, but the Lord would send his Spirit upon all Israel. From the oldest to the youngest, each and every one would know God with the direct intimacy of a prophet (2: 28-29). The Day of the Lord would come with all its supernatural terrors, but the faithful children of God would be safe within his holy city (2: 30-32).

On that Day YHWH will summon the heathen nations, who have afflicted his people, to stand their trial in the Valley of Judgment. Scattered Israel, restored from exile, will exact retribution from her former oppressors (3: 1-8). The pagan hordes will gather for a final onslaught against Jerusalem, but they will be no match for the angelic host who will execute the Lord's sentence on his enemies (3: 9-16a). Throughout this terrible judgment Israel will be protected by her God, and never again will Jerusalem suffer assault or invasion. The land will be blessed beyond human imagination, and while the territories of Israel's enemies lie in ruins, Judah will be inhabited for ever and YHWH will dwell eternally in Jerusalem (3: 16b-21).

What value has all this for us today? Although Joel has obviously modelled himself on prophets of the calibre of Amos, Ezekiel and Second Isaiah, judging by the number of phrases which can be paralleled in their works, his thought is altogether on a lower plane. Where Amos, for example, thinks of the Day of YHWH as a judgment upon Israel Joel appears to look on it as bringing about the vindication of the Jews and the extermination of the Gentiles. He is in fact speaking from the context of the narrow Judaism well after the Exile, fostered by Nehemiah and later especially by Ezra, which exalted Jewish particularism and encouraged nationalistic exclusiveness.

No one can gainsay the artistic skill of Joel in his descriptions both of the plague of locusts and of the Day of YHWH, but what are we to make of his apocalyptic visions? We must admit frankly that the prophet was unable to see the Jews after the Exile as basically anything other than the victimised, if sometimes wayward children of God. In a sense for them the Day of YHWH had already come in the destruction of Jerusalem, and they felt in Second Isaiah's words that in the Exile they had paid "double for all their sins" (*Isa.* 40: 2). The persecution complex which Joel shares with all apocalyptic writers, and which reflects the perennial problem of the continued misfortune of God's people, prevents him likewise from regarding the Gentiles as anything other than the black-hearted enemies of God.

In his defence we may say that it is not so much the Jews as a race

that the prophet is thinking of, but the Jews as the heirs of the Law and the promises, the people of God's choice. As such, their sufferings at the hands of their more powerful neighbours are an affront to the God of Sinai, and consequently their pagan tormentors become the enemies of God's good purposes for the world. The Day of YHWH for them still lies ahead, the final day of reckoning for their crimes against God and his people. We might add that Joel shows none of the triumphant relish in the annihilation of the pagans, such as appears in later apocalyptic (e.g. *Zech.* 9: 15; 14: 12).

Yet when all is said and done, this type of Old Testament writing indicates one reason why a New Testament became necessary. The nationalism of *Joel* must be set beside the universalism of *Isaiah* (2: 2–4; 45: 22–23; 55: 1–5) and *Jonah* (see pp. 294–295), if we are to have a true view of the value of the Old Testament for us today. The new Israel is not merely a continuation of the old but its reformation, fulfilment and completion. What Joel hoped for was not wrong, but it was not enough. Like so many others in the pages of the Old Testament, the prophet saw the truth "through a glass darkly" with all the limitations of his time and circumstance.

In a deeper sense than he knew, he spoke truly when he saw the end of the present age as bringing the victory of God over his enemies, and his Presence with his people Israel eternally. But just as we are guided by St. Peter, in his sermon at Pentecost, to see the Christian significance of Joel's prophecy about the outpouring of the Spirit (*Acts* 2: 14–18), and by St. Paul to see its true meaning (*Gal.* 5: 22), so we are also taught in the New Testament to see that the blessings which Joel predicted are available through Christ for Gentile as well as Jew, for men of all nations who "call upon the name of the Lord", and thus become heirs of the promises made to Israel (*Acts* 2: 21, 39; 10: 45; *Rom.* 10: 12, 13).

AMOS

AMOS AND Hosea are undoubtedly the greatest of the minor
prophets. Chronologically
they are also the first of the
spokesmen of YHWH whose writings have come down to us, and
like all the other prophets whose
pronouncements have been recorded, they cannot be understood
apart from the times they lived
in. The message of the prophets
is in a sense timeless, but it is
always delivered in terms of the
situation in their day.

Both Amos and Hosea flourished around the middle of the
eighth century in the northern
kingdom. To understand their
contribution to the faith of the Old
Testament, the two factors to be
borne in mind are the corrupt
state of society at the time and the
growing power of Assyria. Jeroboam II reigned for forty years
(see p. 199), and Israel was enjoy-
ing such peace and prosperity as
she had not known since the days
of Solomon.

It was popular policy to make
hay while the sun shone. Trade
had increased and money was
plentiful. But most of it found its
way into the pockets of a few and
dire poverty rubbed shoulders
with opulence. Building on a
lavish scale was fashionable. Town
mansions and country estates
gratified the ambitions of the
wealthy grandees but destitution

sat at their gates. Officially religion
likewise prospered. The great
temple at Bethel, ostensibly devoted to the worship of YHWH,
encouraged every aspect of Canaanite religious practice and
claimed it to be the service of
Israel's God. Scrupulous regard
was paid to tithes, festivals, pil-
grimages and sabbath observance.

This was held to be all that
YHWH required. So long as these
pious customs were maintained,
the religious life of the nation was
assuredly in a healthy state.
Whether injustice, perjury and
fraud were rife was no matter.
If the country's economy was in
good heart and true religion was
safe what cause was there for
concern? Least of all was there
cause for concern about Assyria,
who loomed up on the horizon
but who had much elsewhere to
occupy her attention and whose
record of conquest was still in the
making. Furthermore, it was clear
to Israel that YHWH would never
allow his people to be overcome
by a heathen monarch. In short
the subjects of king Jeroboam had
every reason for self-congratulation and optimism.

On to this complacent stage
steps Amos. He disclaims at the
outset any connection with the
time-serving prophets of the state
religion: "I am no prophet, no
member of any prophet's guild; I

am only a shepherd and tend sycomores. But YHWH took me from the flock. YHWH said to me, 'Go and prophesy to my people Israel'" (7: 14–15). So Amos left his sheep and his fig trees at Tekoa, a barren and desolate spot twelve miles south of Jerusalem, and became another of the long line of prophets from the desert who, throughout the progress of Israel from the no-madic life up the ladder of civilisa-tion, sought to remind the people of YHWH of the ancient and austere standards of Sinai.

Probably Amos derived his intimate knowledge of the nor-thern kingdom, where as a Judahite borderer he was of course a stranger, from market days and from the fairs and festivals which were then so common. What he saw there made it impossible for him to remain silent. Seeing that society was in an unhealthy state he sought to find the cause. Ap-parently Amos was not one of those prophets who had a sudden vision of the majesty of YHWH, or whose initial call came to him in an ecstatic trance. It was rather the sheer logic of events that seized him and compelled him to think, and having thought he was not afraid to speak. "Does a lion in the jungle roar, unless he has some prey? . . . When the Lord Eternal speaks who can but prophesy?" (3: 4, 8).

Here was a simple shepherd, forced by the obvious corruption of the times to set himself up as an instrument of YHWH to denounce the age for its crimes, and to fore-tell certain judgment for its dis-loyalty to the God of Moses.

Amos seems to have preached for some time in various places, but his most dramatic appearance was at Bethel. The story is told in 7: 1 – 8: 3 of how, at a great religious festival there, he determined to bring matters to a head and to announce to the people the doom that threatened them for their continued disobedience and im-penitence.

Bethel was the national shrine of the northern kingdom, the royal chapel, and Amos faced his crowded audience much in the same way as Luther did at Worms or Savonarola at Florence. The spirit, the motive and the courage were the same although the time and place were centuries and miles apart. God's judgment on sin, national evils, religious hypocrisy —these are themes common to prophets in every age and these were the lines on which Amos moulded his sermon.

He said in effect: This country is in a parlous state. You have been warned by plagues of locusts and by parching drought that to trifle with the Lord of Creation is fraught with peril. Despite your carefree optimism your society is built on rotten foundations. I have seen YHWH standing on your walls with a plumb line in his hand and he said to me—"This place must be destroyed. What was once straight has become crooked. I can stand no more. This land is ripe for destruction." No one could doubt that the instrument of destruction in the prophet's mind was Assyria.

At this point the priest Amaziah intervened and accused Amos of treason. He was told to keep his prophecies to himself and get back to his shepherding: "You dreamer, be off to Judah and earn your living there; play the prophet there but never again at Bethel, for it is the royal shrine, the national temple". Thus Amos was forbidden the right of public speech, banished to his village and, humanly speaking, but for the piety of his disciples who collected his utterances and recorded them, perhaps at his own dictation, we should have known nothing of this bold man of God who pioneered a new medium of God's revelation to Israel by being the first prophet to have his oracles preserved in written form.

The book of *Amos*, as we have it now, opens with denunciations of Israel's neighbours for their crimes against common humanity (1:1–2: 3). The prophet lashes with his tongue Damascus, Philistia, Tyre, Edom, Ammon and Moab for their barbarous behaviour—massacres of innocent victims, atrocities of all descriptions, oppression, violence and cruelty. He appeals in so doing to the ordinary principles of humanity which are found in every nation. The crimes he condemns are the obvious ones that the mind revolts from.

But he fastens upon these flagrant offences only to turn them deftly into a flank attack on the Israelites themselves (2: 6–16). He rouses their conscience against their neighbours only to show them that their own civil and domestic crimes are equally culpable. Israel may feel that her neighbours are barbarians and may be rightly shocked at their conduct. No such dishonour may stain her own flag but, says Amos, there are crimes of civilisation as well as crimes of barbarism.

It is no pagan horde, but the people of YHWH, who sell an honest man as a slave and a poor man in debt for the proverbial old song; who trample down the feeble like dust and harry the life out of humble folk. It is among the people of YHWH that father and son consort with the same prostitute in the temple, that the humane provision of Mosaic law which ensured the return of a poor debtor's cloak offered in pledge is flouted (*Ex.* 22: 25–27). Rich men loll on these pitiful possessions beside the holy altars, as they debauch themselves with other men's money.

This from the people he had rescued from Egypt and saved from their foes is more than the Lord will stomach, and in graphic and searing terms the prophet warns his listeners that God is not mocked. Neither strength nor speed will save even the doughtiest warrior of Israel when YHWH's judgment falls upon it.

The theme of the next section (3: 1–4: 3) is that heaven's justice is unswerving. Nothing can prevent the collapse of a civilisation that violates divine law. Religion is no insurance, nor is tradition, nor any racial privilege. The stern verdict of YHWH permits of no evasion: "You alone of all men have I cared for: therefore I will punish you for all your misdeeds" (3: 2). The word "therefore" marks a new epoch in Israel's understanding of God. Pedigree and pride of race mean nothing. Responsibility and right conduct mean everything.

Then follows a slashing indictment of the established religion (4: 4 – 6: 14). Amos is not concerned with idolatry, with the worship of the other gods of the Palestinian pantheon, but with the perverted worship of YHWH, through which the Israelites thought that they had safeguarded themselves from all calamity. They are not lacking in religious zeal, on the contrary their zeal outstrips that of their forbears. It is precisely this that Amos condemns. Such assiduous worship, scrupulous observance of ritual and excess of liberality have become a pantomime and a superstition. It is justice and honesty that God demands.

As we have already seen, the seventh chapter describes the clash between Amos and the established religion, while the remaining two chapters (8: 4 – 9: 15) are devoted largely to gruesome forecasts of the devastation and havoc which the Assyrians will wreak on the terrible Day of the Lord. Israel will then learn that YHWH is no mere national godlet to be cosseted and patronised, but the Lord of righteousness and of the nations, Philistines and Aramaeans as well as Hebrews, who will find their longing for the Day of their triumph over the Gentiles turn to anguish, when they feel the hot breath of God's wrath. Many scholars think that the prophecies of Amos end at 9: 8a upon this note, and that the "happy ending" 9: 8b–15 is an appendix by a later hand and out of keeping with the rest of the book.

Amos is the prophet of justice. His standards are rigid and uncompromising, and he has the Israelite desert-dweller's hatred and suspicion of everything connected with civilisation, which is apt to bias his judgment. But on the moral issues between man and man, and on the moral order of the universe, he is on bedrock. Morality is not an accident or a convention; it is the principle on which the universe works. Amos is no philosopher and builds no system. What he sees, he sees by intuition. For him the sequence of cause and effect applies to the whole of life: sow evil and reap destruction, whether you be man or nation.

OBADIAH

NOTHING is known about the identity of Obadiah and it is not even certain when he lived. The most likely explanation is that he was one of those who voiced the sense of frustration and dejection that pervaded the small community of Jerusalem after the Exile—compressed into a tiny area, seeing their former broad lands in the hands of their enemies, and feeling themselves powerless to do anything to change their situation.

The subject of the book—the shortest in the Old Testament—is primarily an expression of the conviction that "the mills of God grind slowly but they grind exceeding small". There was a long story of enmity between Israel and its neighbour Edom, south of the Dead Sea. Tradition traced the origin of the two peoples to Jacob and Esau (*Gen.* 36: 1), and Esau's already bad reputation suffered further from the activities of his descendants (cf. *Heb.* 12: 16).

At the fall of Jerusalem in 587 B.C., Edom like other ancient rivals of Israel made no attempt to conceal its delight, and hastened to exploit its opportunities by occupying Israel's former territory (*Ezek.* 35: 3–15; *Ps.* 137: 7). Now

it had become Edom's turn to be overrun by Nabataean Arabs, and Obadiah sees in this the just judgment of God (1–14). The second half of the prophecy (15–21) looks on the present plight of Edom as a presage of its ultimate fate, and that of the other still triumphant Gentile nations. Judah has already drunk her cup of bitterness, but soon the Day of YHWH will overtake her foes and the golden age will dawn for the people of God.

Amos had seen the Day of YHWH as a judgment on Israel (*Amos* 5: 18). Now with the loss of both kingdoms, the experience of exile and the misery of vassalage to enter on the credit side, it is not surprising to find Obadiah, like Joel, taking the view that Israel had paid her debt, and that those who had so far gone scot-free must likewise pay the price (see p. 287). This is therefore far less a hymn of hate uttered by a nationalistic Jew, than the expression of a deep-seated prophetic conviction that God's righteousness cannot for ever be flouted by godless men, and a recognition that the downfall of Edom is proof that the God of Moses—and of Amos— holds the reins of history firmly in his hands.

JONAH

IN TWO WAYS the book of *Jonah* is unlike its companions in the group of twelve short collections of prophecy which form the concluding section of the Old Testament. Firstly, it is a story about a prophet rather than a compilation of prophetic oracles, and, secondly, it is superficially at any rate very much more familiar to the average person than the others, containing perhaps the best known incident in the Old Testament. It is an extremely readable and vivid story, but unfortunately like much else in the Old Testament it is often sadly misunderstood.

For *Jonah* is not a story about a whale. The incident where the prophet is swallowed by a great fish is not even the most spectacular happening in this short narrative. Much effort has been expended by those who miss the point of the book, to demonstrate either that such an occurrence is physically impossible, or on the other hand that whales have been found with gullets large enough to accommodate a man. How amused the ancient writer of *Jonah* would have been at this attempt to discredit the Bible, or to confound the sceptics, by applying the yardstick of zoological science to a tale which is neither scientific nor even historical but a parable like the Good Samaritan or the Prodigal Son.

The story, as a story, is sheer fun and fantasy. One incredible event follows another in quick succession, but the author's purpose is clear throughout. As Jesus wished us to see in the anonymous Samaritan the perfect type of good neighbourliness and charity, so the author of *Jonah* sought to illustrate the opposite type of character in this picture of a man who is the embodiment of intolerance, bigotry and lack of human sympathy.

But *Jonah* is more than a tale of an unlovable man, it is a challenge to a whole people. It was written, like the book of *Ruth*, soon after the time when Nehemiah and Ezra had instilled into the little Jewish community, returned from Exile, that their only hope of survival as the legatees of the Law and the promises lay in keeping themselves free from contamination by intermarriage or traffic of any kind with Gentiles. This had led to the rigid view that the covenant relationship with God was for his people only. Heathen nations, whether in Palestine or elsewhere, were beyond the pale and beyond God's concern.

In drawing his cartoon of Jonah, as typifying this bigoted attitude, the unknown master who was responsible for this little book was challenging all such views in the spirit of Second Isaiah, who saw Israel's mission in the world as God's light to lighten the Gentiles, and not as a candle to be put under a bushel (see p. 254). The message of God's love, which had been entrusted to his people, and his purpose that all nations should learn of it through their witness and example, runs through this little tale from start to finish, and gives it the right to be classed with those high peaks of Old Testament insight, which reach already through the mists of partial revelation into the clear sunshine of Gospel truth.

The chief character of the book, Jonah (whose name means "dove", a traditional symbol for Israel as in *Ps.* 74: 19), is summoned by YHWH to set out for Nineveh, a byword among strict Jews as the supreme example of Gentile irreligion and infamy (cf. *Nahum* 3). His mission is to proclaim God's judgment upon them, but knowing the Lord's readiness to forgive the penitent, Jonah, fearful that the heathen might repent and be pardoned, and dreading this eventuality, boards a ship which is outward bound in the opposite direction.

The hound of heaven is, however, on his trail. First, the Lord sends a tempest and forces the humane heathen sailors to throw this hoodoo overboard to prevent a shipwreck. Jonah would welcome death but the Lord has not finished with him by any means. A large fish has been commissioned to convey him back to land, where he is once again charged to carry out his original mission (1: 1 – 3: 2.—The psalm in 2: 2–9 is a later addition).

Jonah has now no option but to proceed to Nineveh where, as he had feared, his message of doom had an instantaneous and dramatic effect. In a fit of the sulks Jonah takes up his stance in the offing, hoping against hope that YHWH will not be foolish enough to spare these unspeakable Gentiles. The Lord, by waving his magic wand, induces the prophet to show for the first time a spark of compassion if only for a short-lived plant, whereupon YHWH asks him slyly if there is not much more reason for the Lord to have compassion on this great city with all its guiltless infants and harmless cattle (3: 3 – 4: 11).

So the story very properly ends with a question mark, for the author does not know whether his countrymen will respond to his challenge. There they sit in their walled-in sanctuary of Jerusalem, like Jonah in his bower, brooding over the wickedness of the world as they imagine it, and clutching their faith to their bosom, while the real world, like the decent sailors and the responsive Ninevites, is crying out for the word of God to be preached to them by his reluctant servants. We should be very obtuse if we did not see in this little gem of Old Testament prophecy a challenge also to every branch of the Church today.

MICAH

WHILE THE first Isaiah was guiding the national policy of Judah at the end of the eighth century B.C. (see pp. 250–251), a much less distinguished but no less forceful prophet was making pronouncements on the affairs of church and nation from the point of view of the common folk. This was Micah, a native of Moresheth, a village in the foothills of Judah not far from the Philistine city of Gath. Even more than Amos he had the countryman's suspicion and distrust of town-life, and a deep-seated conviction that civilisation inevitably brought moral and spiritual disaster in its train.

The book that bears his name opens with a judgment on Israel and Judah, in which he sees the Assyrian menace as the hand of YHWH bringing just retribution on Samaria, Jerusalem and the whole land of the promise, because of the sins of God's people (1: 1–16). The crimes of which they have been guilty are, for Micah, primarily the oppression of the weak by the strong, expropriation of the peasants from their land, eviction of helpless smallholders, and enslavement of innocent children. Priests and prophets alike come under his condemnation for their sordid money-grabbing, and their specious assur-

ances that no harm can ever befall the chosen people of YHWH. The holy city has become a monstrous parody of what it ought to be and must pay the price. Yet, beyond its destruction, Micah, like other great prophets, sees hope of a renewal of Israel's life. God will yet reign over a more worthy people (2: 1 – 3: 12).

Almost in Isaiah's words (cf. Isa. 2: 2–5), Micah looks forward to a golden age when, in a world at peace, the nations will turn to Israel for the light and inspiration that come from her knowledge of the true God. Beyond the death of the kingdom as they know it, and the discipline of exile, lies the vindication of God's purpose and the deliverance of his people. Under the leadership of their messianic king, sprung like David from Bethlehem (cf. Matt. 2: 6) and endowed with David's military skill, the enemies of God will be vanquished, and a cleansed and contrite remnant of Israel will offer the service that is due to her Lord (4: 1 – 5: 15).

Meantime, Israel is called to remember the patient love with which God has borne her follies and guided her destiny. In one of the great passages of the Old Testament (6: 6–8), Micah concentrates the message of all the prophets. "What doth the Lord require of thee but to do justly, and to love mercy, and to walk humbly with thy God?" In this quintessence of the prophetic protest against mere formalism in religion, we can see both the incisive character of their emphasis upon the moral aspects of religious faith, and the weakness of an approach that made such high demands upon fallible mortals who were unable to comply with them. Micah can only hope that one day God will somehow make it possible for his people to live together in the obedient relationship that fulfils his will, in a world that has learned to know his power (6: 1 – 7: 20).

The Hebrew text of the book is corrupt, and the oracles, some of which must stem from a later day than that of Micah, are arranged in a fairly haphazard order. This explains the relative impossibility of making much sense of the A.V. as it stands. But the passionate convictions of Micah shine through the obscurity of the text. Whether or no he himself suffered from the oppressions he describes, his social conscience is red-hot with honest indignation, but it is the indignation of a man of faith, who sees society's disorders not as the mere exploitation of the weak by the strong, but as a travesty of the obedience to God which is incumbent upon rich and poor alike. His prophecy of the downfall of Jerusalem (3: 12), which was followed by king Hezekiah's reforms, was quoted in justification of sparing the life of Jeremiah over a century later, when that prophet echoed Micah's sombre forecast (*Jer.* 26: 11–19).

NAHUM

IN THE turbulent story of the Near East in biblical times, no more ruthless and terrible war-machine smashed its way through the greater and lesser states than the imperial power of Assyria. Bloodthirsty and irresistible, its armies ravaged the Fertile Crescent and struck terror into the hearts of kings and commoners alike. Ruled by tyrants who boasted of their merciless treatment of their foes, this military steamroller crushed one after another of the tiny principalities of the Levant, leaving a haunting memory of death, destruction and terror. One of their many victims was the northern kingdom of Israel, which in 722 B.C. met the fate of other similar pocket-states which stood in the way of Assyrian expansion.

The book of *Kings* and the works of the prophets bear eloquent testimony, borne out by the boastful inscriptions of the Assyrian rulers themselves, to the horror which the very name of Assyria, and Nineveh its capital, awakened in the minds of all who had suffered from these brutal war lords and their disciplined savages. Consequently when in 612 B.C. Nineveh met the fate that had befallen so many unhappy cities, and was sacked by the Babylonians and their allies, exultation was widespread, and the fervent hopes of all the small states, which had been trampled in the dust by the Assyrians, were centred solely on the downfall of their oppressor. Their only prayer was that he should never be allowed to rise again. In the event their hope was well founded, and a few years after the fall of Nineveh the Assyrian empire was no more.

The prophet Nahum gives us the biblical version of this general rejoicing. As is to be expected, he sees Assyria's fate as the just judgment of God upon a godless people. In splendidly dramatic verses, which need no comment, he vividly depicts the sack of Nineveh and exults that the fate of other great cities like Thebes (No-Amon) will now be shared by those who had laid them in ruins.

It has been objected that Nahum has no word of pity for Assyria and no word of condemnation for Israel; that he falls far below Isaiah and Micah, who saw the Assyrians as God's means of chastening his people, or even more below Jeremiah, his contemporary, who saw the Babylonians not as a useful stick to beat the Assyrians but as a rod in the hand of YHWH to discipline Israel. This may well be so, although we have no reason to suppose that these few lines exhaust the whole range of the prophet's utterances. On the other hand, if there is any moral order in the universe, a nation with a record like that of Assyria deserved nothing less than annihilation, and Nahum is surely right to regard them as enemies of God and man of whom the world was well rid.

HABAKKUK

NEW INTEREST was aroused in the book of Habakkuk when a commentary on this prophet was discovered among the Dead Sea Scrolls in 1947. Previously there had been considerable discussion among scholars as to whether the Chaldeans or Babylonians, referred to in 1 : 6, were in fact the people who ravaged Judah and ultimately captured Jerusalem in 587 B.C., in which case this book would date from about 600 B.C. The other possibility was that the enemy referred to was the army of Alexander the Great, which would appear to fit the situation better, and would only require a minor change in the word "Chaldaeans" to make it read "Greeks" (Kittim for Kasdim). The commentary found at Qumran would seem to support the latter, which would of course date the prophecy considerably later than 600 B.C. The prophet's words would then become an anxious concern for the fate of the Israelite community and its neighbours, as Alexander's army advanced into the Levant.

Whichever view is correct—and there have been other suggestions as well—it does not alter the main theme of the prophecy. Nothing is known of the prophet himself except his name and a legendary story in the Apocrypha (see p. 326). He is however a man of the calibre of Job, who dares to question God's government of the world and finds an answer in trustful faith. His complaint that oppression and injustice go unpunished in his own experience (1 : 2–4), is met by an assurance from YHWH that evil of this kind will not escape retribution. God will use the invading armies of Babylon (or Greece) to chastise his recalcitrant people (1 : 5–11).

This does not satisfy Habakkuk, however. How can God allow ruthless pagan conquerors to spread devastation among his own chosen folk and their neighbours, who with all their faults are far less guilty than rapacious imperial powers? (1 : 12–17). The reply of YHWH is that these violent plunderers will not escape without scathe. They will meet their deserts. This is the knowledge that must sustain the troubled simple man. He must trust in God's justice though the divine machinery sometimes seems to be at a standstill (2 : 1–20). The third chapter of the book is an independent psalm, in which the prophet proclaims his trust in God's providence through all the upheavals that assail the world (3 : 1–19). Not the least important feature of this profound little book is that Habakkuk's words in 2 : 4 "the just shall live by his faith" (i.e. his loyalty to the Law and the promises of God) become the basis of St. Paul's reinterpretation of the significance of faith in *Rom.* 1 : 17, *Gal.* 3 : 11, and likewise form the prelude to the great panegyric on faith by the author of *Hebrews* (*Heb.* 10 : 38).

ZEPHANIAH

To UNDERSTAND the almost unrelieved gloom of the book of *Zephaniah*, we do well to remember that this prophet made his witness in the early years of the reign of king Josiah, when the religious and social conditions of Judah had reached their lowest ebb, as a result of the baneful policies of Manasseh and Amon, and before the young king Josiah felt himself strong enough to carry through the deuteronomic reformation of 622 B.C., following the discovery of the "book of the law" (see pp. 200–201).

If we then think of Zephaniah as a descendant of the worthy king Hezekiah (1 : 1), who had to live under a regime which had completely reversed the sound policies of his ancestor, and which was a living contradiction of all that the great prophets had fought for, it is easy to see why this man, who shared their views, is so violent in condemnation of his own society, and why nothing less than its destruction seems to him to be its proper fate.

It was at this time, too, that barbarian hordes of Scythians from the north swept through the Fertile Crescent, making havoc wherever they went and molesting even the powerful Assyrian empire. Although he does not mention them by name, it is clearly the depredations of these marauders that the prophet refers to, and he sees in them a foreshadowing of the even more terrible Day of YHWH when God will visit the nations, including Judah, with just retribution (see pp. 270–272). Having depicted this terrifying judgment on Jerusalem (1 : 2–18), Zephaniah foretells the same fate for Judah's neighbours, even for proud Assyria (2 : 1–15).

It seems most likely that the third chapter of this book has had later additions made to it, and that the prophet, having returned to his denunciation of Judah (3 : 1–5) and the other nations (3 : 6–8), looks forward in true prophetic manner to the survival of a remnant of humble folk who will serve God faithfully in a world that is rid of all who violate his laws (3 : 12–13). The vision of the nations united in acknowledging YHWH (3 : 9–10), as well as of the future triumph of Israel (3 : 14–20), stem from a later date and hardly tally with the tone of the major part of the book.

HAGGAI

THE atmosphere which has pervaded the last three prophetic books which we have been studying has been one of war, devastation and doom. In their several ways, Nahum, Habakkuk and Zephaniah were impelled to speak in the name of God against a background of political upheaval, violence and destruction. The next three prophets among the collection of the twelve short books that conclude the Old Testament have a different background and a different message.

They all come from the period following the Exile, when, after the "*Sturm und Drang*" of Israel's fight for its existence, and the clash of imperial powers, the people of God had returned to the homeland after the Babylonian captivity, and sought amid the shattered fragments of their former glory to rebuild their commonwealth in accordance with the divinely given Law. We have therefore to think of the book of *Haggai*, *Zechariah* and *Malachi* as stemming from the period of Israel's rebirth, when, under the guidance of priest and prophet, the little community sought to reorientate its life and mould its future, along the lines which the great prophets, beginning with Amos, had declared ought to have been followed by the people of the covenant from Sinai onwards, but from which they had so grievously and so fatally strayed.

In reading the latter part of the work of the Chronicler (*Ezra— Nehemiah*), we have seen how, from his remote vantage point over two centuries after the events he describes, that pious and zealous recorder idealised the return from exile and the subsequent temper of the Jerusalem community. He could not conceive it otherwise than that the returned exiles were consumed with a passionate desire to restore as quickly as possible the proper ordinances of religion in the spirit and setting enjoined by Second Isaiah and Ezekiel (see pp. 210–212). The books of *Haggai* and *Zechariah* present a more sober picture of what actually happened.

It may be that, as the Chronicler claims, the foundations of the new Temple were laid by the original repatriated exiles in 537 B.C. (*Ezra* 5: 16). If so, there is no indication in the books of *Haggai* and *Zechariah* that any further steps were taken to complete it, until Haggai laid it upon the people's conscience seventeen years later that the ruined Temple was a standing reproach to a community that claimed to be YHWH's chosen folk, and an offence in the sight of God.

In 520 B.C. (i.e. the second year of Darius I of Persia), Haggai calls on governor, high priest and people to set about the task of rebuilding. He accuses them of being more concerned to equip themselves with comfortable homes than to restore the house of God. The drought and famine from which they have apparently suffered he attributes to the wrath of God. So immediate was the effect of his words that in three weeks work on the Temple had started (1: 1–15). A month later he had to appeal to the people again. Many felt that the new Temple could never compare with the glory of Solomon's master-piece. Haggai encourages them with the assurance that the messi-anic kingdom is at hand, and that the treasures of the pagan nations which the Lord will destroy will be available to enrich his house (2: 1–9).

A little later still, he tells them that it was their previous unwilling-ness to take this work in hand that had tainted their service of God and brought on themselves his displeasure. From now on, how-ever, prosperity would reign (2:

10–19). The little collection of oracles ends with the prophet's proclamation of the imminent end of Gentile dominion, and the announcement that Zerubbabel the governor, descendant of David, is the messianic king (2: 20–23).

On a short term view Haggai was of course mistaken. He did in fact get the Temple built in four years (*Ezra* 6: 15), but Zerubbabel was not the Messiah, and when the messianic Kingdom did come in Christ it did not involve the spoliation of the Gentiles and the enrichment of the Temple. Haggai falls below the level of the great prophets in that his chief concern is with the outward fabric of wor-ship, yet when we remember the importance of the Temple as the heart of post-exilic Judaism, the cradle of Christianity, we must recognise our debt to the zeal and passion of this relatively unknown prophet, who stirred up the embers of a languishing faith, and who saw the rebuilding of the Temple as the necessary first step towards the renewal of the religious life of his people.

ZECHARIAH

THE BOOK of *Haggai* deals with one topic only—the rebuilding of the Temple at Jerusalem after the Exile. The prophet Zechariah was associated with Haggai in fostering this enterprise, and thus speaks from the same point in the story of Israel and from the same background. His prophecies, however, cover a wider range of ideas, and the book presents so many problems that no more than a rough impression can be suggested here. It is generally agreed that chapters 1–8 contain the utterances of Zechariah, the contemporary of Haggai, and that the remaining chapters of the book (9–14) come from a later period (fourth to third century B.C.), and deal with a different situation.

Like Haggai, Zechariah found the impetus to his prophetic activity in the general revolt which broke out in the vassal states of the Persian empire in 522 B.C. To the devout Jew, that at once suggested the imminent downfall of the Gentile oppressors and the impending Day of YHWH. Moreover, since it was combined with the presence as governor of Zerubbabel, who traced his ancestry back to David, the conviction in the minds of both prophets was strengthened that the messianic king was in their midst and that at any moment the Lord would show

his hand, terminate the rule of the hated Gentile oppressors, vindicate his chosen people and inaugurate the messianic Kingdom.

It was thus imperative that in preparation for this end event the Temple of YHWH should be restored, so that, as Second Isaiah and Ezekiel had foretold, the Lord should find his kingly throne awaiting him when he returned to reign in Zion and from there execute his majestic purpose for the world (*Isa.* 52: 7–10; *Ezek.* 43: 4–5). Zechariah was therefore moved to add his exhortations to those of Haggai (*Ezra* 5: 1–2), and for two years, from 520–518 B.C., he encouraged the builders of the Temple not so much with promises of material prosperity, like Haggai, but with visions of the glories of the messianic Kingdom that was about to come.

These visions, eight in number, and all represented as taking place in a single night, form the distinctive feature of the first eight chapters of the book. Combined with oracles in the normal prophetic manner, they all seek to assure the people that the messianic age is at hand. Following a call to repentance (1: 1–6), the prophet in vision and pronouncement foretells the return of YHWH to his own city (1: 7–17), the downfall of the Gentiles (1: 18–21), and a Jerusalem greater than ever before (2: 1–13). Under the divinely blessed authority of high priest and prince the Temple will be rebuilt (3: 1 – 4: 14), Jerusalem will be purged of sin (5: 1–11), and YHWH will reign over a world at peace (6: 1–8). Expanding the same themes (6: 9 – 8: 17), the prophecies conclude with the grand vision of nations of the world turning to the Jews to learn from them of God (8: 18–23).

The complicated historical problems that lie behind the apocalyptic utterances contained in chs. 9–14 are beyond the scope of this commentary, but the invincible hope of a downtrodden people, who believed desperately in the ultimate fulfilment of God's purpose for the world through Israel his chosen instrument, shines through the obscurity of the allusions. When prophecy had sunk to such a low ebb that a prophet was ashamed to be recognised as such (13: 4–6), it is not surprising that ritual holiness was regarded as the supreme witness of the people of God (9: 7; 14: 16–21), or that their oppressors should be conceived of as almost synonymous with the powers of darkness, and meriting therefore no less than utter annihilation (9: 15; 14: 12). Yet through it all burns the conviction that in the end somehow the Gentiles must be won for God, and Jerusalem must become the spiritual centre of the world.

For the Christian Church, however, surely the most memorable features of this second part of the book of *Zechariah* must be the two passages which find their fulfilment in the Gospel. When our Lord enters Jerusalem on Palm Sunday riding upon an ass (*Mark* 11: 1–10), he is consciously identifying himself with the messianic king of 9: 9 who selects this symbol of peace and humility. Likewise when YHWH receives from his faithless people thirty paltry pieces of silver as the reward for his services to them (11: 12), there is more than mere mechanical fulfilment in the New Testament account of the price which Judas received for the betrayal of the body of God's Son (*Matt.* 26: 14–16).

MALACHI

THE LAST of the Old Testament books, like its two predecessors, takes us back to Jerusalem some time after the exiles have returned from Babylon. If we have tended to deplore the rigorist policies of Nehemiah and Ezra, and to regret that the more liberal outlook, represented in the books of *Ruth* and *Jonah*, was swamped by the narrow nationalism and hard legalism of men who, from our remote vantage point in time, appear to have been religious bigots, this book of *Malachi* supplies a useful corrective.

It paints a picture, just before the arrival of Nehemiah, of a society where religion and morality alike were treated with scant respect. The need was obvious for a clarion call from an Amos or a Micah. Instead of that comes this collection of utterances of an anonymous prophet, who lacks both the passion and the insight of the greater spokesmen of YHWH, who cannot breathe new vitality into the religious life of the people of God by lifting them up to the heights like an Ezekiel or a Second Isaiah, but who shakes them into an awareness of their shortcomings in such a way that the ground is prepared for the more forceful programme of Nehemiah and Ezra.

As we have seen (pp. 216–217), it was only by the insistence of these

Ezra Nehemiah

two men and their associates on the exclusiveness of the Jewish heritage that the heart of the Old Testament faith was kept beating through the last few centuries of the reign of the old covenant before Christ brought the reawakening. The book of *Malachi* shows the danger that threatened to destroy the religious legacy of patriarch and prophet, and also teaches us to see the purpose of God working out in ways that are beyond human wisdom.

The name Malachi means "my messenger", and in all probability the prophecies contained in this book were originally anonymous, but came to be attributed to the "messenger" of 3: 1. For convenience, however, the author is generally called Malachi. He speaks to a disillusioned people. The glowing promises of Second Isaiah had not been fulfilled. The Temple had been rebuilt but the prosperity and blessedness guaranteed by Haggai and Zechariah were nowhere in evidence. Scepticism and religious apathy went hand in hand with contempt for moral standards. The priesthood itself had lost any sense of its vocation.

The unusual form of question and answer, which is a distinctive feature of this little book, suggests that the day had passed when a prophet had only to say "Thus saith the Lord" to find ready acceptance for his words. Malachi has to argue his case against a battery of querulous and cynical opposition. To the complaint that YHWH has deserted his people he has no better retort than that the plight of Edom is far worse (1 : 2–5). He takes the priests to task for being bored with their holy office, for being content to offer second-rate animals in sacrifice, for bringing their sacred calling into general contempt. Even the worship of the Gentiles is more acceptable to God (1 : 6 – 2 : 9).

The laity divorce their wives in order to marry more attractive young foreign women, who bring their pagan religious customs with them (2 : 10–16). But YHWH will not allow all this to go unpunished. The Day of the Lord is at hand (2 : 17 – 3 : 5). Let the people pay their proper tithes and the fields will burgeon again with no more plagues of locusts to devour the crops (3 : 6–12). As for the faithful few, let them not lose heart. Their faithfulness is not forgotten in heaven, and when the terrible Day of Judgment comes they will have their reward (3 : 13 – 4 : 3).

Malachi, in his eagerness to meet the genuine dissatisfaction of his hearers with the over-simplified traditional doctrine of rewards and punishments in this life, finds an equally oversimplified solution of the world's disorder in an imminent Day of YHWH. In his desire to avoid the mistake of enunciating high principles, which are incapable of fulfilment, he almost seems to reduce the proper service of God to the type of pedantic ritual correctness which eventually produced Pharisaism.

But we must be grateful to him for his noble conception of the office of the holy ministry (2 : 5–7), for his high doctrine of the sanctity of marriage (2 : 14–16), and his recognition of the worth of sincerity in worship even in paganism (1 : 11). The concluding verses of the book (4 : 4–6), in which the Law is regarded as all-sufficient, and the messianic age is foreshadowed by the promise of the return of Elijah as its herald, are indicative of the two streams of thought, legalism and apocalypticism, which mould the minds of the people of God in the intervening period between the Old and New Testaments. Jesus, and, following him, the early Church, saw in the mission of John the Baptist the fulfilment of this prophecy of Elijah as the forerunner of the Messiah and his Kingdom (*Mark* 1 : 2; 9 : 11–13; *Luke* 1 : 17).

THE APOCRYPHA

THE APOCRYPHA

WHATEVER ELSE we say about the books of the Apocrypha it is safe to claim that too few people know about them. Apart from the much quoted passage from *Ecclesiasticus*: "Let us now praise famous men" which is often read at Remembrance Day services, the contents of the Apocrypha are on the whole almost as unfamiliar as the contents of the Koran. The reason for this is not far to seek. Most of the Bibles we possess do not include the Apocrypha, and we have either to buy the Apocrypha as a supplement to the ordinary Bible, or ask specially for an edition which contains it.

It would be too much to claim that a knowledge of the Apocrypha is indispensable for a proper understanding of the Bible, but it would certainly be true to say that, apart from their own intrinsic interest, the apocryphal books which are sandwiched between the Old and New Testaments form a useful introduction to the Gospel, and help to explain many features of the New Testament which have not been prominent so far in our study of the Bible.

Between the last chapter of *Malachi*, dating from about 450 B.C., and the first chapter of the gospel according to St. Matthew, there is a gap of over five hundred years. Part of the reason for such a large gap is of course the method of arrangement of the books. *Malachi* was not in fact the last book of the Old Testament to be written, nor was Matthew's gospel the first of the New Testament writings. St. Paul's letters were in circulation before the gospels and, as we have seen, quite a large proportion of the Old Testament dates from considerably later than *Malachi*—all the section known as the Writings (see p. 142), including the work of the Chronicler (see p. 203), and notably the book of *Daniel*, which brings us down to 167 B.C.

Even at that we are left with a gap of approximately two hundred years which, however, is more apparent than real, because from the time when the book of *Daniel* was written, and even before, right into New Testament days, there was a steady flow of Jewish sacred writing of all kinds—history, wisdom, moral tales, poetry, apocalyptic—in short a continuation of the same kind of writing as we have found in the Old Testament. The question naturally arises as to why this literature was not included in the Old Testament and to that there are various answers.

The process of fixing the contents of the Old Testament was a gradual one. The Hebrew Bible consisted first of all only of the Pentateuch, the most sacred part in the eyes of the Jews, and containing the Torah or Law of God. To this were added in course of time the books of the prophets, and lastly the Writings. There were various official tests for determining which books should be included in the authoritative list or canon, but basically the criterion was the intrinsic value of the book itself. If a book by virtue of its own worth, its hold on the affections of the people, its value as a guide to life and as a treasury of the knowledge of God, had established a position for itself, its inclusion was generally certain.

Those books of the Old Testament that hovered longest on the borderline of acceptance or rejection are precisely those that we should expect to do so—*Esther*, *Ecclesiastes* and the *Song of Songs*. Their religious value was doubted, and *Esther* was eventually included only because of its association with a popular festival, while the wholly secular *Song of Songs*, when regarded as an allegory, could be given a religious significance, and thus become eligible for admission into the sacred canon.

This process of selection and rejection continued over several centuries, and it was inevitable that just as some of the present Old Testament books were almost excluded, so some of the other sacred writings of the times were almost admitted. Obviously a line had to be drawn somewhere, and the Old Testament canon was not finally closed until A.D. 90, when Jerusalem had been captured and sacked by the Romans, when the Jewish people had no longer a national home, and had begun the long tale of their wanderings which only ended with the revival of the state of Israel in our own day.

It was important that an uprooted people, still strongly conscious of their religious background, should have their authoritative scriptures clearly defined, especially since the new sect of Christianity claimed to be the inheritor of the faith and promises of the Old Testament. But the rabbis who met at Jamnia in A.D. 90 to make the final decision had no easy task. The books of the Law and the Prophets were no problem. They had been long since officially recognised. The real difficulty was with those more recent books which had been circulating as sacred writings of one kind or another, after the canon of the Law and the Prophets had been established.

Perhaps the most notable feature of Jewish life since the Exile, apart from the development of Judaism itself, was the steady stream of emigrants from Palestine as mercenaries, merchants, slaves and adventurers who, in the last three centuries of the pre-Christian era, had made their way into all parts of the civilised world. When the Persian empire came to an end in 331 B.C., it was Alexander the Great who brought about its downfall, and through him and the empire he founded, Greek culture became the dominant influence everywhere even after the Roman Empire took command of the world just before the coming of Christianity.

It was in this Greek period that Alexandria in Egypt became the home of a Jewish community second only in importance to Jerusalem itself. There, in the third century B.C., so many Jews were no longer familiar with the Hebrew tongue that a translation of the scriptures into Greek had to be made. This was the Septuagint, which became not only the Bible for the ordinary Jew living outside of Palestine, but also, later, for the ordinary Christian as well. But once removed from the rigid control of the Jerusalem ecclesiastics, the Greek-speaking Jews had fewer inhibitions about adding to the sacred canon of scripture other improving works which seemed to them to have religious value.

The range of Jewish holy scriptures was therefore much wider in Alexandria than in Jerusalem, and it was by and large these later Greek writings, which had been in circulation overseas and not in Jerusalem, that the rabbis rejected when the decision had to be taken in A.D. 90. Since it was the Palestinians and not the Alexandrians who fixed the canon, those books which were supposed to have been written after the time of Ezra, or which could not be attributed to some notable character like David or Solomon, were relegated to the category of Apocrypha i.e. "hidden" from use in public worship.

These fourteen books, which originally constituted the overlap between the scriptures in use by the Jews in Jerusalem and those in circulation among the Jews overseas, are accepted by the Roman Catholic branch of the Church as an integral part of the Old Testament. Reformed communions generally follow the more conservative policy of the Jerusalem rabbis, and omit them from the scrip-

tures, while the Anglican communion relegates them to the position of an appendix to the Old Testament, includes them in the lectionary, and commends them for devotional use and edification.

The books of the Apocrypha, however, by no means exhaust the list of what was written between the two Testaments. More than as many books again have come down to us under the name of the Pseudepigrapha ("false titles"). These are books of the same varied character, which were reckoned to be on a lower plane than the Apocrypha, and indeed to be definitely heretical. They were never admitted into the Bible and no branch of the Church recognises them as authoritative.

The Importance of the Apocrypha

In spite of their unsatisfactory names, which convey nothing about their contents, the Apocrypha and Pseudepigrapha are of considerable importance, in that they shed much useful light upon what would otherwise be a blank period of over two centuries between the Old Testament and the New. They show us how men's minds were moving in the years just before Christ came, and the kind of religious milieu in which the writers of the New Testament grew up.

There is no authoritative quotation from the Apocrypha in the New Testament such as would suggest that the early Christians put it on an equal footing with the Old Testament, and we should therefore be wrong to overemphasise its importance. But we should be equally wrong to disregard books which the major part of Christendom regards as canonical or edifying, and even if it seems to us that the rabbis at Jamnia were on the whole wisely guided, their rule of thumb method of making the final decision was not infallible. There is much in the Apocrypha that has more to say to us than, for example, the book of *Esther*, and although there is little to be found in the Apocrypha which touches the heights of the Old Testament at its best, it is still the knot which ties the two Testaments together and forms the last stage of the preparation for the Gospel.

When we turn from the last page of the Old Testament to the first page of the New, we have moved from a troubled world where the oriental despotism of Persia held the reins, to a world where Roman arms and Roman law ensured peace and a measure of protection for all its subjects. But although civilisation was dominated by a power that was Roman in name, it was the Greek way of life that permeated it. It was in a world that spoke Greek as its *lingua franca* that the gospel writers, Jews as they were, found in that language a common tongue to reach all corners of the empire. It was in cities built on the Greek pattern, with schools and universities, pagan temples and market places, where men, stimulated by Greek philosophers, discussed the nature of goodness and the existence of God, that St. Paul and the early missionaries founded the first Christian communities. The period of the Apocrypha was the period of Greek supremacy, and in these writings we can detect the influence of Greece on the thinking of even that most exclusive of all its subject peoples, the Jews.

Moreover, when we turn to the New Testament from the Old, we are at once brought up against words and ideas which although perhaps implied in the Old Testament have not been fully developed—the Kingdom of God, the Son of Man, Satan, Paradise, Gehenna, angels and demons, and an intense expectation of the catastrophic end of the world. It is in the writings of this far from sterile intertestamental age that we can see these concepts taking shape.

When the New Testament opens, the Temple is still the life-blood of the Jewish people, and pilgrims from far and near, at home and overseas, make their way there to pay their vows and draw near to God in the place of his appointing. The high priest, with permission of the Roman governor, exercises supreme authority over the life of the people. The party of the Sadducees, comprising the privileged priesthood, supports him in uneasy association with the more popular lay party of the Pharisees, the pillars of the Law, often casuistical but basically patriotic and genuinely devout. The synagogues, which were to be found throughout Palestine and wherever ten Jews banded themselves together in any part of the world, were the mainspring of religious life, where the scriptures were read and the word of God was preached.

All of this likewise emerged after most of the Old Testament had been written, and is reflected in the writings of the intertestamental period. The synagogue may have had its origin in the Exile, but it was in the time of the great migration or diaspora in the Greek era, which led to there being twice as many Jews outside Palestine as inside, that its real development took place. Similarly, while the Sadducees probably took their name from Zadok, the priest, in the reign of Solomon, and the Pharisees were the successors of the godly upholders of the Law referred to in the book of *Malachi*, it was in the intertestamental period, in the struggle between the progressive and internationally minded supporters of Greek ways and the conservative defenders of traditional Jewish practice, that the distinction between Sadducee and Pharisee sharpened into the familiar pattern of the gospels.

There is thus every reason for paying some attention to this little known collection of writings called the Apocrypha. We should have to take into consideration the Pseudepigrapha as well, if we wanted to get a full picture of the trends of thought between the two Testaments. Since the latter are, however, generally to be found only in public libraries, and not always there, we must content ourselves with a rapid impression of the Apocrypha, which will at least save us from the error of thinking in terms of a clear break between the beliefs of the tiny dispirited Persian vassal state of Malachi's day, and the beliefs of the robust self-conscious theocracy, which we find occupying a much stronger position and a much larger territory, when Christ is born as a subject of the Roman empire.

I ESDRAS

THE FIRST book of *Esdras* is a narrative work sometimes known as the Greek Ezra. Most of it tells the same story, though not in the same order and with variant forms of the proper names, as the Old Testament book of *Ezra*, with additional excerpts from *Nehemiah* and *II Chronicles*. Its chief interest lies in an intriguing Brains Trust type of popular tale in 3: 1 – 5: 6, which is not found in the Old Testament. Three young men at the court of king Darius undertake to answer the question: What is the strongest thing in the world? Wine, the king and women are in turn defended, but the prize goes to the competitor who, having pled the case for women, exposes the hollowness of his own argument and those of his rivals, and makes an impassioned plea for truth as the strongest thing of all. Grounded in God, "great is truth and mighty above all things". As his reward, the winner, identified as Zerubbabel, is given the privilege of rebuilding Jerusalem.

II ESDRAS

WHILE, STRICTLY speaking, the intertestamental period should end with the appearance of the first of the New Testament writings, it is more correct to think of it as covering roughly the last two centuries of the old era and the first century A.D. Side by side with the Christian writers who were responsible for the books now contained in our New Testament, the Jews continued to produce their own sacred writings, and *II Esdras* or *IV Ezra* is for the greatest part a Jewish composition dating from about A.D. 100.

It is the only apocalyptic book in the Apocrypha, and its importance lies in the fact that it reminds us that the kind of apocalyptic writing, which we have already encountered in the book of *Daniel*, continued and developed until at the coming of Christianity it split into two streams, Christian and Jewish. The best-known example of Jewish-Christian apocalyptic is the book of *Revelation*, while *II Esdras* is a more sober specimen of the purely Jewish apocalyptic which constitutes a large part of the Pseudepigrapha.

The book opens with an introductory section (1:1–2:48), which is obviously a mixture of Jewish and Christian writing. There is a direct quotation from St. Matthew's gospel (1:30; cf. *Matt.* 23:37), and various passages are reminiscent of other New Testament authors. It seems possible that this introduction might be as late as A.D. 150. The book has clearly nothing to do with Ezra, the priest of the post-exilic settlement, although in the common practice of apocalyptic writing it is attributed to him.

These first two chapters were presumably written by a Jewish Christian as a framework for the central section of the book, sometimes called the Ezra Apocalypse, which originally existed without them. The book begins with a genealogy of Ezra (1:1–3), followed by a passage, in familiar prophetic style, denouncing the Jews for their unfaithfulness to God despite his goodness to them (1:4–24). Because of their infidelity, God will turn from them (1:25–33), and Israel's inheritance will be given to others (1:34–40), while its people will be scattered throughout the world (2:1–9). Ezra is commissioned to announce that the "Kingdom of Jerusalem" which should have gone to Israel will nevertheless soon come to the Church (2:10–14). God's new people must lift up their hearts, for evil will now have no power over them (2:15–32). Meantime Ezra looks into the future and sees a great company of the saints being crowned by the Son of God (2:33–48).

The main part of the book (3:1–14:48) is Jewish, and consists of a number of visions which Ezra is supposed to have had, but which are generally reckoned to be of independent origin, and of different dates within the first century A.D. In the first vision (3:1–5:19), the writer obviously feels that the conditions of the time in which he is living were paralleled by the situation after the fall of Jerusalem in 587 B.C. This most naturally suggests that he is referring to the destruction of the Temple by the Romans under Titus in A.D. 70. He states that he is writing thirty years after this date, i.e. A.D. 100.

His problem is to account for the downfall of the holy city and the prosperity of its enemies. In a manner familiar to apocalyptic writers, he therefore pushes this problem back into the days when Babylon triumphed and Israel suffered (ch. 3). The answer comes from the angel Uriel, who suddenly appears and makes it plain to Ezra that no man can understand the mystery of God's ways. He asks him if he can weigh fire, measure the wind or recall a day that is past. If he cannot compass simple things of this nature, how can he hope to understand the hidden plans of the Almighty?

There is so much evil in the world that nothing will come right until the new age dawns, and that will not be long delayed (ch. 4). The signs that herald it will be clear to all: the sun will shine during the night and the moon will shine by day; blood will drop from wood, stones will talk, evil will increase, destruction will be widespread. Then will men know that the end of the world has come (5: 1–19).

In the second vision (5: 20 – 6: 34), the seer depicts pathetically the plight of God's people, and is again told by Uriel that he must leave these matters in God's hands (5: 20–40). He then asks what will happen to the righteous men who have died in the past when the new

age dawns, and he is told that these faithful ones will also share in the Kingdom (5: 41 – 6: 10). Once again supernatural events are foretold as the sign of the coming end (6: 11–34).

As a preparation for each vision, the seer fasts for a week and broods over the questions that perplex him. It should be remembered that the problem that concerned the writer—and likewise all the apocalyptists—was not a new one but a very real one. They knew that Israel was in fact the only nation that worshipped one God devoutly and, according to her lights, sincerely. If therefore she was plagued with misfortune, disaster and political oppression, what would the world think of God? It was genuinely not so much a concern that Israel should have to suffer hardship: the agonising fear was much more that if Israel were annihilated, who would maintain and defend the good name of God?

The Hope that a Messiah will Come

Accordingly in the third vision (6: 35 – 9: 25), the seer asks why Israel, the chosen race, has not been given possession of the world if, as had been so often declared to her, the world had been created to be the preserve of God's people (6: 35–59). Uriel replies that it is sin that has destroyed Israel's chance of entering into her heritage 7: 1–25), but that the good time coming is at hand. It will be ushered in by the Messiah (not Jesus—7: 28), who will reign on earth for four hundred years, at the end of which he and all then alive will die. Then for seven days there will be silence followed by a general resurrection of the dead and the Day of Judgment (7: 26–45).

But the seer is now upset when he reflects how small, in view of the general sinfulness of man, will be the number of souls who will be saved at the Day of Judgment (7: 46–56). The reply of the angel is that this is the "condition of the battle". Every man must shoulder responsibility for his own deeds. Many are created but few will be saved (7: 56–61). Ezra prays for mercy on the wicked in the Day of Judgment, but is informed that they have had their chance (7: 62 – 9: 25).

For his fourth vision (9: 26 – 10: 59), the seer is told to go and wait in a field. There he sits sadly lamenting, when a woman in mourning appears, weeping over the loss of her only son. The seer reproves her, pointing out how much greater is the misfortune of all Israel than her own personal bereavement. The woman, however, refuses to be comforted. Suddenly she utters a loud cry and disappears. In her place arises a vision of a city. Uriel is again at hand to give the explanation, which is that the woman was the eternal heavenly Zion, while her son who died had been the earthly Jerusalem which had been destroyed.

The fifth (Eagle) vision (11: 1 – 12: 39) is in the full classical tradition of apocalyptic writing. The seer beholds an eagle rising out of the sea with twelve wings, three heads and eight smaller wings. One feather after another rises and rules the world, followed by a very complicated set of feather-man-œuvres, including feather-eating and eventually head-eating. Suddenly a lion with a human voice comes roaring out of a wood, and taxes the eagle with having afflicted the world. Gradually the eagle disintegrates and is finally burnt up. In the explanation given to the seer the eagle turns out to be the fourth—Greek—empire of the vision in *Daniel*. Its contortions are the various historical events of the Graeco-Roman age, and the lion is the Messiah who will compass its downfall. The Ezra-Apocalypse proper is rounded off in 12: 40–51, and the next two visions are independent.

The sixth vision (13: 1–58), is of a man rising out of the sea. The man is attacked by a hostile horde, but flies up to a mountain and, breathing out fire on his enemies, burns them up. He then summons a peaceable multitude with which he remains surrounded. It transpires in the interpretation that the man is the Messiah; his enemies are the heathen nations, and the peaceable multitude is the lost ten tribes of Israel, who have been miraculously preserved and will be miraculously restored.

In the seventh and last vision (14: 1–48), which is called the Ezra legend, Ezra hears a voice speaking out of a bush and telling him that his end is at hand. He is instructed to write down all his visions and their interpretations before he dies. Five scribes are allotted to him and he dictates to them for forty days. A sacramental cup guarantees the success of the enterprise. Ninety-four books are written (R.V.: not 204 as in A.V.), i.e. twenty-four canonical books of the Old Testament, which he is instructed to publish, and seventy others which he is told to keep secret.

The concluding chapters (15–16) are reckoned to date from the third century A.D., and have nothing of special interest in them. On the other hand, whatever we may feel about the religious value or relevance of the preceding chapters of II Esdras, there is no doubt that they had a profound importance for the age in which they were written, and in approaching the New Testament this apocalyptic atmosphere has to be taken into account.

However unfamiliar, unattractive or meaningless much of II Esdras may be for us today, here is a moderate sample of a whole library of such works that were produced in the centuries around the transition from B.C. to A.D. II Esdras, although properly belonging to New Testament times, shows the type of Jewish background in which the writers of the New Testament were reared. What was being written down in A.D. 100 must have been at least to some extent reflected in the Jewish environment from which Jesus and Paul came.

The Pseudepigrapha contain apocalyptic works of an even more bizarre and obscure character than II Esdras. Such writings as the Book of Enoch and the Apocalypse of Baruch shed light on the atmosphere of messianic expectancy, of supernaturalism and of despair of this evil world into which the Christian gospel came. Naturally enough amid so much that is speculative, there is considerable disagreement in detail between the various apocalypses of this period, but there is an overriding similarity of outlook with II Esdras, with which we have to reckon in our study of the New Testament.

TOBIT

THERE COULD BE no greater contrast than that between the tortured mind and weird visions of the seer of the Ezra Apocalypse and the placid homely atmosphere of the book of Tobit. If the last book we have looked at has shown us one aspect of the thoughts of many of our Lord's countrymen as the old age drew to a close, above all their sense of the corruption of the world and their hope of its imminent end, this present book reminds us that this was not the only element in their thinking.

For here in the form of a charming and often moving story, better known to theatre-lovers as Tobias and the Angel, is a precious insight into ordinary Jewish family life. The tale is fanciful and the setting is placed back in the days when the northern tribes of Israel had been deported to Assyria. But the date of the book is somewhere in the second century B.C., and the scenes of home life and family affection depicted in it are the product of the work of prophet and priest in inculcating private piety and neighbourly charity in these years of Israel's humiliation.

When we are inclined to think of the Judaism in which our Lord was reared in terms of the harsh and rigid Pharisaism of some of the gospel narratives, we may well reflect that the humane and warmhearted Tobit was also representative of Judaism. Here is a strict and punctilious Jew, who fulfils his religious obligations according to the letter of the Law, but his love of God and of his fellow men, his devotion to his wife and son, and his splendid integrity in thought and deed convey irresistibly the impression that this is how the Old Testament faith at its best must have worked out in practice.

Despite the many flaws in character which the narrow and exclusive point of view of the successors of Nehemiah and Ezra tended to encourage—self-righteousness and bigotry among them —let us not forget this other side of the picture, or fail to see in such genuine piety as that of Tobit and his wife, the prototype of Joseph and Mary of Nazareth and the countless other simple Jewish homes in our Lord's day, of which they became the most significant example.

The story of Tobit is straightforward and needs no comment. Raphael, the guardian angel, and Asmodaeus, the malicious demon, carry us forward to New Testament times, when angels and demons play a large part in popular theology by being the instruments of good and evil, where the Old Testament would in general ascribe these activities directly to YHWH. It is pleasant also to find a dog as Tobias' companion, instead of as mostly elsewhere in the Bible being depicted as a scavenger or used as a term of abuse.

JUDITH

THE NEXT BOOK of the Apocrypha is, like *Tobit*, a work of religious fiction. Its theme, like that of *Esther*, is the power of a woman's wiles to save her people. Judith, the heroine, who cuts off the head of Holofernes, the Assyrian general who was bent on the destruction of an Israelite city, is, however, by no means as blood-thirsty as Esther. She is moreover an extremely devout widow, faithful to the last to the memory of her husband.

Again, like *Tobit*, the story is extremely readable and simple. It is easy to understand how its strong nationalist flavour and its strict religious temper would commend this book to a generation which was fighting for its life under the Maccabees (see pp. 327–329), while striving to maintain its distinctive religious practices against the encroachment of liberal Greek ideas. Although the incident is unhistorical, the intensity of faith in God, combined with meticulous observance of the provisions of the Law on the one hand, and patriotic fervour mingled with hatred of Gentile oppressors on the other, illuminate for us the trend of popular Jewish thought on the eve of the Christian era.

THE REST OF ESTHER

THESE ADDITIONS TO the Old Testament book of *Esther* consist of the difference between the orthodox Hebrew text and the Greek translation. In the Greek text, however, the various items came in their proper place within the narrative of *Esther*. In the English Bible they are printed consecutively as an appendix, and in this form make little sense. Even when inserted into the book of *Esther* and read as they were originally meant to be read, they do little to add to the quality of that work. Their main contribution is to give some religious tone to a book that is notoriously lacking in it, and it would be safe to say that this is the least valuable part of the Apocrypha.

THE WISDOM OF SOLOMON

The Prophets and the Philosophers

THE NEXT TWO books of the Apocrypha are Wisdom books i.e. they come into the same category as *Proverbs*, *Ecclesiastes* and *Job*. The present book, called the *Wisdom of Solomon*, has as little to do with king Solomon as *Proverbs* or *Ecclesiastes*. His name is associated with it by the writer, partly to give it a cachet, and partly because all wisdom scribes considered themselves to be writing in the tradition and echoing the sentiments of that notable exponent of wise counsel. In all probability this book was written by an Alexandrian Jew within the last fifty years before the birth of Christ.

It was perhaps the most popular and certainly the most quoted book of the Apocrypha in the early Church. St. Paul, the author of *Hebrews*, perhaps other New Testament writers, and certainly the Christian Fathers were influenced by this work, but apart from that it can stand on its own merits as one of the few great books in the intertestamental period. *Wisdom* falls into two quite distinct sections (chs. 1–9 and chs. 10–19), so clearly indeed that some scholars have suggested that there may have been two distinct authors. The first part is characteristic of wisdom writings in general, the second part is mainly historical. Both in literary quality and in depth of thought the first part is vastly superior.

When we come to the New Testament, and move from the Palestinian atmosphere of the Old Testament and the gospels to the wider world of the Christian mission, we shall have to notice how the Church had to restate and reinterpret the Jewish thought forms, which had been adequate so long as the people of God had been brought up as Israelites, into words and ideas which were more familiar to cosmopolitan congregations, speaking the Greek language and breathing the air of

Greek civilisation, even if the empire in which they lived was Roman in name and fact. After New Testament times, in the formative period of the Christian creeds and of Christian theology, the process went further, and the historic confessions of the Church, as well as its doctrines, are a blend of the Hebrew origin of the Christian faith in the Bible, and the Greek way of expressing it which was common currency in the first centuries of the Church's life.

One of the most interesting features of the book of *Wisdom* is that in it we find the first scriptural attempt to incorporate the ideas of Greek thinkers into the legacy of the prophets. The writer, who is obviously well acquainted with Greek philosophy, is the first outstanding exponent of the thesis that the best of the Greek world of ideas must be interwoven with the heritage of Israel. But let us be quite clear as to what he does. He is too good a son of the Old Testament tradition to attempt to concoct a new religion called the Religion of Graeco-Israel.

It is much rather that he recognises, as a Jew in Palestine could not bring himself to do, that God had also spoken to the pagans, and that at their best the philosophers and thinkers of the Greek world were reaching aspects of the truth which were as valid as the insights of the prophets. What was needed was to harmonise them, to combine the revealed religion of Moses and the prophets with natural religion, the conclusions of the philosophers. Where these two could be identified, where the ideas of the Greeks could be regarded as an

interpretation or fuller exposition of the faith of Israel, they should not be rejected simply because they did not spring from the soil of Palestine.

Anything in the pagan world of ideas that was contrary to the word that God had spoken to the prophets, or that was incongruous with it, was rejected. What was consistent with it was assimilated. So in this book we find that the writer, in his view of Wisdom, tends to think of it as the immanent principle that controls and orders the universe, much as the Stoics claimed this to be the function of the Reason or Intelligence that keeps the universe in being. So also we find the writer adopting from the Greeks their classification of the four cardinal virtues —temperance, prudence, justice and fortitude (8: 7)—and the characteristically Greek, but so far unbiblical doctrine of the immortality of the soul.

It does not seem as if the author's acquaintance with Greek philosophy goes very deep. Much more likely is it that these ideas were, so to speak, in the air, and to the writer of *Wisdom* they seemed apt and helpful. He has no hesitation in flatly contradicting any Greek notion that is opposed to Old Testament revelation—such as that matter, and, therefore, the human body, are naturally evil—and he pours scorn on any kind of materialistic or hedonistic conception of life, both of which were defended by one or other of the popular Greek schools of thought. He is thus no mere synthesiser, but a man profoundly conscious of the Old Testament tradition, who is prepared to take from Greece only what will better interpret the legacy of Israel. As we shall see, the writer of the fourth gospel, St, Paul, and the author of *Hebrews* follow in his footsteps.

The Pitfalls of Scepticism

A further point of interest is that this book is in a sense a counterblast to the pessimism of *Ecclesiastes*. The author, in the guise of Solomon, replies to the other Solomon, who speaks in the words of the Preacher. It is not unusual to find one book of the Bible written to correct another. *Job* was written in protest against Ezekiel's doctrine that a man received his deserts in this life. *Ruth* was intended to tilt at the prohibition of mixed marriages by Ezra and Nehemiah. So in chs. 2 and 3, the author of *Wisdom*, in castigating the views of renegade Jews in Alexandria who have renounced their religion, might be summarising the point of view of *Ecclesiastes*. He certainly condemns it out of hand.

Where *Ecclesiastes* had grimly pled for acceptance of the element of luck and chance, and emphasised the finality of death, this writer maintains that "the souls of the righteous are in the hand of God". Where *Ecclesiastes* had rejected in disillusionment the value of all wisdom and knowledge (*Eccl.* 1: 18), our author extols the pursuit of wisdom as gladness and joy. The Preacher, as we have seen, succeeded in combining a fairly far-reaching scepticism with a fundamental belief in God. But it

was a dangerous line to follow, and many would be more ready to grasp the scepticism and neglect the leaven of religious belief. This was apparently what the apostate Jews of Alexandria had done, and it is against their misunderstanding of *Ecclesiastes*—or it may be their understanding him only too well—that the author of *Wisdom* directs his fire.

It should also be noted that the conception of wisdom reaches its peak, short of the New Testament, in the mind of this particular writer. He shares the normal Old Testament view of human wisdom, as the kind of prudence that manages the everyday affairs of life wisely, at the same time maintaining that the recognition of the supremacy of God is the mark of the truly wise man. But when he comes to speak of divine wisdom he goes a stage further than *Proverbs* or *Job*. For him Wisdom is almost an independent being. *Proverbs* had spoken of Wisdom in poetic vein as being present at the Creation of the world. This book almost suggests that Wisdom was the world's Creator.

The Greeks would have said that Wisdom or Reason was the abstract absolute principle responsible for all that exists. This writer would say rather that only God can be Creator, but Wisdom is his agent, sharing his nature yet distinct from him (7: 22–8: 7). It is obviously not far from this way of thinking to St. Paul's conception of Christ as the Wisdom of God (*I Cor.* 1: 24).

These three elements should be borne in mind in reading the first nine chapters of this book. The author is bent on showing that within the Jewish faith there is this ideal of wisdom, the highest activity of the human spirit, so sublime that in possessing it a man has within himself something of God, something that makes him independent of the changes of this world, and is of immortal stuff. He wants to show moreover that this is a faith which incorporates the best of the pagan mind. At the same time he is anxious to combat the arguments of his contemporaries who would transform the cool realism of *Ecclesiastes* into an excuse for libertinism.

There was, however, another problem facing the writer in Alexandria, namely the prevalence of pagan supersition, which, in view of the multiplicity of gods and goddesses, shrines and temples, in any city in those days, is not surprising. He therefore devotes the second half of his book to an extremely tedious dissertation on idolatry, in which he recapitulates at length Israel's early history. This part of the book holds little interest for us.

It is, however, in a similar effort to strengthen the faith of his Jewish brethren that he produces the finest passage in the book (3: 1–9), giving the assurance that persecution and even death cannot harm the man who is faithful to God. Only slightly less telling is the comparable passage in 5: 1–16. These two splendid sections, together with the hymn in praise of Wisdom (7: 22 – 8: 7), and the fine passage in 11: 21–26, single this book out as among the greatest writings in the Bible. It may indeed be that 2: 12–20, which outlines the fate that must befall a perfectly righteous man, is a reminiscence of Plato's prophecy in the Republic (*II* 361), or it may be an allusion to the death of some contemporary martyr. Looking back to Golgotha, is it too much to say that it may also have been an inspired intuition? The early Church at all events regarded it as a prophecy of the sufferings of Christ.

ECCLESIASTICUS

THIS BOOK, ALTHOUGH it contains probably the best known words in the Apocrypha (44: 1–14), lacks the purple passages of *Wisdom*, and its general style is so like that of the book of *Proverbs* that we tend to feel that we have read all this before. It is, moreover, a far more haphazard collection of sayings, aphorisms and general good advice than *Proverbs*. Thus it is impossible to summarise it or indeed to detect any progress or plan in it. Yet it is a book not without its own interest and its value as a prelude to the New Testament is considerable.

The name *Ecclesiasticus* was given to the book because it was so intensively used for instruction in the Christian Ecclesia or Church, but as we can see from the title the original name was the Wisdom of Jesus, the son of Sirach, and the author is commonly known simply as Ben Sira. His grandson, who lived in Egypt, translated the book into Greek, and from what he says about his grandfather in the prologue, from what Ben Sira says about himself, and especially from what he says about other people, we can get a clearer picture of the author and his times than of any scriptural writer so far.

He was a Jerusalem Jew, belonging to the class technically known as wisdom scribes, and he wrote this book about 180 B.C. He had his lecture room where people came for instruction (51: 23), and like a good teacher he spent much of his time in study (39: 1–11). Part of his work had been in diplomatic service, involving foreign travel (39: 4). It is no doubt due to these contacts with the wider world of Greek civilisation, that Ben Sira so obviously shares the Greek idea that virtue and knowledge are one and the same thing.

The old Hebrew idea was that God's Wisdom was one thing and man's wisdom another. The Greeks on the other hand, represented wisdom as equivalent to godliness, and under their influence the wisdom books in general adopted this view. But for the Hebrew, wisdom meant not merely rational behaviour, but obedience to the revealed will of God as contained in the Law. Thus there came about the identification of wisdom with the Law: the wise man, and therefore the good man, was the man who feared the Lord, that is, who obeyed his commands as contained in the Law.

This bridging of the difference between the Greek and Hebrew outlook on life is present to a certain extent in all the wisdom literature which dates from the Greek period i.e. *Proverbs. Ecclesiastes,*

Wisdom and *Ecclesiasticus.* But in none of them is it so axiomatic as with Ben Sira, that the wise man is the good man and the wicked man is a fool (1: 1–20). Our author does not, however, confine himself to generalisations. At the other end of the scale, and possibly based on his experience of foreign travel, Ben Sira delivers some homely injunctions on how to behave when dining out (31: 12–21). Perhaps it is with recollections of a series of state banquets that he reflects wryly: " Better is the life of a poor man in a mean cottage than delicate fare in another man's house " (29: 22).

He describes himself modestly as merely rehashing the ideas of other wisdom teachers (33: 16), but obviously there was a common pool of wise saws which the compiler of the book of *Proverbs* was as likely to draw on as Ben Sira. Our author is, however, unfair to himself in this because there is distinct individuality in his teaching. Apart from the general line of wisdom-teaching which he follows, he has an unusually deep understanding of human nature and a very observant eye.

He draws a picture, for example, in 16: 17–23, of the man who believes that he is so insignificant that he can commit any offence at all and God will not notice. He is very conscious of the danger of a long tongue (19: 6–16), and his remarks about gossip are salutary— " If thou hast heard a word let it die with thee; and be bold, it will not burst thee " (19:10). He has some very fine things to say about friendship, such as that " a faithful friend is the medicine of life " (6:

16), or that a new friend is like new wine but an old friend is like a rare old vintage (9: 10).

Ben Sira must have been speaking from experience with temperamental prima donnas when he cautions: "Use not much the company of a woman that is a singer lest thou be taken with her attempts" (9: 4). From experience too must come words like these: "Be not made a beggar by banqueting upon borrowing" (18: 33); "The talk of him that sweareth much maketh the hair stand upright" (27: 14); "As the climbing up a sandy way is to the feet of the aged, so is a wife full of words to a quiet man" (25: 20).

One of his sayings has become proverbial: "He that toucheth pitch shall be defiled therewith" (13: 1). The three most beautiful things that he knows are the unity of brothers, the love of neighbours, and a man and his wife who agree (25: 1). What he has to say about alcohol (31: 27-31) is relevant for any age, likewise his words about doctors, especially that they should be men of prayer (38: 1-14). The fine chapter on the marvels of the created world should also be noticed (43: 1-33).

Behind his apparent preoccupation with the rules of behaviour, Ben Sira is obviously a man of deep religious faith. For him wisdom is religion. It is only by serving God

and his neighbour that a man has any claim to be called wise, and wisdom comes only to the man who keeps God's commandments. Judged by his book this admirable sage seems to have been a teacher who practised what he taught.

Again, in savouring the contents of this book, let us remember that it throws the door wide open for us into the everyday life and thought of the Jewish community as the end of the Old Testament era approaches. Not only so, but while it is too soon in 180 B.C. to speak of the two great parties of Pharisees and Sadducees, which did not emerge until after the Maccabean war of independence (see pp. 328-329), Ben Sira himself is an attractive example of an early Sadducee. His love of the Temple and admiration of the high priest (ch. 50), the absence of apocalyptic expectation or intense messianic hope, of any mention of resurrection or of angels (cf. Acts 23: 8), as well as the significant omission of the name of Ezra, father of the Pharisees, from his list of Israelite worthies, mark him out as a precursor of the party that, after the Maccabean rebellion as also in the gospels, found few who had much good to say of it. Despite that, this book suggests that there must have been many Sadducees who shared Ben Sira's genuine piety and integrity.

BARUCH

THIS LITTLE BOOK opens with a scene in Babylon, where the exiles of 598 B.C. are represented as hearing of the destruction of Jerusalem in 587 B.C. Baruch, known from the book of *Jeremiah* as that prophet's secretary, purports to write this book which is sent together with a sum of money to Jerusalem. The money is to pay for offerings to be made on the altar of the ruined Temple. Prayers are to be said for king Nebuchadnezzar and the exiles, and the book is to be read liturgically on specified days (1: 1–14).

The burden of the book is a confession of the sins that have brought about this disaster (1: 15–2: 10), and a plea for God's forgiveness (2: 11–3: 8). Israel's downfall has been her failure to keep the Law, which is the embodiment of wisdom (3: 9–4: 4), but Jerusalem, the widowed mother, bids her children take heart (4: 5–29), while she herself is comforted with the prospect of the destruction of her enemies and the return of her children (4: 30–5: 9).

It is clear from the historical inaccuracies that the destruction of Jerusalem referred to is not that of 587 B.C., but by a familiar biblical convention is that of A.D. 70 at the hands of the Romans, and that the book in its present form dates from the end of the first Christian century. *Baruch* is interesting as an indication of how religious Jews saw the pattern of sin and judgment recurring as certainly in the historical events of A.D. 70 as in those of 587 B.C. It is noteworthy how closely in this connection this little book reflects the attitude and even the words of the Old Testament prophets and sages. We may notice also that while the new Israel was striking out on its world mission to take the Gospel to the nations, the old Israel was still hoping for the downfall of the Gentiles and the ingathering of the chosen people (4: 31–37), and that while the Church was proclaiming the new life in Christ that death could not destroy, such a fine devotional writing as this could still see nothing beyond the grave (2: 17). It is not surprising in the light of these limitations that Christianity succeeded where Judaism failed.

THE EPISTLE OF JEREMY

ALTHOUGH IN THE English Bible this little homily is tacked on to the end of Baruch to form its sixth chapter, it is quite independent. Again by a literary device, it purports to be a warning written by Jeremiah to the exiles on the eve of their departure for Babylon (v. 1), but it is in fact a general denunciation of idolatry, whether practised by Jews or pagans, written during the Greek period. We may think its language extravagant, in that no intelligent pagan would credit a statue of a god as being anything other than a representation of the deity, and certainly would not believe that images of wood and stone had the power that the author scornfully accuses him of attributing to them.

On the other hand not all pagans were intelligent, and simple folk lived and died in mingled fear and veneration of their idols, as they still do in many parts of the world today. This sermon illuminates for us, in more detail than elsewhere in the Bible, the problem that confronted both Jews and Christians when they proclaimed the truth that there is but one God. It is obviously based on *Jer.* 10.

ADDITIONS TO DANIEL

LIKE THE ADDITIONS to the book of *Esther*, there are included separately in the Apocrypha extra passages which, as the preamble indicates, originally formed part of the book of *Daniel* in the Greek version of the Hebrew scriptures. The first of these, called the Song of the Three Holy Children, consists mainly of a prayer (vv. 3–22), and a hymn (vv. 29–68), which in all probability in origin had nothing to do with the book of *Daniel*, but were given a narrative framework (vv. 1–2 and 23–28), implying that they were uttered by the three men in the fiery furnace in *Dan.* 3. Like Jonah's psalm sung while he was inside the whale, the sentiments hardly seem appropriate to the occasion. The prayer, a confession of national sins, is reminiscent of *Dan.* 9, and the psalm, part of which is familiar from the Book of Common Prayer as the Benedicite, reminds us of *Ps.* 148 with a repeated refrain.

The history of Susanna is a story of virtue vindicated. Two wicked elders who contrive the downfall of a beautiful young woman are exposed by the acumen of Shakespeare's "Daniel come to judgment". The point of this tale from Jewish folk-lore is obviously to teach the power of prayer, and to enhance the reputation of Daniel, who in the Maccabean period acquired the status of a popular hero (see p. 274). The latter motif is also plain in the two following amusing stories: "The History of the Destruction of Bel and the Dragon", where Daniel's quick-wittedness discomfits the priests of the god Bel (cf. *Dan.* 3), and destroys a sacred serpent worshipped by the Babylonians. The prophet Habakkuk, airborne under protest, assists in his triumph (cf. *Dan.* 6). Both of these tales also serve to ridicule idolatry.

We can profit from the devotional spirit of the Song of the Three Holy Children, and as for the rest of the additions to *Daniel*, it is at least of interest to see the type of religious folk-lore which was current shortly before our Lord's day and no doubt also within it.

THE PRAYER OF MANASSES

THIS BEAUTIFUL prayer needs no commendation and little explanation. It will be remembered that the Chronicler has a tradition that Manasseh, the king of Judah who attracts the worst verdict of the prophetic historian of the book of *Kings*, did in fact repent of his sins while a captive in Babylon (*II Chron.* 33: 10–16; see p. 204). This short and moving confession has been composed by some pious writer between the time of the Chronicler and the end of the Old Testament period. It is the shortest, but one of the finest pieces of writing in the Apocrypha. Whether it ever had anything to do with Manasseh or not, the author of it clearly believed that even that unspeakable offender was not beyond the mercy of God.

I AND II MACCABEES

IN READING THE book of *Daniel* we saw (pp. 273–274) that behind the extravagant apocalyptic visions lay a major political and religious crisis in Israel's history. The fourth decade of the second century B.C. seemed to many faithful Jews to herald the death throes of a world that had become so monstrous in iniquity that God could no longer restrain his hand from shattering it. But when Alexander the Great bequeathed to the world the legacy of Greek culture, he set up a chain reaction which instead of bringing the world to an end as the author of *Daniel* expected, transformed the little community of Nehemiah and Ezra into the spearhead of a fighting force which once again made Israel a power to be reckoned with in the Near East.

The first book of the *Maccabees* begins by sketching the career of Alexander, who in 331 B.C. routed the Persians and became master of the world (1: 1–7). This was the beginning of the period which gave the nations at large the benefit of Greek civilisation, but which a century and a half later confronted the Jewish community with a choice which was in effect one between life and death.

When Alexander died his empire was divided (1: 8–9), and the dynasty that ruled in Syria, the Seleucids, eventually took control of Judaea. It was the ambition of the Seleucids not only to bring all parts of their dominion under subjection, but to extend to them the whole rich heritage of Greek culture. The most enthusiastic of these oriental advocates of western ways was Antiochus Epiphanes, who began to reign in 175 B.C. (1: 10).

He had many sympathisers among well-to-do Jews who hailed with relief the introduction of liberal ideas, and there were those among the younger men in Jerusalem who were apparently prepared to undergo a surgical operation to remove the stigma of circumcision as they competed naked in the Greek games (1: 11–15). It was more difficult, however, to sympathise with the modernist policies of Antiochus when they included the spoliation of the Temple, ruthless massacre and destruction, and a determined attempt to eradicate every distinctive Jewish practice and belief on pain of death (1: 16–53).

In 167 B.C., the unspeakable crime was committed of erecting in the Temple a pagan altar to Zeus ("the abomination of desolation" v. 54), accompanied by the public burning of the scrolls of the Law and the prohibition of circumcision. Many chose to die rather than break the ancient covenant (I: 54–64), and it was in the light of these events that the book of *Daniel* was issued, as a summons to all Jews, who loved their sacred heritage, to resist to the death this threat to the very existence of Israel as a holy and peculiar people, chosen by God to witness to his saving purpose.

The first book of the *Maccabees* goes on to describe an incident at Modin where the local priest Mattathias, consumed with righteous rage at the sight of a Jew obediently offering a sacrifice on one of the pagan altars which Antiochus had erected, slew not only the culprit but the king's agent as well (2: 1–26). This was the signal for a general revolt among all Jews who preferred to make themselves outlaws and face certain execution, rather than break the laws of their fathers and depart from the tradition of Sinai.

These were the Hasidaeans, the "pious men", and on the death of Mattathias, one of his sons Judas

Maccabaeus or Judas the Hammer, became the leader of the rebellion which they supported. To begin with, so strict was their observance of the Law that they allowed themselves to be massacred rather than fight on the sabbath (2: 27–70). But this moving witness of patriotic fervour coupled with religious conviction did not last. The patriotism certainly remained, and the rest of the book (chs. 3–16) describes how under the leadership of first Judas (3: 1–9: 22), and then his two brothers, Jonathan (9: 23–12: 53) and Simon (13: 1–16: 24), Jerusalem was liberated, the Temple restored, the Law re-established and the land once again became free.

The narrative is complicated, and the historical details are of little consequence for our purpose. In broad lines it is a story of rival factions among the Seleucids, and of a struggle within Jewry itself, between the patriots and the pro-Greek party under a succession of venal and time-serving high priests. Apart from the value of the book in shedding light upon a chapter in Israel's story about which, apart from the book of *Daniel*, the Old Testament tells us nothing, *I Maccabees* adds a further element to our knowledge of how the stage was set at the coming of Christianity.

The Maccabean war of independence degenerated into a struggle for power among the members of the Maccabee family, who early on had lost the support of the pietists whenever religious freedom was assured. It came to an end in 63 B.C. when Pompey, the

Roman general, was invited to mediate between the factions, and in so doing took control of Judaea in the name of the rising new power which was shortly to become the empire which dominated the world, and under whose auspices Christianity came to birth.

In this book, written somewhere around 100 B.C., we can read of the first impression made by the Romans upon the Jews (8: 1-17), and can see the party lines taking shape which have become clearcut by the time of the gospels. The liberal, aristocratic, pro-Greek faction, which drew its support mainly from the conforming priesthood, developed into the party of the Sadducees, while the patriotic conservative defenders of the old Jewish way of life were the forerunners of the Pharisees. Among the latter in New Testament times, the most martial types known as the Zealots (cf. Simon the Zealot—*Luke* 6: 15), who conducted incessant guerrilla warfare against Rome, were the successors of the militant outlaws who supported Judas Maccabaeus.

It is salutary, having read *I Maccabees*, to turn to *II Maccabees*, which is an abridgment of a larger work (2: 23) and covers much of the same ground. There is, however, this significant difference, that while *I Maccabees* is written from the point of view of an admirer of the Maccabean brothers and their achievements, *II Maccabees*, written rather later, makes a more sober appraisal of the family's dynastic ambitions. Where *I Maccabees* gives the credit for military victories to the vigour and astuteness of the leadership, *II Maccabees* attributes all such successes to the intervention of God, whose chief concern was the safeguarding of his Temple and its worship. Despite the latter author's fondness for the miraculous, and his delight in horrifying details, or perhaps because of it, his narrative, though historically less accurate, is more readable and certainly more entertaining.

NEW TESTAMENT

THE GOSPEL ACCORDING TO ST. MATTHEW

IT IS GENERALLY agreed that Mark's gospel was the first of the four gospels to be written, and that both *Matthew* and *Luke* used *Mark* as a basis. It is therefore advisable to read *Mark* before *Matthew*, and it will be assumed in the following comments on *Matthew* that the section on *Mark* (pp. 349–385) has already been read.

Perhaps fifteen or twenty years after Mark's gospel appeared in the West, the gospel which we know as *Matthew* appeared in the East—probably in Syria. The editor had clearly two main objects in view. One was to supplement Mark's gospel by including the teaching of Jesus which Mark had omitted, the other was to show by reference to the Old Testament how truly and unexpectedly Jesus had fulfilled the deepest hopes and aspirations of the Law and the Prophets.

For this latter reason, Matthew's gospel stands very properly as the first book of the New Testament forming the bridge between Act I and Act II of the divine drama, and for both reasons it very quickly ousted *Mark* as the gospel par excellence of the early Church, and indeed of the later Church, until the comparatively recent interest in getting back to the oldest historical record of the life and work of Jesus brought *Mark* again into favour as the primary witness.

But having read Mark's gospel as the foundation document or original title deed of Christianity, we can turn with profit to read the other gospels in order to amplify our knowledge and deepen our understanding of the significance of the events that Mark first recorded. In the case of Matthew the chief interest for us is, of course, the large amount of space he devotes to the teaching of our Lord. St. Luke also includes the teaching of Jesus in his gospel, and there are over 200 verses containing sayings of Jesus which these two gospels have in common.

Obviously both gospel writers had at their disposal the same sources of information on the substance of what Jesus taught, whether this came from a written document containing principally the words of Jesus—designated by the letter Q for convenience from the German *Quelle*, a source—or simply from oral tradition. Matthew, however, has preserved the sayings of Jesus in a more compact form and for this reason his gospel is particularly valuable.

As a historical account of the ministry of Jesus, however, *Matthew* is less reliable than *Mark*. This gospel has been well described as a revised and enlarged edition of *Mark*, for most of Mark's gospel has been reproduced in *Matthew*, sometimes verbatim. But on occasion Matthew alters or amends Mark's account, if he thinks it is liable to be misunderstood or if it seems to him in some way abrupt or even irreverent.

One of the principal merits of Mark's gospel, from a modern point of view, is that it has a frank and realistic approach which strongly conveys the authentic note of the earliest tradition. Jesus and the disciples are portrayed as above all real men. Jesus is not a demi-god, and the disciples are far from resembling saints in stained glass windows. That is not for a moment to suggest that our Lord in Mark's gospel is portrayed as merely a man among men. From start to finish there is an "mysterious undercurrent", which makes it abundantly plain that he was much more than a great prophet or an inspired healer.

But Mark—no doubt in dependence on Peter's vivid memory—has no hesitation in recording that Jesus was angry or astonished or weary, that there were some things that he could not do and did not know. Matthew, on the other hand, tends to omit facts of this kind, or alter Mark's words in some significant way, if he feels that the earlier gospel is too blunt or candid. Similarly his treatment of the disciples is much more respectful than that accorded by Mark, again no doubt under Peter's influence.

By the second century of the Christian era, there was beginning to appear the type of legendary story about Jesus which always tends to grow up around the life of any saint or holy man. The apocryphal gospels which stem from this period and later, with their wealth of fantastic tales of Jesus' boyhood and miraculous powers, show us how wisely guided the Church was to canonise our four gospels and refuse to recognise any others. But in Matthew's gospel—particularly in some of the miraculous events which he records in connection with the Crucifixion and Resurrection—we can see the beginning of the dangerous process when piety begins to invent details to enhance the reputation of the dead.

The fact that the writer of *Matthew* is content to draw so much of his material from *Mark* makes it quite certain that whoever he was he was not Matthew, one of the twelve apostles. No one who had belonged to the select company of the disciples would be willing to accept the second-hand evidence of John Mark, at best a youth on the fringe of Jesus' followers at the time of our Lord's ministry. An early tradition, however, asserts that Matthew the apostle made a collection of the "oracles" of Jesus, presumably his sayings, and it may well be that the teaching of Jesus, which features so prominently in this gospel, was first written down by Matthew whose name thus became attached to the whole gospel.

Apart from the fact that the first evangelist was obviously a Jewish Christian, we know nothing else about him unless what we can glean of his character and interests from a reading of his gospel. In addition to using Mark's gospel, and drawing like St. Luke upon a common source of information containing sayings of Jesus, this first evangelist also includes certain incidents, parables and words of Jesus which are found nowhere else in the gospels, and which were presumably familiar to the particular Christian community in Palestine to which the writer belonged before the Fall of Jerusalem in A.D. 70. A notable feature of this gospel is also the large number of quotations from the Old Testament, which may well have come from a collection of selected scriptural passages current in the Church in his day, showing how Jesus had fulfilled God's words to Israel.

The Son of David

(1 : 1 – 4 : 25)

CHARACTERISTICALLY, Matthew begins his narrative with the legal genealogy of Jesus as the Son of David, beginning with Abraham and ending with Joseph of Nazareth. By an ingenious piece of mathematical juggling, he finds messianic significance in the fact that the number fourteen—the numerical equivalent of David's name in Hebrew—can be shown as the common factor in the three stages into which he divides our Lord's ancestry (1 : 1–17).

Like St. Luke and unlike St. Mark, he takes as his starting point the Birth and not the public ministry of Jesus (1 : 18–25). Matthew's account, certainly in the language of poetry, though less beautifully moving than Luke's, nevertheless makes the same assertion, that Jesus was not the child of the natural union of Joseph and Mary but that Mary was "found with child of the Holy Ghost". Apart from sceptics who dismiss the whole idea of the Virgin Birth of our Lord as impossible, many devout Christians have felt that this somehow destroys the reality of the Incarnation.

Undoubtedly the Virgin Birth is a difficult fact to adjust to all that we know of biological processes. But do we know everything? Certainly the Virgin Birth is no more of an obstacle to faith than the Resurrection, and science can have nothing to say about either. If our Lord's life on earth ended with the supreme miracle of triumphing over death, is it any less appropriate that his coming into the world should also have been unique? Many of us would find it more difficult to understand how the power that Jesus has exercised over the history of the world and the lives of men sprang from the union of a humble peasant pair, than to believe that God, as at the Resurrection, acted at the conception of Jesus in some mysterious way beyond our understanding.

It does not in any sense detract from the significance of Matthew's use for the first time, as so often in this gospel, of an Old Testament quotation in 1 : 22–23, that the Hebrew word in *Isa.* 7 : 14 means any young woman and not necessarily a virgin. The early Church did not invent incidents in Jesus' ministry to fit Old Testament texts. They used Old Testament passages to illuminate historical happenings. In this case the real meaning of the text is that with the Birth of Jesus, meaning "Saviour", the word Immanuel acquired a new significance. When Jesus was born men could say in all truth: "God is now with us".

The narrative of Matthew's second chapter is so familiar to us from Christmas cards and carols, that we are apt to dismiss it as a pretty fairy story matching the tinsel and glitterwax of the children's parties. On the contrary, when we look beneath the engaging poetic décor, we come face to face with highly probable history. The story is not of three legendary kings but of a group of astrologers, presumably from Babylon, the stronghold of astral observation, who associate the appearance of an unusually brilliant star with the wellknown Jewish expectation of a Messiah.

It was usual to connect a stellar phenomenon of this kind with the birth of some notable person, and there is nothing surprising in men of this type setting out to investigate. Nor is the alarm of wily Herod the Great to be wondered at, still less the mad old king's determination to eliminate any messianic pretender by a massacre of all infants in the Bethlehem area. The flight of the Holy Family to nearby Egypt until after Herod's death, and the reason for their settling in Galilee on their return, apart altogether from Luke's information that Nazareth was their home, are also circumstantially probable.

Matthew, or his prior source, tells all this in deceptively simple words which have never failed to awaken a response in minds that have not grown too dull to sense his artistry. But of course for him and for his first readers it is the Old Testament background that dominates the narrative. Jesus is born in Bethlehem (2: 5–6), where the Son of David should appear (*Micah* 5: 2), and having shielded the new Moses from a similar slaughter of infants by royal edict (*Ex.* 2: 1–10), God calls his Messiah from Egypt (2: 15), as he had delivered Israel his "son" in days gone by (*Hos.* 11: 1), to make through him a new covenant of grace (2: 1–23).

The first gospel, following *Mark*, now plunges straight into the public ministry of Jesus, beginning with his Baptism at the hands of John (3: 1–17). The Temptation of our Lord is described in fuller detail (4: 1–11), indicating the various ways in which the new and greater Joshua (Jesus is the Greek form of Joshua), having crossed the Red Sea in baptism (*I Cor.* 10: 2), endures the forty days of testing in the wilderness, like the Israelites' forty years in the desert, and like Moses' forty days and nights upon Sinai (*Deut.* 9: 9), and Elijah's forty days and nights in preparation for the voice of God on Mt. Horeb (*I Kings* 19: 8), emerging victorious as a more effective Saviour of God's people through his obedience to the Law given to Moses (*Deut.* 8: 3; 6: 16; 6: 13), which the old Israel had failed to keep.

Jesus discards in turn a Messiahship which would offer men the materialistic panaceas that in their weakness they crave for (4: 3–4), or which would compel their belief in him and his mission by some spectacular display of power (4: 5–7), or which would make him master of a greater Davidic empire based on compromise and something less than absolute loyalty to God (4: 8–10). So in his new-found strength, our Lord sets out to fulfil his mission, which is to bring light and life to the Gentiles, as Isaiah had foretold (*Isa.* (9: 1–2), by proclaiming the imminent reign of God over the world, healing the bodies and minds of men, and summoning the founder-members of the new Israel into his service (4: 12–25).

The Sermon on the Mount
(5: 1 – 7: 29)

IT IS TO THESE founder-members of the new Israel that Jesus now addresses the words which Matthew has collected in the following three chapters (5–7). The total of all the sayings of Jesus as recorded in the four gospels cannot possibly exhaust all that our Lord taught his disciples, nor can even the contents of these three chapters, known as the Sermon on the Mount, have been delivered at one time or in one place. Matthew gives us rather a selection of the best remembered and presumably most often repeated sayings of Jesus, and it is more than enough to give us an insight into the mind of our Lord and his intention for his Church.

The first gospel deliberately chooses to place the scene of the Sermon on a "mountain", for is not this the new Moses promulgating a new Law for the men of the new age? Indeed Matthew's whole gospel, with its orderly arrangement into five sections, with five blocks of teaching alternating with five blocks of narrative, clearly suggests the parallel between the

Pentateuch and the five books of the Law of Jesus. This new design for living that Jesus outlines, however, is not intended to contradict the old Law but to clarify, complete and transcend it.

The Sermon begins with an arresting series of paradoxes. The Beatitudes describe the character of those who would be subjects of the Kingdom, and a strange picture they present. All their attributes are the direct antithesis of ordinary secular values: they are the humble in heart, the merciful, the pure in heart and the peacemakers. Such are the men of the Kingdom of God, or Kingdom of heaven, as Matthew calls it. Jesus knows that these are not the martial, self-assertive qualities that ride rough-shod over all opposition. The world being what it is, persecution and misrepresentation are inevitable.

Such has always been the fate of God's servants, as the prophets of old knew to their cost. But the new men of the Kingdom are to take heart and stand firm. Their mission is to be the salt that gives common life its savour, they are to be like a light shining in a dark place or a city perched on a hill. Their task is to form a "spiritual aristocracy", whose acts of mercy and charity radiate through the world (5: 1–16).

Then as a prelude to setting out the terms of the new Law, Jesus makes plain his attitude to the Old Testament dispensation. It is not to be regarded as cancelled, for it is good so far as it goes—but the subjects of the Kingdom must go beyond it. They must not think that the new Law is less exacting than the multifarious obligations that are laid upon the scribes and Pharisees, for the new Law makes even greater demands (5: 17-20).

Jesus then illustrates his point by taking some outstanding examples from the old Law, and showing how, under his new Law, they are given a depth and inwardness which the external fulfilment of the traditional commandments could not approach. The sixth commandment had forbidden murder. Jesus says that the real act of murder is not the actual killing of a man, but the inward feelings of hate and anger. If these are not checked and stamped out, the equivalent of murder has been done (5: 21-26).

Similarly the seventh commandment forbade adultery. Jesus says that adultery is already committed the moment the will to commit it exists (5: 27-32). So with the third commandment against perjury, Jesus says that the real remedy is not to condemn a man for false testimony, but to insist that a man's whole speech should be trustworthy and reliable without the need of special oaths (5: 33-37). The old Law insisted on the justice of retaliation, an eye for an eye and a tooth for a tooth. Jesus says the new kind of men must return good for evil. There must be no limits to their charity towards their neighbours, friends and enemies alike. God shows charity to all men, so must the member of his new family. His perfection must be the perfection of God (5: 38-48).

Next Jesus takes the three common religious duties of the Jewish Church, almsgiving, fasting and prayer, and insists that ostentatious practice of religious obligations is to be shunned. These are matters that should be between a man and his Maker, not grounds for approbation by the world at large. There must be no thought of getting credit for being pious. As a pattern of how to pray Jesus teaches his disciples the Lord's Prayer.

This is given not as the only prayer to be said, but as a guide to the right way to pray. The man who has taken upon himself the new rule of God does not bludgeon the Almighty with petitions on his own behalf. He prays that God's will might be done, and his rule established as fully on earth as it is in the world that is unseen. All that a man needs for himself is to be allowed to take part in that great purpose, and so he asks only for his daily needs to be supplied, his sins to be forgiven, and to be helped to withstand evil (6: 1-18).

The remainder of the chapter (6: 19-34) is really an amplification of the chief lesson of the Lord's Prayer. The man who enters the Kingdom—who accepts the rule of God for himself—has now a new motive for existence, and indeed only one motive, namely to identify himself more and more with the will and purpose of God as opposed to his own private ends. His will is his own to make it God's. So the attractions of materialism take second place (6: 19-21), for a man cannot worship two masters well—God and money (6: 24). His attitude to God must be one of trust and confidence. God who feeds the birds and decks the lilies is not likely to neglect his children. So anxiety about the future is foolish and unnecessary (6: 25–34).

The rest of the Sermon (7: 1–27) rather looks as if it were a collection of odd topics included here for convenience. Jesus insists on self-criticism. A man must not judge his neighbours before he has examined himself—in which case he will not judge at all (7: 1–5). Returning to the question of prayer, the next section (7: 7–12) seems to contradict the Lord's Prayer by insisting that a man under God's new rule must be urgent in his requests, not waiting for God to bestow his blessings, but it is clear from the concluding verse 12 that the things he is to ask for are not for himself.

The Golden Rule is laid down as the norm and as the summary of the whole teaching of the Law and the Prophets. It involves complete self-giving. The Sermon ends with the clear assertion that it is not verbal professions of loyalty to God that count, but doing his will and that alone (7: 15–23). The man who hears these words of Jesus and lives accordingly, is building his house upon a rock; the man who does not is building upon sand (7: 24–27).

What are we to make of the Sermon on the Mount? First of all, it is not a code of behaviour for the world at large. It was addressed to disciples, to those who had already committed themselves to Christ. Even for them it is not a collection of rules, like Jewish Law, but basic principles from which individual situations must be approached. Nor is it meant to be taken literally. "Turning the other cheek" may be done in a more un-

christian spirit than knocking a man down, and to "give to everyone that asketh" can encourage loafers and parasites.

Jesus' teaching is likewise not a programme of social reform, as if he were prescribing a short cut to Utopia, any more than it is a rule of life for a select few who are to cut themselves off from society, and renounce the good material things of the world that the Creator has given to men. It is above all the compass by which the man of the new age must steer his course, knowing full well that no one apart from Jesus himself has ever fully done it. It is in short an impossible standard, as our Lord clearly recognised when he enjoined us to keep praying for forgiveness (6: 12).

No human effort can comply with God's absolute demands. Life in this world with its problems and temptations is too much for human weakness, and the citizen of the Kingdom sees this standard before him, recognising that only once has it been fulfilled on earth in the life and death of Jesus, and finding his own life shown up as a poor and tattered caricature. This has been the experience of all the saints, indeed the more saintly they have been the more they have been conscious of the gulf between what they ought to be and what in fact they are.

So Jesus' teaching remains the impossible, which his followers are nevertheless bound to try to attain. It is the measure of our failure rather than of our achievement, the judgment of God upon our proudest efforts, and it brings us back again and again to the

humility which is the first requirement of a disciple. Jesus' teaching
is thus fundamentally designed not
to hedge us in with rules, nor to
saddle us with an unrealistic programme, which we are incapable
of fulfilling, but to establish the
right relationship between God
and ourselves. It is from this relationship, involving daily confession of failure and acceptance of
forgiveness, that there comes the
kind of behaviour that God requires of us.

The Work of an Apostle of Christ

(8 : 1 – 11 : 1)

IF WE FOLLOW the pattern of
Matthew's gospel, we come now
to the second of his five "books"
of the new Law. The birth stories
(chs. 1–2) form the prologue,
chapters 3–7, covering the preparation of the Messiah for his task,
and the enunciation of the principles of the new life to which he
summons men, constitute the first
"book", ending with the coda in
7 : 28–29. This formula reappears
in similar words at the end of each
of the four succeeding "books"
(11 : 1 ; 13 : 53 ; 19 : 1 ; 26 : 1), until
the epilogue of the Crucifixion and
Resurrection (chs. 26–28) brings
the gospel to an end.

The second book (chs. 8–10) has
as its main theme the missionary
vocation of the Church. As in
book I, Matthew begins with a
narrative section, most of which is
already familiar from Mark's
gospel. After the healing of a leper
(8 : 2–4), Jesus commends a
Roman centurion in Capernaum

for having greater faith than any
Israelite, and prophesies the ingathering of the Gentiles and
God's judgment of the Jewish
people who have proved unworthy
of his choice. He heals the centurion's servant, Peter's mother-in-
law, and many unnamed suffer-
ers—actions which Matthew sees
as the fulfilment of the role of
Isaiah's Servant (*Isa.* 53 : 4), who
"took our infirmities and bare
our sicknesses" (8 : 5–17). Matthew then records the stilling of
the storm and the cure of the
Gadarene demoniac—or rather
demoniacs, for in this gospel there
are two of them (8 : 18–34).

Back in Capernaum Jesus heals
the paralysed man of *Mark* 2 : 1–
12, Matthew following Mark's
account even to the reproduction
of the parenthesis of 9 : 6. Matthew = Levi is recruited into the
apostleship and the question of
fasting is dealt with. Jairus'
daughter and the woman with the
haemorrhage are healed, as are
two blind men and one who is
dumb (9 : 1–36).

The series of narratives, which
are obviously taken by Matthew
to be the prelude and justification
for what follows, ends with a call
from Jesus for "labourers" for
the "harvest" (9 : 37–38). Men are
everywhere in need of healing in
mind and body, ripe for ingathering into the Kingdom, and so our
Lord commissions the Twelve (10 :
1–4), and through them the Church
that they represent, to continue
his work of preaching the Gospel
and curing the sick. They are to
begin with Israel (10 : 5), and
proclaim God's word to his ancient people. Those who spurn

God's messengers will feel God's judgment (10: 5–15).

But the mission of the Church must extend beyond Israel, and it will bring persecution upon the apostles of God. Our Lord foresees too that the preaching of the Gospel will not always mean peace, but that many a home will be disrupted when one of the family becomes a follower of Christ and another rejects him. Yet the servant of the Gospel will be sustained by the power of God, and in giving himself for Christ's sake will find the only kind of life that is worth having. Whoever welcomes such a servant of Christ welcomes Christ himself, and even a tiny kindness to the humblest of Christ's people is not forgotten in the sight of God (10: 16–42).

The Nature of the Kingdom
(11: 2 – 13: 53)

THE SECOND "BOOK" of Matthew ends with a concluding verse (11: 1), and the theme of the gospel now changes in the third section to the general topic of the meaning of the Kingdom. John the Baptist had expected a Messiah who would come with fiery judgment (3: 11–12). It is not surprising therefore that he wondered whether Jesus were indeed the long expected Deliverer. No less than the religious authorities, John had his own conception of how the Messiah should behave. Jesus does not answer his question directly but asks him to draw his own conclusion. If all the signs of the promised reign of God are present—in the healing of men's

bodies and the preaching of the Good News of God's forgiveness —can this be anything other than the Day of the Lord, and can Jesus be any other than the Lord's anointed? (11: 2–6).

John, says Jesus, was indeed the Elijah who was to herald the coming of the Kingdom, the last of the great prophets, yet he belonged to the old age. Now the new age has begun, the decisive battle between God and the power of evil has commenced (11: 12), and the least important member of Christ's flock is heir to an inheritance that even John the Baptist did not share (11: 7–15). Then in words of solemn condemnation, Jesus denounces his own countrymen for their failure to respond to God's call. Like petulant children they want neither John's asceticism nor Jesus' love of men. Not only the cities of the Gentiles but infamous Sodom will fare better at the Day of Judgment (11: 16–24).

In a great paean of thanksgiving, our Lord, in words which might come from St. John's gospel, so profoundly do they express Jesus' consciousness of his unique Sonship, gives God the glory for the gift of the Gospel to men of childlike hearts, and offers them the tranquil confidence which comes from faith in him, and the blessedness of wearing the "yoke" of his service, which means becoming part of him (11: 25–30).

Matthew now records our Lord's conflict with the Pharisees, in the stories of the disciples plucking corn on the sabbath (12: 1–8), and his healing of the man in the synagogue with the paralysed hand (12: 9–13). Again the evangelist draws attention to Jesus' fulfilment of the role of Isaiah's Servant (*Isa.* 42: 1–4) in the healing of vast numbers of sick folk (12: 14–23), and relates the charge of the Pharisees that this must be the devil's work. Jesus counters this accusation as in Mark's narrative, and charges the Pharisees with the unforgivable sin against the Holy Ghost (12: 24–37).

When the Pharisees ask for some "sign" of his Messiahship, Jesus replies that the only "sign" he is prepared to give is that of Jonah at Nineveh, which was a call to repentance, and he contrasts the ready response of the Ninevites with the obduracy of God's chosen people. If we set this saying in *Matthew* beside the version given in *Luke* (*Luke* 11: 29–32), it is clear that both evangelists are using the same written source, and that Matthew and not Jesus is responsible for the comparison of the three days and nights in the whale's belly with the space of time between the Crucifixion and the Resurrection. Nor does it argue for or against the historicity of Jonah—or the queen of Sheba—that our Lord uses these two well known Old Testament characters to make his point (12: 38–42).

Our Lord concludes his charge against Israel by showing the danger of partial conversion. Israel has gone some way towards ridding herself of the major blots on her former record, through her verbal profession of allegiance to the Law, but seven worse devils have entered and possessed her religious life—bigotry, intolerance, prejudice and the rest of the sins of Judaism. Only a complete possession by the Spirit of God—such

as came to the new Israel at Pentecost—can ensure true obedience (12: 43–45). The chapter ends with the visit of our Lord's family, and his proclamation of the great new family of Christ's people (12: 46–50).

Matthew now follows these illustrations of the nature of the new life that Jesus brings to men, life in the Kingdom of heaven under the rule of God, with a series of parables. First, the parable of the sower deals with the preaching and hearing of the word of the Kingdom, the Good News of the new age (13: 1–23). Next, in a parable peculiar to Matthew, Jesus speaks of the wheat and the tares, the good and the bad, that will grow side by side in the world untill the end of time. Despite the best efforts of the Church, the devil will never be idle (13: 24–30).

The kingly rule of God is like the seed of the mustard tree, tiny but of great promise, or like the yeast that leavens a mass of dough. It is like hidden treasure, for a man should sell all he possesses to make it his own, or similarly it is like a priceless pearl. Again it is like a dragnet which collects fish of all kinds, good and bad (13: 31–50). The message of the Gospel is thus God's call to every man, through the words and works of Jesus, to make his decision for or against him as a matter of life and death. Many will respond who will later prove worthless, but the witness of the new community who accept the rule of God will grow and spread despite them. It is a message which is new in form, but as old as God's first word to Adam (13: 52).

The Life of the Church

(13: 54 – 19: 1)

HAVING ROUNDED OFF his third book (13: 53), Matthew turns to the topic of the Church in book four, and both narrative and discourse centre in general on this theme. Jesus' rejection by his own countrymen (13: 54–58), and the murder of John the Baptist (14: 1–12), are related as a prelude to the feeding of the five thousand (14: 13–21). The story of Jesus walking on the water has its effect heightened by the addition peculiar to this gospel of Peter's unsuccessful attempt to emulate him (14: 22–33).

It is of interest to notice how Matthew alters the narrative of Mark, which he is using, in three significant ways in this short section. Jesus is not called the "carpenter" (cf. *Mark* 6: 3) but the "carpenter's son" (13: 55). It is not said of him that he "could" not do many mighty works in Nazareth (cf. *Mark* 6: 5), but that he "did" not do them (13: 58), and the effect upon the disciples when Jesus calmed the storm was not that they were "amazed" and "wondered" (cf. *Mark* 6: 51) but that they "worshipped" him (14: 33). Matthew is obviously concerned that nothing in Mark's account which might conceivably be misinterpreted as derogatory either of Jesus or the disciples should remain uncorrected.

After a summary of healing acts of Jesus in the lakeside area (14: 34–36), Matthew records the controversy with the Pharisees about inward and outward cleanliness (15: 1–20). The daughter of the Syro–Phoenician woman is healed (15: 21–28), and the four thousand are fed (15: 29–39). Still mostly following Mark, Matthew now leads up to Peter's recognition of Jesus as the Messiah (16: 1–16).

He adds, however, not only our Lord's acknowledgment of this as a direct revelation from God, but his commission to Peter to be the foundation stone of his Church. Simon becomes Peter, the rockman, head of the new family of God and with supreme authority over it (16: 17–19). Yet when Jesus goes on to declare the inevitability of the Cross, this rockman shows how far even those with the deepest insight into the mind of the Master fall short of his perfect response to God (16: 20–28).

Matthew continues to follow Mark in the story of the Transfiguration (17: 1–8), in the identification of John the Baptist with Elijah (17: 9–13), in the healing of the epileptic boy (17: 14–21) and in a further prediction of his Passion (17: 22–23), but introduces an incident peculiar to this gospel, generally known as the "coin in the fish's mouth." It is not in fact stated that either fish or coin was found.

Peter is questioned as to whether his master paid the statutory annual temple tax of half a shekel (*Ex.* 30: 11–16). Jesus had apparently paid this tax hitherto but now claimed, whimsically, on the analogy of royal princes not being subject to taxation among the Gentiles, that neither should the children of the new Israel be bound to pay for the upkeep of their Father's house. Our Lord's instruction to Peter

(17: 27) is surely a humorous dismissal of the practice—although he complies with it—as irrelevant in the new age (17: 24–27).

After this narrative section, Matthew has collected sayings of Jesus into a fourth great discourse (18: 1–35), which deals in general with Christian charity within the Church. Our Lord begins with the telling illustration of the child-like trust which is the prerequisite of discipleship (18: 1–4), and goes on to speak of the responsibility of every member of the Church for the weaker brethren (18: 5–6), and of the individual's responsibility for himself before God (18: 7–9). God cares for all his children (18: 10), especially for the ones who go astray (18: 11–14).

Disputes between Church members should be settled between themselves, or, if that fails, by the decision of the whole community (18: 15–19). Two of the greatest sayings of the gospels follow (18: 20–22), on the Presence of Christ wherever two or three of his people are gathered in his name, and on the duty of Christians to forgive their neighbours "until seventy times seven". The parable of the unmerciful servant, found only in *Matthew*, is told as an example of how ready we should be to forgive our neighbour since God has forgiven us so much more (18:23–35).

Messiah Comes in Judgment
(19: 2 – 26: 1)

THE CONNECTING verse between book four and book five (19: 1) indicates that Jesus now leaves Galilee and moves south-ward with Jerusalem as his goal. In our Lord's discussion with the Pharisees on the question of divorce, Matthew makes two additions to Mark's account. The clause in 19: 9 to the effect that divorce is only permissible in case of "fornication" is best understood if we take fornication to mean marriage within the forbidden degrees, in which case the marriage is already null and void. The other addition is Jesus' assertion that there are some for whom voluntary celibacy is the cost of a life dedicated to the service of God, as in our Lord's own case (19: 2–12).

Jesus blesses the children (19: 13–15), prescribes the remedy for the dissatisfied rich young man (19: 16–22), and speaks of the dangers of wealth and the rewards of his service (19: 23–30). The point of the parable of the labourers in the vineyard (20: 1–16), which is found only in this gospel, is that r thing that we can ever do gives us any right to expect preferential treatment from God. Such good works as we are able to perform are done by God through us, and the glory is his, not ours. God's family must share and share alike with each other since God's forgiveness is offered equally to us all.

After a further prediction of his Passion (20: 17–19), our Lord deals with the request of James and John for privileged places in the Kingdom. Characteristically. Matthew puts the plea into the mouth of their mother, but it is clearer here than in *Mark* what was in these disciples' minds. Jesus had just spoken picturesquely of the twelve disciples in the new age, sitting on twelve thrones judging the tribes of Israel (19: 28), meaning that the apostles were to be the authorised representatives of Christ over the New Israel, the Church. It was from some misunderstanding of what this saying implied that the request of the two disciples came, and it was on this point that Jesus had now to enlighten them (20: 20-28). As in *Mark*, the last stage of Jesus' journey to Jerusalem is marked by the healing of a blind man, two of them in *Matthew*, at Jericho (20: 29-34).

Following Mark with few additions Matthew records the Triumphal Entry (21: 1-11), the Cleansing of the Temple (21: 12-17), the cursing of the fig tree (21: 18-22), and the question of the Sadducees as to Jesus' authority (21: 23-27). The striking parable of the two sons (21: 28-32) compares the ecclesiastical dignitaries unfavourably with the "publicans and harlots", and Matthew uses this and the parable of the wicked husbandmen (21: 33-42) to lead up to our Lord's pronouncement of God's withdrawal of his favour from his ancient people, and his choice of a new and worthier Israel, words which united Sadducees and Pharisees in determining to crush him (21: 43-46).

Again in the parable of the wedding feast (22: 1-10), representing the union of the Messiah with his Church, it is not the expected guests (the orthodox Jews) who gather round the table, but those who would normally be regarded as the riff-raff of society (the "publicans and sinners", and the Gentiles). But they also will stand under the judgment of God in so far as they prove unworthy

(22: 11-14). Returning to Mark, Matthew now relates the encounter of our Lord with the Pharisees and Herod's officials on the question of paying taxes to the Roman government (22: 15-22), and with the Sadducees on the question of the resurrection (22: 23-33). The two great commandments, love to God and one's neighbour, are singled out as the heart of the Law (22: 34-40), and the Messiah establishes his claim to be greater than the Son of David of popular expectation (22: 41-46).

The concern of Matthew as a Jewish Christian to justify the supplanting of the old people of God by the new Israel of faith, comprising both Jew and Gentile, has been consistently apparent throughout his gospel. The old people of God had been given every opportunity in the past, but above all now in the messianic time, to fulfil their role as heirs of God's promises. Instead, their persistent obduracy had flouted the authority of God's Anointed, his works of healing and compassion had produced no sign of repentance, and above all their religious leaders had been instrumental in bringing about his Crucifixion.

It is against this background that we must read chapter twenty-three of the gospel, which is a vitriolic attack on the Jewish religious leaders. However strongly Jesus may have felt that those who ought to have been foremost in leading their people and the rest of the world to God were in fact "blind guides", who emphasised ceremonial trivialities and condoned more serious offences, it is unlikely that our Lord would have been responsible for such a general tirade which is obviously unfair to the Gamaliels, Nicodemuses, and Josephs, of whom there must have been many who would have agreed with this condemnation of some of their number.

No doubt Jesus did castigate the Pharisees on particular occasions for hypocrisy and other sins of the spirit, but this sweeping indictment surely reflects rather the temper of the early Church in the days when Christian missionaries found their most active opponents among the rigid upholders of the Jewish Law. Nevertheless the chapter remains as a charge against religious insincerity in every age which we must lay upon our own heart and conscience (23: 1-39).

The last discourse of Jesus (chs. 24-25) with which Matthew concludes his fifth book, makes it abundantly plain that the same condemnation that has been passed upon the Jews, ecclesiastics and laymen, will likewise be passed upon the new people of God if they prove equally worthless. The judgment of the Messiah, which has been the theme of the fifth book, is now extended from Temple and synagogue to Church and world.

Chapter twenty-four is an expanded version of the thirteenth chapter of *Mark*. But by the time this gospel was written Jerusalem had fallen and its Temple had been destroyed. The Jewish-Roman war which Jesus foresaw had left a shattered and desolate country. It is therefore with this new and vivid evidence of the inexorable judgment of God, that Matthew and the early Church in general would see an even deeper signifi-

cance in our Lord's words than would the Roman circle of Mark's readers, and the historical pattern of sin and punishment which had been detected in the events of Israel's history by the Old Testament prophets, as well as by our Lord himself, would conjure up more vividly than ever the ultimate Judgment of God at the end of time.

The threatened judgment on Jerusalem passes as in Mark's version into the Judgment of the Son of Man, the climax of history (24: 1-36). It is likened to the judgment that came upon Noah's world, and we are warned in the parable of the two servants that we cannot play fast and loose with God (24: 37-51). In the parable of the wise and foolish virgins (25: 1-13), which is peculiar to *Matthew*, we are taught that we cannot rely on the good works of others but that each of us must be responsible for himself and must always be prepared for Christ's coming.

The parable of the talents, found also in Luke's version, where the number is ten and not five, is a lesson in the same vein of God's demand upon us to give of our best, to use to the full the gifts that God bestows on us in the service of his children (25: 14-30). As a magnificent climax to his theme of judgment, Matthew pictures the final Assize when the King comes into his own and divides his people. The sublime simplicity and humanity of Christian service are nowhere in the gospels more splendidly evident than here.

Doubtless in Matthew's mind it is charity towards hungry, thirsty, naked and imprisoned Christians by the world at large that receives our Lord's blessing. In a pagan world with tiny Christian communities no other possibility could be envisaged. Today we can see in our Lord's words a wider application. Christ died for all men and all men are his brothers. Christian charity recognises no boundaries of caste or creed, and this word may well be taken as the basic dominical summons to Christian service. To serve others in the name of Christ is to serve him and be with him for ever, which is "life eternal". To refuse, is to separate ourselves from him, which is "everlasting punishment" (25: 31–46).

Passion and Resurrection of Jesus
(26: 2–28: 20)

MATTHEW'S FIFTH book is rounded off in 26: 1. Thereafter, as there was a prologue narrating the Birth of Jesus, there comes now an epilogue relating his Death and Resurrection. There is no need of comment for most of this account. Not only is the narrative straightforward but it also follows Mark's order, mostly in Mark's words. There is the plot to arrest Jesus (26: 2–5), the anointing at Bethany (26: 6–13), the betrayal by Judas (26: 14–16), the preparation and celebration of the Last Supper (26: 17–30), the Agony in Gethsemane (26: 31–46), the Arrest of Jesus (26: 47–56), the first informal Trial (26: 57–68) and Peter's denial of his Master (26: 69–75).

The day of the Crucifixion begins with the formal Trial before the Sanhedrin (27: 1), and Jesus is handed over to Pilate (27: 2). At this point Matthew departs from Mark's narrative to describe the fate of Judas. Now repentant, but too late to undo the mischief, he hangs himself. Another version of his death is given in *Acts* 1: 18, but Matthew sees in the purchase of the potter's field a fulfilment of *Zech.* 11: 12–13. It is comforting to find that he confuses Jeremiah and Zechariah (27: 3–10).

For the rest of the Trial before Pilate and the subsequent Crucifixion, Matthew follows Mark closely (27: 11–66) but adds some details which are found only in this gospel. Pilate's wife warns him as a result of a dream to beware of sentencing an innocent man (27: 19), and Pilate absolves himself of guilt in the matter by publicly washing his hands as a sign of his innocence (27: 24). These may be genuine features of the Trial, or they may be part of the folk-lore of the Jerusalem Christians. This would certainly seem to be true of Matthew's story that at the Crucifixion the earth quaked, graves opened and the dead arose (27: 51–53).

Peculiar to *Matthew* also is the precaution of the priests against the disciples' stealing the body of Jesus, by sealing the sepulchre and obtaining a guard of Roman soldiers from Pilate to guard the tomb (27: 62–66). This again may be authentic, although it seems unlikely that Pilate would agree to such a procedure. It is possibly a story which has its origin in the allegation of the Jews after the Resurrection that the disciples had stolen the body. This seems to be suggested by the sequel in 28: 11–15.

Matthew's narrative of the Resurrection (28: 1-8) intensifies the miraculous nature of the occurrence. On Easter morning two of the women who had been present at the Crucifixion and had seen the entombment visited the sepulchre. There was an earthquake; an angel came down from heaven and rolled back the stone which sealed the tomb, petrifying the guards. The words uttered are those of the angel in Mark's gospel.

As the women in mingled fear and joy are on their way to tell the disciples of what had happened, they are met by the Risen Lord, who more or less repeats the angelic message (28: 8-10). The bribing of the guards by the priests is then recounted (28: 11-15), ensuring that the common explanation of the mystery will be that the disciples were responsible for removing the body.

To many it will appear that Matthew's account of the Resurrection is the least satisfying of the four gospels. Mark conveys in sober language the basic fact that the tomb was empty. The presence of his angelic messenger is simply the normal Jewish way of expressing the conviction that the Resurrection was an Act of God. The remaining two gospels, as we shall see, give us various convincing narratives of the appearances of the Risen Christ.

But Matthew's unlikely story of the sealing of the tomb and the bribing of the guards should not discourage us from treating his narrative of the Resurrection with the respect it deserves. Like the other gospel writers, he affirms the fact that the tomb where the body of Jesus had been laid on the Friday was found empty by some of his women followers on the Sunday morning. How many of them there were, whether two (*Matthew*) or three (*Mark*) is a matter of little moment. Unlike the other gospel writers, however, he tries to convey an impression of the actual Resurrection itself (28: 2-4).

Matthew's account is an attempt to express in theological terms the world-shattering, awe-inspiring character of the event that changed the course of history. Equally theological is the solitary and rather stilted narrative of the encounter of the women with the Risen Lord (28: 9-10), which lacks the realistic note of the remaining gospels, but is this evangelist's way of leading up to the great scene on the mountain top in "Galilee of the Gentiles" (4: 15) with which his gospel ends, when the Moses of the New Covenant gives his solemn charge to the New People of God.

This majestic final utterance of our Lord, here pictured as Risen and in some sense Ascended, and seen by believers and doubters (perhaps the five hundred referred to in *I Cor.* 15: 6), is a fitting conclusion to a gospel which has consistently emphasised the missionary vocation of the Church. Christ's command to his people to go out among all the nations, making new disciples, baptising and instructing, is rightly taken to be the charter of the new Israel, whose Lord is with her "alway, even unto the end of the world" (28: 16-20).

THE GOSPEL ACCORDING TO ST. MARK

Palestine in the Time of Christ

THE RIVALRY BETWEEN the different factions of the Maccabean family had not only brought into disrepute the laudable motives that initially prompted Mattathias and his sons to start the war of independence, but also had given the Romans an excuse to take Palestine under their protection. When Pompey entered Jerusalem in 63 B.C. (see pp. 328–329), it was the beginning of a fateful association between Jew and Roman which ended with the terrible war of A.D. 66, the final destruction of Jerusalem in A.D. 70 and the ultimate dispersion of what was left of the Jews to the four corners of the earth.

At first it did not seem as if this would be the outcome. Rome was a tolerant mistress, and under her auspices the world at the end of the old era enjoyed such peace as it had never known before. Roman garrisons kept unruly elements in check, more by the power of law and order that they represented than by brutal repression. Palestine alone knew no peace. No sooner did the land have respite from the Maccabeans and their dynastic disputes than a new incubus arrived to harass it.

This was the house of Herod the Great, who in 27 B.C. became king of a larger area of Palestinian territory than any Maccabean had ever laid claim to. Unlike the early Maccabeans however, he ruled by permission of Rome, which lost him the support of the Jewish patriots. Moreover, although a Jew by religion, he was only half-Jewish by birth and wholly Greek in his sympathies. Despite the fact that he rebuilt the Temple at Jerusalem and made it one of the wonders of the world, he was highly unpopular both for his subservience to Rome and for the fiscal policy which became necessary to finance his extravagant projects.

His reign left a memory of horror. His acts of repression, intensified by his own mental disorders, led to crucifixions and massacres becoming common practice. On his death in 4 B.C., so great was the aversion of the people towards the reigning house that they besought the emperor in Rome to take the country under his direct protection. Augustus, however, did not accede to this request and the land was divided among Herod's sons. The particular son who became ruler of Judaea, Archelaus, was the worst of the family, and the ten years of his reign (4 B.C.–A.D. 6) were a continuous tale of riot and rebellion.

Eventually Augustus recognised that it would be more prudent to agree to the popular demand, and a Roman official was put in charge of Judaea, while Herod's other sons continued to govern Galilee and the territory beyond. Thus, when Jesus was born, it was Herod the Great who authorised the massacre of the innocents (*Matt.* 2: 16), but it was a Roman procurator, Pontius Pilate, who alone had the power of life and death over all Jews thirty years later.

Politically, then, the background of the gospels is that of this small proud and restless people, once again under the heel of a world empire. A Roman administrator controls Jerusalem, the heart of Judaea, a minor province not more than fifty miles across from the Mediterranean to the Jordan, and less than a hundred miles from north to south between the territory of Antipas, son of Herod the Great, in Galilee, and the barren mountains of the south.

Economically, the land was impoverished by a series of bad harvests, the extravagance of Herod, and crushing Roman taxation. Civil war and rebellion had left a legacy of malnutrition and suffering. Starvation was a real fear in the lives of the smallholders, who made up the greater part of the population. Failure of crops meant inevitably falling into the hands of money-lenders, with the alternative for the younger members of the family of either bondage or brigandage. The number of beggars, mentally unbalanced and physically diseased people who appear in the gospel stories—unusually large for a primarily agri-cultural community—reflects the tragic story of Palestine under Maccabean, Herodian and Roman auspices.

Religiously, the high priest and his supporters in the Sadducean party subscribed to Roman authority, discouraged revolt and made the best arrangements for their own well-being. The Pharisees, including in their number militant rebels like the Zealots, and monastic orders like the Essenes, commanded the support of the vast majority of the population, and ranged from the rigid devotees of the Law, caricatured in the gospels, to the plain devout folk like Joseph and Mary of Nazareth —restive under Roman domination and steeped in the tradition of the Old Testament.

Messiah Has Come

IN THE INTERTESTAMENTAL period, as troubles increased and life grew harder, as foreign oppression from one quarter gave place to similar treatment from another, we have seen how the hope of a dramatic intervention by God and the advent of a Messiah, which had been crystallising since the days of the great prophets, grew in intensity until the apocalyptic end of the present world seemed at any moment due. Although this mood of expectancy was officially discouraged by Sadducees and Pharisees alike—the Sadducees in a desire to preserve the status quo, and the Pharisees on the grounds that only rigid conformity with the terms of the Law would bring the messianic Kingdom in God's good time—it was the fervent hope of every robust patriot that soon Messiah would appear, and like a new David would smash the yoke of the Roman oppressor, while the more religiously minded dreamt of a supernatural Messiah who would come in judgment, cleanse the world of its evil, and by the strong power of God reign over a new and purer earth.

About the year A.D. 30, a small band of Jews, obviously honest and godly working men, created a stir in Jerusalem by claiming that Messiah had come, and that the golden age, the good time coming, which prophet and psalmist had promised for centuries had at last begun. This was not by any means a unique claim. There had been other aspirants to the title of Messiah who had all had their followers. This particular group, however, made startling assertions which had never been made before. Their message was that the Messiah was Jesus, the carpenter of Nazareth, whose preaching and healing acts had drawn the crowds in Galilee and Judaea, who had, as everyone knew, recently been crucified for blasphemy, but whom God had now raised from the dead as they themselves could testify.

The Resurrection was the crowning proof, they claimed, that this was indeed the new and greater Moses who had come to reappraise the Law, and to found a new community within Israel based on allegiance to himself, which every penitent Israelite might join. God's Messiah had been neither a politician nor a soldier, nor had he made a dramatic descent from the skies, but he had in the deepest sense fulfilled all that the scriptures had promised. Now God in his mercy was giving his stubborn people, who had rejected the prophets and crucified the Messiah, this last chance to return to him in repentance and obedience before the final Judgment, when the Messiah would come again to consummate the divine purpose.

The first half of the book of Acts tells the story of how this little band of Nazarenes grew and spread, and the second half of the book records how under the dynamic leadership of Paul of Tarsus, the Gospel was carried out of Israel to the Gentile world, until it reached the capital of the empire, Rome itself. But hardly had the new movement reached Rome than its two chief advocates, Peter and Paul, died martyrs' deaths in the first persecution of Christianity by the Romans under Nero in A.D. 64.

Until then the Gospel had been spread by the preaching of the missionaries. So long as there were those alive who had been with the Master in Galilee and Jerusalem, and who were able to instruct the younger missionaries in the facts of the gospel story and the words of the Lord, there was no need of written records. There is good reason to think that before the deaths of Peter and Paul, a beginning had been made to gather together collections of the sayings of Jesus, as well as groups of stories and parables and a connected narrative of the Passion, in addition to Old Testament passages which bore some reference to the events of Jesus' life and death.

But with the passing of the first generation of eye-witnesses of the ministry of Jesus, with the expansion of the mission and the increasing demand for authoritative guidance for converts and catechumens, as well as the growing realisation that the Second Coming of Christ was not an immediate possibility, the need was felt to have in writing a connected record of the ministry of Jesus, which had previously existed only as illustrative or homiletic material in the sermons of the missionaries.

Mark: The First Gospel

IT IS GENERALLY agreed by New Testament scholars that the first gospel to be written was not *Matthew* but *Mark*, and that this gospel was written in Rome soon after the deaths of Peter and Paul, probably in A.D. 65. From the earliest days of Christian tradition, the writer of this gospel has been identified with John Mark, son of the Mary in whose house the first Christians used to meet in Jerusalem (*Acts* 12: 12). Later, John Mark became an apprentice missionary with Paul on his first tour, and remained associated with him in one way or another until that apostle was martyred.

Of more significance for the writing of the gospel, however, was Mark's association with Peter. Again tradition helps us by describing Mark as Peter's "interpreter", and by telling us that after Peter's death Mark wrote down the narrative of the life and death of Jesus, based on what he had heard from the chief apostle himself. In reading the gospel we shall see from time to time clear evidence of eye-witness reporting, which reflects the part that recollection of Peter's talk and preaching played in the composition of the book.

We shall also find reason to believe that Mark himself was present at the last stages of Jesus' ministry in Passion Week (see p. 382), and as an active missionary Mark would have in any case a fair knowledge of the events of the Galilean ministry and the teaching of our Lord. There is, however, very little of the teaching of Jesus included in Mark's gospel, which suggests that this was already in circulation in written form, and that Mark's narrative was intended to supplement it.

The part that Peter played as the authority behind Mark's gospel accounts for the fact that the other two gospels—*Matthew* and *Luke* —which were written from much the same point of view as that of Mark, and hence all three are called the synoptic gospels, largely reproduce Mark's gospel, in some places verbatim, and always treat it with respect. As we shall see, these two gospels not only include the narratives borrowed from Mark, but add the teaching of Jesus which Mark omitted, and some special material to which apparently Mark did not have access or which he did not choose to include.

Thus, in reading *Mark* first, we are reading the Gospel in its basic and earliest form, written not more than a generation after the events it describes, with people still alive who could challenge its accuracy. Moreover, we are reading something that is merely a written record of what had been preached in public since the first days of the mission in Jerusalem, just after the Crucifixion. We have every reason to feel confident, therefore, that what we are reading is a faithful account of what actually happened, allowing for the missionary purpose of the writer and the fact that no human record is infallible.

Perhaps it is at this point that something should be said about what we are entitled to expect from the gospel writers in general, as well as what we are not entitled to expect. First of all they were evangelists. That is, their main object was not to provide the kind of biography of Jesus that a modern author would be asked to provide. Their aim was to record what Jesus said and did, in so far as it had a bearing on the salvation of men. There are thus many blank spaces in the record—for example the first thirty years of our Lord's life. We are also told nothing of his appearance, education, private conversation or the hundred and one other details that a biographer today would supply.

Secondly, the gospel writers were human, as were the people from whom they derived their information. Although memories in those days were better trained than they are today, and the check by the community on deviations from the fixed form of a story was very rigid, we must always allow for the possibility of misunderstanding, or faulty memory, or intentional modifications of a narrative with a view to improving or clarifying it. Thus while we may reckon that sayings of Jesus, which were in the nature of things short, pithy and often repeated, are likely to be accurately handed down to us, we must always allow for the possibility that an incident that happened only once, especially if it was of a startling character, might not be reported precisely in accordance with what took place.

Thirdly, each gospel writer had a particular circle of readers in mind, and this, apart from the question of what special information was available to him, coloured his presentation of the gospel story. Mark, for example, was writing for a small community of Gentile Christians in Rome, who had just seen their leaders executed, and who were themselves in need of encouragement to hold fast to their faith in face of persecution and mortal peril. He therefore shapes his record of events in such a way as to make it as relevant as possible to the needs of his readers.

When we read St. Matthew's gospel, we are struck by the number of Old Testament quotations and the frequent reference to Old Testament ideas. Obviously one special purpose of that gospel was to persuade Jews that Jesus was indeed the Messiah, the culmination of Israel's hope. Similarly St. Luke's gospel, as we shall see, was directed particularly to the Gentile world at large, with a view to assuring intelligent pagans that this new Christian community was no disguised Jewish sect, but a potentially worldwide movement open to men of all nations.

In view of these considerations since *Mark* is the earliest and shortest gospel which both Matthew and Luke have enlarged and modified, it will be best for us to begin our study of the New Testament with Mark, gleaning from him the general course of events, and then turning to Matthew and Luke to fill up the gaps in Mark's presentation, and to provide us with the substance of the teaching of Jesus which Mark does not include.

The Beginning of the Gospel
(1 : 1–8)

THERE WAS A time in the heyday of "liberal" Christianity last century, when it was thought that by taking St. Mark's gospel and pruning it of all the awkward passages—awkward from the point of view of the scientific understanding of the time—we should arrive at a true picture derived from this earliest gospel of the "Jesus of history", who had been, so it was felt, transformed by the other gospel writers and St. Paul into the "Christ of faith". Unfortunately for the "liberals" and fortunately for us, St. Mark does not allow us to make any such distinction. For him the "Jesus of history" is the "Christ of faith", as the first words of his gospel indicate.

He does not leave us with any illusion about his own attitude to the task which he has taken in hand, which is to tell of the Gospel, or "good news" about Jesus. From start to finish, this story is one not of an inspired teacher from Nazareth, but of an enigmatic and powerful figure who says unlikely things and does incredible things, and who in the writer's view can only be described as the "Son of God". Since Mark is writing for the benefit of Gentiles, this term is more meaningful than "the Christ", the Greek word for the Messiah, which in the wider mission field had come to be used as synonymous with Jesus or as part of his proper name (1 : 1).

For Mark, the beginning of the Gospel was the appearance of John the Baptist. We therefore do not find here stories of the birth of Jesus, as in Matthew and Luke. The ancient world had no great interest in childhood or adolescence, and Mark quite naturally starts his story at the point where Jesus' public ministry is about to begin. Unlike Matthew, Mark is not writing specifically for Jews. He therefore does not go out of his way to show by quotations from the Old Testament, how all that happened in the life of Jesus fulfilled what had been written about the Messiah.

On this occasion, however, the two Old Testament quotations with which he introduces John the Baptist (1 : 2–3) are sufficiently striking to constitute an exception. In *Mal.* 3: 1 the prophet had spoken of the "messenger" who would herald the advent of the Messiah, while Second Isaiah (40 : 3) had used words which aptly described the role of the Baptist. For Jesus, and therefore for Mark and the early Church in general, the Baptist was the Elijah whom men had come to expect as the forerunner of the Messiah, and the Baptist's habitat in the desert, his dress and his message, all suggested that this element of the prophetic promise of the coming of

God's new age had now been fulfilled (*Mal.* 4: 5; *Mark* 9: 11–13; *Luke* 1: 17).

It is noteworthy that where Second Isaiah had pictured the way as being prepared "for our God", Mark has no hesitation in applying these words to the coming of Christ. For him Jesus is Lord and therefore God. John's mission in the desert country beside Jordan was a call to national penitence. Both Matthew and Luke tell us more about it (*Matt.* 3: 1–12; *Luke* 3: 1–18), but Mark contents himself with recording two main facts, apart from a description of the Baptist's prophetic garb and ascetic diet.

The burden of John's message, according to Mark, was that the messianic age was at hand; he himself was merely the herald of God's Messiah. The distinguishing feature of his campaign was an invitation to all who were moved by a sense of guilt, and the impending messianic Judgment, to be baptised by immersion in the Jordan as an outward token of their repentance. He claims, however, that this baptism by water is only the prelude to a more significant baptism, which, as Mark's readers well knew, was the gift of the Holy Spirit which accompanied or followed baptism after Pentecost (*Acts* 2: 38; 8: 14–17).

It was only to be expected that John's unusual appearance and the terms of his message should arouse widespread interest. Genuine prophecy had not only died out, but all prophecy had fallen into disrepute in Israel (*Zech.* 13: 4–6), and in Maccabean times even the best of the high priests was regarded as

holding only a watching brief, pending the reappearance of true prophecy in the messianic age (*I Macc.* 14: 41) as Joel had promised (*Joel* 2: 28).

The Baptism and Temptation of Jesus
(1: 9–13)

AMONG THOSE WHO went down to the banks of the Jordan to be baptised was Jesus. According to Mark he had come straight from Nazareth. The account of his Baptism is short but deeply significant. It is described in terms of a personal experience of Jesus, which must have been retold by him at a later date, and in which heaven itself was opened to him, the Spirit of God descended on him and he heard the voice of God.

It is in the words which Jesus hears, two quotations from the Old Testament, that we can learn what this experience meant for him. He cannot have come to John the Baptist from any sense of guilt, otherwise the rest of the gospel makes nonsense. He can only have come because, during the years of his young manhood in Nazareth, he had become increasingly conscious that unlike any of his contemporaries, religious or lay, his relationship to God was untroubled by any sense of sin or shortcoming. It was direct and free without inhibition or hesitancy, without the arid spells, the self-distrust and doubts of even the greatest of the Old Testament saints.

Moreover, unless the power that Jesus exercised, to which every page of the gospels bears witness, was the product of legend or deception, the young carpenter must have found himself increasingly perplexed by the sense of his growing power which no one else shared. We are surely entitled to think that it must have occurred to one steeped in the Old Testament, as Jesus by his knowledge of it shows to have been the case, to wonder whether he himself were not in fact the Messiah who had been promised to Israel.

John's mission by the Jordan, with its message of the impending advent of the Messiah, would naturally attract Jesus. He would undergo the baptism of repentance not for his own sins, but as one who identified himself with his people, as Messiah would do if he were to come. His experience at the moment of Baptism suggests that it was at this point that Jesus became certain that he was the Messiah. There can be no other meaning in the two Old Testament texts which he quotes from *Ps.* 2 : 7 and *Isa.* 42 : 1.

The first word of God's commission, "Thou art my beloved Son", comes from a psalm in which the messianic king is promised dominion over the whole world. The second, "in whom I am well pleased", is from one of the Servant songs in Second Isaiah. By joining these together, Jesus accepts his commission as a charge from God to be the Messiah of psalm and prophecy, the divine Saviour for whom the faithful among the people of God had longed and prayed, but who at the same time, or perhaps after the Temptation which follows, sets his compass in the direction which his messiahship shall take, the road of the Servant of YHWH, who by his suffering and death will bring the nations to the knowledge of God.

If we may think of Jesus' Baptism as his acceptance of his commission to be the Messiah, we may take the Temptation in the wilderness which follows to be the sequel. There could be many ways of using his powers, many ways of being Messiah. Mark, unlike the other gospels, does not describe these various short cuts to success, although he makes it plain that all of them were the prompting of the devil. In solitude, then, and for some time, Jesus thrashes out the problem that faces him. He comes back from the desert country with his mind made up. The wild beasts or powers of evil have done their worst, but the victory has been with the angels (*Ps.* 91 : 11–13).

Mark's gospel has a notably staccato effect. Few words are wasted, and the air of breathlessness and the number of times the word "straightway" occurs have often been mentioned. Only when we come to the Passion story do we get the impression of a lengthy chronological narrative, otherwise it seems as if Mark strings together incidents, parables and summaries of events in such a way that it is often difficult to know whether this or that happening took place at this or that particular time, or whether Mark has some other reason in mind for including it at that point.

The Kingdom of God
(1 : 14–20)

IN vv. 14–15 he gives a synopsis of the contents of Jesus' preaching when he returned to Galilee. He does not say how long it was after his Baptism, but indicates that in the meantime John the Baptist had been imprisoned, an event which is described at length in ch. 6. The burden of Jesus' message was that "the time is fulfilled", the decisive hour has struck.

When St. Paul in *Gal.* 4: 4 says that "when the fulness of the time was come, God sent forth his Son" he means the same thing. It is astounding to reflect in how many ways the world had been prepared for the coming of Christ. There was a unique spell of world peace which enabled the Gospel to spread, a unique common Greek language which was intelligible in all parts of the world and in which the missionaries could speak and write, a network of imperial Roman roads along which the Good News could travel, and a pagan world morally and socially diseased, yearning for a faith that had the power to give life a meaning.

But it was more than that that both Jesus and Paul meant. It was the decisive hour in the sense of the turning point of history. When Jesus used these words, he claimed that the coping stone was now placed on the house that God had been building for his people, since Abraham responded to his summons and received the promise that in him all the peoples of the earth would be blessed. "The time is fulfilled" means that Act I

of the divine drama, the Old Testament, the story of God's work to rescue men from themselves by the choice and direction of a special people Israel, had now reached its climax. Act II, the supreme intervention of God to bring mankind back to himself, has now begun.

Psalmist, prophet and apocalyptist had not been wrong. True, they had seen only part of the picture. For some, the Day of YHWH and the coming of the Messiah had been thought of in terms of a restoration of Israel's political power under a new David, for others it had involved the dissolution of the existing world and the advent of a supernatural Messiah. But their basic conviction had been right that God would not leave his people to perish, though what God meant by his people was something that only a few of the Old Testament thinkers had been able even dimly to grasp.

What did Jesus mean when he said "the kingdom of God is at hand"? Some have thought that like the apocalyptists, Jesus looked for a speedy and dramatic end to the old world and for his own immediate return as the victorious Messiah. Whatever the early Christians thought about this, there is no evidence in the gospels that Jesus held any such view. Others have thought that Jesus regarded the Kingdom of God as having come once and for all with his own messianic ministry, and that nothing further remained for the future.

A truer view would see in our Lord's words, both here and throughout the gospels, the claim that in his own person God had entered the human stage in a new and distinctive way. God was speaking and acting through his Messiah to call men to repentance, to heal their bodies and straighten their twisted minds. Where men responded in faith and trust, where disease and death were routed, where sin and evil in any form were banished, there the "Kingdom of God", that is, the sovereign rule of God over the whole field of life, had already come into being. Man and nature had begun to swing into the right relationship to God.

But the old world remained with all its evils. So long as human life continued there would be sin, and so long as there is sin there is no perfect rule of God. Consequently the Kingdom is future as well as present, now but not yet, begun but not complete. Only in a new dimension, beyond space and time, the Christian fulfilment of the Old Testament "promised land", can the Kingdom fully come and God's purpose be fully realised.

Thus the call of Jesus to his contemporaries was to throw themselves in penitence and humility on the mercy of God, to believe the "good news" of his forgiving love, which had the power to save men from themselves and from the demonic power of evil that surrounded them, and to offer to God the service of perfect obedience and loyalty which is his due. Wherever men so responded through their encounter with God's Messiah, the Kingdom had already begun to come into being. Jesus himself embodied the Kingdom, and all who became his followers became part of it and of him. The first recruits were four fishermen

on the lake of Galilee, Simon, later called Peter, Andrew, James and John.

A Typical Day in Jesus' Ministry
(1 : 21–45)

MARK NOW gives us what looks like a typical day in the life of Jesus, during this period of his ministry. In the nearby town of Capernaum, Jesus, as was the practice of the Jewish synagogue, was invited to preach on the sabbath. His sermon, however, unlike the normal expositions of the rabbis, was marked by what Mark calls "authority". We can gather what that means when we remember that the habit of the scribes in expounding the Law was to quote the views of the various legal experts on its proper interpretation. Jesus apparently did no such thing, but spoke as one who was his own authority, an attitude even more startling than that of the prophets who prefaced their utterances with: "Thus saith the Lord".

Not only was this unusual assumption of authority evident in what Jesus said. His power extended over disease as well. In the synagogue was a man whose mind was unbalanced (1 : 23), in Peter's house was a sick woman (1 : 30), both of whom Jesus healed. In both cases we get the impression that the cure was instantaneous, and that to bring wholeness of mind and body was regarded by Jesus as of equal importance with teaching, as the mission of the Messiah.

In the gospels, physical disease

and insanity are regarded as the work of demons, evil spirits who are subject to Satan, whose kingdom is in constant opposition to the Kingdom of God. Jesus accepts this view-point as a child of his times. A first century Jew with twentieth century medical or psychiatric knowledge, would be as unreal as a first century Jew with a knowledge of space-travel, nuclear fission or even the geography of this planet.

Humanly speaking, and that is how we must speak of Jesus, the Incarnation means that God became man, at a particular time and in a particular place. The scientific, geographical and historical knowledge of Jesus was therefore that of his own day, just as the fact that he was fully human meant that he was at times hungry, tired and despondent. Where Jesus differed from his contemporaries—and from us—was in his knowledge of God, of the purpose of life, and of the hearts of men, not in his possession of the kind of factual knowledge which is in the last resort of secondary importance.

The basic fact for us in this, as in all the healing stories of the gospel, is that Jesus healed suffering folk. Clearly he did not regard it as the will of God that anyone should have a diseased mind or a diseased body. Pain, like death, is an intrusion and an accident, not part of the fabric of the Kingdom of God. In this story he exorcises the "unclean spirit", in the story of Peter's sick mother-in-law his touch makes her well.

We may notice here for the first time a recurring motif in Mark's presentation of the Gospel. One of the problems of the early missionaries was to account for the fact that Jesus was not recognised as the Messiah by his countrymen, but instead was crucified by them. Mark's theme is that not even the disciples reached this recognition, until Peter on their behalf made the great confession at Caesarea Philippi (8: 29), and that Jesus himself discouraged the use of the designation Messiah in connection with his own ministry, because of the misleading political associations of the word in the minds of so many. The demons, however, who possessed the mentally sick, recognised the Messiah from the start. The supernatural powers of the kingdom of Satan acknowledged the stronger power of the Kingdom of God. Thus this madman, presumably making unintelligible noises, is represented by Mark as hailing Jesus as the Holy One of God, i.e. the Messiah (1: 24; cf. 1: 34; 3: 11).

The little anecdote of Peter's mother-in-law, which suggests a personal reminiscence of Peter himself, seems to imply that Peter's house at Capernaum formed Jesus' headquarters at this stage in his ministry (cf. 2: 1), and suggests a homely scene of an expected meal which was not forthcoming, a tale of sudden illness and apologies, followed by the healing touch of the Master—a well-remembered day for Peter.

The display of "authority" over the demon-world, which had been exhibited in the synagogue (1: 27), was enough to establish Jesus' reputation as a healer throughout the countryside (1: 28). When the sabbath had officially ended at 6 p.m. and the Law permitted the work of transportation, there was a throng of patients brought by their friends to be cured in mind or body. This scene, like many other collective summaries in the gospels, makes it plain that Jesus cured far more people than those who are mentioned in detail, and that the healing ministry of our Lord is recorded largely in terms of specimen cases.

In the very early morning after this exhausting and doubtless typical day, Jesus seeks the solitude which the hillside behind the town provided, to recover in prayer the strength that came from communion with the Father. We may picture a similar pattern of preaching in the synagogues, and healing in the towns and villages of Galilee, as constituting the first stage of Jesus' public ministry (1: 39).

At this point Mark introduces a story of a healing act performed on a leper (1: 40–45) which is in some respects obscure. Leprosy in the biblical sense took various forms, some of them curable. The Law, however, prescribed stringent rules to prevent contagion, and insisted on certification by a priest before the sufferer was allowed to mingle in society in the ordinary way (*Lev.* 13: 45 – 46; 14). In this case the man approaches Jesus, which was forbidden by the Law. The difficulty of the story lies in the fact that Jesus appears to be angry with him. "Straitly" in 1: 43 means "sternly", and some manuscripts instead of "moved with compassion" in v. 41 read "being angry". Why should Jesus be angry?

Was it because the man had broken the Law and come among the crowd? Or was it because the man doubted his willingness to heal him? And did Mark want to emphasise Jesus' respect for the provisions of the Law when they were wise (1: 44), as opposed to his critical attitude when the Law became inhuman, as in the next two chapters? At all events for us the main point is surely that Jesus touched the untouchable and healed him (1: 41). Perhaps Mark wanted to show that the best the Law could do was to certify a man when he was cured, but that Jesus could effect the cure itself.

The Beginning of Opposition
(2: 1 – 3: 6)

MARK NOW relates a series of incidents to show how almost immediately after the beginning of Jesus' ministry, opposition from the religious authorities began to make itself evident. Perhaps these stories of growing conflict (2: 1 – 3: 6) had been collected before Mark included them in his gospel. The first of them is the case of the paralytic, whose friends are so certain of the power of Jesus to heal, that they break open the soft roof of the house, presumably Peter's, and let down the mattress with the sick man (2: 1–12).

This too is not an easy story. Unless Jesus knew that the man's paralysis was the result of his own sin, he seems to imply that suffering in general is caused by sin (2: 5), a view which elsewhere he repudiates (*Luke* 13: 1–5; *John* 9: 2–3). Moreover, he seems to heal the man more to impress the scribes than out of compassion for the man's condition. In addition, it is unlikely that at this very early stage in his ministry, Jesus would use the term Son of Man in what is obviously a messianic sense, and claim the prerogative of God in forgiving sins. This, in the presence of legal ecclesiastics, would surely have resulted in immediate arrest and execution for blasphemy.

It is therefore more probable that the historical incident was a simple case of healing which is covered by 2: 1–5a and 11–12. The rest of the narrative, 5b–10, would then be an expansion of the original story for preaching purposes. The incident would be used by Christian missionaries to show that the healing of the body, which was practised in the early Church, was a sacramental symbol of the healing of the whole man, mind and body, including the forgiveness of sin, by the power of Christ. This was how Old Testament narratives were expanded for purposes of instruction in the synagogue, and it was probably in this form that Mark himself first heard the story. He tells it here to indicate one cause of the resentment of religious orthodoxy at Jesus' assumption of an authority that belongs to God alone.

The second cause of offence (2: 13–17) is introduced by Jesus' call of Levi, a collector of taxes on behalf of Herod Antipas, ruler of Galilee. As such, any man would be generally unpopular, but in the eyes of the orthodox there was the added scandal that by nature of his job he had to mix with Gentiles, and the more material consideration that these collectors were generally dishonest. Thus, in the gospels, "publicans", i.e., tax farmers in the service of the Roman government, are bracketed with sinners.

This particular disciple, Levi, is called Matthew in the first gospel (*Matt.* 9: 9). He may, like Simon Peter, have had two names, as 3: 18 seems to suggest. Jesus' second offence is to go out of his way to mix with Levi and his friends in his house, an action which is condemned by the professional exponents of the Law (scribes), who belong to the conservative Pharisaic party. Our Lord justifies his action by quoting a proverb to the effect that just as a doctor will not hesitate to go wherever there is illness, so the healer of souls must be found wherever ordinary sinful men assemble. Jesus obviously does not mean that there are some "righteous" who do not need to repent (2: 17).

The third point at issue between Jesus and the religious authorities was the question of fasting (2: 18–22). Asceticism of this kind has always been one of the conventional attributes of the "holy man". John the Baptist and the Pharisees complied with it, Jesus and his disciples did not. Jesus likens his ministry and message to the gaiety of a wedding feast. The good news of salvation should bring joy and not gloom, and while the bridegroom is present the guests should rejoice. The day will come when the bridegroom is taken from his guests: then would be the time for fasting.

Did Jesus speak thus of his Death at this early stage in his ministry or was this, like the following two verses (2: 21–22), said at some other time? The general sense is that the new Christian faith must create its own forms of worship and not be tied to past Jewish practice. Patches of new unshrunk cloth cannot be fitted into an old garment without tearing it, and new unfermented wine must be put into new goatskins.

The two incidents that follow are both concerned with sabbath observance, and constitute the fourth ground of conflict between Jesus and the Pharisees (2: 23 – 3: 6). In both cases Jesus appeals to the spirit of the Law against the letter. It was permissible to pluck corn in a neighbour's field provided a sickle was not used (*Deut.* 23: 25). There was no reason, according to the Law, why the fact that this was done on the sabbath should make any difference, unless the obligation to regard it as a day of rest was broken. The narrower type of Pharisee, however, interpreted the law of sabbath rest to make it an offence to do much more than draw breath.

In the present story, the disciples were "reaping" in the eyes of these rigid ecclesiastics, and therefore engaging in forbidden activity. Jesus' reply is to set human need on a higher plane than legal niceties. His illustration from the Old Testament is based on the story as told in the synagogues rather than on the incident as recorded in *I Sam.* 21: 1–6. His final illuminating comment, that the sabbath was made for man and not man for the sabbath, has still not been understood in fanatical sabbatarian circles. The last verse of the story is probably the missionary's and not

Jesus' comment: "So you see the Son of Man is Lord also of the sabbath" (see p. 361).

The other sabbath story has a similar motif. The Pharisees maintained that only if a life was in danger would it have been permissible for Jesus to perform a cure on the sabbath. In this case the patient had nothing more wrong with him than a paralysed hand, which could wait until the next day. Jesus, however, again maintains that human need at any time must not take second place to pseudo-piety and ecclesiastical hair-splitting. Is it a greater sin in the sight of God, he says, to heal on the sabbath than to plot the healer's destruction as the Pharisees were doing?

So ends this series of pen-pictures of the growing opposition on the part of the Pharisees to Jesus, and the reasons for it—usurpation of God's sole prerogative, disregard of the strict interpretation of the Law as commended by the experts in holiness, and a readiness to mix with social and religious outcasts. What begins as silent criticism (2: 6), develops from questioning of the disciples (2: 16) into an open challenge to Jesus (2: 18), and ends in determination to get rid of this unholy innovator (3: 6). In this the Pharisees join forces with the Herodians, the supporters of the ruling house.

The Lakeside Ministry
(3: 7 – 4: 34)

CONTRASTED WITH the malevolent intentions of the authorities, the scene now sketched by

Mark is of Jesus' increasing popularity with the common folk of Palestine. Crowds came to Galilee from all parts of the country, so much so that the local synagogues proved too small, and Jesus began a ministry on the lakeside of Galilee, using a boat as a floating pulpit, partly for that reason and partly because of the hordes of sick and mental cases who crowded round him to be cured. We can imagine what this meant when we notice that the words "pressed upon him" in v. 10 really mean "fell upon him" (3: 7–12).

It was at this stage that Jesus selected twelve men to be his disciples and companions. They are set apart to preach the Gospel and heal the sick. Some of them are already familiar from ch. 1, others are barely mentioned anywhere else but here. The twelve are to become in due course the leaders of the Church in Jerusalem after the Resurrection (see p. 421), meantime we may note that one of them, Simon, has been a militant anti-Roman (Canaanite = Zealot), and Judas Iscariot (= man of Kerioth) is the only non-Galilean. It was no accident that Jesus chose twelve and not eleven or thirteen. The Messiah is building the foundations of the new community, the new Israel which is to undertake the task, which old Israel failed to fulfil, of bringing the world back to God; but it is still the Israel of faith, inheritors of the Old Testament promises, and so the twelve apostles represent the twelve tribes of the chosen people (3: 13–19).

To underline the blindness of the Jews to the true character of Jesus' ministry, Mark now pictures the family of Jesus anxiously setting out from Nazareth to take him back home since they feared he had gone out of his mind (3: 21). Meantime Jesus is once again attacked by Jerusalem lawyers, who seem to have gone down to Galilee on instructions from the authorities in the capital. They recognise his power to cure the insane but put it down to sorcery. It is the devil (Beelzebub = Satan) and not God who is behind him (3: 22).

Jesus' adroit reply to this charge is that evil cannot destroy evil. The king of the demon world who causes disease and insanity cannot destroy his own power by being instrumental in healing them. Only the strong power of God, stronger than the power of evil, can defeat the devil's work (3: 27). Our Lord then makes a memorable pronouncement on the sin beyond forgiveness. God's infinite mercy pardons all sins, even the sin of blasphemy against himself, but for the sin against the Holy Spirit, the sin of calling good evil, of refusing to recognise goodness because of prejudice or malice, for that there is no forgiveness (3: 22–30).

At this point the family of Jesus, consisting of his mother and brothers, Joseph presumably being dead, arrives on the scene. They are pictured calling to him from the back of the crowd that throngs round Peter's house. When Jesus is told of it he dramatically uses their presence to make one of his most moving utterances. We can almost see him throw his arms wide as he gathered his mother and brothers together with all the simple folk of Galilee into the great family of God. "My mother and my brothers are those who do the will of God". The Messiah had dedicated himself to the care of all God's children. The claims of his own family must take second place (3: 31-35).

We are now given a series of parables, imaginative stories which in one way or another illustrate Jesus' proclamation of the Kingdom of God. They are represented here as all being spoken on one occasion to an attentive crowd, from a boat offshore in the lake (4: 1-34). It is clear, however, from the interruptions in the series, that this is rather a collection of these illustrations which Mark has arranged in this way or first heard of in this grouping. The longest and best known is the parable of the sower (4: 3-8).

In this parable Jesus represents pictorially the discouragements and consolations of his ministry. Like the prophets of Israel—or like any modern preacher or teacher —he recognised that most of his hearers were unresponsive, yet where the seed fell on good soil the yield was out of all proportion to what was sown. Like all the parables this one ends in a challenge (4: 9) to his hearers: Which kind of soil does each of them know himself to be, as God is his judge?

The next few verses (4: 10-13) do not imply that Jesus used parables to befog his listeners, as the A.V. seems to suggest. He is quoting First Isaiah (*Isa.* 6: 9-10), who had the same problem of seed falling on poor soil. Jesus tells his disciples that to his inner circle he can speak freely of the full meaning of the sovereignty of God over

the whole of life, of the new Israel, and of his own role in it, but to the crowds who flock to see a wonder-worker and pay scant attention to the message behind his healing acts, the most that can be done is to teach them in this crisp pictorial way in the hope that the point goes home to them. Even at that, they see the point without grasping it, they hear and do not understand, they remain unchanged and unforgiven (4: 12).

The explanation of the parable that follows is perhaps more likely to be missionary exposition than Jesus' own words (4: 14-20). It will be surprising if we do not recognise ourselves among the hardened listeners, on whom the word of God falls as on the hardened paths that divide the fields of Galilee (4: 15); or among the fair-weather Christians, whose faith is as shallow as the thin layer of soil that covers the rocky outcrop of the Palestine hillside (4: 16-17); or among the folk whose good intentions are choked by the briers of selfish anxiety, greed and envy (4: 18-19). Pray God that we may sometimes find ourselves among those who make even a five-fold return (4: 20).

The verses that follow (4: 21-34) are shorter parables or extracts from parables. The same sayings appear in different contexts in the other gospels, which suggests that the original setting of some of the things that Jesus says here has been lost. They all refer in one way or another to the proclamation of the Good News. The light of God's revelation in Christ must be allowed to light all men to the truth, and even if it be not fully understood now it will be in days to come (4: 21–22). The more readily men respond to God's summons, the more they understand and benefit from his message (4: 24–25).

The reign of God is in his gift alone. Men can do and have done nothing to hasten its coming. But the seed has been growing secretly, God's purposes have been maturing through the long story of Israel. Now the time is ripe for harvest. God has come in the person of his Messiah to gather men into the new community of his people (4: 26–29). The life of this new community, now tiny like a grain of mustard seed, will grow and spread until it covers the earth (4: 30–34).

The Power of the Messiah

(4: 35 – 5: 43)

FOUR STORIES are now added showing the power of the Messiah over the demon world. Mark makes no distinction between the stilling of the storm (4: 35–41) and the healing acts of Jesus. All are evidence of his authority over Satan's domain. Jesus uses the same word: "be muzzled", in exorcising the demon who caused the storm, as he does in the case of the demoniac in 1: 25. For Mark this act of Jesus is not a violation of "natural law", but a sign that the Messiah is lord over the sea and all created things.

The detailed description suggests an eye-witness reminiscence, and of course for Mark's readers and for us the lesson is plain. It was lack of faith that caused the fear in the disciples' minds. Since the Master was with them they should have had no anxiety. The presence of Christ brings peace to troubled minds (4: 39). At the same time it is right that we should, like the disciples, have a wholesome "fear" or awe of his divine power (4: 41).

The next story, the cure of the Gadarene madman (5: 1–20), takes place on the other side of the lake of Galilee i.e. in Gentile territory. It has been suggested that the man had been driven out of his mind by Roman ill-treatment, hence the word "legion" in 5: 9. It has also been suggested that the cries of the man, as he was being healed, scared the herd of swine who rushed downhill in a panic and drowned.

It is unlikely that either of these ideas would have struck a first century reader of the gospel as particularly important, although they may help to make the story come alive for us. For Mark and his readers, no sympathy would be wasted on the swine. Humanitarian motives or the property rights of the owners would not concern them. The man is possessed by many demons; their existence is threatened by the greater power of the Messiah; the demons do not wish to leave the locality; they are permitted to enter the swine, unclean animals in any case, and are carried headlong to destruction. The point of the story would be that Satan's kingdom is divided, i.e. that evil is self-destroying. When the Messiah encounters the denizens of the demon world they have no escape, no matter where they take refuge.

The next two narratives are

interwoven in a manner already familiar in this gospel (cf. 3: 21–35), the raising of Jairus' daughter and the cure of the woman with the issue of blood (5: 21–43). Back on the Jewish side of the lake, one of the leading members of the local synagogue approached Jesus with a request to heal his daughter. On the way to Jairus' house a woman with a haemorrhage touched Jesus' garment and was healed.

The story is a vivid one, depicting the woman's faith in the power of Jesus overcoming her hesitation at approaching the rabbi, in view of the nature of her complaint; Jesus' sense of loss of power and the woman's delight at feeling herself cured. Continuing on the road to the house of Jairus, news comes that the child is dead. Despite this, Jesus on arrival removes the professional mourners, and in the presence of the parents and his three closest disciples, Peter, James and John, restores the child to life. If the girl had only been asleep or in a trance (5: 39), the event would not have been worth recording. As it is, it serves as an illustration of the Church's view that through the Resurrection of Christ, death is but a sleep with an awakening.

Bread of Heaven

(6: 1–56)

IN HIS OWN home town of Nazareth Jesus suffers the rebuff that the prophets before him had known. It would seem that he had to wait until the sabbath for an opportunity to address his own kindred, and that their reception of him was cold and unfriendly.

Was he not after all the boy from the joiner's shop? (6: 1–6). It was about this time that the twelve disciples were sent out in pairs on a mission of preaching and healing —a pilot scheme for the later work of the Church. Their message was to be the same as that of Jesus—a call to repentance in face of the coming of the Kingdom. There is an air of urgency about their instructions (6: 7–13), suggesting not so much "holy poverty" as that God brooks no delay.

Almost as if to allow time for the disciples to carry out their whirlwind mission, Mark introduces at this point a lengthy account of the death of John the Baptist (6: 14–29). The story of Salome's macabre request for his head has the character of a popular bazaar rumour. It is introduced to give the reason for Herod's antagonism towards Jesus. His bad conscience about John suggested that this was another trouble-maker like the Baptist.

Now the disciples have rejoined Jesus (6: 30), and it was in a vain attempt to escape the crowds and refresh themselves that they found themselves in what should have been a lonely spot on the lakeside, late in the evening, with a large crowd of hungry folk still hanging on the words of the Master. The feeding of a multitude of five thousand (6: 30–44), on which Jesus insisted, would have been a pointless exercise if it had merely been the satisfaction of physical appetite.

When this story is taken together with the parallel story of the feeding of four thousand in ch. 8, and the otherwise quite inexplicable obtuseness of the disciples on the question of a shortage of bread immediately thereafter, it is clear that this is no ordinary feeding that is referred to, but the sacramental Bread of Life which the Messiah provides, a foretaste of the messianic banquet in the Kingdom of God (*Luke* 14: 16–24). The orderly arrangement of the crowd, together with the breaking and blessing of the bread suggest a eucharistic occasion, and this event has properly been called the Galilean Lord's Supper.

The feeding of the multitude is thus an acted parable, a pictorial fulfilment of the manna from heaven in the Exodus story, by which the new Moses, and indeed the new Elisha (*II Kings* 4: 42–44), gives the pledge that God will always feed his hungry people with the true Bread from Heaven, as St. John's gospel shows us (*John* 6: 1–35). In this case the number of the crowd (5,000) and of the loaves (5), together with the number of baskets (12), surely are meant to suggest the twelve tribes and the five books of the Law. This is the proclamation of salvation for the Jews, just as we shall see the parallel feeding of the four thousand to be the proclamation of salvation to the Gentiles.

If we turn to the fourth gospel again, a comment by St. John illuminates the meaning of 6: 45. It is only by reading between the lines in the gospels, which are primarily theological documents, that we normally get any suggestion of the political ferment which formed the background to the ministry of Jesus. St. John, however, tells us (*John* 6: 15) that there was an attempt at this point to make Jesus king. This reflection of the popular quest for a King-Messiah, a political aspirant who would provide the leadership necessary to overturn the alien regime as the Maccabeans had done, not only explains Jesus' anxiety to avoid the use of the word Messiah, but also accounts for the hostility of the secular authorities. It also explains why on this occasion Jesus removed his disciples from the danger of political contagion or official misunderstanding, and went off by himself to strengthen his purpose by prayer (6: 45–46).

It is in this setting that Mark records the second incident where Jesus calms a storm (6: 47–51). As in all the so-called nature miracles, it is misguided effort to look for some rationalisation, such as that Jesus was walking in the water by the shore, or that there was a shelf of rock near the surface of the lake. Mark records the story as it came to him and we cannot hope to penetrate behind it.

Clearly the narrative, like that of the stilling of the storm (4: 36–41), has a double motif. It teaches that Jesus showed himself by his power over nature to be the Messiah. He exercised the functions of YHWH (*Ps.* 107: 23–30), but the disciples were too dull-witted to see this, just as they had failed to understand the significance of the feeding of the multitude (6: 52). There is the further point, as in the other storm-stilling, that in time of darkest crisis ("the fourth watch" =3 a.m.) when men's hearts fail them for fear, as did those of Mark's readers in Rome at the very time when this gospel was written, Christ comes to his people and says "It is I: be not afraid". Had not Isaiah said that "the wicked are like the troubled sea" (*Isa.* 57: 20)? The chapter ends with a general summary of a vast ministry of healing throughout the whole district. Crowds of sick folk clamoured even to be allowed to touch Jesus' clothes and all who touched him were cured (6: 53–56).

"*Thou art the Christ*"
(7: 1 – 8: 29)

ONE OF THE great problems in the early Church was the question as to how far Christianity should detach itself from its Jewish origins. The first Christians were Jews, and even when the Church had spread its net to include Gentiles, the strict Jewish-Christian element tended to insist that the new Israel should incorporate not only the substance of Old Testament faith, but also the details of Old Testament practice. We shall see in the book of *Acts* (e.g. *Acts* 15) and in St. Paul's letters (e.g. *Rom.* 14), how the missionaries had to grapple with this problem and decide how far the peculiar obligations of Judaism—such as circumcision, ceremonial purity, dietary regulations and the like— were binding also for Gentile Christians, who knew nothing of the Palestinian background of the Gospel.

Thus it was of importance to have Jesus' attitude set out and this is what Mark now records (7:1– 23). As always, our Lord states the principle and leaves his followers to decide on the particular.

Some of the strictest members of the Pharisaic party, apparently again deputed by higher authority in Jerusalem to make trouble, accuse the disciples of failing to perform the elaborate ritual ablutions, which the ultra-orthodox practised, to decontaminate themselves before eating after having been jostled by "publicans and sinners". These elaborate precautions—"the tradition of the elders" (7: 3)—were not enjoined by the Law of Moses, but had been developed by the rabbis in post-exilic Judaism.

Jesus denounces their charge as hypocrisy, and taking the fifth commandment as his text, shows how the "tradition of the elders", far from bringing out the inner meaning of the Law, in fact vitiates it. The obligation under the Law to provide for parents could be evaded by the pious dedication of capital or income to religious purposes, as a gift to the Temple (*corban*), without actually parting with the money. Our Lord points out that Judaism allowed a man to enjoy the reputation of holiness while failing in a fundamentally religious duty to his parents.

Jesus goes further than this, however, and criticises the Law itself. For even without the addition of traditional rabbinical interpretation, Jewish law insisted on ceremonial purity (*Lev.* 11: 4–7). Our Lord challenges this radically, and abrogates the Law on this point, when he insists that it is not what a man touches or eats that defiles him, but the evil things that he contrives in his own sinful heart. And what a list they are ! (7: 21– 23).

Outside Herod's territory now, perhaps because of the tetrarch's hostility, Jesus has an encounter with a Phoenician woman from Syria, and therefore a Gentile (7: 24–30). The story of the cure of her mentally defective daughter, who was not herself present, would be important for the missionary Church in that this is a sacrament of the saving power of Christ even for Gentiles who never saw him in the flesh.

Jesus' mission was primarily to the Jews, to Israel, the children of the promises, but when the Church cast its net outside Jewry it was not acting out of harmony with Jesus' intention. Already in the case of the Gadarene demoniac, fairly certainly a Gentile, we have seen him not only cured but commissioned to tell his neighbours the Good News about God (5: 19). Shortly, we shall read of the sacramental feeding of the Gentiles (8: 1–9) and here, sandwiched between them, is yet another indication that our Lord's horizon was not limited by the bounds of race and creed.

In the words Jesus addresses to the woman in the story, therefore, we must not be misled by the apparently brusque dismissal of the Gentiles as "dogs", into thinking that our Lord so regarded them. The Greek word used is an affectionate diminutive, "puppies", which suggests that his remark was whimsical and friendly. The woman's natural wit finds a ready reply in the same vein, but it is hardly likely that Mark thought of the cure of her daughter as a reward for having a quick tongue. It is rather the faith and persistence of the mother that Jesus commends, as well as her recognition of the role of Israel *vis-à-vis* the rest of the world.

Still on the far side of Jordan, among the Greek settlements of Decapolis, a deaf stammerer is healed (7: 31–37). In the impressive word of healing, "be opened", one of the few actual Aramaic words of Jesus uniquely preserved in this gospel, doubtless due to the influence of Peter, may we not hear our Lord's prayer that the ears of the Gentile world should likewise be opened to the Gospel? For Mark, and for all who had been brought up on the Old Testament scriptures, this unstopping of the ears of the deaf and the opening of the eyes of the blind (cf. 8: 22–25) was as much a sign of the presence of the Messiah as the feeding of the multitude and the calming of the storm (*Isa.* 29: 18; 32: 3; 35: 5.) In this particular context it is the disciples, so far deaf and blind to the identity of Jesus, who are gradually having their ears and eyes opened.

So we come to the second eucharistic occasion in the feeding story of 8: 1–9. The Gentile locality, the repetition of the Gentile number seven (cf. *Acts* 6), the fact that the word used for "basket" is the normal Greek word, whereas the "basket" in the previous story is a peculiarly Jewish word, all suggest that this is the sequel and complement to the Galilean Lord's Supper, and means that the Bread of Heaven is offered to Jews and Gentiles alike.

Mark inserts at this point, by way of contrast with the faith of the Gentiles, a demand from the

Pharisees that Jesus would give some visible and incontrovertible proof that he was Messiah, nothing less would satisfy them that he had the right to set aside the Law (8: 10–12). This adds point to the next few verses which all lead up—as indeed the whole narrative so far has done—to Peter's confession in 8: 29. The Messiah comes unto his own and his own receive him not. Mark and his Roman readers, and we ourselves, looking at the narrative from this side of the Resurrection, know the end of the story before we reach it. The disciples, however, have to be shown groping their way towards a recognition of who Jesus was. No dramatic divine accolade will be given, they must reach their conclusion unaided by heavenly portents.

So in Mark's build-up of the denouement, Jesus upbraids them for their failure to understand the messianic significance of the feeding of the two multitudes (8: 13–21). Like the blind man in the story that follows, their enlightenment was gradual, and this is no doubt why Mark chooses to tell here of the man who passed from blindness to seeing "men as trees, walking" before seeing everything "clearly" (8: 22–26).

The time has now come, and this is the turning point in Mark's gospel, for Jesus to put the all-important question to his followers. These are the men who have been with him day and night, in public and in private. To them he has spoken of mysteries as yet beyond their understanding—and there are harder sayings yet to come—but they have seen his power over

men and his mastery over evil. Who then is this Jesus? It was on the way to Caesarea Philippi that they gave him, in response to his question, the popular estimate of his calibre: John the Baptist come back to life, or a new Elijah sent to herald the Messiah, or a prophet, perhaps the expected "prophet like unto Moses" (*Deut.* 18: 15, 18).

All of these identifications went some way towards giving Jesus a unique status in the eyes not of unbalanced demoniacs or enthusiastic acclaimers of a wonder-worker, but of sober citizens competent to judge. It was left to Peter, with intuitive perception, to give the answer for which Jesus had been waiting: "You are the Messiah" (8: 27–29). Matthew's gospel supplies for us the profound reaction of Jesus to this confession (*Matt.* 16: 13–20).

It is perhaps all too easy for us to treat these words as of minor importance, compared with the more developed estimates of Jesus later in the New Testament, but this is the basis of them all. Son of God, Second Adam, Logos, and the various other ways in which later reflection on the person of Christ after the Resurrection expressed the significance of Jesus, rest in the last resort upon the recognition of these hard-headed fishermen that this rabbi from Nazareth was indeed the one for whom Israel had waited, of whom prophet and psalmist had spoken.

This contemporary assessment of Jesus is of supreme historical value, for it meant that already before the Resurrection the disciples of Jesus ranked him as greater than Abraham, Moses, David or any other Old Testament patriarch, king or prophet. As Messiah he had a unique status—God's accredited representative, his anointed emissary, who was to judge mankind, deliver his people, and bring the world to God. For a religious Jew, who knew that Jesus was neither a militant anti-Roman nor an apocalyptic figure dropped from the clouds, to call Jesus "Messiah" was to put him in a category above humankind, a man among men who was in some strange way akin to God.

Foretaste of Glory
(8: 30 – 9: 8)

CHARACTERISTICALLY, however, Jesus does not wish the title Messiah to be used publicly (8: 30). He chooses rather to call himself Son of Man, that enigmatic title taken from *Daniel* 7: 13–27 and used there of the head of the "people of the saints of the Most High", the redeemed community. Jesus applies this to himself and to the new Israel that he has founded, the "kingdom which shall not be destroyed". But as the supernatural leader of the community of the Israel of God, the Son of Man knows that the way to that future glory is through suffering and death.

It is the path of the Servant of YHWH of *Isa.* 53 that the Messiah chooses, as the only way to bring the world back to God. In these two Old Testament passages—*Daniel* 7 and *Isaiah* 53—Jesus finds the true significance of his messianic vocation. He has

elicited Peter's recognition of him as the Messiah, only to show the disciples what he conceives Messiah's role to be. The shadow of the Cross fell upon the Jordan already at his Baptism (see pp. 355–356).

It is perhaps unlikely that Jesus himself uttered a prediction of his death as precisely as here (8: 31) and elsewhere in the gospel. Suffering, death and beyond death victory—some such conviction Jesus undoubtedly had and the rest of the gospel story confirms it. But our Lord was not given to programmatic prediction in other matters, and it is more probable that the exact description given here of what was to happen is the witness of the Church to the Passion and Resurrection after they had happened.

Such a role as Jesus outlined for the Messiah was, however, far from the mind of Peter and the disciples. This was not their idea of how the Master should come into his own, and the vehemence of Jesus' stern rebuke shows how hard it was for our Lord himself to accept what he knew to be the will of God. Peter's voice was the same voice as Jesus had heard and resisted on the mountain of temptation (see p. 356). This was once more the devil-inspired attraction of short cuts to success (8: 32–33).

From now on we may note an increasing tension in the narrative. Jesus' demands on his followers become more radical. He offers them death on a cross as the reward of discipleship, but beyond that death lies the only life worth having. Self-giving is the gateway to the life that God meant us to have: self-sacrifice is the key to the Kingdom (8: 34–37). Jesus ends with a solemn warning against disloyalty (8: 38), and assures his bewildered and by this time doubtless frightened followers of the speedy fulfilment of his triumph. The Cross is but the prelude to the powerful proof in the Resurrection and Pentecost that God's reign has indeed begun (9: 1).

To confirm this word of the Lord the inner circle of disciples, Peter, James and John, are granted a vision of the glorified Messiah (9: 2–8). In the narrative Jesus is transfigured, Moses and Elijah appear, a cloud overshadows the scene and a heavenly voice is heard. Was this a hallucination, a misplaced story of a post-Resurrection appearance, or an actual event expressed in the only possible way open to devout Jews? Surely this last is the only explanation that does justice to the narrative.

The incredulous disciples have just been told that their Messiah is prepared to die like a criminal on a cross, an idea not only repellent but unheard of in Old Testament prophecy. Something more than words must convince them that beyond this death lies victory. So the chosen disciples, who will be the spearhead of mission after Calvary, have to be given a foretaste of the glory of the Risen Lord. St. Luke, who gives a fuller account than St. Mark (*Luke* 9: 28–36), seems to suggest that what the disciples experienced was a vision, and significantly describes it as concerning Jesus' "Exodus" (A.V. "Decease": *Luke* 9: 31).

As Moses, who was instrumental under God in delivering his people from death to life in the first Exodus, reflected the glory of YHWH on Mt. Sinai (Ex. 34: 29), so the new Moses is transfigured on a "high mountain" before the greater Exodus—the deliverance of the whole world by his Death and Resurrection. The cloud representing the glory of God (*Ex.* 19: 16), the voice from heaven (*Ex.* 19: 19), the tabernacle in which the Lord keeps covenant with his people (Ex. 33: 9), all combine to relate this scene to the greatest moment of Israel's history. Jesus is confirmed as God's Messiah, his future exaltation is foreshadowed, and the old dispensation of the Law and the Prophets, represented by Moses and Elijah, disappears leaving Christ alone and supreme.

Steadfastly Towards Jerusalem

(9: 9 – 10: 52)

LITTLE WONDER that simple men found this far beyond their understanding at this stage. A crucified and risen Messiah was no part of Old Testament expectation. It was only when the Resurrection happened that the injunction of Jesus to say nothing of this experience, like so many more of his cryptic utterances, began to make sense. Even their plain question as to why Elijah had not preceded the Messiah, as scripture foretold (*Mal.* 4: 4–6), received an enigmatic answer. Elijah had indeed come in the person of John the Baptist, and the ill-famed Herodias had been more successful in getting rid of him than Jezebel had been in the case of Elijah (*I Kings* 19: 1–2) (9: 9–13).

From the divine vision of the mountain of the Transfiguration, the Bible characteristically plunges us into the heart-breaking world of pain and suffering. Jesus cures an epileptic boy whose father utters words that every Christian must make his own: "Lord, I believe; help thou mine unbelief" (9: 14–29). Now Jesus concentrates on the instruction of his disciples. He forsakes the crowds and bends all his energies to building up in faith and understanding the Twelve who are to be the foundation members of the new people of God (9: 30).

Much of his teaching at this time centred on his approaching Passion (9: 31–32), but there were other lessons that the disciples found equally hard to accept, such as that true greatness for the follower of Christ means to be foremost in service; that charity given to the humblest member of the Christian family is given to God himself; that Christian work is work for Christ, whether it is done under the auspices of the Church or not; that self-denial is of the essence of the Christian life (9: 33–50).

By a devious route, but always with Jerusalem as the goal, Jesus moves towards the climax of his ministry on earth. This tenth chapter of Mark is full of instruction of supreme importance for the Christian life. Once again Jesus abrogates the Law of Moses, this time on the question of divorce, which was permissible in accordance with *Deut.* 24: 1–4. He penetrates behind this provision of the Law to the basic purpose of marriage, which was a more fundamental law, as the life-long companionship of one man with one woman. Contrary to Jewish practice this makes the husband's obligation to preserve the sanctity of the union as binding as the wife's, an obligation which was inherent in God's plan of creation (*Gen.* 1: 27; 2: 24).

With his characteristic love and tenderness towards little children, Jesus, as well as giving them his blessing, when the disciples would have sent them away in a well-meant desire to shield the Master from their high-spirited attentions, uses a child as a telling illustration of the simple trustfulness which is the foundation of the right relationship to God (10: 1–16).

A rich young man who lived an exemplary life and was rather proud of it, is touched on his one weak spot, his love of money, and forgoes the chance of becoming a disciple. Jesus uses him as an example of the danger of having too much wealth. The reward of Christian service is not success as the world reckons it, but the man who ranks Christ and his Church as his first loyalty finds in the happiness of this greater family, despite all discouragement, a foretaste of the fulness of the life to come (10: 17–31).

There is an illuminating glimpse in 10: 32 of the Master striding purposefully ahead on the way to Jerusalem, with the disciples hanging back timid and bewildered. Once more Christ predicts his coming Passion. How little two at least of the disciples understood of the nature of the Kingdom is indicated by their request for places of privilege within it. Jesus warns them that the way to his throne is one of bitter suffering. They in their time will share it with him, but the hierarchy of the Kingdom is in the hands of God, and is based on the dignity of service. In a memorable saying Jesus puts himself in the forefront as the type and pattern, the Son of Man who makes himself a servant, that all the sons of men may become sons of God (10: 32–45).

Leaving Jericho on the last lap of the journey, Jesus accepts the messianic title, Son of David, in healing Bartimaeus, a blind beggar, but he approaches the city of David with a profoundly different conception of his task from what Bartimaeus or any of the bystanders expected. Jesus comes to the holy city, the centre of the religious life of the people of God, the home of the centuries old tradition of priest and prophet, to take issue in the name of God with the corruption and travesty of Old Testament faith and morality for which Sadducee and Pharisee were jointly responsible, and which kept ordinary folk out of the Kingdom and prevented them from seeing the light of the Gospel (10: 46–52).

Messiah Acts

(11: 1–26)

WHEN WE REACH chapter eleven of Mark's gospel, we have the impression that from this point until almost the end of the book we are given a chronological account of the events of the last week—Passion Week—of our Lord's earthly ministry. From the messianic entry into Jerusalem on what we call Palm Sunday (11: 1–11), to the scene at the sepulchre on what we call Easter Day (16: 1–8), the narrative moves smoothly onward, unlike the sometimes disjointed and abrupt character of Mark's account up to this point.

The fact is that it is difficult on the face of it to establish the length of Jesus' ministry on the basis of Mark's information. He tends to give an impressionistic rather than a strictly chronological record, and if we ignore evidence in the other gospels we might well think that the total length of the ministry of Jesus after his Baptism lasted only a few months. If, however, we turn to St. John's gospel, not only does the ministry of Jesus appear to last from two to three years, but there is reference both to an early period after Jesus' Baptism when he was active in Judaea, and a period at the end when he was again longer in the neighbourhood of Jerusalem and in the territory of Judaea and Transjordan than Mark would seem to suggest.

On the other hand, Mark may well have telescoped his narrative. In 10: 1 there is the suggestion of a longish spell of teaching in Judaea and Transjordan, and there is good reason to think that the events recorded from 11: 1 – 16: 8 actually took longer than a week. Perhaps therefore we ought to reckon with a period of as much as six months between Jesus' departure from Galilee and the Crucifixion, with as much as half of that time spent in and around Jerusalem. That would still leave us, however, with a final short space of time, John says six days (*John* 12: 1), between the Triumphal Entry into Jerusalem and the passover. We may therefore follow Mark's account as covering roughly this last week.

Within these few days Jesus performs three symbolic acts of deepest significance. All of them look back to the Old Testament and all of them show our Lord, as always, adapting the Old Testament to himself and not slavishly tying himself to its literal fulfilment. We have seen already how he has freely reinterpreted Old Testament ideas in his conception of his vocation as Son of Man and Servant of YHWH, and in his identification of the mission of John the Baptist with the promise of the return of Elijah.

The time is now past for concealment of his messianic title. Whatever Jesus' own interpretation of the meaning of Messiah may be, it is as Messiah that he comes to Jerusalem for the final encounter with the kingdom of Satan. Accordingly, having made previous arrangements (11 : 4), our Lord enacts his first messianic symbol by entering Jerusalem seated on the back of a donkey. This, as Zechariah had depicted (*Zech.* 9: 9), was the means by which Messiah when he came would enter Zion, not as a conqueror upon a warhorse but as the prince of peace upon a humble beast of burden. The crowd— perhaps pilgrims for the passover mingling with Jesus' followers— hail him as the new David, crying: Hosanna!—"God save Israel now!" (11 : 1–10).

According to Mark, on this first day Jesus merely entered the Temple, looked round it and returned to Bethany for the night

(11: 11). St. John gives us more detail of the home of Martha, Mary and Lazarus in this little village outside Jerusalem, where Jesus lodged during Passion Week (*John* 12: 1–11), and St. Luke not only gives a fuller account of the Palm Sunday procession but also claims that Jesus went straight to the Temple and threw out the hucksters, an event which Mark reserves for the following day (*Luke* 19: 29–46).

This is the second act of prophetic symbolism in these last days (11 : 15–18), and we may imagine that Luke is right in locating the Cleansing of the Temple on Palm Sunday for it is the sequel to the Triumphal Entry. Herod's Temple, still in process of reconstruction in Jesus' time (cf. 13 : 1), was built on a system of courtyards centring on the tabernacle containing the Holy of Holies. The courts of the priests, the laymen and the women were sacrosanct to Israelites. But by a splendid piece of symbolism, around them was an outer courtyard reserved for Gentiles. The way to the inner courts was barred on pain of death to any Gentile, but it was open to every Gentile to pass the barrier by becoming a Jew. The message was plain, that only through Israel could the Gentiles approach the Presence of God in his appointed holy place, and that God intended them to do so.

In order, however, to ensure that only unblemished birds and animals were offered in sacrifice, and to make certain that only ritually clean Temple coinage was offered in payment of the half-shekel Temple tax, which every Jew had to pay annually, traders' stalls and money exchanges had been permitted in the court of the Gentiles, with considerable profit to Temple revenues. By overturning these booths in indignation and disgust, Jesus was, as Messiah, making a frontal attack on the state religion as Malachi had proclaimed the Lord would do (*Mal.* 3 : 1–3).

The Temple was intended to be a house of prayer for "all nations" (*Isa.* 56 : 7). By permitting this sordid traffic for selfish motives, and making it into Jeremiah's "den of thieves" (*Jer.* 7 : 11), the ecclesiastical authorities were literally and symbolically preventing the Gentiles from approaching God. This action of Jesus was sufficient to rouse the Sadducees ("chief priests"), and bring them into an unholy alliance with the Pharisees against him.

Mark prefaces this account of the Cleansing of the Temple with an action of Jesus on the way in from Bethany on the Monday, of which he records the sequel on the following day (11 : 12–14, 20–21). Jesus is represented as cursing a fig tree which then withers overnight. St. Luke has probably a better version of the origin of this story in a parable spoken by Jesus (*Luke* 13 : 6–9). It is not in character for our Lord to put a curse on an actual tree, but it would be a highly apposite action if the fig tree were to be taken to represent Israel. The Old Testament uses the symbol of both the vine and the fig tree in this connection, and the next chapter begins with a parable of Israel as a vineyard.

The curse on the barren fig-tree is the curse of the Messiah on an Israel barren of the fruit of faith and good works that she should have borne. She was cursed although it was not the season for figs (11 : 13), because God expected her in view of her favoured history to be in advance of the rest of the world in piety and morality, instead of which all she produced was a show of leaves—the semblance of religion without its fruits. It was probably with the same thought in mind that Jesus, having foretold the doom of Israel, included also Mt. Zion and its Temple, a saying which then in course of transmission may have been transformed into a reference to the faith that can remove mountains (11 : 23), and associated with further teaching about true and false prayer (vv. 24–26).

By What Authority?

(11 : 27 – 12 : 44)

MARK NOW records the first of a series of test questions, by which the ecclesiastics try to trap Jesus into making an overt verbal claim to be the Messiah, in order to justify his high-handed action in the Temple. Although in the latter stages of his ministry he has made this claim by implication, it is not until his trial (14 : 61–62) that he openly affirms it. Here he matches a priestly attempt to induce him to claim the authority of God—whereupon they would have accused him of blasphemy—by claiming no less authority than John the Baptist, and leaving them nonplussed, for had not John described himself as merely the harbinger of Jesus? (11 : 27–33).

It is sometimes felt that in St. John's gospel we come face to face with a different Jesus from the Jesus of the synoptic gospels, above all that Jesus speaks there of his own status and of his relationship to God in a way that suggests the pious imagination of a later date, and not the historical utterances of our Lord. But here in Mark's gospel, bearing every imprint of an authentic parable of Jesus, is a claim as far-reaching as anything in the fourth gospel, the allegory of the vineyard (12: 1–12).

With Isaiah's picture in mind of Israel as a vineyard which had produced sour berries instead of the expected good grapes (*Isa.* 5:1–7), our Lord vividly sketches in story form the tragic history of Israel's failure. Given every chance, she had not only refused to make a fitting response to God's loving care, but had killed or maltreated the messengers, whom God had sent throughout her chequered existence as his people, to recall her to his service.

In the end, the owner of the vineyard sends his son—and there was no doubt in the minds of Jesus' audience whom he meant (cf. 12: 12)—but the Son is even more unwelcome than the prophets, and meets his death at the hands of the wicked husbandmen. The judgment of God will not allow this to go unpunished, and old Israel must now give way to others—the new people of God—who will be more worthy tenants of the Lord's vineyard. As for the Son who is cast out of the vineyard, his vindication will come when God, in the psalmist's words (*Ps.* 118: 22), makes the stone which the builders rejected the keystone of the Kingdom.

On a second occasion, an attempt is made to involve Jesus in a capital offence. With patent insincerity, representatives of church and state seek to trap him into a treasonable assertion that to pay the Roman poll-tax was an offence against God. If, on the other hand, Jesus admitted the right of the occupying power to extort tribute, he would forfeit the support of every patriotic Jew.

Once more, however, our Lord was more than a match for his enemies. Sending for a denarius, the silver "penny" which would not normally be allowed within the Temple precincts, and which bore at this time the image of the emperor Tiberius with the words "Divo Tiberio", "to the divine Tiberius", he dismissed the transparent trick-question with words to this effect: If the coin is Caesar's let him have it; but worship, and all that that implies, must be rendered to God who alone is divine. Our Lord endorses lawful obedience to the state, but sets a limit of obedience beyond which the religious conscience must refuse to go. The state must never assume the authority of God (12: 14–17).

Again in a third attempt to discredit Jesus, representatives of the Sadducean party, which accepted no doctrine that did not bear the stamp of ancient authority, and therefore did not hold with any belief in a resurrection of the dead —a fairly new idea seldom mooted in the Old Testament—put to him a question reminiscent of the scholastic hair-splitting of the medieval Church. If there is a resurrection, what happens to a woman who has outlived seven husbands? (*Deut.* 25: 5-6). Whose wife will she be in the life beyond?

Jesus' reply to this is twofold. Firstly, we cannot apply earthly standards to life in a different dimension. Secondly, the Pharisees, who believe in resurrection, are more in accordance with scripture than the Sadducees. Since the Bible in the time of Moses speaks of God as the God of Abraham, Isaac and Jacob (*Ex.* 3: 6), we are to understand that these saints of Israel are not dead but alive with God. If they had established the right relationship with God on earth an accident like physical death could not interrupt it (12: 18-27).

The fourth test question is put by a more sympathetic inquirer, who may have been genuinely perplexed. The problem for a godly Jew in Jesus' day was the multiplicity of laws which Judaism tended to place on the same level, so that sabbath observance came to be rated as equally important with neighbourly charity. There were said to be 613 commandments, and it is amid this baffling profusion that the scribe in the narrative asks for guidance. Jesus singles out two injunctions from the whole corpus of the Law (*Deut.* 6: 5; *Lev.* 19: 18), and combines them in one imperishable summary of the whole Law of God: to love God with one's whole being and to love one's neighbour as oneself. The lawyer, who obviously subscribes to this singling out of priorities, is assured that he is not far from the Kingdom (12: 28-34).

We have seen already (see pp. 178-

179) how little attention our Lord or, following him, the New Testament writers, pay to the commonly held association of David with the Messiah. In the popular mind what Israel needed and what God would send was a Messiah of the type of David, who would restore something of the lost glory of the past, and rescue God's people from under the heel of the oppressive Gentile overlord. Jesus, in this passage (12: 35-37), acknowledges Davidic descent, but shows from scripture itself that if David in the psalms called the Messiah his "Lord" (*Ps.* 110: 1) the Messiah must be more than a new David.

In an implicit contrast between the common people who "heard him gladly" (12: 37), and the ecclesiastical lawyers who had been trying to incriminate him, Jesus trenchantly condemned their vanity and ostentatious religiosity. He focuses attention on the value in the sight of God of genuine devotion and charity, in the graphic and moving incident of the widow's mites. The announcement by the well-to-do of large contributions to Temple funds—made publicly, in Jewish practice—is shown up for what it is worth by the generosity of the poor woman who might well have retained even one mite but instead gave everything to God (12: 38-44).

Watch and Pray

(13: 1-37)

THE THIRTEENTH chapter of *Mark* is very difficult. It has been quoted as proof that Jesus was a deluded prophet who expected the world to come to an end, and who further expected to return shortly after his death as a triumphant Messiah descending from the skies. It has, on the other hand, also been dismissed as Jewish apocalyptic set in a Christian framework, not the words of Jesus but the product of the Christian mission in time of persecution—e.g. A.D. 64—when such apocalyptic writing traditionally would tend to appear.

There is, however, no evidence here or elsewhere in the gospels that Jesus was a self-deluded enthusiast, who spoke or thought of an immediate Second Advent as compensation for the failure of his earthly mission. Nor on the other hand can we divorce Jesus from the Jewish background, including apocalyptic thought, from which he sprang, and it would be odd if the early Christians, who undoubtedly expected the Lord to return in their lifetime, had had no "word of the Lord" to encourage them in this belief.

It was of the very nature of apocalyptic thinking, as we have noticed, to see in the catastrophes of history portents and presages of the Judgment to come. It is equally impossible for human beings to think in any other terms than those of time and space. Consequently the apocalyptists who read the "signs of the times", and saw them as reflections of the eternal conflict between good and evil, were bound because of their conviction of the justice and goodness of God to think of a speedy solution of the conflict.

But although they thought and wrote in terms of an immediate end of the world, and an immediate intervention of God in judgment, behind the time-conditioned nature of their thinking was the deeper realisation that there is order and purpose in the things that happen, however incomprehensible they may seem; that God must be seen in action in the events of history, that evil cannot go unpunished, and that in the end somehow God's good purpose must triumph. Men and nations stand under the judgment of God, and they must live and work as if at any moment that sword of judgment might fall upon them.

This is the basic conviction of Christian as well as of Jewish apocalyptic thinking, and however difficult it may be for us to enter into the mind of the Bible in this matter it is an element in the New Testament with which we must reckon. In this chapter of Mark's gospel, we simply cannot say how far it reproduces authentic words of Jesus, how far it echoes conventional Jewish thinking, or how far it reflects the thought and meets the situation of a missionary Church in dire need of consolation. All three strands appear to be involved, and the best we can do is to try to sift from this chapter what seems most consonant with our Lord's teaching in other places.

Taking the Temple as his starting point, Jesus predicts its destruction (13: 2), and prophesies the troubles that will afflict the Church and the world before the end of history (13: 3–13). The impending conflict between the Jews and the Roman empire, which ended with the destruction of Jerusalem, and which must have been as obvious to our Lord as the fall of Samaria and

Jerusalem were to the Old Testament prophets, is seen as the reflection of an eternal conflict and a foretaste of the ultimate dissolution of the world when the Son of Man will come in judgment (13: 14–27).

The judgment on Jerusalem will fall within the generation (13: 30) –it did indeed happen within forty years of the Crucifixion—but the end of the world and the Last Judgment of all will come when God. wills it and not before. Not even the Son knows when it will be (13: 32), and "the gospel must first be published among all nations" (13: 10). But the life of a disciple of Christ means so to live in readiness for the Master's return at the consummation of human history, that he will find his people alert and ready to give an account of their stewardship with a good conscience (13: 32–37).

The language is figurative and not literal, imaginative and not programmatic. Old Testament ideas, often in direct quotation, conventional eschatology, and enigmatic allusions combine to make this strange chapter complex and puzzling. But for us its general message is plain. Jesus joins the prophets in foreseeing no rose-strewn path for the people of God. The Church will never have an easy passage. Good and evil will remain in conflict until the end of time, and there will be many an occasion when evil disguises itself as good, there will be many a false prophet, many a false Christ.

Yet the Church must carry out its task to proclaim the Gospel to the world, and its members, despite all discouragements, must endure in faith to the end. But there will be an end, and it will be the end that God has purposed, when Christ reigns supreme as Lord of all. The power of his Holy Spirit within the Church which strengthens its life and its people's witness, is the pledge that he will come again in power and great glory, in judgment but also in mercy. Meantime the Christian man goes calmly on with his job but lives as if each day may be his last.

Arrest and Trial of Jesus
(14: 1–72)

MARK REVERTS now, after the ominous discourse of chapter thirteen, to the day to day account of Passion Week. We have seen that there is reason to believe that Mark has compressed the record of Jesus' ministry in and around Jerusalem, and it is also probable that he has done likewise in his narrative of the Arrest and Trial of Jesus. It is likely that the events described between 14: 1, generally taken to be Wednesday of Holy Week, and 15: 1, the Friday of the Crucifixion, did in fact take longer.

Mark gives the impression that the Last Supper was held on the Thursday evening as a passover meal and that the Arrest, Trial and Crucifixion of Jesus were rushed through between then and Friday evening. St. John's gospel, on the other hand, insists that the Last Supper was held before the passover (cf. John 18: 28), and recent evidence would seem to suggest that the Jewish passover was celebrated by different religious bodies on different days, in which case St. John's gospel may be right in encouraging us to think of a longer period of time—perhaps a day or two—between the Last Supper and the regular passover.

Following Mark's chronology, which is, however, not altogether consistent, the stage is set on Wednesday of Holy Week for the arrest of Jesus, when Sadducees and Pharisees combine to contrive his death (14: 1). It was essential that as little public interest as possible should be aroused because, whatever Jesus thought of his messianic role, the authorities were undoubtedly scared of a political uprising (14: 2). The well-known incident of the woman with the alabaster jar of costly ointment takes place in the evening at Bethany (14: 3–9). It is possible that the woman thought of her gesture as a tribute to the King-Messiah, but Jesus accepts it not as a royal anointing, but as the anointing of his body for burial.

It may have been this final rejection of any political action that drove Judas Iscariot to renounce his allegiance and betray his Master. If Jesus was determined to die, this was not what Judas had bargained for, and prudence dictated a speedy withdrawal of his support from the losing side. His usefulness to the authorities was that he knew something of Jesus' plans and habits, and could guarantee to take them to where he could be apprehended without attracting attention (14: 10–11).

In preparation for the approaching passover, and with a pre-arranged procedure to ensure the utmost secrecy, Jesus set the stage for the third significant messianic action since he entered Jerusalem on Palm Sunday (14: 12–16).

Whether it was an actual passover celebration that took place on this Thursday evening, it had all the significance of a passover and more (14: 17–26). Tradition has always associated the place of this Last Supper with the upper room in the house of Mary, the mother of Mark, which later became the first centre of the Christian community in Jerusalem (*Acts* 12: 12).

The tragedy of betrayal is underlined, and although our Lord sees his impending death as the purpose of God for him, Judas' dastardly action is none the less condemned as despicable. Then in the course of the meal, Jesus breaks bread as the symbol of his body about to be broken, and offers the wine of his blood about to be shed. This offering of himself which he is about to make is to be the way to a new relationship with God, the New Covenant or Testament of which Jeremiah had spoken (*Jer.* 31: 31–34).

From the time of the Exodus, the passover had been celebrated as a vivid reminder of God's deliverance of his people. Now again at passover-tide, the Messiah proclaims a greater deliverance not of the Jews only but of all mankind. The Son of Man offers himself as the Passover sacrifice for the sins of men; the shedding of his blood as in the old covenant (*Ex.* 24: 4–8) of the first Exodus (see pp. 101–102), liberates his Risen Life which brings God to man and man to God. In that upper room the Servant of God enacts the giving of himself for the forgiveness of many (10: 45), and foretells his Presence with his people at the messianic banquet of the Eucharist, when they partake of his body and blood in remembrance of him.

Departing from his previous practice earlier in the week, our Lord takes his disciples after the Last Supper across the Kidron valley to the Mount of Olives. Quoting Zechariah's saying about the smiting of the shepherd and the scattering of the sheep (*Zech.* 13: 7), he reassures them with the promise of the Resurrection. Peter and the rest claim that whatever happens they will not desert him (14: 26-31).

The awful horror of what our sins mean to God is nowhere in the whole Passion narrative more apparent than in the scene in the garden of Gethsemane at the foot of the Mount of Olives (14: 32-42). While the disciples drift into uneasy sleep, our Lord wrestles in prayer not merely with the agonising torture of scourging and death by crucifixion, but with the heartbreaking realisation of the malevolence and bigotry by which Godfearing men were plotting his end, the fickleness of the ordinary crowd who would acquiesce in his destruction as readily as they had acclaimed him, and the appalling cowardice of even his closest followers—one of them indeed having betrayed him.

The end of his lonely Agony comes bringing a tranquillity which accompanies him through his Arrest and Trial to the Cross. His plea that he might be spared the cup of bitterness (cf. 10: 38) is not granted. Instead he is given power to say: Not my will but thy will be done. As the sound of approaching footsteps is heard in the garden he rouses the exhausted disciples.

The traitor's kiss of recognition is given in the flickering light of the torches of the Temple police. Jesus offers no resistance and is led away captive, completely abandoned by his terrified followers (14: 43-50).

There would seem to be no possible relevance in Mark's comment on the young man who fled naked from the scene, unless this is a personal note by the author of the gospel that he himself was there (14: 51-52). Is it not more than likely that young John Mark, having seen Jesus leave his mother's house with the disciples after the Last Supper, followed them out of curiosity and was therefore a firsthand witness of the scene?

Jesus is taken, presumably before midnight, to the high priest's house where there seems to have been a first informal Trial. Despite the efforts of the ecclesiastics, they could not find witnesses to produce evidence which would give a semblance of judicial sanction to their determination to have Jesus put to death (14: 53-59). The evidence which they were seeking came from our Lord himself, who now for the first time openly claimed to be the Messiah, and added words from the Son of Man prophecy in *Daniel* 7: 13, which were an unambiguous assertion of his Resurrection and Exaltation.

The high priest—either Caiaphas or Annas, his father-in-law and predecessor in the office (*John* 18: 13-24)—reacted with the conventional signs of horror at this blasphemy, and Jesus was condemned to death (*Lev.* 24: 16). There was no alternative possible: either Jesus was the Messiah, in which case they must submit to his authority, or he was a mad impostor who must be despatched for the sake of peace and prudence (14: 60–64).

Jesus has to submit to horseplay from the bystanders, while in the courtyard below Peter, who had plucked up enough courage to follow at a distance, is vehemently denying that he had ever even heard of Jesus (14: 65–72). A formal trial is held at day-break, by which time the Sanhedrin, the supreme ecclesiastical court, had had time to be summoned and could legally pass judgment. But the death penalty could only be pronounced by the Roman procurator (15: 1).

The Crucifixion
(15: 1–47)

PONTIUS PILATE, representing the Roman government in Judaea, was in Jerusalem for the passover. Normally his official residence was in Caesarea on the coast, but at the religious festivals the procurator went up to Jerusalem, to be in readiness to control any nationalist uprising that might be occasioned on these days when ancient patriotisms were revived. The Roman garrison was quartered in the Tower of Antonia, adjacent to the Temple, and it was here on the Pavement (John 19: 13) before the Praetorium that the final trial of Jesus took place.

Pilate, as a typical Roman official, was not interested in the religious niceties of the case. His concern was with the political aspects of Jesus' claim to be Messiah, and his questioning accordingly emphasised the role of kingship.

He was surprised that Jesus, in pursuance of his acceptance of the role of the Servant (Isa. 53: 7), made no reply to the charges brought against him by the priests.

By ancient custom a prisoner was released at the passover, and Pilate, unwilling to accede to the condemnation of a man who was clearly innocent, offered to release Jesus. Incited by the priests, however, the crowd demanded the release of a notable rebel, Barabbas, and howled for the crucifixion of Jesus. Pilate's own record was such that he could not afford to antagonise the priesthood, much as he hated them, and the sentence of death was passed.

The majesty of Christ is nowhere more evident in the gospel than at his trial. It is not the prisoner who is judged but the venomous ecclesiastics, the fickle crowd and the vacillating procurator. After cruel scourging and a mock coronation in honour of the "mad Messiah", carried out by the Roman soldiers, Jesus is led off to crucifixion (15: 2–20). In his exhausted state, Jesus was unable to bear the heavy burden of the cross-beam, which the criminal had normally to carry to the place of execution, and an African Jewish pilgrim, Simon, whose sons were apparently well known to Mark's readers, was made to carry the cross.

The place of the Crucifixion was then outside the city walls, now, however, within the Church of the Holy Sepulchre, and was called Golgotha or, in Latin, Calvary, the rocky surface being shaped like a skull. A guild of pious women in Jerusalem made it a practice to attend crucifixions, and to offer drugged wine to the criminals to deaden the excruciating agony. Jesus refused to take this. At nine o'clock in the morning our Lord was crucified, with Pilate's impotent thrust at the ecclesiastics inscribed over his head: The King of the Jews.

Two rebels, probably connected with Barabbas, were crucified with him, while the Roman soldiers whiled away the time by gambling for his clothing (15: 21–28). The cross was a low structure, the top being not more than eighteen inches above the heads of the onlookers, so that the mockery of those who passed along the nearby road could be clearly heard by the victim and the crowd. From midday until three o'clock in the afternoon there was "darkness over the whole land". If it was a sirocco, it matched the blackness of the deed (15: 29–33).

At three o'clock Jesus uttered a cry of dereliction: My God, why hast thou forsaken me? If this is taken to be merely the beginning of *Psalm* 22, which then developed into a mood of trust and confidence in God, it reflects also the last word which St. Luke records: Father into thy hands I commend my spirit (*Luke* 23: 46). But surely the cry was a real cry, and the sense of desolation was for a moment at any rate the crowning sorrow of the Passion. This was part of the price of the Incarnation.

The Aramaic words sounded like a call for help from Elijah, supposed in legend to succour people in distress, and a bystander —perhaps a soldier—offered our Lord a sponge soaked in wine to quench his thirst. With a loud cry Jesus died, much sooner than was normally the case at crucifixions, where the sufferer sometimes hung on the cross for days in agony. The Roman guard commander, moved by we know not what, exclaimed more truly than he realised: This was indeed a god-like man. Mark also records that with the death of Jesus the veil of the tabernacle of the Temple was split in two—the barrier that had hitherto kept men out of the Holy of Holies where the Presence of God dwelt was torn asunder (15: 34–39; cf. *Heb.* 10: 19–20).

A number of women who had looked after our Lord's human needs in Galilee, and who had followed him to Jerusalem were present at the Crucifixion. Doubtless from them later came some of the details of the event. Now, on the Friday evening, a member of the Sanhedrin, Joseph of Arimathaea, who was in sympathy with the stand Jesus had taken, secured the body from Pilate, and in the short time available before the sabbath, buried it in one of the rock tombs which abounded in the neighbourhood of Calvary, rolling a heavy cartwheel stone across the mouth of the cavelike sepulchre (15: 40–47).

The Resurrection

(16: 1–8)

THE HASTY deposition and burial had been necessary because of the rigid Jewish regulations for the observance of the sabbath. Three of the women who had been present at the Crucifixion, and who had watched from a distance where the body of Jesus was buried, went on the Sunday morning to perform the last act of homage to the dead by anointing the corpse in accordance with Jewish practice. As they approached the tomb they deliberated as to how they could roll back the heavy stone which sealed the opening.

According to Mark's story they found the stone rolled aside and the body of Jesus no longer there. In its place they encountered an angelic figure (see p. 348), who assured them that the crucified Jesus had risen. They are urged to break this news to Peter and the other disciples, and to prepare them for an encounter with the Risen Lord in Galilee (cf. 14: 28). The women fled from the tomb in terror, "for they were afraid" (16: 1–8).

If there is any point in gospel criticism about which all the experts are agreed, it is that at this point Mark's gospel ends. The rest of the chapter (16: 9–20) is the so-called "Longer Ending" to the gospel, which does not appear in the oldest manuscripts, and which is a second century pastiche of adapted excerpts from *Matthew*, *Luke* and *Acts*. A conclusion to the gospel called the "Short Ending", appears in a few manuscripts of even later date.

The question arises therefore as to why Mark's gospel ends in this abrupt and tantalising fashion. It has been suggested that he was interrupted in the composition of the gospel, or that the fragile papyrus of the original manuscript was broken off. Neither of these solutions seems satisfactory. Is it not more likely that Mark had accomplished the task he set himself to do and terminates his gospel as abruptly as he begins it—though no more abruptly than St. Luke terminates the book of *Acts* (see p. 445)—because this is the note on which he means to end?

The readers of his gospel knew from experience much about the Risen Christ. They knew less about the details of Jesus' ministry. This Mark has traced from the mission of John the Baptist to the Crucifixion, and as he begins his gospel with the proclamation of the coming of the Messiah, he ends it with the proclamation of his Resurrection. Jesus is not dead but alive. The tomb is empty, the Lord is risen. And the fitting note to conclude his story is the awe-struck wonder of the simple women who were the first to come face to face with the greatest of all the messianic acts, the supreme "sign" by which God vindicated his crucified Son and inaugurated the Kingdom "with power" (cf. 9: 1).

The other three gospels supply the details of the appearances of the Risen Christ which Mark's gospel lacks, but, as we shall see, the earliest written evidence of the Resurrection is not in the gospels but in St. Paul's first letter to the *Corinthians* 15: 3–8. Behind that lies the evidence of the book of *Acts*, that within a few weeks of the Crucifixion, the disciples who had fled in terror from the garden of Gethsemane, and who had seen their beloved Master hurried to a felon's death, were boldly out and about in the streets of Jerusalem proclaiming that God had raised him from the dead. It was on this "best attested fact in history" that the Church was founded.

THE GOSPEL ACCORDING TO ST. LUKE

WE KNOW much more about the author of the third gospel than we do about the author of *Matthew*. Both the evidence of the New Testament and unanimous early Church tradition identify him as Luke, the "beloved physician" of St. Paul's letters (*Col.* 4: 14) and companion of his missionary journeys (*II Tim.* 4: 11; *Philem.* 24). St. Luke was responsible also for the writing of the book of *Acts*, which together with his gospel forms a two-volume work dealing with the beginning of Christianity.

That he was a Gentile and not a Jew is obvious from both his books, and by an examination of *Acts* (see pp. 437–438) it can be established that he joined St Paul's team on the second missionary journey at Troas, worked at Philippi for a time as resident evangelist, lived at Caesarea for two years during St. Paul's imprisonment there and accompanied him on his final journey to Rome. Various conjectures have been made to fill out this picture, such as that he first made contact with St. Paul in his professional capacity, that he was a freed slave who dedicated both his books to his former master Theophilus, that he was a ship's doctor and that he was a painter.

These are all more or less speculative suggestions, and the same uncertainty surrounds his early background. The most likely guess is that he may have been a Greek doctor in Antioch, the first great centre of Gentile Christianity. His gospel in its present form dates from about the same time as *Matthew*, around A.D. 80, but there is some reason to think that Luke compiled a shorter edition of his gospel as much as twenty years earlier.

As it stands, Luke's gospel is made up of four strands. More than half of Mark's material has been used by Luke, and he incorporates a large number of sayings of Jesus from a source which was also used by Matthew. In addition to the narratives of the Birth of Jesus (chs. 1 and 2), which are peculiar to *Luke* and which form the third strand, this gospel also contains stories and teaching of Jesus amounting to about half the book which are found nowhere else.

It has been suggested that much of this special material was gathered by Luke during Paul's imprisonment in Caesarea from A.D. 56–58, and that he produced a first sketch of his gospel soon after that, consisting of this information and the teaching of Jesus which he got from the source called Q (see p. 333). Later, when Mark's gospel came into his hands, he wove these three elements together and added the infancy stories to make his present gospel. The collected teaching of Jesus which was used by both Matthew and Luke is generally dated somewhere between A.D. 50–60, so that if this view of the composition of the third gospel is correct, it means that in *Luke* we have not only teaching of Jesus which like that in *Matthew* dates from before the publication of Mark's gospel, but also narratives of the life of Jesus found only here and dating also from before the writing of *Mark*. It should be added, however, that the fact that a narrative or saying can be shown to be "early", is not necessarily a guarantee of its accuracy, any more than a "late" narrative or saying is necessarily less reliable. But there is a reasonable probability that this will be the case.

What is clear beyond dispute, however, is that Luke addresses his gospel to the educated Gentile world. It is the most "scholarly" of the gospels, in the sense that Luke tells us in his introduction (1: 1–4) that he knows of various previous attempts to give an account of the life and teaching of Jesus, and that he is now undertaking to provide an accurate and systematic record based on examination of what has already been written.

His gospel is in fact a Christian apologia for the benefit of the pagan world, showing above all that Christianity is not an obscure Jewish sect but potentially a world-religion, and that far from being a disruptive element in society—which was more than a suspicion in Gentile minds, even in those early days before the Church clashed with the empire—the new faith is on the side of law and order, and is designed to be an integrating factor in the community.

Luke's gospel has been called by Renan the "most beautiful book in the world", and many of us would echo his verdict, remembering how many of the best known stories and parables in the gospels, such as the Prodigal Son and the Good Samaritan, are found only here. The universalist outlook of this gospel, with its wider horizons, its emphasis on the barrier-breaking power of the Spirit, first in bridging the gulf between Jews and Samaritans, then between Jews and Gentiles, is one of its most attractive features.

The interest of St. Luke in social questions has often been noted, as has the prominent place he gives to women in the gospel story. More significant is his emphasis on how much our Lord cared for the black sheep of society, for the poor and for the outcasts, and how often he found the strength and inspiration he needed for his task in prayer and meditation. As we read this gospel we should keep our eyes open for these particular contributions of this evangelist, for with them he enlarges and deepens our understanding of the words and works of Jesus as recorded by Mark and Matthew.

Much of this contribution is made by the narratives and parables which are found nowhere else in the gospels, much, on the other hand, is conveyed by the way Luke tells stories which we have already encountered. Let us not imagine that these are additions he makes out of his own imagination. Rather they are elements in the tradition which were common knowledge, but which this evangelist thought to be of more importance than did the other gospel writers who omitted them. Perhaps St. Luke's greatest contribution of all is the success with which, from start to finish of his book, he conveys the impression that the Gospel is indeed Good News and not bad news, a message not of the power of evil but of the triumph of God's love, and of the joy and not the gloom of Christian belief and practice.

St. Luke addresses his gospel and the book of *Acts* to Theophilus (1 : 3 ; *Acts* 1 : 1). The name means "lover of God", and it has been variously conjectured that this was the real name, or an assumed name for prudential reasons, of a Roman official who had become a Christian, or that Theophilus stands for any "lover of God" among Christian Gentiles. The author makes it plain that the first stage of the gospel's existence was the preaching of the "eyewitnesses (of the events) and ministers of the word", but that now the second stage has been reached of putting down in writing a record of the origins of the Christian faith (1 : 1–4). St. Luke's particular intention is to give a fuller and more detailed account for the benefit of a pagan convert, than would be given in normal catechetical instruction by a missionary.

Birth and Boyhood of Jesus
(1 : 5 – 2 : 52)

IN THESE first two chapters of the gospel, in which St. Luke tells of the Birth of Jesus, we see Luke the poet rather than Luke the historian. The style of this introductory section is so different from that of the rest of the gospel, so thoroughly Jewish in character and so reminiscent of the Old Testament, that the most likely explanation is that Luke found some document containing these birth stories, possibly while at Caesarea, and with his natural sense for beautiful writing, left them largely untouched and incorporated them as a preface to his gospel.

Like the birth stories in Matthew, these chapters are not for the man with the measuring-tape mind. Behind them lies the mystery of the Virgin Birth which we have already discussed (see p. 335), the reticence of our Lord's mother from whom much of this must originally have come, and the genius of a compiler who has combined the mind of a theologian with the soul of a poet to produce this incomparable idyll.

The birth of John the Baptist, as forerunner of the Messiah, is linked with that of Jesus, through the relationship of the mothers of the two infants. Perhaps the story of John's birth was originally part of the tradition current among his followers. The first chapter is memorable for the words of the Magnificat (1 : 46–55) and the Benedictus (1 : 68–79).

The census which took Joseph and Mary from Nazareth to

Bethlehem to be registered, may have been a local affair or it may have been part of a more far-reaching decree, but it is of much less real significance than the symbolism of the manger bed and the adoration of the simple shepherds. Matthew's gospel makes no mention of all this, as Luke's account says nothing of the visit of the wise men or the flight to Egypt.

The third great hymn of praise in these chapters, the Nunc Dimittis (2: 29–32), is spoken by Simeon in the Temple at the Presentation of the infant Jesus. Simeon adds sombre words which point forward to the troubled manhood of the days-old babe and the heartbreak of his mother. Godly old Anna, like Simeon, a type of the devout and faithful Jew, nurtured on the scriptures and awaiting the Messiah, likewise gives thanks to God for the child of Mary (2: 34–38).

Alone among the gospels, Luke lifts for an instant the veil that shrouds the thirty years of our Lord's life between his Birth and his Baptism. This is the well-known incident of the boy Jesus, at the orientally mature age of twelve, sitting at the feet of the rabbis in the Temple, plying them with questions and astonishing them by the depth of his understanding (2: 41–51). This feature, and the boy's reply to his relieved mother's inquiry obviously seemed to Luke to round off this infancy narrative in a fitting manner.

The Christ has been acclaimed at his Birth as the light that will illuminate the world. His coming has been heralded as bringing peace on earth to men of goodwill.

Simeon and Anna, humble shepherds and learned doctors, with Mary his mother, have joined with the angelic host in hailing the incarnate Lord. St. Luke contents himself with telescoping the "hidden years" at Nazareth into one memorable sentence: "Jesus increased in wisdom and stature, and in favour with God and man" (2: 52). It could not have been better said.

"The Acceptable Year of the Lord"
(3: 1–6: 19)

LUKE prefaces his account of the public ministry of Jesus with particulars of the rulers of the various regions of Palestine, and a note on the date of John the Baptist's mission (the fifteenth year of the reign of Tiberius), which gives us the probable year of our Lord's Baptism as A.D. 26 (3: 1–2). A little later he tells us that Jesus was then about thirty years old (3: 23). The dates of the Christian era were not fixed until the sixth century A.D., and the monk who was entrusted with the task made an error in his calculations. Since Herod the Great died in 4 B.C., the probable date of our Lord's birth was 6 B.C. (Matt. 2: 16), and his age at the beginning of his public ministry would thus be thirty-two.

For his narrative from this point on, Luke is dependent partly on Mark, partly on the source which he shared in common with Matthew, and partly on his own special information. As we have already noticed the first two of these three sources, it will be necessary only to comment where Luke introduces significant new elements into the gospel story.

In his account of John the Baptist's mission, for example (3: 2–20), Luke characteristically gives a note of the social concern of John's message (3: 10–14); at the Baptism of Jesus (3: 21–22) he notes that Jesus prayed throughout; and in giving the genealogy of Jesus (3: 23–38), unlike Matthew, he traces his ancestry back beyond Abraham, the father of the Jews, through Noah and Seth to Adam, the father of mankind, "the son of God".

After the Temptation in the wilderness (4: 1–13), our Lord returns to Galilee, preaching in the synagogues there (4: 14–15). Luke expands Mark's account of Jesus' appearance in the synagogue of his own town of Nazareth into an illuminating description of the actual scene (4: 16–30). After the statutory reading of the lesson from the Law, Jesus unrols the Hebrew scroll of Isaiah, and reads as the lesson from the prophets a passage from *Isa.* 61: 1–2.

Our Lord applies this proclamation of the coming Messiah to himself, and declares that this is the decisive hour, significantly omitting Isaiah's words that the "acceptable year of the Lord" is also "the day of vengeance of our God". As he sits expounding the text the reaction of his hearers passes from approbation to hostility, and Jesus draws a trenchant parallel between his reception by his own people and that of Elijah and Elisha, who found a readier response from Gentiles.

In Capernaum Jesus heals the demoniac in the synagogue (4: 31–37), Peter's wife's mother (4: 38–39) and many more diseased in mind and body (4: 40–44). Whatever be the origin of Luke's story of the miraculous draught of fishes (5: 1–11), whether it was originally a post-Resurrection appearance of Jesus (cf. *John* 21: 1–11), or a story told to illustrate Jesus' summons to the disciples to become fishers of men (*Mark* 1: 17), it is in this latter sense that it would be valued by the Church in Luke's day.

The Lord calls his first disciples, with Peter at their head, to gather men into the net. In their own strength they are powerless, but in the strength of Christ the haul exceeds all their expectations. St. Luke himself had seen this happen in the Gentile mission. Returning to Mark's narrative, Luke now relates the healing of the leper (5: 12–15), and of the paralysed man who was let down through the roof (5: 17–26).

Levi, the tax-collector, becomes a disciple, and in his house Jesus is taken to task by the Pharisees for mixing with untouchables, and for failing to behave like an orthodox holy man. Our Lord challenges religious conservatism in words which are always relevant. Which of us has not been guilty of saying: "The old is better" (5: 27–39)? Still following Mark, Luke now recounts the incident of the disciples plucking corn on the sabbath (6: 1–5), the healing of the man with the withered hand (6: 6–11) and the calling of the twelve disciples (6: 12–16). Great crowds gather from all parts of the country to be cured and none is disappointed (6: 17–19).

"To the Poor the Gospel is Preached"

(6: 20 – 9: 50)

LEAVING Mark's narrative at this point, Luke goes on to relate some of the stories and sayings of Jesus which he shares with Matthew, and some found only in this gospel. First of all, he gives a shortened version of the Sermon on the Mount; in Luke's gospel it is the Sermon on the Plain (6: 20–49). Beginning with the Beatitudes, he includes excerpts from *Matt.* 5 and 7 with less emphasis on the contrast between the new Law and Jewish practice, since he is writing principally for Gentiles.

The story of the healing of the servant of the centurion at Capernaum (7: 1–10) is followed by a story, peculiar to Luke, of the restoration to life of the son of a widow at Nain (7: 11–16). Unlike the story of Jairus' daughter (*Mark* 5 : 22–24, 35–43), there is no suggestion that the man may have been in a coma. Unless we dismiss this as a pious tale, or say that the man could not have been completely dead in the medical sense, we have here what amounts to a test-case.

If our Lord was who he claimed to be, we cannot presume to say what he could and could not do. The evidence of the vast healing work of his ministry is irrefutable, and none of these cures is explicable by normal therapeutic practice. Jesus' restoration of the blind, deaf and paralysed, of lepers and demoniacs, is no less miraculous than his raising of the dead. To him sickness and death were alike signs of the power of evil over men which he had come to break, and which would be broken in the fulness of the age to come.

Jesus did not, however, bring the dead back to life indiscriminately. There are only three cases recorded in the gospels. If we may try to fathom our Lord's purpose, we may perhaps think that in each of these cases there was special ground for compassion—the little daughter of Jairus, the son of a widow, and Lazarus, Jesus' personal friend. But the bodies of the dead who were raised to life must in this present age die a second death.

Our Lord's actions in these cases, therefore, may be best taken as visible pledges of the truth that the Church has proclaimed from Easter Day onwards, that by his Resurrection Christ has conquered death for all his people. To be born again into his Body, the Church, through baptism, is to enter upon a life which the physical decay of our frail human body cannot affect. For the Christian, life and death are no longer measured in medical terms. Life means life in Christ, and death means separation from him.

It is in this context that Luke next records the visit of the disciples of John the Baptist, to inquire whether Jesus were in fact the Messiah. They receive our Lord's reply that all the signs of the messianic age are now to hand—men restored to wholeness of mind and body, to new life, to the right relationship with God (7: 17–23). Luke follows this with our Lord's words about the significance of John's mission, comparing it with his own (7: 24–35).

St. Luke now includes one of the wonderful stories which make his gospel so beloved, that of the prostitute who washes our Lord's feet with her tears, and puts to shame the godly Pharisee, who had neglected the normal courtesies of an oriental host towards an honoured guest (7: 36–50). We may be grateful to Luke, also, for the glimpse he gives us in the next few verses of the women who accompanied our Lord and the disciples on their travels, providing their meals and generally looking after them (8: 1–3).

Luke comes back again to Mark's gospel for the next section, and we are given the parable of the sower and other familiar sayings (8: 4–18), the visit of our Lord's mother (8: 19–21), the stilling of the storm (8: 22–25), the cure of the Gadarene demoniac (8: 26–39), the raising of Jairus' daughter and the healing of the woman with the issue of blood (8: 40–56). In all this Luke makes little or no alteration to Mark's narrative, although we may see his professional pride being rather shocked at Mark's comment on the doctors, in the case of the woman with the haemorrhage, that she "was nothing bettered, but rather grew worse" (*Mark* 5: 26). Dr. Luke omits this blunt remark, which he no doubt thought was in rather bad taste.

Jesus now sends out the twelve disciples on their pilot mission as an example to the later Church (9: 1–6), disturbs the guilty conscience of Herod Antipas (9: 7–9), and feeds the multitude of five thousand, the Galilean Lord's Supper for the Jews (9: 10–17).

Luke, who has been following Mark's narrative up to this point, omits a large section from *Mark* 6: 45–8: 26, including the stories of Jesus walking on the water, feeding the four thousand, healing the Syro-Phoenician woman's daughter and disputing with the Pharisees on the question of ceremonial cleanliness.

Perhaps he was pressed for space, perhaps the copy of Mark's gospel which he was using did not contain this section, or perhaps he felt that some of it was repetitive and some unsuitable for Gentile readers. At all events the third gospel passes on now to Peter's confession of Jesus as the Messiah (9: 18–20), and Jesus' solemn words predicting his Passion, Resurrection and Exaltation (9: 21–27). Luke's illuminating version of the Transfiguration (9: 28–36) has already been noticed (see p. 372), and this is followed by the healing of the epileptic boy (9: 37–42), the lesson on the meaning of "greatness" (9: 43–48) and on the danger of religious exclusiveness (9: 49–50).

The Journey to Jerusalem

(9: 51 – 18: 14)

AT THIS point Luke leaves Mark's record aside, and begins the great central section of his gospel (9: 51 – 18: 14), some of which has come from the same source as Matthew used. Much, on the other hand, is found only in this gospel, and it is here that Luke's greatest contribution to our knowledge of the mind of Jesus is made. This whole section stands

under the introductory words of
9: 51—"He stedfastly set his face
to go to Jerusalem", and while it is
difficult to trace the route or
compute the length of time involved, it is more important to
recognise that Jerusalem, and the
Passion that awaits him there, are
in the forefront of our Lord's
thoughts from now on.

Characteristically, Luke records
Jesus' wish to lodge in a Samaritan
village on the way. When he is
rebuffed as a Jew by the truculent
natives, unwilling to forget the
age-old feud, it is rather his angry
and impetuous disciples who earn
his rebuke, than the Samaritans
who are unable to recognise their
Saviour (9: 52–56). Jesus has
equally strong words for those
whose service of him takes second
place after their own affairs (9:
57–62).

In addition to the mission of the
twelve disciples, Luke alone records a mission of seventy (10:
1–16), although the instructions
to the disciples are much the
same as those given to the Twelve
elsewhere. This is surely regarded
by Luke as a foreshadowing of the
Church's mission to the seventy
nations of the Gentile world, based
on the list in *Gen.* 10, as the mission
of the Twelve is regarded as
primarily the Church's mission to
Israel. The return of the triumphant seventy is for our Lord a cause
of exultation, as he sees in their
success the ultimate annihilation of
evil (10: 17–20). He follows this
with the great thanksgiving for the
Good News of the new age (10:
21–24).

The lawyer's question as to
which is the greatest command-

ment, here altered by Luke for the
benefit of his Gentile readers into
a question about eternal life,
gives rise to the parable of the
Good Samaritan, as an example of
what is meant by loving one's
neighbour (10: 25–37). We may
feel that it was easier for the
Samaritan in the story to recognise
his "neighbour" as a wounded
man on that lonely road than for
us in a complex twentieth century
world. But the point of the story is
just that your "neighbour" is
anyone who needs your help.

Luke gives us for good measure
at this point the immortal glimpse
of Martha and Mary (10: 38–42).
Our Lord is not blaming dear,
fussy Martha for being the practical, busy person without whom
life would soon come to a standstill. He is gently telling her to
stop flapping. There is a place for
the Maries also who are ready to
sit down, and think, and listen to
what God is saying. In this sense
theirs is undoubtedly the "better
part".

Jesus teaches the disciples the
Lord's Prayer, a shorter form than
in *Matthew*, and with "sins"
instead of "debts", in response to
their request for instruction in
prayer after they had seen our
Lord himself praying (11: 1–4).
This gives rise to the parable of the
importunate friend (11: 5–8), an
illustration of the words which
follow on the need for constant
conversation with God (11: 9–13).

For the rest of this chapter, Luke
gathers together words of Jesus
which we have already mostly
encountered either in *Mark* or
Matthew: on the charge that he
healed men by black magic (11:

14–23), on the danger of partial conversion (11: 24–26), a new word on our Lord's great family (11: 27–28), a familiar word on the "sign of Jonah" (11: 29–32), and on the Gospel as the light of a man's life (11: 33–36). The Pharisees and ecclesiastical lawyers are taken to task for their failure to distinguish between true and false piety (11: 37–54).

Having urged the disciples to stand fast in their faith and fear no man (12: 1–12), Jesus tells the splendid parable, found only in *Luke*, of the rich fool who followed the gospel of "eat, drink and be merry" (12: 13–21). Luke supplements this with words well-known from the Sermon on the Mount, on the proper attitude of the Christian man towards the material things of life (12: 22–34). The patchwork of sayings which concludes the chapter (12: 35–59), is more easily understood in the fuller version of *Matt.* 24–25, dealing with the responsibility of the Christian disciple, and the need to live under the constant judgment of God with a wakeful conscience; but we may note Luke's own interest in our Lord's inward conflict (12: 49–50) in view of his approaching Passion. It is a foretaste of Gethsemane.

Jesus uses some recent occasion of a clash between the Jews and the Roman authorities, ending in a massacre, and a similarly recent collapse of a building in Jerusalem, which killed several people, to explode once and for all the theory which bedevilled Old Testament theology, that suffering and death are punishment for sin. He offers no explanation of why such things happen, but asserts that disasters of this kind should serve as a warning to us all to put ourselves right with God (13: 1–5). The parable of the fig-tree (13: 6–9) serves to enforce this lesson: as we have seen (p. 376), the parable may be the origin of the incident of the cursing and withering of the fig tree in Mark's gospel.

The issue of the rigid observance of the sabbath crops up again in the new story of a crippled woman who is cured of her deformity (13: 10–17), and the comparisons of the growth of the work of the Gospel with a mustard seed, and with leaven reappear (13: 18–21). Another familiar theme in a new guise is our Lord's warning to his countrymen, that Gentiles will flock into the Kingdom from all quarters to join patriarchs and prophets, but many Jews who expect the right of entry will be turned away (13: 22–30).

The Mind of the Master

JESUS maintains his purpose to bring his messianic mission to a head in Jerusalem, despite warnings against Herod from friendly Pharisees (13: 31–33), and he laments over the intransigence of the holy city (13: 34–35). The fourteenth chapter consists mostly of Luke's own special information. The scene is set at a meal-time on a certain sabbath in the house of a leading Pharisee, where our Lord's healing of a man who suffered from dropsy gives rise to adverse comment (14: 1–6). Jesus takes occasion to use the rivalry of the guests for the most important seats at table, as an illustration of the wrong attitude within the Christian community. Humility is the keynote of life lived under the rule of God (14: 7–11).

Our Lord's words in 14: 12–14 must not be taken as a veto on ordinary hospitality among friends, but as a reminder of the social obligations of the Christian man towards those from whom he can expect no hospitality in return. The parable of the great supper (14: 16–24) has some resemblances to Matthew's parable of the wedding feast (*Matt.* 22: 1–10), but St. Luke makes it much clearer that our Lord is speaking of the messianic banquet in the Kingdom of heaven, life in the presence of God. The outcasts of society (the publicans and sinners), and those beyond the pale (the Gentiles), are welcomed to the feast, and take the places of the originally invited guests (the godly Jews), who for one reason or another decline their host's invitation.

The point of the parable for us is that the service of God is costly and demands sacrifice. All the guests who were invited had good reasons for staying away, but none of them was prepared to put the obedience of God before his own private concerns. It is this lesson which our Lord reinforces in the following words (14: 25–35) on the cost of Christian discipleship and the necessity for self-renunciation.

Luke now adds three parables illustrating God's boundless love. Like the joy of the shepherd who finds his lost sheep (15: 1–7), there is more rejoicing in heavenly places over the repentance of one sinner than over the merits of

ninety-nine pillars of orthodoxy. The story of the poor woman, who sweeps every corner till she finds the lost coin, presses the lesson home (15: 8–10), but it is the superb parable of the prodigal son (15: 11–32) which brings us to our knees. This is the gospel in a nutshell. The elder brother in the parable was undoubtedly originally meant to represent the pious Jews who resented our Lord's care for the less respectable members of society, but the story is timeless. None of us dare assume the role of the elder brother for we are all prodigal sons, stumbling back, when we come to ourselves, into the arms of our Father, who comes running to meet us.

In chapter sixteen St. Luke has collected parables and sayings dealing with the stewardship of money. We may well wonder what such a saying as 16: 18, dealing with divorce, is doing in such a collection, and indeed it is not at all clear what the little block of sayings in 16: 16–18 has to contribute to this context. We have encountered them already in *Matthew* but their appearance here is rather odd. The rest of the chapter consists mainly of two parables which are complementary.

The story of the unjust steward (16: 1–8) is not a commendation of dishonesty, and the steward is not held up for our admiration, except in so far as his active concern for the safety of his own skin is contrasted favourably with the half-heartedness of Christian disciples in their concern for their eternal salvation. In the sayings which follow, our Lord advocates holy worldliness, in the sense of

shrewd (but honest) management
of the world's affairs with which
we are entrusted, including our
own, as the best guarantee that we
shall also be faithful servants in the
things of the spirit (16: 9–12).

On the other hand, our Lord
makes it abundantly plain that we
must know where to draw the line,
and that "mammon", which
stands for material possessions in
general, must never take first place
(16: 13–15). This was the sin of
the rich man in the parable that
follows (16: 19–31). It is sheer
fantasy to treat this story as if it
were a literal description of life
beyond death in heaven and hell,
or as if in the after life the rich are
inevitably condemned to suffer,
and the poor are automatically
compensated for their hardships
on earth.

A parable has always one main
point to make, and in this case it
is a warning, couched in the conventional imagery of the times,
that a rich man who makes money
his god and cares nothing for the
needs of those less fortunate than
himself, will feel the judgment of
God in the life to come. Lazarus
is in a happier state, not because
he was a poor man, but because he
was also a good man as the meaning of his name—"God is his
help"—implies. The five brothers
of Dives, the rich man, are introduced at the end of the parable, to
emphasise our Lord's contention
that the wealthy have had already
ample warning.

In the series of sayings of Jesus
to which St. Luke next turns (17:
1–10), a new and profound utterance of Jesus arrests our attention,
again one of the words to be

written on every Christian heart:
"When ye shall have done all
those things which are commanded
you, say, We are unprofitable
servants: we have done that which
was our duty to do". St. Luke
may be "the scribe of the gentleness of Christ", as Dante called
him, but he also faithfully records
our Lord's uncompromising demands.

The poignant story of the nine
ungrateful lepers, and of the one
who came back to give glory to
God and thanks to Jesus—a constant rebuke to us all—has the
added point that the man who
remembered his debt of gratitude
was a despised Samaritan (17: 11–
19). In the saying that follows (17:
20–21), a common misunderstanding should be corrected. When
Jesus says: "the kingdom of God
is within you", he cannot mean
"within each one of you", for he
is talking to the Pharisees. The
Greek words can equally well
mean: "in your midst", i.e. the
reign of God, represented by his
Messiah, has now begun, and God
is at work among men in a new
way, if they could only see it.

Apocalyptic passages are always
difficult, and it is not surprising
that there has been so much confusion and misunderstanding in
connection with our Lord's words,
both in the early Church and in
our own day. We have already
encountered his cryptic utterances
on Judgment and the Second Advent in *Mark* 13 and *Matthew* 24–
25. St. Luke has two main
apocalyptic discourses, here (17:
22–37), and in 21: 5–36. The
themes are similar throughout, expressed often in the same words.

Jesus speaks here of his ultimate Triumph, after his Passion, which is also God's Judgment of the world, the last event of time. But he sees such events as the Deluge, the destruction of Sodom and the fall of Jerusalem as fitting into this pattern of judgment and bids them be taken as divine warnings. Judgment also falls on individuals with unexpected suddenness. The wise man will therefore always be prepared, for that it will come to everyone is as certain as that vultures gather round a corpse.

The last few verses of this central section of St. Luke's gospel (9: 51–18: 14), where he has told us so much of the work and words of Jesus that we should not otherwise have known, consist of two little pictures drawn by our Lord and preserved uniquely in this gospel. The first is the story of the unjust judge (18: 1–8), who to save himself from the importunate pleas of a widow with some wrong to be redressed, eventually took up her case. This is again a lesson on the need for persistent prayer. If such an unsatisfactory judge is prepared under pressure to pay attention to a petition, is it not plain that a God who cares will be ever ready to listen to the prayers of his people?

The second word-picture is the perfect illustration of the proper attitude to adopt in approaching God. The self-righteous Pharisee, proud of his spiritual achievements, boasting of his piety and religious orthodoxy, is contrasted with the diffident "publican", with bent head and contrite heart, praying: "God be merciful to me a sinner" (18: 9–14). Leaving us with this wonderfully vivid insight

into our Lord's mind, St. Luke now returns to Mark's narrative and takes us through the events leading up to the Crucifixion. He has, however, as we shall see, his own significant additions to make to what Mark has already told us.

The Events of Holy Week
(18: 15 – 24: 53)

THE INCIDENT of Jesus blessing the children—Luke calls them "infants"—is now recorded (18: 15–17), followed by Jesus' meeting with the virtuous but over-wealthy ruler (18: 18–23), and our Lord's words on the snare of riches (18: 24–30). Jesus predicts his Passion (18: 31–34), and heals the blind man at Jericho (18: 35–43). Luke inserts at this point a story which he alone tells of Zacchaeus, the little tax-collector who climbed a tree to get a glimpse of Jesus, and whose whole life was changed by his encounter with our Lord (19: 1–10).

The parable of the pounds, which follows (19: 11–27), is more complicated than the parable of the talents in *Matthew*. It seems as if some contemporary historical allusions have become involved in it. The main meaning, however, can be seen to be the same as that of Matthew's version, that from the Passion of our Lord to the final consummation, his servants in the Church who are entrusted with the gifts of the Spirit in their varying degrees, will have to render an account of their stewardship when he comes.

Covering now familiar ground, St. Luke traces the events of

Passion Week. The Triumphal Entry into Jerusalem is described (19: 28-40), Luke alone adding that as Jesus approached the city he wept over it, as he spoke of its impending destruction (19: 41-44). The Cleansing of the Temple is next recorded (19: 45-46), followed by teaching and controversy there with the religious authorities (19: 47 – 20: 8). The parable of the vineyard, pregnant with meaning, rouses the combined opposition of priests and scribes (20: 9-19).

Questions are put to Jesus on the obligation to pay the imperial poll-tax (20: 20-26), on belief in a resurrection (20: 27-40), and our Lord himself makes pronouncements on the meaning of the Son of David title for the Messiah (20: 41-44), on ostentatious religiosity (20: 45-47) and on Christian liberality (21: 1-4). The apocalyptic discourse of 21: 5-36 is taken from *Mark* 13, but Luke's note at its conclusion (21: 37-38) would seem to confirm the suggestion that "Holy Week" lasted longer than seven days (see p. 380-381).

For the account of the Trial and Crucifixion of Jesus, St. Luke largely follows Mark's narrative, but adds distinctive touches from his special source of information and from his own editorial handling of Mark's material. He describes the plot to apprehend Jesus (22: 1-6), and the preparations for the passover meal (22: 7-13). At the Last Supper (22: 14-34), Luke adds the words: "This do in remembrance of me", which St. Paul quotes in his instructions to the church at Corinth (*I Cor.* 11: 25), and records our Lord's saying: "I am among you

as he that serveth," which St. John represents in action in the washing of the disciples' feet (*John* 13 : 1-15).

Jesus, having warned his disciples about the troubled life that lies ahead of them after his Death, and having dismissed the idea of armed resistance (22: 35-38), leaves the house of the Last Supper and endures the Agony of Gethsemane, Luke alone noting his bloody sweat (22: 39-46). Our Lord is arrested and taken to the house of the high priest, whose servant, wounded in the fracas in the Garden, Jesus had healed, as Luke tells us. While Peter in the courtyard of the house was strenuously denying that he had anything to do with the prisoner, "the Lord turned and looked upon Peter" (22: 47-62).

After the ghastly foolery of the guards, and the Trial by the Sanhedrin, Jesus is taken before Pilate, who pronounces him innocent, despite the trumped-up charge of treason (22: 63 – 23: 4). Luke alone includes an additional Trial, if it can be called a trial, before Herod Antipas, ruler of Galilee, to whom Pilate had diplomatically referred the prisoner. Luke is most likely right in associating the mock coronation of the Messiah with Herod's bodyguard, since Joanna, mentioned in 8: 3, was attached to Herod's household. This exchange of courtesies between Pilate and Herod resulted, ironically enough, in better relations between them (23: 5-12).

Despite Pilate's well-intentioned efforts to spare the prisoner's life, emphasised by Luke, for whom, both here and in *Acts*, the Jews are always the villains of the piece and the Roman authorities paragons by comparison, the priests and the crowd have their way. Barabbas is released and Jesus is handed over to the executioners (23: 13–25). While Simon of Cyrene carries the Cross, Jesus addresses the weeping women who followed behind, foretelling the disaster which fell upon Jerusalem in A.D. 70 (23: 26–31).

St. Luke alone records Jesus' plea for forgiveness for his murderers as he hangs on the Cross, words which moved to penitence one of the two criminals who were crucified with him, and who now receives absolution pronounced by the dying Messiah. A third word from the Cross is also the last: Father into thy hands I commend my spirit. As in *Mark*, Joseph of Arimathaea secures the body of Jesus, and the faithful women see him lay it in the sepulchre (23: 32–56).

St. Luke's account of the first Easter Day begins with the early visit to the tomb by the women, who intended to anoint the body so hastily buried on Good Friday. They find the stone rolled away and the tomb empty. Two angelic figures remind them of Jesus' prophecy of his Resurrection, whereupon they return to the disciples with the news of the empty tomb and are greeted with open incredulity. Peter, to satisfy himself, runs out to the tomb, sees the grave-clothes lying by themselves in the vacant sepulchre and leaves the scene in deep perplexity (24: 1–12).

Two thousand years of the Church's proclamation of the Resurrection may have made it easier for us to accept it as a fact, even if it remains as much of a mystery. St. Luke's evidence is that whatever Jesus had said about his Passion and what lay beyond it, the Resurrection came as a wholly unexpected and startling shock to his followers. It is in this light that the minor discrepancies in the gospel narratives become explicable. Is it surprising for example that the excited women found it hard to remember what precisely they had seen at the tomb except that it was empty?

St. Luke, however, gives us in addition the experience of two of these followers on their way home to the village of Emmaus on the afternoon of Easter Day (24: 13–35), perhaps of all the records of the appearances of the Risen Christ to his disciples the most illuminating. With superb skill St. Luke conveys the picture of these two bewildered travellers, deep in conversation about the events of the last three days, and of the unrecognised stranger who overtook them and patiently expounded the messianic Gospel of the Old Testament.

It was in the familiar word and action of the breaking of bread that at last they knew that it was the Saviour himself who had sat with them in their simple home, and with joy in their hearts they hastened back to Jerusalem to tell the rest of the disciples. Again the mystery of the Risen Lord was revealed to his assembled followers (24: 36–43), and with it came the assurance that this was no ghost but our Lord himself, unmistakably himself but somehow different, with a body that was no longer subject to the ordinary laws of time and space.

Luke concludes his gospel with a charge from the Risen Lord to his disciples to proclaim the Good News to all the world, and a promise of the coming of the Spirit at Pentecost, which is to be described at the beginning of Luke's companion volume, the book of *Acts* (24: 44–49). As a further link with Acts, where the event is more fully described, Luke rounds off his gospel with the Ascension, and leaves us with the picture of the young Christian community, no longer mourning for a dead master, but "continually in the Temple, praising and blessing God" (24: 50–53).

THE GOSPEL ACCORDING TO ST. JOHN

THERE HAS been a remarkable trend among New Testament scholars in comparatively recent years, towards a more positive evaluation of the historical reliability of the fourth gospel, and towards a more conservative view of its date and its author. No one has ever disputed the devotional and theological worth of this gospel. It has always held supreme place among the four evangelists for its profound insight into the significance of the person and work of Christ.

But until fairly recently it was generally held that this was a product of second century reflection on the life and teaching of Jesus, superbly beautiful, but not to be taken seriously as an authentic record of either what Jesus did or what Jesus said. Some of the reasons that led to this conclusion will be obvious to anyone who, having read the three synoptic gospels, turns to St. John's gospel expecting to find a fourth version of the same story told in the same way.

The first three gospels begin with either the Birth or the Baptism of Jesus, and then follow the course of events more or less systematically through the Galilean ministry to Passion Week and the Resurrection. From their record, Jesus emerges as a carpenter of Nazareth who, at about the age of thirty, startles the townsfolk and villagers of Galilee by a teaching and healing ministry which was unique in Jewish history. Claiming the authority of a new Moses, he set himself up in opposition to the accredited religious experts, as the final arbiter on the true meaning of the divine Law by which the life of the people of God had been governed since the days of the Exodus.

By the significance he attached to his healing acts, and by the implications of his preaching, Jesus, from his Baptism onwards, clearly identified himself with the Messiah of Old Testament prophecy, and although he preferred to avoid the title because of its political connotation, it was as the Messiah that his followers eventually acclaimed him. Jesus himself, however, selected certain elements of the common messianic expectation as he thought fit, rejecting those aspects which he did not favour.

His preference for the title of Son of Man, taken from Daniel's vision, as the description of his own role, was associated in his words and actions with the concept of the Servant of God in Second Isaiah's prophecies. Jesus thus claimed to be the divinely appointed Head of a new Israel, who must first pay the price of the perfect obedience of the Servant by his own suffering and death, but who would be vindicated by God beyond the grave, keep tryst with his people through his Spirit, and finally at the end of time be acknowledged by the whole world as Lord and King.

The *leitmotiv* of his message was that the decisive hour had struck, the crisis of history had come, and that the reign of God on earth had begun. Gathering round himself men who were prepared, through their encounter with him, to put their lives under the sovereign command of God in repentance and new resolve, Jesus founded the community of the new age, the Church, a reconstituted Israel based on faith and not on race, for which he foresaw expansion not unmixed with trouble, but for which he predicted ultimate victory.

Is this the kind of picture which the fourth gospel also paints? Superficially there are many marked differences, and it is these differences which led to the historical value of St. John's gospel being called in question. Instead of beginning with the fact that Jesus was born or began his ministry, this gospel begins with the theological assertion that Christ is the creative power behind the universe. There is no record of Jesus' Baptism or Temptation; his ministry takes place in Judaea and Jerusalem more than in Galilee; his teaching is not in the form of the short crisp utterances of the synoptic gospels, but is conveyed in long and subtle discourses; well known synoptic phrases like "kingdom of God" and "Son of David" tend to disappear and to be replaced by concepts like "eternal life" and "Son of God".

In short, the down-to-earth atmosphere of the synoptic gospels seems to have vanished. We are brought face to face with a Jesus whose mind moves in realms of contrast between light and darkness, and between the Church and the world, who speaks of himself as the true Vine, the Bread of life, the Light of the world, whose constant emphasis is on the relationship between himself and God.

When to these and similar differences, and there are many more that could be mentioned, was added the fact that this gospel appeared to be dependent on the synoptic gospels, it is not surprising that scholars tended to discount the evidence of St. John for the actual events of the ministry of Jesus, and preferred to regard the book as the work of some devout Christian of the third or fourth generation. Recent study, both critical and archaeological, has called for a revision of this view.

A papyrus fragment of St. John's gospel, discovered in Egypt and now in the Rylands Library at Manchester, convinced the most radical critics that the gospel could not have been written later than A.D. 100; investigation of some of the sites and place names mentioned only in John indicates that in matters of Palestinian geography, the writer of the fourth gospel was well informed; on matters of chronological detail in which John differed from Mark, it has been discovered that John is sometimes more accurate; and it is now by no means certain that John was dependent on the synoptic gospels for any of his information.

The Author and His Purpose

IN SHORT, the previous view of this gospel as a late theological work, written in Asia Minor by a Gentile Christian to bridge the gulf between the Greek world and the Jewish origins of the Gospel, can now be seen to have been mistaken in some important respects. We are still not in a position to say with certainty who wrote the gospel or when it was written. What we can say is that the gospel bears the mark of having been written by someone who knew his Palestine, whose mother tongue was Aramaic, who was steeped in the thought of the Old Testament, and who may well have been writing his gospel at the same time as the authors of *Matthew* and *Luke*.

If we may go farther, it would seem almost certain that the epistles of *John* are written by the same hand as the gospel. In these letters the author describes himself as the Elder or Presbyter (*II and III John*). But the fourth gospel claims as its author "the disciple whom Jesus loved" (21: 20, 24), and here we must fall back on tradition to help us. From the second century onwards, the "beloved disciple" has been identified with the apostle John the son of Zebedee, who after the fall of Jerusalem removed to Ephesus and died at a ripe old age (cf. 21: 23).

It would seem to be the most probable solution of a vexed problem, to think of the Presbyter as the actual writer of the gospel, but depending on the apostle for his inside information much as John Mark depended on St. Peter. If we are right in identifying the anonymous disciple of 18: 15 with the Presbyter-evangelist, we may think of him as a young Jerusalem Jew at the time of the Crucifixion, originally a Sadducee with an aristocratic background, but now happy to be the follower of the Galilean fisherman who had been the intimate friend of Jesus. As tradition locates the Presbyter likewise at Ephesus, and gives his name also as John, it would be easy to see how the Church would come to fuse the two Johns and to credit the apostle with the actual writing of the gospel.

The fourth gospel is thus best understood as ultimately depending on the information of old John, the son of Zebedee, about the events in which he had played so large a part in his youth, and on his reflections upon their significance. His evidence does not conflict with that of the synoptic gospels; for the most part it supplements them. All the gospels are in some sense theological, in that they all do more than record events. They also interpret their significance. But John's gospel is by far the most theological among them, in that the impact of our Lord upon his contemporaries is described against a backcloth of eternity. It is a portrait of Jesus, rather than a series of photographs.

The historical motive is there as in the other gospels, but it is subordinated more thoroughly to the apologetic motive, to the attempt to show Jesus not just as he was for Jews in Palestine, but as he is at all times for everyone.

The fourth gospel is thus the key to the proper understanding of the synoptic gospels. It is here that, having traced the outline of Jesus' ministry in *Mark*, and having added the special contributions of *Matthew* and *Luke*, we can see our Lord in his true perspective. St. John has so steeped himself in the mind of Jesus, that it is sometimes difficult to tell whether it is our Lord or the evangelist who is speaking.

It is here in the discourses, given privately to the chosen circle, that we can see fully that the fundamental element in our Lord's consciousness was not that he was Messiah, or Servant, or Son of Man, but that he was Son of God. This unique unbroken relationship with the Father, this sense of oneness, is the reality which these Old Testament titles in one way or another seek to express. It is here too that we learn the true meaning of the miracles, not merely as events that happened once, but as sacramental acts which convey eternal truth.

Recent study of the Dead Sea Scrolls has disclosed the fact that much of what for some time had been thought to be Greek ideas in the fourth gospel are in fact Jewish. The repeated contrasts between light and darkness, spirit and flesh, truth and falsehood, which play so large a part in this gospel are not, as they might seem, importations of Greek thought. Like the Dead Sea Scrolls themselves they find their origins in the Old Testament.

Nevertheless the Jewish evangelists who were responsible for the writing of this gospel lived in a Greek world when they produced this book. If therefore we should like to think of each of the four gospels as having a specific purpose, apart from the general aim of bringing men to God through Christ, we can see in St. John a Christian missionary, who is aware of the Gentile world around him, and who is conscious that some ways of presenting the Gospel will be more meaningful to the pagan mind than others, and who chooses his language and reinterprets Jewish thought-forms with that end in view.

The Word Made Flesh
(1 : 1–18)

THE GOSPEL begins with a prologue (1 : 1–18), which is highly important in that it indicates the point of view from which the rest of the book is written. This preface is in a sense a summary of the Old Testament, from the Creation story to the last of the Old Testament prophets, John the Baptist, because the purpose of the author is to show our Lord in what he believes to be his proper perspective. He is not about to record the story of someone who began as a child in Bethlehem, or as the Messiah on the shores of the Lake of Galilee, but of someone who is the human expression of the creative purpose of God.

The first words of the gospel therefore take us back intentionally to the first words of the book of *Genesis*, and to the Creation of the world which was an act of God's love. St. John chooses to call this creative movement of God his "Word". He might equally well have called it his "Wisdom". It is the power which called the universe into being, the purpose that lay behind it, the divine energy which brought order out of chaos and light out of darkness.

When St. John says: "In the beginning was the Word" he means not only the divine fiat: "God said . . . and it was so". He wants us to think of something more personal than a bleak and abstract creative principle, it is rather the saving purpose of God, the beneficent act of love which made life possible at all. The Old Testament had spoken of the Wisdom of God almost as a personal emanation of the divine Being, instrumental in the creation of the world (*Prov.* 8: 22–31), and of his Word which was responsible for the existence of all that is (*Ps.* 33: 6, 9). The apocryphal book of *Wisdom* combines them (*Wisd.* 9: 1–2).

Moreover, it is easy for St. John to speak of this Word of God as the basis of the life of the world, as the light given by God to men, for with one accord the Old Testament prophets testify to the Word that came to them from God, the Word that declared his will to save mankind and to bring men back to himself.

It is against this background that St. John sets the stage for the gospel story. "The Word was made flesh". The loving purpose of God to create, care for and bring into the right relationship with himself the whole cosmos, was expressed once in history in a human life. The divine mind and will became incarnate in Jesus Christ. Without this true Light the world groped in darkness, and, when the Light came, God's own ancient people who might have been expected to be the first to welcome him, "received him not".

But those who have now accepted him as Lord and Saviour have been reborn through baptism into a new relationship to God, that of adopted sons. In Christ they have recognised the glory of the Presence of God tabernacling among men (cf. *Ex.* 40: 34–38), and seeing him they have seen the Father. The Baptist was merely his herald, Moses but the promulgator of the Law. Christ alone is the source of grace and truth, which he now freely shares with his people.

St. John does not return to this idea of Christ as the Word of God for the remainder of his gospel. His main emphasis is on Christ as the Son. But although his thought in the prologue is thoroughly steeped in the Old Testament, it cannot have been absent from his mind that his introduction to the gospel was also couched in terms which would mean something to the Greek reader. The Stoics claimed that the world was created and sustained by the divine Reason, or Logos (= Word). But no Greek philosopher would ever have dreamt of suggesting what is for

St. John the nub of the gospel, that the divine Word could and did become man. It is this fact that he now proceeds to demonstrate.

"The Friend of the Bride-groom"
(1 : 19 – 3 : 36)

ST. JOHN begins his narrative proper with the witness of John the Baptist to Jesus. Having denied any suggestion that he himself was the Messiah, or Elijah *redivivus*, or the new Moses, the Baptist indicates Jesus as the expected Deliverer (1 : 19–29). Implying but not describing our Lord's Baptism, and omitting the Temptation, St. John proceeds to Jesus' calling of the disciples, who, unlike Mark's story, recognise Jesus from the first as the Messiah, and leave off following the Baptist to become the first apostles. Nathanael is usually identified with Mark's Batholomew (1 : 30–51).

The fourth gospel records only seven miracles, or signs of the Messiah, and each of them is intended to convey one or other aspect of the divine revelation in Jesus. First comes the wedding at Cana, at which Jesus turns water into wine (2 : 1–11). Everything in the story suggests that this is neither a conjuring trick nor a kindly gesture to save the face of an embarrassed host. The guests have already had enough to drink, and to supply them with an additional 120 gallons is hardly human wisdom far less divine.

Doubtless there was a marriage at Cana, near Nazareth, which our Lord and his mother attended. But the incident becomes in John's hands a parable of the messianic banquet, in which Jesus replaces the water of Judaism, represented by the jars for ceremonial ablutions (2 : 6), with the rich new wine of the Gospel. When the Messiah's hour is come (2 : 4), he will provide the Wine and Bread of life, symbolised in the Eucharist, with plenty for all and to spare (cf. 6 : 13).

After this short spell in Galilee (2 : 12), Jesus goes up to Jerusalem. There are indications in Mark's gospel which would not only tally with John's picture of our Lord's ministry having involved much more activity in Jerusalem and Judaea than merely Passion Week, as at first sight seems to be indicated, but also with a ministry lasting longer than the few weeks or months which on the surface appear to be suggested by the synoptic gospels.

St. John mentions here (2 : 13) the first of three passovers, pointing to the fact that our Lord's ministry lasted about three years. The reference in 2 : 20 confirms the evidence of *Luke* 3 : 1 that A.D. 26 was the first year of Jesus' mission, since the rebuilding of the Temple began in 20 B.C., and this, together with the references to the three passovers, would give us A.D. 29 as the probable date of the Crucifixion.

In this gospel the Cleansing of the Temple (2 : 14–17) is put at the beginning of Jesus' ministry instead of at the end. In the synoptic gospels it is the direct cause of the violent opposition of the ecclesiastical authorities which led to our Lord's arrest. There may have been two such occasions, but it is more likely that as a supplement to the substitution of the Gospel for the Law in the Cana story, John means us to see this as the symbolic act of the Messiah, which presaged the end of animal sacrifice round which the worship of the Temple revolved. For this reason, unlike Mark's account, the animals are driven out together with the hucksters, and Jesus predicts that if the Temple is destroyed, he will replace it with the new temple of his Body, the Church (2: 18–25).

The story of Nicodemus (3: 1–16) is like everything else in this gospel more than merely an account of a historical encounter. Nicodemus is a learned Pharisee, who comes for a private theological discussion with Jesus. Our Lord, however, turns what might have been a cosy chat into a stark presentation of the fundamental issue. Unless a man is prepared to sink his pride and acquire a child-like heart, there is no point in discussing the proper service of God, for there is no other way to salvation. On man's side it means repentance (in the water of baptism), and on God's side it means the supernatural gift of the Spirit. Human effort cannot achieve it.

Not all the learning of the theologian, or the virtues of a godly life, or the privilege of belonging to the chosen people can put a man right with God. Only by constant attention to the words of Jesus, by standing humbly at the foot of the Cross, the place of healing as in the Exodus story of the serpent (*Num.* 21: 1–9), and by accepting there daily the forgiveness of God, can we know what it means to have

eternal life. It was for this that God in his love sent his Son into the world.

God's gracious purpose is our salvation and not our condemnation. But the choice is in our own hands. If we choose to live in the darkness of unbelief we damn ourselves, and the final Assize merely confirms the judgment we have already passed on ourselves. To "do the truth", to do good in accordance with the light we have received, is proof that our belief is genuine and that it is God who is working in us (3: 17–21).

We are now given an indication of the missions of the Baptist and of Jesus being conducted almost side by side (3: 22–24). The Baptist gives his last testimony to Jesus before disappearing from the record (3: 25–36). He is the friend who has arranged the marriage of the Bridegroom (Christ) with the Bride (the Church), and his task is now accomplished. Christ must "increase" for he is "from above", and the Baptist is humbly and joyfully content to "decrease", i.e. to see his work taken over by one whom he knows to be God's Son.

The Galilean Ministry

(4: 1 – 6: 71)

THE SETTING of the next story is in Samaritan country, when Jesus is on his way from Judaea to Galilee (4: 1–4). This is the familiar incident of the woman at the well (4: 5–42), but again we must see this as implying something more than a casual meeting. It sets indeed our Lord's seal on Christian missionary enterprise. The

Samaritans and the Jews hated each other cordially not only for historical reasons. Each claimed to have the true religion of the people of YHWH, the Samaritans insisting that the scriptures began and ended with the Pentateuch, and that the true temple was not in Jerusalem but on their Mt. Gerizim.

Jesus, weary and thirsty, turns a casual request for water into a profound discourse on the water of life (i.e. the Gospel) which he offers to all. It may be that the woman had had five husbands, as the narrative says, and was now living with a paramour. It is more likely that the reference is to the gods of the five nations which occupied Samaria after the Assyrian conquest and resettlement (*II Kings* 17: 29-31). If this is so, our Lord's point would be that the Samaritans who now claimed to worship YHWH were not his true bride.

At all events the climax of the discussion is the point where Jesus, having discounted the claim of the Samaritan to have the true faith and the true place of worship, and having reaffirmed that the historical line of revelation passed through Jerusalem and the full Old Testament tradition embodied there, goes on to assert that the day has come for the true worship of God no longer to be channelled through the faith and practice of the Jews, but through the response of men to the promptings of God's Spirit wherever they may be. The end of the story is that many of the Samaritans accept Christ as their Saviour, the first-fruits of the gospel of reconciliation offered to the non-Jewish world.

This sign of the readiness of those who were not so hidebound in their prejudice that they failed to welcome their Messiah when he came, is intensified by the story of the healing of the nobleman's son which concludes the chapter (4: 43-54). Jesus has won over Samaritans, now he wins the allegiance of a Gentile court official, who like the centurion of the synoptic gospels (*Matt.* 8: 5-13), displays a faith in the power of Christ which his own people have not shown.

Soon after this, Jesus goes up to Jerusalem (5: 1) and there he heals a helpless paralytic at the pool of Bethesda (5: 2-9). Not only was this act a violation of the Law, since it was performed on the sabbath, but Jesus' words of forgiveness which followed were a usurpation of the authority of God. On both counts Jesus in the eyes of the ecclesiastics deserved to be put to death (5: 10-18).

Our Lord takes this occasion to speak at some length of his relationship to God. He is the bearer of new life for mankind, and all who respond to him pass from the state of being spiritually dead, though they are physically alive, to the true life that is eternal. Thereby they escape the condemnation which the world must face, since by embracing Christ in baptism they have thrown themselves on God's mercy, confessing that they are guilty men and accepting his forgiveness. What awaits them is the final judgment which awaits all mankind, but which need hold no terror for those who have been faithful to their baptismal vows and may expect the Master's acclaim: Well done, good and faithful servant (5 : 19–29).

In the conclusion of the discourse Jesus adduces three witnesses to his status: John the Baptist, God himself, through the mighty works which he enabled the Son to perform, and the testimony of the scriptures which point to the coming of the Christ (5 : 30–47). We may notice in this passage, and this is true throughout the fourth gospel, how difficult it is to say what are our Lord's own words, and how much these words have been modified by reflection on the part of the evangelist on the significance of Jesus, in the light of the experience of the Church.

Again a scene in Galilee, and this time it is the familiar story of the feeding of the multitude (6 : 1–14). It is followed by the significant allusion to the attempt of the crowd to find in Jesus another Judas Maccabaeus (6 : 15—see p. 367). Then comes the story of our Lord walking on the lake and succouring his terrified disciples (6 : 16–21).

The words which Jesus now speaks (6 : 22–59) turn on the recognition by the crowd who had just been fed that he was the new Moses (6 : 14). This is the point of his claim to be the true Bread of Heaven, the lifegiving food of the spirit which is sent from God. The manna of the Exodus in Moses' day, for all that it sustained the people of God on their journey, had no power to confer the life that triumphs over death. Only the body and blood of God's incarnate Son, offered on the Cross and made available in word and sacrament, guarantees eternal life to every believer.

St. John represents this teaching as being too much for many of Jesus' disciples, who promptly left him. Peter, however, in the name of the Twelve, utters words which many of us will want to make our own: Lord, to whom shall we go? thou hast the words of eternal life. It is at this point with the mention of Judas Iscariot, that the narratives selected from the Galilean ministry come to an end (6 : 60–71).

The Judaean Ministry

(7 : 1 – 11 : 57)

WE NEXT follow Jesus to Jerusalem (7 : 1–13), where at the Feast of Tabernacles we are given a composite picture of the conflicting views of our Lord taken by the various factions in the city, which for the evangelist here stands for the verdict of the world at large: some say he is mad (7 : 20), some say he cannot be anything but the Messiah (7 : 31), some say of him: Never man spake like this man (7 : 46). The authorities, however, entrenched behind their prejudices, have made up their minds that he is a public danger and must be got rid of (7 : 14–53).

St. John gives us now one of the great stories of the gospel, that of the woman taken in adultery (8 : 1–11). Of all the trick-questions put to our Lord none is answered more effectively than this, and certainly none which brings more embarrassment to the sly provocateurs. In the sequel the discourse that Jesus delivers crystallises our Lord's rejection by his own people.

To the claim that as sons of Abraham the Jews were also sons of God, Jesus retorts that their refusal to recognise the truth of his teaching shows them to be much more sons of the devil. His final assertion that he existed before Abraham, and his assumption of the name of YHWH for himself ("I am"), roused his hearers to physical violence, and Jesus symbolically turned his back upon the Temple and the false doctrine it had come to represent (8: 12–59).

The gospel takes us a stage further in the next chapter with the long story of the healing of the man who was born blind (9: 1–41). This incident, described with a wealth of detail seldom found in the gospels, but reminiscent in many ways of similar stories in the synoptic record, is, in the hands of St. John, transformed into a parable of the conversion of the Gentiles. The significance of washing in the pool of Siloam is, for John, baptism into Christ, by which the man at long last sees the light.

In the final words of the narrative, the contrast is drawn between Jew and Gentile. Our Lord came into the world that those who were blind might see. In the event those who thought they could see (the Jews), pronounced judgment on themselves and became blind. In particular their religious leaders, the custodians of the truth delivered by Old Testament priest and prophet, showed by their bigoted refusal to recognise the Light of the world that they were the blindest of all.

About three months would seem to have passed since Jesus left Galilee and went up to Jerusalem to the Feast of Tabernacles in the autumn of A.D. 28 (7: 10). It is now towards the end of the same year, about the time of the feast held to commemorate the re-dedication of the Temple after its violation by Antiochus Epiphanes (10: 22). From this period St. John culls the beautiful discourse in which our Lord likens himself to the Good Shepherd (10: 1–18). The best known Old Testament passage in which God is figured as a Shepherd is, of course, *Ps*. 23, but our Lord may also have had in mind *Isa*. 40: 11 and *Ezek*. 34.

In this gracious utterance, the vivid picture of the eastern shepherd and his handling of his sheep, is full of rich allusion to the relationship between Christ and his people. As a shepherd lies at the entrance of the fold to protect his flock, a veritable living door, so Jesus calls himself the Door through which all men must come to God. There is no other way to the abundant life but through Christ. Jews and Gentiles alike are members of the same flock under the same Shepherd, who of his own free choice gives his life for his sheep.

Jesus' words in which he speaks of his people as being given to him by the Father, and of himself and his Father as one, are more than the opposition can bear. There is murder in their hearts, but Jesus will choose his own time. He leaves Jerusalem and continues his mission on the other side of Jordan in Peraea, and apart from a visit to Bethany described in the next chapter, he remains well away from the city (11: 54) until a few days before the passover (12: 1) in the spring of A.D. 29, when he returns to Jerusalem for the last time (10: 19–42).

The simple household at Bethany, just outside Jerusalem, which was the home of Martha, Mary and Lazarus, and which seems to have been the nearest approach to a home that our Lord knew in his earthly ministry, has already featured in the gospel story (*Luke* 10: 38–42). It is the news of the illness of his friend Lazarus that brings Jesus back from Transjordan for a fleeting visit to Judaea. The story is told with a vividness that makes it plain that whatever lessons the evangelist found in the incident, the raising of Lazarus from the dead is the factual basis of the teaching that springs from it (11: 1–46).

The disciples try to dissuade our Lord from risking the danger of arrest by returning to Judaea. Thomas emerges as a man of great courage, however his later reputation as the Doubter may have fixed his character in popular thought (11: 16). Jesus, however, clearly regards the death of Lazarus, which has followed his illness, as provoking a major issue. To restore a dead man to life on the very doorstep of Jerusalem would be to invite violent reaction from the religious authorities, who would at once want to lay hands on someone who was either an agent of the devil or a charlatan.

Jesus sees the fulfilment of his purpose to raise Lazarus as inevitably leading to his own Death (11: 4), and seems to have gone out of his way to make the miraculous character of his action inescapable (11: 6, 15, 39). Our Lord brings Lazarus back to life, but he interprets this as being of much more significance than restoring a dearly loved friend to his family. His action is the pledge that all who are quickened into new life by their encounter with Christ have entered upon life eternal. Lazarus' body will die again, but the real Lazarus, and with him all who acknowledge the power of Christ to raise them from the death of sin, will never die, for Christ is the Resurrection and the Life.

Our Lord's anguish on this occasion (11: 33, 35) is a blend of human sympathy, the cost of healing (a factor which we must never forget in the long tale of our Lord's ministry to the suffering) and the sense of impending crisis. At the end of the chapter the determination of the ecclesiastics to bring matters to a head, and the prophetic words of Caiaphas the high priest, confirm our Lord's assessment (11: 47–57). Jesus, however, withdraws from the Jerusalem area (11: 54) until the time he has chosen for his final confrontation of the authorities at the next passover.

Holy Week

(12: 1 – 21: 25)

THE ANOINTING of our Lord on the Saturday before Palm Sunday, which the synoptic gospels also record, is now attributed to Mary of Bethany, and Judas Iscariot's motive for the impending betrayal of Jesus is put down in advance to his avarice (12: 1–9). St. John also notes that one of the causes of the hostility of the

authorities towards Jesus was the
defection of many Jews from the
synagogue (12: 10–11). Crowds
of pilgrims in Jerusalem for the
passover came out to greet the
Messiah on Palm Sunday, and the
Pharisees note indignantly that
"the world is gone after him"
(12: 12–19).

Among the pilgrims were some
Gentile adherents of the synagogue
anxious to meet our Lord, who at
this point speaks of his Passion
and his glorification, and, in St.
John's equivalent of the Agony in
the Garden, foresees the power of
the Cross to draw all men to him
(12: 20–33). St. John contrasts
this interest of the Gentiles with
the obduracy of the Jews, and sees
in it a fulfilment of Isaiah's words
(*Isa.* 53: 1; 6: 9, 10), while Jesus
utters a stern warning of the Last
Judgment on all who reject him
(12: 34–50).

There follows the sublime acted
parable of the dignity of Christian
service when our Lord washes the
disciples' feet, normally the duty
of a slave. But as is clear from the
narrative, it is more than a lesson
in humility. It is the cleansing
power of the Death of Christ,
appropriated in Baptism, and repeated in the Eucharist (13: 10),
that is for the evangelist the real
meaning of Jesus' action (13: 1–17).

This moving occasion, recorded
only in St. John and bearing all
the marks of an eyewitness account, is followed by the betrayal
by Judas, which is likewise related
with detail that could only come
from the disciple "whom Jesus
loved" (13: 18–38). It is at this
Last Supper in the Upper Room on
Maundy Thursday, from which

St. John omits the words of the
institution of the sacrament as
being common knowledge and
practice, that the next four chapters of discourse (14: 1 – 17: 26) are
represented as having been uttered
by Jesus.

Although we cannot think of
these words as being remembered
verbatim, no mind other than our
Lord's could have conceived them.
St. John may have shaped into this
form, as Matthew has done with
the Sermon on the Mount, recollections of different occasions and
his reflections upon them, but in
their present setting between the
Last Supper and the Cross, they
convey an imperishable impression
of the range and depth of our
Lord's teaching.

These are chapters to be read
and re-read, and nothing in the
New Testament will bring us
nearer to the mind of Christ.
Here are not only great themes—
peace, love and unity—but great
words: "I am the way, and the
truth, and the life" (14: 6); "He
that hath seen me hath seen the
Father" (14: 9); "Greater love
hath no man than this, that a man
lay down his life for his friends"
(15: 13); "I have overcome the
world" (16: 33); "(I pray) that
they all may be one" (17: 21).
Here too is our Lord's teaching
on the Spirit, who will guide the
Church into all truth (16: 13),
and his matchless prayer of self-
consecration as he turns to face his
Cross (17: 1–26).

It is with these words on his lips
that Jesus now leads the disciples
from the Upper Room across the
Kidron valley to the place of his
Arrest (18: 1). The Agony in the

Garden is omitted, having been suggested already in 12: 27–29, and Jesus submits willingly to the guards who lead him off to his first Trial, the informal hearing before Annas, ex-high priest but still the power behind the throne (18: 2–13). For the report of the Jewish Trial that follows we have the authority of the disciple who had access to the high priest's house, perhaps the Beloved Disciple but more likely the evangelist himself (18: 15).

The preliminary inquiry before Annas—who may have had apartments in the official residence of Joseph Caiaphas, his son-in-law and successor in the office—is followed by the formal Trial before the Sanhedrin, while Peter in the courtyard denies his allegiance to Jesus (18: 14–27). At the subsequent Trial before Pilate, the Jews remain outside the Praetorium to avoid ceremonial contamination in view of the impending passover, while the procurator questions the prisoner inside.

We are not told of any eyewitness at the Roman trial. The report may have come from a slave or a soldier, later converted to Christianity. Pilate is revealed as unsure of his own position and terrified of a charge of treason, despite his conviction that the prisoner was harmless. Two of his jesting remarks have become for different reasons immortal: "What is truth?", "Behold the Man!" After the scourging and the mocking, the choice of Barabbas and the final expedient apostasy on the part of the priests, who put Caesar in the place of God, Jesus is led off to Calvary (18: 28 – 19: 16).

From the Cross, Jesus commends his mother to the care of the Beloved Disciple, and with the cry: "It is finished", proclaims his mission accomplished and seals with his Death the salvation of the world. Since the following day, Saturday, was both the sabbath and the passover, the breaking of the legs of the victims had to be carried out, to hasten death by depriving them of any footrest, thus ensuring heart failure.

Jesus, however, was found to be already dead, and the soldier's action of piercing his side, ostensibly to make certain, is intended by the evangelist to indicate that it is from the Death of Jesus that the sacraments of Baptism (the water) and the Eucharist (the blood) derive their efficacy. Thus while the passover lambs are being killed in the Temple, "Christ our Passover is sacrificed for us" (*I Cor.* 5: 7). God's deliverance of the new Israel is accomplished, and the body of the Second Adam, the first-born of the new Creation, is reverently buried in a "garden" (*Gen.* 2: 8) by Joseph and Nicodemus (19: 17–42).

In the narratives of Easter Day, many will feel that St. John's record of the two disciples who ran to the cave-tomb at the instigation of Mary Magdalene is peculiarly convincing. They find the sepulchre empty, and the body and head wrappings lying in a collapsed state in the position where the body of Jesus had been. However the change was effected, and here we must remain in the presence of mystery, the implication is that the resurrection-body of Jesus had passed through the grave-clothes as it was to pass through doors in the later appearances (20: 1-10).

Mary herself, as incredulous as the disciples, is convinced by the Risen Christ, unrecognised at first then joyfully embraced. His dissuasive words: "Touch me not", confirm the lesson that this is the same Jesus, but not the Master of flesh and blood bound by time and space. She must not cling to the Jesus of Galilee, but keep her love for the Risen Lord who will soon be able to be present with all his disciples everywhere (20: 11-18).

The next revelation is to the apostles themselves, who receive the Lord's commission to go out and do his work in the power of his Spirit. He breathes the life of the new Creation into them, as God breathed life into Adam when the old world was made (*Gen.* 2: 7), and gives them authority over the Church to pronounce forgiveness of sins or to ban from the fellowship (20: 19-23). The winning over of Thomas, the doubter whose doubts were intensified by solitude, and who yet came back to the community and there found his faith, has its point in that he calls to our Lord's mind the vast company of those who will not have seen him in the flesh and yet will believe (20: 24-29).

In a sense the evangelist ends his gospel at 20: 30-31, with a reminder of the many others things which might have been included in the record and with a statement of the purpose of the gospel, which is equally true for the whole of the New Testament. The last chapter is more of an appendix to emphasise the continuing Presence of Jesus with his Church and her world-wide mission. In this story of the appearance of Christ to the fishermen by the lakeside, the imagery of evangelism is as clear as in *Luke* 5: 1-10. Seven disciples are present, the Gentile number; without the guidance of Christ they are powerless to gather men into the Church; with his help the net is filled, 153 being then the total number of known types of fish.

This great world Church in embryo, sustained by the eucharistic Bread from heaven (21: 9, 13), is commended to the pastoral care of the chief apostle, now forgiven his three-fold denial of his Master and given a thrice-emphasised charge (21: 1-17). His own death on a cross is predicted, likewise the advanced age of the Beloved Disciple, who is quoted as the authority behind the gospel, which ends by stressing the limitations of any human record of the words and works of Jesus (21: 18-25).

THE ACTS
OF THE APOSTLES

IN THINKING of the whole Bible as a divine drama of the Acts of God in history, we have so far covered the first two acts. The Old Testament—Act I— is the record of what God did through Israel to point the way back to himself. But we had to learn through Israel's experience, that even with the best guidance and the best intentions, the ineradicable twist in human nature leads us inevitably astray.

Act II—the gospels—is the story of what God did to straighten our twisted nature, by himself becoming man and making it possible for all of us to renew our lives in him. The rest of the New Testament, from *Acts* to *Jude*, is the third act of the drama, when we are shown new men in Christ beginning to break down the barriers that had kept us from God and from one another, and gradually, by the spirit and power of Christ, bringing themselves and society more into harmony with the will of God.

Since the Bible is the story of a cosmic breakdown and a cosmic rescue, reduced to the dimensions of a tiny stage, so that our small minds can comprehend it, Act III, although the scenes change faster than in Act II, is still played out on an area of the earth's surface that can be covered in a few hours' flying time.

The two figures who occupy the centre of the stage throughout most of the New Testament are Jesus and Paul, Master and disciple. In the gospels, we have been able to appraise the evidence for the life and teaching of Jesus, and to form some idea of the impact he made upon his first followers and upon the Jewish community in general. The atmosphere is Palestinian, the thought-forms are entirely Jewish and derived from the Old Testament, the scope is no larger than Galilee and Jerusalem.

When we reach the last page of the gospels, the impression we are left with is of a handful of ordinary men and women transformed into a dynamic community by their experience of the Risen Christ. They are the nucleus of the Kingdom of God which came into being with the advent of Jesus. They have been trained by him in discipleship, and charged with the task of spreading the Good News through all the world.

These are no plaster saints but very fallible men and women, barely recovering from the shattering blow that the Crucifixion had dealt to their belief that Jesus was the heaven-sent Messiah, but now convinced that all that he had said of himself was true. They knew now that he was in a unique sense both human and divine, that God was in him as never in any other man, and that the same Jesus who had been crucified a few short weeks before was with them in a much more vital sense than he had ever been when he was on earth. The Kingdom of God had now come, as he had foretold, "with power", and they were no longer a collection of timid, fearful mortals, but men who were conscious of a new exaltation of spirit, which they had never known before. The last verse of St. Luke's gospel gives us a picture of them after the Ascension, continually in the Temple praising God (*Luke* 24:53).

When we turn from the gospels to the New Testament epistles, however, the scene has materially changed. The atmosphere is no longer Palestinian but imperial; instead of consisting of a handful of Jews in Jerusalem, the Christian Church is now thrusting spearheads into every corner of the Mediterranean. It has become a world-wide missionary movement, and its chief spokesman is not one of the twelve disciples but a converted Pharisee, Saul of Tarsus. In short it is taking shape as the Church we now know; its beliefs are being crystallised; it is losing its local setting and becoming universal.

How did this change take place? Certainly no new elements were imported. All the developments of the early Church, both in its universalism and in its theology, were there in embryo already.

There is no gulf between the gospels and the epistles. The Church, as we find it at the end of the New Testament, is the inevitable successor of that handful of men in the Temple described in the last verse of Luke's gospel. This is the new Israel, the new chosen people of God, the *ecclesia*.

But the question that naturally arises is as to how this transition was effected, and what were the stages through which the Church passed from its real foundation on Easter Day. The answer is to be found in the book of *Acts*, which is essentially a bridge between the life of Jesus and the missionary activities of Paul. It is the story of the birthpangs of the Christian Church.

As we have seen already, the book of *Acts* is the second volume of a work in two parts by St. Luke, the physician and companion of St. Paul's missionary journeys. Like the third gospel, *Acts* is dedicated to Theophilus, and much that has been said of Luke, his patron, his interests and his methods is applicable also here (see pp. 386–388). Undoubtedly, for example, the same historical motive lies behind the writing of volume two as of volume one.

Luke wished to continue the story of Jesus' ministry, and to show that the gospel narrative was only what Jesus "began" to do and teach (1:1), and that in this second part of the record of the beginning of Christianity, Jesus was still as active through his Spirit as he had been in the flesh. In this sense the first thirty years of the story of the Christian Church covered by the book of

Acts (roughly A.D. 30–60) are the sequel to the Galilean and Judaean ministry of our Lord.

There is, too, the same purpose in *Acts* as in the gospel, of commending Christianity to the educated pagan world. Following the same line as in the gospel, the new faith is presented as no petty little Jewish sect, far less an irresponsible movement upsetting law and order, but as a religion with universal possibilities, which would cement those very values of justice and social solidarity which the Roman government claimed to uphold.

We have already seen how in the gospel Luke goes out of his way to emphasise that the Jews were vindictively bent on the Crucifixion of Jesus, and that the Roman government, represented by Pilate, tried to restrain them in vain (*Luke* 23 : 4, 14, 22). Similarly in *Acts*, Paul is the victim of Jewish hatred, despite the clemency of Roman governors or other fair-minded judges on two notable occasions (18 : 14–15; 26 : 31–32). St. Paul is, moreover, proud of his Roman citizenship, and confident that his appeal to Caesar will be justly dealt with.

Undoubtedly, too, St. Luke in writing this book was anxious to give St. Paul his proper place. Paul is his hero, and rightly stands head and shoulders above anyone else in the narrative. Not having been a member of the original circle of disciples, Paul's authority could be questioned in a way that would not be possible in the case of Peter. It is therefore one of Luke's aims to show the first-hand nature of Paul's commission, coming directly from Jesus himself, and to underline the primary part he played in the formation of the Church

Since the author of *Acts* is also the author of the third gospel, the date of the composition of both is probably approximately the same, around A.D. 80. Similarly, the careful gospel historian, who used various sources to compile his first volume, may be expected to have used the same technique for the second. If he followed his method of writing the gospel, the material he used would be partly written documents, and partly information which he collected in the course of his missionary work. Is this apparent from the book itself?

The *Acts of the Apostles* as described by St. Luke fall naturally into two parts, chapters 1–12 and chapters 13–28. The first part has as its chief characters Peter, Stephen and Philip, and deals with the spread of the Church from Jerusalem to Samaria, Caesarea and Antioch. The second part has as its chief character Paul, covers his missionary journeys through Asia Minor and Greece, and eventually brings the Gospel to the capital of the Roman empire itself.

For the second part of the book Luke could not have a better source—he was on the spot himself. As Paul's companion, for part of the time he was an eye-witness of the events he describes, and when he was not actually present he was in an excellent position to know what was happening. Thus the second half of the book is more or less based on Luke's travel-diary (see p. 437).

In the first half of the book it would appear that Luke has collected local traditions from the various centres concerned. Thus where events at Jerusalem are recounted, we may assume that Luke got his information from Peter, Mark and other members of the Jerusalem Church. Details of events at Caesarea would come from Philip the evangelist, with whom Paul and Luke lodged when they stayed there (21: 8). As for the Antioch narratives, if Luke was not himself a native, what happened in this first centre of Gentile Christianity was sufficiently important to be common knowledge. The summaries of sermons delivered by Peter in the early days of the mission would need no special channel of information; they are shortened versions of normal missionary preaching.

The Gospel of the Holy Spirit

THE BOOK OF *Acts* is sometimes called the Gospel of the Holy Spirit, for the obvious reason that St. Luke sees the whole growth and movement of the Church as directed and empowered by no other agency. But the Spirit works through ordinary men and women. Hence this book, properly called the *Acts of the Apostles*, is a story of action, of human personalities. It is history told through human lives. The rise of the Christian Church is traced not in anti-quarian chronicles, but in the life stories of Peter and Philip, of Barnabas and Paul. So is it with the difficulties with which the apostles have to contend, the superstition, idolatry and black magic which permeated the pagan world. These are not described as theories to be disproved, but are incarnated in personal encounters between the missionaries and their opponents.

It is this conception of history as the interplay of personalities that gives the book its remarkable vividness. We are plunged straight into the teeming life of the ancient Near East, with its mixture of Jew and Gentile, its crowded streets and market places, its mobs and ghettoes, its fashionable women and imperial officials, its magicians and intellectuals, and, confronting it all, a handful of men afire with a new message and endowed with superhuman courage.

For some people the miraculous character of some of the events described in the book of *Acts* presents a problem. It is perhaps less of a problem when we recognise the extraordinary atmosphere of these early days of the Church. However we interpret the coming of the Spirit at Pentecost (2: 1–13), it was clearly a supernatural happening which sent the apostles out into the streets of Jerusalem and far beyond, as men gifted with new power and conviction.

Jesus had promised that he would send his Spirit, and his Spirit had come upon them. Almost all the miracles in *Acts* are healing miracles, and the simplest explanation is to take them at their face value as the power of the Risen Christ working through the apostles, and continuing the work of healing which he began in Galilee. Jesus was no longer with them, he was *in* them, and in his name they were able to rout disease and death as he had done himself.

When we think of the enormous field covered in the story of these first thirty momentous years in the life of the Church, the theological problems, the missionary expansion, the difficulty of reconciling a Jewish faith with a Gentile world, the multiplicity of activities, the varied characters of the apostles, their successes and their setbacks, let us marvel at the skill with which Luke summarises it all in a book that can be read through at a sitting.

The literary master of the gospel is no less skilful here. The two main points which he wishes to make, that a Jewish sect became in thirty years essentially a world religion, and that the man mainly responsible for that was Paul of Tarsus, are the two facts which, as we reach the end of the book, remain uppermost in our minds. To achieve this result St. Luke weaves his tapestry with consummate art, selecting typical incidents, providing a suitable background, suppressing all irrelevancies and keeping the theme of his design constantly before our eyes.

As for the historical reliability of the book of *Acts*, it may be said that as an overall picture of the first stage of the Church's story it is irreplaceable. But we have good reason to think that Luke is more than an impressionist painter. It may be noted, for example, how much more detailed is the chronology of the second half of the book, where Luke was an actual eyewitness, than is the case in the early chapters. Luke could easily have supplied the same type of apparently accurate time-table in the first half of his book, but he prefers to leave things deliberately vague. He will not invent what he does not know.

Another mark of an authentic historian is that he does not gloss over the fact that the early Church was no society of paragons. Luke notes their covetousness, their tendency to schism, their discontent, their Pharisaism. Even his hero Paul is not white-washed, and his lamentable quarrel with Barnabas is faithfully recorded.

Again, a mark of the reliability of Luke's record is that the theology bears all the signs of the earliest stage of Christian thinking. Jesus is still largely the Jewish Messiah, for Luke is telling the story of the days before the mind of Paul or John has been busy with the deeper significance of who Jesus was and what he did. This is the stage where the Church was content to say that in knowing Christ men knew God, without trying to define their experience in theological terms. So Luke depicts the evangelistic approach of the earliest missionaries as empirical: "Repent and believe the gospel and you will find that what we are saying is true. You too will be filled with the Holy Spirit as we are, and know this new kind of exhilaration and joy in fellowship."

It was not until the genius of the Church's greatest theologian, who is also the chief character of this book, set itself the task of analysing this experience, and sought to find its meaning within the framework of God, man and the universe, that the faith of the

Church became concrete, rational and defensible. But for all that Paul is Luke's hero, it is no part of the historian's self-appointed task to incorporate Paul's theology in the narrative of Acts. Even if as a practical layman he understood the range and depth of Paul's thought, his object was simply to tell how the Good News spread from Jerusalem to Rome, and he left it to Paul's letters to achieve their own object.

The Ascension and Pentecost
(1 : 1 – 2 : 13)

IN THE FIRST few verses, St. Luke recapitulates the substance of the last chapter of his gospel. He reminds his readers of how the apostles, at first incredulous of the fact of the Resurrection of Jesus, had gradually become convinced by the appearances of the Risen Christ, first to one then to another, that the Lord was not dead but gloriously alive. The forty days for which these appearances lasted would have significance for St. Luke, or indeed for anyone familiar with the Old Testament, because they presented a parallel with the duration of the giving of the Law on Mt. Sinai.

It is quite clear that much of what our Lord had said during his ministry about his Passion and Resurrection had been only dimly understood. St. Luke suggests now, as in his gospel (24 : 44), that it was the instruction of the Risen Lord himself to the disciples that clarified their minds as to the true meaning both of Jesus' words and of the Old Testament scriptures,

and gave them the programme of action for the new Israel, as Moses had done for old Israel.

In the light of this the apostles are anxious to know how soon the mission of the new Israel will be accomplished, and they are told that it means first proclaiming the Gospel in Jerusalem, and from there extending their evangelism to the farthest corners of the earth. This they could not do without new power from God, and they are bidden to await the coming of his Holy Spirit which will make their task possible (1 : 1-8).

The Ascension of our Lord is described with typical restraint. It is a pictorial way of saying that when our Lord had made it plain that the Resurrection was a fact, and had convinced a sufficient number of his followers that this was so, the appearances ceased. The cloud and the angelic figures are the natural biblical accompaniment of divine mystery, conveying the message that Jesus is no longer confined to Galilee but is enthroned and exalted in heaven, from where he is able by his Spirit to be present with his people, and from where at the end of history he will be revealed as Lord of all (1 : 9-11).

It is in the strength of this conviction and this promise that we now find the nucleus of the Church in the days between the Ascension and Pentecost, gathered together in the upper room, doubtless the same large apartment of Mary's house in Jerusalem which had been the scene of the Last Supper. There they met for prayer—the eleven, the ministering women, and our Lord's own family. The narrative suggests the intensity of their expectancy, encouraged no doubt by eager study of the scriptures (1 : 12-14).

But meantime the Church had as its first task the restoration of the damaged authority of the Twelve. The place of Judas, the traitor, must be filled. His unhappy demise is here described as death by dropsy, although in Matthew's gospel it is recorded that he hanged himself. Despite St. Augustine's valiant effort to reconcile the discrepancy by suggesting that the rope broke, it is perhaps better to think that by the time both Luke and Matthew came to write their records it was no longer certain how Judas had died, except that he had come to a bad end.

Peter is clearly leader of the community, which numbers over a hundred, and it is at his instigation that Judas' successor is chosen. The symbolism of maintaining the twelve tribes of the new Israel is too important to be overlooked. It is noteworthy that the chief qualification of the new apostle is that he should have been a first-hand witness of the historical events of Jesus' ministry, and that his task is primarily to declare his knowledge of the Risen Lord. Two men are shortlisted, and after prayer, they draw lots. Matthias becomes the twelfth apostle but neither he nor his rival is ever mentioned again (1 : 15-26).

The story of Pentecost, the first Whitsunday, marks the end of the period of waiting, of reflection, of doubt and despair turning to conviction and expectancy, and heralds the launching of the mission to Jerusalem, which took the Twelve and their associates out from the seclusion of the upper room and into the conflicts and stresses of the public proclamation of the Gospel. This is the basic fact, coupled with the equally basic fact that they went out as men transformed, with a new sense of power and exhilaration and with quite incredible courage.

The narrative of 2: 1-13 describes a communal religious experience shared by the apostles, presumably within the precincts of the Temple, such as has been repeated in some degree at various times and among various groups within the Church since New Testament days. The disciples became ecstatics in a way which is already familiar from our knowledge of early Old Testament prophecy (see pp. 190-191), and which has been experienced in the history of fervent evangelistic revivals in later times. It is clear from 2: 13, where cynical bystanders concluded that the apostles were intoxicated, that this was the first occurrence within the Church of the phenomenon known as *glossolalia* or "speaking with tongues", i.e. men in the grip of deep religious emotion uttering unintelligible noises and behaving in a way which non-participants would view with mixed feelings. Some would see it as undoubtedly proof of divine possession, others would regard it with distaste or scepticism.

That this was a common feature of early Church life is indicated by references such as *Mark* 16: 17; *Acts* 10: 46; 19: 6, and by St. Paul's efforts to keep it within bounds in his letter to Corinth (*I*

Cor. 14). To those within the Christian community it was regarded as a certain sign that the Holy Spirit had taken possession of a believer, as was indeed the case. However uncongenial the idea may be to the more conventional branches of the Church, it is still true that in negro Christian communities, among others, this is as genuine a sign of the presence of the Holy Spirit as the more contemplative experience of the mystic, or the orderly inward response of the churchman to the word and sacrament.

The importance of Pentecost, however, is that this was the first of such evidences of the presence of the Spirit in the Church, the climax of the period of waiting for the promised power. St. Luke sees in it a variety of theological undertones. It is something that can only be described in terms of wind and fire, symbols of God's power and judgment. It is also the first token of the barrier-breaking miracle of the Gospel, which here symbolically abolishes the obstacle of language, the equally symbolic punishment for human pride, which since the days of the Tower of Babel had kept men apart. Pentecost turns the Tower of Babel upside down (see pp. 38–39).

There was no need for a miracle of language. Practically all those present were Jews from overseas, either now resident in Jerusalem or visitors in Jerusalem for the festival, who could understand Greek or Aramaic. But Luke suggests that the new language of God's love in Christ which lay deeper than mere words, and which by the time *Acts* came to be

written had won men's hearts and minds in all parts of the civilised world, was born in the power of Pentecost. In the Jewish Year, Pentecost commemorated the giving of the Law on Sinai, and was celebrated fifty days after the Exodus—Passover. St. Luke as a Christian sees Pentecost as the divine gift of the Spirit, fifty days after the Christian Exodus-Passover, the Crucifixion and Resurrection. Pentecost was also for the Jews the festival of the firstfruits of the harvest (*Lev.* 23). For Luke it is the festival of the firstfruits of the Spirit within the Church, the beginning of the welding together of mankind into one great family of God by the reconciling power of Christ himself, ascended but now in Spirit present with his people everywhere for ever.

The Mission to Jerusalem
(2: 14 – 5: 42)

PETER, AS spokesman, addresses the crowd whose attention has been drawn by the ecstatic behaviour of the apostles, in the first recorded sermon of the Christian mission. St. Luke gives us the précis only (2: 14–40). He begins by disclaiming any possibility that the apostles have been drinking, and invites his listeners to see in their conduct rather the fulfilment of the words of *Joel* 2: 28–32 predicting what would happen in the messianic age. The long expected outpouring of God's Spirit and nothing less had caused this revival of "prophecy".

It is worth noting that Peter quotes Joel's words in full, including the supernatural wonders, implying that these too have in effect been seen in the "miracles and wonders and signs" of Jesus. Following our Lord himself, the early Church used apocalyptic language not literally but symbolically. For Peter and the rest, the mighty works of Jesus culminating in the Resurrection were clear proof that the "last days" foretold by Old Testament prophecy had begun. In one sense the Day of the Lord's judgment was yet to come, but in another sense it had already dawned. Now was the time therefore to heed Joel's warning before it was too late (2: 14–21).

Peter's presentation of Jesus in this first stage of the mission is, in Luke's version, wonderfully realistic: Jesus, as everyone present knew, had by all that he had done shown that God was using him to do his work, to confront men with the truth and to undermine the power of evil. Yet despite every evidence of his divine commission, God's own people had handed him over to the lawless Gentiles to be crucified. That this was no mere human choice but part of the divine plan was clearly shown by the fact of the Resurrection. God had raised him from death, because his Messiah could not be subject to Satan's thrall.

David's words (Ps. 16: 8–11), said Peter, have been marvellously fulfilled. He was not speaking of himself when he said that death and decay were not to be his fate, because David's tomb with his mouldering bones is known to all. He was obviously speaking of the new David, and of his empty tomb, and we have seen this Risen Jesus, who is now exalted with God and has poured out this new power which you see and hear.

Again, continues the apostle, David's words have come true (Ps. 110: 1) when he foretold that Messiah would sit at God's right hand, for Jesus of Nazareth, the Crucified, is now by the Act of God exalted to be Lord and Christ. The climax of Peter's sermon is a call for repentance, with baptism into the new community as a sign of God's forgiveness, and the promise of the same experience of the Holy Spirit as has been vouchsafed to the apostles. The time is short but the opportunity is there for all who choose to seize it (2: 22–40).

If Peter's use of the Old Testament here strikes us as somewhat artificial, it is nevertheless in keeping with the way the early missionaries in general were forced to handle the scriptures when they were addressing Jews. They were trying to convince people who had already made up their minds that the infallible Word of God clearly indicated what Messiah would be like when it pleased God eventually to send him. Ecclesiastics and ordinary folk alike were satisfied that according to the Old Testament a felon's death on a cross was no part of the picture.

But the apostles had lived with Jesus, and they had seen and listened to the Risen Christ. For them the problem was solved. They were convinced now that what had happened was in the deepest possible sense "according to the scriptures", that Christ was indeed the climax of the whole story of God's dealings with Israel. Nevertheless they were often hard put to it to produce chapter and verse for their conviction, apart from *Isa.* 53, which, of course, until Jesus adopted the role of the Servant as his own had never previously been associated with the Messiah.

If the events of Jesus' life, his Death and his Resurrection had been a mechanical fulfilment of Old Testament prophecy, the missionaries' task would have been an easy one. But the Word made flesh was greater than the Word in writing. God had acted in Christ in such a way as to give the scriptures of the Old Testament a significance which went deeper than any verbal parallelism.

The whole gamut of the Law, the Prophets and the Writings had been preparing the way for the Gospel by outlining the pattern of God's ways with mankind, but it is not surprising that when the Son of God came, human wit, left to itself, failed to recognise him. Indeed one of the ablest Jews—St. Paul—who had no doubt at all about what the scriptures meant, and felt that he had all the answers to the presumptuous claims of these Galilean illiterates, had to be turned inside out by the Holy Spirit before he would admit that God refused to be bound by human estimates of how precisely he would achieve his purpose for the world's salvation.

Nevertheless, we are told that on the occasion of Peter's first sermon, if Luke is not compressing events which covered a longer period, up to three thousand responded to his appeal and were baptised into the Church, moved no doubt more by what they had seen than by the apostle's rather unconvincing scriptural arguments.

The marks of the new community are described as obedience to the teaching of the apostles, a common fellowship, eucharistic celebration, and meetings for prayer. A sense of awe prevailed in face of the signs of divine power working through the Twelve, and voluntary sharing of possessions was practised. Continuing, as good Jews, their religious obligations in the Temple, they also gathered in each other's houses for sacramental occasions. The hallmark of their fellowship was a joyfulness and patent sincerity which won the sympathy of all, and their numbers increased from day to day (2: 41-47).

The healing of a well-known crippled beggar by the apostles, effected in the manner of the gospel cures, but now by the authority of Christ (3: 1-11), provides the occasion for Peter's second sermon (3: 12-26). Such a cure, he claims, would have been impossible for ordinary men like the apostles. But the God of Israel has vindicated his Servant Jesus (A.V. = "Son" v. 13), the Holy and Just One, the Author of life, and it is through faith in his power to heal that the cripple is now restored.

The suffering and death of the Messiah had been foretold by scripture (*Isa.* 53), Peter went on, although the Jews did not recognise it, but that did not mitigate the crime of the Crucifixion. God in his mercy, however, had given them this one further chance of repentance before the Judgment. They have killed the promised prophet "like unto Moses", and for that the penalty is death, were it not that God, remembering his covenant with his chosen people, now offered them first before all others this opportunity to become reconciled with him.

While popular support for the new preaching increased (4: 4), opposition also began to gather. In this the Sadducees took the initiative since the Temple was within their jurisdiction. They were constitutionally opposed to messianic movements of any kind which might disturb the status quo, but in addition any doctrine of resurrection was against their convictions, and the identification of Jesus with the new Moses was outrageous. They therefore put an end to Peter's sermon and clapped the apostles in the guard-room (4: 1-4).

Peter's defence on the following day is an uncompromising declaration of allegiance to Christ as the only way of salvation (4: 5-12). Surprised at the "boldness" and fluency of ignorant Galilean fishermen, but faced with the incontrovertible fact of the cripple's recovery, and popular support for the apostles, the authorities could do no more than forbid them to mention the name of Jesus in public and let them go (4: 13-22).

This first great victory for the cause is acclaimed by the whole community and their exultation issues in another pentecostal experience. Reference is made again to the policy of pooling resources which prevailed at this early stage,

a policy as unrelated to monastic practice as to any form of communism. Barnabas appears for the first time in the record as a model for this willingness of the "haves" to share with the "have-nots", in contrast to the unsavoury pair whose scandal is next related (4: 23-37).

The fact of the sudden deaths of Ananias and Sapphira is on the face of it quite credible. What is not credible is any suggestion that the leader of the Christian community deliberately brought about their end. The narrative is obviously compressed and perhaps for this reason tends to give a false impression. It may be that the dramatic collapse and death from shock of a husband and wife, who were later discovered to have perpetrated a fraud, was related as a terrible warning to others.

As it stands, the crime of the unfortunate pair was clearly not that they refused to co-operate in the system of voluntary sharing, but that they ostentatiously claimed to have made a great sacrifice, and in fact secretly retained some of the proceeds of the sale of their property. Their sin was hypocrisy which Peter rightly regards as lying to God (5: 1-11). We get an impression at this stage of many genuine cures being performed by the apostles, as well as of a fair amount of superstitious respect for their powers. Solomon's Portico, a colonnaded cloister just outside the Temple, seems to have been the centre of this healing mission (5: 12-16).

Once again the Temple authorities try to stamp out this disturbing new movement, and the apostles are imprisoned for the second time. The "angel" who set them free may have been a secret sympathiser among the guards, which would explain the dismayed concern of the Sadducees as to where this insidious doctrine would end (5: 17–24). Meantime the apostles were back in the Temple proclaiming the faith, and on being re-arrested were again brought before the authorities.

In reply to the high priest's charge, which among other things betrayed a guilty conscience about the Crucifixion, the apostles once more boldly affirmed their allegiance to Christ as Saviour. They were saved, by the intervention of Gamaliel, from the consequences of what must have seemed to the Sanhedrin their insufferable blasphemy in claiming exclusive rights over the Holy Spirit (5: 25–42).

Gamaliel, under whom Paul had studied (22: 3), was the leader of the Pharisaic party, and a man of great reputation both for his learning and his wisdom. In this case he counsels moderation. There had been many such movements, he reminds the council, which had proved to be but nine-days' wonders. If this new group is of the same kind it will die a natural death. If on the other hand it is God-inspired nothing can stop it. The apostles are flogged as a cautionary measure, forbidden once more to continue their mission, and liberated. Next day they are back in their accustomed place proclaiming the faith, popular feeling and the opposition of the Pharisees being too strong for the Sadducees. Proud to share the sufferings of their Master, the apostles continue their work in public and in the house-churches, proclaiming that Jesus is the Christ.

"The Blood of the Martyrs . . ."

(6: 1 – 8: 40)

THIS splendid picture of the young Church, contained in the first five chapters of *Acts*, may be too good to be true but it is not too good to be possible. We have been dealing with a small localised community in the first flush of a new enthusiasm, in the very place where the Lord had taught, healed, appeared to be crushed but, miraculously, triumphed over the worst that men could do against him. Little wonder that there is this idyllic quality about the earliest stage of the Church's story; exhilaration is the keynote, devotion and self-sacrifice are crowned with success, problems are few and opposition is negligible.

It is not clear how much time has elapsed between the end of chapter five and the beginning of chapter six. There is obviously a new situation, which calls for new tactics, and we may suppose that the events now to be described take place a year or two later. Numbers have grown considerably and there are two factions within the Church, the native born, Aramaic - speaking, Jerusalem Christians (Hebrews) and the overseas, Greek-speaking, Jewish Christians now resident in Jerusalem (Grecians). There is also a well defined social class known as the "widows", who are dependent on charity and are to be found in both camps. Common ownership has apparently proved impracticable.

Trouble about the fair distribution of food, as between the two groups of needy widows, leads to the appointment by the Twelve of seven auxiliaries (6: 1–6). It may be that there were seven centres of distribution which one or other of the newly appointed stewards was to supervise. It is more likely that Luke sees significance in the Gentile number, and looks on this as the first sign of a breakaway from the exclusively Jewish origin of the faith.

At all events the seven men have Greek names, and two of them, Stephen and Philip, almost immediately distinguish themselves as liberal in outlook and prepared to adopt a more radical line. It seems, therefore, that more was involved than a mere delegation by the Twelve of the humdrum task of administering the soup-kitchens, leaving them to carry on with the preaching work of the mission. The appointment of the seven would appear rather to be a concession to the claims of the overseas Jews to have some share in the government of the Church. At this stage they are not designated as "deacons", and indeed their solemn commission by prayer and the laying on of hands, as Moses commissioned Joshua (*Num.* 27: 18, 23), suggests rather their being set apart for the full office of the ministry. It is not clear from the Greek text whether it was only the Twelve or the whole congregation who took part in the ordination. The community certainly chose and nominated the candidates as being men "full of the Spirit and of wisdom".

The appointment of the seven sets the stage for the emergence of Stephen (6: 7–15) as the first evangelist to make a clear distinction between Judaism and Christianity, and to mark, as it were, a halfway stage between the conservatism of the Twelve and the radicalism of St. Paul. There is reference to further progress in the Church's growth, including the access of many of the Jewish priesthood, presumably of the lower orders of the hierarchy. Disputations take place in one or more of the synagogues of the city frequented by overseas Jews, in which Stephen argued in defence of the Christian interpretation of the scriptures. It is fascinating to speculate whether one of his chief opponents in the synagogue attended by Cilicians was an equally zealous advocate of his beliefs, Rabbi Saul of Tarsus, more generally known by his Greek name, Paul.

Failing to refute Stephen's arguments, the Jews secured his arrest under an indictment of blasphemy, and accused him before the Sanhedrin of claiming that Jesus could destroy and rebuild the Temple (cf. *Matt.* 26: 61), and of overturning the law of Moses. Stephen's speech in his own defence appears to be an innocuous review of Old Testament history (7: 1–53), but its purpose is clearly to undermine the accepted foundations of Jewish religion, by admitting the charges to be true and questioning the official view of both the Law and the Temple.

His case is that God appeared to Abraham first, not on the holy soil of Palestine, but in Mesopotamia, and that Israel became the chosen people before the rite of circumcision was instituted (7: 1–8); the appointed meeting place between God and his people was the Tent in the wilderness, and it was Solomon, not God, who wanted a Temple (7: 44–47); even Isaiah condemned the Temple and spoke of the inwardness of true worship (7: 48–50); the Jews' treatment of Moses and the prophets in the past had made it inevitable that when Messiah came they would treat him in the same way (7: 51–53).

The reaction of the Sanhedrin to this provocative speech was one of unbridled fury, which was intensified when Stephen daringly proclaimed Jesus as the divine Son of Man. The parallelism between Stephen's trial and subsequent death and that of Jesus is emphasised by his prayer for his murderers and his commendation of his soul to his Lord. Thus died Stephen, the first Christian martyr, and Luke skilfully introduces as a witness, and no doubt instigator of the stoning of Stephen, a young rabbi whose name was Saul. St. Augustine said that it was Stephen's prayer for his persecutors that started the questions in Paul's mind which led to his eventual conversion (7: 54–60).

This throwing down of the gauntlet by a notable spokesman of the young Church led to a violent persecution which, however, was the means of driving the Christians not underground, but out of Jerusalem, and from there through-out Palestine, so that the Gospel instead of being suppressed was proclaimed wherever they went. For the first, but by no means the last time the blood of the martyrs was the seed of the Church. Foremost among the persecutors was Saul of Tarsus, who behaved with all the venom and cruelty of the worst kind of religious intolerance. Only the Twelve, and presumably the rest of the more conservative native Jewish Christians, remained unmolested (8: 1–4).

The mission of Philip the evangelist, one of the seven, is now recorded as the first step towards a wider conception of the Church. His work among the hated Samaritans is blessed with a rich harvest, and crowned, on the visit of Peter and John, with ecstatic evidence of the presence of the Spirit. Simon Magus, the sorcerer, who tried to buy this apparently magic power of the apostles, affords an early glimpse of the superstition with which the Church had to contend (8: 5–25).

A further step in the expansion of the Church is taken, when Philip admits by baptism into the fellowship a Gentile adherent of the Jewish faith. This vivid picture of a highly intelligent Ethiopian official, puzzling over the meaning of Isaiah's prophecy of the Servant, and being given a satisfying answer by a Christian missionary, must have been included by St. Luke as a typical example of the accession of many such devout pagans, who found their previous attraction to Judaism now superseded by the more powerful persuasiveness of the Gospel (8: 26–40).

The Conversion of Paul

(9: 1–30)

THE NEXT few verses record the most important event in the whole history of the Christian Church, the conversion of Paul. No single man has done more to make Christianity a world religion, and certainly no single man has had a greater influence on Christian thought. It is a mark of Paul's greatness that he has been so often maligned and misunderstood as the man who perverted the simple Gospel of Jesus into an involved and complicated theological system. Nothing could be farther from the truth. No one has ever been closer to the mind of Jesus or has more clearly seen the significance of what our Lord said and did.

Luke has already introduced him as the most violent and able opponent of Christianity in the first stage of the Church's story. Paul will tell us himself, later in Acts and in his letters, of his birth in the Greek city of Tarsus in Cilicia, a province of Asia Minor, as the son of a loyal Jew who enjoyed the privilege of Roman citizenship; of his training as a rabbi and a tentmaker; of his study under Gamaliel in Jerusalem. No rabbi was more zealously conscientious in his endeavour to live up to the demands of the Law upon his private life, no one was more proud of his Jewish ancestry and of the heritage of Israel.

It is a measure of his zeal that he emerges in Luke's narrative, first as the instigator of Stephen's death, and now as the Grand Inquisitor, determined to root out this poisonous new heresy which had disclosed itself under Stephen, not as the harmless folly of simple Galilean fishermen, who believed they had found the Messiah, but as a blasphemous affront to the infallible Law of God as delivered through Moses to his people.

It must be crushed not only as a dangerous attack on the authority of the divinely ordained ecclesiastical hierarchy, and an insidious attempt to vitiate the claim of Temple and synagogue to be the sole channel of access to God, but above all as an outrageous perversion of the scriptures by which these people sought to prove that their misguided carpenter-founder who had properly died a criminal's death was in fact the glorious heaven-sent Messiah of psalm and prophecy, who would one day appear.

St. Augustine has hinted (see p. 428) and modern psychology can help us to understand, how doubts began to grow in the mind of this bigoted Pharisee. How could Stephen die with a prayer for his murderers on his lips? Did the unremitting attempt to live up to the impossible demands of the Law bring a man closer to God and to salvation? Did the scriptures not indeed say that the Servant of God must suffer to conquer, and was this not perhaps part of the true messianic hope? Could it be the will of God to harry these defenceless Nazarenes? What had happened to the dead body of Jesus?

All this is conjecture, as is the impression that as his doubts increased Paul's fury redoubled, as he hastened north as far as Damascus with letters of authority from the high priest to root out any followers of the Way, as Christianity was called in those early days, and bring them back to Jerusalem for trial (9: 1–2). What is not conjecture but plain fact, is that he entered Damascus a stricken, broken man, physically blind, mentally shattered, to become, on his recovery, the humblest of the Christian family, the slave of Christ, and the most fearless and able protagonist of the faith he had tried to exterminate.

It is trifling with religion, psychology and common sense to attribute what happened on the Damascus road to hallucination, epilepsy, sunstroke or hysteria. There is no evidence that Paul ever suffered from any of them. Nothing less than a miracle could have revolutionised the life of this eminently sane and balanced rabbi. His own testimony is that Christ laid hold of him (*Phil.* 3: 12). He came face to face with the Risen Saviour, as the apostles had done after the Resurrection, and he knew in that moment that Jesus of Nazareth was indeed the Messiah.

Luke's story of his conversion (9: 3–9) supplies the details which are substantially the same as Paul's own accounts later in *Acts* (22: 6–11; 26: 12–18). The sequel in terms of his reception into the Christian community in Damascus with the moving words: "Brother Saul", and this to the terror and scourge of the believers, can tell us nothing of the agony of remorse that Paul must have endured, as he reflected on the purpose with which he had set out and the crushing blow which his pride and self-esteem had suffered (9: 10–19).

The narrative of *Acts* is neces-

sarily compressed, and Paul himself tells us that immediately after his conversion he went into retreat, doubtless to try to clarify his own mind (*Gal.* 1: 17). It was probably some time later, when he had rethought his position, that he returned to Damascus as a Christian missionary, which naturally brought upon his head the concentrated fury of his former Jewish associates (9: 20–25) and ended in his ignominious escape over the city wall in a basket.

Moreover he adds in the same autobiographical passage in his letter to the *Galatians*, that it was not until three years later that he had his first meeting with the apostles in Jerusalem (*Gal.* 1: 18). It would be on this two-weeks visit that Barnabas came to his aid, and vouched for him with the naturally cautious Twelve, who knew him only by his bad reputation. This visit too ended in a hasty departure because of Jewish opposition, and Paul was sent back to Tarsus for his own safety (9: 26–30).

Meantime, Luke having brought his hero on to the stage and established his right to be called the thirteenth apostle, with an equally direct commission from Christ, returns to the story of developments in the mission, which made it necessary for Paul to return, this time to hold the stage until the end.

The Mission to the Gentiles
(9: 31 – 13: 3)

WITH THE conversion of Paul and the dispersal of the more liberal elements, the Palestinian

Church had a period of peaceful development (9: 31). Luke records two notable cures performed by St. Peter, Aeneas a paralytic at Lydda, and Dorcas, an active church worker at Joppa, who were both restored to life and vigour (9: 32–42). Peter's host at Joppa is mentioned specifically because tanning was an "unclean" profession in the eyes of Jewish orthodoxy. Simon's house was "by the sea side" (10: 6), not for health reasons but to keep him as far as possible away from the punctilious upholders of the ceremonial Law. In lodging with him, Peter is breaking down another barrier (9: 43).

The story that follows (10: 1–48) of the conversion of Cornelius, is told at such length that it is obvious that Luke considers it to be highly important, as indeed it was. Philip had preached to the Samaritans, and an Ethiopian had under his guidance become a Christian. The significance of Cornelius is that he was not only a God-fearing Gentile, like the Ethiopian eunuch, but a Roman army officer, and that he and his friends were baptised into the faith on the instructions of Peter, the chief apostle and head of the Church.

Everything in the story, apparently a series of coincidences, is designed to show that there was no chance in the matter at all, but that God was guiding Peter against his will to admit the right of Gentiles to enter the Church on equal terms with Jews. A heaven-sent dream of a variety of animals, all pronounced technically "clean" by divine revelation, is taken by Peter to mean that the dietary laws of *Lev.* 11, and hence the strict ceremonial distinction between "clean" Jews and "unclean" Gentiles, are no longer valid for Christians.

The historical basis of the story may be that this Roman, an adherent of the Jewish synagogue in Caesarea, had had his interest in the new faith aroused by Philip, the evangelist, who was now resident there (8: 40). Hearing of the visit of the leader of the Christians to Joppa, Cornelius invited him to address a meeting of his friends. In retrospect the circumstances have probably taken on a more dramatic character.

In the summary which Luke gives of Peter's sermon on this occasion (10: 34–43), the main new point compared with Peter's previous sermons is that he now recognises that a man who reverences God and seeks to do his will, whether Jew or Gentile, is acceptable to him. This recognition is spectacularly confirmed when the predominantly Gentile gathering becomes ecstatic in the power of the Spirit. Baptism into the full fellowship of the Church had to be the obvious conclusion to this Gentile Pentecost (10: 44–48).

The sequel to this important development was that Peter, on his return to Jerusalem, was taken to task by the strict Jewish Christian faction within the Church for consorting with Gentiles. Peter has to convince them with a full account of the incident, that this had not been done on his own initiative but by the inescapable leading of God. Luke is once more guilty of anticipating future developments, when he pictures the right-wing Jewish Christian party as accepting Gentile Christianity at this stage as a *fait accompli*. It is clear both from the subsequent narrative and from Paul's letters, that a mission to the Gentiles was not contemplated by the Twelve at this time, and that resistance to the idea of Gentiles within the Church continued on the part of the Jewish Christians for some considerable time (11: 1–18).

Nevertheless events, or rather God's Holy Spirit, proved too strong for religious conservatism, as has happened time and again in the subsequent history of the Church down to the present day. The Christians who were driven out of Jerusalem, at the time of the persecution arising out of Stephen's witness, had scattered far and wide taking the Gospel with them. Some of these liberal Jewish Christians, when they reached Antioch, the great eastern metropolis of the empire, a city of half a million people and the capital of Syria, had already begun a mission to the Gentiles.

Cautious as ever, perhaps necessarily so, the Jerusalem church sent Barnabas to investigate, and he, himself a Cypriot, and therefore less parochial than most of his colleagues, recognised that what was happening at Antioch, was the work of God. Shrewdly reckoning that there was only one man capable of exploiting this promising situation, Barnabas fetched Paul from his obscurity in Tarsus, and for a whole year between them they built up the church at An-

tioch as the first centre of Gentile Christianity. It was here, too, that for the first time the Nazarenes, or followers of the "Way", were given the nickname of "Christians", which like "Quakers" and "Methodists" of later days soon became an honoured title proudly acknowledged (11 : 19–26).

Luke is now rounding off the first part of his account of the origins of the Church. He has sketched admirably the territorial spread of Christianity in the Levant, and the progressive victory of the liberalising and universalist view as opposed to the narrower attitude of the Jerusalem Christians, who would have kept the Church tied to the apron strings of Judaism, and thereby, humanly speaking, would have condemned it to eventual extinction as an ineffective sect of the Jewish faith.

He has given us a glimpse of the organisation and practice of this first stage of the Church's existence: the Twelve as the supreme authority, and under them a variety of ill-defined subordinates, evanglists, prophets and elders. The Eucharist and Baptism are well-established, house-churches are the normal place of meeting, *glossolalia* is a frequently attested evidence of the Holy Spirit but so also is the excellence of character of a man like Barnabas (11 : 24).

The stage is being set for the beginning of the second period of growth, when Paul and his associates embarked on the gigantic task of taking the Gospel to the whole of the known world. As a preliminary to this, Luke records the persecution of the Jerusalem church by Herod Agrippa I, grandson of Herod the Great, and last king of Judaea, whose short reign from A.D. 39–44 interrupted the line of Roman procurators by whom Judaea was governed during New Testament times (12: 1–2).

The apostle James was martyred, the rest of the Twelve had either already taken flight or did so then. Peter himself was imprisoned, but once again sympathisers among the prison guard came to his aid and he was able to escape, perhaps to Antioch (Gal. 2: 11), having nominated James, the brother of Jesus, as head of the Jerusalem church (12: 3–24). From now on there are two chief centres of Christianity: the mother church at Jerusalem, presided over by the ultra-orthodox James, whose leanings towards Judaism made him even more acceptable to the Jewish authorities than the Twelve, and the progressive young church of Antioch, which from this point becomes the power house of the new evangelism and the real headquarters of the Church.

Thus after the dispersal of the Twelve, we find Paul and Barnabas returning to Antioch having visited Jerusalem with a gift from the Antioch church for the famine-stricken community there (11: 27–30; 12: 25). With them they take John Mark, later the author of the gospel, whose mother's house was still the chief meeting place of the Jerusalem church (12: 12). They had not been long in Antioch before the church there commissioned the three of them, Paul and Barnabas as fully-fledged missionaries, young Mark as an apprentice, to set out on their first missionary journey (13: 1–3).

Paul would by this time be about 44 years old. Fourteen years had elapsed since his conversion in A.D. 32, most of which time he had been engaged in missionary activity in Syria and Cilicia, his own native province (Gal. 1: 21). Now he sets out with the world as his parish, the accredited leader of the mission to the Gentiles, as had been agreed with the Twelve before Herod Agrippa's persecution scattered them (Gal. 2: 1–10).

Luke's narrative in this second half of Acts needs little comment. With deft strokes of his brush he paints an unforgettable picture of Paul and his associates, battling against the bigotry of fanatical Jews and against indifference, ignorance and superstition among the Gentiles, yet despite these and many other obstacles—not least ill-health and physical danger—the courage of this small band of indomitable men carries the Gospel through country after country to the very heart of the empire. Paul himself is tireless. Preaching, teaching and travelling, working at his trade to support himself, arguing and pleading in synagogues and public places or wherever the opportunity arose, for the next twelve years he gave himself no quarter.

On top of this and all his care and concern for people, and for the progress of the communities he founded, came his correspondence —letters to churches and letters to friends. Dashed off at odd moments as circumstances allowed, these letters are his great legacy to the Church. Of those that have been preserved, ranging from profound theological argument to happy personal greetings, the least we can say is that they form an indispensable companion to Luke's story. We ought not to regard them as disembodied utterances, to be studied as chapters in a textbook of theology, but ought rather to read them in their proper place in Paul's story—and in a modern translation—as part of the living growth of the New Testament Church. In this way we shall not only avoid the mental indigestion which we should undoubtedly suffer if we began at *Romans* 1 and read straight through to *Philemon*—an artificial sequence based on length—but we shall also illuminate the story that Luke has to tell in *Acts*, and see more clearly why the name of Paul holds the place it does in Christian history.

First Missionary Journey
(13 : 4–15 : 35)

SETTING OUT from Antioch in A.D. 46, the three missionaries made their way via Cyprus to the south coast of Asia Minor. Paul suffered from what he calls a "thorn in the flesh" (*I Cor.* 2 : 3; *II Cor.* 12 : 7), which may have been recurrent malaria. This might explain why he left the swampy terrain of the coast and headed north into the mountains of the interior. What is not explained is why at this point Mark left the party and returned to Jerusalem—was it homesickness, faintheartedness, a quarrel, or did he not approve of Paul's attitude towards the Gentiles? (13 : 4–13).

At all events Paul and Barnabas proceed to another Antioch, an important town in the province of Galatia. Here they would find the mixed population common to cities of the empire, native Asians, Greeks, Romans and a colony of Jews. It was Paul's practice in his campaigns to approach the local synagogue first of all, partly because of his conviction that the Jews, as the people of the promise, should be given every opportunity to embrace what he believed to be the true faith of Israel, as embodied in the scriptures and fulfilled in Christ, and partly because the fringe of Gentile adherents of the synagogue provided a natural avenue, through the Old Testament faith with which they were familiar, not only to their becoming Christians themselves, but also to Paul's establishing contacts with their pagan compatriots.

His sermon on this occasion may be taken as typical of his normal missionary preaching directed to Jews, claiming that Jesus was the long expected Messiah as the scriptures abundantly showed, and that only by believing in him and in forgiveness of sins through him, could men find the salvation that obedience to the Jewish Law could never provide (13 : 14–41). Jewish opposition and Gentile response provoked Paul into a public declaration that, having given the Jews an opportunity which they had rejected, he would now confine himself to evangelising the Gentiles. This too became his common practice (13 : 42–49).

The mission to Pisidian Antioch ended, like so many subsequent campaigns, with the expulsion of the missionaries at the instigation of outraged orthodox Jews. A similar pattern of events evolved at Iconium, their next centre (13: 50 – 14: 5). The following few verses give a fascinating glimpse of the superstitious backwoods of Asia Minor, where the inhabitants spoke an unknown dialect and mistook the apostles for gods in disguise (14: 6–18).

Jewish venom, however, pursued them even there, and Paul was stoned and left for dead. Yet on his recovery he had no thought of retreat, but continued to the next town and, having established a Christian cell there, he retraced his steps visiting the little churches he had founded and arranging for some kind of rudimentary organisation to carry on the life of the community. Thus ended the first tour which may have lasted anything up to two years, and the apostles returned to Antioch to face a major crisis (14: 19–28).

The orthodox Jewish position was that unless a man was born a Jew, or as a Gentile proselyte became, in effect, a Jew by circumcision and full observance of Jewish Law, he could not share in the Old Testament promises made to Israel. Most Gentiles who were attracted by Judaism were drawn to it on ethical and monotheistic grounds, and refused both circumcision and compliance with ceremonial law. They preferred to remain merely sympathetic adherents of the synagogues, like Cornelius and the Ethiopian eunuch.

The most conservative section of the Jewish Christians, however, who had simply added the belief that Jesus was the Messiah to a full acceptance of Judaism, were insistent that any Gentile who became a Christian should come into the membership of the Church on the same terms, involving circumcision, observance of Jewish dietary laws, and avoidance of contact with their former Gentile associates wherever possible.

This view, which was to some extent shared by all members of the Jerusalem church, was of course quite intolerable to Paul. It was alarmingly clear to him that if this were to be insisted on, Christianity would die a natural death or the Church would be split in two. A compromise must somehow be reached. It appears that in the absence of Paul and Barnabas on the first missionary tour, some of the stricter members of the Jerusalem church had come to Antioch, and had propounded this extreme view to the consternation of the Gentile Christians there (15: 1).

It was decided that a delegation led by Paul and Barnabas should go to Jerusalem to thrash the matter out. This was the occasion of the first General Council of the Christian Church at Jerusalem in A.D. 49, described in 15: 2–29, and by the grace of God Paul won the day. Not only did Peter support the liberal universalist outlook, based on his own missionary experience, but even James, spokesman of the ultra-Jewish party within the Church, and to all accounts a man with the habits and mentality of John the Baptist, subscribed to it. Some minor reservations were made, but in principle the victory had been won by Paul, and the decision of the

Council was embodied in a decree, armed with which Paul and Barnabas returned to Antioch (15: 30–35).

This did not mean that the problem was solved once and for all. It was to be a live issue within the Church for many years to come. Nationalism dies hard, and the tradition of a thousand years is not readily thrown aside. But history was on the side of the catholic principle, and when Rome and not Jerusalem became the centre of Christianity, its international character was assured.

An example of how hard the Jewish Christian outlook died, and which gives us some idea why so much of Paul's controversial writing in his letters is concerned with this very problem of the place of Jewish practice in the Christian Church, is to be found in an incident which no doubt made the Council of Jerusalem inevitable. It is referred to in Paul's letter to the *Galatians* (2: 11–21). It appears that Peter, not for the first time in his life, went back on his word. Having mixed freely with the Gentile converts in Antioch at the common meal which included Holy Communion, he took fright when some of the stricter partisans from Jerusalem raised objections, and retreated to the old Jewish position of segregation. Even Barnabas was affected.

Paul apparently did not mince matters, but took Peter to task in front of the whole congregation and rated him soundly for his inconsistency. It was a mark of the greatness of the two men and of their Christian charity, that they were able to give and take

hard knocks and still remain brothers in Christ. About this time Paul wrote, from Antioch, a letter to the churches he had founded in Galatia on the first missionary journey. If we read the epistle to the *Galatians* at this point it provides an admirable commentary on the whole problem (see pp. 468–472).

Apparently these young churches were being upset by the same type of Jewish Christian conservatism as Paul himself had had to face in Antioch, and for which he had publicly rebuked Peter. His argument in the letter is that Jewish Law had its uses, but it had now been superseded by the new and greater Law of Christ. Under his Law all Christian men, whether Jews or Gentiles, stand equal and free before God.

Second Missionary Journey (15: 36 – 18: 22)

NOW THAT this vexed question had been officially settled, Paul's next task was to communicate the decision of the Council of Jerusalem to the young churches of Galatia. This he decided to do in person, armed with the document, and to extend it into a second missionary tour. Barnabas is to be his companion, but Barnabas insists on taking his cousin John Mark, and this Paul will not have. No one who had put his hand to the plough and turned back, as Mark had done on the first journey, was fitted for a missionary role. Happily, Paul later on had cause to revise his opinion (*Col.* 4: 10–11; *II Tim.*

4: 11), but in the meantime the quarrel was hot and the apostles decided to separate, Barnabas taking Mark with him to Cyprus, while Paul, replacing his old associate with Silas or Silvanus, a leader of the Jerusalem church (15: 22), set out overland for Galatia (15: 36–41).

He was now on the great Roman road that stretched from Antioch to Ephesus, and the time was probably the autumn of A.D. 49. Although Luke passes swiftly over the early part of the journey, it may have involved weeks or months of hard work, preaching and organising. The route of the two apostles took them through Tarsus, and the gap in the Taurus mountains, by which means they reached the churches of the first missionary journey in the reverse order. At Lystra, Mark's place in the team is filled by Timothy, a youth who was later to become one of Paul's stoutest henchmen, and to whom two of the New Testament letters are addressed (16: 1–5).

It seems as if the journey was dogged with misfortunes and obstacles of one kind or another. Having left the towns of the first tour behind, the most natural route would have been to follow the Roman road straight through to Ephesus. Whatever diverted them from it, and likewise why they were thus prevented from evangelising the promising fields of Mysia and Bithynia, is unknown to us (16: 6–8).

Instead of any of their plans coming to fruition, they found themselves in the end on the shores of the Aegean sea at Troas, which for all its history as the site of ancient Troy was nevertheless an apparent dead-end. Yet on looking back, Paul and his companions could not regard this frustration of their plans as anything other than the guidance of the Spirit, for it was by their going to Troas that the Gospel first came to Europe.

At Troas, a fourth member was added to the party, Luke, the "beloved physician", writer of the third gospel and of this book of *Acts*. At least this is the most obvious explanation of the fact that the narrative now changes from the third to the first personal pronoun (16: 10), beginning the so called "we-passages" in *Acts*, which suggest not only that the writer is now present himself, but that what follows is more or less his travel diary.

Luke may have been a doctor practising in Troas, who was summoned to attend Paul in one of his bouts of illness. It has been suggested that it was due to Luke's persuasion, assisted by a vivid dream, that Paul concluded that it was God's will that he should cross the sea into Macedonia in Europe, a venture into unknown country and among unfamiliar people (16: 9).

Crossing the Aegean, the missionaries found themselves again on a great Roman highway which stretched from the Hellespont to the Adriatic, and it was in the towns along this road that Paul and his companions preached the gospel and founded Christian churches. The first halt was at Philippi, ten miles from the sea. Thanks to the presence of Luke, the narrative of this visit is extremely vivid (16: 11–40).

We are shown the apostles making their way to the riverside, where, for lack of a proper synagogue, the few Jews and their adherents met for prayer; Lydia, the hospitable Gentile business-woman; the crazy young clairvoyante; the imprisonment of the dauntless apostles who sang psalms in their cell; the earthquake and the panic-stricken jailor; Paul standing on his dignity as a Roman citizen. What a pity it is that Luke went no further than Philippi. The use of "we" now reverts to "they", indicating that he remained as resident evangelist to consolidate the work of the apostles. It is odd to think that a church that became Paul's favourite, the only one which he allowed to give him financial assistance (*Phil.* 4: 15–16), and to which he later wrote perhaps his most affectionate letter, should have started under such unhappy auspices, and with a successful business woman, a medium and a jailor as its foundation members.

Continuing down the imperial highway, and passing through towns which had no Jewish colony, the apostles next stop at Thessalonica, where there was a synagogue (17: 1–9). From the letters which Paul afterwards wrote to this church, it would seem that the campaign lasted longer than the three weeks indicated by Luke, and that Paul found himself a job at his own trade of tent-making to pay his way (*I Thess.* 2: 9), which appears to have been his normal practice.

The pattern of the campaign here and at the next town, Berea (17: 10–14), seems to have been the familiar one of an approach through the synagogue; some success with Gentile adherents; violent opposition from bigoted Jews, leading to an enforced and speedy departure on the part of the chief missioner. Silvanus and Timothy are left behind in Macedonia to carry on the work, while Paul himself goes on to Athens.

If we may read between the lines, it would seem as if Paul was a sick man at this time. He has to be escorted by ship to Athens by some of the local people, and on arrival there at once sends for Silvanus and Timothy. They apparently came, but Paul felt that the needs of the Macedonian churches were greater than his own and sent them back, remaining in Athens alone (*I Thess.* 3: 1). It is an odd contrast to think of Renan's "ugly little Jew who had no taste for beauty", wandering among the temples, statues and porticos of Athens, the home of poets and philosophers, and the most cultured city of the ancient world.

Even in Paul's day, when its heyday was past, it must have been a place of dazzling loveliness. Paul, however, did not see it with the eyes of a modern tourist, but with the critical eye of a religious reformer. He saw it as Savonarola saw Florence, or as Luther saw Rome, as a beautiful shell with death at the heart of it. He saw it as a city of souls groping in darkness for the truth. He shared the view of the satirist that it was easier to finds gods there than men, but Paul felt that that was something to weep over and not to laugh at.

"His spirit was stirred in him,

when he saw the city wholly given to idolatry". To Paul, the one thing that mattered, belief in a righteous God and in his service, was nowhere to be found. Instead of that he encountered idle philosophising, frivolous living, and an altar "To the Unknown God". So Paul, not content with the usual approach through the synagogue, frequented the market place, where the lively Athenians were still, as in the days of Demosthenes, interested in "nothing else but either to tell or to hear some new thing".

His talk came to the ears of the philosophers of the city, Epicureans and Stoics are specifically mentioned by Luke, and he was invited to state his case formally and publicly before the light and learning of Athens, the councillors of the court of the Areopagus, the guardians of religion and education. They did not expect much from him, and although he did his best, meeting them on their own ground, and including a quotation from their own poets, they laughed him out of court whenever he mentioned the Resurrection.

Paul's argument was cleverly constructed, a more intellectual version of his other recorded speech to a purely Gentile audience (14: 15–17), but it convinced no more than one or two of his hearers. The others politely said that they would hear him some other time. Thus the apostle left Athens with the wind completely out of his sails, a discouraged and despondent man (17: 15–34).

To leave Athens and go to Corinth, was like moving from Cambridge to Manchester. Athens was the provincial university town, Corinth was the great commercial metropolis. It was a seaport of half a million people about fifty miles from Athens; it had a large Jewish colony, a cosmopolitan population, and its reputation for profligacy was proverbial in the ancient world. To this rather terrifying proposition came Paul at the beginning of A.D. 50, still smarting from his failure at Athens, and, as he said later, "in weakness, and in fear, and in much trembling" (*I Cor.* 2: 3).

He found work with a Jewish couple, Aquila and Priscilla, tentmakers like himself, and refugees from Rome after the expulsion of the Jews in the reign of Claudius, in A.D. 49, which was occasioned, as Suetonius tells us, because of riots connected with one "Chrestus". This was most likely the same kind of trouble between Jews and Jewish Christians as we have encountered in *Acts*.

In Corinth Paul stayed for a year and a half. Again reading between the lines, it would seem that Paul's depression was not properly banished until Silvanus and Timothy arrived from Macedonia. They brought such good news of the progress of the churches there, that he not only launched into the Corinthian campaign with renewed vigour, but also wrote the first of his two letters to Thessalonica, to express his delight and answer some of the problems that concerned the young church there. Both *I Thess.* and *II Thess.* should be read at this point, since the second letter followed the first, after a short interval, to clear up some mis-understandings (see pp. 487–493).

When the approach through the synagogue at Corinth failed, Paul turned his back on the Jews, left the house of Aquila and Priscilla in token of his action, though they remained fast friends, and went to live with a Gentile next door to the synagogue. The cause prospered and the church grew, a notable convert being the ruler of the synagogue, but, as Paul says later, the church at Corinth comprised "not many wise, not many mighty, not many noble (*I Cor.* 1: 26). Indeed he goes considerably far-ther, and suggests that the church was built out of the dregs of Corinthian society (*I Cor.* 6: 9–11).

In the summer of A.D. 51, as we learn from an inscription at Delphi, a new Roman proconsul was appointed over the province of Achaia, of which Corinth was the capital. This was Gallio, a brother of Seneca, the philosopher. The Jews took this opportunity to bring up the old charge against Paul of preaching an illegal re-ligion, as they had done at Philippi (16: 21) and Thessalonica (17: 7).

Gallio, however, was too good a Roman official to interfere. "He cared for none of those things", religious disputes were none of his business, and he chased the Jews from the tribunal without even hearing their case. Some months later, in the spring of A.D. 52, Paul left Corinth for his fourth visit to Jerusalem. With him went Aquila and Priscilla, as far as Ephesus, where he left them, and continued his journey to Caesarea and Jerusalem. Having celebrated the passover there, he returned to his headquarters at Antioch (18: 1–22).

Third Missionary Journey
(18: 23 – 21: 17)

PAUL STARTED out on his third missionary tour in A.D. 53, primarily to fulfil a promise (18: 21). Passing through the familiar country of the first two journeys, and visiting en route the churches he had founded, he came eventu-ally to Ephesus, chief town of the province of Asia, which was to be his headquarters for the next three years (20: 31). Some time before he arrived, a certain Jewish-Christian evangelist from Alex-andria, by name Apollos, had reached Ephesus, and had made a reputation for himself as an eloquent and learned preacher.

But his gospel was the Gospel with a difference. The Christ he preached was Christ without the Resurrection; the baptism he advocated was, like that of John the Baptist, a simple rite of immersion as a token of repent-ance. It would seem that he proclaimed Jesus as the Messiah, but knew nothing of the signifi-cance of his Death and Exaltation. Unknown to him too, was the ecstatic gift of the Holy Spirit, associated with baptism.

Aquila and Priscilla, however, took him in hand and instructed him, and shortly afterwards he moved on to Corinth. There he was of great service to the church, but, as we learn from *I Cor.* 1: 12, one unfortunate result of his skill as a preacher was that he attracted a popular following which tended to think of itself as "Apollos' church", not an unknown phenomenon in modern Protestantism. Luke's mention of him here is valuable, in that it indicates another problem with which Paul and his associates had to contend in those early days, the existence of well intentioned but inadequate presentations of the Gospel, which made some kind of control within the Church desirable and necessary (18: 23 – 19: 7).

Paul's stay at Ephesus, after the normal overtures through the synagogue had proved fruitless, seems to have been mostly concerned with the exposure of black magic. Luke's account of the events of Paul's stay there, short though it is, conveys vividly the superstitious outlook which prevailed in these pagan cities. That one man should have been able to do so much to combat it, is one of the marvels of the story of Christianity.

We are given a glimpse of astrologers and itinerant magicians, preying on a credulous populace, and, fighting against it, this solitary little Christian missionary, preaching during the midday siesta in a lecture room, obviously with considerable success. Not only is there a dramatic episode, where these practitioners of the black arts consign their cabalistic parchments to the flames, but also, as we learn, the faith spread throughout the whole province. Ephesus was to become in the next hundred years one of the greatest centres of the Christian Church, chief of the seven churches of Asia referred to in the book of *Revelation,* and much of the groundwork must date from these years of hard work by Paul and his deputies in the city and province generally (19: 8–20).

It was while he was busy in Ephesus that bad news reached him from Corinth. Remembering its reputation as the cesspool of Greece, and the fact that many of the earliest converts came from the lowest stratum of society, it is not surprising to find that after Paul's departure, some of them had fallen back into pagan practices. Paul apparently wrote them a strong letter which has been lost but to which he refers in *I Cor.* 5: 9. Part of it may be contained in *II Cor.* 6: 14 – 7: 1.

He received a reply to this letter, referred to in *I Cor.* 7: 1, raising a number of questions on which the church of Corinth needed his advice. But, in the meantime, he had received further bad reports of conditions in the Corinthian community, which called for firm handling. Accordingly, with these two ends in view, he wrote, sometime in A.D. 54, the letter which we know as *First Corinthians* (see pp. 455–462). To read this letter at this point is to realise how vast were the odds against which Paul was fighting, how intensely practical was his approach to the Christian life, and how superbly sure he was of the hand of God in all that was happening, despite the setbacks.

It would seem, however, that this letter was too kindly, at all events it did not have the desired effect. Matters remained unsatisfactory at Corinth, and Paul appears to have paid a flying visit, alluded to by implication in *II Cor.* 12: 14, a much less pleasant occasion than his original campaign, followed by a sharp letter referred to in *II Cor.* 7: 8, part of which may be embodied in our present *II Cor.* 10–13 (see pp. 466–467). If this is so, it provides a most fascinating glimpse of Paul defending himself and his authority as an apostle. Apparently the Corinthians were listening to mischief-makers who were slandering Paul's behaviour and motives, and in these chapters we are brought very close to this extraordinary man and his mind as he mingles irony with reproach, tenderness with severity and pride with humility.

But of all this Luke has nothing to say. We should not even know that Paul had paid that elusive short and painful visit to Corinth (*II Cor.* 2: 1), which preceded the "severe" letter, if the apostle had not told us himself. The true picture of him is thus of fully occupied days at Ephesus, working at his trade, holding meetings in the city, sponsoring evangelistic expeditions into the surrounding country *and* keeping in touch with the churches everywhere. This last point was certainly one of the secrets of the success of his work, and it was not the least of his daily burdens (*II Cor.* 11: 28).

About this time he began to think about going to Rome, visiting Greece and Jerusalem on the way. Before this decision materialised, an exciting event took place, which sheds another ray of light on the background and conditions under which the Gospel spread. Luke is at his best in describing the riot in Ephesus. The temple of Diana was the pride of the Ephesians, and one of the seven wonders of the world. Pilgrims came from far and near to pay homage at the shrine, not of the chaste huntress of early Roman days, but of a repulsive-looking goddess of fertility.

The craftsmen of the city, silversmiths and coppersmiths, did a thriving trade in making small images of the goddess and selling them as souvenirs to pilgrims. Numbers of these have been found, some as far away as the ruins of Pompeii. But now there is a slump; Paul's campaign against superstition has been too successful. The climax comes in a highly excited mass meeting, which Paul is dissuaded with difficulty from addressing. Fortunately, however, Ephesus was blessed with a diplomatic town clerk. When the apostle writes in his letter to the Corinthian church (*I Cor.* 15: 32) of having fought with wild beasts at Ephesus, he was probably thinking of mobs like this one (19: 21–41).

Soon afterwards Paul left Ephesus. In his letter to the Romans, written a little later, he mentions an imprisonment (*Rom.* 16: 7), and it is possible that he may have spent some part of his three Ephesian years in prison, and may have despatched from there some at least of the letters which are generally thought to have been written later from prison in Rome (see p. 473). At all events, after leaving Ephesus, he visited the Macedonian churches again.

While in Macedonia, word was brought to him that the Corinthian church had taken matters in hand, punished his calumniators (*II Cor.* 7: 6–7), and that now everything was going splendidly. So Paul writes again, his fourth letter to Corinth, which is our *Second Corinthians*, though possibly only the first nine chapters (see pp 463–466). In it he explains why he has been unable to come to them, and expresses his happiness that all is now going so well. This is an intensely personal letter. It gives us some idea of how deeply concerned the apostle had been about the situation in Corinth, and it supplies the autobiographical background of which the compressed narrative of this period in *Acts* tells us nothing.

Paul followed this letter shortly afterwards with his third visit to Corinth, where he stayed for three months. His tireless mind was now stretching even beyond Rome to Spain, and in his great letter to the Christians at Rome, which was written while he was at Corinth, and which should be read as the most searching and profound exposition of his thought (pp. 447–454), the "gospel according to St. Paul", he tells them of his intentions (Rom. 15: 22–29).

But first he had a special task on hand. For some time he had been organising and encouraging the young churches to contribute money for the relief of the mother church at Jerusalem. Luke does not make much of this in *Acts* (cf. 24: 17), but it is obvious from Paul's letters of this period, both from his direct requests for help and his repeated refutation of the charge that he was collecting money for his own benefit, that he attached great importance to this common effort as a means of emphasising the solidarity and unity of the Church, and probably also of establishing better relations with the Jews (*I Cor.* 16: 1; *II Cor.* 8, 9; *Rom.* 15: 25).

So he leaves Corinth, returning to Jerusalem by a longer route, since he had heard of a plot to kill him. This was probably planned to take place on a pilgrim ship, which would be crammed with fanatical overseas Jews, bent, like Paul, on celebrating Pentecost at Jerusalem. He therefore travels by land back through Macedonia, collecting Luke, who has been all the while at Philippi, as we may deduce from the reappearance of the travel-diary "we" in 20: 6, and being joined at Troas by a number of delegates from the young churches, who were obviously charged with the task of taking the contributions of their respective communities to Jerusalem (20: 1–6).

At Troas, a certain Eutychus, unable to keep awake during an inordinately long Pauline discourse, falls out of a window but mercifully survives; at Miletus, near Ephesus, Paul gathers the Ephesian church together and takes farewell of them in a moving address, and in a manner that shows the affectionate relationship that existed between the apostle and his flocks (20: 7–38).

He appears to have a premonition of what will happen to him in Jerusalem, and this is intensified by various warnings he receives on the way. The whole journey, once more gaining in vividness from Luke's own presence, reminds us irresistibly of that other journey, where Paul's Master set his face steadfastly to go to Jerusalem, and one of the greatest tributes to the bravest disciple of Jesus is the record of these deeply touching scenes at Miletus and Tyre, where Paul must have felt that his work had not been in vain. So the third journey comes to an end, and Paul, for the fifth and last time since his conversion, enters within the walls of the holy city (21 : 1-17).

Paul's Last Journey
(21 : 18 – 28 : 31)

FOR THE remainder of the book of *Acts*, the narrative is much more detailed owing to Luke's actual participation in the events he describes. While it is of interest, as an account of the behaviour and attitude of Jews and Roman officials towards the Church, and of Paul's own thoughts and experiences, the apostle himself is in no position to further the expansion of the Church by his own efforts, and the dynamic tempo of its development up to this point is inevitably slowed down.

We are told of the cautious suggestion of James, and the other officials of the Jerusalem church, that Paul should ostentatiously demonstrate his respect for Jewish Law, and of the failure of their scheme. A howling mob of fanatical Asian Jews set upon Paul in the Temple, and he barely escaped with his life by the intervention of the Roman garrison quartered in the Temple area.

Despite Paul's efforts to justify himself, in his speech to the crowd from the steps of the Antonia Tower, the scene of Jesus' trial before Pilate, his defence of his association with Gentiles only served to infuriate the mob further.

His Roman citizenship helped him once more, and instead of being left to the tender mercies of the Jews, he was sent for his own safety under escort to the Roman procurator of Judaea at Caesarea (21 : 18 – 23 : 33). A trial was staged under the presidency of this man, Antonius Felix, which was inconclusive, as were further interviews with the procurator and his wife Drusilla, a daughter of the Herod Agrippa who had murdered the apostle James and persecuted the Jerusalem church (12 : 1-2). Both the procurator and his wife had unsavoury records, and Felix was soon afterwards summoned to Rome to stand trial himself for using unnecessarily harsh repressive measures in dealing with Jewish rebels (23 : 34 – 24 : 26).

It was two years—presumably owing to the lengthy process of Roman justice—before a successor was appointed. Meantime Paul was a prisoner, and the only man who seems to have profited from these two years at Caesarea, A.D. 56-58, was Luke, who no doubt used his time to the best advantage, and built up the knowledge from local sources at Caesarea and nearby Jerusalem which he afterwards embodied in his gospel.

The new procurator, Porcius Festus, seems to have been a man of a different stamp from his predecessor, and to have been an exemplary Roman official. A fresh trial was held immediately, at which the Jews brought forward the new and dangerous charge of treason. Whether through anxiety about the effect of this on the procurator, or from weariness with the protracted nature of local justice, Paul at this stage made a dramatic appeal to Caesar. Every Roman citizen had the right, if he had the money, to appeal to the emperor's court in Rome, the equivalent of an appeal to the House of Lords, and Paul must have had promise of financial support, as Felix apparently knew (24: 26).

Before being sent to Rome, Paul had another opportunity to state his case on the occasion of an official visit by Herod Agrippa II, only by courtesy called king in Judaea, since he was technically merely an adviser there on Jewish affairs to the Roman government. Festus' verdict was that Paul was mad, and Agrippa's reaction was to ask him if he was trying to convert him. Both apparently privately believed that there was no truth in the Jewish charges, and no reason why Paul should remain in custody. But he had appealed to Caesar, and to Caesar he had to go (24: 27 – 26: 32)

Luke's description of the voyage to Rome is a masterpiece, and the contrast between this lively narrative and the matter of fact way in which years of Paul's previous life are passed over, studded as they were with a whole series of adventures every bit as exciting (cf. *II Cor.* 11: 24–27), makes us regret over and over again the absence of a pen like Luke's accompanying the apostle all the way. Setting out from Caesarea in the autumn of A.D. 58, and having no alternative but to winter in Malta, Paul's party landed at Puteoli in the bay of Naples in the spring of A.D. 59, being met by representatives of the Roman church as they approached the city along the Appian Way (27: 1 – 28: 15).

So Paul had achieved one of his great ambitions, to visit the capital of the empire, albeit not in the role of a travelling evangelist, but as Caesar's prisoner awaiting trial. He was manacled to a soldier, but apparently was allowed to lodge in a house of his own. Here he lived for two years from A.D. 59 to A.D. 61, but not by any means in idleness. According to Luke he had a constant stream of visitors, keeping him in touch with the work and progress of the churches. This we know too from the letters which he wrote during this imprisonment to the churches of Ephesus, Philippi, Colossae and to his friend Philemon (see pp. 473–486 and 503–504).

At this point, however, Luke's narrative ends with surprising abruptness. It may be that he had planned a third volume which was never written, or that he wrote a third volume which has been lost, or that both the gospel and *Acts* were designed to serve as a brief for Theophilus to be used in Paul's defence. It is equally possible that Luke, like Mark, ends where he means to end, and that having brought the apostle of the Gentiles to the capital of the Gentile world, as a literary craftsman he felt, as many since his day have also felt, that this was the perfect ending with St. Paul still the prime mover of the Gentile mission, still able to direct though unable to travel, with the door wide open into the future and the Holy Spirit still guiding the people of God (28: 16–31).

For the rest of Paul's story we have to fall back on tradition. It was generally believed in the early Church that in the great persecution of the Christians in Rome by Nero in A.D. 64, both St. Peter and St. Paul were martyred. But there have been many scholars who have held that Paul's two years of imprisonment ended in his acquittal, or, in his release without a trial, and that between A.D. 61 and 64 he went far afield on missionary journeys, visiting Spain as well as old and new churches in the eastern Mediterranean.

In support of this there is the evidence of early tradition, and there are appropriate references in the letters to *Timothy* and *Titus* (*I Tim.* 1: 3; 3: 14; *II Tim.* 4: 13, 20; *Tit.* 1: 5) (see pp. 494–502). Many modern scholars, however, do not admit these epistles on grounds of style and contents to be genuinely Pauline, although most would agree that there are fragments of Paul's writings within them. Thus this problematical last journey of all must remain an open question. If it did take place, we cannot reconstruct it.

THE EPISTLE OF
PAUL TO THE ROMANS

IF, DISREGARDING the advice given on pp. 433 – 434 we prefer to read the New Testament right through from *Matthew* to *Revelation*, we should recognise that, when we reach the epistle to the *Romans*, we have arrived at the point in the New Testament, comparable to the book of *Job* in the Old Testament, where it is imperative that we should use a modern translation such as the New English Bible, or Phillips' or Moffatt's versions, if we do not want to find ourselves floundering in a morass of words. It is comforting to remember that it is not only in the present day that the letters of St. Paul are often difficult to follow. Even in New Testament times it was felt that they contain "some things hard to be understood" (*II Pet.* 3: 16).

Of none of his letters is this more true than the epistle to the *Romans*, which Coleridge called "the most profound work ever written". Unlike most of Paul's letters, it does not deal primarily with some particular problems which are exercising the local church, or with specific matters which the apostle feels should be brought to its attention. Paul had never visited Rome when he wrote this letter from Corinth (see p. 443), but he was anxious to establish relations with a church which he shortly hoped to include in his itinerary, and to use as a base for further activity.

In so doing he pens what is in effect his *credo*, the distillation of over twenty years' reflection on the nature and meaning of the Christian faith. Time and again in the history of the Church, it is to this particular letter that men have turned to reset their compass, when they were disturbed by the sense that the contemporary presentation of the Gospel was inadequate or erroneous. So it was with St. Augustine, with Luther and with Barth.

Writing to people who have committed themselves to Christ both from Jewish and pagan backgrounds, Paul's concern is to show that no matter from which side of the fence he may have entered the Christian community, the problem for every man is the same—to be in the right relationship with God. Neither Judaism nor paganism can build a ladder to bridge the terrifying emptiness that separates man, steeped in his earthbound pride and folly, and burdened with his own and society's guilt, from the utter holiness and perfection of an eternally transcendent

God. Only what God himself has done, by stooping down to our level in the person of Jesus Christ, can lift us up to the heights where God dwells, to find there the true fulfilment of our being as members of his family.

For Paul, the problem is intensified inasmuch as that until his conversion on the Damascus road, he had believed with passionate conviction that the answer to mankind's predicament had been given once and for all to Israel. To the progeny of Abraham, fortified by the Law and the Prophets, God had offered the unique privilege of being his covenanted people, and his chosen instrument to lead the world back to himself. Now, however, Paul has to reconcile the historical role of Israel with his Christian conviction that all believers, Jew and Gentile, are equally brothers in Christ before God and enter the Church on equal terms.

He is too conscious of the continuity of God's revelation of his will and purpose, from the days of Abraham to the coming of the promised Messiah, to suggest that the legacy of the Old Testament could be ignored. Only by stressing that the Church is the new Israel, inheriting both the promises and the vocation of the old Israel, can he do justice at the same time to the witness of the Old Testament and to his proclamation of Jesus, the crucified carpenter, as the unique Son of God, who makes it possible for all who are united to him by faith to share his sonship and call God "Father".

What Christ has done— Justification by Faith

(1:1–4:25)

HAVING introduced himself, and identified himself with his readers as sharing in the common cause of furthering the Gospel, Paul speaks of his long-felt wish to visit Rome. As the apostle to the Gentiles, he has an obligation to proclaim the Gospel in the cultural centre of the empire, as well as in the backwoods of the provinces. Although it had its origins in Palestine, this Gospel, which he is proud to preach, is a Gospel for the whole world (1: 1–16).

Paul then goes on to state what is in effect the theme of his letter, and his interpretation of what Christianity is all about. Using the word "righteousness", in its Old Testament sense of God's activity in the world to save men from the power of evil in themselves and around them, he claims that in the Life, Death and Resurrection of Jesus (the "gospel"), this "righteousness" of God has now been supremely revealed. All that we have to do is to accept this Act of God, by which he has himself bridged the gulf that divides us from him, counting us innocent for Christ's sake although we are guilty, and thus doing for us what we are unable to do for ourselves. The distinctive Christian attitude is therefore one of humble and thankful trust in God, and dependence on what he has done through Christ, in short, "faith" (1: 17).

Having outlined his theme in this compressed form, Paul now proceeds to develop it in detail. First, he shows how paganism comes under God's condemnation. Although they had ample evidence in the created world of the Supreme Being who sustained it, the Gentiles had steeped themselves in superstition and idolatry. In consequence, morality had for them ceased to have any meaning; sex perversion and anti-social behaviour, personal failure and public scandals flouted what conscience clearly indicated as the proper way of life (1: 18–32).

Paul then points out that the Jews are in no better case than the Gentiles. They may think that as the people of the Law they are in a favoured position. This is not so. God condemns evil wherever it exists—in Gentiles who disregard their natural recognition of the difference between right and wrong, or in Jews who violate the laws of God revealed to them through Moses (2: 1–16). Jews who pride themselves on their moral superiority should look at their own dubious record. There is no merit in the sight of God in circumcision, unless it is matched by inward consecration. A good pagan is better than a bad Jew (2: 17–29).

It has been the will of God to select Israel, as the people to whom he entrusted the revelation of his nature and purpose in the Old Testament. But in so far as the Jews have failed to comply with God's standards, they have cut themselves out of the divine plan meantime, and stand side by side with the Gentiles as guilty sinners facing the Last Judgment (3: 1–20).

It is to men in this situation that God has now given new hope, a hope indeed that has been foreshadowed in the Old Testament, but that has now become a reality through Christ. God offers free pardon to guilty sinners—and that means every man alive—not because of anything they have done or can do to deserve it, but because of what Christ has done. God treats guilty men as innocent, and delivers them from the shackles of their sins, when they commit themselves utterly to Christ. The right relationship to God, achieved once only in the perfect obedience and self-dedication of Christ, becomes possible through the mystery of the Cross, for all who identify themselves with Christ by incorporation into his Church. The gulf had to be bridged: God himself had to bridge it: now any man may make his way from death to life in the strength of God's Son (3: 21–31).

Then, with special reference to the problem of the Jews, who claimed to be in a privileged position *vis à vis* the Gentiles because of their descent from Abraham, Paul embarks on a complicated argument, to prove that Abraham was not in effect the classic example of how obedience to the Law made a man right with God. On the contrary, it was because Abraham was pre-eminently a man of faith, who trusted God implicitly, that God accepted him and chose him to be the "father of many nations". This obviously could not mean the Jews only, but must mean all men everywhere who similarly commit their lives to God. Abraham is thus "the father of us all", Jews and Gentiles, in that he is the prototype of all who are now willing to respond to God as he did, and share his unquestioning faith (4: 1–25).

What Christ Does— Santification

(5: 1 – 8: 39)

THIS NEW status, which we as Christians acquire through faith in what God has done through Christ to restore our true relationship with him, gives us both the inward peace that comes from the knowledge that we are forgiven, and also the certain hope of ultimately reaching the fulfilment of our destiny in the nearer presence of God. Because of this confidence, we can face whatever changes and chances befall us, knowing that we are in the safe keeping of a God who loves us.

The proof of his boundless love is that Christ died for us, while we were still poor guilty creatures. Now, therefore, we can be sure that having rescued us from our plight, and given us a fresh start, God will enable us to grow into true sonship through the power of the Risen Christ, and so escape final condemnation at the Last Day (5: 1–11).

Then, taking Adam as the representative of mankind without the Gospel, Paul describes the plight of the whole human race before the coming of Christ. Held in thrall by pride and disobedience, mankind could expect no other fate than death, the symbol of its corruption and failure. But now God has reversed the process. By

sending his Son as a man, but unlike the race of Adam without Adam's sin, being indeed man as man was meant to be, the whole prospect for the human race has been transformed. The slate has been wiped clean, the tyranny of sin and death has been broken, man's future holds hope in its hand and not despair. The perfect obedience of the divine Son of Man cancels the disobedience of all the fallible sons of men, and through him the finality of death is turned into the promise of eternal life (5: 12–21).

But if God in his love has done all this for us, forgiving our sin and cancelling our guilt, and if none of this is a reward for our own efforts to live the good life, but simply the boundless mercy of God, is there any point now in our striving to do what is right and just? Paul's answer to his own question is that when we commit ourselves to Christ, and become incorporated by baptism in his Body the Church, we recapitulate in ourselves Christ's Death and Resurrection. We die to the past, to our old selves, and rise to a new life centred in him. (Paul is, of course, thinking of the symbolism of adult baptism by immersion.) We are no longer slaves of sin but slaves of Christ, and his power which has conquered sin is available to help us to defeat temptation (6: 1–14).

Paul emphasises at some length the difference between life, after we commit ourselves to Christ, and life as we lived it before, comparing it with passing from the service of sin to the service of righteousness, or with being wedded first to the Law and then to Christ. Whatever the metaphor, his main contention is that we have entered a new relationship with God, which no longer involves a frantic attempt to comply with moral standards, but rather involves our putting ourselves at God's disposal to be used as God sees fit. In this the Holy Spirit is our guide (6: 15 – 7: 6).

In case it should seem that the preceding paragraph of his letter had suggested that Old Testament laws, from which the Christian was now freed, must therefore be regarded as sinful, Paul is at pains to explain the function of the Law. It shows up sin for what it is, and without it we should not recognise that we are in fact sinners. But it also stimulates our desire to sin, in that all forbidden things become doubly attractive.

Paul then speaks of his own experience. As a youth he was carefree, because he did not see his behaviour against the background of the Law. When he accepted the Law as his standard, at once he became conscious of sin and moral failure. This was, however, clearly not the fault of the Law, which is good in itself, but of the tendency to sin which is in every man from Adam onwards. Paul recalls the frightful struggle which he endured before his conversion, accepting the rightness of the moral law with his mind, but unable to live up to it because of his own moral weakness. It was from this dilemma of a divided personality that Christ had delivered him (7: 7–25).

Thus it is on a note of triumph that Paul ends this main part of his letter. Christ liberates us from the power of sin, which leads inevitably to our spiritual death. The moral demands of the Old Testament Law are not strong enough to straighten our twisted natures, but God has made this possible through Christ. When God's Son took a human body, exposed himself to the power of sin and defeated it, he won the battle in principle for all mankind.

The man who commits his life to Christ in the Church, finds that his outlook is changed. He no longer lives as he did, because his whole personality comes under the power of the Spirit of God. For the Christian, therefore, death is past when life in the Spirit begins, and the subsequent dissolution of the physical body is incidental (8: 1–13).

When we put our lives in God's hands, we become his children, and there is no place in this relationship for our former fears. The very fact that we are moved to call God "dearest Father", should prove to us that it is God's own Spirit teaching us that sonship of God is our true inheritance. This we share with Christ, as we also share his suffering (8: 14–17).

As we see the toll of suffering in the world around us, the prevalence of decay and death in the natural order, let us remember that the whole process is moving towards a mighty climax. We have already a foretaste of what this glorious end will be, in that we live in two worlds at the same time. While still in this present world, we have been given a glimpse of the new heaven and new earth, which we shall only truly know when we enter into our full inheritance in the nearer presence of God. Meantime we have not merely the hope of this great consummation to sustain us, but God himself helps us to grow into the right relationship to himself, through his own Spirit within us which responds to him (8: 18–27).

So as we reach out towards God in the life of the Church, we find that he enables us to turn all that happens to us to good account. It is in God's eternal purpose that all men should become like Christ, sons of the great family of God. Through none of our own doing but purely by God's love, we find ourselves within this family, treated as sons, with the best yet to come. In face of this what have we to fear? We know that we are sinners, yet the great Judge of all accepts us as we are. Christ alone could condemn us, but in fact Christ is our defender.

Nothing can separate us from Christ's love: nothing that the world can do to us can really harm us. The mysteries of the universe, the unknown future, the chances of life and the certainty of death—none of these things can ever come between us and the love of God, as we know it in Jesus Christ (8: 28–39).

Old and New Israel

(9: 1 – 11: 36)

AFTER THIS great paean of praise, Paul devotes the next section of his letters (9: 1 – 11: 36) to a problem which, for a converted Jew of strictly orthodox background, who found himself

now assuring the Gentiles of God's acceptance of them as his children, was bound to be perplexing and disturbing. This was, of course, the fact that the vast majority of his fellow Jews rejected the Gospel, and refused to recognise Jesus as the Messiah.

It was unthinkable that a people who had been chosen as God's own, who had entered into a covenant relationship with him, who had been given the scriptures and the promises of God's blessing, who had indeed humanly speaking borne the Messiah, should now be cut out of the divine plan which Paul has just been outlining (9: 1–5).

The apostle begins his answer by distinguishing between the Jewish nation and the Israel of God. It was not to the lineal descendants of Abraham that the blessing of God was promised. Abraham had had a son before Isaac was born, but Isaac was chosen to inherit the promise. Similarly Jacob and not Esau, his older brother, was selected to be his father's heir. It is thus not by human standards of privilege or merit that God chooses or rejects his people (9: 6–18).

If God sees fit to pass over his ancient people Israel, because of their unfitness for the task he had planned for them, and selects instead a new Israel, this is in keeping with his actions in the past and has indeed been forecast by the prophets (9: 19–29). Despite their devotion to the Law and their zeal for God, the Jews lacked the one thing essential, faith in the Lord Jesus Christ and his Resurrection (9: 30–10: 21).

True, says Paul, we must not

forget Isaiah's "remnant" (see p. 250), the faithful handful of Jews who, by the grace of God, have become Christians, but, in the providence of God, the rejection of the Gospel by the Jews as a whole has led to the far greater gain of opening up the possibility of salvation to the pagan world. Let the Gentiles beware of treating lightly this opportunity that God has given them, and let them remember their debt to the old Israel. But Israel's blindness is only for a time. God had not discarded his ancient people, and in the end the Jews too will be gathered into the Christian Church (11: 1–36).

Christian Behaviour
(12: 1 – 16: 27)

THEN, HAVING concluded his masterly assessment of the significance of Jesus, and the meaning of the Good News, Paul turns to its implications, and shows its consequences for Christian behaviour. Because of what God has done for us in Christ, "therefore" (12: 1), says the apostle, here is what we must do for God, and, for most of the remainder of the letter, Paul draws our attention to the practical obligations of the Christian life. He calls on all of us, his fellow Christians, to dedicate ourselves wholeheartedly to God, and to remember that each of us has a definite part to play in the work of the Church, whatever our particular gift may be. Brotherliness, charity, and forgiveness among ourselves are to be our response of

gratitude to God for his mercy (12: 1–21).

The state and its officers are to be respected, for civil authority is divinely constituted to preserve good order. Paul had no reason to complain of Roman justice in his own case, and it was not until the persecution of the Church under Nero, almost ten years later, that the state came to be regarded as the enemy of God and not, as here, his servant. Paul is, of course, not enjoining obedience to the state or its officers on the part of Christians, irrespective of whether it exercises justice or maintains the common good.

He then echoes our Lord's teaching on loving our neighbour as summing up all the commandments, and stresses the importance and urgency of right behaviour in face of the imminence of the end of this present age (13: 1–14). The next topic is one which, although more acute in the early Church, to some extent concerns us even today, namely whether ascetic practices, or regard for certain holy days, should be a matter of dispute in a Christian community. The underlying principles of Paul's argument are still valid: that we recognise an area of freedom in Christian behaviour and agree to differ without malice, and that in exercising that freedom we show respect for the scruples of others (14: 1–23).

After further remarks on Christian behaviour in general, and on Christ as Saviour of both Jew and Gentile, Paul strikes a more personal note. As chief missioner to the Gentiles, he can with all modesty claim to have traversed the known world to bring the Gospel to pagan lands. His next ambition is to visit Rome on his way to Spain. Meantime his immediate task is to take the offering of the younger churches to Jerusalem, for the relief of the mother church, with some misgivings, rightly, as it transpired, as to his reception both by the Jews and by his Jewish fellow-Christians (15: 1–33).

It is thought by some scholars that the epistle ended at this point, and that the last chapter, among other things so full of personal greetings, was more likely to be originally written to Ephesus where Paul was well known, than to Rome where he had never been before. In that case the last chapter may have served as a covering letter, attached to a copy of *Romans* which was sent to Ephesus. It is equally possible that all those mentioned in the last chapter were in fact in Rome at the time, and that this sixteenth chapter is a striking illustration of Paul's concern for all the churches, and of his pastoral care for Christian friends and acquaintances everywhere.

Among the greetings are some to names that can be identified elsewhere in the New Testament, others are to unknown members. After a warning note on mischief-makers, and greetings from Paul's associates in Corinth, this remarkable letter ends with a doxology (16: 1–27).

THE FIRST
EPISTLE OF PAUL
TO THE CORINTHIANS

S T. PAUL'S mission to Corinth
has already been described
(pp. 439–440), and also the
circumstances which led him to
write four letters to the church
which he had founded there (pp.
441–443). In no other New Testament writing are we brought into
such close touch with the day to
day life and problems of a Christian community in the first century,
as in the second of these letters
which we know as *First Corinthians*. Remembering the background of the membership, it is
difficult to know, as we read this
letter and its sequel, whether to be
more astounded at the dauntless
faith and magnificent courage of
the apostle, who might have given
up in despair, or whether to be
more heartened that it was upon
such unpromising foundations that
God built a world Church.

Cliques, Immorality and
Lawsuits
(1 : 1 – 6 : 20)

P AUL BEGINS, in the normal
manner of a letter in those days,
with a greeting and an expression
of thanksgiving (1 : 1–9), and then
proceeds to deal with the first
major blemish in the community's
life. He had heard that instead of
being bound together in Christian
fellowship, the church was split
into cliques, one group claiming to
be supporters of Paul himself,
presumably as founder of the
congregation, another group pro-
fessing to be followers of Apollos,
the eloquent preacher from Alexandria (*Acts* 18 : 24 – 19 : 1; pp.
440–441). A third group preferred
to call themselves Peter's party—no
doubt the more Jewish element,
who stressed their allegiance to the
leader of the Twelve—and a fourth
group, probably rather sancti-
moniously, declared themselves to
be followers of none but Christ
himself.

It does not seem that there was
any deep-seated divergence of
belief, rather do we get the
impression of people who were
prepared to turn the church into
a party political arena, behaviour
which might easily result in
schism. Paul's concern for the
unity of the Body of Christ, and
his horror at any suggestion that a
variety of fallible human leaders
could possibly replace the sole
divine authority of Christ, is

apparent in every word of his rebuke.

He is happy that only a handful of the converts had actually been baptised by him, so that no one could accuse him of trying to found a private sect. He glories in his own limitations as a preacher, in that the stark message of the Cross had been left to make its own powerful impact upon men's minds. No skilled philosopher's arguments, to which all Greeks were well accustomed, could disguise the fact that the preaching of a crucified Messiah made nonsense to the self-styled intellectuals among the Gentiles, and outraged the deepest convictions of the Jews (cf. *Deut.* 21 : 23 ; *Gal.* 3 : 13).

God, however, does not work by human standards. It is not the powerful or clever or strong whom he chooses for his purposes, otherwise they might think that the credit was theirs alone (1 : 10-31). Paul cites himself as an example of a man of no great gifts, who was moreover far from well at the time of his mission to Corinth, but whose powerful effect upon his hearers was clear proof that nothing but the Spirit of God working through him could have achieved what he did (2 : 1-5).

As distinct from the barren speculation of intellectuals, he says, there is a type of knowledge which is communicated by Christian missionaries, and which any simple mind can understand. This is the knowledge of God and of his purpose to refashion the world, which Christian believers are enabled to share through the gift of God's own Spirit (2 : 6-16).

But this insight into the ways of God is no automatic possession conferred upon converts to Christianity. Men have to grow to spiritual maturity before they can claim to fathom the mind of God. So long as the Corinthian church members squabble among themselves, and foster a sectarian spirit, they are no better than the pagans. It matters little under whose instruction we first learn the truth about God, says the apostle. The Church has only one foundation, Christ himself. Whatever a preacher or teacher builds on this foundation is his responsibility, and he will be judged by it at the final Assize. The Church is God's Temple, and the small community at Corinth is part of it. Woe betide anyone who tries to disrupt its unity. Its members can have no other master but Christ (3 : 1-23).

Church leaders, Paul goes on, are simply servants of Christ, not to be deterred by every breath of criticism, but facing all the time the ultimate judgment of God. No leader should be given undue importance, since whatever gifts he has have been given him by God. As for the Corinthian church members themselves, their complacency and self-satisfaction contrast ill with the plight of Paul and his fellow missionaries in Ephesus, despised, ill-treated, overworked, looked on as the lowest of the low. Yet as their father in God, Paul still begs them to set their house in order. Timothy has been sent to pave the way for a visit from the apostle himself. Let them see to it that the occasion will be a happy one (4 : 1-21).

Paul next turns to a flagrant case of incest within the congregation. The man must be excommunicated at once. One case of corruption of this kind can poison the whole community. Have they forgotten that they have been delivered from their pagan past, that a new age has dawned? What grounds for pride in their church can they have, when this sort of conduct is condoned? The apostle reminds them that in his first letter he had cautioned them against mixing with people of low moral standards. He did not mean pagans, he meant so-called Christians. Men who do not accept Christian standards can be judged by God alone, but the Church must discipline its own members (5: 1–13).

The thought of Church discipline reminds the apostle of another Corinthian failing of which he has heard, their tendency to refer every trifling dispute among themselves to the pagan law courts. In his letter to the Romans, Paul upholds the authority of Roman law in major matters involving real or imagined injustice (*Rom.* 13: 1–7). His reference here is obviously to minor affairs, which ought to be settled within the Christian community by friendly arbitration. It is a Christian act to suffer a wrong, it is not a Christian act to be guilty of the very sins which God has given us a chance to put behind us for ever (6: 1–11).

The fact that Christ has made us free, says St. Paul, does not mean that we can now follow our instincts. This is particularly true in the case of sex. Our bodies are to be treated with reverence, because the Spirit lives in each one of us and each of us has an eternal destiny. Sexual intercourse can never therefore be merely a matter of physical satisfaction, since it is the sacrament of the union of two personalities, like faith-union with Christ. Since our bodies are temples of the Holy Spirit, they are not our own to do with them what we like, they belong to Christ whose servants we are (6: 12–20).

Marriage, Freedom and Restraint

(7: 1–11: 1)

ST. PAUL now proceeds to deal with questions which have been raised by the Corinthian church members in their letter to him. The first group of answers is connected with sex and marriage. In all that the apostle says, it is important to remember that he shared the general conviction of the early Church that in a few years the present world would pass away, and that in the consummation of the New Age, of the beginning of which Christians were already conscious, human relationships which now depended on physical factors and biological urges would in some way be spiritually transformed.

He therefore commends celibacy, with marriage as a second-best. Once a marriage has been contracted, however, sexual intercourse must form an integral part of the union, except by mutual consent. Divorce is not permitted for Christians by Christ's command (*Mark* 10: 11–12). Even where one partner becomes

Christian and the other remains a pagan, Paul's advice is against breaking up the marriage. Rather let the Christian partner influence the other for the sake of a Christian home. If such a marriage proves eventually unworkable, separation is allowable.

Distinctions like the differing traditions of Jew and Gentile, or the status of freeman and slave, are unimportant in view of the approaching End. Marriage at such a time is an added distraction. Referring next to an odd practice, later abandoned, St. Paul rules that if a man and woman find themselves under too great a physical strain, having elected to live together in "spiritual" wedlock, which amounted to living in an unnatural brother-sister relationship in the same house, they ought to get married. Widows are of course free to remarry, but Paul reckons that widowhood in the circumstances is preferable (7: 1–40).

When St. Paul turns to the next question on which the Corinthian church has asked for his advice, we are to remember that in any pagan city the vast variety of shrines, each with its deity and associated animal sacrifices, led to the fact that Christians buying meat in butchers' shops, or attending social functions, which were often held in some temple, could hardly avoid eating meat which had been dedicated to one of the heathen gods or goddesses. It looks as if the Corinthian Christians, in opposition to the strict Jewish-Christian view, were claiming that this could not possibly do them any harm, since they knew that the

pagan idols had no reality behind them.

St. Paul agrees in principle, but stresses that a Christian must act from love as well as from knowledge. Should a Christian find himself in a situation where his justifiable exercise of liberty in this matter would encourage a more scrupulous fellow-Christian to follow his example, and afterwards to endure the misery of a guilty conscience, he would be acting more in accordance with the mind of Christ if he respected his neighbour's inhibitions and abstained. (We do not need great perception to see the application of this in the twentieth century) (8: 1–13).

Paul now instances his own behaviour as an illustration of the self-imposed discipline which is incumbent on every Christian. As an apostle, he has every right to feel free to do what any other Christian teacher does. Yet for the sake of a more effective ministry he fasts, remains celibate, and refuses to accept the maintenance that any preacher is entitled to expect.

Instead of flaunting his freedom from Jewish Law he has conformed to it in order to win the Jews for Christ. Conversely, when among Gentiles he has stressed the irrelevance of Jewish Law, although he was only too conscious that a Christian must live under law—the Law of Christ. In short he has been prepared to accommodate himself to everybody, and to show himself no mercy, in order that he might be better able to do the one thing that matters—to lead men to Christ (9: 1–27).

Then in order to dispel any

illusion the Corinthians might have that they were in no danger of succumbing to the weaknesses of lesser men, St. Paul reminds them, by quoting incidents from the Exodus story, that the Christian sacraments are no automatic protection against sin. The Israelites of old had their experience of the Presence of God, and foreshadowings of Holy Baptism and the Eucharist, yet all this did not prevent them from falling a prey to idolatry and immorality, or from meeting their deserts. Let the record of the Old Testament be a warning (10: 1–12).

God gives us power to resist temptation, says the apostle, but for our part, we must never forget that the sacrament of Holy Communion makes us one with Christ and with one another. To show even a semblance of reverence to a pagan god, is to be false to Christ and to encourage the powers of darkness. Paul sums up the whole question as follows: our neighbour's good must be our criterion, and this is a higher law than our own freedom. That is what is meant by eating and drinking—or doing anything else—to the glory of God. Let Paul's example be our guide as Christ's is his (10: 13–11: 1).

"Decently and in Order"

(11: 2–14: 40)

PASSING NOW to matters connected with the public worship of the Church, the apostle deals first with the question of whether women should have their heads covered at divine service. In commending the existing practice that women ought to be veiled, Paul's argument is so tied up with synagogue tradition, first-century customs and obscure interpretation of the Old Testament, that it has little relevance for today. He does not appear to convince even himself with his reasoning, and concludes by justifying his position from the fact that it is generally "the done thing" (11: 2–16).

The chief importance of his next topic is that it gives us our oldest evidence for the pre-Pauline institution of the Lord's Supper, and for its regular celebration in the early Church. It was, as we have seen, the practice in pagan cities to hold feasts under religious auspices in the temples, and it would seem that in Corinth this had encouraged the transformation of solemn eucharistic occasions into unseemly brawls. In the earliest days of the Church, the celebration took place in house-churches during or after a social meal, the *agapé* or love-feast. Eventually the two parts were disjoined, but in the meantime the apostle makes a valiant attempt to ensure that the sacramental part is conducted with reverence and decorum, and traces various ills in the community to the improper observance of these sacred occasions (11: 17–34).

Underlying what the apostle says in the next three chapters (12: 1–14: 40), is the practice of "speaking with tongues" (*glossolalia*), which from the day of Pentecost had come to be regarded as indisputable proof that a person in the grip of such religious ecstasy was possessed by the Holy Spirit (see pp. 421–422). Apparently the Corinthian church was making too much of this, and had raised questions about it in the letter which Paul had received. His object now is to put this phenomenon in its proper perspective.

In their pre-Christian days, he says, the Corinthians had known religious ecstasy of a pagan kind. As Christians they must recognise that where ecstatic utterance proclaims Jesus as Lord, it is the operation of the Holy Spirit. But this is only one of many ways in which the Spirit of God is active within the Church. Indeed all the work and worship of the Church, teaching, healing, believing, preaching, as well as this gift of "tongues" is nothing but the Holy Spirit in action.

All of these have their place in the Church, which is the Body of Christ, and all are as essential to each other as are the various parts of the human body. Thus there are apostles, preachers, healers, administrators, ecstatics and all have their part to play. As in the case of the human body the less spectacular roles may well be the more important (12: 1–31).

But, goes on the apostle, in the unsurpassable thirteenth chapter, there is a higher gift of the Spirit than any of these that have been mentioned, and, without it, all the other gifts of oratory, insight, faith and self-denial are worthless. It is the gift of Christian love, patient, kind, unselfish and generous. All other gifts of God are limited to this world and therefore imperfect. This is true of our knowledge of God, of all human proclamation of his will and purpose, and of religious experience.

They belong to our childhood stage in the Christian life, and will be superseded when we come face to face with God in the full maturity of the life to come. All that we shall take with us to him is our faith, our hope and our love—and of these by far the greatest is his gift of love (13: 1–13).

Returning then to the question at issue, St. Paul discusses the value of ecstatic utterance. Doubtless it is the work of the Spirit and is the outpouring of an emotional response to God. But it is unintelligible and benefits no one, unless the utterer is able to explain what his babbling means. Outsiders will simply think that he is mad. Preaching, on the other hand, is of far more value in winning men for Christ by appealing to their minds as well as to their emotions. Above all let the worship of the Church be orderly and dignified, and this, in accordance with Paul's Jewish upbringing, excludes women from taking any active part in the service (14: 1–10).

Christ's Resurrection and ours (15: 1–58)

THE LAST great topic of the letter is of supreme importance. It would seem as if some of the Corinthians doubted whether there was any possibility of a bodily resurrection after death. St. Paul not only gives his views on this point at some length, but also gives us, in addition, our earliest evidence of the Church's belief in Resurrection of Jesus, based on what the apostle claims to have been told when he became a Christian.

As a prelude to dealing with the question of whether there is a resurrection for ordinary men, the apostle begins by citing the historical basis for any such hope. From the outset, the missionary message of the Church had been that, as the Old Testament witness foreshadowed (*Isa.* 53), Christ died for our sins. Also in fulfilment of prophecy he rose from the dead (*Ps.* 16: 10; *Hos.* 6: 2), and subsequently appeared to Peter (*Luke* 24: 34), to the Twelve (*Luke* 24: 36), to a crowd of five hundred (presumably in Galilee or, as some think, at Pentecost), to James the Lord's brother, who was thereby changed from unbelief to become the leader of the Jerusalem church, and then to all the apostles. But for Paul this was more than second-hand reporting, for the Risen Lord had finally appeared to him, the arch-persecutor of the Church, in that shattering moment on the Damascus road (15: 1–11).

This then is the ground of our belief. If there was no Resurrection of Jesus there can be no resurrection for us, and if there is no resurrection for us our preaching is a mockery, those who have died in the faith have been duped, and we are still unreconciled with God. But Christ has indeed risen, St. Paul affirms, and has opened the gates of death into the life beyond for us all (15: 12–21).

Paul then, as he more fully develops the thought in his letter to the Romans, contrasts man as he is (Adam) with man as he is meant to be (Christ). For man as he is, the natural end is death, physical and spiritual. Since the coming of the New Man, this prospect of death has been transformed into the certainty of life eternal for all who become part of him as members of his Body, the Church.

Christ was the pioneer of victory over death, and at the end of this age, when he comes again, those who are united to him will share that victory. Beyond the Judgment, when sin and evil and death itself have been destroyed, the Son who has been the means of reconciling the world to God, will take his proper place in subordination to the Father who is supreme sovereign over all (15: 22–28).

St. Paul then, almost in parenthesis, touches on what appears to have been a custom among the Corinthian Christians of baptising by proxy on behalf of some, presumably members of the same family, who had died unbaptised and might therefore, it was thought, miss their chance of being incorporated into the fulness of Christ's Kingdom at his Advent. This practice, says the apostle, makes as little sense as his own daily contempt for physical death, if there is no resurrection. Rather let us live for the satisfaction of the moment, if existence in this world is all that we have to hope for, for what we believe will always determine how we act (15: 29–34).

Then the apostle faces the obvious question! How can we picture such an apparently incredible happening as dead bodies coming to life again? Paul ridicules any suggestion that our physical bodies could be restored to their former state, and uses the analogy of sowing seed, which "dies" in order to produce a variety of plants. There is continuity between the seed and the plant, but no resemblance. Again, there is no comparison between the splendour of celestial bodies like sun, moon and stars, and even the most splendid thing that exists on earth (15: 35–41).

These illustrations, says the apostle, may help us to imagine the transformation which necessarily takes place, when a body which has been a mouldering corpse is raised to new life in another dimension. What we now know are our "material" bodies, but what we shall be given are our "spiritual" bodies. Life in the presence of God is so different from life on earth, lived on a different plane and subject to higher laws, that we can only talk of it within the limits of our human understanding, but we may say that as we are now cast in the mould of mortal man (Adam), then we shall be fashioned according to the pattern of the Man who is eternal (15: 42–50).

St. Paul then, envisaging the end as soon about to happen, summarises what he has already said in his letter to the *Thessalonians* (see pp. 488–490). When the great Day comes, the dead will be raised. and those who are still alive at the time will be changed to fit them for a new type of existence. Having this faith, what have we to fear from death or the grave? The power of sin and the tyranny of the Law have both been broken.

Christ has conquered them all and so, through him, have we (15: 51–58).

Final Messages
(16: 1–24)

FROM THESE great heights St. Paul characteristically comes down to practical matters. He counsels the adoption of a freewill offering scheme, in preparation for the collection for the hard hit mother church in Jerusalem by which he set such great store (see p. 443), indicating by his words that the "first day of the week" was already taking the place of the sabbath as the Lord's Day among Gentile Christians. Outlining his future plans, he bravely gives as a reason for staying on at Ephesus meantime not only that there is much opportunity, but also that there is much opposition (16: 1–9).

Timothy, apparently a diffident character, is commended, and Apollos is revealed as tactfully declining to encourage his supporters at Corinth by his presence, despite Paul's generous insistence. Then with a final admonition, various warm personal references and affectionate greetings, the apostle concludes the letter with his blessing. The Aramaic words: *Marana Tha*—Come, Lord!, not only link the young Gentile church with its Palestinian origins, but also remind us of the keen expectancy with which the early Christians looked for the speedy return of Christ (16: 10–24).

THE SECOND
EPISTLE OF PAUL TO
THE CORINTHIANS

BETWEEN THE dispatch of *First* and *Second Corinthians* lies, as we have seen (p. 441), a story of worsening relations between the apostle and his troublesome flock at Corinth, necessitating a brief unhappy visit and an angry letter. The combined effect of these would seem to have been successful in removing the main causes of misunderstanding, but if we are right in thinking that only the first nine chapters of *Second Corinthians* constitute this fourth and last letter to Corinth (see p. 443), we can detect in them, behind the apostle's obvious satisfaction that disciplinary action has been taken, a certain wariness which was absent from *First Corinthians*, for all its blunt criticism. The Corinthian church is clearly still an explosive mixture, which has to be handled with great care.

Reconciliation
1: 1 – 2: 17

AFTER A preliminary greeting, Paul begins his letter by referring to a recent crisis which had made him despair of his life. Whether this was similar to the riot at Ephesus (*Acts* 19), or whether it was a serious illness, is not clear. At all events, his ex-perience of God's comfort in his hour of need enables him now to encourage the Corinthians to turn to the same source of strength in the difficulties which they are facing (1: 1–11).

He then proceeds to defend himself against charges of insincerity, and in particular of failing to pay a promised visit to Corinth (cf. 12: 14). His recent sharp letter, which he had written with a heavy heart, had been intended to save such a visit from becoming a repetition of the painful occasion, when he had descended upon them in wrath from Ephesus. Now that the church had taken matters in hand, and disciplined the man who had been chiefly responsible for the smear campaign against Paul, the apostle was more than ready to consider the matter closed (1: 12 – 2: 11).

As he had waited at Troas, he says, on his way from Ephesus to Macedonia, to learn from Titus, who had been the bearer of the "severe" letter to Corinth, what the reply of the church there would be, his anxiety had been intense. Now, however, his relief bubbles over in thanksgiving to God for the irresistible advance of the Gospel of which he is, by Christ's command and by God's grace, proud to be a minister (2: 12–17).

The Christian Ministry

(3:1–7:4)

IS THIS MERE arrogance, he asks, or does he need some official commendation to justify his claim to be a true apostle? Surely the changed lives of the Corinthian churchfolk are the best proof that God has set him apart to do his work. And what a glorious vocation it is to be the messenger of the Spirit in bringing to men the new life and light of the gospel! (3:1–6).

The old covenant given through Moses was in some sense a reflection of the glory of God, but the New Covenant in Christ far excels it. To be a minister of God under the Old Testament dispensation was in itself a noble calling, even if it did not succeed in bringing men into the right relationship with God as it professed to do, but to be called to the ministry of the new order which achieves this very thing is the most glorious vocation of all (3:7–11).

The veil that covers the scrolls of the Law in the synagogue, Paul goes on, is a symbol of the veil that still prevents the Jews from recognising the truth about God, as it has been revealed in Christ. For Christians, on the other hand, nothing now stands between us and God. We are enabled by the power of the Spirit to grow into true sonship of God, being transformed more and more into the likeness of Christ as we open our hearts to him (3:12–18).

A true Christian minister, continues the apostle, can have no truck with underhand behaviour or with any distortion of the scriptures. His appeal is to every man's conscience, and only by deliberately closing their eyes to the truth—which is the devil's work—can men fail to be enlightened. If the minister himself is poorly equipped for his task, the wonder is that God can achieve so much with such indifferent material. So whatever trials and setbacks afflict him, the true servant of Christ is never in despair. In some deep mystical sense he is sharing in Christ's suffering and death, so that he himself, and others through him, may share in Christ's life. Thus amid the frustrations of day to day affairs, he is not only day by day inwardly renewed, but also keeps his hopes high by anchoring them to things that are unchanging and eternal (4:1–18).

After all, says the apostle, this vulnerable thing that we call our body is but a flimsy tent which will one day have to be dismantled. But God has prepared for each of us a more permanent dwelling-place, which awaits us when we die. Here in this life we often long to experience this new kind of existence, which means being more fully united to Christ. But whether here or hereafter, the service of Christ must be our chief concern, and we shall be judged hereafter by what we have done here and now (5:1–10).

St. Paul then, with one eye on his opponents in Corinth, as indeed has been the case throughout these chapters, maintains that all his missionary activities have been motivated by his love of Christ. Considerations of status and technique are no real criterion, in judging those who have committed themselves to Christ as his ministers. God has made new men of them, bringing them into a new relationship with himself. As such, the apostles of Christ are commissioned to proclaim the good news that God has made the same kind of new relationship possible for everyone. He offers to sinful mortals a free pardon for the sake of the perfect obedience of Christ, who identified himself with them that they, by identifying themselves with him, might grow into the same pattern of obedience (5: 11–21).

So, adds St. Paul in conclusion, as ambassadors for Christ, his true ministers must be indifferent both to hardship and opposition, to persecution and personal attack (6: 1–10). This splendid and moving digression, which began at 2: 14 and ends at 7: 4, is partly a noble defence by the apostle of the purity of his own motives against detractors and calumniators, whose attack as we can surmise must have ranged from the charge that he was not properly authorised, to accusations of high-handedness and irresponsibility.

It is, however, much more for us today at the same time a magnificent exposition of the high vocation of the ministry of the Gospel, whether clerical or lay, into which Paul throws flashes of insight and profound understanding of the significance of the Christian life for the whole Church, which are among the greatest treasures of his letters (e.g. 3: 2–3; 3: 6; 4: 6, 7–10, 18; 5: 17, 19, 20; 6: 4–10). He rounds off this great section, before resuming the more detailed narrative of his recent activities at 7: 5, with an appeal to the Corinthian church to be as warmly responsive and open hearted with him as he is with them (6: 11 – 7: 4).

There would seem to be much to be said for regarding what appears to be another short digression (6: 14 – 7: 1) within this passage, as part of a previous letter, and not as properly belonging originally to this, the apostle's fourth letter to Corinth. It is a warning against idolatry, and the danger of associating with pagans and their worship, such as might better fit an earlier stage of St. Paul's relations with this church. Many scholars believe that this may be part of Paul's first, and otherwise lost letter to Corinth referred to in *I Cor.* 5: 9. A single stray sheet of papyrus containing this fragment might easily have been incorporated here in error by the editor of the Pauline correspondence in the possession of the Corinthian church.

Christian Stewardship

(7: 5–9: 15)

NOW AT LAST Paul takes up again the thread of his narrative (7: 5), at the point where he broke off (2: 13) to enlarge on the true nature of the ministry of the Church. He speaks of the relief which Titus' arrival in Macedonia with good news from Corinth had given him, in the midst of much anxiety and worry. Part of his trouble was apparently the local situation, no doubt Jewish opposition, but more important was the question of whether his sharp letter to Corinth might have been a mistake. Paul's deep distress over his estrangement from one of his congregations, and his disappointment that they should have been ready to listen to unfounded charges against him, stand out as clearly in each line of this chapter as his delight that now his faith in his little community has been amply justified (5: 5–16).

The apostle now turns to the delicate matter of raising money for his cherished scheme of relieving the needs of the mother church in Jerusalem (see p. 443), and at the same time binding the younger churches together in a common purpose. A year earlier the collection had been started (*I Cor.* 16: 1–9), but no doubt partly due to the unhappy relations between Paul and the Corinthian church in the meantime, nothing more had been done about it.

There is a marked difference between the confidence with which Paul launched the project in his previous letter, and the diffident and careful way in which he raises the matter now. The example of the Macedonian churches, who could ill afford the money, is cited as a pattern to be followed. The apostle deprecates any suggestion that the collection is compulsory, and tries throughout to emphasise that Christian liberality is merely part of our proper response to the love of God, as in the great words of 8: 9. To avoid any suggestion of personal gain, Paul entrusts the arrangements to Titus and two other representatives, perhaps Luke and Timothy. This whole passage is indeed the great charter of Christian stewardship (8: 1 – 9: 15).

The Angry Letter
(10: 1 – 13: 14)

IT IS DIFFICULT to imagine anyone continuing reading this letter from this point through the last four chapters (10–13), without his being jolted into an awareness that they form a very odd sequel to what has gone before. We have seen the apostle, despite his gingerly handling of a recently strained relationship, doing his best to consolidate the much happier situation at Corinth, expressing his deepest gratitude that the main obstacles to a proper association between pastor and people had been removed, and voicing genuine affection and benevolence towards the whole community.

To think that he would suddenly switch to the defensive, and, without mincing matters, open the flood-gates of his wrath, mingling threat with indignation, requires some more plausible explanation than that he is now, without warning, addressing a small and troublesome minority who have to be brought to heel. A much more satisfying solution is to treat these four chapters as part of the angry letter referred to in 7: 8, which followed Paul's abortive visit to Corinth referred to in 2: 1, and which preceded his final friendly letter, which we have just read in chapters 1–9. Such a fragment of a previous letter, like 6: 14 – 7: 1, may well have been found among the archives of the Corinthian church, and could easily be tacked on at the end of Paul's last letter to Corinth, by an editor who rightly felt that this invaluable insight into the mind of the apostle must be preserved at all costs.

We find Paul strongly defending himself against the charge that he is not "spiritual" enough to be a true apostle (10: 1–6), and that for a man of such insignificant appearance and lack of eloquence he has too high an opinion of his own importance (10: 7–11). He derides the self-advertisement of his opponents, and asks to be judged himself only by what God has enabled him to do already in Corinth, and may yet enable him to do further afield (10: 12–18).

He accuses the chief trouble maker at Corinth, who had apparently made a deep impression on the congregation, of presenting a version of the Gospel, which is not only out of line with the Christian faith as proclaimed by genuine missionaries everywhere, but is also untrue and dishonest. Would the Corinthians, Paul asks, have been more impressed with his own claim to be a true apostle, if he had subsisted on their charity, instead of working for his living with occasional help from Macedonia? (11: 1–15).

Then in a magnificent outburst of indignation, and excusing himself for boasting like a fool, Paul sets out his apostolic qualifications in comparison with those of his rivals. His moving and startling account of what he has suffered for the Gospel's sake not only makes us realise how little St. Luke has been able to tell us in his brief summary of Paul's life in *Acts*, but also gives us some measure of the indomitable courage and endurance of this physical "weakling" (11: 16–33).

No less illuminating for our understanding of this incredible man is his account of a memorable mystical experience which took him into the forecourt of heaven, one of many glimpses of the divine reality which enabled him to accept his recurring bouts of illness —perhaps malaria or migraine— together with all his other misfortunes, as gateways to a deeper fellowship with Christ (12: 1–10). Surely, concludes the apostle, there has been ample evidence, in his ministry of healing at Corinth, that God's blessing was upon his work, and, if the Corinthians complain that his financial independence deprived them of the right to support their founder, this is odd reasoning indeed (12: 11–13).

Paul now turns to speak of his projected third visit to Corinth, which, as we have seen (2: 1), he failed to pay until sometime later (*Acts* 20: 2–3). He maintains his intention to continue to be self-supporting, and refutes the charge that he has manipulated to his own advantage the fund for the relief of the Jerusalem Christians. With some misgiving he wonders whether his visit will heal or merely widen the breach between himself and the Corinthian church folk (12: 14–21).

Yet, come what may, discipline must be maintained within the Church, and Paul is determined to exert his authority as an apostle. His last words to his recalcitrant flock in this vexing situation are to re-emphasise that his chief concern in the whole unhappy affair is not his own prestige, but the health and wellbeing of the Christian community in Corinth (13: 1–10). His final message (13: 11–14), with its buoyant tone and cordiality, fits in more readily as the conclusion of the letter contained in chapters 1–9.

THE EPISTLE OF PAUL TO THE GALATIANS

THIS GREAT manifesto of the freedom of Christian men is, as we have already noted (see pp. 435–436), the product of the most hotly debated controversy within the early Church. Was Christianity destined to remain essentially Judaism with some added ingredients, tied to Jewish practice and orientated on Jerusalem, or was it rather to be forward-looking and outward moving from its spiritual home in Old Testament faith and ethics into the uncharted tracts of the Gentile world?

Paul himself was quite clear in his mind that the former course meant inevitably death to the Gospel of Christ, and that only by offering to the pagans a faith that was free from the restrictive practices of Old Testament ceremonial law—circumcision and dietary regulations in particular—was there any hope of Christianity making headway. To achieve this he had to fight a running battle throughout most of his missionary service, not only with the conservative Jewish-Christian leaders of the church in Jerusalem, but with their supporters, itinerant and static, who raised the same issue on the lower level of the local churches.

It was such a conflict of opinion within the little Christian communities which Paul had founded in the Roman province of Galatia, on his first missionary journey (see pp. 434–435), which evoked this letter. The apostle has returned to Antioch, having completed this, the first of his tours, when the news reaches him that some advocates of the thesis that no Gentile can become a Christian without first becoming a Jewish proselyte, had been spreading this doctrine among the churches of Galatia—Pisidian Antioch, Iconium, Lystra and Derbe—with disturbing results.

Combined with this, was a campaign of denigration of Paul himself, as being of less than true apostolic status compared with the Jerusalem leaders of the Church, who had been actual disciples of Jesus. Pending a definitive ruling on the Jewish-Gentile issue, which was subsequently settled in principle at the Council of Jerusalem (*Acts* 15), Paul writes this letter to the Galatian churches in defence of his own point of view, and of the validity of his own apostolic status.

It is a most important contribution, not only for its autobiographical details, and for the insight it gives us into the apostle's own very human reactions to what must have been a highly exasperating development, but also because this letter strikes the first notes of the theme which Paul later expounded at length in the epistle to the *Romans*. Here, however, we see Christian theology being created, not in a mood of calm reflection, but in the heated and often passionate defence by a sorely provoked, hard-working missionary of convictions which mattered more to him than life itself.

Apostle by Divine Commission
(1 : 1 – 2 : 21)

THE LETTER opens abruptly and without Paul's usual cordiality. Right at the outset, the apostle asserts his direct commission from Christ and from no human authority, apostolic or otherwise. Passing quickly to the attack, he charges the Galatians with disloyalty. They have turned away from the true Gospel and let themselves be persuaded by false and misleading propaganda (1 : 1–10).

Then in support of his claim to have derived his authority straight from God, and not from the apostles at Jerusalem, Paul launches into a narrative of his life. He tells how, in his pre-Christian days, his fanatical allegiance to the faith of his fathers made him the arch-persecutor of the Church. From that moment on the Damascus road, however, when his vision of Christ had convinced him that the crucified carpenter, whose death damned him in the eyes of all orthodox Jews, was on the contrary God's Messiah, he needed no further commission to become a minister of the Gospel.

Only on two occasions since then had he had any contact with the apostolic dignitaries in Jerusalem, once three years after his conversion, another time several years later. Both visits were friendly and informal, with no suggestion of anything other than approval on the part of the Jewish-Christian leaders for the work that Paul was doing among the Gentiles. They were informed of the line he was taking in his preaching, namely that the Gentiles need not observe the Law, and no attempt was made at any time to make him alter it in favour of a more Jewish-Christian approach.

Far from that, it was recognised that Paul was of equal status with Peter, the one as head of the Gentile mission and the other of the Jewish mission. Indeed on one notable occasion, when Peter in a moment of weakness violated the agreement that Gentiles should not be expected to observe Jewish Law, Paul had taxed him publicly with spiritual dishonesty (1 : 11 – 2 : 14).

This leads the apostle into an enunciation of his own basic understanding of the meaning of the Gospel, which he later develops at length in *Rom*. 1–8. As opposed to any view which maintains that a man can establish the proper relationship with God only through observance of levitical Law, Paul asserts that nothing other than faith-union with Christ can achieve that. To turn back from this new relationship, and become a slave of legalistic obligations, is to exchange life for death. The man who commits himself to Christ has in effect passed from death to life, the new life that comes from the power of Christ working in him. To accept this gracious gift of a loving God, is to realise how futile is any attempt to get right with God by any human efforts (2 : 15–21).

"Our Wills Are Ours To Make Them Thine"

(3 : 1 – 5 : 6)

HOW CAN the Galatians, asks the apostle, be so stupid as to want to don the strait-jacket of the Law from which Christians have escaped? When they have come to understand the meaning of the Cross, known the power of the Spirit in themselves and seen its effect upon others, how can they confuse Christian faith with Jewish legalism? Even Abraham, father of the Jews and founder of the people of God, obtained this grand position and achieved the right relationship with God, because he was a man of faith and not because he meticulously observed the Law (3 : 1–6).

The promise that God made to Abraham, says Paul, that through him all nations would be led to the full knowledge of God, is therefore now operative for all who share the same kind of faith. Gentiles, who accept in faith the offer of God's forgiveness, are the true heirs of the promise made to Abraham, not the Jews who rely on lineal descent and their fulfilment of the Law to save them. Indeed, those who expect to achieve salvation through obedience to the Law

are accursed rather than blessed, since scripture itself maintains that nothing less than total obedience to the Law—which as Paul has always maintained is impossible—is sufficient to make a man right with God (3 : 7–12).

But Christ, continues the apostle, has now made the Law null and void. If the Law was right in treating Christ as a felon, and inflicting the death that according to *Deut.* 21 : 23 put him beyond the reach of God's mercy, then clearly the Gospel is untrue. But by raising Christ from the dead God declared the Law to be no longer valid, and by identifying himself with sinful men, in the first instance Jews, and bearing on their behalf the ultimate penalty of disobedience of the Law, Christ set them free from their obligation to observe it. Having nullified the Law by his Death and Resurrection, he has now made it possible for all who are united with him by faith, both Jews and Gentiles, to by-pass the Law and live by the power of the Spirit (3 : 13–14).

The promise of blessing, says Paul, was made to Abraham and his "seed". This cannot mean all Jews—since, as Paul maintains, the word used in *Gen.* 17 : 7 is singular and not plural—but the one representative Jew, the Messiah (and thus also all who commit their lives to him). Moreover, such a promise cannot be affected by the laws of Moses, which come into effect several centuries later, and are simply designed as an interim dispensation until Messiah should come. Men under the rule of Law could not avoid being guilty of sin and conscious of their guilt. The Law was therefore, as it were, our childhood guardian, leading us by the hand to our meeting with Christ, who made a new kind of relationship to God possible, and brought the usefulness of the Law to an end (3 : 15–25).

But now, argues St. Paul, by faith in what Christ is and what he has done, men and women of all races, and of every social class are offered the opportunity to become the inheritors of the promise made to Abraham. By faith and baptism they become part of Christ and part of each other, caught up into the family of God (3 : 26–29). Just as children, before they are of an age to inherit the fortune their father has left in trust for them, are subject to the jurisdiction of the trustees, so men, both Jews and Gentiles, were at the mercy of the fates until in God's good time he sent his Son, as a man like themselves, to free them from this bondage by his own victory over it, and to make it possible for them to enter into their proper inheritance (4 : 1–5).

We know, the apostle proceeds, that we are now God's sons, because through the Spirit of Christ within us we are able to call God our Father. How then can men who have entered this intimate relationship with God turn their backs upon it, and revert to some kind of superstitious veneration of rules and regulations? How can the Galatians forget how they had welcomed St. Paul, sick man as he was (see p. 434), for the sake of the Gospel of freedom which he brought them, and now listen to men who offer a spurious substitute religion? (4 : 6–20).

The Jews, says Paul, are like Ishmael, born into slavery—the slavery of the Law—and doomed to banishment. Christians are like Isaac, inheritors of the promise to Abraham, and born by the grace of God into the freedom of true sonship. To submit to circumcision and accept the obligations of Judaism means for a Christian not the acquisition of added holiness, but the loss of Christ and all his benefits. Christian life means accepting the rule of love, not the rule of law. The Christian in faith-union with Christ is neither better nor worse for any outwardly imposed obligation, such as circumcision. He is freed from all such restraints in order that his life should be governed by love to God and man (4 : 21 – 5 : 6).

"Whose Service is Perfect Freedom"

(5 : 7 – 6 : 18)

THIS IS THE thesis which the apostle now proceeds to expand, having appealed once more to the good sense of the Galatians and given some trenchant advice to the trouble-makers. Christian freedom must not be confused with licence. It means serving one another in love, for we too are in a sense under law, namely that we must love our neighbours as ourselves. But the true Christian does not live in accordance with a set of rules. His life is a spontaneous response to God's love, which means that under the guidance of the Spirit he is enabled to avoid the wrong kind of behaviour, and to become more like Christ in his attitude and actions (5: 7-25).

St. Paul concludes his letter with some practical counsel on Christian forgiveness, and the obligation upon Christians to help one another, and to support their teachers. Having so far dictated the letter, as was customary, he adds a characteristic note in his own hand. A last thrust at the Judaisers and the futility of circumcision is rounded off with a triumphant assertion of the all-sufficiency of Christ, who makes all things and all men new. To be reborn into this New Creation is to be the true heir of the promises to Israel, now embracing Jew and Gentile, the Israel of God. So the apostle, whose bruised body witnesses to his selfless service of his Master, ends this powerful, moving letter, which goes far deeper than the superficial first century issue of Judaism versus Christianity into the real nature of Christian freedom, which is the service of God (5: 26 – 6: 18).

THE EPISTLE OF
PAUL TO THE EPHESIANS

ST. PAUL HAD spent three crowded and eventful years at Ephesus (see pp. 440–442), and the measure of the success of his mission, as well as of the affection he had awakened, is to be seen in the touching farewell between the apostle and the leaders of the Ephesian church at Miletus on his last journey to Jerusalem (*Acts* 20: 15–38). Yet here is a letter addressed to these same Ephesians, which lacks any word of greeting to a single one of these well-loved friends, which indeed suggests that writer and readers are unknown to each other (1: 15; 3: 2), and which closes with an unusually formal benediction: "Grace be with all them that love our Lord".

To account for this, and other difficulties of thought, style and language, it has been strongly argued that this letter was not written by St. Paul, but by a later disciple who knew his master's mind and reflected his thought. This is not impossible, and it might suggest that the early Church was richer in anonymous inspiration than we imagine. Most scholars, however, take the view that the letter was written by St. Paul, and account for its impersonal character by suggesting that it may have been a circular letter addressed in general to the churches in Asia, with a blank space in 1: 1 for the insertion of the appropriate name. In support of this it may be noted that some of the best ancient manuscripts omit the words "at Ephesus" in that verse. This may indeed be the "lost" letter referred to in *Col.* 4: 16.

The letter is obviously written from prison, forming, with *Philippians*, *Colossians* and *Philemon*, what are generally known as the "Captivity Epistles". This imprisonment is normally identified with St. Paul's final two years of captivity in Rome (*Acts* 28: 30), although other spells in prison in Caesarea and Ephesus have been canvassed.

The arguments on all these questions are complicated, but they make little or no difference to our understanding of the letter. We shall not go far wrong if we think of St. Paul in prison in Rome near the end of his ministry, writing this letter at the same time as the letter to the church at Colossae, and the private message to Philemon, in this case dealing not with the problems of any particular church—as in *Colossians* —but unfolding his mind, for the benefit of all the churches in the Ephesus mission field, on the great theme of Christ and his Church.

Many people will feel that this is the greatest of all St. Paul's letters. It is not always easy to follow, but the difficulty lies mostly in lifting our small minds up to the heights to which Paul's own mind soars. Here is none of the heat of controversy but rather a deep devotional spirit, as if the apostle himself were awed by the sublimities about which he was writing. More clearly than most of Paul's letters, *Ephesians* falls into two sections, theological and practical, and it shows how completely the apostle linked faith and action as two sides of the same coin.

The New Family of God
(1: 1–3: 21)

THE OPENING note of the letter, after the initial greeting, is one of thanksgiving to God for all that Christ means for the Church. The purpose of God from eternity has been to make it possible for men to become his true sons, and to gather them into one great family of mutual love. This he has now begun to do through Christ, who by his Life, Death and Resurrection has enabled us to be delivered from all that kept us apart from God, and to enter into this new relationship.

More than that, we now know that it is God's plan to bring not only the Church but the whole cosmos into perfect harmony with himself through Christ, and it is our inestimable privilege as members of the Church to share this knowledge, and to look forward to sharing also in the realisation of God's purpose. You who have responded to the Gospel, says St. Paul, already know, by experiencing the power of the Holy Spirit in your own lives, something of the glorious future which lies ahead (1: 1–14).

The apostle's thanksgiving for all that he has heard of the faith and good works of his readers, merges into a prayer that they might come to an even deeper knowledge of God, to grasp the wonder of what it will mean to live in perfect fellowship with him, and to realise even now what the power of God can do in their lives. There are no limits to such a power, which was able to raise Christ from the dead, and exalt him high above any other dignity that we can imagine, either here or hereafter. It is this Christ, supreme over all, whom God has made head of the Church, which is his Body, and whose life is more and more fully expressed within it (1: 15–23).

Now we know what it means to pass from death to life, from the living death of self-centredness to the new life which is centred with Christ in God. Nothing that we have done or could have done, but only the love of God towards us, has made this possible. He has made new men and women of us, so that we might carry out the work he summoned us to do (2: 1–10).

Remember, says the apostle, that it is not so long ago that you Gentiles were beyond the pale, you had never heard of Christ, and you had no share in the heritage of Israel, the people of God. But now by virtue of Christ's work, you Gentiles and we Jews are brought together in Christian fellowship before God. Christ has made peace between us and has broken down the barrier which divided us, and which was symbolised by the wall of the Court of the Gentiles in the Temple at Jerusalem. It was the Law that kept us apart, but Christ's Death and Resurrection made the exclusive claims of the Law a dead letter, and created the possibility of a new type of man, neither Jew nor Gentile, but Christian (2: 11–16).

This then is the Gospel, the good news—that the Gentiles who knew nothing of God, and the Jews who knew something of God but not enough, are now both able to reach the full knowledge of God on equal terms together. There is no longer any distinction. All Christian men are equal members of God's family. The Church is like a great shrine in the making, a true Temple, where Christ is the foundation stone, apostles and prophets form the base, ordinary Christians constitute the interlocking fabric of the walls, and the whole edifice is the dwelling place of the Spirit of God (2: 17–22).

It is for preaching this Gospel, continues St. Paul, that I now have to write to you from prison. You know how by God's grace I became the apostle to the Gentiles, and how he revealed to me, and to his other servants in this great work, what had never hitherto been understood, that the Gentiles are to stand on an equal footing with God's own chosen people, the Jews. No human wits or human power could have given me this knowledge or the strength to proclaim it.

For this reconciliation of Jew and Gentile in one Church is, as all the world can see, the first step in the eternal purpose of God to bring the whole cosmos into the same unity and harmony with himself through Christ and his Church. Since this is the scope of the divine plan, do not be distressed that you have brought this suffering upon me (3: 1–13).

So, adds the apostle, as he comes to the end of the doctrinal part of his letter, as I think of this great new family of God, I pray that our heavenly Father may strengthen you by his Spirit, and that you and all his people may learn more and more the endless riches of Christ's love, that the Church may be filled with the Spirit of God, to whom be all glory (3: 14–21).

Family Life

(4: 1 – 6: 24)

ST. PAUL NOW turns to the practical implications of this great vision of the role of the Church in the world. Christians must set an example of humility, patience, tolerance and charity. God has made us one great fellowship, let us strengthen our unity by fostering peace amongst ourselves. Let us never forget that the Church is one and not many, sustained by the same Spirit of God. We all share the same hope, the same Lord, the same faith, the same baptism, the same heavenly Father who is above and within all that he has created (4: 1–6).

But, of course, each of us within the Church has a separate function. Christ, who came down amongst us, and has now been exalted, so that the whole universe should be filled with his Presence, has given each of us a special gift which we are to use for the enrichment of the life of the Church. The aim of all this is nothing less than that the Church should grow and mature, until it expresses the wholeness of Christ in its life. We are not children, to be carried away by every new idea, and to be taken in by every plausible tongue. Rather we must hold fast to the truth we have received, and grow up into the fulness of the Body of Christ, each of us making his own contribution, depending on him who is the Head (4: 7-16).

Therefore there must be a clean break with the past. Have done with all illusion, ignorance and sensuality. The Christian life means a changed life, a total re-making of our nature into what God intended it to be. Since we are all bound together in one Christian fellowship, there can be no room for lies or for harbouring grudges. Dishonesty, a foul tongue, spite and ill-temper—these are offences against God's Spirit, which is within us. But kindness, generosity and a forgiving heart—these are no more than our just debt to God, who has forgiven us (4: 17-32).

Since we are God's children, our Father must be our pattern, and that means showing to each other the same kind of costly love as Christ has shown to us. Casual sex relationships, greed and filthy talk will bring God's punishment, let us make no mistake about that, so let us keep away from people who say that these things do not matter. There is as much differ-ence between behaviour of this sort and the conduct of a Christian man, as between darkness and light. The light of Christ's truth in which we now live, shows up human conduct in its true colours (5: 1-14).

Christian behaviour springs from a realisation of who we are and why we are here. So we must use our time to the best advantage, and try to know the will of God in our own lives. Resorting to drink in the hope of finding inspiration or exhilaration is a dangerous ex-pedient. Too easily it becomes a habit. The man who seeks and finds his inspiration in the service of God, will want to express him-self rather in singing God's praises or in offering silent praise and thanksgiving within his own heart (5: 15-20).

St. Paul now turns to home life, and outlines the general attitude that ought to govern relationships in a Christian household. The underlying principle is mutual recognition of status, with re-sponsibilities corresponding to rights. Wives are to recognise their husbands as head of the house, as Christ is Head of the Church. But by the same token husbands are to love their wives as Christ loved his Church, which means self-giving to the uttermost for the sake of a perfect marriage. A man must love his wife as he loves himself, and Christian mar-riage, which is the fusion of two personalities, reflects the bond between Christ and his bride, the Church (5: 21-33).

Children, likewise, are urged to obey their parents and respect the commandment to honour them.

But parents have a responsibility to treat their children with understanding, and to bring them up in a Christian way. A Christian slave will recognise his duty to serve his master well, just as a Christian employer will ever be mindful of his obligation to treat his slaves well, remembering that he will be held to account by God before whom master and slave are alike (6: 1–9).

Then in a great closing passage, St. Paul, his imagination caught, as some think, by the sight of a Roman legionary on duty in the prison, but finding his imagery in the Old Testament, describes the resources of the Christian soldier, in his constant battle against the forces of evil and the powers of darkness. Nothing less than the whole armour which God provides will suffice—truth, integrity, the power of the Gospel, the knowledge of salvation, the word of God, faith and prayer (6: 10–18).

Finally the apostle, calling himself "an ambassador of Christ—in chains", asks for his readers' prayers that his work for the Gospel may continue. Tychicus, who is entrusted with this letter, and with the letter to the Colossians (*Col.* 4: 7), will give them all further news. The letter ends with the apostle's blessing (6: 19–24).

THE EPISTLE OF PAUL
TO THE PHILIPPIANS

THERE COULD be no greater contrast than that between the general tone and contents of the letters to the Ephesians and to the Philippians. The one is formal, carefully thought out, and maintains a consistently exalted level of theology and ethics throughout. The other is affectionate, almost chatty, unsystematic, and directly concerned with the affairs of a local congregation. Yet *Philippians* has purple passages which strike the deepest Pauline note, and give us some of the apostle's finest insights. Indeed it is perhaps the best example of how some trifling issue in the life of a little Christian community sparks off in St. Paul's mind the kind of profound reflection which makes him the most creative thinker in the early Church.

Despite an inauspicious beginning (see pp. 437-438), the apostle's relations with the church at Philippi had always been extremely cordial. It was his first missionary venture outside Asia, he had subsequently visited it on more than one occasion (*Acts* 20: 1-6), his "beloved physician", Luke, had been its father in God, and, as we can read from this letter, it was the only one of his mission stations that he allowed to give him financial help. The

church at Philippi was clearly no problem child like that at Corinth, nor fickle like the churches of Galatia, and the warmth of Paul's regard for its people makes this perhaps the pleasantest of all his letters.

It was also in all probability the apostle's swan song. Written from prison, like *Ephesians*, *Colossians* and *Philemon*, it does not fall into that group which were sent by the hand of Tychicus to the province of Asia, but has its own special *raison d'être*. There is some dispute, as in the case of these other Captivity Epistles, whether the prison was in Ephesus, Caesarea or Rome, with perhaps more justification in this case for thinking that it may have been in Ephesus.

Nevertheless, the traditional view that *Philippians* was written during Paul's final imprisonment in Rome, and later than the other three, seems to fit the facts better than any other. The occasion of his writing this letter was particularly happy. The apostle's friends at Philippi had learned that he was in prison, had raised some money among themselves, and had sent it to Rome in charge of one of their members, Epaphroditus. Unfortunately, the messenger became seriously ill while in Rome, but when he had recovered and was ready to return home to Philippi, St. Paul took the opportunity to send this letter with him, conveying his thanks and good wishes to the Philippian churchfolk.

Jesus Christ is Lord
(1: 1 – 2: 30)

IN HIS opening greeting, the apostle associates with his own name that of Timothy, who probably wrote the letter at Paul's dictation, and was known to the Philippians from the early days of the mission, addressing himself to the Christian community, including its leaders. "Bishops", called "presbyters" or "elders" elsewhere in the New Testament, and "deacons" are of course, at this stage in the history of the Church, not the equivalent of modern representatives of these orders, but office-bearers in the local housechurches (see p. 501).

Then follows, in accordance with the pattern of letters in Paul's day, a thanksgiving, in this case for the knowledge that the Philippians had always been behind him, either on the mission field or now as he faces his trial. He can think of no better prayer for them than that they should continue to grow in Christian love and understanding, until the coming of Christ (1: 1–11).

Paul now reassures his readers that his imprisonment has not hindered the work of the Gospel in Rome. On the contrary, the local missionaries have taken fresh heart from his example of evangelising even among his guards.

Some, if the truth be told, resent the great reputation of this newcomer to Rome, and cannot forget that it is they who have borne the heat and burden of the early days of the Roman mission. No matter, the Gospel is being preached, and that is all that counts.

The apostle now speaks of his impending trial. It may issue in life or death, and sometimes he wishes that he were dead for the sake of closer communion with Christ. But he knows that God still has work for him to do on earth, and so looks forward to a reunion with his friends at Philippi. Let them give a good account of themselves, and resist all attempts by the supporters of pagan religions to suppress them (1: 12–30).

Then, apparently with reference to something he had heard of party-strife and spiritual pride in the congregation at Philippi, St. Paul makes a noble and immortal plea for unity and humility. The supreme example that should ever be before the eyes of all Christians is that of Christ himself, who did not hesitate to shed his divine status, not only becoming a man. but making himself the Servant, of whom Isaiah had spoken, living and dying in perfect obedience to God, and enduring the last humiliation of a Cross.

It was for this, the perfect obedience and humility of the Son of Man, that God has now exalted him above the whole universe, ultimately to be acknowledged by all as Lord and King, under God the Father. This is the kind of obedience that is expected of Christ's people. God has put into our hearts the desire to serve him, and has given us the strength to do it. It is for us to follow our Lord's example, in responsibility before God (2: 1–13).

The lives of Christian men and women should be like bright lights, shining out in the darkness of the surrounding pagan world. Paul hopes that he will live to see the Second Coming of Christ, and that he may then feel that the progress of his Philippian church is such that he will be satisfied that his work has not been in vain. If life is not granted to him, his death will be joined with the offering of their faith as a worthy sacrifice to God (2: 14–18).

Timothy is to be sent to Philippi soon, to pave the way for Paul's own visit. Epaphroditus too, now recovered in health, who had brought the money for Paul from Philippi, will shortly be on his way home (2: 19–30).

Rejoice!

(3: 1–4: 23)

IT WOULD almost seem as if Paul may have meant to conclude his letter about this point, and that either after an interruption or because some new information has reached him, he decides to take up another topic. Implying that he had already written to Philippi on this subject, the apostle refers to the danger of being taken in by "holier-than-thou" Judaisers, who insist that Christian faith is inadequate for salvation, without the merit that accrues from observing Jewish ceremonial law, particularly circumcision.

St. Paul counters this by claiming that it is Christians, and not Jews, who witness to the true significance of circumcision, which is merely an external symbol of an inward commitment to God. But if it comes to a competition in superficial sanctity, says the apostle, who has a better claim than he himself—every inch a Jew, and a most godly Pharisee to boot?

Yet all these so-called advantages he has thrown aside as worthless, for the sake of knowing Christ and becoming part of his Body. All his moral and spiritual achievements, on which he once prided himself, he now regards as less than nothing, since he has found the only way to the right relationship with God through committing his life wholly to Christ. To know the living Christ, and to have suffered and died with him, in the hope of living in perfect union with him for ever—this, says the apostle, is all that now matters (3: 1–11).

Not that he reckons to have reached the full maturity of Christian life. But he is content to run his race, growing into a fuller understanding of his first encounter with Christ on the Damascus road. Not looking back, or calculating how well he has done, he presses on to the winning post for the prize of the full knowledge of God in Christ. This, he says, is the true Christian attitude (3: 12–16).

St. Paul then urges his readers to take their example from his own way of living, and warns them against those Christians who confuse freedom with licence. A Christian must regard himself as already a citizen of heaven, from where Christ is soon to appear.

When he comes, the chains that bind us to this earth will be broken, and we shall be transformed into his likeness (3: 17–21).

In closing his letter, the apostle refers to a personal quarrel between two prominent women in the Philippian church, characteristically making it the occasion of a final splendid homily on toler-ance, the need for prayer, and for thinking about the big things that really matter. His last words of thanks to the Philippians for their financial help are an illuminating comment on the spiritual resources which had sustained him throughout his missionary life, and were still adequate in this his most critical hour (4: 1–23).

THE EPISTLE OF PAUL
TO THE COLOSSIANS

ONE OF THE many dangers to which Christianity in its earliest stages was exposed came from within the local churches themselves. It consisted of attempts to "improve on" the original gospel as proclaimed by the missionaries, by insisting that it was not rigid enough, or effective enough, or perhaps exciting enough, and that Christianity needed strengthening and deepening and widening, if it were to become an adequate means of salvation.

The main thrust of this movement came from the Jewish Christians, many of whom no doubt felt that not only had venerable and worthy Old Testament practices been recklessly thrown overboard, but that there was also something to be said for the point of view of the extremists, who argued that what had been thrown overboard must at all costs be retrieved.

It was clearly because so strong a case could be made out for the thesis that, without universal circumcision and observance of levitical law, Christians could neither compete with the Jews in public demonstration of personal sanctity, nor safely claim to be the legatees of the Old Testament promises made to Israel, that St.

Paul found it necessary to thunder so violently against it, as, for example, in his letter to the Galatians.

But a similar danger presented itself from the side of the Gentile Christians, and although the full effect of this threat was not felt until after Paul's day, the first shadows fall across the New Testament writings. Thus we find not only St. Paul, but St. John and the author of *II Peter*, striving in their letters to the young churches to root out this insidious development, which, just as much as the efforts of the Judaisers, sought by the addition of extraneous ingredients to "improve on" the apostolic faith, and make it more intellectually respectable and spiritually satisfying.

It was in response to information that a situation of this kind had arisen in the Christian community at Colossae, that Paul wrote this letter. The church there was not one of those which Paul himself had founded. He had never even visited the town, which lay about a hundred miles east of Ephesus, in the province of Asia. It lay off his route when he travelled from Pisidian Antioch to Ephesus on his third missionary tour, and it had apparently been founded by Epaphras, one of Paul's disciples, in the campaign that evangelised so much of the country round Ephesus, during the three years that Paul lived there (see pp. 440–442).

While Paul was in prison in Rome, Epaphras joined him, and brought news of the church at Colossae and its special problems. It is not altogether easy to say precisely what form the Colossian "heresy" took. Since the churchfolk there were well aware of it, St. Paul does not need to describe it, and we can only gather from his argument a general impression of what it may have been.

Clearly it was a product of an age which had seen the breakdown of the old barriers between East and West in the empire that had been founded by Alexander the Great, and was now Roman in name and government. When the gods and goddesses of ancient Greece and Rome became discredited, the way was opened for a fusion of eastern religions with western philosophy. Endless variations on this theme were possible, and it was in a pagan world, which sprouted new faiths like mushrooms, that Christianity had to stake its claim.

The particular issue at Colossae appears to have been an attempt, doubtless well-meant, on the part of some Christians, to enrich the teaching they had received with elements from paganism, and also in this case from Judaism. Ordinary Christianity was apparently not good enough. It lacked philosophical depth. Respect must be paid to the mysterious cosmic forces that govern man's existence. Between God and man, influential angelic beings held sway, and must be given the worship that is their due. Pagan asceticism to mortify the flesh, and Jewish ritual observance to discipline the soul, seem also to have played a part in this strange attempt to make Christianity more attractive to religious highbrows.

All this might seem to be little more than the passing eccentricity of a small group of Christians in a remote province of Asia Minor, were it not for the fact that it provoked St. Paul into what is without doubt his most comprehensive statement of the significance of Jesus, and his rebuttal once and for all of any attempt to fit Christ into some kind of composite religion.

But the Colossian heresy was much more than a local aberration. Its more developed form, Gnosticism, of which this was an early precursor, threatened to shake the Church in the second century from its pristine faith. It is one more mark of the genius of St. Paul that he foresaw this danger in these small beginnings, and in this letter indicated how it could and must be overcome.

The Cosmic Christ

(1: 1–29)

AFTER A friendly greeting, St. Paul gives thanks to God for the steady progress in Christian witness of the Colossian church, part of a growing response to the truth of the Gospel all over the world. Epaphras, who first acquainted them with the Christian message of salvation, has recently rejoined Paul and brought him this good news. Paul's prayer for the little congregation is that they may grow by God's grace into full understanding of the Gospel, and its implications for their daily living (1: 1–12).

In what follows, St. Paul is addressing himself to the problem of meeting the arguments of the Colossian "heretics". He does so by claiming for Christ supreme power under God over the universe, and over any supernatural forces which may be thought to affect man's destiny. His thought connects with what St. John says of Christ in the first chapter of his gospel (*John* 1: 1–14), as well as with the Old Testament ideas of the creative Word of God in *Gen.* 1, and the Wisdom of God in e.g. *Prov.* 8.

God, says the apostle, has delivered us from the powers of darkness into the light and life of Christ. We are now freed from the fear of all those hostile forces that dominated our existence, and from the burden of our own guilt. For Christ is God in action. He is the creative purpose that shaped the universe, the meaning of its existence, supreme over all orders of being, the unifying principle that underlies the whole cosmos.

This same Christ, continues St. Paul, is embodied in the world in the Church, of which he is the Head. By his Resurrection he inaugurated the new age in which the Church now lives, and of which she acknowledges him to be the Lord. It is the will of God that the whole universe should find its fulfilment in him, since God chose to express himself fully in Christ, and to restore the right relationship between himself and the universe through him. This he did by the perfect obedience of Christ, culminating in his sacrificial offering of himself in death, the supreme act of love which broke the power of evil, and gave the world a fresh start (1: 13–20).

This reconciliation, says the apostle to his readers, applies to you too. Now you are no longer cut off from God by your past misdeeds, for he has put you on a new footing by virtue of Christ's Death. But this new relationship is only effective so long as you stand fast in the faith as you have received it, and refuse to be coaxed away from the path you have now begun to follow (1: 21–23).

As a minister of this gospel, St. Paul goes on, I am now in prison. But I bear this affliction gladly, because it enables me to share the suffering which Christ still endures in his Church, until the final fulfilment of God's purpose. My call from God to be his minister was for your sake, so that I might make known the secret which by the will of God has now at last been disclosed: that Christ is in you Gentiles, giving you all the glorious hope of becoming fully the sons of God that you were meant to be. This is my message from God, not for the few but for you all (1: 24–29).

Dying and Rising with Christ
(2: 1 – 4: 18)

THE APOSTLE then goes on to speak of his concern for the Colossian church, and their neighbours at Laodicea, and all Christians who are as yet unknown to him. His prayer for those Asians, who are surrounded by the diversity of pagan mystery-religions, is that they should know that the only true mystery is Christ, the key to all wisdom and knowledge. Only by being fully grounded and rooted in Christ, will they be able to resist the allurements of futile speculation and man-made mysteries.

Christians must have no truck with belief in a variety of supernatural beings who control their destinies. The whole power of the supernatural world and ultimate reality itself are concentrated in Christ. He is all that we need. As for circumcision, it only becomes meaningful when in conversion and baptism a Christian sloughs off his old unregenerate nature, and by reproducing in his own life the Death and Resurrection of Jesus, enters into a new relationship with God within the fellowship of the Church. By his Cross, Christ has freed us from the demands of a Law that we could never fulfil, and thus exposed as powerless the malign forces that held us in their thrall (2: 1–15).

By the same token, continues St. Paul, petty rules of diet and rigid observance of holy days are irrelevant. So are ascetic practices, angel-worship and pseudo-mysticism. This type of self-styled holiness is spurious, because it is not centred on Christ, who alone can integrate the faith and practice of the Church.

Men who have turned their backs upon the past by dying with Christ, cannot possibly let their lives still be dominated by materialistic rules and regulations of this sort, no matter how impressive it looks to the outside world. On the contrary, those who know what it means to rise from death to new life with Christ, must have their anchor in heaven and not on earth. The true life of the Christian is even now, despite his involvement in the concerns of the world, united with Christ in the ultimate reality of God's being. When this world passes and Christ is finally seen to be Lord of all, the life of the Christian will also be seen to be the only true life, and will then find its complete fulfilment in a new dimension (2: 16 – 3: 4).

On this note St. Paul ends his breath-taking analysis of the status and significance of Christ, and what that means for Christians— the more breath-taking when we remember that it was written by a man on trial for his life in the vast unfriendly pagan capital city, to not much more than a handful of his supporters in a remote part of the empire. The Church, for which he makes such fantastic claims, cannot have numbered then more than a few thousand souls from Rome to Jerusalem.

For the rest of his letter, Paul outlines the ethical implications of what he has just been saying. Most of it is already familiar to us from the letter to the Ephesians (see pp. 475–477), which seems to have been written after *Colossians*, in an attempt to provide for the churches in the province of Asia in more generalised and systematic form the teaching contained in this letter. In both *Ephesians* and *Colossians*, however, it is equally plain that St. Paul regards Christian behaviour as the inseparable counterpart of Christian faith. Dying and rising with Christ is no mere theological word-play, it is the basis of personal conduct and character.

Put to death the old self, says the apostle, with all the evil things that stained the past, the sins of the flesh and the sins of the spirit. As new men in Christ—and that means the disappearance of all distinctions of race and class—cultivate the Christian virtues, above all, love. So in the home, the new life issues in new attitudes on the part of husbands and wives, parents and children, employers and slaves (3: 5 – 4: 1).

Finally, after some general admonitions, St. Paul refers to Tychicus, the bearer of the letter (and of *Ephesians*), and Onesimus, his companion on the journey to Colossae, who, as we shall see in the letter to Philemon, needed all the praise that the apostle gives him here. The letter closes with greetings from a variety of Paul's friends, who were with him in Rome, including St. Mark, and St. Luke, the evangelists (4: 2–18).

THE FIRST
EPISTLE OF PAUL TO
THE THESSALONIANS

JUDGED BY the brief account in the book of *Acts* of the Thessalonian mission, Paul's efforts on this occasion could hardly be said to have resulted in unqualified success. The apostle appears to have thought so too, and his low spirits on arrival at Corinth were attributable not only to ill-health, and his failure to make any impression on the philosophers of Athens, but also no doubt to a deeper anxiety as to whether methods of evangelism, which had been effective in Asia Minor, would work as well, or at all, in the west (see pp. 437–439).

A by-product of his relief when Silvanus and Timothy arrived in Corinth, with the news that the Macedonian mission had produced results far beyond the wildest expectations, was this first letter to the church at Thessalonica. Neither this nor the second letter, which was despatched soon afterwards, can be reckoned among Paul's greatest writings. Many would say that, apart from the Pastoral Epistles (see pp. 494–502), which are in any case of doubtful origin, the Thessalonian correspondence is the least interesting and relevant section of the Pauline letters.

These two brief communications, addressed to the congregation at Thessalonica, do not handle majestic themes like *Romans* or *Ephesians*. On the contrary, their main concern is with questions which seem to us to be no longer major issues, and which are in any case dealt with in a way which awakens little response in twentieth century minds. This, however, as in the case of the letter to the Hebrews (see p. 505), is a superficial judgment, and while no one could claim that the Thessalonian letters match *Hebrews* in importance, they shed much light on the tensions and anxieties of the early Church, and the prodigious difficulties that the missionaries had to overcome. But perhaps most of all, they underline the unquenchable hope in the growth of the Church, and the ultimate victory of the cause of Christ, which motivated St. Paul himself, and which he was able to communicate to the unpromising material that made up the first Christian congregations.

The apostle begins his letter by greeting the members of the little community at Thessalonica in his own name and those of Silvanus and Timothy, who were with him in Corinth when the letter was written, and who had both been involved in the Thessalonian mission. He gives thanks to God as he recalls the initial response to the Gospel message, a response which clearly showed that the Holy Spirit was powerfully at work. The faith of the Thessalonians had endured despite persecution, and had become a talking-point far beyond the confines of Greece.

Even strangers, before the missionaries have a chance to tell them, speak of the wonderful transformation that has taken place, changing men, whose religion was sheer pagan idolatry, into servants of the true and living God, waiting expectantly for the end event of human history, when the Lord Jesus will come again to reign over his people (1: 1–10).

The Second Advent

THIS IS THE first mention in the Thessalonian letters of what is in fact their distinctive feature. The Second Advent of Christ, what it will mean and when it will happen, seems to have been almost an obsession among the Christians of Thessalonica. Although so much emphasis is placed upon it in these letters, as compared with the later letters that St. Paul addressed to the young churches, this does not necessarily mean either that the missionary message at Thessalonica was different from that given elsewhere, or that St. Paul's views changed as time went on.

The Second Coming, or to give it its Greek name, the Parousia, was a constant element in the faith of the early Church, and the speedy end of the present age with the return of Christ, the Last Judgment, and the final establishment of the rule of the Messiah, is taken for granted by St. Paul and every other New Testament writer. If Philippians is Paul's swan song, his expectation of the Second Advent is as keen at the end of his days as now, in the full flush of his missionary activity (*Phil.* 1: 10; 4: 5).

It would appear, however, that the Thessalonian church found particular aspects of this belief puzzling, and for this reason St. Paul devotes more space than usual to this topic. In what he says, he seems to be repeating the Old Testament phrases in which Jewish Christians, brought up on the apocalyptic language of the prophets and the intertestamental period, applied to Christ what had been said in the scriptures about the Day of the Lord, with the descent of YHWH to earth in judgment (see pp. 270–272).

For Jewish Christians, certain that in a real sense the old age had passed and the new age foretold by the prophets had begun with the First Advent of Christ, conscious too of living in the midst of supernatural events, the greatest being the Resurrection of Jesus, it was natural to think that God, having shown his hand so dramatically in the works of Christ and the apostles, would speedily bring the old evil order to a spectacular end and usher in the new order in a way that would convince all mankind, and not only the small groups of believing Christians, that Jesus was Lord and King of all the nations.

We should be wrong, therefore, to take what St. Paul says in these letters about the Parousia, as necessarily a programme which he expected literally to be fulfilled. The Old Testament language, which he uses with regard to the end of the world, is as much the language of symbol and poetry as the Old Testament description of the beginning of the world in Gen. 1. Both the beginning and the end of everything are beyond human understanding, and can only be suggested in pictorial form as the biblical writers clearly indicate.

We should also be wrong to think that the early Church laid all the stress upon an immediate Second Advent. When Christ did not return, the Church does not seem to have been unduly disturbed, suggesting that her basic concern was not with the time-factor, but with the sense of the nearness of God in judgment and the certainty of Christ's victory.

We should therefore do well to remember the original meaning of the word Parousia, which is "presence", and its later use meaning the "visit of a king". The Church believed that the King had come, that he was already present with his people through the Holy Spirit, but one day sooner or later the King must be acknowledged by the whole world; his Triumph over evil, sin and death must be absolute. Then at last the purpose of God in creation would be fulfilled, and the new age, in which Christians already live by faith, would finally begin. In this sense the expectation of St. Paul and of the Thessalonians, underlying the unfamiliar Old Testament imagery, is still the faith of the twentieth century Church.

Problems at Thessalonica

ST. PAUL, then, having touched on this topic, returns to the narrative of his mission at Thessalonica. Obviously, since his departure, mischief-makers have been busy — presumably, from what follows, they were Jewish agitators—suggesting that he was a smooth-tongued charlatan of doubtful morals. He therefore reminds the Thessalonians of his work among them, his care for them, his refusal to accept any financial help, and his insistence on taking a job to support himself (2: 1–9).

Then he speaks of the persecution they have suffered at the hands of their own countrymen, who have treated them as badly as the Jews have treated the Christians in Palestine. Paul does not mince his words as he denounces his compatriots. He suggests that it is due to their machinations that he has been unable to revisit Thessalonica. However, he had sent Timothy in his stead, and now Timothy had returned with the splendid news of the little congregation's Christian witness. Paul still hopes to pay them a visit, but meantime he must deal with the particular problems they are facing, and of which Timothy has told him (2: 10–3: 13).

He pinpoints issues on which the Thessalonians are falling short of

Christian standards: sex behaviour, hospitality and idleness. It was never easy for converted Gentiles, living in the sex-ridden atmosphere of a pagan city (see pp. 523–524), to break completely with past habits, and to remain faithful to their wives or to avoid pre-marital promiscuity. Mutual help and hospitality were also essential in every Christian community, many of whose members came from the lowest strata of society. Refugees and travellers from other centres were also constantly in need of food and shelter.

The third problem was, as far as we know, a Thessalonian peculiarity. As part of their end-of-the-world obsession, it appears that some of the church members had downed tools, and not only expected others to support them as they waited for the Second Advent, but also kept their more sensible neighbours off their work by fussing around with their excited speculations. Paul has to deal with this more fully in his second letter (4: 1–12).

In keeping with his unusually frequent references to the Second Advent (1: 10; 2: 19; 3: 13) in the previous part of his letter, the apostle now turns to the questions that chiefly perplexed the Thessalonian Christians. Firstly, when the Lord Jesus comes again what will happen to those Christians who are already dead? St. Paul, who at this stage clearly expects to be alive himself when Christ returns, a view which he no longer held by the time he came to write *Philippians* (*Phil.* 1: 20–26), reminds then of the traditional teaching of the missionaries on the subject of the Parousia, in words replete with Old Testament allusion and imagery. But through this poetic framework, he expresses his own personal conviction that those who die "in Christ" before his final Triumph, remain "in Christ" until they are finally welcomed into his Presence to be with him for ever (4: 13–18).

The second point that worried the Thessalonians was the obvious question as to when the Parousia would take place. It might be possible for Old Testament prophets and New Testament apostles to speak of the Day of the Lord as liable to come at any time, without being very much concerned as to when the world as they knew it would cease to exist. The answer in their case is, of course, that they were so firmly anchored to the world beyond sense and sight that the time-factor ceased to be important. For simple folk, however, like the Thessalonians and ourselves, the problem is not so easily solved.

St. Paul deals with the point by reasserting that the Day of the Lord, the end-event of time and history, would come as the prophets and the Lord himself had said, suddenly and unexpectedly. But Christians, who live in the light of the Gospel and in accordance with its precepts, have nothing to fear. If we are protected by the armour of God—faith, hope and love—against the temptation of the world, the flesh and the devil, and practice obedience to God, it makes little difference when we are called on to give an account of our lives to our Maker. For the essence of the Christian life is a relationship with God through Christ, which is not affected by the death of the body, but on the contrary is deepened and enriched in the fuller freedom of the age to come (5: 1–11).

The apostle rounds off his letter with various cautionary remarks. The Thessalonian members should treat the office-bearers in the congregation with more respect, settle their private quarrels, and generally achieve a better tone in their community life. They are not to look askance at what they might feel to be exaggerated or unpalatable forms of Christian witness or behaviour, though at the same time they must not accept everything that passes for Christian evangelism as genuine (5: 12–22). The letter ends with a prayer and a blessing (5: 23–28).

THE SECOND
EPISTLE OF PAUL TO
THE THESSALONIANS

PROBABLY only a few weeks later, Paul has to write again to the same people, either because his first letter was misunderstood, or because he had heard that the Second Advent hysteria had become worse. Much of the second letter covers the same ground, in the same language, as the first. Persecution has apparently intensified at Thessalonica, yet despite that, the congregation is standing firm.

Paul comforts the little community with the assurance of divine justice, and affirms that retribution will fall upon the enemies of the Gospel in the final Judgment, just as surely as the faithful followers of Christ will reap their reward. But it should be noted, that although once more Paul transfers the imagery of the awe-inspiring Day of YHWH from the Old Testament to the New, and pictures Christ as Judge in the same terms of fiery vengeance on the wicked as the Hebrew apocalyptists had done, his thought is far removed from the traditional Christian conception of the Last Judgment in sculpture and fresco, where the smug satisfaction of the saved is matched by the writhing torments of the damned.

For Paul, salvation meant union with Christ in this world, with the hope of a more perfect union hereafter. Conversely, the greatest punishment in the case of those who rejected the Gospel, or persecuted its followers, would be, in the apostle's view, separation from God for ever. It is the difference between being and not-being, and Paul is quite clear that it depends on what we do in this life, whether we may look forward to eternal life or whether we cut ourselves off from God for ever (1:1–12).

Turning now to what is obviously the main reason for his letter, Paul tries to make it plain to the Thessalonians that there is no reason whatever for their belief, however they reached it, that the Second Advent is all but upon them. In what is undoubtedly the most obscure passage in the whole of the New Testament, he reminds them, with some impatience, of what he had already told them during the original campaign about the various things that must happen before the end of the world takes place.

We may draw a veil over the attempts of biblical commentators, ancient and modern, to make sense of this passage. St. Augustine was the first to confess failure, and we may be well advised to follow his example. St. Paul obviously assumed that the Thessalonians knew what he was talking about. Perhaps they did. But it is at least not surprising that they had to be told again, and it is doubtful whether they were even then much enlightened.

If we might venture to sift out of this enigmatic pronouncement what meaning it has for us today, we might say that the basic thought in the apostle's mind is that the world will never, until the end of time, provide an easy passage for the Church or the Gospel message. The wheat and the tares of our Lord's parable (*Matt.* 13: 24–30) will always grow side by side, because man's rebellious spirit refuses to recognise the authority of God.

The Church is bound to preach the Gospel among the nations, and to hope and pray and work for the extension of Christ's Kingdom throughout the world. But evil is strongly entrenched, and the battle that has to be waged is of cosmic dimensions. Christianity will always suffer setbacks, and may even have to fight for its very survival, but the outcome is in the hand of God, and that outcome is the final victory of truth over falsehood, good over evil, Christ over Antichrist (2: 1–12).

Then, after an interlude in which he gives thanks for the eternal purpose of God that men should be saved, prays for the continued progress of the Thessalonian church, and expresses his confidence in their growth in Christian discipleship, the apostle turns to the second main concern of his letter. This is the problem of absenteeism, already referred to in his previous letter, but now apparently intensified.

St. Paul, with all the indignation of a man who had not only never spared himself in his evangelistic work, but had combined it with working at his trade so as to be a burden to no one, denounces shirkers who sponge off their neighbours for allegedly religious reasons, in this case the expected arrival of Doomsday. Give them nothing, he says bluntly, and hunger will bring them to their senses.

Yet his last word, almost as if he feels that he has been too harsh, is to remind his readers that even the black sheep in the congregation are still members of the family (2: 13 – 3: 18).

THE FIRST EPISTLE
OF PAUL TO TIMOTHY

THE TWO letters to Timothy and the letter to Titus, generally known as the Pastoral Epistles form a little group by themselves among the Pauline letters. It is an open question, however, whether they were actually written by St. Paul or by one of his disciples. The balance of modern opinion is in favour of the latter solution, for a variety of reasons.

The situation and movements of the apostle, as described in these letters, cannot be fitted into the narrative of the book of *Acts* (see p. 446). Consequently, if Paul wrote them, we must assume that the two years of imprisonment in Rome (*Acts* 28: 30) ended in his release without trial, or in his acquittal after trial, that he then embarked on further missionary journeys, to which the first letter to Timothy and the letter to Titus refer, before being imprisoned in Rome for a second time, where he wrote the second letter to Timothy. On this view the later imprisonment was final, and ended in the apostle's condemnation and death.

There is no good reason for dismissing the possibility of such a fourth missionary tour, even if there is no biblical evidence of it outside these letters, and no Church tradition to support it. Nor would it be proof that St. Paul did not write these letters to say that their theme, church organisation and discipline, smacks more of a later generation, when the need was to consolidate the faith, than of the creative first generation, when Christian theology was being hammered out by a master mind, whose characteristic teaching as we know it from the other epistles is not found here.

Nor is it a fatal objection to Paul's authorship to say that the type of "heresy" which is denounced in these letters is a more developed form of that which we have already encountered in *Colossians* (see p. 483), suggesting a gap of some decades, rather than three or four years. Scholars, who find themselves forced to the conclusion that Paul did not write these letters, are more impressed by the absence of characteristic phrases, by the sentence-construction, and other significant linguistic differences between these letters and the remaining ten epistles acknowledged to be genuinely Pauline, than by any of the above objections, to which some kind of satisfactory answers can be found.

But the cumulative effect of the arguments against Paul's being the author of these letters is considerable, and although it does not remove all the difficulties, it is probably best to think of the Pastoral Epistles as being written towards the end of the first century by one of the apostle's disciples. His purpose is to strengthen the resident ministry of the Church, to standardise its teaching, and to check any deviations from the apostolic faith as it had been handed down.

He is not being dishonest in writing under the name of his master, for it is Paul's mind and purpose that he is interpreting. Moreover, it is highly probable that he has worked into his letters fragments or notes of actual Pauline correspondence to Timothy and Titus, particularly the personal references such as in *II Tim.* 4. He is obviously moved by a pastoral concern for the churches, and anxious that the leadership of the various congregations should be as effective in his own day as it had been when men like Timothy and Titus had built up the Christian communities of which they had been given temporary oversight, under the guidance and inspiration of St. Paul himself.

The Apostolic Delegate

THE FIRST of the three letters purports to be written by St. Paul to Timothy, his younger colleague, who had been so closely associated with him in the mission field, from the time when Paul had recruited him for missionary service at Lystra, to take the place of John Mark on the second of his campaigns (*Acts* 16: 1–3). Timothy is now being delegated to organise the churches at Ephesus, and immediately it becomes ob-

vious that one of his tasks, and indeed one of the chief purposes of the letter—as indeed of all the Pastoral Epistles—is the safeguarding of the traditional apostolic faith against a specific type of "heresy".

This seems to be a more advanced variety of the same kind of "superior" Christianity as had already caused trouble at Colossae. As we can gather from what the Pastor says about it, it was a mixture of fantastic speculation ("old wives tales"—*I Tim.* 4: 7), secret ritual, ascetic practices and Jewish legalism. It is not so important for us to know precisely the nature of this "heresy", as to recognise once more how imperative it was for the leaders of the Church to attack with all the power at their command, as a travesty of the universal Gospel, any brand of Christianity which claimed to be for the select few.

According to the narrative, St. Paul, on leaving Ephesus for Macedonia, had left instructions with Timothy to put a stop to the attempt by some Jewish-Christian teachers there to indoctrinate the congregations with this mixture of Judaism and elementary Gnosticism. Instead of proclaiming the straightforward Gospel, they were losing themselves and their hearers in religious jargon, and confusing their minds on issues of moral conduct with their demands for ultralegalistic scrupulosity.

Christianity, says the Pastor, stands or falls by its claim that salvation is achieved through Christ alone. This is the Gospel, that eternal life comes by committing ourselves wholly to him, and accepting his sovereignty over all that we do. Two notable local defaulters failed to live up to this standard and were banned from the fellowship (1: 1–20).

Instruction is now given to Timothy for the maintenance of sound doctrine and wholesome behaviour within the congregations, firstly in the conduct of public worship. Prayers must be offered for all ~~men~~, particularly for rulers and those in authority, not only that society may be "quietly and godly governed", but also because it is the will of God that all ~~mankind~~ should be saved through the self-sacrifice of Christ (2: 1–7).

Public prayer and public teaching are masculine activites; women, dressed in sober attire, must be content to listen and learn. Their contribution to the life of the Church should be made through their good works and through caring for home and family. (Many women might accept this role without agreeing to the Pastor's rather thin argument that the prior creation of Adam implies male superiority, and that women are clearly inferior to men as teachers because Eve was more easily taken in by the serpent) (2: 8–15).

To Me this is not Paul

Minister and People

IT WOULD seem that at this stage the ministers or bishops of the local congregations were not held in high esteem. Thus it is apparently necessary to insist that they must be monogamous, well-behaved and charitable, as well as being able to balance their household budgets and control their own families. They must also not bring their congregations into disrepute by their unseemly behaviour. The outside world, adds the Pastor, is always only too ready to judge the Church by the failure of the parson (3: 1–7).

Similarly, the subordinate office of deacon in a congregation must be held by men whose characters are above reproach. Deacons, like ministers, must be screened before they are appointed, and the same scrutiny applies to their wives, of whom a similarly high standard is demanded. The implication seems to be that the deacon may be promoted to take charge of the congregation if his record warrants it (3: 8–13).

In parenthesis, we are told that the apostle expects to return to Ephesus shortly, but that in the meantime he wishes to give this guidance for the proper ordering of the Church, which is the household of God. We are then given a little type of creed which seems to be a fragment of a hymn. The heart of our faith, it says, is our belief in one who became a man amongst ~~men~~; who triumphed over suffering and death by his Resurrection in the power of the Spirit, an event which was attested by divine messengers; and who now, exalted to his rightful place, is proclaimed as Lord of all and believed in by men in every nation (3: 14–16). *world*

Yet despite this glorious Gospel in which we believe, the letter goes on, we have never been encouraged to think that it will not be undermined. This is what is happening now, through the machinations of those pernicious propagandists, who insist that celibacy and abstinence from specified kinds of food are essentially binding upon all who want to be first-class Christians, although we know very well that God instituted marriage, provides every kind of food, and indeed offers the whole created world, for man's benefit. Let us rather accept all these things with thankfulness (4: 1–5).

Timothy is then encouraged to instruct the churches along these lines, to distinguish between superstition and true religion, between self-discipline and pointless asceticism. What matters most is to have a firm faith and confident hope in a God who cares for all, above all for those who give themselves to him. Further, Timothy is not to be worried because of his youth. He is to set a good example in all things, and continue with the regular conduct of public worship by virtue of his ordination (4: 6–16).

Next, instructions are given on dealing with various groups within the Church. Widows are singled out for particular mention, since they constituted a special class requiring to be supported, preferably by their families, or, if not, by the Christian community. In the latter case, their names are to be placed on a roll for the distribution of charity. The two conditions widows must fulfil for this privilege are, to have been active in good works, and to be over the age of sixty. Widows of less than sixty are regarded as rather flighty and unreliable, and are recommended to remarry (5: 1–16).

Elders or presbyters (i.e. minis-

ters), who are especially effective preachers or teachers, are to be paid twice the normal stipend and are to be protected against frivolous accusations, but they are not to be spared if they are proved guilty. The best safeguard is to make careful inquiries before ordaining them to the ministry. In an aside, Timothy is enjoined to be less rigorous with himself, and to drink wine for the good of his health. The difficult problem presented by Christian slaves in pagan households can only be solved if the slaves remember that the good name of the Church is in their hands. If on the other hand the household is Christian, the slave must not take unfair advantage of the fact that he is his master's equal in Christ (5: 17 – 6: 2).

Concluding his letter, the Pastor comes back to the point from which he started, with a denunciation of the heretical teachers. Their chief concern is to make money. This leads him to reflect on the true Christian, who is content with the basic necessities of life, contrasted with the man who is a prey to the perilous temptations of avarice. Timothy is exhorted to follow in the footsteps of the Lord, to whom he pledged allegiance at his baptism —the Christ who suffered and died for him—until in God's good time he will come again. Then with a final word, as an afterthought, urging the wealthy to share their riches, the Pastor again impresses on Timothy the need to maintain the traditional teaching of the Church, and with this the letter ends (6: 3–21).

THE SECOND EPISTLE
OF PAUL TO TIMOTHY

IF THIS letter was actually written by St. Paul, it is the last that he ever wrote, at least the last that has been preserved in the New Testament. The apostle is in prison in Rome, and this time, unlike his state of mind when he wrote *Philippians*, he does not expect any other outcome but death. On the other hand, if, as seems more likely (see pp. 494–495), the letter was written by a Pauline disciple, he creates a greater impression of a genuinely Pauline letter in the second epistle to Timothy than in the first, and has incorporated not only characteristically Pauline phrases, but almost certainly also extracts from Paul's actual correspondence.

It would seem to meet the case best to think of a Church leader, towards the end of the first century, anxiously viewing the rise of heretical teaching in his day, and living at a time when the Church was beginning to experience the waning of the zeal and enthusiasm of its earliest days, seeking to improve the situation by adopting the device of a letter from the apostle Paul to Timothy, in which Paul foretells the troubles which the Pastor knew at first-hand. Thus the letter, although ostensibly addressed to Timothy, is in effect an appeal from an apostolic leader of the Church to all Christian communities, but particularly to the ministers, to set their house in order, to retain what is true and fight what is false, and, despite strong opposition, to defend the faith at all costs.

The letter begins with an affectionate and fatherly greeting to Timothy, indicating a warm and long-standing personal relationship between the apostle and the younger man's family. Timothy, who is represented as rather diffident and timid, is encouraged to be bolder in his evangelism and more courageous in his personal witness. The Good News of the renewal of the life of the world is no human invention, but the proclamation of what God has purposed from eternity, and has now revealed to men through Christ. The Church is caught up into this great purpose, and relies on no human power to safeguard its message. As Paul's disciple, Timothy is the custodian of the teaching that has been handed on to him, and the need for faithful servants of the Church is illuminated by the wholesale defection from the apostle of many of his strongest supporters (1: 1–18).

So Timothy is exhorted to pick his lieutenants carefully, in order that proper Christian instruction can be given throughout the

✗ churches. The ministry of the Word is a full-time job, and congregations must maintain their pastor. Why should they do so? So that the Gospel may be preached, the Gospel of the Resurrection of God's Messiah, and all that that means for the salvation of the world. I may lie here in gaol, says the apostle, suffering for the Gospel's sake, but the proclamation of the Good News cannot be stifled (2: 1-10).

Then, as in *I Tim.* 3: 16, we are given an excerpt from what looks like an ancient confession of faith in the form of a hymn, a simple verse which may have been taught to young believers in a time of persecution. The themes are the transition from death to life, from suffering to victory, which summarises Christian experience and Christian hope, followed by a demand for loyalty and faithfulness like Christ's own (2: 11-13).

The apostle contrasts this with the empty words of the heretical teachers. One type of this teaching is mentioned, apparently maintaining that the doctrine of the resurrection of the dead means rising to new life with Christ, and claiming that this has already happened in the experience of each Christian convert. But, adds the writer, we cannot be surprised if the Church, like any dwelling-house, is a mixture of furnishings of varying value. Let us all strive, he urges, to be among the most cherished possessions of the Master of the House (2: 14-21).

Timothy is next cautioned against any kind of behaviour which would impair his influence as a Christian minister. Theolo-

gical flights of fancy accomplish nothing and lead to dissension. The true servant of the Gospel must always have in mind the winning back of those who have been led astray by wrong ideas. This can only come by patience and tolerance, never by violent arguments (2: 22-26).

The apostle now utters a warning that the last days of this present age will be a time when every kind of evil will be rampant, and false teachers posing as godly men will spread corruption. Moses in his own day had to contend with Egyptian sorcerers, but their end was as certain as will be the end of these heretical teachers (3: 1-9).

On the other hand, Timothy has had the benefit of the apostle's example and instruction. He has seen him triumph over all adversity and opposition. No true Christian can expect to escape persecution. So long as Timothy remembers what he has been taught, and the teacher who taught him, and above all so long as he turns for strength and guidance to the scriptures on which he has been reared, he will be able to meet every problem that confronts him and every antagonist who opposes him (3: 10-17).

Timothy is urged with all the means and skill he possesses, to proclaim the Gospel constantly and teach its truths, the more so since the Coming of Christ is near. Let him not be surprised to find men ready to listen to any kind of nonsense, and turning a deaf ear to the Gospel. In such a situation he must remain calm and unflurried, press on with the task of evangelism despite all opposition, and get on with his day to day duties (4: 1–5)

In the last section, surely unmistakably the voice of Paul, the apostle speaks of his approaching end. He has reached the winning-post and now looks forward to the prize—the crown of life eternal. He gives Timothy various personal messages, asking him to come to him bringing a warm cloak, and his books and papers. He writes of his disappointment that at his first appearance in court not one of his friends came forward to support him, but yet he was not alone for his Lord, who had never left him, stood by his side and gave him all the strength he needed. Now as he faces death, he knows that whatever men may do to him his future is to be with Christ for ever (4: 6–22).

THE EPISTLE
OF PAUL TO TITUS

WE HAVE already encountered Titus in connection with the affairs of the church at Corinth (see pp. 463, 465). Now we are given to understand that, due to his successful handling of these matters, he had been temporarily seconded for the purpose of strengthening the life of the churches in Crete, a position analogous to that of Timothy in Ephesus. If Paul was the founder of these Cretan Christian communities, it must have been during his problematical final journey.

This letter is strongly reminiscent of the first letter to Timothy and, like it, it is more probably a pastoral directive, written by a later Church leader, and designed for wider use among the churches, than an authentic letter of St. Paul to a fellow-worker (see pp. 494-495). The same themes recur, including church organisation, the necessity for sound teaching and refutation of false doctrine, and guidance on Christian behaviour.

It seems clearer in this letter than in *I Tim.*, that elders, or presbyters, and bishops were synonymous in the New Testament Church. Further than that it is difficult to go. The Pastor is more concerned with the good character of the presbyter-bishops than with a definition of their office.

The simplest solution would appear to be that as a carry-over from the Jewish synagogue, elders or presbyters were appointed to supervise the Christian communities. This function of oversight led to the use of the word "episkopos", or overseer, as an alternative title. Both terms are used to describe the minister in charge of a congregation.

It was not until the second century, and beyond New Testament times, that a bishop came to have something approaching his modern status and function. None of the main Christian denominations of the present day can claim that its pattern of ecclesiastical government reproduces that of the New Testament Church, but the three main systems, episcopal, presbyterian and congregationalist, can with equal right claim to be derived from it.

Thus after the opening greeting, the first charge that is laid upon Titus is to appoint presbyter-bishops in the various churches in his area, and their qualifications are described in much the same way as in *I Tim.* 3. One of their main purposes is to check the spread of false teaching, particularly from Jewish Christians, again an echo of *I Tim.* 1 and 6 (1: 1-16).

Then follows some guidance on what is expected of various groups in the congregations—the young and middle aged of both sexes and also the slaves (2:1–10). Through the coming of Christ, the letter continues, we have been shown the Christian way of life and the demands it makes upon us. We now look forward to his coming again, we who are liberated by him from the thraldom of evil, and eager to be used in his service (2:11–15).

Titus is to teach his people to respect authority and to be good citizens, remembering that those who are Christians now were once guilty of the same behaviour as the pagans. Only because of the mercy of God, and by no merit of our own, we have been reborn as true sons of God by baptism and the power of the Holy Spirit. Thus, renewed and strengthened, we may look forward to the promised inheritance of eternal life, which is offered to all who in faith commit themselves to God (3:1–7).

Christians have an obligation to work for the common good. By the same token, they should not waste their time in profitless theological arguments. Anyone who obstinately persists in maintaining ideas contrary to the teaching of the Church should be left to his own devices. The letter ends with various greetings and a reminder that Christians must never be drones (3:8–15).

THE EPISTLE
OF PAUL TO PHILEMON

W̲E MAY describe the inclusion of the letter to Philemon in the New Testament as a happy accident. It is not addressed to any church, it contains no exposition of doctrine and deals with no common problems. On the contrary, it is a private note on a personal matter written by St. Paul to an old friend, the only example we have of what must have been a steady stream of correspondence from the apostle to his wide circle of associates and acquaintances within the young Christian communities.

It was, in a sense, tacked on to the letter to the Colossians. We are told (*Eph.* 6: 21–22; *Col.* 4: 7–9) that the man who was entrusted with the delivery of the letters to Ephesus and Colossae, Tychicus, was accompanied by one Onesimus, and it is this Onesimus who was the cause of the letter to Philemon being written. From it we learn that Philemon was a well-to-do citizen of Colossae, whose house was big enough to be the meeting-place of the little Christian congregation there. There was an obvious bond of affection between Paul and Philemon, the basis of which was the fact that Paul had been responsible for Philemon's conversion, perhaps while the latter was on business in Ephesus.

Philemon had a slave who had robbed his master and decamped, none other than Onesimus, who had made his way to the capital of the empire and somehow contacted St. Paul. It may not be too fanciful to think of a headstrong youth with an eagerness to see the world, restive under the restraints of slave-status in the small-town life of Colossae, tempted to steal his passage money to Rome, and once there having repeated the experience of the Prodigal Son, seeking out his master's old friend Paul, as the one sure refuge for a worried and frightened boy.

At all events, we gather from the letter that under Paul's influence Onesimus became a Christian, and that Paul developed a genuine fondness for him and found in him a willing helper. But repentance and service were not enough. Onesimus was still legally a thief and a runaway slave, and must make his peace with his master and take his punishment, as well as making his peace with God.

Accordingly, the apostle sends him back with Tychicus to Colossae, but adds his personal appeal to the generosity of Philemon, in a letter which is not only a masterpiece of tact, but gives us a precious glimpse of this great-hearted apostle caring as deeply for one of life's casualties as Jesus his Master had done before him.

The letter itself presents no difficulties. Paul admits the just rights of Philemon over his slave, but counters them with a Christian plea for mercy. We may take it that the presence of the letter in the New Testament implies that his appeal was successful, that Onesimus was pardoned, and that Philemon made the letter public and added it to the library of apostolic writings in the house-church at Colossae.

It may be wondered in these days why St. Paul at no point questions the right of Christians to own slaves. Neither here, nor in his letters to the Ephesians (*Eph.* 6: 5–9) and the Colossians (*Col.* 3: 22 – 4: 1), does he say what may seem to us now to be obvious, that slavery as an institution is incompatible with the Gospel. Part of the reason is that the lot of a slave in Paul's day was generally better than that of millions of peasants and industrial workers in the world today. Slaves might not only be trusted members of a household, but might also hold responsible positions in business, public administration and the professions.

Part of the reason is also undoubtedly that slavery was too much an integrated feature of society to be questioned by anyone at the time. It took almost two thousand years for the Christian conscience to awaken to its wrongness and to abolish it. But when St. Paul in this letter put the relationship of Philemon and Onesimus, master and slave, on to the new plane of Christian brotherhood, he enunciated a principle which in the long run was bound to end the ownership by one man of another man's life, with absolute rights over the whole of his being.

We may also see in this little letter the supreme example in the New Testament of the Gospel of reconciliation in practice. An ex-Jewish rabbi, to whom all Gentiles were once untouchables; a wealthy Gentile patrician, to whom an itinerant Jewish preacher in a Roman prison would normally be an object of contempt, and to whom a runaway thieving slave was a dangerous animal to be beaten or put to death; a rootless slave without hope of human sympathy, or even human justice—in all conscience, humanly speaking, an impossible trio, yet all three are caught up through their common allegiance to Christ into an entirely new relationship, where each acknowledges the other as one of God's adopted sons, and a brother for whom Christ died.

THE EPISTLE
TO THE HEBREWS =

(more conservative sect of Jewish-Christians possibly in Rome.

THE LETTER to the *Hebrews* is probably one of the least familiar writings of the New Testament, even to those who claim to "know their Bible". People tend to be put off by what appears to be the inordinate amount of space which is devoted to Jewish ritual, animal sacrifice and priestly practice. From the Christian point of view, the writer seems to be flogging a dead horse, since, we suppose, these matters are no longer a problem for us whatever they may have been to the original readers of the letter.

Moreover, the emphasis on Old Testament history, and the conclusions that are drawn from it, are not at first sight conducive to our being impressed by the relevance of the letter for our time, nor indeed is the use of Old Testament texts particularly convincing. It would, however, be a thousand pities if we let ourselves be put off by these superficial impressions, because not only is the epistle to the *Hebrews* one of the most important books of the New Testament for giving us a proper understanding of the significance of the work of Christ, but it is also a timely and topical manifesto for our own day.

It can hardly be called a letter, and indeed it reads much more like a sermon. It seems to have been credited to St. Paul for want of a better solution, and ever since Origen, in the third century A.D. remarked: "Who wrote the epistle God only knows for certain", it has been practically universally agreed that the author was not St. Paul. Paul was primarily interested in the moral aspect of the Law, and not in what went on in the Temple at Jerusalem. The basic element in his faith was a mystical union with Christ, which this letter never mentions.

If it was not Paul, who was it? Endless suggestions have been made, the most likely being Luther's guess that the writer was Apollos, the eloquent preacher from Alexandria (*Acts* 18: 24–28), but it is best to speak in terms of an anonymous "Author", and to reflect that the early Church had more men of genius and profound insight than the accredited few writers with whose names we are familiar.

The letter is addressed to the "Hebrews", which in the New Testament sense means the more conservative section of Jewish Christians (cf. *Acts* 6: 1), but from various references in the text it is clear that it is only a small group of such people that is being addressed. The general view is *purpose - to show that for Christians the only certainty is the living Christ & to show the Priesthood of Jesus.*

that this group formed part of the Christian community in Rome—perhaps meeting in a particular house-church—and that the Author was writing to them from Alexandria, the greatest Jewish centre outside Palestine.

The Purpose of the Letter

THE READERS are apparently living at a time when a threat of organised persecution on the part of the state is causing some anxiety, a more serious attempt to make them renounce their Christian allegiance than any previous attacks upon them. The most likely date is shortly after A.D. 60, before the violent onslaught on the Christians instigated by the emperor Nero in A.D. 64, but long enough after the establishment of the Church in Rome to make the Christians, who did not conceal their contempt for pagan religion and their hostility to pagan standards of behaviour, an unpopular element in society which could be harassed with impunity.

But the Author's concern is not simply to encourage his readers to resist all efforts to force them to give up their Christian faith. For this letter is yet another example of the burning problem of the early Church, which was how far Christianity was to be tied up with its Old Testament origins. The danger in this case, however, does not come from Jewish Christian propagandists, trying to impose Jewish practice upon Gentiles, as in the Galatian churches, but from the nostalgic yearnings of Christians, who had once been Jews, for the ancient practices and traditions among which they had been reared.

Not only so, but they seem to have felt that in turning their backs on the old certainties, the hard-and-fast legal system of Judaism where everything was crystal clear, and in trusting themselves to the more nebulous guidance of the Holy Spirit, they were like men adrift in a vast uncharted ocean. The Author would endorse Chesterton's view that "there are no certainties but dead certainties". His purpose is to show that for Christians the only certainty is the living Christ, that we must take our courage in both hands and venture out into the unknown future, trusting in God alone.

He maintains that to turn back from this Christian freedom to the superficially solid ground of Old Testament legalism is to exchange reality for shadow. Christians must never look backwards to forms of religion that were good enough in their own day but are now inadequate. Their task and vocation is to evangelise the world, to refuse to take refuge in the little closed circle, where theological hairs are split and where the pious practice of ancient rites guarantees spiritual satisfaction, but rather to go out where Christ is and do battle with him for the souls of men.

Side by side with this practical purpose, the Author's aim is to point to Christ as the only way by which men reach the right relationship with God. The gulf which exists between, on the one hand, man burdened with the guilt of his own wrong choices and, on the other hand, the holiness of a just and righteous God, can only be bridged by one who is himself God and man. human.

The whole effort of Old Testament ceremonial Law—the priesthood, the sacrifices, the dietary regulations—was a desperate attempt to bridge this gulf from man's side only. Yet in its very dependence upon the role of priest and sacrificial victim, it pointed the way to a divine Priest and a voluntary Sacrifice which God himself provided. When the sacrifice was no longer the meaningless offering of the blood of slaughtered animals, but the offering of perfect obedience on behalf of man, by a Mediator who united in himself the divine and the human, then at last the bridgehead was established. God had stretched his arm across the gulf to pull men over to himself.

On the other hand, in no other New Testament writing can we see so clearly how the events of the Gospel were foreshadowed in the Old Testament. We are shown that Old Testament religion was questing for the truth, which was ultimately revealed in Christ, through its insitutions of priesthood and sacrifice. Moreover, in the great conception of the covenant, the pattern of the Exodus, the conviction of the twin reality of God's judgment and God's mercy, the Author shows us the underlying unity that binds Old and New Testaments together as a record of the Acts of God.

We may be thankful to him, too, for putting a question mark against our attachment, like that of his readers, to the deeply rooted traditions of our own particular brand of churchmanship. He would ask us whether we, like the small group of Jewish Christians in Rome, are not more concerned to discuss the peripheral niceties of faith and order, than to grapple with the vast problem of a Christless world.

Especially now, as we balance on the precarious knife-edge of international politics, and stand at the threshold of hitherto unimagined exploration of apparently infinite and impersonal space, we do well to remind ourselves, under the Author's guidance, that "here we have no continuing city, but we seek one to come", and that meantime what we are called to do is to "run with patience the race that is set before us" looking to Jesus the pioneer and perfecter of our faith, who is "the same yesterday and today and for ever" (13: 14; 12: 1–2; 13: 8).

The Law and the Gospel

(1: 1 – 4: 13)

The letter begins with a magnificent affirmation of the significance of Jesus. In Old Testament times, the prophets grasped one aspect or another of the nature and purpose of God, but now, at the decisive moment of history, God's own Son has come among men to express in what he did and said, all that we need to know or can know, about God's will for us and for the world. It is this Son, the fulfilment of all the hopes and promises of Israel, the creative power that shaped the universe, the human embodiment of the essential being of God, who has made us at one with God by his offering of himself, and has now taken his rightful place as Lord of all (1: 1–3).

What follows is a string of Old Testament texts, designed to prove that Christ is superior to angels. The clue to this surprising change of tack is to be found in the traditional Jewish belief that the Old Testament Law had not been delivered by God directly to Moses, but that he had received it from angels (*Acts* 7: 51–53; *Gal.* 3: 19). Since the readers of this letter were treating the provisions of the Jewish Law as equally binding upon Christians, the Author's purpose is to show by the use of scriptural texts that the Messiah is superior to angels, and that therefore the Law for which they were responsible has been superseded by the gospel (1: 4–14).

This explains his next point, which is that if it was a punishable offence to break the old Law, it would be absolutely disastrous to disregard the new Gospel, which has been attested in so many unmistakable ways as God's great new Act for man's salvation. When the psalmist said that man, who was "for a little while made lower than the angels", is now lord of creation (*Ps.* 8), he can only have meant the Son of Man, since it is obviously not true that ordinary mortals are masters of their fate (2: 1–8).

On the other hand, Jesus, who is now Lord of all, endured incarnation, humiliation and death, so that having shared and triumphed over suffering and mortality, he might take the sting out of death, and be able through his experience of our plight to lead us to God with understanding and sympathy (2: 9–18). Even Moses, the father of the Law, was but a servant

among the people of God; now, however, the Son and heir of the household of God has come, and we are all summoned to follow him (3: 1–6).

We Christians, says the Author, have started out on a New Exodus, with Christ as our Leader and Deliverer. Our goal is the promised land, which for us is life in the presence of God. Let us be warned by Israel's failure at the first Exodus, not to lose heart and always to trust in God's providence. The Old Testament tells us of two incidents in the Exodus story, where through lack of faith the Israelites were punished by not being allowed to enter Canaan, which was for them the promised land (*Ps.* 95: 7–11; *Ex.* 17: 1–7;) *Num.* 13–14).

The Author goes on to make the point that Canaan could not have been the ultimate promised land that God purposed for his people. For Christians it still lies ahead, and means the full communion with God ("rest") of which the worship of the sabbath is a foretaste. To turn back from this great pilgrimage to which the whole Church has been summoned, through lack of courage or lack of faith, is to endanger our chance of ever reaching our goal (3: 7–4: 13).

In a sense the Author has until now been clearing the ground, and paving the way for what is in fact the main subject of his letter, the priesthood of Jesus. He has mentioned this once or twice already, without explanation, indicating that among the various attributes of Jesus in the early days of the Church, such as Messiah, Son of

Man, Wisdom of God, Word of God, Son of God—all of them based on Old Testament ideas–the conception of him as the new and greater High Priest was also a familiar part of Christian belief.

Remember that the Author was writing to Jewish Christians, who were apparently suffering from a sense of deprivation, in that the Church, following the direction of Jesus himself, regarded levitical law as no longer valid or binding on either Jewish or Gentile Christians. For Jews living overseas, who were unable except by special pilgrimage to take part in the sacrificial ritual of the Temple at Jerusalem, the next best thing was the meticulous observance of the kosher and other dietary regulations, which, they felt, kept them within the provisions of the old covenant and secured their participation in its benefits. Conservative Christian Jews, including the readers of this letter, were anxious to carry over this link with Old Testament tradition into Christianity.

But, in addition, it would seem that those particular readers were attaching great importance to the loss of the good offices of the Jewish high priest, who once a year on the Day of Atonement, carried out a ritual whereby the sins of ignorance and omission committed by the whole people were symbolically confessed over a scapegoat, which was then driven off into the desert and destroyed (*Lev.* 16). These strictly brought-up Jewish Christians appear to have felt that here was a hard-and-fast assurance of forgiveness, a cover-plan which made men right with God, and

with which Christianity offered nothing comparable.

The Author's task is therefore to show that nothing has been lost in dispensing with this side of Old Testament Law, and that indeed Christianity provides an infinitely more effective means of forgiveness. If, as was indeed the case, the whole object of the Old Testament practice of sacrifice, and the function of the priesthood, was to restore the broken relationship between God and man which resulted from sin, what the Author has to show is that not only did the Jewish practice fail to achieve its object, but also that Christ effects in the fullest sense all that the Temple, with its priesthood and its ritual, had been striving in vain to accomplish.

The High Priesthood of Jesus

(4: 14 – 9: 14)

SO HE BEGINS his main theme by recapitulating what he has already said about Jesus as the perfect High Priest. Now at the very Throne of God, Jesus, from our knowledge of him, ensures that our prayers will be heard and that mercy will be shown to us, since he knows the needs of human kind, having shared our life and its temptations but, unlike us, not having yielded to them. Since this is the kind of God with whom we have to deal we need have no fear (4: 14–16).

Jewish high priests, says our Author, had to be ordinary fallible mortals, so that they entered sympathetically into the plight of the people they represented before

God. Moreover, their office was none of their own choosing, but depended on their priestly caste, in accordance with God's appointment of Aaron and his descendants. Jesus, however, fulfilled these two conditions more adequately than any high priest could ever do. Not only was he directly appointed by God as his divine representative on earth (*Ps.* 2: 7; cf. *Mark* 1: 9–11), but the priestly office of the Messiah was of a higher order than that of Aaron (*Ps.* 110: 4). Further, by his experience of human suffering, epitomised in the Agony of Gethsemane, he learned the cost of perfect obedience, and the price that has to be paid by those who commit themselves absolutely to the service of God (5: 1–10).

The Author has likened the priesthood of Jesus to that of Melchizedek, but before he goes on to explain what he means, he breaks off into a digression. He takes his readers to task for being more anxious to discuss the difference between Jewish and Christian teaching, than to follow out the implications of their Christian faith in action (5: 11 – 6: 3). He speaks further of the danger of apostasy, the irretrievable step of publicly renouncing and cursing Christ through fear of persecution, but adds that the past record of his readers gives every reason to expect that none of them will betray his Saviour (6: 4–10).

Their danger is much more that of slackness and lack of enthusiasm for the active missionary enterprise of the Church. Why should they be discouraged by opposition? Have they not the pledge of God

in scripture, that the whole world will be brought back to the obedience of God by the work of the Church, and does not that give them a firm anchor in heaven? This is the goal towards which the whole Church must strive, confident that the way has been pioneered by Christ himself, the eternal High Priest who leads us into the Presence of God (6: 11–20).

So the Author comes back to Melchizedek, and launches into what must seem to anyone today to be a very far-fetched effort to show why the priesthood of Jesus is superior to that of the Temple in Jerusalem. Let us not forget, however, that this kind of argument was not only normal in those days, but was the only kind of argument that would convince the Author's readers. His main point is that the *Genesis* story of Melchizedek's blessing of Abraham (*Gen.* 14: 18–20) shows that his priestly status was higher than that of the levitical priesthood, since both Levi and Aaron were descendants of Abraham and were therefore in principle blessed by Melchizedek.

Further, much later, the Messiah (*Ps.* 110: 4) was heralded as a priest of the type of Melchizedek, indicating that when Messiah came, the existing priesthood and the Law that ordained it would be superseded. With the coming of Christ the old Law and priesthood, and indeed the old covenant-relationship between God and his people, have been declared to be insufficient. Thus, as opposed to a priesthood consisting of fallible mortal men, constantly engaged in trying to bridge the gulf between guilty men and God by the day to day sacrificial ritual, we have now a Priest who is himself sinless and eternal, who has made the one perfect sacrifice of his own obedience, and who alone can make us at one with God (7: 1–28).

There can be no comparison, continues the Author, between a ministry of reconciliation exercised by earth-bound priests in an earthly sanctuary, and the ministry of Christ, which brings men to God on the initiative of God himself (8: 1–5). This heavenly ministry, whereby we are enabled to have access to the Father through the Son, makes possible a new relationship with God, the New Covenant which Jeremiah envisaged (*Jer.* 31: 31–34).

In looking forward to such a new relationship, the prophet, under divine inspiration, clearly condemned the old relationship, the first covenant based on the Law of Moses, as inadequate. What God was promising was that the time would come when compliance with written codes would no longer be the means of salvation, but when salvation would depend upon a direct knowledge of God and acceptance of forgiveness of sin freely offered (8: 6–13).

Under the old dispensation, the means of approach to God for ordinary folk was through the ministrations of the priesthood in the Temple at Jerusalem. But for all its elaborate arrangements (9: 1–5), all that it achieved by way of making men at one with God was that only once a year, on the Day of Atonement, one man, and he a sinful mortal called to the office of high priest, was allowed to enter the Holy of Holies, the symbolical

dwelling place of God. All that he hoped to do even then was, again symbolically, to wipe out the sins that men did not know they had committed—inadvertent failure to comply with dietary laws and other peripheral offences (9: 6–10).

But now under the new dispensation, we have a High Priest, who does not merely hold out hope of forgiveness but who offers us the experience of it. Christ has entered once and for all the real dwelling place of God, with the offering of his own life, thus making God and man at one for ever. If the involuntary sacrifice of mere animals was supposed to get rid of some kind of superficial uncleanness, what must be the effect of Christ's voluntary offering of his own sinless life to God?

The answer that the Author gives is that Christ's life of perfect obedience, surrendered on the Cross, was a spiritual sacrifice which is eternally valid. Sacrifice has as one of its objects the restoration of a broken relationship, atonement or at-one-ment. Christ's sacrifice restores the broken relationship between God and man, because he unites both in himself, and because his Spirit has the power to remake our lives. By lifting the deadweight of moral failure from our shoulders, Christ enables us to respond to God as we ought (9: 11–14).

Atonement by Blood

(9: 15–10: 18)

THE NEXT passage of the letter is one which has occasioned much misunderstanding. The Author's words (9: 22) that "without the shedding of blood there is no forgiveness", have given rise to travesties of New Testament teaching, suggesting that there is some almost magical significance in the use of the word "blood" in connection with the Atonement, as a bloody sacrifice either to appease an angry God, or to buy off a powerful Devil.

We merely need to look at the Old Testament narratives of the establishment of the covenant between God and Israel (*Gen.* 15; *Ex.* 24: 4–8), to see that it is not the blood of the sacrificial animal that is important but the life of the animal, which was identified in olden days with its blood. The important point in the covenant ritual was the liberating of the animal's life by its slaughter, and the idea was that this liberated life acted as a mediator between the two parties to the covenant, thus uniting them. Whether the contracting parties passed between the two halves of the severed animal, or whether some of its blood was sprinkled on both parties, the purpose was the same (see pp. 47, 101–102).

The Author is now speaking of Jesus as the mediating or unifying factor between God and man in the New Covenant. But it is not his blood as such that produces this effect, it is his Risen Life, which is liberated by his Death. The perfect obedience of Christ, epitomised in his voluntary Death, has cancelled out the accumulated guilt of the people of God and made it possible for those in old Israel who were faithful to God, as well as those in the new Israel

who commit themselves to him, to share together in the full realisation of eternal life in the Presence of God.

All Old Testament ritual of atonement, whether by Moses, or by the priesthood, on behalf of themselves or the people, subserved the purpose of keeping the covenant pact with God intact. Through transgressions against any provision of the Law the proper relationship with God was felt to be broken, and the individual or the nation had to be brought back into the right relationship. Since, under the old dispensation, this was effected by animal sacrifice, it was on the whole true to say, as the Author claims, that without the shedding of blood there was no forgiveness (9: 15–22).

In the ritual of the Day of Atonement, continues the Author, the high priest symbolically cleansed the sanctuary with the blood of the sacrificial animals. But nothing less than Christ's offering of himself once and for all could sweep away the cloud of human sin that created a barrier between earth and heaven. And as the high priest, having effected the atonement in the sanctuary, reappeared before the people, so Christ will at the end of time appear once more to reign supreme for ever (9: 23–28).

The Author now concludes the great theological passage which began at 8: 1, and which is indeed the heart of the epistle. Perfect knowledge of God and unbroken fellowship with him belong to the age to come. Through what Christ has done, we can have a foretaste of this perfect relationship here and now. But the Law and all its ritual stands self-condemned as insufficient.

If men had felt under the old dispensation that the Day of Atonement, and other ritual acts, could lift the burden of guilt from their minds they would long ago have ceased to repeat them. Their sense of sin remained, however, because animal sacrifice cannot bring forgiveness to a guilty conscience. The best that these legal and ritual observances could accomplish was to remind men that they were sinners, separated from God.

It was thus the purpose of God to provide the perfect mediator, the only possible bridge between guilty man and a righteous God, by sending his Son as man, to live man's life in utter obedience, and by this perfect offering of himself not only to supersede all man's imperfect attempts to get right with God, but also to win for all who identify themselves with Christ a new status of sonship, forgiven and free and at one with God. The Author leaves us with a picture of the serene and exalted Christ, his work of reconciliation accomplished, now awaiting his final Triumph (10: 1–18).

Onwards and Upwards
(10: 19 – 13: 25)

UNTIL NOW the Author has been consistently using pictorial language to describe what Christ has done for us. Since he was arguing his case with men who were most familiar with Old Testament ritual, as practised in the Temple at Jerusalem, his analogies and metaphors have been drawn from that quarter. For us this is largely unfamiliar territory, but we might arrive at the same point if we imitate the Author's habit of painting pictures, but using less out-of-the-way imagery.

His problem so far has been basically this: How can men who are painfully conscious of their own failure, and the accumulated guilt of society which they share, ever hope to become the kind of people they know they ought to be, the kind of people they feel they were meant to be. His answer has been that no man-made solution is possible. God has, however, stretched out a hand to us, in Christ, to pull us out of the morass and place our feet on solid ground. But the solid ground is only the beginning of the uphill ascent that we must tackle next. What we know is that Christ has climbed the path before us and awaits us at the top.

It is with the practical business of climbing the hill that the rest of the letter is mainly concerned. The Author assumes that we have repented of our failure, committed ourselves to the service of Christ by baptism, and are now involved in active Christian work and mutual help (10: 19–25). He repeats his earlier warning against treating lightly the sacrifice that Christ has made. No one can do this and expect to escape God's judgment. Yet the record of the readers gives the Author grounds for confidence that, having set their feet upon the new way, they will not turn back (10: 26–39).

This leads him into the splendid passage on faith. Faith means trusting in God, come what may. It is only faith that enables us to believe that the universe is God-controlled, and in a long recital of the Old Testament saints and martyrs he shows that it was only faith in the unseen purpose of God, despite all evidence to the contrary, that enabled Abraham, Moses and these other great souls of old Israel to earn the right to be called God's people (11: 1–40).

Now as we struggle forward in the race of life these ancient heroes of the faith encourage us by their achievements. They, like us see Jesus at the goal, the supreme example of faith, beckoning us on until we with them are gathered into God's eternal Kingdom. If the way be hard, remember that in this race of life God puts us on our mettle, and expects us to help one another (12: 1–13).

In a last magnificent outburst, the Author contrasts the gloom and terror of life under Law, with the exhilaration of being caught up in the great company of the saints of old and new Israel, living amid the light and liberation of spirit that suffuses the Church on earth and the Church in heaven. With this great vision of the New Jerusalem as the end of our journey, let us nevertheless remember that there is no automatic progress towards it. We journey daily under the judgment of God, and we treat our great new privilege lightly at our peril (12: 14–29).

The final chapter of the letter begins with familiar exhortations to comply with Christian standards of charity, fidelity and generosity and to obey the instructions of the leaders in the congregation. But in the heart of all this there is a passage which is in a way the crux of the whole letter (vv. 8–16). Our allegiance must be to Christ, who is unchanging and eternal, for our strength comes from God alone, and not from compliance with any dietary regulations.

The altar which we are concerned with is in heaven, where Jesus has for ever made it possible for us to approach God through him. But since Jesus was driven out of Israel by his own people, and died beyond the confines of their holy city, our place is with him in the wider world, sharing his suffering. We must follow him in the spirit of Abraham, not knowing where our road may lead us, but knowing that our final goal is beyond this world. Meanwhile our proper response of gratitude to God for what Christ has done, is that we should offer ourselves in worship and good works, and in loving our neighbour as ourselves (13: 1–25).

THE EPISTLE OF JAMES

THERE IS A group of seven short letters in the New Testament, called the general or catholic (i.e. universal) epistles. They consist of the writings known as *James, I and II Peter, I, II and III John*, and *Jude*. Unlike St. Paul's letters, they are not "occasional" correspondence, that is, written at a particular time, to a particular church, to deal with a particular situation.

They are rather addressed to the whole Church, to all the Christian communities everywhere, on matters of general interest to them all. *II and III John* are not quite in this category, but they are tacked on to *I John* and are usually reckoned to fall within this group. The first of these letters in the order of the New Testament books is the epistle of *James*.

This letter has never quite recovered from the bad odour into which it fell when Luther, who described Paul's epistle to the *Romans* as "the chief book of the New Testament and the purest gospel", denounced the letter of *James* as "a right strawy epistle". Luther may have been right about *Romans*, but he was surely quite wrong about *James*. His objection to it was that it lacks theological fibre. It does not emphasise the redeeming work of Christ and justification by faith, but concentrates attention on the practical business of daily living.

Indeed, James would seem to be bent on contradicting Paul, when he says that "Faith without works is dead" (2: 26), but in reality there is no contradiction at all. James means by "faith" empty professions of belief, creeds that are mere lip service, in the same sense as the saying of Jesus: "Not every one that saith unto me Lord, Lord shall enter into the kingdom of heaven; but he that doeth the will of my Father which is in heaven" (*Matt.* 7: 21).

No one would have agreed with him more than St. Paul. The kind of "works" which Paul condemns, is the hopeless attempt to win salvation by observing all the niceties of Jewish moral and ceremonial law. Whereas the kind of "works" that James regards as indispensable, is the practice of Christian behaviour that Paul binds together inseparably with the possession of Christian faith.

Who "James" was is not by any means certain. The writer calls himself simply, "James, a servant of God and of the Lord Jesus Christ" (1: 1). Four people bearing the name are found in the New Testament, two of them being apostles—James, the son of Zebedee and brother of John, and James, the son of Alphaeus, known as James, the younger. Since the writer does not claim to be an apostle he can hardly be one of these; moreover James, the son of Zebedee, was beheaded as early as A.D. 44 (*Acts* 12: 2).

Nothing is known of the third James (*Luke* 6: 16), except that he was the father of Judas; but the fourth man, James, the brother of Jesus (*Mark* 6: 3), may very well have been the author of this letter. Whether he was a full brother of Jesus, or a son of Joseph by a previous marriage, is not clear. What we are told is that he, like the rest of the Nazareth household, naturally could not believe that God's Messiah had been brought up in their family circle (*Mark* 3: 20–33), but that he was converted by an appearance of the Risen Christ (*I Cor.* 15: 7), and later became leader of the mother-church in Jerusalem.

There are many traditions about him, all pointing to his strong Jewish sympathies, as indeed does the New Testament itself (*Gal.* 2: 12; *Acts* 21: 18–26). He was called James the Just, on account of his moral rectitude, is said to have been a strict Nazirite, to have spent so much time in prayer that his knees were as hard as a camel's and to have been martyred for his faith about A.D. 62.

Such a man might certainly be the author of this letter, with its strong Old Testament flavour, reminiscent at times of the wisdom scribes, at times of the prophets, combined with its allusions to the Sermon on the Mount, and its background of early Church theology and organisation. On the other hand, it is odd that the leader of the Jerusalem Christians should mention the name of Jesus only twice, and that when he re-

fers to endurance of suffering, he takes Job as his example and not Jesus (5: 11), and turns to Elijah for an illustration of the power of prayer (5: 16–18).

It is also difficult to understand why, if the brother of Jesus was the author, this letter was not universally accepted as part of the canon of the New Testament until the fourth century. If he was, this writing, which is more a collection of moral instructions than a normal letter, must have been composed before James's death, probably around A.D. 60. Many scholars, however, prefer to think of it as the work of some otherwise unknown James, a Jewish-Christian leader of the Church later in the century.

Practical Christianity

THE EPISTLE has been described as an "ethical scrap-book". It has no connected line of thought like a Pauline letter, and no doctrinal emphasis. It is practical throughout. The questions with which it is concerned are those of everyday life—the need for patience, the dangers of an unguarded tongue, the claims of Christian brotherhood. James's teaching is summarised in 1: 22— "Be ye doers of the word, and not hearers only".

He rages like a veritable Amos at the injustices of the rich against the poor, against inconsistency and hypocrisy. He exalts the wisdom of the good man, like a wisdom scribe of the Old Testament, but the good life is for him the "royal law": Thou shalt love thy neighbour as thyself. James is a man with a hatred of shams and pretences; his indignation and scorn in face of any insincerity constitute the most striking feature of his homily.

James addresses his letter to "the twelve tribes which are scattered abroad", which may mean particularly Jewish Christians wherever they may be, or simply the Christian Church regarded as the New Israel. He speaks first of the value of trials and temptations of various kinds, as an essential element in the building up of Christian character. God gives us the wisdom we need to overcome them, if we ask his help honestly and sincerely (1: 1–8).

Prosperity and adversity have nothing to do with the quality of a man's character. What matters is that our lives should be linked with God. And let us not blame God for the temptations that assail us, they come from within ourselves, and if we give in to them we end in spiritual death. God, on the other hand, wills nothing but our eternal life. All that is good in this world comes from his unchanging goodness.

He has given us the chance to be his sons and daughters and has shown us what we must do. To be responsive to him means not only recognising the truth, as God has revealed it to us in Christ, but also acting upon it. Keeping company with God is not merely a matter of church attendance, but involves practical help for those in need, and real self-denial (1: 9–27).

There is no place for class distinctions in the Christian Church.

God overturns our estimates of human worth. The only true criterion is to love our neighbour as ourselves. If we fail in this we fail in everything. We may talk about our "faith", but unless it issues in works of mercy it is worse than useless. Nor can we evade the issue by saying that some are cut out to be devout and pious, whereas others express their religion in service.

Religion that is not service is not religion at all. There is no merit in assenting to Christian doctrine if we do no more than that. We have only to look at the Old Testament, to see that the real reason why Abraham's faith is extolled is that he was the kind of man who was prepared to sacrifice his son, because he believed it was the will of God. Even Rahab receives honourable mention for assisting Joshua's spies. In other words, faith without deeds to back it up is an empty shell (2: 1–26).

Few of us should set ourselves up as instructors of others in matters of religion, for we are all human and fallible, and the spoken word is a powerful and dangerous weapon. Surely our claim to be teachers of others must depend on whether we exhibit Christian behaviour—honest, reasonable and charitable—and a modest and peace-loving demeanour (3: 1–18).

If we are at loggerheads with one another, the root of the trouble is in our own unworthy passions and our failure to pray aright. We cannot have it both ways—self and God. Yet God will always enable us to do his will if we give him the chance. Sincerity and humility before him are the gateway to eternal life. No man who takes the royal law seriously, and tries to love his neighbour as himself, can ever presume to judge his fellow men (4:1 –12).

Next, James has a word to say to the business man who makes his plans for the future lightheartedly, without a thought of his dependence on God for his very existence, and a much sterner warning for those who have built up a fortune on injustice and exploitation of their workers. For ordinary folk, the watchword must be endurance of all trials and adversities in the spirit of Job, remembering that we shall all be held to account by a just but merciful Judge (4: 13 – 5: 11).

Cursing our lot will not help us in time of trouble, but prayer will. Confession to one another, and intercession for one another, work together with medical resources for the healing of mind and body. There are no limits to the power of prayer, as the story of Elijah shows us. The surest way of saving our own souls is to be concerned about the souls of others (5: 12–20).

THE FIRST
EPISTLE OF PETER

THE NEXT of the seven general epistles is addressed, like *James*, to Christian communities scattered over a wide area. This time, however, the area is defined as Asia Minor, and to judge from the tone of the letter the background of the readers has been not Jewish but Gentile. There is less doubt also as to who the author of this letter may have been. He describes himself as "Peter, an apostle of Jesus Christ", and while, as we have seen, this is no guarantee that the authority of St. Peter is not being claimed for a document which some later writer believed to represent the mind of the chief apostle on these matters, there are good grounds for thinking that this is in fact a letter written by St. Peter himself.

Perhaps to say "written" is to say too much. In 5: 12 there is mention of Silvanus as the actual writer, and if this was the Silvanus of Paul's missionary journeys, and if Peter left him free to paraphrase his ideas in his own way, it would account for the fact that the letter smacks strongly of St. Paul's style and way of thinking, as well as explain how an Aramaic-speaking fisherman could write such polished Greek.

But Peter's name has always been associated with this epistle,

and there is no convincing argument to make us think otherwise. We may also accept the tradition that St. Peter met his death in the persecution launched against the Christians in Rome by the emperor Nero in A.D. 64. This letter bears all the marks of having been written when such a violent persecution was in the air, and the description of the place of writing as "Babylon" (5: 13) reflects the early Christian attitude to Rome, as the successor of the fateful city of bitter Old Testament memories, "the mother of harlots and abominations of the earth" (*Rev.* 17: 5).

The purpose of the letter is to comfort and encourage Christians, who are already suffering some degree of persecution for their faith. St. Peter's argument is that these afflictions, which are only temporary, have a cleansing and enriching effect, in that those who suffer are drawn into closer fellowship with Jesus, and so become progressively more like him. They are to take Christ as their example, who suffered and gave his life for them; he triumphed over death, so therefore will they, and their sacrifice, like his, will not be in vain.

The crown of glory which the faithful will receive makes what they have to endure now seem trifling. But just because there is this glorious prospect open before them—so much more real and significant than the momentary trials through which they are passing—so they must be exemplary in their behaviour as husbands, wives, slaves or whatever they happen to be. The way to convince their enemies of the truth of their faith is by their own Christlike behaviour.

The whole letter is a buoyant message of hope. We can well imagine its effect upon dispirited and fearful folk, harried by a hostile state and tempted to renounce their faith. St. Peter lets them see their situation in its Christian perspective. He shows them the permanence of Christian values and the certainty behind Christian hope, not only by holding up Christ's own suffering as a pattern, but by reminding them that they are now through him subjects of an eternal Kingdom, which is the only one that really matters. The deepest level of Christian experience is to suffer with and for Christ.

Perhaps the first part of the letter (1: 3 – 4: 11) was originally an address delivered to candidates for baptism, at all events Peter begins by reminding his readers of what it means to be born again as Christians into a new life, which is eternal and indestructible. Whatever trials may now beset us must be regarded as a testing of our faith, and of our hope in that full fellowship with Christ which lies ahead, but of which already we have partial knowledge (1: 1–7).

This new relationship with the unseen Christ, the very essence of the Christian life, was the major theme of Old Testament prophecy. But the prophets saw, too, the part that suffering would play as a prelude to the triumph of the Messiah over all that sought to destroy him, and this as we now know through the Gospel is true also for ourselves. For the Gospel tells us that Christ's offering of himself, the price of his perfect obedience, makes it possible for all who turn their backs upon the past and commit themselves to him, to share his obedience and loving service and, in the end, also his Triumph (1: 8–25).

Partakers of Christ's Sufferings

SINCE WE have been born again into Christ, we must be nourished by his Spirit, and avoid everything that is harmful to our proper growth. It is God's purpose that we should together form a Church, a spiritual temple—each one of us a living stone built into and around the great corner-stone, Christ himself—and as the new priests of God we have to offer a new kind of sacrifice, namely our own lives. By God's grace, the role of old Israel is now ours. Past disobedience forgiven, we Christians are now called to be God's new chosen folk, dedicated to his service and summoned to witness to his great mercy. For those who reject this role, Christ is a stumbling-block rather than the keystone of the living structure (2: 1–10).

As Christians, we are but pilgrims passing through this world; our true allegiance is elsewhere. But at the same time we must behave in such a way that the world recognises that this is so. So far as conscience allows, we are subject to the law of the land like everyone else, whether we are free men or slaves, and must take the punishment we deserve if we break it. But the distinctive mark of the Christian is his acceptance of undeserved suffering, as a true follower of Christ, who has not only left us his example, but by taking our sins upon his own shoulders and suffering on our behalf has brought us back to God. So even a slave, bearing humiliation in the spirit of Christ, can witness for him and win others to the service of the Master (2: 11–25).

A Christian wife, too, can witness for Christ and convert a pagan husband, by the silent example of her attitude to life and by the standards she adopts for herself. The Old Testament has much to teach us of the power and place of women in the home. Christian husbands also must love and respect their wives as sharing equally in the true companionship of Christian marriage. In short, whoever we are or wherever we are, the Lord's words and the Lord's ways must always be our guide (3: 1–12).

No real harm can ever befall us if we are bent on following Christ. We may indeed suffer for our allegiance to him, and have to justify our actions, but it is better to suffer with a clear conscience than to sin. If anyone ever suffered unjustly it was our Lord, yet see what his Passion and Death have done for mankind!

The Death of his body was but the prelude to his mighty acts as universal Saviour. Even before his Resurrection, while he was in the state of death, his spirit was proclaiming salvation to those whose disobedience had brought God's punishment on the world in the days of Noah. Thus to the dead Christ has given new hope, but also to the living, for the Ark and the few in it who reached safety, borne up by the waters of the Flood, foreshadowed the salvation that is now offered to all through the water of baptism. Not, of course, that baptism alone effects our salvation, but it is the sign of God's forgiveness, and seals our response to him through the power of the risen Christ, who has triumphed over death and evil, and reigns now in glory (3: 13–22).

Therefore whatever suffering we have to undergo, let us endure it in the spirit of Christ. If we do this, the effect on us is that sin has no longer any attraction for us. We have, in all conscience, had our share of vice and folly, and our former associates take it amiss that we are no longer prepared to join them. But they too will come under God's judgment which is universal, for even the dead, as we have seen, are now offered the chance of responding to the Gospel and sharing in the new life with God (4: 1–6).

So, in the light of our final Assize, let our lives be governed by moderation, prayer and charity. Hospitality is a Christian virtue to be practised ungrudgingly. Whatever our gifts may be, let us offer them for the common good, and let all that we do be done in the spirit of Christ to the glory of God (4: 7–11).

The trials that now beset us are no more than we ought to expect.

Let us rather rejoice that we are privileged to share Christ's suffering, and look forward to share also in his Triumph. To be vilified as "Christians" is an honour: to be brought to book for some crime that pagans would be guilty of is unforgivable. God's judgment will fall first upon us as Christians. Let us draw a veil over the fate of those who have flouted the offer of salvation. If it is decreed that physical suffering is now to be our lot, let us accept it and trust in God (4: 12–19).

Finally, St. Peter, recalling that he is himself a minister of the Gospel, and one who, unlike his readers, had seen the actual Passion of Christ and glimpsed his future glory, appeals to his fellow ministers to be genuine shepherds of their flocks until the coming of the chief Shepherd himself. By the same token, humility and not arrogance should mark the demeanour of the younger element in the congregation (5: 1–7).

But one and all must be constantly on guard against the temptation to compromise their faith. They are part of a great Christian fellowship of those who suffer for their loyalty to Christ. So with a blessing, a mention of Silvanus, greetings from the congregation in Rome, and from John Mark who was with him, the apostle brings this moving letter to a close (5: 8–14).

Perhaps a special word should be said about 3: 19 which is the only New Testament reference—except perhaps *Eph.* 4: 9—to the clause in the Apostles' Creed: "he descended into hell", and which gave rise to the concept, beloved of writers of medieval mystery plays, of the Harrowing of Hell, or Extraction of Souls from Hell.

For us today the message of these words must surely be St. Peter's basic conviction, that those who have died without the knowledge of the Gospel, even the worst of them—and we might add, whether before Christ's day or since—are not beyond the mercy of God. The choice of accepting or rejecting salvation cannot be limited by the accidents of time and place. Just as the myth of the Deluge expresses God's unchanging condemnation of Everyman's disobedience, so the myth of Christ's "preaching to the spirits in prison" affirms the universal possibility of Everyman's rescue from the consequences of his waywardness.

THE SECOND
EPISTLE OF PETER

THERE IS general agreement among scholars that the letter called "The Second Epistle General of Peter" was the last book of the New Testament to be written, and that therefore St. Peter, the apostle cannot have been its author. The writer, however, in well-known biblical fashion, composes this letter embodying what he clearly believed to be the opinions of the apostle, and so identifies himself with him, going out of his way, indeed, to provide corroboration for apostolic authorship by quoting gospel incidents involving St. Peter.

Not only do the tone and style of the letter differ widely from those of *First Peter*, but the situation envisaged in it is one which fits the second century rather than the first. No Christian writer refers to *Second Peter* before A.D. 200. It was regarded as of doubtful origin for a long time after that, and was finally admitted, only after considerable hesitation, into the canon of the New Testament. It must have been written at a time when the letters of St. Paul had been collected and were generally known (3: 15–16), and it is based on the letter of Jude (see pp. 533–534) which itself cannot have been written much before A.D. 100.

For these and other equally good reasons, the date of the letter would seem to be somewhere about A.D. 150, and the unknown author was merely doing what many of his biblical predecessors had done, in claiming in good faith the authority of a greater name than his own for his homily, since he was confident that this is what St. Peter would have said had he been alive to say it. He writes this letter to Christian congregations in general, to deal with a problem which was of major concern to earnest churchmen then, and, we might add, which is no less relevant to our own day.

We have already seen in St. Paul's letters, that one of the many dangers that threatened Christianity in its early days was a lowering of moral standards. The Jews had been brought up for centuries on a strict moral code. When they became Christians, whatever other errors they were guilty of, the moral backbone that the Law had given them made it unlikely that their chief weakness would lie in the direction of sexual laxity.

Spiritual pride, obsession with tradition, theological hairsplitting —these were the Achilles' heel of Jewish Christians, but not libertinism. For Gentile converts to Christianity, however, sex relationships presented a real problem. Reared in an environment where promiscuity was the norm, and surrounded still by those who regarded sex as being in the same category as food—to be taken as required—it was difficult, and sometimes impossible, for Gentile Christians to maintain the uncompromising standards of faithfulness in marriage and pre-marital chastity which the Gospel demanded.

There was, however, the added danger that the teaching of St. Paul might easily be misinterpreted or wilfully misunderstood. While he had, on the one hand, insisted on the need for self-discipline in matters of sex, he had also emphasised the freedom of the Christian man from the suffocating restraints of the Law. If salvation was no longer to depend on striving to fulfil the obligations of a rigid moral code, but on self-commitment to God under the guidance of the Holy Spirit, many might respond finely to the challenge but the less scrupulous might well argue that the Spirit's guidance coincided with their own biological urges.

Thus Paul's idea of the liberty of a Christian man could be perverted to mean the licence of a Christian man. In the letter to the Colossians, and in the Pastoral Epistles, we have seen the beginning of the Gnostic heresy which maintained, among other things, that since knowledge of the truth was all that was needful to obtain salvation, what we do with our bodies is a matter of indifference. Whether we mortify the flesh or indulge it, Christianity means thinking the right thoughts, not doing the right things. By the second century this insidious propaganda had reached

serious proportions and it is against this menace—now in our own day once more a live issue—that the letter before us is directed.

The writer begins by reminding his readers of the new power that has come into their lives, which makes it possible for them not only to avoid the poison that permeates society, but also progressively to share in the life of God himself. Since God has done this for them, let them not fail to make the proper response. He warns them, speaking as St. Peter, of his appointed end (*John* 21: 18–19), and promises that they will not be left without guidance. (This may be a reference to St. Mark's gospel, or to the various apocryphal books attributed to Peter in the second century).

Unlike the nonsense which is being talked by the false propagandists in their midst, the apostolic teaching which they have received, about the Second Coming of Christ in judgment, has been handed down by men who saw the glory of the Lord already at his Transfiguration, and heard the voice of God commending Jesus as his Son. What they heard then was but confirmation of what the prophets of Israel had always foretold (1: 1–19).

Yet not every prophet in Old Testament times spoke a true word from God, and similarly not all so-called Christian teachers are genuine spokesmen for Christ. Some will be won over to their side because they appeal to men's lower natures, others will be taken in by their unscrupulous exploitation of human stupidity.

They will, however, get their deserts in the end, like the fallen angels (see p. 534), and the godless world of Noah's day. Like the people of Sodom and Gomorrah, they will pay the price for their dissolute behaviour, while those who follow in the footsteps of Noah and Lot will be helped to withstand temptation. These impious men, with the morals of the farmyard, drunken lechers whose god is money, claim to make men free of all restraints, but in fact make them slaves like themselves of their own passions. Far better that men like these had never borne the name of Christ, than thus to drag it in the gutter (1 : 20 – 2 : 22).

Do not be misled, continues the writer, by those who say that the Church's teaching about the Day of Judgment is a myth, and that the promise of Christ's coming again is fantasy. As surely as the waters of the Flood destroyed the old world, the fire of God's Judgment will consume this apparently solid and secure earth that we know. God's patience is great and mankind is given every chance, but Judgment there will be and the Day will come when least expected Be ready for it, he says; fix your hope on the new creation and on God's reign of righteousness.

All this is clear, concludes the author, to those who read St. Paul's letters with proper understanding, although many deliberately misrepresent him. So be on your guard against those who try to undermine your faith and keep close company with Christ (3 : 1–18). Thus it transpires that the writer's basic point is that if the ordinary Christian man is to be healthy and wholesome in mind and body, he must live his life as if at any moment he might be called upon to settle his account with his Maker.

THE FIRST
EPISTLE OF JOHN

THE NEXT three of the seven short general epistles in the New Testament are ascribed to "John", and at once a connection with the gospel suggests itself. The style, the themes and the very words remind us irresistibly of the serenity and profundity of the fourth evangelist. The second and third epistles of John are slight contributions of little consequence but they provide, as we have seen (see p. 403), the clue to the authorship of all the Johannine literature.

Both claim to be from the pen of one who describes himself as the Presbyter or Elder, and it seems most likely that this man, known to be a disciple of John, the apostle, reproduces the mind and reflections of the old saint. If we follow Church tradition, we may think of the apostle John, the son of Zebedee, leaving Palestine after the fall of Jerusalem, settling in Ephesus, and becoming the acknowledged leader of the church there, and indeed of the churches in the province of Asia generally.

It matters little whether the apostle himself, or the Presbyter, or a disciple of both, actually composed this first letter. Whoever it was, he speaks with the authority of one who is a father in God to the people he addresses. He writes as a pastor and a friend to the churches which come under his spiritual oversight. Whether we regard the letter as an appendix or sequel to the gospel, it was probably written before the end of the first century.

The letter may be read in two ways. We may treat it as a beautiful little piece of devotional writing, in which the author states and restates certain great Christian truths, and lets his mind play around such themes as eternal life, the love of God and brotherly charity. But dominating all else, his major theme is the centrality of Christ. It is as if he is holding up in front of his eyes an image of Jesus, turning it round and looking at it from every angle, letting the light play upon its features and directing its reflection on to every aspect of daily life. The great passage on brotherly love (4: 7 – 5: 5) shows how clearly John regards belief in Christ as the very mainspring of practical living.

The second way in which the letter may be read is to see it in its original setting, as one of the early Christian counterblasts against those travesties of the Gospel which are grouped together under the general heading of Christian-Gnosticism, and which represent the danger to the apostolic teaching, which came from the exotic mixture of philosophy and religion resulting from the meeting of East and West at the beginning of the Christian era.

Colossians, the Pastoral Epistles, Second Peter, Jude and this letter, all in one way or another indicate the battle that had to be waged to save Christianity from becoming part of the indeterminate mixture of mysticism, fantasy and superstition that threatened to swamp it. This first epistle of John was originally a spirited, and indeed violent, attack upon a particular variety of these Gnostic ideas.

It appears that in Ephesus, about A.D. 95, a certain teacher with Gnostic sympathies, by name Cerinthus, was propagating a private brand of Christianity so successfully that he won over some of the leading Christians to his side. They seceded from the Church to form a sect of their own, and made considerable headway in attracting pagan supporters.

In addition to the normal attitude of Gnosticism, that knowledge (*gnosis*) of God is all that matters, and that conduct is therefore of little importance, people who shared gnostic views also claimed that true religion is a thing of the spirit, and can have nothing to do with the material world. All that is material is evil; all that is spritual is good. This made the Incarnation a real problem for Christians who had leanings in the direction of Gnosticism. If matter is evil, how could God take on a human body?

Their answer to that was that Christ only seemed to be human. He was not a real man. This here-

sy, known as Docetism, was defended by Cerinthus, who added as his own special contribution the view that Jesus and Christ were two different beings. Jesus, he claimed, was an ordinary man of no significance until the moment of his Baptism. At that point the heavenly Christ descended upon him, and remained until the completion of the revelation that he had come to communicate. Thereupon the supernatural Christ left Jesus, who became a man again and as such was crucified. His death, however, signified nothing, since Christ had by that time left him.

Fantastic nonsense of this kind, produced from that extraordinary hotch-potch of ideas which surrounded the beginning of the Church, has little or no relevance for us today. But this epistle of John can be read as a commentary on it, and as a protest against this type of spurious Christianity. It is well to remember that aberrations like this had to be fought tooth and nail, if the faith was not to become merely another of the odd brands of religious philosophy which were current at the time.

Faced with the fact that some members of the churches under his care had already formed dissenting bodies holding these views, John writes this letter to stop the rot going further. He not only protests with vigour against the absurdity of this pseudo-Christianity, but aims to present the faith in its true character to all who are disposed to dabble in "advanced" ideas.

The burden of his reply is that: "Jesus Christ is come in the flesh" (4:2), not as two separate beings but one, and as a real person not a hybrid. The teaching of Jesus is not a mystery that only experts in religious philosophy can fathom; it is summed up in the one word, love—love of God and love of man, and love of both because God first loved us. This is the heart of the matter. For Christians there is no opposition between the spiritual and the material, only between good and evil. If we wish to be attuned to God, it will not come by seeking to probe the secrets of the Absolute, but by doing his will.

So it comes about, as so often in the Bible, that in trying to cope with a specific problem, in this case a dangerous tendency to woolly thinking, a man of God is given insights which he passes on to us, and which reach far beyond the immediate situation into imperishable verities valid for all time. The sonorous and impressive opening words, strongly reminiscent of the beginning of the fourth gospel, declare the author's conviction about the unchanging truth of the faith he stands for.

New Life from God through Jesus Christ

IN THE name of the apostles, says John, I proclaim the good news of God's offer of life to all—life which means eternal fellowship with him, who was made visible and concrete in the words and works of Jesus. Through him we know that God is light and not darkness, moral perfection and not evil and corruption, so that those who claim to know God but whose lives show that they are still living in darkness are none of his (1:1–6).

To live in God's light means living in true fellowship with one another, accepting forgiveness of our sins through Christ, and following in his footsteps. This is the old Gospel which is ever new; through it we have passed from darkness to light, from hate to love, from sin to forgiveness. We cannot claim to love God and live like pagans (1:7–2:16).

The world that we know will pass away, indeed the signs of its end are at hand in these godless men who have turned their backs upon Christ and his Church. They profess to have special insights, but no man who denies that Jesus is the Christ can know anything about God. Stand by the Gospel that you have been reared on. It is all that you need. Keep company with Christ, and the Day of Judgment will find you unafraid (2:17–28).

Living a Christ-like life is sure proof that we have been made new men through him. Out of his boundless love, God has called us to be his children. We do not yet know fully what that means, except that when we see God face to face we shall be like him. Let us therefore not blur the distinction between right and wrong. Wrongdoing is of the devil, and if our lives are truly bound up in God there is no loophole left for sin to enter (2:29–3:9).

Loving one another is the very heart of the Gospel, the proof that we have passed from living under the power of hate and death—like Cain—to living under the power of love and life, like Christ, who showed his love by offering his life for us. Here is our pattern of self-sacrifice, whether it be in great things or in small. It is deeds that count, not words. When we are helping our neighbour, we may be sure that we are right with God. Even if we think we are not doing enough, let God be the judge, but if we know that we are doing all we can, we are in the right relationship to him and his Spirit is ever with us (3 : 10–24).

But we must be careful, says John, in parenthesis, to distinguish between those who speak the truth in the power of God's Spirit and those who say what is untrue, the spokesmen of Antichrist, such as those who have now left the Church. The test is whether they believe and proclaim that Jesus Christ was made man. This is the truth that will prevail, because it is truth from God, and will be believed by all who are his people (4 : 1–6).

So, continues the author, returning to his theme, love is the root of the whole matter. Caring for and about each other brings us into the very Presence of God, because God himself is love. No other motive could have made him send his only Son amongst us, to give us the opportunity to live as he meant us to live. Let us not define love by any human standards. It is something divine, that moved the Father to send his Son so that the power of sin over us might be destroyed (4 : 7–10).

Love for one another is our proper response to God's love for us. Indeed, although God is invisible to mortal eyes, he actually lives in us, when we allow his love to grow in us and to issue in love for each other. We know that we are united to God because of the presence of his Spirit within us. But we have also visible proof of his Presence in that his Son became man for our salvation, and if we are convinced of this we are also united to God by sharing in the result of his love towards us (4 : 11–16).

So if love becomes the ruling principle in our lives, we are in fact living in union with God, and the Day of Judgment can hold no terror for us. Love to God and love to man are two sides of the same coin. If there is no charity in our hearts and in our actions towards our neighbours, our claim to love God is a living lie and a defiance of our Lord's own commandment (4 : 17–21).

We are all God's children, if we accept that Jesus is the Saviour of the world, and if we love the Father we must love his children also. But loving God means living in obedience to his commandments, which include loving our neighbour, and we are given power to keep them by God himself, who promises that we shall be victorious over evil through Christ (5 : 1–5).

Let us have no half-baked faith, says John, with an eye particularly on the sectarians; Jesus did not become the Christ at the moment of his Baptism, and it was as the Christ that he died to be our Saviour. We have threefold evidence of this—the Holy Spirit, who was clearly seen in the words and works of Jesus, and who is now active in the life of the

Church; the divine commission of Jesus at his Baptism, and our own baptismal regeneration; the power of the Cross, and the grace conferred by the Eucharist. This is all God's Word to us, and our own experience confirms it, though we may of course choose to reject it. In short it comes to this, that God has given us the possibility of life in the fullest sense through his Son Jesus Christ. Without him we have nothing (5: 6–12).

But I am writing this letter, says John, to those who have committed themselves to Christ, and who therefore may be sure that this abundant life is theirs. So we can say our prayers knowing that they will be granted, including our prayers for our fellow-sinners—although one who is guilty of outright apostasy may be past praying for.

However, we can be sure that no one who has fully pledged himself to God can continue in a life of sin, for even although we live in the midst of temptation, we have Christ at our side. It is through him that we know we have found ultimate reality and ultimate truth, and this knowledge and fellowship is something that death cannot destroy. Anything less is caricature and illusion (5: 13–21).

THE SECOND
EPISTLE OF JOHN

IT IS SURPRISING that the second and third letters ascribed to John have survived at all. Each of them was probably written originally on a single sheet of papyrus, and the contents can hardly be described as of sufficient importance to warrant special care in their preservation. If we are right in thinking that they are written by the same hand as *I John*, the simplest explanation would be that the second letter, which is addressed to a congregation, and the third letter, which is addressed to an individual, were attached to the copy of *I John* which was already in the possession of this particular Christian community. We do not know the name of the community or the identity of the individual. It would be reasonable to assume, however, that the church addressed in the second letter was in the Ephesus area, over which John had oversight, and that the recipient of the third letter was a leading member of the congregation.

The second letter may be described as a postscript to *I John*, possibly written some time later, but echoing its sentiments and applying them to a local situation. From the opening words onwards, John, addressing this particular community as "the elect lady", i.e. a church chosen by God, makes it plain by his emphasis on the "truth" which is the common bond between them, i.e. the apostolic faith, that his main concern is with deviations from the traditional gospel.

He repeats his assertion of the first letter that brotherly love is the mark of the Christian, as opposed to the disdain for ordinary mortals which "advanced" thinkers affected, and that there must be no traffic with heretical teachers who deny the Incarnation. Any such travelling missionaries, apostate Christians, who claim that it is possible to know God without accepting the full doctrine which the Church holds about Christ, should not be officially welcomed or given any hospitality by the congregation. The letter closes with the promise of a visit and greetings from the church to which the writer is attached ("thy elect sister").

THE THIRD
EPISTLE OF JOHN

PERHAPS AT the same time as the previous letter was sent to the congregation, this personal message was addressed to Gaius, one of its prominent members. If so it reveals a piquant situation. Presbyter John has learned from visiting members of this congregation of the generous hospitality shown by Gaius to itinerant evangelists sponsored by him.

On the other hand the resident minister of the congregation, one Diotrephes, had treated some of John's friends with scant ceremony and had encouraged others to do likewise, even to the point of trying to expel from the church those who did not agree with his tactics. In addition, he was stirring up feeling against the Presbyter in a most unpleasant way.

John writes now to Gaius to commend Demetrius, presumably the bearer of the letter and the leader of the party of missionaries now being sent out again, hoping to see him soon—and incidentally threatening also to deal with Diotrephes. The likeliest explanation of this fascinating glimpse of an apparent clash of personalities may be that this was something deeper, providing indeed a valuable commentary on the teething troubles of a growing Church.

The apostolic age was all but past. St. John as the last survivor of the Twelve had delegated to the Presbyter the oversight of the congregations in the Ephesus area. Thus the Presbyter, like Timothy and Titus, although not an apostle might be called an "apostolic man".

But meantime the local congregations were expanding and developing a spirit of independence, which meant that while they were prepared to accept the authority of an apostle they were not necessarily prepared to acknowledge the authority of his nominee. Diotrephes may thus be an example of a local minister who felt that the Presbyter should limit his jurisdiction to the congregation over which he presided.

On the other hand, it is possible that Diotrephes was one of the Christian-Gnostics, referred to in *I and II John*, who had gained control of a congregation, and regarded Presbyter John and his orthodox missionaries with understandable hostility. In this case Gaius would be the leader of the orthodox minority in Diotrephes' congregation, and the obvious person for the Presbyter to write to, asking for hospitality for his approved evangelists. In either case the letter is an intensely human document.

THE EPISTLE OF JUDE

MOST PEOPLE, having read the epistle of Jude, would agree that there is probably no other point in the New Testament where we are more inclined to sigh for what we have lost and wonder what we have gained. The writer of this letter apparently interrupted a letter of another kind—of which, if he ever subsequently completed it, there is now no trace—to pen this indictment which he felt to be of extreme urgency (v. 3). We may gather from the few lines where he is not engaged in denunciation, that the letter that might have been written could have been one of the highlights of the New Testament.

We may be grateful for the splendid benediction (vv. 24–25), and the fine words in v. 21, but for the rest of the vituperative contents most of us can probably raise little enthusiasm. Yet is this a fair judgment? Here is a Church leader who is passionately concerned for the purity of the faith, and the good name of the Christian communities. Both are obviously being threatened by unscrupulous propagandists, and Jude does not mince his words. Second thoughts on this letter may well persuade us that in the Church of our own day indifference may pose as Christian charity, and that tolerance is not always a Christian virtue.

If the writer was, as he claims to be, Jude, the brother of James, the implication is that the James in question was the head of the Jewish-Christian church at Jerusalem, and that Jude was therefore a brother of Jesus (*Mark* 6: 3). On the other hand, anyone speaking of the faith "once delivered unto the saints" (v. 3), suggests a later generation, as does the situation described in the letter. We are, therefore, probably on safe ground in thinking of this as a trumpet-blast from an unknown Church leader to some unspecified congregations around A.D. 100, which, as we have seen, was substantially echoed in the letter known as *Second Peter* (see p. 523).

After an initial greeting, the writer claims to have been deflected fron his original purpose of writing a different kind of letter by, as it would seem, the receipt of news of the dangerous activities of some people, posing as Christian teachers, in congregations for which the author assumes some responsibility. The trouble seems to be the now familiar Gnostic view that morals have nothing to do with religion. Some influential people, tainted with gnostic ideas, were apparently advocating and practising sexual promiscuity and perversion and thereby degrading Christian liberty to the level of pagan licence (vv. 1–4).

The author reminds his readers of the fate of evildoers in the past —the Israelites at the time of the Exodus who were punished for their sins by death (*Num.* 14: 29, 37), the angels who fell from grace (*Gen.* 6: 1–4), and who, according to the intertestamental book of Enoch, were cast into the abyss, there to remain in chains until the Day of Judgment, and the citizens of Sodom and Gomorrah, who suffered the fire of the Lord's vengeance (*Gen.* 19: 24).

He draws on another book from the Pseudepigrapha, the Assumption of Moses, to provide an example of how even archangels do not presume to arrogate to themselves the authority of God, as these charlatans now do, who flout all authority, live like animals and invite the same condemnation as their Old Testament counterparts, Cain, Balaam and Korah (vv. 5–11).

With a variety of analogies, the writer pours out the vials of his wrath upon these unworthy pastors, and draws once more on the book of Enoch to maintain that it was just such men for whom that prophet envisaged the necessity of supernatural judgment. Even the apostles—which and where the author does not say—had foretold such an outburst of godlessness in the last days.

On the other hand, Christians who maintain the true faith may await the Judgment with confidence. For them it will mean eternal life with God. Meantime, their task is to rescue any waverers, but to shun those who are too obdurate to be influenced. And, thus, with one of the great blessings of the New Testament, this passionate outburst ends (vv. 12–25).

THE REVELATION OF JOHN

WITH THE *Revelation of St. John the Divine*, i.e. the theologian, we reach what is in more senses than one the Bible's last word. But since we have been thinking of the whole Bible as a drama, of which the Old Testament forms the first act, the gospels form the second, and the rest of the New Testament constitutes the third, it is best not to include *Revelation* as part of the drama proper, but as a kind of epilogue which balances the prologue in *Gen.* 1–11.

For in a sense the divine drama which the Bible records is still going on. Act III is even now being played out. The book of *Acts* and the New Testament letters cover the beginning, and set the plot in motion for the last stage of its development. With the rebirth of the old Israel of Act I through the new dynamic of Act II as the Israel of God in Act III, the scene is laid for the growth and activity of the Church in the power of Pentecost, until God's purpose for the world is complete.

So far, Act III has lasted for almost two thousand years, a long time if we think in terms of the span of a human life, but less than an instant in terms of the divine economy. A long time, too, if we let our thoughts dwell on the disunity and ineffectiveness of the Church, on its failures and its crimes, its compromises and its inadequacies. A short time, on the other hand, if we give full weight to the power of evil in and around us, to human inertia, pride and stupidity. For this is the material, inside and outside the Church, with which God's Spirit has to work, and he will only work by love and not by compulsion.

When we are in a despondent mood, and talk of the modern world as the new Dark Ages, with materialism as rampant on this side of the Iron Curtain as on the other, when we gloomily think of our civilisation as post-Christian, and see the Church retreating as often as advancing, let us take heart from what the Church has in fact accomplished. Men may from time to time revert to the law of the jungle, and savagery is not far below the surface in every one of us, but can any man deny the evidence of history?

In these short years of the Church's infancy, saintliness and courage, care and concern have made their mark. Lives have been changed, fear has given place to hope, new light has shone in dark places. The Church has no need to apologise for its total record of social service and its defence of the cause of the weak and helpless, the wayward and unfortunate, though it may well be ashamed that it has so often left its consecrated servants to fight its battles for so long alone.

But wherever Christian men and women in the name of Jesus battle against ignorance and injustice, prejudice and superstition, Act III of the divine drama still goes on, and each of us is offered a part in it, in however minor a role. This is the ultimate challenge of the Bible to every new generation and to everyone born within it: He that is not with me is against me.

We may well, however, ask at this point two pertinent questions. One, if the divine drama is still being played out, if God is still in action in the world, through those whom he calls into his service and who respond to his call, why are the work and witness of Christian saints and scholars, poets and moralists, not equally worthy of inclusion in the Bible? Are the Confessions of St. Augustine, Thomas à Kempis' Imitation of Christ, Bunyan's Pilgrim's Progress, and the acts of modern apostles like Kagawa and Schweitzer not of the same order as the writings of the New Testament men, and the stories of St. Philip, St. Stephen, and St. Paul?

Briefly, the answer is that the Bible contains the definitive record of the Acts of God in a particular setting and at a particular point in history, which brought into existence the instrument of God's plan to renew the whole life of the world and to bring everything into the right relationship with himself. It is not as if God has ceased to act, but rather that he has given us in the Bible all that we need to know, to enable us to co-operate with him in what he is still doing.

We had to be shown in the prologue to the drama the truth about ourselves, and from Act I we had to learn that, left to ourselves, our best intentions will always be defeated by our twisted natures. The highest moral standards and the most devout aspirations are not enough to lift us out of a morass which is of our own making. Act II declares that only God himself can do that, and that he has done it. Act III is the record of the beginning of the reconciliation of the world to God, and at the same time the end of the special disclosure of God's plan and purpose, which we needed in order to assist in its accomplishment.

The gulf between God and man has been bridged by God himself in the person of the new kind of man, Jesus of Nazareth, who is God expressed in terms of a human life. By our allegiance, loyalty and commitment to him and what he stands for, and by drawing on the divine resources of the community which he instituted —in worship and prayer, in availing ourselves of the ministry of the word and sacrament—we too can begin to become new men and women, and share in a life which the accident of physical death cannot destroy.

In Act III the foundations of this new kind of life are communicated; we are shown how it works out in practice; and we are left with a pattern of Christian faith in action, which we are invited to make our own. But having given us this the Bible very properly comes to an end. All that has followed in the last two thousand years is secondary and derivative. The greatest Christian saints, thinkers and social reformers have created nothing new. The faith once delivered has been their inspiration and their guide. They have restated and reinterpreted, but none of them has ever claimed to be anything other than a servant of Christ and an unworthy imitator of the apostles.

This raises our second question, namely, that if we look at the Church and the world, in the light of what the Church might have done and what the world might have become, we may well ask what guarantee we have, that all the efforts of the Church through its members will make any permanent impact on what too often seems to be the discouraging and indifferent mass of humanity. What is to be the end product? Have we any reason to hope that not in this century or this millennium but in the end, whenever that may be, the Bible has not been leading us up the garden path with rosy prospects which will never be fulfilled? It is to this question that the book of *Revelation* supplies the answer.

The Epilogue to the Divine Drama

THIS IS indeed, therefore, the epilogue to the record of the Acts of God. Its message is, above all, that whenever we become disheartened by the apparent failure of the Church either to do its proper job, or to achieve what the New Testament obviously regards as its mission, we should

take comfort and renew our hope from this God-given picture of the end of the story, beyond space and time, and, far more, beyond the limited horizon of ordinary mortal creatures.

Sad to say, however, the book of *Revelation* has been more mishandled by religious cranks than any other book in the Bible. It has been used to foretell the future like a biblical Old Moore's Almanac, it has been treated like Joanna Southcott's box, as a repository of world-shaking secrets, or else it has been hailed as the key to the rise and fall of every political adventurer up to the present day.

Certainly the book is an odd one; its language is cryptic, its symbolism is bizarre and sometimes grotesque. But the clues to its proper understanding are, firstly, that it is the child of Jewish apocalyptic and, secondly, that it is a tract for the times. Let us take the second point first.

It is perfectly plain from 1 : 1, 3 that the writer expects his prophecies to be fulfilled immediately, and not centuries ahead. These prophecies, as we shall see, concern the impending end of the world and the creation of a new heaven and a new earth. Only such an event, the writer felt, could meet the situation in which he lived, a time, as we can gather, of bitter persecution and red martyrdom.

Like *Hebrews*, this book was written to encourage resistance among Christian people, to strengthen the resolution of waverers and to comfort the faithful. The writer of *Revelation*, however, adopts the outlook of Jewish apocalyptists, foretells the end of the world as the only solution of the ills from which his readers suffered, and holds out to all persecuted Christians the hope of future blessedness.

The closest affinities of *Revelation* are not with anything else in the New Testament, but with the books of *Daniel*, *II Esdras*, and the host of apocalyptic productions that flourished between 200 B.C. and A.D. 100. At the turn of the eras, the flow of such writings divided into two streams—Jewish and Christian—and this is the only specimen of Christian apocalyptic which has been included in the canon.

Remembering, then, that the author is writing for his own generation and not for some unspecified future age, let us look at the situation that made such a book necessary. The Roman empire was held together by various expedients, one of them being the practice of enforcing the worship of the emperor upon all subject peoples. This was dictated more by political opportunism than by religious motives.

As Rome's internal problems increased, and the difficulties of administering her far-flung empire multiplied, not least due to the incompetence of successive emperors, the need for enforcing this simple token of submission upon all her subjects became the greater. Throughout New Testament times, however, as we have seen, the Christian Church was expanding rapidly. It had soon ceased to be regarded as a sect of the Jews and had come to stand on its own feet.

Nero had launched a persecution against the Christians in Rome in A.D. 64, but this was more than anything else a madman's cover-plan for the fire which destroyed much of the city. A few years later, however, Vespasian issued an edict which condemned to death all who refused to worship the image of the divine emperor. Christians could avoid taking part in pagan ceremonies at the risk of social ostracism, but they could escape paying divine honours to the emperor only at the risk of death.

In the reign of Domitian, who like Nero was both cruel and mad, persecution raged not only in Rome but throughout the empire. This was in A.D. 93. From the numbers of Christians who were being martyred for their refusal to substitute a crazy despot for the God and Father of the Lord Jesus Christ, it seemed to many within the Church that the last days had come. One such was the author of the book of *Revelation*.

His tract is, therefore, a summons to all Christian believers to resist to the death the blasphemous mockery and superstition of calling a man God. So appallingly evil have the times become, that the writer cannot envisage the world continuing much longer. He sees this wholesale persecution of the faithful as the work of Antichrist, whose appearance heralds the beginning of the end. Soon, very soon, Christ will come again in Judgment. The enemies of God will be punished, and those who are faithful to the end will receive their reward.

The similarity of *Revelation* to

the book of *Daniel* and other apocalyptic writings is obvious. Persecution calls them forth, and a cataclysmic end to the present world is the only solution they all have to offer to the evils of their day. Beyond this catastrophe, however, they hold out the promise of a glorious future for all who have taken their stand for God in full awareness of the cost.

Revelation, which is from the Latin equivalent of the Greek form "apocalypse", is therefore, like all apocalyptic writing, primarily a message of comfort and encouragement, in which the writer undertakes to reveal or unveil for his readers the great things that are about to happen by the hand of God, to requite them for their present afflictions.

All that is known about the author is that his name was John, and that he was exiled for his faith on the island of Patmos, a penal settlement in the Aegean. Many ancient and modern authorities have identified him with John, the apostle, but he does not himself claim this title, calling himself merely a prophet, and no two documents could be less alike than the fourth gospel and the Apocalypse.

The date of writing that seems most likely is sometime in the reign of Domitian, say about A.D. 95, when general persecution raged, and emperor worship was an issue of prime importance everywhere. Those to whom the message is addressed are the seven churches of the Ephesus area in Asia Minor.

The book itself is a strange mixture of visions, symbolism, cryptic numbers, apocalyptic jargon and Old Testament allusions. Sublime glimpses of heavenly glory are mingled with what is, apparently, sub-Christian gloating over the downfall of the damned. It is impossible to read *Revelation* with full understanding without the assistance of a more detailed commentary than can be provided here, but the author's thought can be sketched in broad outline.

The Power of Evil

JOHN CLAIMS to have received a revelation of what is about to happen from Christ himself, with instructions to communicate its contents to the churches. Beginning with a greeting and an ascription of praise, he tells how, on the island of Patmos, he had a vision of Christ in glory presiding over his Church. He is charged to write to seven particular churches —representative of the whole Church in their varying degrees of strength and weakness—with a reassurance that whatever may happen to them here on earth, their essential destiny is in the Lord's hand (1 : 1–20).

We are then, in letters addressed to the seven churches, given a picture of the Church as a whole in John's day as it faced the challenge of persecution—courageous but lacking enthusiasm as at Ephesus; harassed, despoiled and at the mercy of its enemies as at Smyrna; too ready to compromise like the church at Pergamum, or too tolerant of unwholesome influences within the congregation as at Thyatira (2 : 1–29).

John has little to say in favour of the church at Sardis, which he describes as spiritually dead; on the other hand, the Philadelphian church has a good record, and is commended for its faithfulness despite its small numbers, while the church at Laodicea is condemned for its complacency and half-heartedness. Like an Old Testament prophet, he calls for repentance and reform before it is too late, but to all who respond and to those who have remained faithful throughout, he passes on Christ's promise of sharing in his Triumph when he comes (3 : 1-22).

From this picture of the Church, then, as now, a grey mixture of honest effort to live up to its high calling, and depressing failure to achieve it, surrounded by indifference and hostility, and in places fighting for its life, the Seer turns to paint in startling contrast the scene which he has been privileged to glimpse of the serene majesty and overpowering splendour of Almighty God enthroned in heaven.

Like so much else in this book, the language is not descriptive in any literal sense, but impressionistic. Words can only hint at what is indescribable in human terms, and we are here in the realm of the poet, the painter and the composer, not of the historian or the scientist. The theme is one of worship and adoration, of the sovereign Creator receiving the praise and honour that are his due (4 : 1-11).

In his vision, John sees the sealed book which holds the secret of the destiny of mankind, and which lies in the hand of God.

No one but Christ is worthy to take this book and disclose its contents—or, as we should say, to interpret the purpose of Creation —and it is as a Lamb that the Seer pictures him, the symbol of our Lord's offering of himself to bring all men to God. Self-sacrifice, John would tell us, is at the very centre of the being of God, and it is as the Saviour of the world that Christ is worshipped by the whole universe (5 : 1-14).

It may seem to be a contradiction of this splendid vision of an omnipotent Creator whose power lies in self-giving love, to turn to the next theme of the writer, which is the opening of the seven seals of the book of destiny by Christ, and the unleashing of war, revolution, famine and pestilence upon the earth—depicted as the notorious Four Horsemen of the Apocalypse. There is, however, no contradiction.

This is God's Judgment on man's rebellion against his good purpose. When mankind rejects the guidance of natural law and revealed law, whether in the pagan or Jewish-Christian world, the moral order of God's universe exacts its toll. In a sense, as the writer suggests, it is Christ who brings disaster upon mankind, because it is defiance of all that he stood for that produces its own inevitable consequences.

So in this sixth chapter with its grim picture of man's inhumanity to man, bringing chaos, oppression, bloodshed and death, it is right that men should cry for mercy from "the wrath of the Lamb", for the gospel never encourages us to think of God's love as sentimental obliteration of the difference between good and evil. God is love, but if we prefer hate we pay the price (6: 1–17).

Six of the seven seals of the book of destiny have now been broken, all recognisable effects of man's rebellion in every age. Before the seventh seal is broken, the writer swiftly interposes another element in his total picture, the promise of final vindication and victory to the victims of man's ruthless disregard for the laws of God, who commit themselves to Christ and find in him the life that is eternal. John doubtless had in mind the persecuted Christians of his day facing certain martyrdom, but the great words of vv. 14–17 have brought strength and comfort to the bereaved in every age (7: 1–17).

With the breaking of the seventh seal a new series of disasters afflicts the world, each new onslaught being heralded by the blowing of a trumpet. Some of these disasters suggest natural causes reminiscent of the plagues of Egypt (8: 1–13), others—the locusts and the horsemen—suggest the demonic forces of evil. The writer's main point would seem to be that men are judged by their reactions to such impersonal catastrophes, as surely as they are in times of war and other man-made havoc, and that even these natural calamities are powerless to shake the obdurate into an awareness of God (9: 1–21).

John is building up his picture for the ultimate clash between good and evil, Christ and Antichrist. In preparation for this final revelation, he is given further insight into the divine purpose (10: 1–11), and in the symbolism of the Two Witnesses (the Law and the Prophets), whose words were rejected by their countrymen but who were vindicated by the Resurrection of Christ, he declares God's Judgment on his chosen people the Jews, expressed in terms of the fall of Jerusalem in A.D. 70 (11: 1–13).

Yet although the Devil has succeeded in alienating the people of the promise from the God who called them to his service, the divine purpose cannot be thwarted. The old covenant has passed into the New Covenant, and with the triumph of Christ the sovereignty of God over the whole world has been assured for ever (11: 14–19).

In vivid imagery, mythological in character in keeping with so much of this book, John sketches the background of the cosmic conflict between good and evil, Christ and the Devil. Out of this wayward people of God comes the Messiah. His very existence is threatened by the power of evil, and the community which bore him, Israel, now transformed into the Church, is in peril of her life.

But the battle between the Church and the Devil is not determined on earth. It has already been settled in heaven. The Ascension of Christ meant the downfall of Satan, and every act of Christian sacrifice confirms it. Now, according to John's picture, having been driven from the presence of God, the Devil becomes the enemy of all who seek to do God's will, using every weapon he can find to defeat the purpose of the Creator (12: 1–17).

In John's day no Christian could be in any doubt as to what instrument lay closest to Satan's hand. Like the author of *Daniel*, who saw in Antiochus Epiphanes and his blasphemous parody of true religion the very incarnation of evil (see pp. 273–274), John now, in the full apocalyptic tradition, describes the Roman empire as the Beast from the realms of chaos and darkness which Satan uses to harry and destroy the people of God.

His picture is of the overweening power of a world-state, incarnated in such emperors as Nero and Domitian, caricaturing the worship of God with its demands for worship of its rulers; a false faith bearing all the outward marks of genuine religion, and claiming for itself the total allegiance of its subjects. If John had set out to describe the character of the twentieth-century totalitarian state and its diabolical power over its people, he could not have penned a more apt indictment (13: 1–18).

The Victory of Truth

FROM THIS open warfare against the Gospel, with its inevitable toll of martyrs, John turns for a moment to lift the veil from the sequel. The martyred host, who have refused to bow the knee to Caesar, are gathered together in the presence of the Lamb. On the surface, the Beast has won and the Church has ceased to exist. But now God's Judgment is declared to be about to fall on all who have chosen to sell their souls to this travesty of the truth.

Let us not treat the Seer's vivid imagery of the torments of the damned any more literally than his visions of the bliss of the redeemed. Yet we cannot refuse to take with all seriousness his conviction about the inevitability of retribution. As in the rest of the New Testament, the Seer's belief is that the worst punishment that can befall beings who are created to be sons of God is to be separated from him through their own actions, it may be, but for his mercy, for ever (14: 1–20).

Turning back from his vision of the result of the Last Judgment, the Seer now describes the prelude to the Judgment itself. While the martyred Church in heaven celebrates its deliverance through the new Exodus, and rejoices in full fellowship with God, the fate of its persecutors is being prepared. The seven vials of the wrath of God are poured out bringing fresh disasters —all of them representing the inexorable consequences of the abuse of power by a godless civilisation. The stage is set for the final clash between good and evil at Armageddon (15: 1 – 16: 21).

For John this cosmic battle is prefaced by the destruction of the city of Rome—mistress of the pagan world, epitomising irresponsible power, inhumanity, and hatred of all that the Gospel stands for. Rome is the reincarnation of Babylon, persecutor of the people of God, the antithesis of justice and the synonym for vice. In a magnificent taunt-song, the Seer contrasts the lamentations of those who have profited from the achievements of this crystallisation of ruthless materialism, with the exultation of all who knew her as the arch-enemy of the spirit of Christ (17: 1 – 18: 24).

In the scene which follows, depicting joy in heaven over the downfall of the oppressor of the Church, let us remember that, as elsewhere in the Bible, the faithful and the unfaithful are as sharply distinguished as white and black. For John, as for Old Testament prophets and apocalyptists, there are in this context no shades of grey. Those who have taken their stand on the side of God and who have suffered for their convictions, are by that very fact acclaimed as saints, as surely as their opponents are treated as children of the Devil.

While we may hesitate to make so sharp a distinction, we can recognise why in a period of mortal danger, crisis and persecution, the issue appeared more clear-cut than in less agonising times. In the heavenly rejoicing over the annihilation of Rome, the Seer celebrates the victory of God's purpose over the power of evil that perpetually seeks to thwart it, and which in his day was embodied in the claim of the state upon the total allegiance of its subjects.

With the defeat of the chief enemy of the Gospel, the way is clear for the final union of Christ and his Church, the Lamb and his Bride. But first there is the last battle of all between the forces of Christ, here pictured as the fifth horseman of the Apocalypse, the Word of God, and the hostile powers of paganism, ending in their extermination and the imprisonment of their master the Devil (19: 1 – 20: 3).

From this point, until the end of the book, there are difficulties in the sequence of events which have led some commentators to suggest a rearrangement of the text. However, unless we are looking for a programmatic description of the end of the world—which would be out of keeping with the rest of the book—we need not be unduly disturbed by occasional inconsistencies. The Seer is hinting, suggesting and sketching, not prognosticating.

He thinks of the martyrs for the faith as being in a category by themselves. They alone are to share in the messianic millennium—perhaps a parable of the life of the Church as it should be on earth—following which comes the final overthrow of Satan and the Last Judgment. After the general resurrection of the dead, all men are judged on the record of what they have done or what they have failed to do. Having served their purpose, death and the place of the dead are consigned to the same fate as the Devil and his minions (20: 4–15).

Then in a new dimension, beyond space and time, the Seer pictures the perfect fellowship of the people of God with the Creator whose service they have entered. Suffering, sin and death are past, and in the heavenly New Jerusalem those who have been faithful to God live for ever in his Presence, and man at last re-enters the Paradise from which since Adam's Fall he has been estranged. The Seer's last words are that what he has described is about to happen, and he ends with a call to his hearers to live in expectation of the speedy Coming of Christ (21: 1 – 22: 21).

As in other biblical apocalyptic literature, the Seer's predictions of the immediate end of the world did not come true. But if his conviction as to the method by which the Church would be vindicated was wrong, he was nevertheless right in maintaining that somehow God would rescue his people. The Church, contrary to John's expectation, did in fact survive and in time proved stronger than the Roman empire, and doubtless such writings as *Revelation* did much to encourage it to stand fast in the testing days of persecution.

But to find the permanent value of the book of *Revelation* we must look behind the apocalyptic scaffolding into the heart of the writer's thought. His world-view is that beyond the rise and fall of empires, the afflictions of the righteous and the chances and changes of fortune, lies the purpose of God, a good purpose which will in the end prevail. The war between good and evil is never-ceasing, but in the end, says John, the outcome is sure. We live in a planned universe, he maintains, not in a mad chaos, and within that plan is the vindication of goodness and the punishment of evil.

The glimpses he gives us of the world beyond sense and sight are as circumscribed as any human thought on the subject is bound to be, yet we are uplifted by their magnificence and encouraged by the truth that they hint at. We know that the walls of the New Jerusalem will not be of jasper, nor will its pearly gates lead into streets of gold, but when John tells us that the glory of God will illumine it, that its lamp will be the Lamb, that his servants will serve him and see his face, we acknowledge that this is indeed a word from God, and a fitting end to what the Father of the Lord Jesus Christ has to say to us in the Bible.

77 10 9 8 7 6 5 4 3